Contemporary Social Problems

The Dorsey Series in Sociology
Advisory Editor
Robin M. Williams, Jr.
Cornell University

Consulting Editor
Charles M. Bonjean
The University of Texas at Austin

Contemporary Social Problems

ROBERT R. BELL
Temple University

1981

THE DORSEY PRESS   Homewood, Illinois   60430
Irwin-Dorsey Limited   Georgetown, Ontario   L7G 4B3

362.042
B435c

ISBN 0-256-02412-X
Library of Congress Catalog Card No. 80–70083
Printed in the United States of America

1 2 3 4 5 6 7 8 9 0 MP 8 7 6 5 4 3 2 1

To Wendy L. Jones, Ph.D.
with whom I share sociology,
tennis, and marriage

Preface

The study of social problems has always been a basic part of American sociology. In the early days of American sociology the major interests were in social problems relating to the cities, immigrants, poverty, crime, breakdown of the family, and so on. Over the years, many of these problems came to be the substantive areas of sociology and represent a major part of course offerings in sociology.

Sociologists, like almost all professionals, are specialists. The field is too complex for any sociologist to be an expert in all theories, methods, and substantive areas. Any sociologist who starts to write a book on social problems quickly realizes he must learn a great deal about substantive areas that are not a part of his specialization. In many ways the most interesting part of writing this book was reading and preparing the chapters about which I knew the least: for example, the chapters on work, urban areas, and ecology. In those chapters more directly related to my specializations the problems were to limit what could be presented in one chapter.

There are a variety of theoretical approaches that are used in the study of social problems. I have chosen to use primarily, but not exclusively, a conceptual approach that attempts to examine a social problem as a process. Essentially the interest is in the rise, development, and establishment of a social problem in contemporary American society. This means that some problems discussed are emerging while others are clearly recognized as being a part of our society.

I have tried to include a wide range of social problems of interest and importance to undergraduate students. I have avoided a lot of sociological jargon, in the hope that students will find this book more comprehensible.

I wish to thank Dr. Wendy L. Jones (Fox Chase Cancer Research Center, Philadelphia) for her help. She helped to frame the conceptual approach and critiqued all the chapters.

Robert R. Bell

Contents

PART FIVE CRIMINAL BASED SOCIAL PROBLEMS

PART ONE

Introduction

Chapter 1

An Anatomy
of Social Problems

Societies long have had to deal with various conditions and events seen as problems. There have probably always been some conditions defined as bad and treated as inescapable conditions of society. For most of history some conditions have been seen as inevitable and untouchable. But beginning in the 18th century the fatalism of the past was increasingly replaced by a view that problems could be alleviated or solved. It no longer seemed necessary to wait for the one available solution—divine intervention. The view came to be that rationality and directed social change would solve social problems. This optimism has come to be a part of the American ideology, which holds that social problems can be resolved if only given the time and effort and money. The fact that this often has not proved true hasn't greatly altered the optimism.

In general our interest is in how social problems come to gain social importance. Before something can be considered a social problem it must be recognized as negatively defining some significant group of persons or behavior in society. Many areas of activity that some persons see as problems are never identified as social problems. This is because they are neither severe nor widespread enough to be defined as socially significant. Our interest is to discover why some problems are so defined while others are not.

Social problems occur in society through the interaction of individuals. A social problem, at whatever stage of development, is a dynamic process because some change is always taking place. A problem may emerge as a social problem, be relatively stable for a while, and over time begin to fade away. Even during the time when a social problem appears to be relatively stable, there always are some changes occurring because the problem consists of what people do with and to each other.

There are a number of theories related to defining social problems. The disorganization approach assumes that a social problem exists as an objective condition or arrangement that is a part of the structure of society. When it is seen in that way, it is defined as intrinsically bad or even as being malignant in contrast to normal or healthy society. Herbert Blumer suggests that social problems are fundamentally the products of a process of collective definition. He sees this to be the case rather than the problems existing independently as a set of objective social arrangements with an intrinsic structure. For Blumer, and other symbolic interactionists, social reality is made up of social acts, and it is these acts that should be the focus of research rather than social structures and institutions.[1] The interactionist stress is on process and that is the focus we take in examining the nature of social problems. For example, if our interest is in poverty as a social problem, it is not in the economic structure of poverty but rather in how people define poverty and act toward it, and in how they are influenced by one another's definitions of poverty and its consequences.

Our approach is to look at the settings of social interaction where something is considered to be a social problem. The interactional nature of the problem will often focus on different values or different ways of acting. Or persons may have difficulties in carrying out such basic processes as exchanging words, gestures, and cues of approved or condemned behavior. "Thus, people may be troubled, and may engage in troubling behavior, because they are unable to agree on the meaning of 'the world,' proper conduct, or even basic concepts, and because of inherent limitations in the human ability to communicate and order communication."[2] When people interpret one another's actions and respond in socially appropriate ways, they "create" rather than "discover" reality. Often the nature of the interpersonal setting where a social problem occurs includes multiple realities. For example, the world of drug use created by the police is very different from the world created by the drug user.

Our interest in this chapter is to look at the how and the why of the interactional process—how and why people act and are reacted to. John I. Kitsue has argued that a sociology of social problems must take the perspective of the individual as a starting point and focus on the definitions and claims-making activities as the basic subject matter. He says, "We examine how individuals and groups become engaged in collective activities organized and directed toward establishing institutional arrangements, recognizing punitive conditions as problems, and attempting to relieve, ameliorate, and eliminate them."[3]

Social deviance is behavior that violates institutional expectations—the expectations that are shared and recognized as legitimate in a society. This definition suggests that deviant behavior is a reflection of how persons perform and of the structure of the groups within which they perform. In other words, deviance has both an individual and group perspective, although the usual pattern for analysis is to look at the interaction of deviants within a social setting.

Deviance theory argues that persistent deviance is not an individual or group creation but rather has a history in particular locales. This means that many areas responsible for deviance have existed for some time and have contributed to a history and to certain systems of deviant behavior. This time factor is an important influence on social deviance because when deviance persists it often becomes patterned (although not all deviance is systematic, nor is all systematic deviance socially organized). There may be systematic individual deviance where there is no interaction among the participants. That is, many deviant patterns are practiced by solitary individuals.

In a general sense, social deviance may be thought of as a part of social problems. Basically the stress of defining deviance is on what people do, and how, and in what ways it is defined as deviant. The study of social problems includes the concerns found in the study of deviance but is also interested in broader social questions about the structure and function of society. While all social deviance may be thought of as a social problem, not all social problems are social deviance.

The reason for these brief comments on social deviance is that this book, like almost all social problem texts, will include some substantive areas that are social deviance. The traditional topics such as social problems of the city, poverty, and population are included. But also usually included are the common areas of social deviance like drugs and homosexuality. The difference in presenting these two areas is that in discussing social problems a somewhat greater stress is placed on structure and function, whereas in those areas thought of as social deviance, the stress is more on the person and social interaction. But these different stresses are a matter of degree and are not absolute. In the substantive areas we will look at all areas as social problems and, wherever appropriate, we will also consider the social deviance dimension.

Basically the conceptual approach to be used in this book is that social problems may go through three developmental stages. However, many problems do not go through all three stages. The first stage is the interactional process where there is an emergence of a definition of a social problem. Many problems may never get beyond this stage. The second stage is the development of various publics that attempt to deal with the social problem. At this stage conflicting solutions are proposed; there are a number of social problems that do not go beyond this stage. The third stage is where *institutionalization* takes place. Only a few social problems reach this stage. Once a problem is institutionalized, there is no guarantee that it will remain so. At any time a social problem may be moving through the developmental processes either towards institutionalization or towards disappearance as a social problem. Its disappearance as a social problem may be the result of its disappearance altogether, or as a result of becoming acceptable, and therefore no longer being seen as a problem. But for the most part, our conceptual approach is to look at social problems as they develop through any of the three stages. This means that the conceptual approach can have a more meaningful application for some social problems than others. There is more to say with regard to a social problem that is receiving a great deal of public attention because those who want to define it are vocal and visible—for example, abortion or drug use—while other social problems are less visible or controversial because they have become accepted, as with crime or mental illness. Still others may have less visibility because they are disappearing as social problems; for example, illegitimacy or premarital sexual behavior.

THE EMERGENCE OF A DEFINITION

In examining various social problems in later chapters we will look at their historical origins and how they have survived or failed to survive as social problems over time. Some social problems have been around a long time; for example, crime or minority group conflicts. Others have been a social problem in the past, come to be seen as less serious, but later return as a social problem. Poverty is an illustration of a social problem with this kind of history.

The intensity of a social problem for society can also vary greatly. For example, homosexuality is seen as less of a social problem today than a few decades ago, while violence appears a more intense social problem today than in the recent past. Also, for those social problems that continue to exist for a long period of time, the alleged causes and cures often change. To illustrate, in the past mental health problems were often seen as caused by sin and the treatment was repentance. In contrast, today the cause is usually explained as psychological and the cure is medical-psychiatric treatment.

A society is rarely confronted with the inevitability of some objective condition being defined as a social problem. If we look at any phenomenon defined as a social problem at different times in a given society or in different societies, we can see there is nothing inherent in a phenomenon that necessarily makes it a social problem. A social problem is not the result of some intrinsic malfunctioning of a society but rather comes about through a process of definition whereby a particular social condition is selected and identified as a social problem. As Blumer points out, a social problem does not exist for a society unless it is recognized by that society to exist. "It is a gross mistake to assume that any kind of malignant or harmful social condition or arrangement in a society becomes automatically a social problem for that society."[4]

There are many difficulties in defining a social problem. For example, there is a very subjective result when persons who are influential define a social problem. Whatever subjective elements go into the definition they tend to call for punishment of the "offenders." There are usually negative statements about those persons defined as the social problem and what should be done about them. Malcolm Spector and Kitsue suggest that we may define social problems as the activities of groups asserting complaints and that the definers claim some organization which attempts to change the conditions. The emergence of a social problem is contingent on the organization of group activities to define some conditions as a problem and to state that it should be eradicated, ameliorated, or in some way changed. These groups usually have strong notions on how this change is to be brought about.[5]

In general, the more severe the definition of the social problem, the stronger the nature of the proposed solution. What that usually means is the stronger the punishment for those held to be responsible for the problem. At the first stage we often find there is strong disagreement that a social problem exists and therefore needs solution. By the second stage there is usually agreement that a problem exists and strong points of view on what ought to be done about it. By the third stage there is a high level of agreement that a problem exists and on the response. At the third stage, there are social agencies trying to enforce actions to control the social problem or to deal with its consequences.

We can say that all problems that come to be seen as social problems must go through the first and second stages (and often into the third stage). But some dangerous or threatening actions never make it to being a social problem—for example, smoking of cigarettes or white collar crime. Some problems may get to the second stage of conflicting solutions but drop out as social problems. This would be true of hippies and militant students in the late 1960s as social problems.

Of crucial importance at the first stage is those who are defining something as a social problem—how much power and influence do they have? For example, various groups periodically go around saying the world is coming to an end on a given date but they are heeded because they have no social credibility. Or sometimes groups may have a good deal of influence about some condition being a problem but opposition groups may cancel out their influence. Such would be the case with attempts at gun control laws that can't match the political clout of the anti-gun control lobby.

A Naming Process

The emergence of a problem defined as significant involves a naming process whereby groups of some social significance define the problem. The problem comes to be heard among those who share the belief that it is a social problem. The naming process is influenced in a variety of ways. Frequently what is defined as a social problem, as well as the kinds of definitions that go with the condition, is a result of social class or power differences in society. For example, it is often the welfare worker who defines for the poor, the physician who defines for the woman wanting an abortion, or the priest who defines for the woman seeking birth control help. Often those with power define both the problem and the ways to deal with it. Inherent in the thinking that defines many social problems is the assumption that some persons are better able to decide for others than those persons are able to decide for themselves. This is a kind of "playing God" syndrome which is very often based not on fact but on subjective evaluation and the power to control or influence conditions seen as social problems. This also often explains why many people are hostile to those in power—the powerless are treated like children and told what would be best for them.

Basically the ultimate measure of whether or not an act is a social problem depends on how those who are socially significant in power and influence define the act. No act would be a problem in its social consequences if no significant elements of society defined it as such. And in any given society, what the response to the act will be is always problematic and situational. Those who commit an act must do so in a social setting where their behavior will be defined as a problem if there is to be social consequences from that behavior.

There is clearly a high level of relativity to what will be defined as a social problem and the sanctions that will go with the definitions. As suggested what is defined as a social problem varies with time. One reason for differences in response to a social problem over time is that a society will, on some occasions, direct its attention to some conditions and not to others. This is seen in the varying level of concern over time directed at gambling, drug use, and so forth. Differences in response may also be determined by who commits the act and who has been defined as being harmed. For example, the middle class often defines as juvenile delinquents lower-class boys, but not middle-class boys, although the behavior of both groups may be similar. Another variation in defining a social problem may be the consequences of the

© George W. Gardner

The "right" to bear arms

act. A young woman is generally not strongly condemned for having premarital sexual experience; however, if she gets pregnant she may be subjected to strong social criticism.

Because there is never universal agreement on whether or not something is a social problem, there is always the potential for conflict. People look at the world from viewpoints reflecting different value systems, and often what becomes the prevailing view of what is right is determined by the relative power of the definers. The definition of social problems is always the definition by some group or groups. It is incorrect to conceive of a social problem apart from its definers. As J. L. Simmons points out, "Everyone, square or hip, straight or criminal, is outraged by something."[6] Therefore it is useful to ask about a given problem what group defines that action or condition as a problem?

The above points suggest why the defining of a social problem is a naming process. Regardless of the features of the act, the behavior must be defined as a social problem by some important or significant elements of society or it will not be seen as a problem. However, the person whose action is defined as a social problem may or may not define himself in the same way. The relationship between a social problem and the broader society is a basic one. It has sometimes been assumed that if the broader society defines social acts as social problems, then they are. While this may be true for the broader society, it is not necessarily true from the perspective of those whose action is defined as a social problem. They may not accept the definitions, or they may define themselves and their actions from very different perspectives.

Reality is never absolute but often is defined by the beholder. Multiple realities mean that people often see the same things in different ways, respond in different ways, and treat what they see in different ways. We may not recognize there are different realities which leads us to believe that only what we see is true and all other views are false. Often in looking at social problems, a point of view becomes rigid because it is assumed to be the only right one.

When persons find their actions defined as social problems and these definitions do have some impact on them, they can respond in a variety of ways. They can accept the definition or they can deny it. They can hide or run away. They can fight the definition or ignore it. When people are aware that their actions or conditions are defined as a social problem and find the definition significant to themselves, they are involved at a particular level of interaction. This is different from individual deviance where the act may be defined as deviant but the person is not known to the definer and therefore doesn't have to react. For example, some physicians are drug addicts, but their deviancy is unknown to others so there is no interactional context for them.

Individual Responses

Persons who are defined as actors in various situations regarded as social problems react in different ways. Some groups refuse to have their actions defined as a social problem. For example, many homosexuals do not accept the definition that homosexuality constitutes a problem. However, when sanctions are brought to bear, they can constitute moral and/or legal consequences. Moral sanctions are easier to reject. The moral beliefs and laws against homosexuality often are not significant to the homosexual lifestyle, so the people involved can easily reject them. By contrast, drug users are often subject to both moral and legal harassment which is much more difficult to counteract or ignore because the legal system can invoke severe punishment.

When the sanctions against a social problem are primarily moral and the defined group can pretty much ignore them, this can be very frustrating to those doing the defining. Often when this occurs there is an attempt to strengthen the moral condemnation by having new or stronger laws passed. For example, many who are morally opposed to homosexuality want stronger laws against that activity. For some social problems the battleground may be in the legal arena. This is the case with abortion where the pro-abortion forces want more liberal laws and the anti-abortion groups want to repeal the more permissive laws of recent years.

Usually the emergence of a social problem at the second stage is accompanied by attempts to deal with it. Bur rarely is this left to one group for any extended period of time. Other groups develop interests and each may have a different impact on those defined as social problems as well as other interested parties. As suggested, power becomes very important at this stage because it determines the exposure and impact of a certain viewpoint. So various powers and vested interest groups are concerned with the emergence of the problem and suggested treatments. One thing a vested interest group may try to do is change the distribution of something defined as a problem. For example, historically the attempts to control drug use have been to influence its distribution. Powerful agencies may develop as a result of this approach. The approach is rarely one of attempting to eliminate the social problem but rather to control it. For example, the Federal Narcotics Bureau attempts to control the distribution of drugs and police departments attempt to control drug-related crime.

Often those agencies that attempt to control a social problem have no strong motive to reach a final solution because the existence of the social problem is necessary to maintain that agency. Quite simply, no social problem means no job. In other instances, the continuation of a problem becomes justified on the basis of the "good" it does. For example, one argument used against making the sale of tobacco illegal is that it would put thousands of persons in the tobacco industry out of work. So it is argued it is better to continue to sell cigarettes. This logic suggests that cancer is better than unemployment.

"Causes"

As various groups define something as a social problem the focus is usually on the individual actors involved. That is, the problem is often defined in terms of the individuals who contribute to it. The drug problem is basically defined as those persons who use drugs or the crime problem as those who commit specific types of crimes. The definition of a social problem in terms of contributing actors often allows the definers to hold the actors responsible for the social problem. This is the pattern of "blaming the victim." To illustrate, a person living in poverty may be personally defined as lazy rather than as a victim of the economic system. A homosexual may be labeled as personally sick and weak rather than as exercising a legitimate choice of sex partner. Or the rape victim is sometimes seen as contributing to her own rape rather than being a victim of a society that socializes many males toward violence and aggressiveness.

What is of sociological importance is that rarely is society seen as responsible and rarely is it subjected to any real criticism. It is true that sometimes statements are made that our permissive society is responsible for all kinds of problems, but those statements often come from persons with little prestige and power and therefore have little real impact. It is not as if there are viable options to our society that would eliminate almost all social problems. Most modern large industrial countries, whether capitalist, socialist, or communist, have pretty much the same social problems.

With society not being blamed, the individual is not the only scapegoat for most social problems. What has frequently come to be blamed is one institution—the family. Most people belong to families, but the families are not organized collectively in any way. So they are easy to criticize and have no means of fighting back. The family often gets blamed for such social problems as delinquency and crime, drug and alcohol use, mental illness, all kinds of sexual deviance, the aged, sex role conflict, and so forth. Furthermore, it is often not the family in general that is blamed but rather the modern woman. Because she often no longer stays home she is seen as "causing" many of the above social problems, though the blame may be somewhat less today than in the past.

Sometimes the definers of social problems themselves are caught within the fabric of some social problems because many problems cut across all levels of society. The person concerned with some social problems may have to define and handle those persons who are close to him and are defined as a part of the problem. Often when a social problem is close to the definers, they see those who suffer as "victims." They are usually not seen as victims of the social system or personal inadequacies, however, but more typically as the victim of "bad" influences, company, or circumstances. The person who has a spouse who is an alcoholic or a son who is a drug addict usually sees them as victims. It is possible that as more persons are personally affected by a social problem, they will change their definitions of the seriousness of the social problem. This appears to have been the case in the liberalizing of marijuana use. A few years ago it was seen as a social problem involving junkies, blacks, and lower-class people by persons in power. But when their children or they, themselves, or people in power were arrested on charges of drug possession and some were given severe jail sentences, the definitions as to the seriousness of the social problem were rapidly reduced. As a result, the legal punishments were greatly reduced in many states.

Because of the interactional nature of social problems the definers must always be seen as a part of the problem. Something only becomes a problem when people see it as threatening and undesirable. For a social problem to emerge there must be people saying that something is wrong and that it is threatening in some way. Furthermore they want it stopped or at least removed from where they are confronted with it. Given the fact that nothing is inherently a social problem, the reaction of significant groups is crucial. But just as this must occur for something to emerge as a social problem, a loss of interest and concern can lead to the disappearance of a social problem. For example, such may be true at this time with regard to premarital sex where there is little strongly organized criticism among groups with social power or influence.

Significant Groups

There must be some socially significant groups declaring an action or condition to be a social problem, but there must be more. There must be some response through interaction with other groups in society. This means that one group's feelings about the social problem must receive endorsement and support from others. There must be some dialogue taking place in society. This can occur through institutional support that something is a social problem as with Catholic church support against legal abortion. It can also be through the mass media who can publicize a social problem and can greatly contribute to its emergence. Recently the mass media, especially television, have contributed a great deal to violence being seen as a social problem. They have made it highly visible.

Without institutional or mass media support, a social problem may never really emerge. Smoking is a good illustration: many Americans believe it is bad and dangerous but they get little institutional support and practically none from the mass media. Social drinking does not become a social problem because many people do it and they don't want to be criticized or have controls placed over their right to drink.

In some instances a behavioral area does not become a social problem because the actors who are engaged in it are able to take a position that their behavior is right and proper. To own a gun or to drink socially is presented as a right of the individual and there is created a forceful rhetoric of individual freedom. When this rhetoric is generally accepted by society, no social problem is defined as existing. By contrast, other problems can become social problems even when those who are engaged in the behavior say they have a right to do what they want but their right is not accepted by the broader society. Such is the case with homosexuality.

There are other possible influences on the potentiality of a problem coming to have social significance at the first stage. Often whether or not a social problem will move on to the second stage is related to its being defined as severe, which depends in part on how long it lasts and whether it recurs. For example, the use of addictive drugs is more of a social problem than nonaddictive drugs because they are seen as more severe and as having been around for a longer time. They are also seen as having more severe consequences in their users.

Also, the number of persons involved in an area helps determine whether or not it will be defined as a social problem. In general, when the behavior of only a few people is defined as a social problem, they are usually seen as cases of individual pathology or deviance. It is only as greater numbers are seen to be involved that their acts or conditions are defined as a social problem. Mental illness is felt to be a more important social problem than the use of prescription drugs, not only because the problem is seen as more severe, but also because there are far more people defined as mentally ill.

In most cases, any group defined as a social problem represents a minority in society. Being a minority usually means less power and less chance to have impact on society. Therefore, being a minority group (whether delinquents, homosexuals, drug users, the poor, etc.) is a reflection of less power because they have little or no chance to attain a majority position. The combination of less power and smaller size usually destines the minority group to remain a social problem.

In summary, it is basically at the first stage that groups in society seek to define and gain social acceptance for some area to be seen as a social problem. This is a necessary condition before it is possible for that problem to move into the second stage.

CONFLICTING SOLUTIONS

This stage is often characterized by a battle between vested interests seeking to gain increased social significance and control of the problem. There is usually an attempt to gain acceptance of proposed ways of dealing with the social problem. We want to examine some of the influences that contribute to the acceptance or rejection of the symptoms of the social problem, as well as influence what should be done about the problem.

Public opinion. Basically public opinion is a reflection of how much society is concerned about a problem and also about suggestions for dealing with it. Often public opinion is subject to manipulation. Frequently what is most important is the influence that the mass media is directing at the problem. For example, in the late 1960s the mass media, especially television, played a major role in shaping public opinion to believe that marijuana was a severe social problem. The media accepted the value that marijuana was bad and then made the case against it as strong as possible by using whatever evidence supported the argument. The mass media rarely attempts to present a problem as objectively as possible. They make a value judgment, usually conservative and in agreement with their sponsors (advertisers), and attempt to significantly influence the acceptance of a particular social problem. Also by their decision *not* to publicize a problem, such as gun control or cigarette smoking, they implicitly support them as nonsocial problems.

Public opinion is also greatly influenced by the stand that various institutions take on a problem. This means that some institutional groups, that are well organized can play a strong role in the acceptance or rejection of something as a social problem. Such is the case in abortion being seen as a social problem because of the influence of the Catholic church or gun control not being a social problem because of the resistance of the American Rifle Association. These kinds of groups can elicit tremendous influence because they can bring pressure to bear not only on public opinion but also on legislators.

Public opinion is further influenced by the awareness of a social problem. Probably far more Americans are aware of crime as a social problem than they are of poverty. This is not because they personally see or experience either, but rather because they hear far more about crime than poverty. The mass media directs far more attention to crime than it does poverty. Often because people hear little about poverty, they really don't see it as a significant social problem. Yet, because they hear a lot about crime they see it as far more a common problem than it really is.

Vested interests. Implied in the discussion of public opinion is that vested interests often operate to influence the acceptance or significance of a social problem and also to influence the possible solutions adopted. The vested interests usually determine the stress and the strength that a given social problem will have. But in most interests there are divergent values. Blumer says that a social problem is always a focal point for the operation of different and conflicting viewpoints. It is the interplay of those interested that constitute the way in which society deals with any one social problem. Blumer also suggests that it is this interplay at the second stage where the problem becomes the object of discussion, of controversy, and of diverse claims. "Those who seek changes in the area of the problem clash with those who endeavor to protect vested interests in the area."[7]

Vested interests means that specific values are in operation. This clearly implies that competing groups see their respective views as significantly different. To be seen as different from one another is the major reason for their remaining apart and not merging together. As earlier suggested, vested interests disagree on the reasons for the existence of a social problem and proposed solutions to deal with it. For example, if a group believes in moral right and wrong in defining sexual behavior, then many areas of sexual behavior have the potential to be defined as a social problem. Society may define certain sexual behavior as bad and therefore a problem and as something threatening to society. Different groups may basically agree that "sexual promiscuity" is a social problem, but they may represent different vested interests in what should be done about it. Some may want a return to traditional values, others to greater religious education and control, and still others to tougher laws or better application of existing laws.

In general, social problems are defined as more severe when they are seen as affecting "innocent" people rather than only if they are seen as affecting those defined as deviant. The drug user or the homosexual is seen as dangerous not just because of what each is doing to himself but because they are seen as a threat to the "moral fiber of society—a threat to all that is good and decent." Also those persons who are actively involved in the control of drugs have a vested interest best served by making the social problem appear to be as broad and as dangerous as possible.

Sociological input. Vested interests also come from sociologists in their study of social problems. Values enter into what gets selected for study. Sociologists have, from the beginning, placed a major substantive stress on various soical problems. Frequently problems are studied because they are easy to get at. Often this is because accessible areas are funded for research or sometimes because the actors in the problem area want help. There is also the politics of research. Research funds are usually reserved not only for specific areas but often for projects that will take a specific direction. For example, there may be money to study unwed mothers but not to study teenagers with satisfying sex lives. Teenage pregnancy is often seen as a social problem and one needing correction. Whether or not it is a social problem is not the question. The question is—what's the solution?

Sociologists continue to devote much of their attention to studying the unhealthy, the unhappy, the misfits, and the social failures. There often appears to be an embarrassment about studying successful people. This is more than the obvious problem of defining who are happy

and successful people. Even when definitions are acceptable, it is almost as if there is a fear of being self-indulgent and self-satisfied if it is recognized that some people are more positive and successful in their lives than are others. It seems to go against an ethic that life is problematic and difficult at best—and often miserable at worst. Many sociologists appear to feel more comfortable with their conscience by staying with the "less fortunate." Often this is more satisfying because they don't see themselves as having pathologies and social ailments so they can seek to understand and help the less fortunate. It is not that people with problems should be ignored, but rather that along with them successful persons are also worthy of study. They are worthy of study not only in their own right, but also to help better understand various social problem areas.

Among many psychologists and sociologists there are other kinds of resistances to studying the successful or happy individual. One is the resistance to the notion that the individual has any real control over his or her own destiny. These are perspectives that see the individual as being impinged upon by external influences and forces. The person is what he is because of those forces, and little credit is attributed to him as the giver of meaning to the external events that he interacts with and acts toward. The second perspective is that success or failure for the individual is determined externally. For example, one has a happy marriage because he meets the social dimensions seen as constituting marital success.

Sociologists are rarely ever involved in the study of the emergence of a social problem. Thier involvement comes about only after social problems are recognized by society. Blumer observes that sociological recognition follows in the wake of societal recognition and veers with the winds of the public identification of social problems.[8] The conventional sociological approach has been to assume that a social problem exists basically in the form of an identifiable objective condition in society. The societal definition gives the social problem its nature, lays out how it is to be approached, and shapes what is to be done about it. "A sociologist may note what he believes to be a malignant condition in a society, but the society may ignore completely its presence, in which event the condition will not exist as a social problem for that society regardless of its asserted objective being."[9]

Causes of Social Problems

A major part of any claim for public support is a strong and reasonably convincing statement about the causes. Alleged causes often differ among various interest groups and need to be identified in part because from defined causes come the particular solutions interest

National Library of Medicine

A long history of blaming women

groups advocate. It is therefore important for a vested interest group to be able to establish a claim of understanding the causes so it can get on with its "solutions."

In the Western world, the oldest and most common view of the causes of social problems has been one of individual pathology. That is, something wrong exists in the individual. At an earlier time, the deviant person was thought to be possessed of the devil, while later on he was believed to have genetic defects. Because his "problem" was seen as inside him he was punished, destroyed, or removed from society. Under the biological or genetic interpretation of deviance it was believed that something inherent in the deviant set him apart from others. For example, for many years, criminals were sometimes defined as biologically distinctive in one way or another. However, in recent years the explanations of why individuals are social problems have for the most part shifted from genetic explanations to explanations based on illness. That is, the view has moved from seeing criminals as morally or biologically defective to seeing them as having psychological limitations or incapacities. Often society has shifted its view on how the individual should be dealt with from punishment to medical treatment.

A common view of individual responsibility is that the person defined as a social problem is willfully aggressive against the norms of society or is too weak to follow the norms that most people do. If the person is willfully aggressive, for example, and commits criminal acts, then the treatment will generally be punishment and imprisonment. On the other hand, if he is a drug addict, which often means that he is defined as a weak-willed individual, he will be treated in a repressive manner. He is typically not allowed to have legal drugs, and must then seek them out through illegal sources. Thus, one possible consequence of the "cure" of not allowing him to get legal drugs is to intensify the problem. He is placed in a position where it will probably be necessary for him to resort to deceit and crime in order to support his drug habit.

As previously suggested, the mass media often have a close relationship with the causes of some social problems. It seems clear that the amount of exposure that the mass media, and especially television, give to almost any activity influences how it will be viewed and the importance attached to it. Television can be a direct cause. For example, there is some evidence that coverage of certain kinds of violence may lead some viewers to engage in similar behavior. But it may also be a cause in a more indirect way by bringing the social problem to public attention and illiciting new responses. In the late 1960s the hippies were made to be socially "important" primarily through the mass media. To a great extent they became a social problem because the mass media made them one.

Just as there are many theories attempting to explain the causes of social problems, so too there are many attempts to suggest what might be done to cure them. It is almost always true that when cures are suggested, the assumption has been made that a cure is needed. That is, one might imagine that the first level of consideration would be to find out whether a cure in an area is needed—but this is usually not a serious consideration. Sometimes the person defined as a part of a social problem assumes without serious question that a cure is needed for his problem. When that person agrees to the cure recommended, he is agreeing with the definer who has designated him as needing help. For example, when a homosexual male seeks out psychiatric help to try to rid himself of his homosexuality, he is agreeing with those who have defined him and his behavior as a problem.

As earlier discussed, most views about the cause of social problems are on the personal, rather than the social, level. Therefore, most suggestions for cures are aimed at individual alteration rather than social change. For example, as Leslie T. Wilkins points out, "If one takes the view that crime is identical with sin, it is likely that one will restrict one's thinking to remedial measures affecting only the individual."[10] Therefore, most curative theories follow the lines of trying to affect the individual, through force, medical treatment, or education.

It would seem clear that social problems cannot be explained by any simple cause and effect basis because they represent a diverse phenomenon with complex causes. "Sometimes there is a biological anomaly, sometimes a disrupted home, sometimes bad companions, sometimes too little legitimate opportunity, sometimes too much pressure, and so on."[11] Complex causes often make people uncomfortable since they want simple explanations. That is why when some group comes along with a simplistic "cure," it often gains rapid support. For example, that murder can be greatly reduced by returning to the use of capital punishment may be a simplistic cure.

Just as it is hard for many Americans to believe that the causes of social problems may be very complex, it is also hard to accept the fact that for many social problems there are no real cures. This is in part due to the belief that American "know-how" can find a solution to almost anything. This belief explains why many Americans willingly turn to all sorts of "quacks." Many believe that those who say they have a solution must have one because they believe that there should be a solution. People are often attracted to a simplistic view of how to resolve problems. This is reflected in such things as *Reader's Digest* articles, "Dear Abby" columns, and television commercials. People are constantly being told and accept new "miracle drugs" that never reach the market, to "stand firm and your children will respect you," or that romantic problems can be solved by using a new deodorant. But cures to social problems may be nonexistent or very complex—rarely are they simple. It may also be that some cures work only for some people; for example, Alcoholics Anonymous works for some but not all alcoholics. It may be that the passage of time "cures" more social problems than any psychological, social, or medical programs.

It sometimes happens that when one problem is alleviated or cured, that very success may contribute to the emergence of a new problem or may exacerbate another. For example, a major social problem has been sexism in the United States. As this has been somewhat decreased and women have achieved some greater opportunities, the new rights have not always been areas they would define as desirable. Not only have they achieved greater opportunities for education and occupation, but they have achieved greater chances to become drug addicts or alcoholics.

At the second stage, there is always some jockeying around for influence and power with regard to any social problem. As one group attempts to mobilize support for its solutions, others are saying we have a better way. One group may be arguing that the solution to the drug problem is to legalize the sale of nonaddictive drugs, and another

"Remember the good old days when problems had solutions?"

group may say the laws should be made tougher. Still another group may be saying an educational program for the young is the answer. Therefore, different interest groups are coming up with different solutions and in most instances are saying their solution is the only good one and the only one that will work.

In recent years there has come to be an increasingly important dimension involved in the struggle for defining a social problem and possible solutions—the organization of persons who have been defined as a social problem. Examples are the development of Gay Liberation groups to fight against homosexual discrimination and Gray Panthers to fight age discrimination. These groups develop a structure and a rationale for themselves and basically stress their rights to be what they are and to not be discriminated against. These groups do not argue for cures but rather for acceptance. What is most striking about this trend is that traditionally those actors defined as social problems had to cope with the definition individually, but increasingly there is the opportunity to deal with it from the greater strength of collective action.

We generally talk about social problems as if they were uniform throughout the United States. When we examine specific social problems later in the book we will look at some variations in regional differences. For example, the South and Southwest have a record of greater violence than does the rest of the country. Homosexuality is responded to very differently in San Francisco than it is in a small Midwestern city.

In summary, the second stage is where the social problem is reasonably well established, although it may have to fight constantly for recognition. Most important, this is the time for various vested interest groups to argue for their priority in influencing the social problem and to come up with their ways of solving it with their solutions.

INSTITUTIONALIZATION

Most social problems never reach this stage, but for those that do, it is a time where there is a high social acceptance that a problem does exist and that it is a significant one. There also continues to be various agencies to deal with the problem. Often the agencies are based on the emergence and stablizing of laws, norms, and related social roles. Examples of this level of social problem would be delinquency, crime, and mental illness.

Laws

The enactment and application of laws are a basic part of this stage and therefore we will look briefly at the importance of laws. The concept of law implies rules characterized by regularity. A law is a rule of human conduct that most members of a community recognize as binding on its members. However, the extent to which a law is binding varies greatly. Laws have the police power of the state behind them. Laws always imply a formal government context of power and authority, although the existence of power and authority doesn't necessarily mean that they will be used. A society may feel strongly about something and yet feel that social ends may be better met by having the controls remain informal and general rather than by having them enacted as formal laws with a more precise application. This is because many rules (such as the Ten Commandments) function primarily as ideals or as positive models toward which people should strive.

The law makes an important distinction in defining what is illegal. In a number of situations, what is illegal is not being something, but rather is possessing or doing something. For example, it is not illegal to be a drug addict, a homosexual, or an alcoholic. For the drug addict, what is illegal is the procurement or possession of illegal drugs. For the homosexual, it is various homosexual acts that are illegal. And for the alcoholic, it is public intoxication or driving an automobile while under the influence of alcohol which are illegal.

There is no necessary relationship between the degree to which something may be viewed as a social problem and its control by the law. For example, the use of marijuana is probably much less dangerous than the use of alcohol or cigarettes, but the laws against marijuana use are severe while the laws about the consumption of alcohol or cigarette smoking are few and weak. Often a society exaggerates the dangers of the things it wants to control. Once again, a good illustration is the overstated dangers of marijuana.

The important point is that something doesn't have to be dangerous to society for it to be against the law. Some acts may be criminal or deviant not because they are dangerous, but because they are legally proscribed as such. In fact, the law may be irrational in that the members of the society cannot explain it, but the law is real nevertheless. Or a law may be arbitrary because it is imposed by a strong minority and may even lack general support and be actively opposed. Such has been the case with the Sunday "blue laws." Also, studies show that a strong majority of Americans favor stronger gun control laws but they don't get them because of the opposition of a strong minority. There are some laws that may represent the consensus or perhaps even a majority, yet be opposed by a large number of the population; for example, the antigambling laws in many states are flaunted. Where there is strong social disagreement, what often happens is that the enforcers of policies become ambivalent in their enforcement because the public is often indifferent toward particular social problems.

It seems clear that with a few possible exceptions, the more intense the enforcement of laws the greater the effect the laws will have on deviance. Pittman points out that this can be seen in the treatment of drug addicts in America. Even though addicts may never encounter any law enforcement agency personally, they cannot help but be constantly aware of the law's presence. The fact that they must buy drugs in secret is the result of law enforcement. Also the high price and low quality of illegal drugs are a result of social policies. Furthermore, the addict typically must resort to illegal behavior to support his habit.[12]

It is possible that in the near future laws will be increasingly influenced by a new and emerging view toward some social problems. This view is that people should be legally punished only for acts that are socially dangerous, independent of their moral character. This viewpoint makes a distinction between public and private morality, as well as between illegality and immorality. It would restrict the law to those acts which offend against public order and decency or subject the ordinary citizen to what would be offensive or injurious. It argues that laws do not create good people. This view can be illustrated in the area of sexual behavior. Such sexual activities as rape, exhibitionism, solicitation, and so forth would continue to be against the law. However, private sexual activity between consenting adults would no longer be subject to legal control.

In the eyes of some people, laws have a special and almost mystical quality in that to break them is to do more than go against the specific law—it is to show basic disrespect for laws. Sometimes the person using illicit drugs is seen as doing something more than purchasing something against the law. He is saying that the law is not acceptable and does not apply to him. Sometimes when a person says in effect "so what" to a law, many persons are upset. In either of the above cases the law abider finds his laws not taken seriously and this can be threatening to his view of them. He must often explain why the person breaks the law. So he may come to believe that people break laws or ignore them because those people are bad, evil, sick, vengeful, incompetent, and so forth.

Sometimes social problems and their solutions become almost unquestioned reality. Generally, this would be true of violence or the use of hard drugs. But as the problems become more political, their reality becomes more questioned because alternative causes and/or solutions are often presented. The interest groups that got pushed out at the second stage may try to work their way back in. One way of getting back in is to get attention by saying that the solutions that have been accepted are no good or not working. This can be effective in gaining attention. For some years the treatment of even the most serious of all crimes was imprisonment, and it was not strongly questioned. However, some interest groups that were mainly eliminated at an earlier time have been able to say, and be listened to, that the prison solution is not working. These were the groups interested in a return to capital punishment for serious crimes and they have regained a great deal of influence in recent years.

Other Social Controls

Some social problems are common to all societies, but what comes to be unacceptable is based on how a society views a given activity. Social problems and deviant behavior are common and natural to society. There is always a relationship between individuals engaging in particular patterns of behavior and the community which defines the behavior. We know that different societies may define the same thing in different ways. For example, norms about premarital chastity for the female may fall anywhere along a continuum from high permissiveness to high authoritarian control.

In most instances most people in society are socialized effectively to the approved values of society, and as a result they control their own behavior and don't have to have external sanctions brought to bear. Basically all social systems depend on a successful socialization system to insure conformity. But when self-control does not work, and the individual violates the rules, external sanctions are often used. The prime mechanism for controlling behavior is the application of sanctions. To reward proper and punish improper behavior may not only correct improper behavior but also teach the individual what is expected in the future so he may direct and control his own behavior.

There is often an inconsistency in applying social controls. It is sometimes not what is being done (the act) but who is doing it (the actor) which determines the degree to which social control will be applied. For example, there are white-collar criminals who are using computers to steal and when caught receive light sentences. Other examples are Richard Nixon and his colleagues who were caught in the Watergate crimes but received no legal punishment or very mild sentences.

There are a variety of roles that are developed in a given social problem area by the third stage. These are the roles not only of the social actor involved in the problem but also the roles of those in the social system who are charged with finding cures. For example, there are the roles of the criminal, police, courts, prisons, and so forth. Furthermore, the person filling the role defined as a social problem is rarely, if ever, filling only that role. The man has many other social roles to handle. For example, the alcoholic may also be a husband, father, employee, church member, friend, and so forth. Sometimes those roles come into conflict with one another. The alcoholic at times cannot effectively be an employee or a parent. He may fail behaviorally as an alcoholic and at other times be caused to fail because he is socially defined as an alcoholic.

However, to point out that persons in social problem areas often have role problems and confusion is not to say that they are always unhappy and would like to change their style of life. The ideology of the broader society often assumes this to be true, but the facts suggest otherwise. The degree of frustration or unhappiness will often be determined by the kind of activity they are involved in. As Lemert points out, persons who deviate because of such things as stuttering, systematic check forgery, alcoholism, and drug addiction are marked by the almost total absence of any durable pleasure. "Instead their lot is one of gnawing anxiety, pain, unhappiness, and despair; in some cases ending with deterioration or suicide."[13] By contrast, many

United Press International Photo

Nixon leaving the White House a free man

others appear, by any reliable measure, to be just as happy as the non-social problem population. Very often the person considers his behavior to be quite reasonable and rational, and from where he sits, with his needs and attitudes, what he does is quite logical. For example, many homosexuals are as happy or happier than many heterosexuals.

In general, it can be said that whatever the solution, it is never as big as the social problem. A solution that would be as big as the problem would eliminate it. Social problems never reach the level of a "polio solution." With the discovery and application of polio vaccines, polio ceased to be a medical problem in the United States. Vested interest groups often argue they have a "polio solution" but they never do. This means that any group that gains strength as the source for dealing for a social problem can be sure of their power for only a limited time. The fact that they always fail to completely solve the social problem means that competitive solutions are fighting to be heard. But when they come up with their solutions, and get a chance to take over the social problem, they too almost always fail. This is because most of our social problems appear to be inherent to all industrial social systems.

A social problem is often posed on an abstract level. On that level, solutions are offered that in reality have no way of being achieved. For example, in the 1960s poverty was attacked under the rhetoric of "a war on poverty" which meant the goal was to wipe it out. But that was nonsense because the basis of poverty rests in the social system and the system was never seriously questioned. Rather, selected aspects of poverty had war declared on them. This was done through such things as free lunches for children from low-income families, job training for some unskilled workers, and so on. This was like trying to heal a badly fractured leg by applying a band-aid. The point is that the solutions are never made on the same level as the problems.

Social problems are often dealt with by breaking them down into smaller parts. For example, if the problem can be seen as better nutrition for children from low-income families, then a free lunch program can do something toward easing that problem. But this makes the social problem appear to be too minor and the interested groups insist on thinking much bigger. To talk about something like waging war on poverty, crime, or drug addiction is basically meaningless. However, it does get attention and often this satisfies the real end—of getting elected to office, getting increased appropriations or justifying an agency.

Conclusions

In general, what can be said about the individuals at the three possible stages of social problems? At the first stage actors don't see themselves as social problems because of the uncertainty of the definitions. At this stage it is being argued whether or not there is a social problem. For example, cigarette smokers generally don't see themselves as a part of a social problem. At the second stage people know that a significant part of society see them as a part of the social problem. They may or may not see themselves in that category. For example, very heavy drinkers may not see themselves as alcoholics. Or sometimes at the second stage people become a part of an interest group and implicitly they recognize they are different, if not a social problem. At the third stage, people may see their social problems as a part of social reality. Because the problem is well accepted by society, people may accept that for themselves. In fact, some may come to see themselves as others do, as being bad or evil. They may recognize a sense of inevitability about being so defined. Sometimes persons found guilty of serious crimes accept the view of themselves as criminals and all that it implies in terms of their actions and their future.

Many social problems are interrelated and the focus on any one is arbitrary as to what it includes and what it excludes. For example, poverty is a major factor related to delinquency, crime, drug use, the aged, and so forth. Or violence has an overlap with mental illness. It may also be that some social problems are seen as contributing to other social problems. It is probable that social problems which produce or exacerbate other social problems are more serious or critical to society than those which have less effect. For example, poverty can be seen as leading to more mental and physical health problems, higher rates of alcoholism, family disruptions, crime, and so forth.

Yet, even though there is a great deal of overlap among social problems, each one has some unique history of its own. To illustrate, drug use can't be explained completely in terms of poverty, or crime, or any other social problem. They may all contribute, but the history of a given social problem means that unique things happened at different times in its development. Therefore, it is important in the chapters ahead to look not only at what social problems share in common but also at what makes each unique.

We take the position that given the values of American society there are no major social problems that will be solved. It might be possible by changing the social system but that is not likely to happen. And as suggested, even if the system could be changed, we know of none that could be introduced that wouldn't also have social problems—many the same and some different. The best that can be achieved is that some social problems are alleviated. As earlier suggested, social problems are very much a part of the political arena. Many people have a vested interest in maintaining some social problems and others want them to continue to be distributed in the population the way they are.

Social problems will continue to be a part of life. There continues to be optimism that a solution can be reached but it also may be that in the future a generalized apathy could emerge as people become more and more cynical by repeated failures to solve social problems. Robert Nisbet suggests that while our extreme social problems will be reduced in the future, because of the spread of knowledge and of a humanitarian ethic, other problems will undoubtedly take their place.[14]

In summary, we have suggested three stages through which a problem may emerge and become social. As described, some potential problems never get beyond the first stage where there is an emergence of a social problem, such as cigarette smoking. Others get into the second stage of conflicting solutions as with drugs. Others get into the institutional level of the third stage as is true for juvenile delinquency. In the substantive chapters ahead we will look at each social problem as related to the three stages. All of them will have been through the first stage and will be in either the second or third stage.

NOTES

1. Herbert Blumer, "Social Problems as Collective Behavior," *Social Problems* (Winter 1971), p. 298.

2. Amitai Etzioni, *Social Problems* (Englewood Cliffs, N.J.: Prentice-Hall, 1979), p. 15.

3. John I. Kitsue and Malcolm Spector, "Social Problems and Deviance: Some Parallel Issues," *Social Problems* (June 1975), p. 593.

4. Blumer, *"Social Problems,"* pp. 301–02.

5. Malcolm Spector and John I. Kitsue, "Social Problems: A Reformulation," *Social Problems* (Fall 1973), p. 146.

6. J. L. Simmons, *Deviants* (Berkeley, Calif.: Glendessary Press, 1969), p. 19.

7. Blumer, "Social Problems," p. 303.

8. Ibid., p. 299.

9. Ibid., p. 300.

10. Leslie T. Wilkens, *Social Deviance* (Englewood Cliffs, N.J.: Prentice-Hall, 1964), p. 13.

11. Simmons, *Deviants*, p. 51.

12. David Pittman, *Alcoholism* (New York: Harper and Row, 1967), pp. 110–11.

13. Edwin M. Lemert, *Human Deviance, Social Problems, and Social Control* (Englewood Cliffs, N.J.: Prentice-Hall, 1967) p. 55.

14. Robert K. Merton and Robert Nisbet, *Contemporary Social Problems*, 4th ed. (New York: Harcourt Brace Jovanovich, 1976), p. 756.

SELECTED BIBLIOGRAPHY

Blumer, Herbert. "Social Problems as Collective Behavior." *Social Problems* (Winter 1971), pp. 298–306.

Etzioni, Amitai. *Social Problems*. Englewood Cliffs, N.J.: Prentice-Hall, 1976.

Hadden, Stuart C., and Lester, Marilyn. "Looking at Society's Troubles: The Sociology of Social Problems." In *Understanding Social Problems*, by Don H. Zimmerman et al., pp. 4–31. New York: Praeger Publishers, 1976.

Kitsue, John I., and Spector, Malcolm. "Social Problems and Deviance: Some Parallel Issues." *Social Problems* (June 1975), pp. 584–94.

Lemert, Edwin M. "Beyond Mead: The Societal Reaction to Deviance." *Social Problems* (April 1974), pp. 457–67.

Manis, Jerome G. "Assessing the Seriousness of Social Problems." *Social Problems* (October 1974), pp. 1–15.

Merton, Robert K., and Nisbet, Robert. *Contemporary Social Problems*. New York: Harcourt Brace Jovanovich, 1976.

Spector, Malcolm, and Kitsue, John I. "Social Problems: A Reformulation." *Social Problems* (Fall 1973), pp. 145–59.

PART TWO

Institutional Based
Social Problems

Chapter 2

Ecology, Energy, and Pollution

The most basic problem for human survival is to ensure that the environment be able to sustain life. Very early in their evolution humans demanded more from their environment than simply survival. They wanted other material things that provided higher and higher standards of living. To meet those increased material needs, people have altered the environment and depleted natural resources. In this chapter we want to examine the resources in the environment which human beings have drawn upon. Some of these resources have been affected by the changing and increasing uses of energy and the resultant problem of residual pollutants. Ecological problems are social problems because decisions of usage and waste disposal are determined by human values. Now the social problem question is not whether there is a severe ecological problem at hand, but rather how great it is and what can be done about it.

An ecological problem can center around a wide variety of misuses of the physical environment. Our major concerns will be with depletion of natural resources and the effects of pollution on the physical environment. Threats and dangers to the physical environment are not something new in history. The first dangers appeared when expanding populations resulted in the emergence of urban living and the developments of new technologies. It is often observed that early cities in Mesopotamia had, as a part of their developing technology, constructed large irrigation systems that diverted water from rivers. Initially this led to increased crop yields, but eventually the continual evaporation of water pulled salts to the surface of the soil. Later, the salt concentration became so great that no crops would grow and the area has since that time remained an arid wasteland.

Ancient agricultural practices also had a negative impact on the environment. For example, it is claimed that overgrazing is responsible for the barrenness of much of the interior of the Old World. The damage occurred perhaps three or four thousand years ago; since that time the land destruction has never been reversed. "The dry lands of the center of the Old World are permanently and sadly diminished in their utility."[1] It is likely that when Pericles was building the Parthenon the land along the Mediterranean had rich forests. But the stripping of the forests and centuries of land erosion has altered the land and sharply reduced the annual rainfall.

In human evolution, the first significant breakthrough in controlling the use of energy (other than that provided by the individual) was with the use of fire. Fire came to be the major means of burning off land for farming and pasturage. Later, the burning of fuels became the major source of energy for the world. Gradually, as people learned to utilize carbonaceous fuel—first wood, then coal, petroleum, and natural gas—they multiplied their available energy many times over. Expanding use of those energy sources has allowed the earth to support an increasing number of human beings.

For most of history the burning of wood has been the major source of energy. Wood was used for heating, cooking, and the beginnings of industry up until the middle of the 16th century. In Tudor England, the first energy crisis developed. By 1540, the local woodlands in eastern England were becoming depleted and the price of firewood doubled and doubled again by 1580. The fuel crisis affected the poor first and the hardest. City dwellers became so desperate for wood that they pillaged the surrounding countryside, tearing down fences and ripping out hedges. A new source of energy was needed and it was found in coal. British coal production rose from perhaps 50,000 tons per year in the 1540s to at least one million tons in 1680. But the switch to coal brought to the city a new problem—pollution.[2]

With the settlement of North America, one of the major problems was clearing land; initially almost all power was limited to human energy. Other environmental problems quickly emerged. The very first settlement, Jamestown, the first capital of Virginia, had to be abandoned because the accumulation of wastes polluted and contaminated the water supply.

The ways in which the lands were used also quickly led to problems. The available land seemed unlimited to the early settlers, and there was no concern with overusing the land because other land was available. Carl O. Sauer points out that in Europe, the manner of living was constrained by conditions of the land, but in the new country the land was to be exploited for profit. He points out that an early illustration of this overuse was the wearing out of land in Virginia by tobacco planting. The westward movement of Virginians was conditined largely by the destruction of land through tobacco. "The opening of the 19th century with the initiation of upland cotton planting set the South definitely on its way to the permanent crisis in which it now is."[3]

It was not until the beginning of the 20th century that there was any significant governmental concern with the environment. Theodore Roosevelt was the first president to actively promote the conservation of resources and wildlife. In 1905 the United States Forest service was made responsible for protecting national forests and for replanting destroyed areas. For the first time the nation's waterways and the problems of flooding and soil erosion came under study. Roosevelt also encouraged the states to set up their own conservation commissions. But it was soon clear that most states were much less able to resist encroachments on their public lands by private interests and to protect the public domain than was the Federal government.[4]

It was not until the Dust Bowl of the 1930s that federal legislators showed any sensitivity to the dangers of unregulated use of renewable resources; they enacted the Soil Conservation Act. But the thousands of conservation laws that have been enacted since then have done little to prevent ecological disruption. "Most conservation laws are part of an 'Administration Handbook' telling corporations how to apply for resource extraction rather than controlling them."[5]

It was during Franklin D. Roosevelt's administration (1930s) that

Soil erosion and the Dust Bowl of the 1930s

United Press International Photo

the Federal government became the primary watchdog over the environment. The Tennessee Valley Authority (TVA) created employment for thousands, reduced the flooding of the Tennessee River and created new hydroelectric power supplies. The Roosevelt administration also instituted federal programs concerned with protecting soil, clearing forests, dredging rivers, and generally trying to upgrade the environment. But at the same time new plants and factories were being built that contributed to the increasing problems of pollution and misuse of resources.

NATURAL RESOURCES

All of our natural resources come from the environment around us and are a part of a system balanced through the evolutionary process. Upsetting that balance results in a chain-effect altering of the system not caused by natural evolution. The earth functions as a biosphere where the surface layer of the earth and the surrounding atmosphere sustain all life. Land, air, water, and energy are basic to the maintenance of all living organisms. Biologists talk about *ecosystems*. An ecosystem is an interconnected web of living and nonliving things. Their interrelations lead to a relatively stable equilibrium. This can be a relationship between forms of life, or interaction with a lake or forest, or even the earth itself. As an example of a simplified ecosystem, Barry Commoner describes the relationship, and need for balance, between rabbits and lynx in Canada. When there are many rabbits, the lynx prosper. But as the population of lynx increase, they ravage the rabbit population and reduce it. As a result rabbits become scarce and are not sufficient to support the numerous lynx. As the lynx die off because of lack of food, the rabbits are hunted less and increase in number. The cycle is continuous. Disbalance could enter the system if, during one swing, the lynx managed to eat all the rabbits. With no more rabbits, the lynx might die off and the entire system would collapse. The more complex the ecosystem, the more successfully it can resist a stress or disbalance. For example, in the rabbit-lynx system, if the lynx had an alternative source of food they might survive the sudden depletion of rabbits.[6]

An ecosystem is generally never stable for very long in nature. On a large scale, floods or fires can bring about rapid change. The tendency is generally to maintain a stable equilibrium, but the ecosystem can also be upset by bringing in an alien species. Alternately, the elimination of a native species can also disrupt the system by removing the natural enemy of other species. "In India, where some snakes are poisonous, it is common to kill any snake seen. As a result India loses one fourth of its grain crops to rats and mice."[7]

There are four interrelated ecological concepts that are a part of ecosystems. (1) *Interdependence*, meaning that everything is related to and depends on everything else. This may be indirect but nevertheless the removal of one part will negatively affect all other parts. (2) *Diversity*, meaning there is a wide variety of different life and life support parts to the system. In general the greater the diversity of species, the greater the probability of survival for any one species. (3) *Limits*, defining the finite growth for any organism. There are limits on numbers of a given species an environment can support. (4) *Complexity*, referring to the intricacy of the relationships between the various parts.

In general the view of mankind toward the environment sometimes may have been fearful, but rarely was it respectful. In the 19th century, the idea of man's control over nature or even man against nature was closely linked with the idea of infinite and inevitable progress. Technology and invention were seen as evidence of success. "The optimism was based on material progress, on the idea that this high rational civilization in its onward movement not only advanced itself but was also producing humanized environments which went along with it."[8] We want to look more specifically at America's natural resources and what is happening to them.

Except for a few forms of microorganisms, all forms of life take oxygen directly from the air or from quantities of air dissolved in water. Water is also directly absorbed and converted by living things. The purity and availability of water sets limits for all forms of life. The availability of energy needed to maintain life rests on a complex set of interrelationships and the passing on of energy through various living organisms. The primary source of all energy is the sun. Most plants convert solar energy into food through the use of water and chlorophyll. Animals cannot use the sun's energy directly, but get it through eating the food that plants manufacture or by eating other animals.

Humans have drawn from nature vast amounts of natural resources. These have been the fossil fuels, metals, and other minerals. These are all nonrenewable resources, which means they exist in a finite amount. Turner points out that there may someday be substitutes for fossil fuels, but there can be no substitutes for the depletion of nonrenewable resources. "Life simply cannot be sustained without air, water, and soil."[9]

Water. Water is constantly on the move. It is found in the atmosphere as vapor where it condenses and falls to the earth as some form of precipitation. It goes underground or runs off into streams, rivers, and eventually into the oceans. It evaporates into the atmosphere, and the cycle starts again. Seventy percent of the earth's surface is ocean water, and the oceans serve as a filtering system where all kinds of debris—mineral and biological—are dissolved, decomposed, and transformed into life-supporting substances. "It is the universal global sink, a vast septic tank from which clean water returns to man, beast, and plants by way of evaporation and precipitation."[10]

While the oceans cover 70 percent of the earth's surface, the resources of energy and oxygen needed for plant and fish life are concentrated in thin bands along the shore lines of the main continents. Ultimately all sea life depends on diatomes, a one-celled algae, that can survive only in well-lighted waters to a depth of not more than 250 feet. The marine organisms that feed on the diatomes live in shallow waters, especially in marshlands and saltwater estuaries. The estuary serves as a nursery and spawning ground for many species of fish eaten by humans. The estuaries serve as a nutrient-rich medium that is the base of the food chain for the larval states of many marine forms during that critical part of the life cycle. Ninety percent of our total seafood harvest is dependent in one way or another upon estuarine environments.[11]

The tidal-marsh ecosystem is an interface where the water and the land meet, and it is there that the nutrients tend to concentrate. In the temperate zones it is a place dominated by grasses that play a very important role in the total marsh ecosystem. Each year about half the grasses that fall into the marsh are decomposed by bacteria. As a result of this bacterial action, the total protein content of the grass vegetation is actually increased. But much of this land has been lost. "Of the 27 million acres which are important as fish and wildlife habitat in the 27 states sharing the estuarine zone, about 7 percent—close to 570,000 acres have been eradicated."[12]

Sixty percent of the United States population lives in a band 250 miles wide along the Atlantic, Pacific, and Gulf shorelines. Two thirds of the factories that produce pesticides, two thirds of those turning out organic chemical products, about 60 percent of those making inorganic chemicals, 50 percent of the petroleum refining plants, and two thirds of the pulp mills are located in the coastal states. "These estuaries, are becoming places where the pollutants merge and concentrate, often with deleterious effects on terrestial and aquatic wildlife."[13]

Many forms of life associated with the oceans have been wiped out. Sauer points out that the seas and their shorelines have been wantonly stripped of many mammals and birds without compensating substitutions. "The killing of the sea otter, for instance, has simply removed from our coasts the most valuable of all fur-bearing animals, whose presence could not diminish in the least any fishing or other marine activity of man."[14] There is strong evidence that whales may be heading toward the same extinction.

Historically, the availability of water has been a major influence in the location of settlements. This has occurred because of the necessity of water for survival and also because water provided a means of transportation. The availability of water often sets limits to population density. For example, in Australia most of the country has never been settled because there is no water. With rare exceptions, the availability of water determines the founding of settlements and the extent to which it will develop. A limited water supply also has meant that farming and grazing are constantly threatened by droughts. Every few years in Australia there are serious droughts and a great loss of livestock. Because of the lack of water, fire is also a danger. Every year there are large areas of land ravaged by fire.

In the United States, water supplies have become a problem for some cities. For example, in New York City there was a serious water shortage in 1965 because there had been two years of relatively light rain and the reservoirs were low. Cities like Houston and Phoenix are faced with water problems. These are cities with rapidly expanding populations which are almost entirely dependent on water from un-derground. In these areas the water levels underground are going down, and that water supply is not being replenished. These cities are going to have to seek new sources of water.

Minerals.   Minerals are nonrenewable. While there are fairly adequate supplies of some minerals, others are rapidly disappearing. For example, most gold in the United States has now been mined. While the middle of the last century saw the great gold bonanza in the West, the gold fields of today attract only tourists. Commoner points out that if all metals were valued as much as gold, the problem of mineral depletion would be solved for a very long time. "Depletion of metal is not so much governed by the amount of metal used as by the value placed on it and therefore its degree of reuse."[15] For example, while almost all gold is saved or reused most iron is never reused.

Land.   It can take as long as 1,000 years to produce one inch of topsoil. In many places in the world, topsoil is being lost at the rate of several inches per year because tilling has exposed it to wind and water erosion. The fertility of the land is also linked to its usage. Soils develop slowly by weathering. Sauer points out that in the old world peasant agriclture, because animals grazed in close proximity to crops, the animal manure kept the soil reasonably fertile. But in the United States, with more specialized farming, row crops and bare fields in the off season have resulted in a diminution of the organic matter in the soil. In addition, surfaces were eroded through the action of rains.[16]

It is estimated that a little over one acre of farmland is required to produce the minimal amount of food required for one individual. Presently most of the world's available land is being cultivated. Most attempts to increase the productivity of land requires tools and methods that in cost are beyond the reach of many poor countries. Moreover, the best fertilizers come from petroleum, which has gone up astronomically in cost.

In the United States, the average person today uses about as many calories, protein, and other foods as in 1946. But food is now grown on less land with the use of more fertilizers and pesticides than in the past. In another sense, Americans are less dependent on what can be grown because their clothes are more likely to be made of synthetic fibers than of cotton or wool.

One of the great resources of the land is forests. Forest lands serve a variety of important functions. They not only provide timber, but are also the habitat of wildlife and meet many recreational demands of humans. Forest lands also manufacture a major portion of the earth's oxygen supply. Forests absorb rain and release it slowly, as well as providing ground cover against erosion. It is estimated that when the first settlers arrived in America about 40 percent of the land was covered by forest. Today it is slightly more than 20 percent.

Through most of American history the forests were cleared to provide more land for farming. As a result, many forms of animal and bird life were destroyed because they were dependent on the forest lands for food and shelter. There are also many forest plants that depend on trees for shade, and they too disappear. Destruction of forests for agricultural reasons drastically alters the ecosystem. Deforestation and cultivation tend to decrease the air temperature, reduce the rainfall, increase the runoff of water, and promote soil erosion.

ENERGY

The need for energy and its uses is ubiquitous; it permeates almost every activity and every enterprise. Seventy-five percent of all energy used comes from oil and natural gas, both of which are finite and short lived nonrenewable resources. But whether provided by fuel-fed machines, by beasts of burden, or by people, work must be done in every production process, and work is generated only by the flow of energy. There is no way in which this thermodynamic imperative can be avoided. While the labor of people or animals may be substituted for certain inanimate forms of energy, this can be done only for certain production processes. For example, the possibility of ever flying from New York to Rome in a plane powered by human or animal labor is essentially zero.[17]

The United States's consumption of energy has doubled about every 12 years in recent history. About 97 percent of the primary energy comes from nonrenewable fossil fuels. About 38 percent is from the solid fuels (coal), with consumption rising relatively slowly. About 45 percent of the consumption is oil, with the consumption rate doubling about every decade. Almost 20 percent is the use of natural gas and that consumption rate is doubling about every 7 to 8 years.[18]

Around the world some estimates suggest a steady 4 to 5 percent annual increase in total world energy demand until the year 2000. This would mean doubling the supply available for use. If we take the figures for electricity—by far the most rapidly growing form of energy—American forecasts suggest an increase of at least 300 to 400 percent over the next 20 years. "Other developed economies are growing even faster, although from a lower base. The Japanese use of electricity, for instance, has been increasing by 15 percent a year."[19]

In the United States, at the present time, automobiles consume about 15 percent of the total energy used. This is about the same as all other forms of transportation put together. About 41 percent is used in industry and much of this is in hidden uses, in the refining of steel, aluminum, and other raw materials, the processing, molding, shaping, and joining of countless things. The rest of the energy is consumed in roughly equal parts in homes on one hand and in offices, shops, schools, and hospitals on the other hand. "Energy for space heating is the biggest single category both in residential and commercial establishments, amounting in all to about 18 percent of our energy supply."[20]

Oil. The process of oil formation, as with coal, is very slow. No oil has been found in sediments that are less than 15,000 years old. This is because the process of oil development *sometimes* takes a very long time, possibly hundreds of thousands of years.[21] Today, oil is the main source of fossil energy being consumed, and the supply may last only another 70 to 80 years. About two thirds of the world's ultimately recoverable liquid oil reserves, and more than half of current reserves, are in the Persian Gulf region. Most of the rest is divided between the USSR and the Western Hemisphere, with a small supply in Africa. It is thought that any substantial deposits, as yet unfound, will not greatly alter the time when physical depletion of oil will occur. "If oil consumption continues to double every decade, then a doubling of world reserves will delay depletion by only a decade."[22]

In only 50 years the United States has already discovered and consumed more than half the producible oil that was created over hundreds of million years. The United States consumes about 6 billion barrels of oil per year. The United States now produces about half and imports the other half. The immense cost of importing this oil is one of the principal causes for the balance of payments deficit, the declining value of the dollar in overseas money markets, and the high rate of inflation. The known reserves of oil in the United States are about 31 billion barrels. If the United States continues to extract 3 billion per year, the reserves will last us about 10 years. The off-shore fields are potentially important but they have not been proven.[23]

As the oil reserves decrease in the United States, the problem is less one of complete depletion than a question of economy. The oil will become too costly to produce. "We will exhaust not our oil, but

United Press International Photo

Exploration for off-shore oil

our ability to pay for acquiring it."[24] With each barrel of oil taken out of the ground, the next barrel becomes progressively more expensive. Inevitably, as a nonrenewable energy source is depleted, the cost of producing it rises faster and faster as more is produced.

Over the years the increasing demands for oil have been related to the production of more material things based upon the use of oil. The development of automobiles as the major means of transportation in America has called for huge amounts of oil. This is an expensive use of energy. For example, the energy required to move one ton of freight one mile by rail now averages about 624 Btu. (British thermal units). Trucks require about 3,460 Btu. per ton-mile. "This means that, for the same freight haulage, trucks burn nearly six times as much fuel as railroads and emit about six times as much environmental pollution."[25]

Modern agriculture also requires huge amounts of fossil fuels. The oil is used not only in powering farm equipment but in many of the fertilizers. Amory B. Lovins points out that this is a trade-off in forms of energy. We must often supply several times as much chemical and mechanical energy as we recover in the energy provided by the food.[26]

Basically the problem with the oil shortage is that a solution, if found, must come from alternative sources of energy. It is very doubtful that there are any huge new supplies of oil yet to be found around the world. The conservation of oil is important but it is only a small part of any answer to the energy shortage. "Oil conservation would be the answer only if there were a continuous but limited supply."[27]

Coal. About 56 percent of the world's ultimately recoverable coal resources are believed to be in the USSR and Eastern Europe, another 20 percent in the United States, 9 percent in the People's Republic of China, 8 percent in Canada, 5 percent in Western Europe, 1.4 percent in Africa, 0.8 percent in the oceans, and 0.18 percent in Central and South America. The world's supply of coal is expected to last for at least another century. However, as it is likely to be used more and more rapidly as other fuels are reduced in availability, this forecast may prove inaccurate.

In the United States, coal continues to be the major energy source in the development of electricity. Almost 50 percent of our electricity is generated by burning coal, 30 percent comes from using oil and natural gas, while the rest is derived from hydroelectric or nuclear plants. It is likely that the use of coal will be greater in the future for producing electricity because of the low contribution being made by nuclear energy.

TABLE 2–1

Production of Electricity in the United States by Source (In percentages)

	Coal	Oil	Gas	Nuclear	Hydro	Other
1971	44.3	13.6	23.2	2.4	16.5	0.05
1974	44.5	16.0	17.2	6.1	16.1	0.1
1976	46.4	15.7	14.4	9.4	13.9	0.2
1978	44.2	16.5	13.8	12.5	12.7	0.2
1979	45.8	16.2	11.9	13.5	12.5	0.2

Source: Adapted from "U.S. Energy Department," *The World Almanac* (New York: Newspaper Enterprises, 1980).

There are many problems related to the mining of coal. It is one of the dirtiest and most dangerous of all industrial occupations. In dig-

Mike Jaeggi

The results of strip mining

ging for deep coal, the miner's working life is threatened by the dangers of exploding mine gases, cave-ins, and flooding. Even when the miner survives to retirement he is apt to be incapacitated or have his life shortened by a lifetime of inhaling coal dust. Over the last 25 years, more than 6,500 men have been killed in mining coal.

Coal is also a dirty fuel to burn. At the turn of the century, when coal was widely used, the clouds of smoke from the factories and steam engines blackened the English midlands and industrial towns in the United States. "Not only soot and ash goes up the chimney if we let it, but also oxides of sulfur that damage plants and human lungs."[28]

Strip mining is another way of getting coal. While this is less dangerous for the miners, it has far greater costs for the environment. In strip mining, huge bulldozers and shovels strip away the earth and scoop out the coal beneath. This is relatively cheap and fast and very profitable. But the land is left almost useless. While over 3 million acres of land have been strip mined in the United States, only about one third has received any reclamation at all. Even in that one third, little has been done and most of the reclaimed land is not used.

Natural gas.   Cheap reserves of natural gas may be slightly closer to depletion than those of oil. Some estimates of natural gas reserves indicate that the world supplies will be exhausted before the end of this century. Even though the use of natural gas got a later start than oil, the recent demand has increased greatly. Gas is also limited by the fact that it is far more expensive to transport overseas than oil. But the cost of natural gas, like that of Middle Eastern oil, has very little to do with the cost of discovery and extraction. "It depends more directly on what the consumer can be made to pay."[29]

It has been argued that the supply of natural gas in the United States peaked in 1972 and has been declining ever since. Natural gas is a finite resource and is nonrenewable; increases in price will not expand the resource. Owen Phillips points out that rapidly increasing the prices can "only make producers more enthusiastic about extracting the remainder more quickly."[30]

Nuclear energy.   This is not a major source of energy anywhere in the world. In the United States, after 25 years and many billions of dollars worth of research and development, nuclear power has only just passed firewood as an energy source. Great Britain, the country most dependent on fission, generates only a tenth of its electricity in this way. Lovins points out that nuclear energy does not represent a large reservoir of cheap energy capable of being mobilized very simply and quickly. "It is, on the contrary, one of the most complex and unforgiving technologies known to man."[31]

The question of safety in nuclear fission is in the end not limited by human care or ingenuity but rather by inescapable human fallibility. The limit is not the human ability to solve problems on paper but rather to translate paper solutions into action. Lovins argues that nuclear safety is not a mere engineering problem that can be solved with sufficient care, "but rather a wholly new type of problem that can be solved only by infallible people. Infallible people are not now observable in nuclear or any other industry."[32]

When one compares the dangers of nuclear energy with coal mining, it is obvious that mining has been infinitely more dangerous in the past. No one has been killed in the production of nuclear energy, but thousands have in the mining of coal. But it is the potential danger of nuclear technology that creates risks unlike those of any other technology. The potential loss from a nuclear accident could be thousands of lives and a vast contamination of the environment.

Lovins suggests that the fallibility of producing nuclear energy might express itself in several ways. These are the problems of containing radioisotopes within the nuclear fuel cycle, containing them after they have been rejected as wastes, and containing strategic materials. These "fallibility problems" can be expected to increase if reactors proliferate. ". . . salesmen outrun engineers, investment con-

Ken Firestone

A nuclear energy protest

quers caution, boredom replaces novelty, routine dulls commitment, and less skilled technicians take over."[33]

The production of nuclear energy is dependent on uranium, and uranium supplies are very limited. If the United States started to use uranium to meet all energy requirements in this country, the supply would run out in about ten years. From this perspective, nuclear energy is not a potentially great source of energy.[34]

Another problem with nuclear energy as a source is that American nuclear power plants operate on a once-through basis. Materials are not recycled and therefore wastes accumulate rapidly. "Reliable figures are difficult to obtain, but presently there seems to be about 2,500 tons [waste in] storage and a further 1,000 tons are being added each year."[35]

It appears clear at the present time that nuclear energy has failed to become a major source of energy in the United States. Certainly the industry has failed to produce cheap electrical power. It is about 20 percent higher than the cost of power from the new coal-fired plants. As a result, public utilities have been sharply cutting new orders for nuclear power plants. They fell from 34 in 1973 to an annual average of four in 1975–77. In 1978 only two new plants were ordered and a number were canceled.[36]

Nuclear energy is becoming less and less a viable alternative for solving energy problems. Even its supporters don't see much of a future. "In November 1977, John O'Leary, Deputy Secretary of Energy, said that if we continue with the status quo, 'the nuclear option is dead.' And in fact, since then it may have died at Harrisburg."[37]

To some extent, the death knell for nuclear energy has been the result of organized resistance. Since the end of the Vietnam war, there has been a need for many Americans to find some acceptable outlet for their need to resist. As a result, part of the antiwar group moved quite easily into the antinuclear area. But probably the most significant blow was the Three Mile Island accident in 1979, which made clear to Americans the potential danger from nuclear energy plants.

Solar energy.   Commoner argues that solar energy could at this time rapidly invade the energy market. He sees solar energy as coming in a wide variety of possible forms. In forested areas Commoner sees solar energy in the form of solid fuel (wood), while in agricultural areas as a liquid fuel (alcohol made from grain), or as a gaseous fuel (methane made from manure or plant residues). In rainy, mountainous areas, it would be used as hydroelectric power; in moderately or intensely sunny places, as a photovoltaic electricity; in breezy places, as wind generated electricity; and almost everywhere as direct heat.[38] At the present time hydroelectricity provides only about 2 percent of the world's primary energy, and geothermal energy is far less.

Commoner also argues that the solar devices that make economic sense are also the most compatible with the environment. "Solar collectors, photovoltaic cells, and windmills simply transfer solar heat from one place to another."[39] But there are many limits in the use of solar power. The basic problem is that the radiant energy from the sun is diffused. "Therefore to capture even supplementary micropower for domestic use means, for example, that the roof of a house virtually has to be covered with solar panels. To provide megapower for heavy industry or to run a whole city, solar collectors would have to cover many square miles."[40]

The Energy Crisis.   The energy crisis became a social problem for many Americans in early 1974 when they found they couldn't get gasoline for their automobiles. A. Clay Schoenfeld points out that there was little or no interest by newspapers in energy resources until 1971. But in 1974, the coverage shot up during the shortage of gasoline. After that, the energy coverage declined until 1977 when President Carter's "moral equivalent of war" claim returned the energy issue to the newspapers.[41] Interest again decreased until the gasoline shortage of 1979.

As suggested earlier, the limited reserves of fuel clearly show there is an energy crisis. Both oil and natural gas are short-lived resources that can easily be exhausted in the lifetime of those who are young adults today. Because we receive 75 percent of our energy from those sources, much of our lives is based on the continuation of that energy source. That energy is used not only to power automobiles and heat homes, but also to extract other raw materials from the ground, "to manufacture furniture and fertilizers, cement for housing, steel, aluminum, and plastics. Energy derived from oil and natural gas is used in the brewing of beer, and in building the machines that make other machines."[42]

There is no evidence that the future loss of oil and natural gas as energy resources will be quickly replaced by other sources of energy. While there have been some advances in the conversion of oil shale, solar energy, geothermal energy, and the use of solid wastes, they have not been great. In 1974, projections were that those sources could fill only 13 percent of the energy demands of America by the year 2000. In 1980, however, the projected percent would be even lower.

In general, the government policy has been not to take the energy shortage seriously. In part government officials know that to put controls on energy usage is politically unpopular. But for most politicians, as for most Americans, there is the tacit assumption that a new source of energy will turn up to save America and lead to even faster growth. This is to a great extent based on the American myth of inevitable ingenuity—the myth that whenever something is really needed an answer will be found. However, such innovations are nowhere in sight. There is always the assumption that there is an answer, but in the energy shortage there may be no answers and therefore no new solutions.

Much of what makes the energy shortage a social problem is its economic consequences. Many of the harmful consequences of the nonrenewability of energy resources are economic. The progressive depletion of the supplies of energy sources leads to a rapid rise in the cost of production and therefore in their price. In turn, the high price of energy intensifies inflation, reduces the standard of living, hinders new industrial investments and aggravates unemployment. The end result is a serious threat of economic depression.[43]

Commoner argues that the energy crisis is the result of the social mismanagement of the world's resources. Because it is social it can be resolved "and man can survive in a humane condition when the social organization of man is brought into harmony with the ecosystem."[44] This assumes that man is socially and psychologically capable of putting aside greed and vested interests for the purposes of sacrificing for the good of all. The occasions when this has happened are few and far between.

Lovins writes that the many technologies that would increase the energy supply are slow, costly, and risky. Therefore, industrial societies should immediately undertake lasting and fundamental—not merely temporary and cosmetic—measures to conserve energy in all sectors and forms, and particularly to minimize the consumption of oil and natural gas. Political imagination and strong moral leadership will be required.[45] Again, these are hardly realistic expectations in present American society.

It appears to be a very strong possibility that the energy crisis will become an increasingly severe social problem. The conservation of present energy sources and the development of new ones will be relatively insignificant. As a result, in a few years, more and more American styles of life dependent on huge amounts of energy will deteriorate. This would greatly increase the possibilities of war, either with other countries over energy supplies or within this country over the control of what energy is still available.

POLLUTION

As discussed earlier, pollution is not a new problem. There has long been the pollution of water with waste and the air with smoke. But in the past there was relatively little that was used and then discarded. The glass and the cloth people had was often used and reused. They did throw away ferrous metals that would rust away in time, paper and wood that would burn, or cloth that rotted away quickly.

In the past, waste usually became a part of an ecological cycle. In that system no waste accumulated because nothing was wasted. A living thing that is a natural part of an ecosystem cannot, by its own biological activities, upset the ecosystem. Human beings, as animals, are no less tidy than other living organisms. However, they pollute the environment because they have broken out of the closed, cyclical network in which all living things function. As a result they introduce foreign substances into the ecosystem that cannot be absorbed.

Technology has been the overwhelming cause of pollution. This is true even though only about one third of humanity has entered the technological age. Around the world, rivers are catching fire, burning bridges over them. Many lakes and inland seas, the Baltic and the Mediterranean, are under threat from untreated wastes which feed bacteria and algae. This exhausts the water's oxygen and threatens marine life. Dust and particles in the atmosphere are altering the earth's temperature in unpredictable ways. The United States is making a great contribution to pollution. "With only one fifteenth of the world's population, the United States extracts 35 percent of the world's minerals and energy and accounts for one half of the industrial pollutants emitted into the world ecosystem."[46]

However, technological pollution is not just a characteristic of American society. For example, pollutants that are found in waters in the Soviet Union are similar to those in the United States. There is no evidence that the technologies introduced into the USSR after World War II were very different from those that have dominated United States production. "In general, the modern technologies of the Soviet Union appear to be as counterecological as those introduced into the United States economy."[47]

There are two basic types of pollution. First, *nondegradable* pollutants are materials and poisons, such as aluminum cans, mercury salts, and DDT, that either do not degrade (return to the ecosystem's cycle) or degrade very slowly in the natural environment. The nondegradable pollutants not only accumulate, but often become "biologically magnified" as they move through biochemical cycles and along food chains. Frequently they combine with other compounds in the environment to produce additional toxins. Second are the *biodegradable* pollutants such as domestic sewage. These can be rapidly decomposed by natural engineered processes. Problems can arise with degradable pollutants when the imput into the environment exceeds its decomposition or disposal capacity. For example, "current problems of sewage wastes result mostly from the fact that cities have grown much faster than treatment facilities."[48]

TABLE 2–2

Solid Waste Generation, Resource Recovery, and Disposal by Type of Material, 1976 (In millions of tons, except as indicated)

Gross waste generated	144.7
Per person per day (lbs.)	3.68
Resources recovered	9.2
Per person per day (lbs.)	.23
Net waste disposed of	135.5
Per person per day (lbs.)	3.45
Paper	42.3
Glass	13.5
Metal	12.2
Plastics	5.1
Food waste	23.0

Source: Adapted from: U.S. Department of Commerce, Bureau of the Census, *Statistical Abstract of the U.S. 1980* (Washington, D.C.: U.S. Government Printing Office, 1978), p. 214.

It has been pointed out that American ideology about the relationship of man to nature leads to many problems of the misuse of nature. Some of the ideological assumptions are as follows: (1) Man is the source of all value. What man wants is a reasonable goal. (2) The universe exists only for man's use, and anything that gets in his way will be removed. (3) The primary purpose of man is to produce and to consume. (4) Production and consumption must increase endlessly. (5) Natural resources are unlimited. (6) There is no need for man to adapt himself to the natural environment since he can remake it to suit his own needs. (7) A major function of the state is to make it easy for individuals and corporations to exploit the environment to increase wealth and power.[49] We want to look next at the different kinds of pollution.

Air pollution. The survival of the human race depends on the atmosphere remaining in essentially the same state it has long been. The air can carry substances that are harmful or even lethal. An excess of any such substances means pollution of the air. Most pollutants get into the air as a result of burning. Even though city dwellers seldom light their fires anymore, their daily lives are still dependent on the process of combustion. "The spotless electric stove ultimately derives its heat from the burning of coal, and something has to burn to make the television set function."[50] Electric utilities often use low-grade fossil fuel which gives off sulfur oxides. About 30 million tons of these oxides are released every year and, when mixed with chemicals found in the air, turn into sulfuric acid.

Cities have the greatest pollution problems. These are not only from coal and oil burning, but also from dust introduced into the air. The urban masses of concrete and asphalt are warmer, drier, and dustier than the country. In fact, the city may be 10 to 20 times dustier than the countryside. One consequence of this is that the dust reflects sunlight back into space and reduces the energy absorbed by the ground. The city has 30 percent less sunshine and 90 percent less ultraviolet radiation. The city also has much more fog than the surrounding countryside.[51]

Over one third of the pollutants released into the air comes from autos. The major chemical of the exhaust is carbon monoxide, which is highly toxic. Nitrogen oxide is also given off which gives a brown tinge to the air. The sun often causes oxides to combine with waste hydrocarbons coming from car exhausts, and this forms peroxyacetyl nitrate which causes eyes to smart and also can damage the lungs. The automobile makes a further contribution to pollution in the form of pulverized rubber and asphalt, generated by abrasion of tires upon the street.[52]

The process of *inversion* refers to a temporarily stablized state of pollution. Temperature inversions most often happen in warm climates where heat from the sun warms the upper levels of the atmosphere. When air is still, it tends to develop into an upper zone of warm air and a lower zone of cold air. Because this is a reverse of the usual situation, it is called inversion. Normally the warmer air would move away, but because the air is still it sits there. And since cold air is denser than warm air, vertical circulation is prevented under these conditions. If the city is built in a valley and surrounded by mountains, the air is further trapped because it cannot move horizontally. An inversion can hold an air mass over a city for several days.

Los Angeles is a good example of a city that often suffers from inversion. It is in a valley surrounded with mountains, and therefore the weather can be locked in for several days. Of all American cities, it is the most dependent on the automobile. Jonathan H. Turner writes that the entire metropolitan area is built around motor transportation, "thereby creating a deadly smog problem while making alternative transport systems politically and economically unfeasible."[53]

One well documented case of the damage that can result from pollution inversion occurred in Donora, Pennsylvania in 1948. Donora is a steel mill city. At that time a thermal inversion trapped all the fumes from the steel mill, a sulfuric acid plant, and a zinc plant. More than 40 percent of the town's population of 14,000 became ill, and 20 died over the four days the inversion lasted.

In London, in December of 1952, there was an anticyclone over the city. This brought in a dense and two-tiered cloud cover, high barometric pressure, and slow, clockwise winds around the edges of about a 200-mile radius. Inside the mass the air stagnated. New pollutants from the continued use of energy added to the dead air hanging over the city. With time, what was a light fog turned into a thick, yellowish layer of smog. It got so bad that motorists could not drive and even pedestrians had to feel their way along the buildings. This lasted for five days before the wind increased enough to blow the polluted air away. More than 5,000 people died as a result of that inversion.

It has been clearly established in recent years that air pollution is related to a variety of health problems. Continuous exposure to air pollution can lead to such illnesses as bronchitis, emphysema, and lung cancer. It can also cause severe eye, nose, and throat irritation. Most of the statistical studies of the effects of air pollution on health show that it disproportionately affects the poor, children, and the aged and infirm. The most striking effects of air pollution on health appear when the victim's health is already precarious. It has been calculated that the risk of lung cancer from breathing New York City air is about equivalent to the risk of smoking two packs of cigarettes a day.[54]

Eugene P. Odum points out that as human mortality from infectious diseases shows a sharp decrease, the mortality and sickness from environmentally related respiratory diseases and cancer have shown an equally sharp increase. He estimates that a 50 percent reduction in air pollution in urban areas could save $2 billion annually in the aggregate cost of medical care and work hours lost because of sickness. This "does not count the 'cost' of human misery or death and disability caused by automobile and industrial accidents."[55]

Water pollution.   Many cities continue to be a major source of water pollution because their sewage systems are an elaborate combination of pipes laid one hundred years ago and modern treatment facilities. But the most pressing problems of water pollution come from industrial waste. Rivers and lakes have long been the dumping grounds for many industries. It is not only the waste that is introduced, but also that many industries depend on water for cooling in their production. They often take water from rivers and return it both polluted and heated.

The balance of life in the water depends on the supply of oxygen in the water and also on proper levels of nitrogen and phosphorous. Chemicals put into the rivers and lakes by industry drastically reduce the oxygen-carrying capacity of the water. When heat is put back into the water this can raise the temperature as much as 20 or 30 degrees. Most aquatic life is cold-blooded and, when the water temperatures go up beyond their capacity for metabolic adjustment, they die. The serious impact of this can be realized when one knows that fish are especially valuable as food because they provide a major part of the world's supply of protein.

Lake Erie has often been presented as a striking example of what pollution can do to a large body of water. Lake Erie has been a major natural resource for a region with a half a dozen large cities and a population of about 13 million. In the past, the area had a large and varied industry ranging from rich farm lands to profitable fisheries. However, the process of creating that wealth led to changes. Pollution has been so great that the original ecosystem has been greatly altered. Most of the beaches that were once used have been closed by pollution. In the summer, great piles of decaying fish and algae stack up on the shore. The water is thick with oil and one of the tributary rivers has even burst into flame. "Lake Erie's living balance has been upset and if the lake is not yet 'dead,' it certainly appears to be in the grip of a fatal disease." [56]

Water can also be polluted by chemicals from fertilizers. The wide use of nitrate and phosphate fertilizers affects the quality of water. Both irrigation and rain can cause the runoff of large amounts of these chemicals into rivers and lakes. The fertilizers will often work in the water in the same way as they do on land. Because they encourage growth, they create algae blooms which became huge masses which grow rapidly and then die. One consequence is that the decay of the blooms uses up oxygen that may kill off fish by depriving them of their oxygen needs. The dead algae usually settles to the bottom. It has been estimated that in some parts of Lake Erie there may be a layer of algae as much as 100 feet thick. The runoff of chemical fertilizers into lakes, rivers, and underground waters also can lead to the pollution of drinking water.

United Press International Photo

Soapsuds on Lake Erie

Oceans are also coming to be increasingly altered by pollution. Recent studies show that the ocean's phytoplankton, which provides the earth with 80 percent of its air, is accumulating chemical substances that may eventually prove toxic to vital life forms.[57] In addition, as discussed earlier in the chapter, there has been the destruction of many estuaries because of pollution.

Land pollution. In general the pollution of land results from the introduction of the chemicals used as pesticides. Land can also be worn out because of poor crop planning, or land can be ruined by erosion caused by air and water. Even though the United States is a recently settled country, it leads the list of exploited and dissipated land wealth countries. Consequently, a great need for chemical fertilizers and pesticides exists.

Anytime that a toxic material is introduced into either air, water, or soil, that material will reappear in the other two. This interdependence also extends to all creatures living in the three elements. Because the toxic materials are nondegradable they are not lost but move from one element to another or into various forms of life.

In the past insects posed a serious problem in farming. To deal with this problem, pesticides were developed which were relatively simple chemical compounds such as lead arsenate. These killed only a narrow range of insects, and they were biodegradable into relatively harmless residues. But then came the development of DDT which was far more lethal, long lasting, and killed a wide spectrum of bugs. But

DDT does not readily biodegrade and remains as a stable compound for many years. DDT settles into the ground, enters water supplies, and with time pollutes the oceans.

In American agriculture, pesticides have often been used to maintain single crop agricultural production. This has simplified the ecosystem. One consequence has been to increase the vulnerability of the ecosystem to diseases and pests, which results in an increasing reliance upon the use of chemicals. In the case of DDT, when some organisms are eaten by other larger organisms in food chains that embrace thousands of species, the chemicals are passed along the chain at nearly full strength.[58] DDT can also be spread by the wind in much the same pattern as radioactive fallout. "When DDT is sprayed in the air, some fraction of it is picked up by air currents as pollen is, circulated through the lower troposphere and deposited on the ground by rainfall."[59] Migrating birds and fish can also transport DDT for thousands of miles.

Noise pollution. In recent years there has been an increasing awareness of danger from noise. It is not just that loud noises are often an irritant, but they can sometimes damage a person's hearing. For example, it has been demonstrated that the continuous loud playing of music, popular in recent years, can lead to severe hearing problems. Odum writes that it is now clear that high intensity sounds such as those emitted by many industrial machines and aircraft, if continued for long periods of time, are not only disturbing to humans, but can also permanently impair hearing.[60]

There has been some attempt in recent years to provide protection against noise. There is a great need for enforced zoning and planning that separates noisy industrial areas and highways from space where people live. "In metropolitan areas, green belt vegetation, and open space in general, may have as great a value in sound amelioration as in air purification."[61]

Some Consequences of Pollution

The possible damage from pollution is great. It kills plants and many forms of life. It is hazardous to health and erodes and dirties everything around us. A major part of the pollution problem is that technology produces many things that can't be degraded. This is true of DDT, which moves through a food chain, and a beer can, which has no purpose after it is emptied.

There are three choices in dealing with waste materials. First, they can be dumped untreated into the nearest environmental setting such as the air, a river, lake, soil, well, or ocean. Second, they can be contained and treated within an area designed for environmental waste.

These can be seminatural ecosystems such as oxidation pounds, spray-irrigated forests, and land fills. Those settings will do most of the work of decomposition and recycling. Third are the more recent methods of treating waste through artificial chemomechanical regeneration systems.[62]

The economic costs of pollution are confusing because they are not usually made explicit. Modern industrial societies do not normally include in their production costs the spewing of effluents into the air or the overloading of the land with solid waste. "Thus they pass as a hidden and heavy cost to the community where it is either met by higher taxation and public spending or by the destruction of amenity."[63] As Boulding observes, when somebody pollutes something and somebody has to clean it up, "the cleanup is added to the national product and the pollution is not subtracted! That is ridiculous."[64]

In general, the cost of pollution can be measured in three ways. First, we can measure the loss of resources through unnecessary wasteful exploitation, as for example, the destruction of fish through the pollution of rivers. Second, we can measure the cost of pollution abatement and control, like the millions of dollars passed on to the automobile buyer for some kinds of emission control over exhaust fumes. Third, we can measure the cost of loss of human life and of poor health, as for example, the relationship of air pollution to many respiratory health problems.[65]

REASONS FOR POLLUTION AND RESOURCE DEPLETION

In this section we want to look at some of the relationships between social factors and pollution. It is a combination of the rapid expansion in populations along with the technological explosion that has brought about environmental pollution. It is generally agreed that increasing affluence of persons in technologically advanced countries has contributed more to pollution than the rise in population. People are not willing to give up the material niceties of life.

In the underdeveloped countries, which make up over 40 percent of the world's population, the shortage of available food and resources is associated with chronic pollution and disease caused by human and animal wastes. By contrast, in the affluent or developed nations, agro-industrial chemical pollution is now more serious than organic pollution. "In addition, global pollution of air and water mostly emanating from the developed countries threatens everyone."[66]

A continuing increase in populations will continue to have great significance for pollution. If a standard of living remains constant, a population that doubles itself will also double its pollution. If the number of "things" people possess or use up increases, so does the potential destructive power of the useless remains. Old automobiles don't simply fade away, yet their metal content is seldom recycled. As Shirley Foster Hartley points out, pollution is also a result of the time lag in "our recognition of the problems created by people pollution and our lack of concern or inability to remedy the problems."[67]

While the production of needs, food, clothing, housing, has just about kept up with the increase in the population in the United States, the kinds of goods produced to meet those needs have changed drastically. New production technologies have replaced old ones. Soap powder has been replaced by synthetic detergents and natural fibers (cotton and wool) have been displaced by synthetic ones. Often steel and lumber have been replaced with aluminum, plastics, and concrete. The products of the new technologies do not readily return to nature.

Technology

The American commitment to technology has been so great that rarely are the costs examined. Our technological commitment is also reflected in the great demand for raw materials. While about 6 percent of the world's population is in the United States, this country uses about 30 percent of the annual world consumption of industrial raw materials. Many of these must be imported, but as more countries become industrialized they are going to be less willing to export their natural resources.

To a great extent the technological development in the United States over the past 150 years has been possible because of cheap energy. But as the energy resources deplete and become exorbitant in cost, so do the technological problems and costs. The wider prosperity of the past has been due to the expansion of technology which has been based on enormous supplies of energy. Energy is at the root of productivity, of the ability to make "more for less"[68] Yet the costs may be rapidly becoming too great.

The technological process clearly links energy use with pollution. The economy of a society extracts stock resources such as oil, coal, and gas. These resources are used to create energy which, in turn, powers the continually expanding and productive technologies of industrial societies. The conversion of energy produces goods, and their consumption is accompanied by the discharge of enormous quantities of waste materials.[69]

Few societies have ever dealt directly with the question of what the consequences of technology might be for the depletion of resources or for pollution. Those who make relevant decisions often have little incentive, responsibility, or authority to consider the possi-

bility that a technological application might have undesirable consequences. In general the trend has been to apply technology as long as
it can be expected to yield a profit, and to assume that any harmful
consequences which might ensue either will be "manageable or will
not be serious enough to warrant a decision to interfere with the
technology."[70]

Commoner argues that environmental degradation usually results
from the introduction of new industrial and agricultural technologies.
Ecologically the technologies are faulty because they are designed for
singular problems and fail to take into account the inevitable side effects that result. This is inevitable because in nature, no single part is
isolated from the whole ecological fabric. While technology can design
a useful fertilizer or an efficient nuclear bomb, it cannot cope with the
total system into which the fertilizer or the bomb intrudes. As a result
there are such disastrous ecological surprises as water pollution or radioactive fallout.[71]

Vested interests are the curicial forces in both the depletion of natural resources and in pollution. The major problem in pollution control is the vast economic and political power of large polluters. Water
pollution exists mainly because polluters have more influence over
government than do those they pollute. So long as they have the
greater power there will be pollution. They only way that new laws
will work is if the scales of influence over government are tipped in
favor of the public. Unless that happens, the requirements the government sets will be constantly violated and the penalties rarely in-
voked.[72]

"Now they say we can't dump our industrial wastes in the river
anymore! My God! What's a river for?!?"

Reprinted by permission The Wall Street Journal

There is a lack of effective voices that can be made heard in opposition to potentially harmful technological developments. On the one hand, the vested interests of technology are the utilitarian values reflected in business and industrial interests which are related to the accumulation of profit and exploitation of natural resources. On the other hand, the public mainly argues that the environment should be adapted to, rather than exploited. The Sierra Club and the Audubon Society are conservation groups that have been around since the beginning of the century but they have relatively little power or influence.

The common view of environmentalists has been to picture them as antibusiness and antiprogress. Beginning with the vicious press attacks by the chemical industry in 1962 on Rachel Carson and her book *Silent Spring,* the environmental movement has come to be seen by many conservatives as anti-American. Schoenfeld observes that in the 1960s the conservation movement was seen by most as "out there." During that period the symbols of conservation were Smokey the Bear and contour plowing. But in fact, in the 1960s the environmental problems were as much urban as rural. Moreover, the new breed of ecologists was viewed with great distrust by many because they were seen as espousing a kind of counter-culture that some people considered subversive. The ecologists called into question the sanctity of the GNP (Gross National Product) as a measurement of economic well being.[73]

James S. Bowman suggests that persons who are concerned with the environment are not clear in their minds about the implications of their attitudes. They understand and believe that an environmental ethic is not isolated from fundamental social values and see that there are inconsistencies between environmental values and traditional (growth) values. As long as they do not see that environmentalism is a social battle, they are not likely to see a need to change people's values. "Under such conditions, these environmentalists may be more a part of the problem than a part of the solution."[74]

As discussed earlier, the concern of business for conservation has been very limited. Phillips writes that some utility companies and oil companies, particularly Exxon, have made a few belated and usually half-hearted attempts to encourage conservation. Attention through the mass media has been sporadic and sometimes confused because of misinformation. "The energy crunch is much worse than is generally believed and very much worse than most industry lobbyists would have us believe.[75]

The use of unlimited natural resources has long been a basic part of America's industrial development. When capital came to replace property as the source of power in society, entrepreneurs were able to raise capital by showing that they would be able to make profits on investments. One way in which this was done was through the free use of rivers and air that could be used for production and to get rid of waste. Basically American factories pollute because their profits are based on processes that create pollution. However, this is a commitment more to technology than to a political ideology. This is indicated by the fact that the existing environmental record in socialist countries is not much better than that of the United States.

The American economic system is based not just on continual levels of consumption but on constant attempts to bring about greater and greater consumption. This is primarily the function of advertising. But when there are continually increasing demands for industrial and agricultural goods, this stimulates higher levels of production requiring the use of greater amounts of energy. And these influences are reciprocal. Once an extensive productive system exists, this system encourages consumer demand and sustains the cultural values as well as the structural arrangements in the society that give rise to an industrial form of economic organization.[76]

With regard to pollution, the economics seem clear. The technology required for pollution controls, unlike ordinary technology, does not add to the value of the output of saleable goods. Therefore, the extensive technological reform of agricultural and industrial production that is required for the environmental crisis cannot contribute to the growth of productivity.[77] Business will have little motive to contribute to the costs of products that are not reflected in the profits.

The costs of saving the environment will be very high. It could call for as much as $50 billion per year for at least a decade just to restore the environment to an acceptable level of health. It would probably call for as much of an expenditure after that just to maintain the ecological balance. This means that pollution control would cost money in higher taxes and higher prices. It would also eliminate many jobs in industry and would make "luxuries" of many goods and services heretofore taken for granted. It would also require a willingness to save, conserve, and recycle.[78] There is certainly no evidence at this time that Americans would be willing to make those kinds of sacrifices. The energy crisis and the dangers of pollution will have to become far more severe than they are now before there will be any great social concern.

Government Influence

In one respect the federal government has made a direct contribution to the destruction of the environment. For example, some of the projects developed by the Army Corps of Engineers have been catastrophes for the ecosystem. A few years ago a series of canals were constructed in Florida that resulted in the lowering of the water table in the Everglades; this led to the destruction of much of the area's wildlife.

Politics and government control of pollution are often closely linked. Frequently, the very government agencies that have been created to protect the public become advocates for the industries they are supposed to control. The Atomic Energy Commission was set up to promote and to regulate the nuclear power industry. But it has generally stressed the promotion of, and paid limited attention to the dangers and threats in the use and handling of, nuclear fuels.

Turner suggests several reasons why the antipollution codes have not been effective. First, the conservation and antipollution laws have been written in ambiguous language. When this has been coupled with the court systems favoritism of economic interests, government agencies have been reluctant to press charges. Second, the existing antipollution laws usually carry weak civil penalties and are seldom backed by criminal sanctions. Third, the vast majority of laws attack the symptoms, but not the sources, of pollution. Typically, they require treatment of pollutants after they have been created. The Clean Air Act did not assert that the internal combustion engine had to be replaced, but only that the ultimate emissions of the engine would have to be reduced. Fourth, many state antipollution laws have a "grandfather clause" that allows industries that polluted before the enactment of the law to continue their harmful activities.[79]

The weakest link in pollution abatement strategy is the inadequate legal protection of environmental quality and the consumer. As mentioned, the greatest economic rewards and the strongest legal protection have been given to those who produce, pollute, and exploit natural resources. Not only is environmental law inadequate at the local and national levels, but it doesn't even exist at the international level, despite the obvious need to protect the atmosphere and the oceans.[80]

Public Opinion

As mentioned earlier there was a dramatic increase in public awareness of environmental problems in the late 1960s and early 1970s. That increased awareness was linked to the Santa Barbara oil spill, the passage of the National Environmental Policy Act and the first Earth Day. Since that time, interest has decreased. One study done in California in 1978 found that although respondents were deeply concerned with inflation and taxes, they continued to believe in the support of environmental protection. In 1979 a Wisconsin study reported that about eight out of ten people were interested in environmental issues and nearly seven out of ten believed that taxes should be used to support a flow of environmental information.[81] These studies report support in the abstract. It is doubtful if there would be high public support if it meant more taxes or a lower standard of living.

There is evidence to suggest that the environmental movement is somewhat elitist in that it is an upper middle-class social movement especially for Democrats. This suggests why it is often seen to be antibusiness. Bowman suggests that in middle- and upper-class suburbs, something like recycling can be enthusiastically supported because it is nonideological. But when the ecological issues are seen as consequences of both consumption and production values, which call for a reexamination of social goals, then any consensus on environmental issues rapidly disappears. "It is a manifestation of the familiar pattern of concentration on the consequences of the problem, rather than the problem itself."[82]

Bowman goes on to suggest that the environmental cause could be reclaimed by more conservative conservation organizations who see compromises with "growthists" necessary for their organizational survival. If this occurs, then the values of industrial consumer America will remain prominent. This would lead to a "tidier" kind of pollution instead of an unequivocal commitment to environmental quality. It may be argued that ecology has run its course through the public's "issue attention cycle" into the postproblem stage, "where the problem becomes institutionalized and therefore, by definition, serious change is not to be expected."[83]

Phillip Althoff suggests a similar fate for pollution control. He argues that it is not enthusiastically embraced by all sectors of the general public and can often be viewed as antagonistic to the maximization of energy resources. As a result, it may fall by the wayside. He says, as too many fail to recognize, that the stages in both the environmental and energy games are the same—"individual prosperity in the short run and individual survival in the long run."[84]

At this time the political interest in pollution and energy is minimal. This is mainly because inflation and unemployment are seen as far more severe problems. The general lack of public enthusiasm for these issues has given politicians a basis for doing little or nothing. For the most part, politicians rarely lead but wait to follow. Phillips suggests that the lack of political interest may exist because very few realize the depth and inevitability of the problem even though they know a problem exists. In part, this is so because they are subjected daily to the powerful lobbying interests. "Energy represents very big money, and big money has big lobbying power. Elections come up every two, four or six years."[85]

THE FUTURE

While the energy and pollution picture is not completely black, it is a very dark gray. For example, there has been some reduction in the use of gasoline since the oil shortage during the summer of 1979. Some cities have shown improvement in the quality of air. There are also some rivers and lakes which have had waste reduced enough so there is a return of some marine life. DDT has been outlawed and strip mining is more carefully watched. But even these minor gains are under constant pressure to be revoked. For example, there are presssures to open up more strip mining and to relax the restrictions on auto emissions.

Commoner, one of the leading conservationists, writes that, based on the available evidence, he believes the present course of environmental degradation is so serious that if it is continued, it will destroy the capacity of the environment to support a reasonably civilized human society.[86] This is what makes environmental problems among the most serious of all social problems. If they are not alleviated, they could lead to the destruction of civilization as we know it. This could happen because the lack of energy would end our technologically based lives. Alternately, it could lead to wars in which most of the world is destroyed in the fight over control of what resources are still available.

In this chapter our interest has been in two interrelated social problems. First, the problem of energy resources. It is clear that the world is rapidly becoming faced with an energy shortage. This is because the fossil fuels are finite and as they are used up, cannot be replaced. The main attempt to solve this problem has been with the development of nuclear and solar forms of energy. Second, the problem of pollution, especially in the air and water, has become of great importance around the world. This pollution leads to other problems, especially those affecting health.

NOTES

1. Carl O. Sauer, "Theme of Plant and Animal Destruction in Economic History," in *Environ/Mental: Essays on the Planet as a Home*, by Paul Shepard and Daniel McKinley (Boston: Houghton Mifflin, 1971), p. 53.

2. Owen Phillips, *The Last Chance Energy Book* (New York: McGraw-Hill, 1979), pp. 22–23.

3. Sauer, "Plant and Animal Destruction," p. 54.

4. William G. Carleton, "Government's Historical Role in Conservation," *Current History* (June 1970), p. 326.

5. Jonathan H. Turner, "The Ecosystem: Interrelationships of Society and Nature," in *Understanding Social Problems,* by Don H. Zimmerman et al. (New York: Praeger Publishers, 1976), p. 306.

6. Barry Commoner, *The Closing Circle* (New York: Bantam Books, 1972), pp. 31–34.

7. Zai Whitaker and Romulus Whitaker, "If They're Killers, What Good Are They?" *International Wildlife* (May/June 1977), p. 16.

8. Clarence J. Glacken, "Man against Nature: An Outmoded Concept," in *The Environmental Crisis,* by Harold W. Helfrich, Jr. (New York: Yale University Press, 1970), p. 132.

9. Turner, "Ecosystem," p. 296.

10. Barbara Ward and Rene Dubas, *Only On Earth* (New York: Horton, 1972), p. 196.

11. William A. Niering, "The Dilemma of the Coastal Wetlands: Conflict of Local, National and World Priorities," in Helfrich, *Environmental Crisis,* p. 147.

12. Ibid., p. 144.

13. Ibid., pp. 143–44.

14. Sauer, "Plant and Animal Destruction," p. 56.

15. Commoner, *Closing Circle,* p. 119.

16. Sauer, "Plant and Animal Destruction," p. 57.

17. Barry Commoner, *The Politics of Energy* (New York: Alfred A. Knopf, 1979), p. 27.

18. Amory B. Lovins, *World Energy Strategies* (New York: Harper, 1980), p. 17.

19. Ward and Dubas, *Only On Earth,* p. 126.

20. Phillips, *Last Chance,* pp. 56–57.

21. Ibid., p. 15.

22. Lovins, *Strategies,* p. 25.

23. Phillips, *Last Chance,* p. 5.

24. Commoner, *Politics of Energy,* p. 27.

25. Commoner, *Closing Circle,* p. 169.

26. Lovins, *Strategies,* p. 18.

27. Phillips *Last Chance,* p. 7.

28. Ibid., p. 88.

29. Ibid., p. 47.

30. Ibid., p. 48.

31. Lovins, *Strategies,* p. 73.

32. Ibid., pp. 62–63.

33. Ibid., p. 63.

34. Kenneth E. Boulding, "Fun and Games with Gross National Product—The Role of Misleading Indicators in Social Policy," in Helfrich, *Environmental Crisis,* p. 165.

35. Phillips, *Last Chance,* p. 98.

36. Commoner, *Politics of Energy,* p. 45.

37. Ibid., p. 45.

38. Ibid., p. 54.

39. Commoner, *Closing Circle,* p. 57.

40. Phillips, *Last Chance,* p. 103.

41. A. Clay Schoenfeld, Robert F. Meier, and Robert J. Griffin, "Constructing a Social Problem: The Press and the Environment," *Social Problems* (October 1979), p. 46.

42. Phillips, *Last Chance,* p. 6.

43. Commoner, *Politics of Energy,* p. 30.

44. Commoner, *Closing Circle,* p. 298.

45. Lovins, *Strategies,* p. 125.

46. Turner, "Ecosystem," p. 298.

47. Commoner, *Closing Circle*, p. 278.

48. Eugene P. Odum, *Fundamentals of Ecology*, 3d ed. (Philadephia: W. B. Saunders, 1971), p. 434.

49. Scott Paradise, "The Vandal Ideology," in *Environ/Mental: Essays on the Planet as a Home*, by Paul Shepard and Daniel McKinley (Boston: Houghton Mifflin, 1971), pp. 222–25.

50. Walsh McDermott, "Air Pollution and Public Health," in *Man and the Ecosphere*, Readings from *Scientific American* (New York: W. H. Freeman, 1971), p. 137.

51. David Gates, "Weather Modification in the Service of Mankind: Promise or Peril?" in *Environmental Crisis*, pp. 36–37.

52. McDermott, "Air Pollution," p. 139.

53. Turner, "Ecosystem," p. 302.

54. Commoner, *Closing Circle*, p. 74.

55. Odum, *Fundamentals*, p. 433.

56. Commoner, *Closing Circle*, pp. 91–92.

57. Turner, "Ecosystem," p. 305.

58. Ibid., p. 304.

59. George M. Woodwell, "Toxic Substances and Ecological Cycles," in *Man and the Ecosphere*, Readings from *Scientific American* (New York: W. H. Freeman, 1971), p. 134.

60. Odum, *Fundamentals*, p. 448.

61. Ibid., p. 449.

62. Ibid., p. 438.

63. Ward and Dubas, *Only on Earth*, p. 49.

64. Boulding, "Fun and Games," p. 161.

65. Odum, *Fundamentals*, pp. 432–33.

66. Ibid., p. 432.

67. Shirley Foster Hartley, *Population: Quantity vs. Quality* (Englewood Cliffs, N.J.: Prentice-Hall, 1972), pp. 165–66.

68. Ward and Dubas, *Only on Earth*, p. 10.

69. Turner, "Ecosystem," p. 304.

70. Harvey Brooks and Raymond Bowerd, "The Assessment of Technology," in *Man and the Ecosphere*, Readings from *Scientific American* (New York: W. H. Freeman, 1971), p. 211.

71. Commoner, *Closing Circle*, p. 185.

72. David Zwick and Marcy Benstock, *Water Wasteland* (New York: Grossman Publishers, 1971), p. 395.

73. Schoenfeld, Meier, and Griffin, "The Press," p. 41.

74. James S. Bowman, "Public Opinion and the Environment," *Environment and Behavior* (September 1977), p. 409.

75. Phillips, *Last Chance*, pp. 52–53.

76. Turner, "Ecosystem," p. 295.

77. Commoner, *Closing Circle*, p. 269.

78. Turner, "Ecosystem," p. 310.

79. Ibid., pp. 306–7.

80. Odum, *Fundamentals*, p. 444.

81. Schoenfeld, Meier, and Griffin, "The Press," p. 53.

82. Bowman, "Public Opinion," p. 407.

83. Ibid., p. 410.

84. Phillip Althoff and William H. Greig, "Environmental Pollution Control: Two Views from the General Population" *Environment and Behavior* (September 1977), p. 455.

85. Phillips, *Last Chance*, p. 130.

86. Commoner, *Closing Circle*, p. 215.

SELECTED BIBLIOGRAPHY

Althoff, Phillip, and Greig, William H. "Environmental Pollution Control: Two Views from the General Population." *Environment and Behavior* (September 1977), pp. 441–56.

Bowman, James S. "Public Opinion and the Environment." *Environment and Behavior* (September 1977), pp. 385–416.

Commoner, Barry. *The Closing Circle.* New York: Bantam Books, 1972.

Commoner, Barry. *The Politics of Energy.* New York: Alfred A. Knopf, 1979.

Lovins, Amory B. *World Energy Strategies.* New York: Harper, 1980.

Odum, Eugene P. *Fundamentals of Ecology,* 3d ed. Philadelphia: W. B. Saunders, 1971.

Phillips, Owen. *The Last Chance Energy Book.* New York: McGraw-Hill, 1979.

Shepard, Paul, and McKinley, Daniel. *Environ/Mental: Essays on the Planet as a Home.* Boston: Houghton Mifflin, 1971.

Chapter 3

Urban Areas

There is a long tradition of associating social problems with the city. A rough distinction can be made between two levels of social problems that are identified with the city. First, there are problems inherent to the city itself, such as crowded living conditions. Second, there are problems which occur with high frequency in the city, although they also occur in rural areas, such as problems of delinquency or crime. In this chapter we will look at both of these kinds of problems. Additionally we shall focus on some social problems which occur in the suburbs.

Historical Background

Over the centuries as the city developed there have been changing definitions of its positive and negative effects on human welfare. In the far distant past the patterns of human subsistence to meet daily needs for survival were met by small groups. It was not until it was possible for some persons to produce a surplus that the town and later the city could emerge. The rise of cities therefore required a new and more productive agriculture. When this occurred, a new form of social organization emerged. Some persons could appropriate for themselves part of the food supplies that were being produced. These groups, "religious and governing officials, traders and artisans—could live in towns, because their power over goods did not depend on their presence on the land as such."[1]

It is probable that the first real urban settlements emerged between five and six thousand years ago in the Middle East and in Asia. Those first cities were quite small because the agricultural techniques

Historical Pictures Service, Inc., Chicago

Tenement life in New York in the past

were still very crude and it was not possible to produce much of a food surplus. The size of early cities was also limited by primitive means of communication and transportation as well as poor sewage and sanitation. From then until the emergence of industrialization, the vast majority of nonrural people lived in towns and small villages.

The modern city did not develop until about 1750. This occurred as a result of the discovery of sources of energy (coal and oil). Davis writes that in Western Europe, starting almost at the zero point, the development of cities not only reached the stage that the ancient world had achieved but continued beyond that. Cities kept expanding rapidly because of improvements in agriculture and transportation, the opening of new lands and new trade routes, "and, above all, the rise in productive activity, first in highly organized handicraft and eventually in a revolutionary new form of production—the factory run by machinery and fossil fuel."[2] The large modern city rests on an industrial base. It has come to depend on the high production of mechanized agriculture, on highly developed means of transportation, and on a vast range of nonagricultural jobs created by industrialization.

During the 18th and 19th centuries, as the cities of Europe and America were developing, they were received with mixed feelings. On one hand the great industrial production and wealth of the city had a tremendous impact on the lives of many. But at the same time the growth of the cities were often very rapid and with this growth came poor housing conditions. There emerged an anti-urban point of view that saw the city as threatening and often destructive to the individual, as well as to society. We will look more at this view shortly.

The historical emergence of cities in the United States can be seen as closely linked to the means of transportation available. The first great cities of the East—Boston, Philadelphia, and New York—are all major seaports. With the westward expansion, the cities that developed were on the great inland rivers—Pittsburgh, St. Louis, and New Orleans—or on the Great Lakes—Chicago, Detroit, and Cleveland. Later, with the development of railroads, cities were built or expanded along major rail junctions, such as Kansas City and Denver.

The cities expanded because of industrialization and transportation. But they also needed huge increases in population to fill the new industrial jobs. Initially, there was a great rural to urban movement of workers who left the farms and came to the cities. But the cities really expanded in size with the great flow of immigrants. The flow of immigrants through the 18th century had been mainly English, Scots-Irish, and Germans who came to settle on farmlands. In the early part of the 19th century came large numbers of Irish and the second wave of Germans; both of these groups became primarily city dwellers. By the middle of the 19th century, the Irish-born made up 25 percent and the German-born 16 percent of the population of New York City. After the Civil War there were large numbers of immigrants from southern and central Europe—Czechs, Hungarians, Polish, Russians, and Ukrainians. These were mostly peasants brought in as contract laborers to work the factories in the Northeastern cities. Around the turn of the century Jews and Italians came in large numbers and they also settled in the cities.

The growth of the cities has continued until recent years because of the movements of various populations. While the first moves were by the native whites, followed by the great influx of foreign-born immigrants, the most recent large internal movement (following World War II) has been by blacks. All of these groups have sought economic opportunity. In all groups there was the belief that what could be found in the city would be better than what was left behind. Generally, this was true—not because what they found was so great, but rather because what they left behind was so bad.

Historically, unskilled laborers have comprised the bulk of migrants to the city because the factories built as a part of the industrial revolution were based on low-skilled jobs. Those industrial needs were met in the earlier decades by the peasants with little or no skills applicable to the industrial marketplace. Since the 1920s, with the strong restrictions against immigrants, those jobs have been filled through internal migration. Generally, the recent movement has been by blacks coming from the rural South to southern and northern cities. There also have been southern whites moving to Chicago and Detroit, and in the West Mexican Americans have moved to West-Coast cities.

As suggested, the urban phenomenon has been worldwide, although developing at different times and rates in different countries. Overall, the world is becoming increasingly urban. In 1850, only 2 percent of the world's population lived in cities of over 100,000 population. In 1900 it was 6 percent and by 1970 it was 24 percent. In recent decades the concentration of populations in urban areas has become a relatively uniform pattern of change throughout the world. By 1975, almost 30 percent of the world's population lived in towns and cities of more than 20,000 people.[3]

In part the urban expansion has been related to the development of transportation systems that allow many cities to draw upon a worldwide market. The great increases in transportation and trade have enabled urban populations to draw from an ever widening area. In many respects it can be said that today the hinterlands of many cities are the entire world. Such modern countries as Britain, Holland, and Japan could not maintain their urban populations entirely from their own territory.[4]

Since 1800 the urbanization of the world has continued, and there is no evidence of its slackening. This suggests the evolution is far from being over. What percentage of a population can be urban is difficult to say, but at present in most countries there is still room for further numbers to move to the cities. In the United States about 70 percent of the population is urban dwellers while in countries like Australia and Holland the rate is getting close to 90 percent. "The three fourths of humanity who live in underdeveloped countries are still in the early stages of an urbanization that promises to be more rapid than that which occurred earlier in the areas of northwest European culture."[5]

TABLE 3–1

Standard Metropolitan Statistical Areas (SMSA) of the Five Largest U.S.
Cities, by Rank in 1970 and Projected Rank in 1980

| | *Rank* | | *Population* | |
SMSA	*1970*	*1980*	*1970*	*1980*
New York	1	1	9,974,000	10,054,000
Los Angeles–Long Beach	2	3	7,041,000	7,359,000
Chicago	3	2	6,978,000	7,610,000
Philadelphia	4	4	4,822,000	5,246,000
Detroit	5	5	4,435,000	4,891,000

Source: Adapted from: Metropolitan Life Insurance Company, *Statistical Bulletin, 56*
(December 1975), p. 5.

The largest cities in the world today are: Shanghai, 10,820,000;
Tokyo, 8,643,000; Mexico City, 8,628,000; Manila, 7,800,000; Moscow,
7,632,000, Peking, 7,570,000; New York, 7,481,000; Sao Paulo,
7,198,000; London, 7,111,000 and Seoul, 6,884,000.[6]

URBANIZATION IN THE UNITED STATES TODAY

In this section we want to look at the city as a social problem. What is
it about American cities that makes them a social problem? In other
words, what is it about the nature of cities that causes the people who
live in them to suffer from social problems? We need to first look
briefly at how cities expanded in the past.

Historically, annexation was a common event. Before 1900 this
method provided the essential source of city growth, as the city expanded to include areas at the edge. Brian J. L. Berry says the end of
the last century was the heyday of civic boosterism and rivalries between cities, and almost all metropolitan cities added large population
areas. But by the turn of the century the desire for autonomous suburban public services led to widespread defeat of annexation proposals.[7]
From 1900 to 1940 the total city growth by annexation declined steadily
from 3.4 percent to 0.8 percent. But in more recent times there has
been some increase in annexation and the percentage of city growth in
the 1960s was 6.2 percent.[8] The annexation of suburban areas slowed
down the overall loss of population by the city. The decline also was
reduced by the movement into the cities of blacks and other lower income groups.

The great economic and material growth of America was based on
its highly profitable development of industrialization. The development of vast industries called for concentrations of the population
which led to the development of larger and larger urban areas. The ra-

tionale for the cities during the vast industrial growth was almost entirely based on the gains that were being made in the name of capitalism. This meant that what was good for industrial development was all that really mattered. The fact that cities inevitably had problems as more and more persons were brought together was ignored or seen as secondary to the material gains of industrialization. Through roughly the first half of this century the powers that be were able to define the city as successful and to define the problems as minimal and manageable. Attempts to deal with such urban problems as poverty, crime, ethnic discrimination, and so forth were sporadic and stop-gap measures. Basically this was because there were no power blocks defining the city as having serious social problems.

However, in the 1920s some changes began to take place, and groups began to speak up about the social problems of the city. But their effect on social change was minimal because they had little influence relative to the power groups of industry, business, and later labor unions who wanted to maintain the city as it was. This continues to be true today, where little power for significant change in the city exists. As we shall see the changes that have occurred in the city have been the result of the emergence of what many believed to be a better means of living and producing goods and services—the suburbs.

To say that 50 years ago the developing interest in the problems of the city could not equal the power of the vested interests is not to say that movement was unimportant. One important effect it had was to bring a new focus of understanding of the city and to try to provide a body of knowledge about city living. In one sense it was almost inevitable that negative views of the city would emerge among intellectuals and academics. This occurred because most of these people were from small towns and rural areas. Their interpretations often were influenced by nostalgia for the rural past and suspicion of the urban present.

The emerging concern with the city provided American sociologists with an increasingly important area of life to study. It can be argued that the city provided sociology with the focus for making a great stride forward as an academic and research discipline. Many of the early social problems studied by sociologists became the substantive areas of post World War II American sociology, such as delinquency, crime, poverty, minority groups, family problems, etc.

In the 1920s and early 1930s the great influence was among a group of sociologists sometimes referred to as the "Chicago school." Under the influence of Robert Park, Ernest Burgess, and Louis Wirth urban sociology reached a high peak of prestige and prominence. In general it was argued that within the city social behavior was related to physical environment. Therefore in areas of physical deterioration there would be found social disorganization as indicated by high rates of delinquency, marital breakdown, etc. Leslie Kilmartin points out that this is different from the focus placed on the study of cities by European sociologists. They saw the development of the city much more as a product of wider economic and social change than did American sociologists.[9]

The studies of the 1920s and the 1930s did more than look at what was happening in the city. They also studied the negative consequences of urbanization for rural and small town life. The students of small town life tended to reinforce the picture of the looming specter that was pointed out by the Chicago school. "Namely, that throughout America—in big-city neighborhoods and in small rural towns—the social structure and sentiments of local community were dissolving."[10]

The dominant theme about the city's impact on the individual was the alleged loss of intimate ties in urban life. The most influential sociologist at the time was Louis Wirth. In 1938 he published *Urbanism as a Way of Life,* which became a sociology classic. Wirth argued that for those living in the cities, coming from very diverse origins and backgrounds, many of their common folk traditions of kinship and friendship would be absent or relatively weak. In the urban community, Wirth believed, such conditions as competition and formal control mechanisms would become substitutes for the bonds of solidarity that were relied upon to hold a rural society together. He saw the development of acquaintances in the city which were relationships based on utility rather than intimacy or kinship. This meant that the interaction of acquaintances had minimal personal qualities and were primarily a means for achieving private ends. Acquaintances were typically means-to-ends rather than ends in themselves.[11]

Wirth believed that urban inhabitants probably have more acquaintances than those living in rural areas. But given the vast number of people living in cities, of all those with whom one came into contact, one would only know a very small percentage. "Characteristically, urbanites meet one another in highly segregated roles. They are, to be sure, dependent on more people for the satisfactions of their life-needs than are rural people and thus associate with a greater number of organized groups, but they are less dependent upon particular persons, and their dependence upon others is confined to a highly fractionalized aspect of the other's round of activity."[12]

In general, the historical heritage from the earlier sociological view of the interpersonal nature of the city was that close forms of association had been pretty much destroyed. The intimacy of community was seen as replaced by the industrialized and bureaucratic controls that often had the effect of driving people to isolation and alienation. While it was seen that new forms of association developed, they were not broad based and personal but rather narrow and specific and appealing to the rational interests of the individual. Albert Hunter says that the view came to be that the "world was no longer one of people in communities but rather one of people against society."[13]

Frequently the assumed impersonal nature of the city was made even more so by the views that prevailed about rural areas and small towns. These views have long been influenced by romantic and nostalgic recollections of rural life. Often stress was placed on a positive view of how every one knew everyone else and ignored the fact that this meant a powerful means of social control and loss of privacy for the individual. In rural areas the relations between persons may be more a matter of style than substance. The friendly greetings and exchanges between people in a small town may be little more than that. The fact that most of them know each other doesn't mean they interact with one another in a significant way. In fact, one study of isolated farmers and ranchers in rural Montana showed those people not to be very well off in terms of friendship. In fact the study found them to be domineering and selfish and found a marked association between the isolated outdoor life and mental illness.[14]

In the 1950s there emerged among some American sociologists a reaction against the negative views of the city for the individual. This was especially so in studies dealing with kinship and other interpersonal relationships of city dwellers. Those sociologists argued that the nuclear family was very important within a modified kinship group and, contrary to general belief, played a very important part in the lives of urban dwellers. However, as Geoffrey Gibson observed, most of the literature on kinship relationships during that period was really little more than the literature on parent-child interchanges.[15] The basic question is how much physical closeness, interaction, and mutual aid between outsiders has to be present before one can say the nuclear family is not isolated. Another problem was that rarely did the studies examine the quality of kin relationships. The attempts to quantify relationships had the result that numbers of hours of visiting are seen as equal and comparable units. But one might visit a parent for one hour and have a significant exchange in conversation that is far more meaningful than sitting with the parent for hours watching television. In almost all cases those studies were interested in the quantity of relationships rather than in quality and meaning.

We want to look briefly at some more recent research and what it suggests about the interpersonal nature of city living. In the past the individual was fitted into a specific role in life. As James S. Coleman points out, during the Middle Ages the whole adult person was specialized; for example, a soldier could not even marry, but was to be totally a soldier. The modern fragmentation of men into many roles was not common to the Middle Ages. Over the years the development of specialized voluntary organizations, each containing only a "part" of the individual, came about slowly and with difficulty.[16]

Various studies suggest that community size and density have little consequence for a person's feelings of belonging, his community participation, or his feelings about the community. Persons who live in large and dense urban areas have no weaker or more limited informal and kinship ties than do the residents of smaller and less densely populated areas. "By contrast, the single most important variable leading to stronger social bonds is length of residence." [17] Having lived for some time in a community leads to the development of a series of life experiences identified with the community and often a sense of identification.

Another research study found no association between size of community and a sense of personal incompetence. The person living in a large city felt as able to cope with the issues of life as the person living in the country or small town. It was concluded that fundamental dimensions of personality, such as a sense of control, were not affected by the gross differences of town and country. Therefore, the attribution of alienation to "urbanism as a way of life" seems incorrect. [18]

The heterogeneous and impersonal nature of the city has a great deal to offer many individuals. However esoteric a person's interests, the city provides an opportunity for finding an outlet or others who

"Don't think 'overcrowded'—think 'the richness of urban life.' "

share that interest. This is well illustrated in the areas of social deviancy where the city provides both the opportunity and relative privacy of indulging an interest that may be defined as immoral or often even illegal. Frequently the small town or rural area forces the individual into isolation because of lack of opportunity, lack of privacy, and more conservative values.

There have been many studies and a vast body of literature on the development of communities and neighborhoods within the city. These have very often been seen as providing the interpersonal setting for living in the impersonal larger city. The evidence is clear that many communities do provide a closeness for its members. William L. Yancey and Eugene P. Eriksen point out that local facilities also contribute to the stability and cohesion of neighborhoods by providing service, space, and activities which are not only necessary "for the development of an autonomous community, but also facilitate the development of informal networks among community members."[19]

People who live in the city can choose their friends and associates from within or outside of the neighborhood as they choose. The neighborhood or community in the city provides the opportunity to choose to be locally anonymous and yet to still not be isolated because of the availability and ease of contacts outside the immediate neighborhood. Claude S. Fischer suggests that village life makes neighboring mandatory. But in cities, this type of neighboring is no longer mandatory.[20]

McGahan points out that the more recent studies of urban life have questioned the extent to which the city contains impersonal and secondary relationships. "In addition to demonstrating the extreme importance of kin and friendship relations to urban residents, contemporary research has also pointed to variation in neighborhood intimacy within the urban community."[21] There are wide differences between communities and neighborhoods in any given city. Another study reports that the urban dweller often develops a greater number of close friends than does the small town resident. In part this may be true because of somewhat fewer ties to kin among city residents. "If kin and friend ties are considered together, it appears that the affective support may be as great for individuals residing in an urban area as for those in a rural area."[22]

Social class has been found to affect interpersonal relationships in neighborhoods. In general the evidence suggests that lower-class persons have fewer intimate friends and engage in less visiting among their friends. The lower-class person tends to limit his social interaction mostly to his immediate family. By contrast, persons in the higher social classes tend to range outside the family as well as outside their neighborhoods. Irving Rosow found that in general, middle-class people have significantly more friends than those in the working class.

"At the same time, working-class people are far more dependent on their place of residence for friendship formation and their social life. Yet, despite this local dependence, old middle-class respondents have more friends in their neighborhood or section of town."[23]

In summary, the findings from studies of the interpersonal nature of the city have been turned around. They have moved from the impersonal view of the 1930s to the argument for many "significant and close" relationships of the 1950s and 1960s. However, the more recent research suggest that neither point of view is a clearcut one. It does appear that for many people who live in the city there is the opportunity to make and maintain close interpersonal relationships. Certainly the city provides many options for the individual. But it is doubtful that very many urban dwellers have the highly intimate and close ties often described of the rural and small town past. But it is also true that the city cannot be held as responsible for the social problems of isolation and alienation as it has in the past.

THE CITY AS A SETTING FOR SOCIAL PROBLEMS

We want to next look at some social problems that are identified with the city. These are problems not necessarily assumed to be caused by the city but are problems found more frequently in cities than in rural areas. In general, our concern is to discover what is it about the structure and institutions of the city that contribute to the increased frequency and variety of social problems?

It has been argued that the city has become increasingly specialized in jobs that call for higher levels of education and training. This has occurred at the same time that the residents of central cities have been increasingly characterized by poor educational backgrounds. This means that people employed in the cities very often don't live there, and this is related to such problems as unemployment and poverty. Inner-city unemployment rates are more than twice as high as the national average "and even higher among inner-city residents who have traditionally been employed in blue-collar industries that have moved to suburban locations."[24] The centers of cities are undergoing change as a result of being more specialized places of work. They are becoming less and less places to live and more places of retail trade. This means that increasingly only low-income families continue to live close to the centers of cities.

The institutions of the inner city have also undergone change. The political pattern has been one of developing support for public programs, emphasizing public assistance as well as housing programs at subsistence levels. Along with this has been governmental social control through the juvenile courts, the mental health system, and related institutions. In brief, "the regulation of the poor seems to be becoming essentially a central-city phenomenon."[25] The rapid expansion of governmental agencies has been very costly. And the public service demands of the central city have greatly increased at the same time as their fiscal ability to support public services has been diminishing. This is not because metropolitan resources are insufficient but because the largest part of those resources has been delegated to the politically autonomous outer rings of the city. "In short, metropolitan expansion in the absence of political reorganization has created an unfair distribution of economic resources and service costs between the cities and suburbs and is a major cause of the financial crises facing central cities today."[26]

The loss of income for central cities is also reflected in their shifting populations. There is the loss of tax dollars because of the white collar migration to the suburbs. At the same time that the tax base is reduced, the inner city costs go up. This is so because those that stay or move in tend to be poor, minorities, and the aged, all of whom need an increasing number of public services such as housing, welfare, police protection, and health care.

Many cities have tried to compensate for the loss of income by people moving to the suburbs through the application of city wage taxes. However, most cities have not as yet used this as a method of tax collection. One of the highest is an income tax of 4.3125 percent applied by the city of Philadelphia on all persons who work in the city whether they live there are not. Berry writes that although partial payments are made by suburban dwellers to central cities through various forms of income tax, user charges, and sales taxes, these sources do not generate the necessary revenue to cover the additional costs.[27]

The movement out of the city to the suburbs has taken both people and jobs from the city. For example, from 1970 to 1975 New York City lost more than a quarter of a million jobs, thus further narrowing its tax base. Also, as the higher-income persons move to the suburbs, their houses are taken over by the less affluent who cannot afford to keep them in the same condition, thereby contributing to the deterioration of the neighborhood. The landlord makes money from high rents and minimal upkeep, and as the property values go down, this further reduces the city's tax revenues.

In recent years the cost of housing has gone up in both the city and the suburbs. However, the housing values of the inner city neighborhoods have risen much slower than those in the suburbs. Because many of their jobs have moved to the suburbs, a number of inner-city residents are caught in a bind. For example, many inner-city white ethnics find themselves not only physically removed from employment chances but also residentially trapped because of the high cost of suburban housing.[28]

Over the years the city has used zoning as a political tool. With zoning it is not only possible to annex land and subdivide it, but also to maintain economic as well as racial segregation. For example, the economic cost of new housing can be controlled by establishing minimal lot sizes that are required for building new houses. Housing values can also be affected by altering the kinds of industrial uses permitted in the area. Often vice is zoned into specific areas, and this happens much more often in black rather than white residential areas.

With the movement of populations out and the influence of zoning laws, the center of the city can be affected in ways that are ongoing and may even be cumulative. For example, when people move away from areas near the center of the city, this reduces the influx of nighttime visitors. Having fewer nighttime visitors means it is more difficult to assure shoppers, concert goers, tourists, and conventioneers that the downtown area is safe for recreation and late hour activities.[29] The reduction of those sources of city revenue further deepens the problem, because the city resources continue to go down.

In recent years there have been attempts in many cities to redevelop and restructure historical and attractive aspects of the center city so that affluent residents will move back in. For some time there have been some areas of center cities that have had expensive high rise apartment houses. These are important, although very limited, kinds of housing that appeal to persons wanting and able to afford the life style of living in the center of the city. In writing about New York City in the 1960s, William M. Dobriner talked about how high above the lower-class "barrios" of Manhattan lived the other "element." "They are the upper-middle- and upper-class executives and professionals who find all the work and play they can handle conveniently located within a few city blocks."[30]

The city satisfies most of the interests of persons who live in the more expensive high rise apartments. The apartments themselves do not appear to serve as neighborhoods for the residents. One study of a high rise apartment complex in New York City found it characterized by a high degree of anonymity and isolation. The study found that only 8 percent of those surveyed could recognize everyone on their floor and only 2 percent knew the names of every tenant on their floor. Many of the residents said they had no interest in knowing neighbors and this was especially true of working couples, childless couples, and unmarried men and women.[31]

During the 1960s in the United States there developed many attempts at alternative living arrangements. There have often been attempts to cut costs with various sharing plans by utilizing space in

United Press International Photo

High-rise apartments in Chicago

large old houses found in many cities. Often the cooperative venture has included renovating the houses for more efficient and comfortable living. Through the 1970s many of the more radical forms of communal living ended and it appears that today's communal or cooperating living patterns are typically based more on economic considerations than on ideological commitments.

In the 1970s, in some of the large cities, a new focus on center city living emerged. This has been the taking over of residential areas by the affluent middle and upper classes. They have bought old houses that continued to be structurally sound and renovated the insides. This is obviously limited because the costs are very high. But where this has been done the real estate values have gone up greatly and new businesses catering to the new residents have been founded, such as various kinds of food and drink specialty shops, clothing boutiques, restaurants, and so forth.

Certainly the future for the city does not look good. The city will probably continue to lose population relatively and sometimes absolutely. As it does so the city populations will become poorer and more dependent on government agencies. But what can be done by agencies will be reduced as the city tax base erodes with more industry, commerce, and jobs moving to the suburbs. The cities will continue to bear the cost of providing both daytime cultural and commercial amenities and nighttime facilities for entertainment and vice for suburban visitors. We can expect increased suburbanization of most types of economic activity along with the migration of middle- and upper-income groups. This will probably be matched by continued declines in center city blue-collar jobs and with their partial replacement by more highly skilled white-collar functions. "At the same time, the resident populations of many central cities will become increasingly dominated by minority groups, the aged, and the poor. Unemployment and poverty will obviously worsen."[32]

As suggested, the range of social problems associated with the city is very wide. There has come to be for many a view of the unmanageability of focusing on the problems of the cities because they include such diverse phenomena as air pollution, civic ugliness, and poverty. "Indeed, urban problems are almost synonymous with the social problems of contemporary American society.[33]

It is a common view among Americans to look at the city as a source of most social problems. People who live in large cities generally define themselves as living amidst actual or potential problems. In a study of over 1,000 Boston homeowners it was found that their major concern was not with such problems of the physical environment as pollution, housing, and transportation. Rather they were most concerned with threats to the social environment such as violence, crime, rebellious youth, racial tension, and delinquency.[34] In June 1975, a national sample of city dwellers were asked: "What do you regard as your community's worse problems?" The greatest proportion mentioned crime (21 percent) and this was followed by unemployment (11 percent). These were followed by transportation problems, education, housing, and high taxes.[35]

Certainly crime is a characteristic of the large city (see Chapter 17).

In the six largest cities in the United States the rate of reported robberies was 756.2 per 100,000 people in 1973. The rate declined sharply
with city size, to 60.9 in cities of 10,000–25,000 population, less than
one tenth of the big-city rate.[36] But the mass media, especially television, creates a distorted picture of violence and crime in the city. The
crimes that get coverage are the most serious one, and they create an
illusion of being much more common than they are in fact.

We know that over time the characteristics that may eventually
define something as a social problem exist but are not given any major
importance or force. But at some point in time these characteristics
may be picked up, publicized, and gain a great deal of force. As discussed, up until the 1930s there had been a great interest in the city as
a social problem setting. But around World War II and during much of
the 1950s there was relatively less concern with the city. In fact, some
of the family studies mentioned earlier were given as evidence that in
those areas all was reasonably well in the city and that people really
did have close and meaningful kin relationships. In general, the 1950s
were a period of high complacency with limited concern with the
social problems that were to burst forth in the 1960s. But the 1960s saw
the explosion of concern with civil rights and the new black militancy;
it was also the decade when poverty was "rediscovered" (see Chapter
4). By the mid-1960s there was a great awareness of the problems of
the city. Many of those were linked to the social problems of racial
conflict and poverty, but many were about the deteriorating material
and fiscal nature of the city. This was referred to in 1968 by the Johnson administration as the "urban crisis." This led to a great deal of
rhetoric but little concrete action, and for the most part the problems
of the city continued to grow.

For many residents one solution to the problems of the city was to
get out if they could. Certainly a big part of the migration to the
suburbs in the 1960s was to try to escape the problems of the city. The
problems of the city were further extended by the constant expansion
of conflicting interests in the city. More and more the city has been
characterized by special interest groups. For example, the unionization of municipal employes, such as police, garbage collectors, public
transportation employes, and others, often leads to severe problems
for those who use and depend on those services. There are also other
conflict groups in the city: for example, religious groups fighting
against birth control information and abortion in the city hospitals, or
neighborhoods resisting new housing for minority groups.

Gerald D. Suttles points out that the American urban crisis has
taken so many different forms that it is often difficult to see its basic
continuities. "At various times our attention has been riveted on
growing racial segregation and conflict, the centrifugal drift to the
suburbs, the job-residence mismatch, and most recently the urban fiscal crunch."[37]

We next will look briefly at some major social problems that have their focus in the cities. This is done briefly because most of them are treated in separate chapters as specific social problems.

Minority groups and segregation. (See chapter 6.) Ethnic residential areas have developed over time as different groups have arrived in the city. Each of these ethnic groups has something distinct about itself, its roles, and its needs. As a result these groups of people occupy different constellations of roles, and have quite different needs, demands, information, facilities, and modes of behavior.[38] Ethnic heterogeneity is a consequence of the distribution of peoples in the city, resulting in much of the urban community being divided by visible social group differences.

Many of the ethnic areas of the city today are three and four generations old and while many of the young do move away, many of the old patterns continue to be maintained. These areas are more than just a group of persons sharing a common ethnic background. They also include the institutions of the ethnic group such as religion, formal and informal organizations, and leisure time activities.

Blacks and segregation. (See Chapter 5.) The slum areas of the city are overrepresented with blacks. The slums represent poverty in its most dramatic and visible form. The heavy concentration of blacks in these areas is a result of low income and highly restricted housing opportunities. For most poor blacks, moving to the suburbs is not a realistic alternative. In fact, studies point out that blacks who live in the suburbs are not much better off than their city counterparts. So while there is little reason for optimism about rebuilding the ghetto economy, the suburbs are no panacea for the needs of blacks in housing and employment. Elliot Zashin argues that "dispersion in the suburbs would undermine recently achieved political gains and the possibility of community-controlled institutions that many blacks appear to want."[39]

There appears to be a clear pattern of inner city housing limitations for blacks. For example, once an urban area begins to swing from predominately white to predominately black occupancy, the change is rarely reversed. The pattern of black residential expansion is from the core of the city outward and they move into areas already characterized by high residential mobility.[40] There is really no free market for black housing. The black population in the city has increased faster than living space has become available. This has meant that even when new areas open up, the demand is so great that crowding is an inevitable result.[41] There are also Chicanos, Puerto Ricans, and poor whites with several problems with living in the city, but the blacks are the largest group.

A major problem for the black is decent housing and it is only if that can be met that other kind of problems may become important, as is evident in blacks' views about living in racially mixed neigh-

TABLE 3–2

Black as a Percent of Total Population Inside and Outside Metropolitan Areas, by Size of Metropolitan Area: 1960, 1970, and 1975   (Data shown according to the definition and size of metropolitan area in 1970)

Type of residence	1960	1970	1975
United States	10.6	11.1	11.3
Metropolitan areas [1]	10.7	11.9	12.5
Central cities	16.4	20.5	22.6
Central cities in metropolitan areas of			
1 million or more	18.8	25.2	27.6
Less than 1,000,000	13.2	14.9	16.8
Suburbs	4.8	4.6	5.0
Suburbs in metropolitan areas of			
1 million or more	4.0	4.5	5.1
Less than 1,000,000	5.9	4.8	4.8
Nonmetropolitan areas	10.3	9.1	8.8
In counties designated metropolitan since 1970	(x)	7.7	(NA)

Note: Standard metropolitan areas as a statistical concept were first used in the 1950 census. However, data for 1950 have not been reconstructed according to the 1970 definition of metropolitan areas.

Source: U.S. Department of Commerce, Bureau of the Census, "The Social and Economic Status of the Black Population," *Current Population Reports* P–23, no–80 (Washington, D.C.: U.S. Government Printing Office, 1979), p. 15.

X = Not applicable.
NA = Not available.

[1] Excludes Middlesex and Somerset Counties in New Jersey.

borhoods. That is, decent housing may be more important than the racial mix of the neighborhood. If given a choice, many blacks would prefer to live in homogeneous neighborhoods, but a considerable number would also prefer mixed neighborhoods. The problem comes with different views of what is an appropriate mix of blacks and whites. Blacks would regard as desirable a neighborhood racially mixed at about 50:50. But whites would regard that as undesirable. In one study of white respondents, 70 percent said they would move if blacks entered their neighborhood in "great numbers" and the tipping point may be as low as 15 to 20 percent.[42]

In the 1950s there were attempts to deal with housing problems in the city by eliminating slums. This was the advent of massive public housing programs based on the notion that the growing problems of the city could be traced to the slums. This view was that the slums acted like a social swamp in which sloth, drunkenness, racial conflict, and disorder festered and grew. And the assumption was that if one eliminated the slum, then one would greatly improve the social health of both the residents and the city at large.[43] After a number of years it became clear that tearing down the slums and building new housing or moving occupants did not greatly improve their housing nor did it reduce their poverty or the related social problems. Amitai Etzioni writes that "slum clearance did create new housing, but much of it was too expensive for the former residents of the area; thus it created serious social dislocation, increased alienation, and led to larger welfare rolls."[44]

Education. One major issue in education in recent years has been the attempt through busing to attain a better racial balance in the schools. In general, this has been the attempt to bus black children into predominantly white schools. The initial concern with desegregation of schools was with the elimination of the dual school system of the South. But the 1960s saw the rise of interest in the North in busing. In many cities, especially Boston, this has been bitterly opposed by many whites.

The second major problem with education in recent years in the city has centered around school finance. The costs of public schools rose dramatically in the 1960s and 1970s. At the same time there emerged a lack of confidence reflected in an increase in the rejection of school bond issues and tax increases. Along with fiscal disillusionment there has also been a related crisis in the authority and control of

School busing in South Boston

schools. Increasingly school policies have been contested by federal and state governments and by the courts. The rapid emergence of teacher unions has given them great power and contributed greatly to the costs of education. In many areas parents have gained new power through community school boards. Coleman writes that the resulting "state is an unstable one, it is a transition stage between a past form of organization with its accompanying legitimate realms of authority and a new form of organization that will differ in substantial ways from the old."[45]

A common problem in many city schools is violence; in many cities police are assigned to the schools to attempt to maintain some order. Often the high schools, in many suburbs as well as cities, function primarily as custodial rather than educational institutions. When typically students must stay until they are 16 years of age, many feel they are in school against their will. In some schools, teaching most academic content has been abandoned, and the aim has become one of maintaining a minimum of order and discipline. Often the students, with no commitment to the academic nature of the school, and often bored and hostile, turn to violence and vandalism. This is most common in the poorest areas of the city where the children have the least educational motivation and the physical plant of the school is often run down and antiquated.

DEALING WITH URBAN PROBLEMS

Given the long concern with city problems, what overall attempts have been made to deal with them? Over the years cities developed with very little planning or projecting of needs. Even the layout of streets has often been haphazard. While initially many American cities set up a grid pattern for their original inner cities, as they spread and took in new areas the road system was adopted as it existed and the result was no particular pattern.

Berry and Kasarda write that historically American city planning has tended to be supportive of private interests and resources and a mosaic culture rather than the production of alternative plans aimed at the common good. The United States has not been characterized by the construction of planned new towns and cities. The first ones that did develop, at the end of the last century, were company towns built to serve specific industrial enterprises.[46] In general the belief has been in local autonomy, and so historically there was little federal government influence in planning or regulating cities and their growth. There is no government body that can be credited with the development and execution of a national urban policy. In the past, if there were any conscious public objectives they were on the one hand to encourage growth, apparently for its own sake, and, on the other, "to provide public works and public welfare programs to support piece-meal, spontaneous developments impelled primarily by private initiative."[47]

City planning has generally been vague and inconsistent. Most often it is the result of politics rather than being based on any reasoned plan. The power of interest groups becomes paramount. For example, highways are built, not for the city residents, but rather for the commuter. Urban renewal gets rid of what some power groups define as undesirable, but undesirable for whom? For example, slums may be destroyed to allow urban universities to expand. But usually equal or better housing is not provided for those displaced. In fact, urban renewal has destroyed ten times as much housing as it has replaced.

Suburban Development

The emergence of suburbs is often thought of as a recent phenomenon but the suburbs have been around a long time. The suburbs seem to have been present in the earliest cities. For example, Egyptian cities had areas of "suburban" villas at some distance from the city center. "The suburb from the 11th to the 18th century developed in two directions. One was as a home for merchants and traders, often immigrants, and the other was the villa dwellings of the wealthy city dwellers."[48]

David Thorns goes on to say that the suburbs increased steadily in importance during the 18th and 19th centuries. As cities came more and more to be seen as undesirable places to live by higher income groups, they looked outside the city. "This move to the suburbs was given further impetus and rationale by the Romantic Movement which extolled the virtues of the countryman and countryside in sharp contrast to the wickedness and vice of the city."[49]

In the United States the growth of the suburbs came later than in many parts of Europe. It is more a feature of the 20th century than the 19th. The period between the Civil War and World War I was the time of great expansion and so the cities were growing at very high rates. But by the 20th century the suburbs were also growing rapidly. In both New York and Boston their suburbs were growing faster than the cities towards the end of the 19th century.[50]

In the United States the movement to the suburbs was to escape from the city and was a result of being pulled toward a rural ideal of life that would provide more room and lead to more attractive living. To move from the city was to have an individual living unit and to have a piece of ground around it. These were ends that were often too expensive for many to achieve in the city.

There was a great boom in suburbanization following World War II, and to a great extent this was due to the mass distribution of the automobile. The high speed automobile replaced the streetcar as the major means of transportation. This allowed for a greater dispersal of the concentrated central population and the dispersal encouraged the further use of motor vehicles in the expanded metropolitan area. However, while suburban population growth has primarily characterized recent decades, almost half of all 1970 incorporated suburbs of at least 2,500 population were found in the 1900 census.[51] Often the growth has not been through the development of new suburbs but rather the expansion of old ones.

In the period from 1920 to 1950 suburbs were differentially changing their status, although persistence of status was also evident. The suburbs with gains in status were primarily in older metropolitan areas with dense center cities. In the 1950 to 1970 period, suburban persistence emerged—most suburbs retained a very high stability of relative ranking in social status.[52]

The urbanization of America reflects a spread of mass suburban culture. This is seen in the nationwide similarities of subdivision developments and the uniformity of freeway construction and patterns of community growth around the freeway exits. There has also been a blurring of the distinction between small town and suburb within the metropolitan area. "And the ubiquitous blighting of the older suburban highway strips by franchises serving the same menus from California to Maine."[53]

Rates of suburban increase.   During the period from 1950 to 1960 the suburbs accounted for nearly 97 percent of the population increase of the 108 standard metropolitan areas in the United States. This growth was generally the greatest in the largest areas. "For example, in the areas of over three million the growth rate of the cities was 1.7 percent as against 98 percent for the suburbs, whereas for those of under 100,000 the figures were 26 percent for the cities and 74 percent for the suburbs."[54]

The expansion of the suburbs was more than people moving into new housing. It also included great developments in the service needs as well as in business enterprises. Between 1954 and 1977, over 15,000 suburban shopping centers and regional malls were constructed to serve the expanding metropolitan population. "By 1978 those shopping centers and malls accounted for more than one half of the annual retail sales in the United States, and the trend shows no sign of abating."[55]

When people move to the suburbs their ties to and dependency on the city do not end. As suggested earlier, this contributes greatly to the operating costs of the city. The commuting population in particular exerts strong effects on police, fire, highway, sanitation, recreation,

Mike Jaeggi

A suburban subdivision

and general administration costs of central cities. The per capita expenditures for central city services have been found to be at least as sensitive to the size of the suburban population as to the size of the central city population itself.[56]

Berry and Kasarda suggest a more subtle means by which suburban populations exploit center cities is by not carrying their fair share of welfare costs in the metropolitan areas. Through the use of zoning and discriminatory practices, the suburbs have been able to keep most of the low income and poorly educated people in metropolitan areas confined to the central cities. "Suburban areas are therefore able to avoid the costs of public housing, public health, and other welfare expenses that impose a heavy burden on the operating budgets of many central cities."[57]

The response to the emergence of suburban living has not been seen as an unmixed blessing. The suburb has had both its admirers and its critics. For some it is seen as a mixture of town and country which can be a viable community in which the advantages of both rural and urban living can be combined. For many the suburban life style is seen as an escape from the problems of the city—an escape from crime, poverty, minority groups, alcohol and drugs, and as a better and safer place to rear children.

By contrast the critics of suburban life see it as a dull landscape that combines many of the worst features of rural and urban living. Often the suburb is criticized as the producer of conformity which has made for too much "togetherness." In one respect the conformity argument is not too meaningful when it is realized that most of the new suburbs are very homogeneous and therefore attract people who are drawn to live there because they are much like those already there. Often, if people's interests and values change and they can afford it, they seek out new areas to live where people will fit their new needs. They seek out a new reference group with which to conform.

As indicated above there are clear differences between many suburbs. John R. Logan talks about "residential," "industrial," and "working-class" suburbs. He found that the working-class suburbs have lower-status populations than residential or balanced suburbs. These suburbs also tended to be older, larger, and further located from the central cities. They had high population densities and had grown less in the past decade. "Indeed, employing suburbs were shown to have many of the characteristics of central cities."[58]

Social class levels have a clear impact on suburban living. The movement of middle-class blacks to the suburbs has been minimal. And movement that has occurred has resulted in decentralization, but not desegregation, of the black population. "Likewise, there are pockets of the poor who have migrated to the suburbs, often concentrated in pockets of poverty either in older industrial suburbs or in the interstices between suburbs."[59] There also tends to be ethnic residential segregation in the suburbs. Foreign-born and second-generation groups, "despite their movement into the suburbs, display a noteworthy degree of residential segregation."[60]

Also of great importance to suburbanization has been the movement of industry that has followed the same general patterns of migration. For many industries there were the push factors of obsolete inner-city structures, lack of inexpensive space for expansion, increasing taxes, deteriorating public services, and rising crime rates. At the same time were the pull factors of suburbs with available land and cheaper taxes. Between 1947 and 1972, metropolitan central cities in the United States lost a net total of 1,146,845 manufacturing jobs while the suburban rings gained 4,178,230.[61]

During the decade of the 1960s, while the labor force living in suburban areas increased 40 percent, the total suburban employment increased 48 percent. The fiscal benefit of industrial and commercial growth can be translated into lower taxes and/or improved public services. Low taxes in turn make the community attractive as a location for additional homes and businesses and the demand for building sites rises. Competition forces up the market value of land, and as land prices rise, "working class households find it increasingly difficult to pay the price of homesites in the community."[62]

The industrial and residential mix of the suburb is not always desirable for the residents. While the tax provided by the industries does contribute to better financed schools, police, and related services, there are also costs. Often industry means poorer roads because of their deterioration by truck use, and there is also often heavy traffic congestion and noise to deal with.

The basic overriding problem of the city is increasingly coming to be financial. The city does not have the means of providing for the needs of city residents nor even the basic upkeep of city facilities and services. As a result, the deteriorating conditions contribute to a greater exacerbation of other social problems—poverty, minority conflict, crime, and so forth. There appears to be no willingness to treat the city as a major problem deserving of a high national priority. It seems safe to predict that the city will continue to be an ever increasing social problem in itself as well as for the other social problems that are found there.

It may be as the energy crisis becomes more severe people will be forced to tighten their community boundaries. More and more people are planning their vacations to stay at home, especially during the times when gas shortages make taking a long trip a real gamble. And the overall consumption of gas relative to automobiles has decreased indicating that on a day-to-day basis people are driving less and staying closer to home.

The emergence of the city has been closely linked with industrialization. The city is often seen as a social problem and also many of the social conditions are identified with the city, that is, poverty, minority conflict, crime, and so forth. In recent decades the city has gone through many changes. This has been especially true of center cities that have lost many of their economic resources and seen rapid population change. There has also been the movement out of the city to the suburbs that has taken not only people but jobs. In recent years there has been some indication of a movement back into the city.

NOTES

1. Kingsley Davis, "The Origin and Growth of Urbanization in the World," in *Neighborhood, City and Metropolis,* by Robert Gutman and David Popenoe (New York: Random House, 1970), pp. 121–22.

2. Ibid., p. 124.

3. Bryan R. Roberts, "Comparative Perspectives on Urbanization," in *Handbook of Contemporary Urban Life*, by David Street (San Francisco: Jossey-Bass, 1978), p. 592.

4. Davis, "Origin and Growth," pp. 124–25.

5. Ibid., p. 129.

6. *Information Please Almanac 1978* (New York: Information Please Publishing, Inc., 1978), p. 105.

7. Brian J. L. Berry and John D. Kasarda, *Contemporary Urban Ecology* (New York: Macmillan, 1977), pp. 183–84.

8. Ibid., p. 185.

9. Leslie Kilmartin and David C. Thorns, *Cities Unlimited* (Sydney, Australia: George Allen and Unwin, 1978), p. 11.

10. Albert Hunter, "Persistence of Local Sentiments in Mass Society," in Street, *Handbook*, p. 141.

11. Louis Wirth, "Urbanism as a Way of Life," *American Journal of Sociology* (July 1938), pp. 11–12.

12. Ibid., p. 12.

13. Hunter, "Persistence," pp. 137–38.

14. Myron Brenton, *Friendship* (New York: Stein and Day, 1978), p. 38.

15. Geoffrey Gibson, "Kin Family Network: Overheralded Structure in Past Conceptualization of Family Functioning," *Journal of Marriage and the Family* (February 1972), p. 15.

16. James S. Coleman, "Community Disorganization and Urban Problems," in *Contemporary Social Problems*, 4th ed., by Robert K. Merton and Robert Nisbet (New York: Harcourt Brace Jovanovich, 1976), p. 578.

17. Morris Janowitz and David Street, "Changing Social Order and the Metropolitan Area," in Street, *Handbook*, p. 111.

18. Claude S. Fischer "On Urban Alienation and Anomie: Powerlessness and Social Isolation," *American Sociological Review* (June 1973), p. 325.

19. William L. Yancey and Eugene P. Eriksen, "The Antecedents of Community: The Economic and Institutional Structure of Urban Neighborhoods," *American Sociological Review* (April 1979), p. 253.

20. Fischer, "Urban Alienation," p. 322.

21. Peter McGahan, "The Neighbor Role and Neighboring in a Highly Urban Area," *The Sociological Quarterly* (Summer 1972), p. 265.

22. Alfred M. Mirande, "Extended Kinship Ties, Friendship Relations and Community Size: An Exploratory Inquiry," *Rural Sociology* (June 1970), p. 265.

23. Irving Rosow, "Old People: Their Friends and Neighbors," *American Behavior Scientist* (September–October 1970), p. 65.

24. John D. Kasarda," Urbanization, Community, and the Metropolitan Problem" in Street, *Handbook*, p. 42.

25. Diana Pearce and David Street, "Welfare in the Metropolitan Area," in ibid., p. 324.

26. Kasarda, "Urbanization," p. vi.

27. Berry and Kasarda, *Contemporary Ecology*, p. 226

28. Kasarda, "Urbanization," p. 43.

29. Gerald D. Suttles, "Changing Priorities in the Urban Heartland," in Street, *Handbook*, p. 533.

30. William M. Dobriner, "The Growth and Structure of Metropolitan Areas," in Gutnam and Popenoe, *Neighborhood*, p. 202.

31. Jacqueline M. Zito, "Anonymity and Neighboring in an Urban High-Rise Complex," *Urban Life and Culture* (October 1974), p. 25.

32. Berry and Kasarda, *Contemporary Ecology*, p. 243.

33. Gutman and Popenoe, *Neighborhood*, p. 17.

34. Sidney Kronus, "Race, Ethnicity and Community," in Street, *Handbook*, p. 227.

35. Coleman, "Disorganization," p. 569.

36. Ibid., p. 570.

37. Suttles, "Changing Priorities," p. 519.

38. Dennis C. McElrath, "Urban Differentiations: Problems and Prospects," in Gutman and Popenoe, *Neighborhood*, p. 385.

39. Elliot Zashin, "The Progress of Black Americans in Civil Rights: The Past Two Decades Assessed," *Daedalus* (Winter 1978), p. 258.

40. Morton Grodzins, "The Metropolitan Area as a Racial Problem," in Gutnam and Popenoe, Neighborhood, p. 483.

41. Ibid., p. 486.

42. Zashin, "Progress of Black Americans," p. 256.

43. Pearce and Street, "Welfare," p. 328.

44. Amitai Etzioni, *Social Problems* (Englewood Cliffs, N.J.: Prentice-Hall, 1976), p. 98.

45. Coleman, "Disorganization," p. 572.

46. Berry and Kasarda, *Contemporary Ecology*, p. 367.

47. Ibid., p. 371.

48. David Thorns, *Suburbia* (Suffort, Great Britain: Paladin, 1973), p. 35.

49. Ibid., p. 37.

50. Ibid., p. 62.

51. Avery M. Guest, "Suburban Social Status: Persistence or Evolution?" *American Sociological Review* (April 1978), p. 251.

52. Ibid., p. 262.

53. David Street, "Conclusion: Life in Urbanized America," in Street, *Handbook*, p. 629.

54. Thorns, *Suburbia*, p. 65.

55. Kasarda, "Urbanization," p. 35.

56. Berry and Kasarda, *Contemporary Ecology*, p. 225.

57. Ibid., p. 226.

58. John R. Logan, "Industrialization and the Stratification of Cities in Suburban Regions," *American Journal of Sociology* 82 (1977), p. 334.

59. Pearce and Street, "Welfare," p. 322.

60. Janowitz and Street, "Changing Social Order," p. 103.

61. Kasarda, "Urbanization," p. 37.

62. Logan "Industrialization," pp. 337–38.

SELECTED BIBLIOGRAPHY

Berry, Brian J. L., and Kasarda, John D. *Contemporary Urban Ecology*. New York: Macmillan, 1977.

Fischer, Claude S. "On Urban Alienation and Anomie: Powerlessness and Social Isolation." *American Sociological Review* (June 1973), pp. 311–26.

Gutman, Robert, and Popenoe, David. *Neighborhood, City and Metropolis*. New York: Random House, 1970.

Logan, John R. "Industrialization and the Stratification of Cities in Suburban Regions." *American Journal of Sociology* 82 (1977), pp. 333–47.

Street, David. *Handbook of Contemporary Urban Life*. San Francisco: Jossey-Bass, 1978.

Wirth, Louis. "Urbanism as a Way of Life." *American Journal of Sociology* (July 1938), pp. 1–24.

Yancey, William L., and Eriksen, Eugene P. "The Antecedents of Community: The Economic and Institutional Structure of Urban Neighborhoods." *American Sociological Review* (April 1979), pp. 253–62.

Chapter 4

Work

To be a part of the work force is common to almost all men and an increasing number of women. There may be only a relatively small minority of adults who have an occupation that highly satisfies them. Most people probably accept their work or actively dislike it. In this chapter the social problem focus is on two levels: first, on the kinds of problems that people have with their work; second, on the problem of unemployment on both the social and personal levels.

Work, in the most general sense, refers to all things that must be done if a society is to survive. Work also implies a division of labor. No one does everything to meet his own survival needs. Even in the most primitive society there is some division of labor; some persons provide food, some prepare it, some serve as protectors, some care for children, and so forth. As human technology developed, the division of labor became more complex. Over time, work became more than doing things, and it often came to be defined as having a value of its own. Societies and individuals have developed a variety of attitudes and values about work.

With the early colonization of America there was a positive social definition of work. Among the early Puritans in New England there was a strong doctrine about work—work was the highest duty of man. Idleness was seen as evil and worldly success was seen as a good indication of salvation. The early belief was that labor was a service to God and to work hard was to serve God. Calvin preached that work was the will of God and that people should seek out the work which brings the greatest success to them and to society.

Early in American history the professions came to be seen as a "calling." This meant that those in the professions had a moral obligation to perform to the best of their ability, since for them to do anything less was to shirk their duty to God. The notion of an occupation being a "calling" continues in some instances to this day. For example, the "service to others" ethic is sometimes focused in such professions as the clergy, medicine, and law. From the beginning in the United States work often had, at least among the professions, a quality of virtue beyond the intrinsic value of the work itself.

Historically, the kinds of work that people have done has changed greatly. During the colonial period 95 percent of the population lived on subsistence level farms. In the northeastern part of the United States the mercantile system of the 18th century led to small businesses that were operated by self-employed tradespeople. These people worked as merchants, craftsmen, and artisans. Early in the 19th century, however, industrialization was very rapid. For example, while in 1810 there were only 75,000 persons employed in manufacturing, the number had increased to 750,000 by 1840. Industrialization meant that work became increasingly separated from home and the worker had to abide by the job discipline that set the location of work and the hours to be there.

The early religious views about work fit very well with the emerging notion of capitalism. Basically, capitalism refers to a deliberate pursuit of personal profit and this was linked to values associated with personal salvation. Capitalism made self-interest a morally acceptable and socially desirable end. Capitalism was also based on the notion of free competition among buyers and sellers, but this has from the beginning been much more honored in the abstract than found in reality. Government has been influential in affecting the marketplace through the use of tariffs and other controls, such as supports for the prices of some commodities as well as the control of some trade.

Capitalism's view of labor also fit well with the development of industrialization. Under the notion of capitalism, labor was to be replaced by machines whenever it was cheaper to do so. This was done in terms of profit and regardless of the social consequences it might have, such as increasing the number of unemployed. In more recent years automation has sharply reduced the number of workers needed in many such primary industries as agriculture and mining.

The most basic shift in the work force over the years has been from a rural to an urban one. Historically, industrialization and urbanization have gone together. In 1820, 72 percent of the labor force was in farm occupations and the rest in nonfarm ones. By 1900 the percent in farm occupations had dropped to 38 percent and by 1970 to only 3 percent.[1] That only 3 percent is now needed to meet the food needs of the rest of the population is due to the industrialization and mechanization of farming. There has also been over the years an increasing percent of the population in the work force. In 1820 only 44 percent of all persons age ten or over were in the work force. By 1900 this had increased to 50 percent and in 1970 to 56 percent. The increase is largely a reflection of the increasing number of women who have entered the work force.

Many of the early social problems associated with industrialization have been reduced or have disappeared. For example, the initial problems of industrialization such as low wages and sweatshop exploitation have been greatly reduced. This has largely been due to labor unions, government regulation, and greater managerial concern. But there continues to be some significant differences between various work groups largely due to unionization. The highly unionized workers in both blue-collar and white-collar occupations receive relatively high wages, considerable fringe benefits, and some protection against health hazards and layoffs, while workers in small nonunion enterprises (such as laundries and small restaurants) and on large industrialized farms receive little in any way."[2]

One important effect of industrialization on the worker was the introduction of the assembly line. This involved a series of different workers, each doing the same operation over and over. Their total combined efforts would produce the finished product. Often the large basic object (for example, the automobile) is placed on the line, and as it moves parts are added to it. Each step for the individual worker is broken down to the simplest and fewest possible motions. The costs to the worker on the assembly line are boredom, monotony, and no interest in or identification with the finished product.

Since the end of World War II the American economy has moved from the industrial era to what has been called a "postindustrial period." The postindustrial period is characterized by the increasing use of computers and automation and a decreasing need for human labor in industrial production. Increasingly there is "the employment of a greater proportion of the labor force in professional, technical, and service occupations."[3] Many of the unskilled and semiskilled jobs have been eliminated. This trend will be discussed further later in the chapter.

THE NATURE AND STRUCTURE OF WORK

As suggested, occupations are structured and distributed through society in a variety of ways. In general, jobs are classified into professional, white-collar, blue-collar, and laborer categories. These categories describe a social and economic hierarchy in society. They represent a herarchy in terms of the income and prestige associated with them. For example, white-collar workers typically differ from professionals in that they are more often employed by others, use practical skills, and have less work autonomy. The blue-collar job

Working in an automobile assembly plant

usually calls for training but no higher education. The labor category typically calls for no special training, skill, or formal education.

In recent years the white-collar category became the large single job grouping when it passed the blue-collar in 1966. White-collar includes professional, managerial, clerical, and sales personnel and in 1974 made up 48 percent of the labor force.[4] The increase in this group was largely due to the clerical and professional fields. Clerical workers now compete with the skilled and semiskilled workers as the largest occupational group in the labor force. The category of blue-collar has remained relatively stable since about 1910 but the composition has changed. The semiskilled, skilled, and craftsmen categories have increased proportionately while the unskilled has decreased. In this age of increasing specialization there are a large number of specific occupations. The Dictionary of Occupational Titles which is published by the U.S. Department of Labor, lists 21,741 different jobs. This is in contrast with 323 occupations listed in 1850.

The professions are the high status occupations in America. In general, an occupation is considered a profession if a high level of education is required and if the knowledge required is systematic and theoretical rather than applied. A profession has considerable autonomy and typically has its own means of regulating qualifications and legitimate conduct. Often this means the profession polices itself through examinations, licensing, and granting titles. The best examples of professions are medicine, law, academics, and so forth.

The huge corporations or business firms, as well as such service institutions as hospitals and universities, have an expanded distribution of workers from top to bottom. What this has meant is an expanded middle range of workers who do not have the professional status of those at the top or the relatively low status of those at the bottom. For example, in some businesses there are many middle level employees in positions that demand no special skill. "They are hired not to provide a specific service or specialized knowledge, but rather to advance the interests of the firm in whatever way they can."[5]

Before the industrial revolution in the United States many businesses were small or operated by the self-employed. Over the years the ideal of being self-employed has been common in America. For many middle-class Americans, to be an owner of one's own business or an investor or landlord is thought to be in control of, rather than to be controlled by, the economy. It means that a person can manage time and money, not as someone else wants, but as that person chooses. However, the self-employed have been decreasing in the United States. In 1880, 37 percent of the labor force was self-employed but by 1970, only 10 percent was. This means that most persons in the work force are employes.[6]

The self-employed person is in an extremely high risk job category. In many small businesses, for example, owning and operating a service station, the failure rate in some years has been as high as 50 percent. Not only is there a high risk of failure but many small businesses, especially in the retail service areas, demand very long hours of work for a relatively low economic return. Furthermore, the return is highly influenced by even minor economic downturns. While the ideal of being self-employed is common to Americans, so too is the risk of failure for those who try.

On one level the ideological opposite to self-employment is government bureaucracy. This level represents a part of the expanding occupational opportunity for Americans. From 1950 to 1970 the fastest growing sectors were the nonprofit institutions (for example, hospitals and universities) and government. In 1970, there were about 6 million federal employes, about half of whom were in the armed forces. There were about 10 million in state and local government. "Almost one third of all the new jobs added in these two decades were provided directly by some form of government employment."[7] By 1976, there were 15,012,000 persons employed at some level of government.[8]

In the American economic system the amount one earns on a job contributes to the individual's prestige. However, money itself is not the sole means of attaining prestige. The way money is earned also contributes to the overall prestige of the individual. For example, a professional athlete may earn ten times as much as a physician but does not have nearly as high a prestige. In a society that places a high regard on work, it is ironic that money acquired from not working can also have high prestige for the individual. Inherited money generally brings the recipient prestige. One study found that inheritors at all economic levels were named by their acquaintances as examples of persons standing socially higher. They found it widely believed that inherited money gives a special ease to life and people with inherited money are thought to be "more comfortable with money."[9] But not all kinds of money acquired without working carry prestige. Just the opposite is true for people who receive welfare. They lost prestige in the eyes of society.

TABLE 4–1

Average Weekly Earnings of Nonagricultural Workers by Years (Gross average weekly earnings)

Year	Current dollars	1967 dollars
1973	145.39	109.23
1975	163.53	101.45
1977	189.00	104.13
1979 (May)	216.45	101.00

Source: Adapted from "Bureau of Labor Statistics," *The World Almanac* (New York: Newspaper Enterprises, 1980).

We want to look a little more at social class and its relationship to work. In general, a person's social position and relative power flow mainly from his position in the economic system. This is also true in the work situation. The essential feature of power in organizations is the ability of persons to control resources, capital, and other people's work. "Indeed, for most people, being 'higher up' means precisely this; the ability to control one's work and the work process of others."[10]

Richard P. Coleman suggests that for most Americans, occupation seems to be playing a less important role in determining social standing than it did in the past. This view suggests that being a blue-collar instead of a white-collar worker once mattered but doesn't anymore.[11] It may be that in surveys many people say occupational differences don't matter but they really do. The American value system of equality often makes it difficult to suggest that differences do matter. Various social stratification studies suggest that many Americans do make distinctions between social class levels and do attach significant differences to different levels.

William H. Form suggests that the internal stratification of the working class may be increasing. In his research of workers in four countries, he found that many skilled workers felt that their problems were quite different from those of less-skilled workers. As a result, "with increasing industrialization, the skilled may become less excited about either a working class social movement or joining the middle-class status groups of society."[12]

The minority group status of the blacks places them in a disadvantaged position in the labor force (see Chapter 6). They are disadvantaged in being underrepresented in the higher status occupations and overrepresented in the lower status ones. In 1977, 52 percent of all white workers were in white-collar occupations while this was true of only 35 percent of "blacks and others."[13] The number of blacks in managerial jobs has more than doubled over the past 15 years, but they still represent only 4 percent of the employees in such jobs (blacks represent about 10 percent of the total population). It is similarly true that the black's proportion of total professional employment has also nearly doubled, but still represents a low figure. Their entrance into the professions has not been uniform. The greatest increase has been in physicians, engineers, and accountants, whereas the least has been in college and university teaching. Black women have lost a part of their share of the total employed professional women, "because of the vast movement of educated white women into the labor force."[14]

Blacks have made significant socioeconomic improvements in recent years. They have narrowed the gap between themselves and whites but have by no means entirely closed it. Peter M. Blau writes that when the expanding high-status occupations are mostly filled by middle-class whites, that creates a labor demand that can help blacks in the lowest strata to move up. They can move to clerk or skilled worker, two occupational groups into which blacks have disproportionately moved in recent years.[15]

The black worker is a part of what has been defined as a split labor market. This refers to a difference in the price of labor between two or more groups of workers with constant efficiency and productivity. "A racially (black/white) split labor market began with slavery."[16] Edna Bonacich writes that even compared with the immigrants that came to the United States after World War I the blacks were more "exploitable." This was because they were desperately poor, with the result that jobs and wages that seemed distasteful to nonblacks often seemed attractive to them. Also from their experience of paternalism in the South, they were not used to intervening organizations, like unions. There had been a long history of discrimination and hostility by white labor which led black workers to be very wary of joining white organizations.[17]

There was a great migration of blacks northward during and after World War I. This occurred not only because economic conditions were bad in the rural South, but also because there were positive inducements being offered by industrial employers in the North. Labor recruiters were sent into the South. In part the recruitment was a product of labor shortages caused by the war and the decline of European immigrants. But "it was also evident that employers saw in this black industrial reserve a population which could be used to keep out unions and displace troublesome and increasingly expensive white labor."[18] Traditionally, even when sought out, the black has been discriminated against in getting various jobs and discriminated against in earnings when he did get a job similar to that of the white.

The work force is also influenced by values about sex roles and employment. In general, work is the area of life where "masculine" traits are thought to fit best. For modern man, work has often become the adult arena for proving his masculinity. The dominant American beliefs about work make it the setting for the man's "proving" his moral worth. "Apart from economic reward, men are taught to value work primarily as an opportunity for successful competition."[19] For most American men their work is their major adult role commitment. It is for them the one area of life where accomplishment is measured and rewarded by the public marketplace. And, until recent years, the main role in adult life for the woman was wife, mother, and housekeeper; but this is rapidly changing.

As will be discussed in Chapter 9, when women enter the work force, they typically enter in a subordinate relationship to men. For example, men are more likely to do the hiring and firing, determine pay, and supervise than are women. It is also true with respect to job characteristics "that men get more authority for similar levels of occupational status and sex labeling of job held than women, at least in the access to higher levels of supervision."[20]

Since World War I the work force has changed greatly through the influx of women workers (see Chapter 10). But whatever the label or measurement used, when compared to men, women's jobs are second rate. For example, they earn less. In 1974, only 4 percent of all employed women earned $15,000 a year or more in comparison to 29 percent of all employed men. A similar difference can be seen if women's income is compared to that of men by educational levels. For 8 years of education, women earn 57 percent of what men do. For 12 years of education it is 57 percent, and for 4 years of college or more, it is 62 percent of what men earn.[21]

The recent changes in the work force were first characterized by an

Arthur Grace/Stock, Boston, Inc.

A traditional division of labor

increasing influx of married women and later with an increase in mothers working outside the homes. The most rapid recent increases of mothers in the work force has been among young mothers. In 1960 only 14 percent of women with at least one child under six years of age was in the work force, but by 1976 this had increased to 40 percent.[22]

Another recent change in the work force has been the number of persons holding more than one job. During the recession period of the 1970s, women gained the biggest share of multiple jobs which suggests that women are working harder than ever before. The biggest increase of women entering the work force has been among white married women. This means an increase in the number of two income families. This phenomenon is "growing faster among whites than blacks, who traditionally have had the largest proportion of two-worker families."[23]

Dual-job holding increased from 3.0 percent in 1950 to 5.3 percent in 1957 and has remained at about that level. Of those who had a second job, in 1974, 38 percent of the men and 18 percent of the women were self-employed on their second jobs. "Although 32.1 percent said they had more than one job in order to meet regular expenses, the second largest group (17.9 percent) said they did it because they enjoyed the work."[24]

While over the years there has been a decline in the length of the work week, this has been offset by dual-job holding. In addition, many people work overtime. For example, 40.1 percent of employed men ages 25–44 worked overtime on a given job, and another 8.2 percent had two or more jobs. They averaged 39 hours in their primary jobs and 13 in their secondary ones. "It may be true that the only occupational segment for which working hours have actually decreased are white-collar jobs such as clerical and low-level administrative positions."[25]

Long hours of work are a frequent characteristic of many in the professions. Both executives and professionals often pay for their job freedom and prestige by working 70-hour weeks. There may be a variety of costs for these people. When they retire they may have more adequate financial resources, but may be bereft of psychological ones. Also, if they lose their jobs the emotional costs can be severe.[26]

There have been changes in the labor force related to age and education. The labor force has been getting younger. In part this has been due to the youth bulge of the late 1960s and early 1970s. But it has also been due to a decline in labor force involvement of older people and an increase in teenage labor force participation. Education serves to keep younger persons out of the work force by forcing them to stay in school, usually until 16 years of age.

The labor force is becoming somewhat more educated. During the 1970s the median education level stayed at about the same level, 12.6 years. But there was a bigger and more significant increase for blacks from an average of about 10 years up to and including some college.[27] Over the past 20 years it is doubtful that the great majority of jobs really have any need for an increased amount of education. It is probable that about four out of every five jobs require no more than a high school education. However, about 60 percent of the recent high school graduates as well as many older people are going into higher education. In the 1950s and 1960s the assumption was that we would need to educate more people to higher levels to meet technological expansion. But this is clearly no longer the case.

There are two general problems related to educational preparation for occupations. One is that the high school diploma acquired by over 90 percent of the younger generation is less and less a sign of educational achievement. Many high schools simply move the person through and hold them to minimal standards of achievement. The result is that many high school graduates are "functionally illiterate." They often can't handle jobs that require even minimal levels of ability to read and write.

The second problem is that the education system turns out many people who are "overeducated" for the jobs available. There is increasingly a lack of harmony between the needs of the occupational world and products of colleges and universities. In general, the best educated today, other than teenagers, are the persons with the most difficulty finding jobs. Ph.D.s in fields like English and history are being turned out at rates of four or five for every job available. Some employers have come up with the concept of the "overqualified." This applies to people who won't be hired because they have education and sometimes other qualifications much greater than the job calls for. The rationale for not hiring them is that they will leave for a better job if they can and that they will be unhappy doing something they are overqualified to do. This increasingly large group of overeducated people may become a greater problem for society. On the individual level they feel a sense of frustration, since they followed the dominant American value that education was the best preparation for a successful adult life but have not reaped the promised rewards. This leads to a great deal of bitterness. Institutions of higher education don't appear to be overly concerned with this and, in fact, because of decreasing enrollments, are aggressively seeking as many students as possible. This is especially true in graduate departments which want to maintain their vested interest in having graduate students even though when they finish there will be no jobs for them.

An important part of the work force is based on the wide variety of businesses that have been a dominant result of the capitalist system. Even though there have been increasing numbers going to work in government and nonprofit institutions, the business world is often the centerpiece when people think of the work force. But in recent years the American feelings about business institutions have changed. One study reports that from the late 1960s to the mid 1970s the number of people having a great deal of confidence in business dropped from 55 percent to 15 percent. Also a Gallup Poll which asked people to describe their level of confidence in those institutions which comprise the United States' power structure ranked educational institutions and/or organized religion first, then the military, Congress and Supreme Court, and organized labor. Business was ranked last of all.[28]

Since the end of World War II business has changed greatly in the United States. It has shifted from a preponderance of single-product, relatively small businesses to a preponderance of huge firms that have diversified products. "The single product firms have declined from about 30 percent of the total Fortune 500 in 1949 to under 10 percent by 1969."[29] Increasingly there is an attempt to sell a corporate image rather than a particular product identification. For example, in television commercials the name of conglomerates (usually initials) are being pushed with a description of all the things they make and sell.

What the work force is hired to do is based on the needs of society. The ideal of capitalistic belief is a marketplace based on supply and demand. The assumption is that products will sell only so long as there is a demand for them. Of course, supply and demand never operate alone because they are influenced through such forces as advertising, government regulations, import controls, and so forth. It is also generally assumed that whatever the state of the distribution of occupations there is a labor supply to fill them. But, as suggested, often the demands of the marketplace don't fit the demands of the labor force. We want to look next at how individuals relate to their worlds of work.

THE INDIVIDUAL AND THE WORK WORLD

When we talk about the number of persons in the work force we are talking about large numbers. In 1974 the total labor force was 93 million. However, the percentage of all men in the work force declined from 87 percent in 1951 to 79 percent in 1974. But employed women, during the same period increased from 35 to 46 percent.

Work, in and of itself, is emotionally as well as economically necessary for most of the adult male population. Work structures their time, provides a basis of many relationships with others, and often gives them a sense of personal worth. This is reflected in the fact that retired men are very likely to say they miss some aspects of their work. "Americans consider work a primary source of feelings of worth, of being a member of a community deserving of respect. Americans have a greater tendency to rely on the work community to provide engagement and sociability."[30]

In general, there are two sets of conditions that appear to be important for individuals to feel good about their jobs. One is what goes with the work—pay, sanitation, safety, and their relationships to supervisors and fellow workers. The second is an interest in what they do. Generally to be happy with a job they must find it challenging and receive some sense of accomplishment. For many Americans, work contributes to self-respect, but not just any work and under just any conditions. For many, work is expected to provide more than just material rewards. "At the very least, work should be a source of pride, and it should contribute to the realization of cherished personal values."[31]

The importance of the job is limited for many workers. Job satisfaction is something sought and most often found in the professions and the more demanding white-collar jobs. It is much less common for the blue-collar or industrial worker. David Thorns writes that for most of them work is not the central life interest. Furthermore, many of them do not value the informal associations with fellow workers and so the work place is relatively less important.[32]

What makes a good job? There are some differences by various kinds of jobs. One study of younger persons of college age found relatively few differences in the job criteria for blue-collar, white-collar, and college trained professional respondents. The blue-collar respondents saw pay as somewhat more important than the others, but they also had almost as high a value about the work being meaningful.[33] Another study found that men more than women felt strongly about pay. But the importance of pay to a good job appears to go down for men as they get older. "Such an effect is partly due to increasing earnings with age but also to a change in values and responsibilities and a growing concern for security as people grow older."[34] Often the younger worker has almost unlimited dreams about his or her future earnings. But as the workers get older the realities of their future become clearer and their earning expectations more realistic. Many older workers may see money as less important to the job because they see themselves as less locked in to that dimension of the job. They may see such things as vacations and retirement benefits as more important to it being a good job.

Often the higher the status of the job for the individual the greater the personal commitment. Persons at top levels tend to make strong personal commitments to their work because their self-esteem depends on accomplishment and recognition. There is a strong pressure on them to evaluate their success not only in terms of the job they hold but in terms of their total career. "That is, in terms of where they are in an anticipated sequence of ever-increasing accomplishment and recognition."[35]

There have been various studies conducted asking workers if they would choose the same job if they could start over. As would be expected, white-collar workers are more likely to say they would than blue-collar workers. One study reported that 70–93 percent of the professionals, 41–52 percent of the white-collar and skilled blue-collar workers, and 16–31 percent of the less skilled blue-collar workers would choose the same kind of work. "One of the things 'wrong' with many blue-collar jobs is not so much the work itself as the fact that they are socially defined as lower than white-collar jobs, even at the same rate of pay."[36]

Rosabeth Kanter writes that over the past 20 years a large number of studies have indicated that the approximate percentage of the labor market that reports job satisfaction has remained relatively steady at about 80 percent. She goes on to say that quit rates have fluctuated inversely with unemployment. "Interesting work overtook steady work as the most important thing employed workers said they wanted from

"I find this work truly fulfilling in many ways—there's the exercise, the sense of accomplishment, and, most important, the opportunity to make lots of noise."

their jobs."[37] It has also been found that people were most satisfied with their jobs when their supervisor was helpful and supportive and was willing to allow worker autonomy. The nature of the relationships with managerial figures was at least as important to workers as the type of work they performed. Job satisfaction came from freedom to do their job and the feeling that their jobs were secure, clean, free from undue pressures, and presented an adequate challenge.[38]

One recent study did find somewhat of a drop in worker satisfaction between 1973 and 1977. The number of workers who believed their job skills would be useful and valuable declined from 68 percent in 1973 to 62 percent in 1977. "Likewise, in 1977, 36 percent of the workers reported underutilization of their skills, compared to 27 percent and 25 percent reporting underutilization in 1969 and 1973, respectively."[39]

The other side of the coin in reactions to the job are factors which lead to job dissatisfaction. Age is one factor in that younger workers have the highest rates of expressing dissatisfaction with their jobs. The younger workers also have the highest rates of job seeking and unscheduled absence from work. "They were the largest population group by age among the third of the labor force that changed occupations between 1965 and 1970."[40] In general the most dissatisfied workers are the ones who earn the least. The young, along with blacks and women, are the most unhappy with their earnings.

One condition of how people feel about their work is what they would do if they didn't have to work. One study asked: "If by some chance you inherited enough money to live comfortably without working do you think you would work anyway or not?" About 80 percent reported they would work anyway. "They might not want to continue to work at their particular job, but money aside, they could not think how they would fill their time except by work."[41] Robert S. Weiss further says that it is only in middle-class occupations that the great majority of men say they would continue to work even if it was not economically required.[42]

Interest in working then is based on more than money. For example, although only a small proportion of sales workers and managers earn more than skilled blue-collar workers, they are much more likely to say they would continue working at their jobs even if they no longer needed to work because of the money. Many white-collar jobs appear to provide enough support to an individual's sense of worth to make the job itself, and not just the fact of working, of value to the person.[43]

An important aspect of people's relationship with the work situation is the way they see work meeting their needs over time. Kanter suggests that what seems to define the issues around work in the United States today more than anything else is the fact that people continue to want more benefits even as they get more. So there is a lag between the realities of work possibilities and expressed or latent jobholder concerns.[44] This is reflected in the worker's getting more vacation time and wanting even more. In many ways gains for the blue-collar worker in terms of involvement with his work have been minimal. The blue-collar or service workers know they haven't gotten very far. This is reflected in the fact that many blue-collar workers, "even those who feel satisfied with their work when all things are taken into consideration, hope for more for their children."[45]

FIGURE 4–1

Reports of Work-Related Problems in 1977

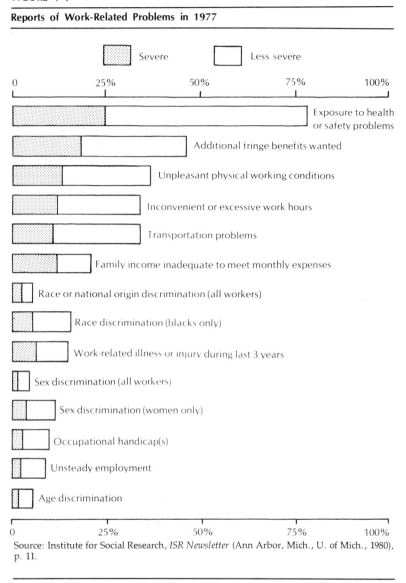

Source: Institute for Social Research, *ISR Newsletter* (Ann Arbor, Mich., U. of Mich., 1980), p. 11.

Still another measurement of work problems is what work and the work environment does to the health of the individual. There are some jobs that are clearly dangerous to the physical health of the worker. For example, coal mining kills hundreds of persons every year. This is either directly through mining accidents or more indirectly in drastically shortening the miner's life span because of lung diseases caused by working in the mines. In recent years there have been increases in absence from work attributable to physical diseases. Peter Warr reports an increase of 22 percent over the past 15 years. However, the increase in physical health problems is not nearly as high as mental health causes. Warr reported for the same 15-year period an increase of absence of 152 percent for men and 302 percent for women due to neurosis and psychosis.[46]

Absence from work because of psychoneurosis, psychosis, nervousness, debility, and headaches is increasing faster than any other form of certified absence.[47] Work satisfaction is highly correlated with mental health. Persons unhappy with their job are most likely to have mental health problems (see Chapter 15). There is evidence that work dissatisfaction is associated with family conflict as well as the use of alcohol and drugs. Mental health rates are also related to levels of work. For example, good mental health is highest among those in the more skilled jobs and lowest for those engaged in repetitive and semi-skilled work. "Job satisfaction and the extent to which individuals saw their world as giving them the chance to use their abilities were consistently important correlates of psychological health."[48]

The importance of involvement and sense of influence on their work is also important to the psychological well-being of the worker. Warr and Toby Wall write there is "extensive evidence that people want immediate participation and that increases in this respect can enhance their well-being at work."[49] One problem with worker involvement in what they do is that many things produced are no longer seen as valuable to the worker. They may often have a sense of being involved in wasteful commodities and services, which diminishes their perception of the value of their own work.

In general the workers' involvement with the job fits two work themes common in America today. Kanter suggests that one theme can be described as cultural or expressive. This is the concern for work as a source of self-respect and nonmaterial rewards. It includes challenge, growth, personal fulfillment, and meaningful work. It is an opportunity to advance and to accumulate and to lead a safe and healthy life. She writes that the second theme can be called political. This is the concern for individual rights and power. It is the seeking of a further extension of the principles of equity and justice into the work place and into the industrial order. It is also the seeking of equality in the form of concrete legal rights.[50]

Alienation.   There has long been a concern with how the worker fits the work force and how the work fits the individual. Beginning with the technological and political revolutions of the late 18th century there has developed for many persons a sense of estrangement from the world. This has been referred to as man's alienation from himself and from others. Alienation can be the clash between the person's self-image and the kind of person work forces him to become. Many jobs force the person to pretend to be something he is not. As a result the person may feel alienated from what he does. Often the alienation the worker feels is due to a feeling of powerlessness, of having no control over what he does.

But how creative really are human beings? There is a romantic notion that inside everyone there is a creative person who will burst forth if given the chance. But there really is no evidence that this is the case. It may be that creativity is confused with having a say in what kind of work one does. As discussed earlier, people do want an input and some degree of freedom in carrying out a job. But to think of this as an urge to express an inner creativity seems a bit far fetched. Furthermore, most work in any society, whether it be capitalist, communist, or socialist, is boring and repetitious. The many things that have to be done every day in any society for its survival leave no room nor opportunity for creativity. This, as a level of social problem, may sometimes be altered but never eliminated.

Vested interests.   The world of work has a variety of viewpoints, orientations, and vested interests. The businessperson, the administrator, the worker, the family, the government, and others all have vested interests they pursue. Over the years there has been a constant struggle to satisfy one's vested interests. The most basic conflict of interests in American society has been between those who own commodities and services and those who do the producing. For most of American history the power struggle was one-sided with the owners and managers in control, but this changed with the successful emergence of the labor movement.

The 1920s and 1930s were major periods of conflict, with the labor movement gaining increasing strength. After World War II the passing of protective legislation swung the balance of power more to the side of labor. When this happened, there were three general options available to capitalists. First, they could relocate part of the industrial process overseas and by doing so acquire cheaper labor. Second, they could relocate internally in parts of the country where labor was cheaper and organized labor had not penetrated. Third, they could mechanize and displace jobs that previously had been filled by cheap labor.[51] These were all options that some businesses followed.

The impact of the American union movement has not been as significant as that in many other industrial countries. The American labor unions, together with employe associations, include only about 30 percent of nonagricultural employment. This contrasts with over 50 percent in Great Britain and 35 percent in Japan and Germany. In Scandinavian countries the percentage probably ranges from 60–80 percent.[52] Since 1960, union membership as a proportion of the nonagricultural labor force has declined. But during the same period collec-

TABLE 4–2

Work Stoppages (Strikes) in the United States

Year	Number of stoppages	Workers involved	Man days idle
1950	4,843	2,410,000	38,800,000
1955	4,320	2,650,000	28,200,000
1960	3,333	1,320,000	19,100,000
1965	3,963	1,550,000	23,300,000
1970	5,716	3,305,000	66,414,000
1975	5,031	1,746,000	31,237,000
1978	4,161	1,617,000	36,841,000

Source: Adapted from "Bureau of Labor Statistics," *The World Almanac* (New York: Newspaper Enterprises, 1980) p. 63.

tive bargaining was extended to new work sectors. "In a number of states, collective bargaining was extended to health services workers and public employes, and there has been an increase in public employe unionism since World War II."[53]

In contrast to other countries, the value commitments of the American labor movement have been different from those in other countries. For example, in Australia the labor unions are much more directly involved in politics. They are also more directly active in social issues. In recent years Australian unions were active in anti-Vietnam war activities and in protests against the mining of uranium for use in atomic energy. The role of the unions in the United States has primarily been concerned with raising wages, improving work conditions, and gaining fringe benefits. The means of doing so has been through the use of collective bargaining. "The unions have never offered any serious challenge to management's prerogative of setting basic goals and policies."[54]

John T. Dunlop points out that American labor unions have not only failed to show interest in codetermination of policies with management but have been hostile to the idea. They have also traditionally looked unkindly toward stock ownership as a means to interest workers in management. American unions regard collective bargaining as an adequate means of influencing management.[55] In fact unions have acquired a vested interest in the smooth running of business enterprises. They often provide the very important function for management of "stabilizing" the labor situation. "Moreover, the unions themselves have become large, bureaucratic structures over which the average worker has as little power as he has over management."[56]

In his study of workers in four countries, Form concludes that the inability of factory workers in advanced industrial societies to bring about change indicates that they lack unity and consensus on political goals. This is true because industrial workers are not a homogeneous group, but rather a stratified group with strong divisions between skilled and unskilled workers. The more industrialized the society becomes, the more distinctive the stratification of skills are in the worker's plant and community involvement. "Skilled workers become increasingly active in various social systems of the society, more differentiated from the unskilled in their behavior, and more independent in their politics."[57]

Form goes on to suggest that the greater work solidarity of the skilled appears to be a natural outgrowth of working in a less restrictive technological environment. He says that in union politics, the skilled are able to put their greater solidarity to work. The skilled are less involved in kinship networks and in the social life of neighborhoods, but they participate more widely in community affairs. "They are more interested and more knowledgeable about both community and national interests."[58] This suggests that unions today represent a much more heterogeneous group than in the past. And certainly the values of many labor union members are more closely attuned to traditional management values than to traditional labor ones.

The use of the strike

The ultimate weapon in the emergence of labor unions has been the legal right to strike. This is often a powerful weapon which is effective even as a threat when it is not actually used. There has been a slight increase in the number of strikes and lockouts in the United States from 5,117 in 1952 to 5,600 in 1976, an increase of 9 percent. However, for the same period of time there has been a decrease of 29 percent in the number of workers involved and a decrease of 36 percent in the number of work-days lost due to strikes and lockouts.[59]

UNEMPLOYMENT

While the way the worker relates to his job is an important social problem, the inability to get a job is an even more basic problem. Unemployment describes the condition of those who want to work but can't find jobs. It is not only an important social problem for those who can't work, but it is also problematic because society must come up with some form of support of the unemployed through either welfare or unemployment compensation taken from the taxes of others. More indirect, but also important, is the fact that unemployment is related to such social problems as crime, poverty, and family difficulties (see Chapter 4).

The percentage of the working population unemployed was 8.7 in 1930. It rose to 23.6 percent during the Depression in 1932, fell to 1.2 in 1944 during World War II, and rose back up to 7.3 percent in 1977.[60] In recent years the rates of unemployment have been going up in all occupational categories. Among white-collar workers it has gone up the least, from 3.8 in 1971 to 4.6 in 1975, an increase of 21 percent. But among blue-collar workers it went from 7.4 in 1971 to 11.5 in 1975, an increase of 55 percent.[61]

The unemployment rates are higher for women, blacks, and the young. In 1979, for white women 20 years of age and over, the rate was 52 percent as compared to white men with a rate of 3.3 percent. For black men 20 and over, the rate was 8.4 percent and for black women in the same age group it was 9.9 percent. For white teenagers, 16 to 19 years of age, the unemployment rate was 14.3 percent and for black teenagers, 36.9 percent.[62]

Unemployment can also be related to problems of health (see Chapter 14). For example, unemployment has long been associated with hospitalization for depression. One study of the health of workers who had been notified that their company was being shut down permanently found significant increases in physical complaints immediately after the news was received, immediately after the plants shut down, and again after protracted unemployment.[63] Of course, unemployment may be a reflection of poor health. The person who has had

TABLE 4–3

Unemployment Rates, May 1979   (Percent of group's civilian labor force)

White, Total	5.0
Men, 20 years and older	3.3
Women, 20 years and older	5.1
Both sexes, 16 to 19 years	14.3
Black and other, Total	11.6
Men, 20 years and older	8.4
Women, 20 years and older	9.9
Both sexes, 16 to 19 years	36.9
Married men, spouse present	2.5
Married women, spouse present	5.2
Women heads of household	8.9

Source: Adapted from "Bureau of Labor Statistics," *The World Almanac* (New York: Newspaper Enterprise, 1980).

serious physical or mental health problems may not be able to work or, if able to work, may not be hired because of his medical history.

Unemployment is an enevitable consequence of technological change. Over past decades hundreds of thousands of jobs have disappeared because of technical development. For example, in the 1930s thousands of men were hired to dig ditches, but that job was made obsolete with the development of digging machines. In general, it is the unskilled and semiskilled jobs that have in the past been made obsolete through technological development. As we shall discuss shortly, this trend is increasingly true of many white-collar jobs.

Are there any solutions to unemployment? Theoretically the only solution is for a society to create jobs. This was done during the Depression of the 1930s when the federal government funded programs to build and repair public properties which led to the hiring of many workers. But many of these lower skilled jobs have disappeared, so there is no need for them. It is doubtful that society will destroy all the ditchdigging equipment so men can once again dig ditches. The unions have sometimes used "feather bedding" practices to protect workers. This is the maintenance of persons on the payroll even though their jobs have disappeared and there is nothing else for them to do. Probably the "best" bet for reaching a low unemployment rate is to have another heavy involvement in a war. But even then it is doubtful that the low unemployment rate of World War II could be matched because many jobs then filled have disappeared because of technological change. It would seem that not only will unemployment not go down significantly in the future, but rather it will continue to go up. Society may have to live with an increasing percentage of unemployable people because there is no need for whatever skills they have to offer.

It is clear that the American work force is a changing one. The major force in the changing of work in recent years has been automation and computerization. Automation refers to the linking together in a continuous process a variety of production operations. For example, in the production of chemicals, only a few workers may be needed, mainly to monitor the automation and make sure it is functioning correctly. With the use of computers, there can be electronic data processing to record, store, and utilize information. Office computer systems now handle bookkeeping inventories, ordering, accounting, and billing. They have made obsolete thousands of clerical jobs.

In part the rise of automation came because of its much greater efficiency in saving the user both cost and time. But the move to automation was not made simply in response to technological innovation. It was; at least in part, a response to rising labor costs. In the steel industry rising wages led to an increase in capital relative to labor. "Similarly in meat-packing, high wages for unskilled and semi-skilled labor, in part due to strong unions, have accelerated automation and the substitution of equipment for labor."[64]

One consequence of automation is that it alters the hierarchy of jobs in a given occupation. Research into American manufacturing establishments suggests that automation increases the proportion of managers, supervisors, and other white-collar workers in an establishment.[65] It is the lesser skilled jobs that automation typically makes obsolete. Automation increases traditional craft skill, but it is applied to maintenance problems rather than production work. This means that more repairers are needed to maintain equipment. "In the largest oil refineries and heavy chemical plants, there are as many or more maintenance employes than production employes."[66]

Alienation among workers appears more common the larger the factory because the worker is further removed from any sense of personal contribution to the overall work enterprise. Team production often helps reduce meaninglessness because the workers more easily develop a sense of purpose when working together than individually. An increased sense of purpose and function in work for the blue-collar employe may be a product of automation. "This technical system brings about smaller factories, production by teams rather than individuals, and integrated process operations."[67]

Robert Blauner has argued that automation has contributed to greater social integration of workers. Historically, one of the most significant factors underlying class conflict in the factory has been the differences in the nature of work performed by production workers and management. But the work of the blue-collar process operators through automation becomes similar to that of the white-collar work-

Milt & Joan Mann

The age of automation and the computer

ers. The automated work is clean, includes record keeping and other clerical tasks, and involves responsibility.[68]

As discussed, automation is not only replacing the blue-collar worker but also the white-collar one. For example, there are now banks of typewriters that can be operated by automation. It is of interest that often there is an attempt to disguise the fact that something is being done through automation because it will seem too impersonal and people will not respond. Many letters are typed through automated methods to look like they were done by individual typists and stamps are used instead of metered mail to give it a more personal touch. In fact, there is a machine made that puts stamps on envelopes off center and tilted to one side so that the recipient will think some human tongue actually licked the stamp and placed it on the envelope.

The changes in the work force do not look good for the future. As suggested, unemployment will remain high and probably increase. It is likely that more and more jobs will be eliminated both in the blue-collar and white-collar areas. Also, as discussed earlier, the institutions of higher education are out of step with occupational needs. This means that the highest status occupations, the professions, are increasingly going to be negatively affected.

One other way in which the work world of the United States is being influenced is through what has become a world work market rather than a separate one for each country. In fact, the United States is a member of the world economy where its competitive position is increasingly precarious. For example, many American factories are outmoded and inefficient compared with the newer ones in countries like Japan and Germany. The United States is dependent for many essential raw materials on countries that are organizing cartels to control the prices, such as the oil producing countries. Furthermore, many American products have become too expensive to compete on the world market.[69]

Leisure.   One of the consequences of the changes in the work force has been an increase in the leisure time of the worker. Work and leisure time is generally linked to the family. In recent years the family as the unit of work has changed drastically with the woman also working outside the home. Leisure time is usually family based, whether the decision is to do something together or separately.

During the last century the average length of the work week in the United States decreased steadily. Vacations have become longer, there are more paid holidays and job entry is postponed longer by going to school. Between 1890 and 1970 the average work week declined by about 14 hours in this country.[70] But in terms of actual free time what does this mean? Women have less free time since more of them have entered the work force. On a weekly basis, employed, married men work an average of 51.3 hours (including commuting) and have an average of 34.6 free hours per week. The employed, married woman averages about 39 hours of work but performed an average of 33 hours of housework (against an average of 11.5 hours for their husbands). "In general, working women have approximately 10 hours less free time than do their husbands."[71]

There is also an uneven distribution of leisure time by occupation. One quarter of all managers, proprietors, and officials, and over half of the farmers and farm workers put in an average of 60 or more hours of work per week.[72] Men in upper strata occupations have often lost out on leisure time. Even though their work lives are shorter and vacations longer they work more hours week after week. It is probable that many men in the professions choose to work. In other words, it is something they would rather be doing than anything else like being with their families.

Money becomes an important factor in the use of leisure time. Often the people with the most leisure time are the ones without the money to do much with the time. A few years ago the woman working outside the home, especially in the middle class, was seen as bringing in a supplementary income; that is, one the family was not dependent on for the daily costs of living. One common use of her income was for leisure-time activities. But this has changed in recent years, and more and more the two-income family uses the combined income to meet the daily costs of living. For example, at the present time a majority of all families that buy a house are dependent on a combined income to get a mortgage.

Americans have often shown an ambivalent attitude about leisure time. Great importance has been attached to earning a respectable living, and therefore most American workers have always preferred to take their share of increased productivity in the form of greater income rather than increased leisure time.[73] This is also reflected in the overwhelming willingness of the American worker to give up leisure time on the weekend for the time-and-a-half and double-time that can be earned by working overtime. Kanter suggests that the tendency to exchange income for more leisure was probably ended by the mid-1930s. From then on workers took production gains in money rather than in more leisure time.[74]

There has also been in recent years some increased commitment to the value of leisure time. This is often reflected in the notion of families doing something together or of individuals pursuing various interests that will broaden their lives and give them more personal satisfaction. This view suggests that work provides for greater and more rewarding leisure, and that leisure will make the person better and more satisfied with work. However, the persons and families with the greatest education, training, and motivation for a diversity of leisure experiences are the ones with the least amount of time to pursue them.[75]

As suggested, many who have leisure are forced into it because they are marginal to the economy. These people would generally give up their leisure for work if they could. Furthermore, the shorter work week has simply encouraged many to take a second job. The frustration with leisure time is sometimes seen with the retired worker. He would often work if he could because he gets little satisfaction from his enforced leisure time. The man who says he can't wait to retire so he can fish often finds fishing a bore within a few months.

As suggested, leisure time for many is acquired at the sacrifice of income. But very often the American values regarding leisure time require money. A great deal of our leisure time is consumer oriented. One kind of leisure time promoted strongly in recent years has been travel, and this is expensive. Other kinds of activities, such as do-it-yourself projects, also tend to cost money. In 1976, the average American household spent 6.6 percent of its total income on recreation. But other items not included such as eating out, tobacco and alcohol, some clothing, personal cosmetics, and transportation could lift the overall figure to about 10 percent.[76]

The American value system regarding the use of leisure time is then generally rooted in the commercial marketplace. This is true whether it be sports, gardening, home crafts, vacations, or travel. All of these activities involve the investment of money. The great American involvement in spectator types of leisure time also involve money. Because the leisure time pursuits are big business, they compete strongly for the leisure time dollar.

Often leisure time is really work. The amount of physical effort the person has to put into leisure may be greater than what he does on the job. There is also the common belief that leisure time should be pleasurable. For example, going on a vacation is to be a rewarding experience, but often it is not. When this happens the person often feels very shortchanged because "it shouldn't be that way."

In conclusion, the needs of the work force have undergone great change. One consequence has been to eliminate many people with certain skills for whom there is no place in the work force. Furthermore the jobs that people do have don't always meet their individual needs or give them any sense of satisfaction or personal fulfillment. Given the probability of increased unemployment and no indication that jobs will become more satisfying to the individual in the future, it can be predicted that work will continue to provide a setting for a major social problem in the United States.

For the middle class in America, work has been highly valued. Work differs in what it demands and who is qualified to do what. People have differing opportunities and positions in the work force as determined by such factors as sex and race. Individuals vary in the degree and reasons they have for being satisfied with their work. How people feel about their work is related to what they will give to the job and what they receive in turn. There are differing vested interests in work as reflected in management and unions. One very basic social problem related to work, and becoming more common, is unemployment.

NOTES

1. *Information Please Almanac 1978* (New York: Information Please Publishing, Inc., 1978), p. 62.

2. Robert S. Weiss, Edwin Harwood, and David Riesman, "The World of Work," in *Contemporary Social Problems*, 4th ed., by Robert K. Merton and Robert Nisbet (New York: Harcourt Brace Jovanovich, 1976), p. 606.

3. Frank Lindenfeld, "Work Alienation and the Industrial Order," in *Understanding Social Problems*, by Don H. Zimmerman (New York: Praeger Publishers, 1976), p. 96.

4. U.S. Department of Labor, Bureau of Labor Statistics, *Handbook of Labor Statistics* (Washington, D.C., U.S. Government Printing Office, 1975), p. 41.

5. Weiss, Harwood, and Riesman, "World of Work," p. 629.

6. Lindenfeld, "Work Alienation," p. 98.

7. Ibid., pp. 101–2.

8. *Information Please Almanac 1978*, p. 64.

9. Richard P. Coleman and Lee Rainwater, *Social Standing in America* (New York: Basic Books, 1978), p. 51.

10. Wendy C. Wolf and Neil D. Fligstein, "Sex and Authority in the Workplace: The Causes of Sexual Inequality," *American Sociological Review* (April 1979), p. 235.

11. Coleman and Rainwater, *Social Standing*, p. 48.

12. William H. Form, "The Internal Stratification of the Working Class: System Involvements of Auto Workers in Four Countries," *American Sociological Review* (December 1973), p. 709.

13. *Information Please Almanac 1978*, p. 58.

14. Rosabeth Moss Kanter, "Work in a New America," *Daedalus* (Winter 1978), p. 50.

15. Peter M. Blau, "Implications of Growth in Services for Social Structure," *Social Science Quarterly*, (June 1980), p. 21.

16. Edna Bonacich, "Advanced Capitalism and Black/White Race Relations in the United States: A Split Market Labor Market Interpretation," *American Sociological Review* (February 1976), p. 36.

17. Ibid., p. 38.

18. Ibid., p. 42.

19. Marc Feigen Fasteau, *The Male Machine* (New York: Delta, 1976), p. 116.

20. Wolf and Fligstein, "Sex and Authority," p. 250.

21. *Information Please Almanac 1978*, pp. 99–100.

22. Ibid., p. 99.

23. Kanter, "Work in America," p. 48.

24. Ibid., p. 57.

25. Ibid., p. 57.

26. Weiss, Harwood, and Riesman, "World of Work," p. 631.

27. Kanter, "Work in America," p. 49.

28. Nancy Needham Wardell, "The Corporation," *Daedalus* (Winter 1978), p. 101.

29. Ibid., p. 98.

30. Weiss, Harwood, and Riesman, "World of Work," p. 608.

31. Kanter, "Work in America," p. 58.

32. David Thorns, *Suburbia* (Suffort, Great Britain: Paladin, 1973), p. 24.

33. Daniel Yankelovich, *The New Morality: A Profile of American Youths in the 70s* (New York: McGraw-Hill, 1974), p. 104.

34. Peter Warr and Toby Wall, *Work and Well-Being* (Middlesex, Great Britain: Penguin, 1975), p. 43.

35. Weiss, Harwood, and Riesman, "World of Work," p. 630.

36. Lindenfeld, "Work Alienation," p. 109.

37. Kanter, "Work in America," p. 52.

38. Weiss, Harwood, and Riesman, "World of Work," p. 623.

39. "Job Satisfaction Has Decreased," ISR Newsletter (Ann Arbor: Institute of Social Research, 1980), p. 10.

40. Kanter, "Work in America," p. 49.

41. Weiss, Harwood, and Riesman, "World of Work," p. 609.

42. Ibid., p. 624.

43. Ibid., p. 628.

44. Kanter, "Work in America," p. 67.

45. Weiss, Harwood, and Riesman, "World of Work," p. 628.

46. Warr and Wall, *Work and Well-Being*, p. 145.

47. Ibid., p. 21.

48. Ibid., p. 121.

49. Ibid., p. 113.
50. Kanter, "Work in America," pp. 53–54.
51. Bonacich, "Advanced Capitalism," p. 47.
52. John T. Dunlop, "Past and Future Tendencies in American Labor Organizations," *Daedalus* (Winter 1978), p. 80.
53. Kanter, "Work in America," p. 51.
54. Lindenfeld, p. 113.
55. Dunlop, "Tendencies," p. 90.
56. Lindenfeld, "Work Alienation," p. 113.
57. Form, "Internal Stratification," p. 697.
58. Ibid., p. 709.
59. *Information Please Almanac 1978*, p. 63.
60. Ibid., p. 63.
61. U.S. Department of Labor, Bureau of Labor Statistics, "The Employment Situation: August 1975," (Washington D.C.: U.S. Government Printing Office, 1975), p. 3.
62. The World Almanac (New York: Newspaper Enterprise, Inc., 1980), p. 48.
63. Weiss, Harwood, and Riesman, "World of Work," p. 620.
64. Bonacich, "Advanced Capitalism," p. 48.
65. Blau, "Implications of Growth," p. 10.
66. Robert Blauner, *Alienation and Freedom* (Chicago: University of Chicago Press, 1964), p. 169.
67. Ibid., p. 24.
68. Ibid., pp. 179–80.
69. Weiss, Harwood, and Riesman, "World of Work," p. 606.
70. Lindenfeld, "Work Alienation," p. 104.
71. William Kornblum and Terry Williams, "Life Style, Leisure, and Community Life," in *Handbook of Contemporary Urban Life*, by David Street (San Francisco: Jossey-Bass, 1978), p. 65.
72. Lindenfeld, "Work Alienation," p. 105.
73. Weiss, Harwood, and Riesman, "World of Work," pp. 608–9.
74. Kanter, "Work in America," p. 57.
75. Kornblum and Williams, "Life Style," p. 64.
76. *Information Please Almanac 1978*, p. 65.

SELECTED BIBLIOGRAPHY

Dunlop, John T. "Past and Future Tendencies in American Labor Organizations." *Daedalus* (Winter 1978), pp. 79–96.

Form, William H. "The Internal Stratification of the Working Class: System Involvements of Auto Workers in Four Countries." *American Sociological Review* (December 1973), pp. 697–711.

Kanter, Rosabeth Moss. "Work in a New America." *Daedalus* (Winter 1978), pp. 47–78.

Kornblum, William, and Williams, Terry. "Life Styles, Leisure, and Community Life." In *Handbook of Contemporary Urban Life* by David Street. San Francisco: Jossey-Bass, 1978, pp. 58–89.

Lindenfeld, Frank. "Work Alienation and the Industrial Order." In *Understanding Social Problems*, by Don H. Zimmerman et al., New York: Praeger Publishers, 1976, pp. 96–125.

Warr, Peter, and Wall, Toby. *Work and Well-Being*. Middlesex, Great Britain: Penguin, 1975.

Wolf, Wendy C., and Fligstein, Neil D. "Sex and Authority in the Workplace: The Causes of Sexual Inequality." *American Sociological Review* (April 1979), pp. 235–52.

Chapter 5

Poverty

For a society to maintain itself its members must have those things necessary for basic survival. But basic survival needs are the bottom line and all individuals want more—a little more to a great deal more. In the money economy of the United States persons must acquire the money to buy the needs of life—food, shelter, clothing, and so forth. People who do not have the means to buy or acquire what a society defines as minimal suffer from poverty. What this minimal level is and what solutions might eradicate poverty are questions which have no clearly accepted answers.

While the conditions that constitute a level of poverty may remain relatively constant over a period of time, the persons falling below that level may or may not be defined as living in poverty. In the United States poverty has sometimes been seen as a serious social problem and at other times has been ignored—at least to the extent that there was little social awareness of the extent of poverty or few concerted efforts directed at resolution. This can be seen by looking at some historical views about poverty in the United States.

POVERTY OVER TIME IN THE UNITED STATES

In the 18th century in the United States poverty was not seen as a social problem. There was a clearly defined social structure with the rich and the powerful at the top. Those at the top often received deference from those at the bottom, and during times of social need, those at the top provided some help for the poor. Solutions arose locally in response to a particular need, but generally poverty was seen as a natural condition of life. Initially poverty was accepted as inevitable and as the fate of most of the masses. "The American philosophy stressed that in a society where there is work for all, nobody needs to go hungry."[1]

A general view of the poor was that they lived that way because of their own inadequacies. It was often seen as their "nature" to be poor. Later the view was that many were living in poverty because they had fallen to temptation. They were sinful. As a result, from the perspective of the well-to-do, the poor needed to be protected from temptations. In England, one solution was to put them in workhouses. There they were subjected to religious remedial discipline through long hours of work.

American views on poverty can be understood only through the high social value placed on work. Probably no other society has ever placed a greater emphasis on the significance of work than during the 19th and 20th centuries in America when work came to be exalted for its own sake. "The development of Protestantism, with its Calvinistic emphasis on worldly success, industriousness, individual initiative, thrift, deferred gratification, and the moral obligation to work, led to the formulation of a dominant and pervasive work ethic."[2] (See Chapter 4)

Therefore, with the strong American belief in work, the person living in poverty was seen as going against a major value. If he failed in the economic struggle, it was his fault due to idleness, bad habits, intemperance, vices, and other human weaknesses defined as responsible for his condition. So poverty was an individual matter and only the individual could overcome it. But change did occur and Hanna Meissner writes that around the middle of the 19th century, "under the impact of industrialization and urbanization, criticism of the purely individualistic approach to poverty became more and more frequent."[3]

Over time in the United States the definition of poverty has changed as a reflection of changing values. For example, in the 1920s the general view was that America was about ready to rid itself of any poverty problem. This was expected to happen through the "natural" processes of the market which would bring forth such abundance that America would become the land of milk and honey. This high optimism contributed to the stock market crash of 1929 and made the following economic depression of the 1930s even more difficult for many Americans to understand and to accept.

The depression of the 1930s was the worst ever suffered in this country. Up until the depression there was a fairly clear division of labor insofar as the poor were concerned. There were immigrants, industrial workers and their families, who were considered the worthy poor since their poverty was seen as either temporary or the result of an uncontrollable misfortune. But there were also the unworthy poor who were that way because of willful laziness or moral degeneracy.[4] Then, during the depression there developed increasing awareness that some poverty was due not to the individual but to social conditions. A new way of dealing with poverty was introduced in the 1930s by the Roosevelt administration in recognition that the individual approach to fighting poverty was not enough and much more drastic measures were called for. It introduced new social inventions such as "the Civilian Conservation Corps, to provide work for youth between the ages of 17 to 23, the National Youth Administration to support needy students with part-time work, the work relief programs for the unemployed, and the Social Security Act."[5]

The depression of the 1930s ended with World War II. That war, which called for massive industrial efforts, led to near full employment. The percentage of women entering the work force was greatly increased. With the high employment of World War II, it was com-

Unemployment during the 1930s' depression

monly believed once again that poverty was virtually eliminated. "The general image was one of an affluent society with the highest standards of living in the world which gave everyone its fair share."[6]

During the first half of the 20th century there were many attempts to explain the causes of poverty. As suggested, these were often linked to sin and willful laziness. But poverty was also often linked to other social problems. For example, in the decades of temperance agitation before the Prohibition Era in the United States, there was much interest in drunkenness among the working class and in linking the explanation of excessive drinking with poor living standards. Many other consumption habits have also been tied to poverty, "among them: unsophisticated shopping, purchase of luxuries, big families, unhealthy diets, excessive use of installment purchase, failure to save, and gambling."[7]

As mentioned in Chapter 1, sociologists in America have from the beginning had a strong interest in poverty, which is reflected in a long history of research into this area. The history of poverty research usually represents moral points of view. On one hand the lay researchers of the 19th century felt that the poor were personally and politically immoral and undeserving. On the other hand the social scientists who took up research in the 20th century saw the poor as suffering from individual pathologies and from social disorganization. The poor were seen as deficient rather than undeserving, but often the implication was that the deficiencies had to be corrected before they were worthy of help.

The lower class, defined as the very bottom of the social structure, is by definition suffering from poverty. Furthermore, the general view of the professions that deal with the lower class is that they are problem people. In the discussion ahead we will use lower class to mean those experiencing poverty, whose conditions are generally defined as a social problem at the present time in the United States.

Who are the poor? They are not a set, stable population. While there clearly is a hard core of persons who remain poor from generation to generation, there is also a continuous flow of persons in and out of poverty. For example, in 1967 there were 22.3 million persons defined as poor, but by 1968, 7.3 million of those had left poverty and 5.6 million new persons had entered poverty. The geographical concentration of the poor has changed in recent years. In 1959, the majority of poor people (56 percent) lived in rural America. Today, over 60 percent of the poor live in the cities.

Part of the problem of identifying the poor is the difficulty of defining them. The most commonly used measurement of poverty is one developed by the Social Security Administration during the 1960s and adjusted each year for increases in the cost of living. This is an arbitrary measurement and there is no agreement that it really draws a line between poverty and minimum economic adequacy. Zahava D.

TABLE 5–1

Percent of Persons, Families, and Unrelated Individuals Below the Poverty Level, 1977

All Persons	11.6%
White	8.9
Black	31.3
Spanish origin	22.4
North and west	10.0
South	14.8
Inside metropolitan areas	10.4
Inside central cities	15.4
Outside central cities	6.8
Outside metropolitan areas	13.9
All families	9.3
Husband-wife	5.3
Male householder, no wife present	11.1
Female householder, no husband present	31.7
All unrelated individuals	22.6
Male	18.0
Female	26.1

Source: Adapted from U.S. Department of Commerce, Bureau of the Census, "Characteristics of the Population below the Poverty Level: 1977, *Current Population Reports*" P–60, no. 119 (Washington, D.C.: U.S. Government Printing Office, 1979), p. 2.

Blum and Peter H. Rossi suggest that this disagreement will continue indefinitely for two reasons. "First, because no index and no cutting point will do everything that every party in the dispute would desire, and second, because social change will not acquiesce to the preservation of any index."[8] The poverty level in 1978 was $5,170 income a year for a family of four.

A general statistical picture can be drawn of the poor in the United States. At present there are about 8 million families and 5 million individuals who have incomes at the poverty level. Of these, about three quarters are white. About one fourth of the families are headed by a woman and about one fourth headed by a person who works full time but earns insufficient income. Another 1.5 million family heads work full time but are laid off for parts of the year. Another one fourth have an aged head of the family. Of the total number of poor about 40 percent receive public assistance. While about 40 percent of the poor live in rural areas they get less than one twelfth of the federal funds.

THE SOCIAL SETTING OF POVERTY

In this section we want to look at some of the social variables related to poverty. We want to look first at some of the ways in which the poor are defined. As we suggested, poverty is hard to define and there is often disagreement. Blum and Rossi found that for many writers there are two kinds of poverty. On the one hand are the respectable poor. These are people like the middle class except that they have less income. On the other hand are the "disreputable" poor. These people not only have limited incomes but they are believed to have different values and standards from middle-class Americans.[9]

The disreputable poor are seen at the very bottom of society. One study of social class in two large American cities found that people made the distinction between two lower-class groups. The respondents saw the disreputable as being the welfare class and its members were criticized for usually or always being dependent on public aid and charity for their income. The people at the higher level or the more respectable poor were given their higher status because "they're never on welfare" or "only occasionally."[10]

The above study also interviewed persons in the lower class as to how they viewed themselves. They found that these individuals also saw the lower class as divided into two groups and they almost invariably discriminated between two types of people at the bottom. One category consisted of people who were poverty stricken and/or on welfare and were physically and morally clean. This is where they would put themselves. The other group, and the lowest, were people who were not clean.[11]

At the bottom level, however poverty is defined, there does appear to be a hard-core group. These are people who remain unemployed and whose poverty tends to persist from one generation to the next. These people may be unemployable because of poor health, mental incompetency, or lack of skills. There are some people who have given up on ever getting work. These are often not even counted among the unemployed because they don't get on the records unless they are looking for a job. The basic problem is that many people who are born into great poverty become locked into the system. Their health is often bad because of malnutrition and poor medical help. They develop few skills because education is not a part of their socialization. For them there is realistically no viable way to break out of a trap of poverty.

Very often poverty is associated with not being employed, but that is not always the case. Many poor people work and for those who don't, their lack of work is associated with more than no earnings. Often the view toward the poor is that work is necessary for maintaining their personal integrity. "The implicit assumption is that poor, unlike middle-class people, do not really want to work. If given a subsistence welfare income, without a work requirement, it is assumed that able-bodied poor people would lapse into indolence."[12]

The belief that the lower class doesn't want to work is a misconception of the middle class. Leonard Goodwin suggests that this misconception "permits middle-class persons to believe that they are fun-

Poverty and the family

damentally different from lower-class welfare receipients with respect to work orientation."[13] Another study found that a commitment to work among a sample of poor persons was as strong as among employed white- and blue-collar workers. The persons studied did not want to remain idle and accept public assistance and many expressed moral indignation against people who did not want to work. "The fascinating aspect we encountered was the seeming internalization of the dominant work ethic, with its negative stereotype toward people who accept welfare, by a group of extremely disadvantaged people."[14]

Even the hard-core unemployed often have a positive view about working. One survey found that 84 percent of the sample of hard-core unemployed responded positively to working even if they could live comfortably without it. "Even long-term welfare mothers and their teenage sons continue to have a strong work ethic, associating their self-esteem with work just as strongly as the nonpoor and the working poor."[15]

Often work is not a solution to poverty. Working can be expensive. Costs include transportation, clothes, child care, meals, and work-related expenses. A family can have someone working and still be very poor. In 1978, of the 5,290,000 U.S. nonfarm families who fell below the government's official level of poverty, fully 60 percent had at least one working member, and 87,000 of those families had four or more working members.[16]

A problem for the poor concerning money is that they not only have less of it but when they spend they often get less value for their money than middle-class spenders. What the poor pay for housing in proportion to what they get is often much more than in the middle class. Food often costs more because they buy from small stores with a greater markup rather than from large supermarkets with lower prices. This happens because large stores often won't do business in the poor areas. Even when they do, such large stores in poor areas often charge more for food items than they do in their middle class neighborhood stores. The higher prices have been explained as necessary because they have a low volume of sales per customer and their loss through theft is higher.

The poor are also victims of installment or credit buying. Because they can't accumulate capital they tend to buy with a small down payment and many monthly payments. For example, if the retail price for a television set is $300, a middle-class person may shop around and by paying cash get the set for $250. The poor person buying the same set will often purchase it from a small store on the installment plan and pay the list price plus interest, easily paying $350 for the same television set.

Some writers talk about the lower class as wasteful in their use of their resources. This is obviously a value judgment but is legitimate if one is trying to assess the use of money to meet basic demands of life. Alternately, it can be argued that poverty "causes" the wasteful consumption of alcohol. If people spend a significant part of their earnings on alcohol, they are being wasteful in taking away from basic needs. Therefore, wasteful spending can deplete a family's resources until their income is inadequate. In these cases it is wasteful consumption, rather than low income, that causes a family's poverty. And often even when incomes start below the poverty level wasteful expenses can further exacerbate the situation.

People at all social class levels share in common relationships in American society. The things they share in common are very great, but there are obviously some significant differences. As suggested, values of the lower class affect how they react to work and to poverty. Often there is not only the potential but the reality of value conflict. A person who accepts the American value of work but can't find a job is caught in a significant conflict. The failure to work may be seen as his own fault or the fault of society.

For many poor people the values and norms they have learned are impossible for them to meet. Among the lower class, deviance from some social values and norms is often tolerable. Lee Rainwater suggests that one of the great discoveries that lower-class people make, which middle- and working-class people find hard to understand, is that it is possible to live a life that departs significantly from the way you think life should be lived and that this can be done without ceasing to exist, without feeling totally degraded, and without giving up all self-esteem.[17] In part this can be done through a subcultural set of values which are special to the group and supportive to its members.

Given the relative deprivation of being in the lower class with very little income, it is understandable that the poor often feel frustration and react negatively to the rest of society. Rainwater reports that all investigators who have studied lower-class people seem to come up with similar findings to the general effect that the lower-class view involves conceptions of the world as a hostile and relatively chaotic place. The poor often see the broader world as a place to be always on guard and be careful of trusting others and where the reward for effort is always problematic.[18]

In everyday life, there is a functional autonomy of the lower class which serves both their interests and those of the larger society. The lower class often requires breathing room free from the oppressive eye of conventional society and the application of conventional norms. At the same time conventional society is free from the necessity of facing up to the pain and difficulty the lower class often must live with. "Conventional culture is relieved of the necessity of confronting the fact that norms are constantly flaunted and that the social mechanisms that are supposed to ensure observance of the norms cannot operate effectively."[19]

Rainwater goes on to argue that the lower-class world is defined by two tough facts of life experienced by people from the day they are born until their death. These are deprivation and exclusion. The lower class is deprived because it is excluded from the average patterns of life for the American working and middle classes. "It is excluded because it is deprived of the resources necessary to function in the institutions of the mainstream of American life."[20]

In general, those living in poverty lack the same kinds of social organization found in the middle class. For example, the literature on poverty and the poor describes the areas inhabited by the lower class as severely lacking in community organization. This is not to argue that areas where the poor live are characterized by social disorganization, because many individuals living in poverty are connected with each other through networks of kin and peers. "However, organizations concerned with community affairs, both internally and in dealing with the larger society, are relatively rare."[21] Even contact with kin is less than that found among the middle class. Numerous studies show that the poor visit with relatives and neighbors less than do those in the more affluent communities.

Blum and Rossi, after reviewing a variety of studies, write that lower status individuals are much less likely to vote, belong to organizations that take positions on political issues, discuss political issues with their friends, write or talk to congressmen or other public officials, contribute money to a political party or to a candidate, or attend meetings at which political speeches are made.[22] Generally, the poor feel their efforts at influencing any political policy will have no effect. Furthermore, the notion of entering the political process at any stage has never been a part of their life style.

Life among the poor is often very limited. It is limited psychologically, socially and geographically. Therefore, this restrictive view of life suggests that the position of the poor in the social structure limits their outlook to what goes on around them to the local and immediate setting. One result of this is to restrict their knowledge and experience of broader options and to reduce any sense of control over their own destinies. Because most of the world is distant and unreachable, feelings of alienation and low self-esteem often develop. Russell L. Curtis, Jr., and Louis A. Zurcher report that persons in lower social class levels are much more likely than middle- and upper-class people "to display marked incidences of apathy, feelings of isolation, low self-esteem, alienation, and anomie."[23] Blum and Rossi also report that "the sense of powerlessness, inability to control one's fate, and detachment from the larger society is shown in a number of studies. A number of studies confirm that anomie is more prevalent on the lower levels of the socioeconomic ladder."[24]

The Family and Poverty

There has long been a concern about the effects of poverty on all aspects of the family. Over the years many studies have shown the negative effects of poverty on marriage, sexual behavior, children, aging, and so forth. In general, the literature has argued that the lower the social class level, the greater the incidence of family disorganization and the greater the sense of alienation from the larger society. This has meant for the lower class higher incidences of mental disorder, rates of mortality, incidences of physical disorder, and crime and delinquency rates.[25] In other words, poverty and the family have been linked to many other social problems.

TABLE 5–2

Poverty by Family Status, Sex, Race, 1978

	Percent
Total Poor	11.6
In families	10.2
Head	9.3
Related children	16.0
Other relatives	5.9
Unrelated individuals	22.6
In male-headed families	6.2
Head	5.5
Related children	8.5
Other relatives	5.0
Unrelated male individuals	18.0
In female-headed families	36.2
Head	31.7
Related children	50.3
Other relatives	15.8
Unrelated female individuals	26.1
Total black poor	31.3
In families	30.5
Head	28.2
Female	51.0
Related children	41.6
Other relatives	17.4
Unrelated individuals	37.0

Source: Adapted from *"U.S. Bureau of the Census,"* *The World Almanac* (New York, Newspaper Enterprises, 1980) p. 84.

Rates of desertion and divorce are highest for the lower classes. Marriage as a relationship of interpersonal satisfaction and as an economic arrangement is much less common among the poor. Very often the economic function of marriage is drastically undercut by the inability of the man to work and fill the breadwinner role. For the woman, marriage is a greater risk than in the middle class because there is no guarantee that her husband can successfully be a wage earner. Marriage often provides fewer emotional satisfactions. One study found that being married made no difference to people whose income was below the poverty line; it did not relieve worrying, feeling lonely, or reporting unhappiness or dissatisfaction with their lives.[26]

Very often to talk about the poor family is to talk about a female-headed family. Almost half of all poor families are headed by a woman. There has been a great deal of research related to the one-parent family with emphasis on the impact of the female-headed family structure on the children. In general, if other social variables are held constant, the children in this family structure have no special problems or negative consequences. It is often assumed that in the fatherless family the mother must assume the role obligations of both parents and that this burden leads to disorganization. The research findings on the impact of the mother playing duel parental roles are not very significant. One study suggests that the potential problem in the fatherless families is the inadequacy in the areas of the provider role.[27] If there are adequate funds, many of the problems no longer exist. Sally Bould goes on to say that being a lone adult heading a family is not, in and of itself, problematic for a sense of personal fate control. "Unless some secure and reliable form of nonwork income is available in adequate amounts, the price of staying home and relying on income such as welfare or child support may be high in terms of a sense of personal fate control loss."[28]

What are the sources of income for the low income female-headed family? One study of female-headed families on welfare, where the absent father had agreed to make child support payments, found that the median earning of the absent father was $8,200 per year, while the mothers had a median income of only $3,456 per year, including their welfare payments. Bould suggests that income which has a clear legal, moral, and practical right is important in giving mothers the freedom and autonomy to plan their own lives, as well as the lives of their children, with some sense of assurance and certainty.[29]

Even though the husband usually has a legal responsibility to contribute to the support of his children he very often does not. Moreover, the longer he is separated or divorced from his family, the less likely it is that he will pay anything. This is true even though almost all states have laws where husbands can be held criminally liable for nonsupport of their children. Even in this situation, most laws have been written to favor the man. For example, most states require that nonsupport be proved "willful" and that the wife or children be "in destitute circumstances." "But even in these cases law enforcement agencies are slow to act, and in some counties warrants for noncompliance just pile up and even traffic cases get higher priority."[30]

Often the poor woman has no choice but welfare even if there is a husband with legal responsibilities to help with financial costs. It is also common for a woman to choose welfare rather than marriage. However low the welfare payments, they are constant while a job held by her husband often is not. The woman has control over the welfare

FIGURE 5–1

Characteristics of AFDC mothers aged 15–44, 1975

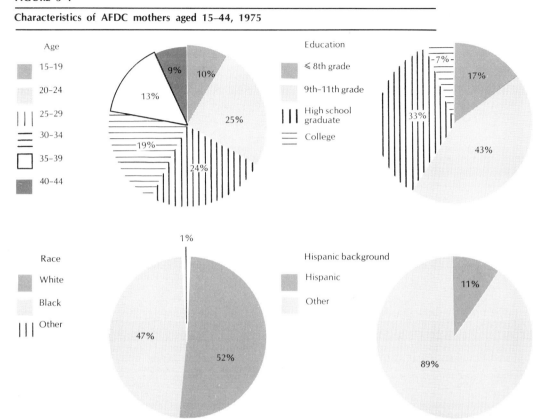

Source: The Alan Guttmacher Institute, "Abortions and the Poor: Private Morality, Public Responsibility," New York, 1979, p. 9.

income since it is paid directly to her. Because most women who are poor have children, they have very limited options for work. If they have young children there is generally no care available for them while the mother works. Because the woman can only work limited hours, she is often further discriminated against with lower pay because she can't go after the better jobs that call for regular work hours.

Not only has the woman head of a household been economically isolated, she also has often been restricted in her activities because of little money and the demands of dependent children. The world of the female-headed family when extended outward is mainly a world of women and children. Very often the women turn to female relatives and friends for emotional support. What this also means is that poverty in America is largely a problem of women and children. There is increasing evidence that many female-headed families are poor not simply because they were poor before divorce, but that divorce is an important cause of that condition.[31]

We want to next look more specifically at some of the problems of poverty that are associated with children. Poverty is very closely linked to whether or not the newborn infant will survive. The death rate is 50 percent greater for infants born to mothers below the poverty level than for women at higher income levels. An infant born to poor parents in the United States has twice as much risk of dying before his first birthday as does the nondisadvantaged child, and his chance of dying before the age of 35 is four times greater.[32]

On the average, the poor are susceptible to more diseases and this is true as well for newborn infants. Among the poor the death rate for newborn babies is nearly three times greater for tuberculosis, six times greater for dysentery, and three times greater for measles than is true for the rest of the population. The death rates for the poor are also twice as great for vascular lesions, about five times greater for influenza and pneumonia, two times greater for bronchitis, and three times greater for infections of the newborn.[33]

Among poor women there are also higher rates of death and serious medical complications in the process of giving birth than among middle-class women. It is estimated that of the approximately 3.5 million births which occur annually in the United States, at least .5 million are by women who have received inadequate prenatal care or none at all. It is estimated that about half of the expectant mothers in poor families go through pregnancy without the required medical attention. "Nationally, a black mother's chance of dying from the complications of pregnancy is four to five times greater than a white mother's."[34]

Once the child is born the hostile conditions that endanger its survival are replaced with new ones. These can be the dangers created by the social conditions of life. The mortality of the young child may be due to the hazards and constraints of inferior housing, poor sanitary conditions, lack of adequate food and clothing, or inadequate medical care. The social environment of poverty may negatively affect the unborn child through the mother. Those in poverty are often vulnerable to stressful situations which result in poor health and, as a result, the poor health of the mother may negatively affect the unborn child.

For the children of the poor who do survive, their special problems are not over. The very fact of growing up in a poverty situation can have negative influences on them. Often the child growing up in poverty starts school with many handicaps in speech ability, listening ability, and in perception in general. "It is therefore not surprising that in many schools in the slums third grade pupils are on the average already one year behind in reading ability."[35]

© Michael Weisbrot and Family

Poverty and children

For women trapped in poverty the situation does not usually improve as they get older, but rather becomes worse. As poor women get older they are less apt to have a husband. They also typically have few marketable skills. So despite all the American myths about women controlling the wealth, women over the age of 65 are the single poorest group in our population. Of these women only the most destitute are eligible for welfare. And millions of old, unmarried women survive on Social Security benefits that average 82 percent of what their husbands would have received had they outlived them. Over one quarter of all unmarried women over 65 have no assets at all.[36]

Blacks and Poverty

The unemployment rates of inner-city blacks persists at a level of about 15 percent for adults and more than 30 percent for young people.[37] It is also the case that black migration has added to the welfare rolls of Northern cities. However, in the cities, the blacks who are most likely to be poor and on welfare are those born and raised in that city. One study found that only recent arrivals from the South were found to have rates of poverty and welfare dependence as high as blacks born and raised in their city of residence in 1970.[38]

For blacks in the city, poverty is also linked to residential areas in which they live. But the standard of their housing has improved. The Census Bureau rated the housing of 73 percent of all non-whites in 1950 as substandard but by 1970 this was true of 23 percent of their housing. Yet, even with this improvement, in 1970 blacks were still four times more likely than whites to live in substandard units, and three times more likely to be overcrowded.[39]

The earlier mentioned study of social class in two large American cities looked at some differences among the lower class by race. They found that most whites in the lower-class sample refused to call themselves lower-class, and this was even true of those at the bottom level. But most blacks accepted a lower-class designation for themselves, whether on the bottom or not. White lower-class Americans avoided identifying themselves as lower class in several ways. The most common was to point to slum-dwelling blacks as a group far lower in status.[40] (For further discussion of blacks and other groups, see Chapter 6.)

VIEWS ABOUT THE POOR

How one group or level of society defines another can vary greatly. Traditionally the middle and upper classes have looked at the poor as clearly beneath them. But in general the poor have been ignored unless they were seen as a problem for the higher classes. Two factors have influenced the higher classes to define the poor as problematic; either (1) the poor are threatening to the higher classes in their social behavior or (2) the poor are economically costly to the higher classes. Often when the middle and upper classes react negatively toward the poor it is because the upper classes think the poor cost them money. In such cases the reaction is against the welfare system rather than poor people, but the hostility is aimed at the poor.

There is some evidence from polls regarding how the poor are viewed by the American public. A Gallup Poll asked: "In your opinion, which is more often to blame if a person is poor—lack of effort on his own part, or circumstances beyond his control?" Thirty-three percent answered "lack of effort"; 29 percent "circumstances"; 32 percent "equal"; and 6 percent had "no opinion."[41]

Not all people who are poor are stigmatized by society in general. Stigmatization is not an automatic result of low income but rather is related to some imputation of moral character. "Thus, some forms of poverty are considered romantic, as, for example, the poverty of hippies, students, and aspiring adults."[42] Usually stigma enters when being poor is associated with being on welfare. In general, any person known to be on welfare as a way of life is defined at the lowest level.

The Coleman and Rainwater study found that for these people, labels such as "chiselers," "freeloaders," and "parasites" were commonly applied. "A special aggravation is the notion that life on welfare "is not so bad these days," that "some people do very well on welfare," that many on welfare indeed "live better than people who work.""[43] It is when the poor are seen as getting something for nothing that moral indignation toward them is the greatest. The hostility is not at their being poor but rather their "using" the poorness.

A common view of the poor is that they have "chosen" their way of life. Even though many people can see horrors associated with living in the slums, there is, nevertheless, a common image that people at the bottom are indifferent to their condition or at least do not seem to mind it enough to be willing to put out the effort to escape it. The impressions held by many toward the poor represent two basic themes. "One is that people at the bottom have very little or nothing in the way of occupational competence to offer prospective employers and the other is that they are too indolent and indifferent to bother."[44]

In recent years, with the many studies of the poor, there has been some disagreement in how happy they are in their circumstances. Some researchers have extolled the spontaneity of expression among the poor, while others have ascribed the same phenomenon to a lack of impulse control. Some see the poor as having a fine and warm sense of humor, while others regard their humor as bitter and sad. Some claim that the poor desperately try to change their condition, sinking into apathy when it becomes clear that the odds are greatly against their being able to do so. Other researchers deny that a strong desire for change exists.[45] These differences may be a reflection of a heterogeneous nature of the poor. Alternately it may be due to differences in researchers' interpretations and value systems. It would seem that in general the life of the poor has to be negative because there is relatively little in their lives to be enthusiastic or satisfied about. On the other hand, what pleasure they do find is relatively unknown because researchers don't define certain activities as pleasurable.

Goodwin suggests that middle-class persons tend to locate the problem of lower-class poverty in the psychology of the poor. Thus to improve the lot of the poor means their psychology must be changed. Hence, solutions are often cast in terms of getting the poor into a proper state for participating in the menial jobs that are available to them. Solutions that might involve major changes in society, such as radical improvement in education and job market opportunities for lower-class people, are rarely suggested.[46] This is because the cost of introducing such programs would make them impossible at this time.

In the 1960s and into the 1970s a cultural explanation of poverty emerged. In this explanation, the "culture of poverty" was seen as a consensus pattern and value system held by the poor and different from dominant cultural patterns. In general, the view was that the poor adapt to poverty by resorting to illegal activities which in their culture of poverty are legitimate. The outlook on life characteristic of the poor was said to furnish them with psychological comfort and at the same time forestall rebellion.[47] Rossi and Blum found from a review of the literature that those traits used to define the culture of poverty are found among the very poor with only somewhat greater frequency than was true of those somewhat above them in social class status. The point is that the "poor do not display characteristics *qualitatively* different from those immediately above them in the stratification hierarchy, and so on up the ladder."[48]

Rossi and Blum concluded that all told, the empirical evidence from examining the literature did not support the notion of a culture of poverty in which the poor were distinctively different from other layers of society. Nor did the evidence from intergenerational-mobility studies "support the idea of a culture of poverty in the sense of the poor being composed largely of persons themselves coming from families living in poverty."[49]

As earlier suggested, poverty has been linked to many other kinds of problems. Basic to the lives of the individuals are the associations between poverty and health. We may look first at the physical health of the poor (see Chapter 14). Up until the first part of the 20th century the bad health of the poor was evidenced by the high incidence of infectious diseases related to crowded, unsanitary, and debilitating conditions. These conditions remain and the resultant problems are not based solely on the incidence of infectious diseases.

Being poor frequently sets up conditions for poor health. Poor people very often live below a subsistence level and in this setting starvation and malnutrition can occur. Not being able to afford the proper foods can result in a weakened condition. Having to live in a polluted area can lead to respiratory diseases. Bad housing can also be related to disease-carrying refuse and rodents. A few years ago, in some of the slum areas of Philadelphia, it was estimated that there was a rat population of 5,000 for every city block.

The poor frequently view health differently than the middle class. There tends to be among the poor greater anxiety over illness and this stems from less knowledge of medicine and the greater consequences of disease for their lives. "The greater fear of medicine and the consequences of disease leads to less utilization of medical facilities."[50] And too, poor people will often slight their health problems in the interest of dealing with what they see as more pressing problems, "such as seeing that there is food in the house, or seeking some kind of expressive experience which will reassure them that they are alive and in some way valid persons."[51]

Rainwater found that just as poor people become resigned to a conception of themselves as persons who cannot function very well socially and psychologically they can also become resigned to bodies that do not function very well physically.[52] The lifestyle of many poor people affects their view of their health. Living in understaffed households, each individual receives relatively little preventive health attention. When a person is sick, it is more difficult to care for him. When the main adult provider is sick, he is in a poor position to care for himself or to seek medical care. Therefore the attitude toward illness in this kind of situation is a fairly tolerant one. "People learn to live with illness rather than use their small stock of interpersonal and psychic resources to do something about the problem."[53]

There is a good deal of evidence that the poor have more severe health problems than do other groups. Some evidence suggests that relative to levels of disability, the use of medical services remains lower among the poor. It has also been found that among the poor, the incidence of such chronic conditions as heart disease, high blood pressure, arthritis, and visual impairment is four to eight times as high as among higher income groups. The rates of orthopedic impairment among the poor is more than twice the national average.[54]

Not only do the poor have more medical problems but they deal with them in different ways. For example, in a given year three times as many people are at home recovering from some chronic ailment among families with incomes of less than $4,000 than among those with more. Chronic problems lead to different courses of treatment. Chronic and acute conditions result in twice as many days of restricted activity among the poor. The poor spend twice the number of days confined to their beds, one fifth more days in the hospital, nearly twice the days away from work, and somewhat greater number of days out of school because of illness.[55]

The process whereby the poor have greater needs for medical care is a complex one. Because they are poor, they are more vulnerable to illness, and this more drastically affects their disability and reduces their income. "Lowered socioeconomic status probably affects access to medical care and other favorable environmental factors, and limitations of access may further result in unnecessary disability and an earlier death."[56]

The poor actually go to the hospital less than other groups, but when they do go they remain for a longer period of time and require more time for convalescence. For many poor people the hospital emergency room serves as a neighborhood physician. In poor areas there are few physicians available, and the poor often cannot afford those who are available. The other choice for many poor is to use the outpatient clinics of hospitals. Rainwater points out that many poor people are used to dealing with medical personnel only in the context of large institutions and have had little chance to develop any personalized relationships with a physician. They are more often used to receiving poor service in low-cost or charity clinics and hospitals. "They expect to wait long hours in order to receive medical service and be shabbily treated by those with whom they deal."[57] Emil Berkanovic suggests that many poor people are culturally unable to make use of many health services because they lack the experience and information to make use of most health care systems.[58]

In recent years the poor have been helped by Medicaid and Medicare. Before their introduction, the poor had significantly lower rates of physician visits and hospital treatments than did higher income groups. After their inauguration, the poor actually exceeded other groups in their use of medical services. "In 1964, members of poor families averaged 4.3 visits to a doctor, while members of families who were not poor averaged 4.6 visits. By 1973, physician visits by the poor had risen to 5.6 a year, while visits by other persons stood only at 4.9."[59] However, this improvement for the poor has not carried through in the quality of their treatment. Despite the evidence of more frequent visits to physicians made possible by Medicaid and Medicare poor persons are still treated within the framework of welfare medicine and still live on a day-to-day basis within the environment of poverty.[60]

In the areas of mental health the poor also have more problems than the higher income groups (see Chapter 15). In general, the poor have more frequent mental illness, more medical treatment, and their illnesses are longer and more serious. The incidence of emotional disorders and mental illness among the poor, who are exposed to numerous stresses, is estimated to be between five and six times greater than for those with higher incomes. "The poor are less likely to get timely and adequate help and more likely to wind up in the desolate warrens of the state mental hospitals."[61]

In one study of those interviewed in low income groups, 65 percent described themselves as "worried and nervous," 58 percent said they were "lonely and depressed," and 39 percent reported "having difficulty sleeping." "The poor have a high incidence of nervous tension, back trouble, ulcers, headaches, sore throats, bad coughs, indigestion, constipation, and exhaustion. They trail the affluent only in disorders which they cannot afford, notably sunburn and allergies."[62]

The poor are not as able or willing to recognize psychological problems as are the middle class. And when they do recognize mental health problems they tend to draw hard and fast lines between normality and being "nuts" or "crazy."[63] When the poor are treated for mental illness, health professionals define their problems as more severe than the problems of the higher classes. The poor are more often diagnosed as having psychoses while mental illness among the nonpoor more often takes the form of the less serious neuroses. In addition, the poor are more often treated in state institutions rather than by private practitioners.[64]

"SOLUTIONS" TO POVERTY

As earlier suggested, for most of human history poverty was ignored or seen as the natural lot for many. It was not until the 19th century that attempts to directly help the poor were introduced. The first social service agencies in the United States developed in urban areas, and they tried to help some of the poor. These organizations were private and were often church sponsored. They offered the poor some food and shelter. Attempts to help the poor with personal problems consisted of religious admonitions. Help was intermittent, a kind of "Lady Bountiful" approach, where the poor were given Christmas baskets and the rest of the year were on their own.

John B. Williamson writes that in the 19th century the stigma associated with receiving public support was usually viewed as necessary so as to discourage dependency and keep the relief rolls within reasonable limits. The stigma associated with being the recipient of public relief undoubtedly peaked during the 1870s and 1880s, the heyday of Social Darwinism. "The intensity of the stigma declined during the early part of this century. There is reason to believe that the lowest point was reached during the Depression and that there has been some increase since then."[65] Up until recent years the blame for poverty almost always was placed on the individual. They were poor because of sin, evilness, sloth, laziness, and so on. But in more recent years there has come to be some recognition that poverty may be built into society and that individuals really have little effect on their economic status.

The most important governmental breakthrough in helping some poor people came in 1935 with the Social Security Act. This established two systems of economic help. One introduced social security through social insurance where persons were required to contribute and have rights to receive benefits. This was extended to the unemployed and the aged. The second was public assistance which calls for no contribution from the individual, the federal government would pay benefits on the basis of the person's demonstrated need. Initially both these plans were seen as temporary and it was believed they would end when the Depression ended. However, not only have they remained, but they have been somewhat expanded, and continue today.

The basic purpose of Social Security is to provide some minimum

Reprinted by permission The Wall Street Journal

"After we take from the rich, why can't we skim
a little off the top before we give to the poor?"

level of support for people over 65. In theory this is to be supplemented from other sources to allow for a more comfortable income. The way to augment Social Security is through working, but there are two obstacles. First, there are few full- or part-time jobs that will take an employee over 65. Only one in four men and less than one in ten women over 65 participate in the labor force. Second, persons who are on Social Security and earn through employment more than $5,000 (in 1980) a year will have their payments reduced by one dollar for every two earned above that amount.[66] There are other discriminations. For example, wives who have worked cannot draw the full benefits of their own social security and many single older persons who consider remarrying would suffer a loss of some of the income they currently receive.

But these government programs have been helpful to many. The effect of social insurance payments and public assistance reduced the incidence of poverty for families in 1971 from 20.9 percent to 12.0 percent even though only 80 percent of the poor received such benefits. "Social insurance and public assistance payments helped 6.4 million families escape poverty in 1971."[67]

The War on Poverty

In 1965, President Lyndon B. Johnson declared war on poverty. This was presented with a great deal of drama and with high expectations. It was supposed to be a many-pronged effort to do away with poverty through government programs. But what was called a war on poverty proved to be nothing more than a few minor skirmishes. The initial budget for the fiscal year of 1965 was $947.5 million. The bulk of those funds went toward education, training, social services, and work experience for youth.[68]

There was initially a high degree of optimism that something could be done but this quickly faded away. The Vietnam war drained the resources, and during that period there were violent protests in the political and social institutions. Increasingly crime in the city became the major concern, and as a result concern about poverty was quickly forgotten. Yet, the war on poverty did have some impact. Even though it was politically motivated and was ultimately politically undercut, it did affect some aspects of urban social welfare. The new multiservice neighborhood centers created in its aftermath reflected in their personnel more indigenous people, "mostly as paraprofessionals, than would probably have been hired otherwise."[69] Joseph Helfgot writes that the millions of dollars spent in the name of the poor largely benefited the middle class, supplying employment to thousands of professional elites, be they black, Spanish speaking, or white.[70]

We want to look more specifically at welfare payments. These include money or services provided to the poor by the government. They are generally seen as something given rather than something earned, and therefore welfare payments often are accompanied by stigma. The public approach necessary to get welfare also contributes to its stigma, since welfare recipients are denied the degree of privacy available to others.[71] But stigma is also associated with assigning the victim the blame for his own situation. Being poor is attributed to personal defects and the blame is on the individual rather than on society. The stigma is associated with the acceptance of public assistance because this separates the person from the ordinary class of people who are usually self-sufficient and for whom status is determined largely by occupation.[72]

Williamson further suggests that being poor is really the root of the low status that goes with receiving help. Programs restricted to welfare recipients tend to be higher in stigma than similar programs open to nonwelfare recipients as well. "More generally, a program such as Social Security, which is not restricted to the poor, carries less stigma than a program designed explicitly for the poor."[73]

The amount of money spent on all types of social welfare in the

United States is great. In 1976 the total social welfare expenditures were 12.3 percent of the gross national product. The federal dollars that are spent are broken down as follows: social security, 44.3 percent; public assistance, 14.8 percent; health and medical care, 5.8 percent; veterans, 5.7 percent; and education, 26.1 percent.[74]

Often there is great resentment toward those receiving welfare if others believe that the person could work but won't. But from a practical point of view, it may be smarter for the person to take welfare rather than work. First, many believe that a person would be foolish to work hard in a low status job for about the same amount of money he can get on welfare. Second, most of the jobs available are low level and low paying. Third, there may be a desire to work but only if it can be meaningful employment.[75]

There is evidence that for many persons who are on welfare there are negative feelings and a sense of stigma. One study found that the woman who earned her family's support was more likely to be better

A part of the welfare system

USDA Photo by Fred S. Witte

off than the mother who stayed home and depended upon unreliable, unstable, controlling, or stigmatizing sources of income. "A welfare dollar is not the same as a work dollar, the former is stigmatizing, the latter is not."[76]

Politics have long been involved in views about welfare. In general, for the conservative, poverty is seen as a result of character defects which stop the person from actively participating in the market economy. The way to deal with the problem is to remove welfare programs which stop them from entering the work market. This view is not very accurate because many of the poor are not able to work, due to age and lack of skills. The conservative view assumes a system in which all persons who want to work can find jobs. However, this is not true of the economic system—there is not a perfect correlation between available jobs in society and job skills of its available members.

The politically liberal position is that the bureaucracy and welfare programs are being used ineffectively. Generally, the liberal assumption has been that poverty can be eradicated by rewarding individual effort through provision of opportunities for upward social mobility and economic gain. Implicit in this view is the belief that the system needs modifications to ensure that the poor can find sufficient escape routes from poverty. From this perspective poverty exists in spite of society, not because of it.[77]

The radical point of view finds the sources of poverty in society itself, and poverty results from class inequality. "Thus poverty exists because America is as it is, and so long as power and institutional networks remain as they are, there will be no change."[78] The only way that poverty would be done away with would be through a new social and economic system. This is impossible because there is no known system which in practice does away with poverty.

Certainly attempts to deal with poverty will continue to be handled in the same fashion by the government. What will continue to be used will be the piecemeal solution or the placement of a few bandaids on the economic body when it gets hurt. For example, when poverty is linked with poor children having "poor" attitudes and values that keep them from succeeding in the American system, the solution is to try and give them new school programs and make them middle class. But this is never a complete new program but rather the introduction of a few small programs. The socialization of the poor child is not changed. Rather, he may be taught a few new skills, for which there is usually little demand by society.

It appears that poverty will continue to be a part of American society for decades to come. Quite simply there are no ready solutions. A solution implies a balance between the demands of a society in its work force and the availability of the exact number of persons with the exact skills to do those jobs. Increasingly, American society will have to determine how large an unemployment group it can accept and care for. It must be recognized that because of minority group status or age, many persons are going to suffer from poverty. To what extent is society willing to make their lives more tolerable? Poverty is the kind of social problem that can be handled only by degree and not through elimination.

Poverty has long been a problem in American society but in recent years, because of much greater public awareness, has come to be a social problem. The poor are not a set and stable population but undergo some changes in composition. The relationship of poverty to the family, to the one-parent family, and to the elderly has been examined. There have been attempts by society to deal with poverty through welfare systems with varying degrees of success. Poverty is closely related to a variety of other social problems; for example, health problems, poor housing, minority conflict, and crime.

NOTES

1. Hanna H. Meissner, *Poverty in the Affluent Society*, rev. ed. (New York: Harper & Row, 1973), p. 1.

2. H. Ray Kaplan and Curt Tausky, "Work and the Welfare Cadillac: The Functions of and Commitment to Work among the Hard-Core Unemployed," *Social Problems* (Spring 1972), p. 470.

3. Meissner, *Poverty*, p. 2.

4. Diana Pearce and David Street, "Welfare in the Metropolitan Area," in *Handbook of Contemporary Urban Life*, David Street (San Francisco, Calif.: by Jossey-Bass, 1978), pp. 326–27.

5. Meissner, *Poverty*, p. 21.

6. Ibid., p. 39.

7. Ivan Light, "Numbers Gambling among Blacks: A Financial Institution," *American Sociological Review* (December 1977), p. 892.

8. Zahava D. Blum and Peter H. Rossi, "Social Class Research and Images of the Poor: A Biographical Review," in *On Understanding Poverty*, by Daniel P. Moynihan (New York: Basic Books, 1969), p. 349.

9. Ibid., p. 350.

10. Richard P. Coleman and Lee Rainwater, *Social Standing In America* (New York: Basic Books, 1978), p. 190.

11. Ibid., p. 191.

12. Leonard Goodwin, "How Suburban Families View the Work Orientations of the Welfare Poor: Problems in Social Stratification and Social Policy," *Social Problems* (Winter 1972), p. 338.

13. Ibid., p. 345.

14. Kaplan and Tausky, "Welfare Cadillac," p. 481.

15. Rosabeth Moss Kanter, "Work in a New America," *Daedalus* (Winter 1978), p. 54.

16. *Philadelphia Inquirer* (May 25, 1979), p. 21.

17. Lee Rainwater, "The Problem of Lower-Class Culture and Poverty-War Strategy," in Moynihan, *Understanding Poverty*, p. 328.

18. Ibid., p. 241.

19. Ibid., pp. 246–47.

20. Ibid., pp. 247–48.

21. Blum and Rossi, "Social Class," p. 356.

22. Ibid., p. 358.

23. Russell L. Curtis, Jr., and Louis A. Zurcher, Jr., "Voluntary Associations and the Social Integration of the Poor," *Social Problems* (Winter 1971), p. 342.

24. Blum and Rossi, "Social Class," p. 392.

25. Peter H. Rossi and Zahava D. Blum, "Class, Status and Poverty," Moynihan, *Understanding Poverty*, p. 40.

26. Lillian E. Troll, Sheila J. Miller, and Robert C. Atchley, *Families in Later Life* (Belmont, Calif.: Wadsworth, 1979), p. 53.

27. Sally Bould, "Female-Headed Families: Personal Fate Control and the Provider Role," *Journal of Marriage and the Family* (May 1977), p. 347.

28. Ibid., p. 348.

29. Ibid., p. 349.

30. Riane Tennenhaus Eisler, *Dissolution* (New York: McGraw-Hill, 1977), p. 49.

31. Ibid., p. 105.

32. Selig Greenberg, "The Legacy of Neglect," in *The Fourth World*, by Leo Hamalian and Frederick R. Karl (New York: Dell, 1976), p. 191.

33. Robert L. Eichhorn and Edward G. Ludwig, "Poverty and Health," in *Poverty*, Meissner, p. 173.

34. Greenberg, "Legacy," p. 190.

35. Meissner, *Poverty*, p. 133.

36. Eisler, *Dissolution*, p. 104.

37. William Kornblum and Terry Williams, "Life Style, Leisure, and Community Life," in *Street Handbook*, p. 80.

38. Harry H. Long, "Poverty Status and Receipt of Welfare Among Migrants and Nonmigrants in Large Cities," *American Sociological Review* (February 1074), p. 51.

39. Elliot Zashin, "The Progress of Black Americans in Civil Rights: The Past Two Decades Assessed," *Daedalus* (Winter 1978), p. 255.

40. Coleman and Rainwater, *Social Standing*, p. 206.

41. Chandler Davidson and Charles Gaitz, "Are the Poor Different? A Comparison of Work Behavior and Attitudes among the Urban Poor and Nonpoor," *Social Problems* (December 1974), p. 230.

42. Amitai Etzioni, *Social Problems* (Englewood Cliffs, N.J.: Prentice-Hall, 1976), p. 31.

43. Coleman and Rainwater, *Social Standing*, p. 195.

44. Ibid., p. 197.

45. Blum and Rossi, "Social Class," p. 352.

46. Goodwin, "Suburban Families," p. 346.

47. Etzioni, *Social Problems*, p. 28.

48. Rossi and Blum, "Class, Status, and Poverty," p. 42.

49. Ibid., pp. 43–44.

50. Blum and Rossi, "Social Class," p. 362.

51. Rainwater, "Lower-Class Culture," p. 260.

52. Ibid., p. 263.

53. Ibid., p. 261.

54. Greenberg, "Legacy," p. 196.

55. Eichhorn and Ludwig, "Poverty and Health," pp. 174–75.

56. David Mechanic, *Medical Sociology*, 2d ed. (New York: The Free Press, 1978), p. 194.

57. Rainwater, "Lower-Class Culture," p. 269.

58. Emil Berkanovic and Leo G. Reader, "Ethnic, Economic, and Social Psychological Factors in the Source of Medical Care," *Social Problems* (Fall 1973), p. 249.

59. Paul Starr, "Medicine and the Waning of Professional Sovereignty," *Daedalus* (Winter 1978), p. 185.

60. William C. Cockerham, *Medical Sociology* (Englewood Cliffs, N.J.: Prentice-Hall, 1978), p. 39.

61. Greenberg, "Legacy," p. 193.

62. Ibid., p. 197.

63. Eichhorn and Ludwig, "Poverty and Health," p. 179.

64. Etzioni, *Social Problems*, p. 27.

65. John B. Williamson, "The Stigma of Public Dependency: A Comparison of Alternative Forms of Public Aid to the Poor," *Social Problems* (December 1974), p. 215.

66. *The World Almanac* (New York: Newspaper Enterprise, Inc., 1980), p. 49.

67. Charles E. Starnes, "Contemporary and Historic Aspects of Officially Defined Poverty in the United States," in *Understanding Social Problems*, by Don H. Zimmerman et al. (New York: Praeger Publishers, 1976), p. 47.

68. Ibid., p. 63.

69. Pearce and Street, "Welfare," p. 329.

70. Joseph Helfgot, "Professional Reform Organizations and the Symbolic Representation of the Poor," *American Sociological Review* (August 1974), p. 490.

71. Williamson, "Stigma," p. 214.

72. Ibid., p. 214.

73. Ibid., p. 226.

74. *Information Please Almanac 1978* (New York: Information Please Publishing, Inc., 1978), p. 70.

75. Kaplan and Tausky, "Welfare Cadillac," p. 476.

76. Bould, "Female-Headed Families," pp. 347–48.

77. Ray C. Rist and Colleen J. Svares, "Poverty and Internal Colonialism," in Zimmerman, *Social Problems*, p. 168.

78. Ibid., p. 169.

SELECTED BIBLIOGRAPHY

Blum, Zahava D., and Rossi, Peter H. "Social Class Research and Images of the Poor: A Biographical Review." In *On Understanding Poverty*, by Daniel P. Moynihan. New York: Basic Books, 1969, pp. 343–418.

Bould, Sally. "Female-Headed Families: Personal Fate Control and the Provider Role." *Journal of Marriage and the Family* (May 1977), pp. 339–49.

Davidson, Chandler, and Gaitz, Charles. "Are the Poor Different? A Comparison of Work Behavior and Attitudes among the Urban Poor and Nonpoor." *Social Problems* (December 1974), pp. 229–45.

Helfgot, Joseph. "Professional Reform Organization and the Symbolic Representation of the Poor." *American Sociological Review* (August 1974), pp. 475–91.

Kaplan, H. Ray, and Tausky, Curt. "Work and the Welfare Cadillac: The Functions of the Commitment to Work among the Hard-Core Unemployed." *Social Problems* (Spring 1972), pp. 469–83.

Long, Harry H. "Poverty Status and Receipt of Welfare among Migrants and Nonmigrants in Large Cities." *American Sociological Review* (February 1974), pp. 46–56.

Meissner, Hanna H. *Poverty in the Affluent Society*. Rev. ed. New York: Harper & Row, 1973.

Pearce, Diana, and Street, David. "Welfare in the Metropolitan Area." In *Handbook of Contemporary Urban Life* by David Street. San Francisco, Calif.: Jossey-Bass, 1978, pp. 319–51.

Starnes, Charles E. "Contemporary and Historic Aspects of Officially Defined Poverty in the United States." In *Understanding Social Problems,* by Don H. Zimmerman et al. New York: Praeger Publishers, 1976, pp. 36–68.

Williamson, John B. "The Stigma of Public Dependency: A Comparison of Alternative Forms of Public Aid to the Poor." *Social Problems* (December 1974), pp. 213–28.

Chapter 6

Minority Groups

Probably from the beginning of time, as groups of humans wandered about the face of the earth and made contact with one another, judgments about each other were made. Such judgments perceived that one group was better or worse in some way. It is also probable that groups were distinguishable in some way which was seen by others as significant. The distinctions might have been based on the foods they ate, the weapons they used, the clothing they wore, or their religious beliefs. Often definitions of differences led to such feelings as fear, hostility, superiority, and so on.

As countries developed and social systems became more complex there often came to be regional differences as well as differences between countries. The base line in defining any minority group relationship is of two groups, distinguishable in some way, with at least one defining the other as inferior. The group doing the defining has constructed reasons for doing so. Frequently it has been the need for a scapegoat, someone to blame for problems, inadequacies, and failures the dominant society feels. In some societies, where there is a long term prejudice against some groups, the original reasons may be lost in the historical past and the prejudice functions as accepted wisdom. But whatever the reasons the prejudice that defines the group as a social problem perpetuates itself around real or imagined differences between the dominant and minority groups.

The extent to which the minority group is maltreated and disvalued varies greatly. In some cases the power of the majority group (as well as its motivation) may be minimal and therefore have little real effect on the minority group. This is increasingly true with reference to religious minorities in the United States. The treatment by the majority group can range from social rejection in specific situations to the practice of genocide—killing the minority members. In this chapter we want to first look at some concepts related to minority group relationships and secondly at some specific minority groups in the United States.

Concepts of Minority Group Relationships

Racism.   This refers to the definition of some group of people as observably distinct and inferior. For example, the black is distinguished by skin color and then defined as inferior because of skin color. Skin color has most often been used as a means of racial identification because it is observable and cannot be changed. In America, highly elaborate rationales were created to "explain" racial differences, to explain why blacks were different and inferior. For most of history racial explanations have been accepted.

At the start of the 20th century in the United States, racist thought was generally respectable among all social classes and in all sections of the country. It was respectable because it fit the generally accepted biological explanations of human behavior. It was not until the 1920s and 1930s that the "scientific" backing that racists had long used was finally revoked.[1]

James W. Vander Zanden suggests there are three stages that take place for racist ordering to arise. First, people must differentiate between groups in a population so that persons are placed in distinct social categories based on visible features. Second, competition takes place between groups for things valued in the society and this helps to generate prejudice. Third, the groups are unequal in power so that the most powerful group is able to actualize its claim to an unequal and larger share of the socially valued things.[2]

Racism can be applied on two levels. First, there is individual racism which consists of overt acts of discrimination or violence committed by individuals. In contrast, institutional racism is less overt, more subtle, and less identifiable in terms of specific individuals committing the acts. For example, institutional racism results in a dual labor market. Blacks are primarily concentrated in a secondary labor market offering low wages, dead-end employment, and few avenues of escape into better jobs.[3] This is also the labor market for Chicanos, Puerto Ricans, and some poor whites.

There have been many studies of persons who are racist and they clearly suggest that prejudice toward one minority group tends to be highly correlated with attitudes toward other minority groups. "Numerous studies of racist attitudes, segregationist voting, lynchings, and school desegregation in the South have shown that hostility towards blacks tends to be inversely related to urbanism, education, occupational status, income, and economic prosperity."[4] Racism is most typical of the white population that has the least. William Tabb found that the groups expressing racist views most openly were those competing directly with blacks for jobs and status. "Such racial antagonisms spring from a competition system which pits individuals and groups against each other."[5]

Prejudice.   This is a negative attitude held by the individual toward some group of people. As an attitude it involves a state of mind. Prejudice is different from discrimination which entails overt action. Prejudice often leads to the action of discrimination but it need not. Prejudice represents a set of negative images. "These images are usually stereotypical, involving simplistic, crude, and rigidly held conceptions of the attributes of individuals placed into a prejudicial category."[6]

Feelings of prejudice vary throughout the United States but the differences are relatively small. Russell Middleton writes that the South has had significantly higher means of all types of prejudice except anti-Catholic prejudice, but the regional differences are generally not great. "It is only in the case of anti-black prejudice that the South has a substantially higher mean score than the non-South."[7] Variation in degrees of prejudice are more closely linked to social class. In general, the higher the social class, the less the prejudice. However, this does not mean the higher social classes are not prejudiced, only to a lesser degree. The somewhat less prejudice of the higher social classes is probably due to their higher education and their being less in competition with minority groups in any occupational or economic ways.

Discrimination.   Discrimination is overt behavior. Discrimination is the most commonly used concept for denoting the differential treatment of persons on grounds that are rationally irrelevant to the situation. "When someone refuses to hire a fully qualified black candidate for a job because of the candidate's race, that person has practiced discrimination."[8]

In recent years federal laws have been passed making it illegal to discriminate against persons in hiring practices. Nevertheless, underlying and very often defying the laws are informal practices of discrimination and *de facto* forms of discrimination that are not formalized by the law. For example, housing discrimination is against the law, but the poverty level of many blacks along with their living in ghettos, leads inevitably to widespread exclusion of blacks from white suburban housing. "Thus, laws can allow people to co-affirm current 'liberal' beliefs, while participating in a set of racist institutional arrangements."[9]

As suggested above, most discrimination is institutionalized and therefore is not highly visible. Oftentimes it is sanctioned by cultural values and regarded as natural, and is therefore difficult to recognize.

United Press International Photo

Racial discrimination in the 1950s

"For example, discrimination against women has been an integral part of America's ethos for a long period of time. Yet perceived discrimination is relatively recent." [10] In general, attacks against prejudice are made on ethical grounds. To discriminate against persons because of skin color, religion, or sex is seen by many as morally wrong. It is seen as depriving those persons of rights they should have. It is always putting their minority status first and their human rights second.

What does the dominant group gain by discrimination? Not only does the dominant group enjoy more advantages than the minority group, but the minority group is commonly one source of the dominant group's advantage. The subjugation of one group confers privilege on the other group. Moreover, discrimination may have a payoff on the personal level. It may enhance people's feelings of self-worth by allowing them to believe they are "better" than other people. Often the person who has achieved little with his life will feel superior to the black simply because that person is black and he is not.

There are several ways in which groups in a society can be subjected to racism, prejudice, and discrimination. Often minority groups have been segregated. Segregation can range from near total exclusion from the rest of society to partial desegregation in selected areas, as for example, in education or certain occupations. There have been some instances where segregation has been the choice of the minority group. For example, the Amish, a religious order, have long kept themselves separate in their living styles from the rest of society. This is because their religious values dictate a life style different from that of the general society.

Cultural pluralism is another way in which society deals with minority groups. Pluralism is a process whereby people with different cultural backgrounds live together relatively harmoniously and peacefully and allow each the expression of their own distinctive ways of life. Examples of this occur in Switzerland and in Singapore where there are four languages officially recognized and each language group retains their cultural distinctions. Yet, these four language groups are not completely equal in power, status, and general influence.

In the United States there has come to be some notion of cultural pluralism in recent years related to ethnic groups. This is reflected in the hyphenated groups—i.e., Italian-American, Spanish-American, etc. The view is held by the ethnic group itself that it wants to maintain some identification of pluralism. This is reflected in the argument that schools should teach the child two languages. They should not only be taught English, but if they are of some Spanish-American group, they should learn Spanish. This is a deliberate attempt to maintain a cultural distinction and a resistance to becoming assimilated fully into American society.

Assimilation is a process whereby groups with different ways of thinking and acting become fused together and lose their previous identity. Richard D. Alba suggests that usually there is a distinction between two different kinds of assimilation. There is *acculturation*, which is the acquisition of the culture of the natives, and social or structural assimilation, the integration with them at the primary level, including marriage. It is often assumed that acculturation can occur without social assimilation. "Individuals can participate in ethnically heterogeneous secondary relationships—for example, on the job by virtue of their sharing a common culture and return home to the ethnically segregated worlds of neighborhood, friendship and family. Thus, ethnicity survives as long as there are ethnic communities."[11] We will look more at ethnicity shortly.

Historically, the American pattern has been for immigrants to become assimilated. During the first hundred years of the United States this was easy because most immigrants were from Great Britain. These groups, especially as they spread to different parts of the United States within a few generations, quickly became assimilated. It has been suggested that as non-English immigrants, to the United States became assimilated into American culture they contributed a richness from the cultures of origin. But this is most often a romantic exaggeration. Certainly there has been some influence on speech, food, clothing, and so on, but for the most part assimilation has meant giving up what was different from the American culture.

Minority Conflict

Given the inherent conflict nature of minority group relationships there has long been an attempt to explain the nature of the conflict. There have been a number of theories developed to explain this conflict on the personal and interpersonal level.

Frustration-aggression theory argues that people are goal directed and they become angry and hostile if their desires are frustrated. If they don't know who or what is blocking them, they turn their hostility toward some scapegoat. Usually the scapegoat is someone available who is unable to resist or fight back. This is supported by the general findings that unsuccessful people show the greatest amounts of prejudice. Discontent of any kind may find an outlet through frustration-aggression. While the need to put down others may be psychological, the target or prejudice is determined by the values of society.

Another closely related psychological theory is the *social-neurosis* explanation. This views race prejudice as a symptom of a maladjusted, neurotic personality. It is argued that it is found among people who are insecure, troubled, and discontented. But this theory appears to be exaggerated and makes prejudice symptomatic of more than it really represents for most individuals.

There has also been an interest in the *authoritarian personality* as an explanation for prejudice. These are people who come to view the world in a good-bad fashion. They are described as being submissive toward those they see as having power over them and aggressive toward those they see as beneath them in status. "Lacking insight into their inner feelings, they project their own unacceptable impulses on the minorities whom they regard as beneath them."[12] James G. Martin reports that in studies of authoritarianism it is especially evident among "(1) the less educated, (2) the aged, (3) the rural, (4) members of disadvantaged minorities, (5) people of lower socioeconomic status, and (6) those who have been reared in an authoritarian family environment."[13] The classic example of the authoritarian personality was Adolf Hitler.

Middleton argues that there are significant limitations to the personality theories of prejudice. This is made worse by the fact that there are significant differences between the South and non-South regarding prejudice against blacks, yet there are not such differences between these areas for other types of prejudice. "If prejudice were a simple function of personality predispositions one would expect each of the types of prejudice to behave in essentially the same way."[14]

There have also been theories that have a more sociological base attempting to explain prejudice. These theories are often based on the notion of *intergroup conflict.* This means that conflict develops because the dominant group has greater privileges and power and attempts to justify its position by claiming some kind of superiority. Sometimes the explanation is in terms of relative deprivation; i.e., the gap between what those in power have and others have and how those others feel about how little they have. At other times some form of *social disorganization* is used to explain prejudice. This theory suggests a breakdown of some imporfant norms so that one group must do without some things. There may be conflict in trying to get the norms restored by the minority and the dominant group refusing to do so.

Ethnicity

In this section we want to look at the relationship of ethnic background to experiences with prejudice and discrimination. Ethnicity describes characteristics of a group and may include language, religious beliefs and practices, institutional norms and values, expressive styles, special foods, or so on. In the United States ethnic location patterns "are not a result of a random process but are based in the immigrant group's time of arrival, route of travel, and ethnic cohesions."[15]

The emerging definition of ethnicity has varied greatly over time. As a result, the period of the time a given group entered the United States partly determined the reaction they were given. At certain points in time they have been wanted and at other times not. The extent to which they were isolated often removed them from the consciousness of the majority with the result there were fewer negative or positive feelings about them. In general the reaction to ethnic groups is determined by their visibility and whether or not they are seen as a threat by others.

Andrew M. Greeley points out that an ethnic group is a human collective that is based on the assumption of a real or imagined common origin. The ethnic group came into being when the peasant commune broke up. It was essentially an attempt to keep some of the values, "some of the informality, some of the support, some of the intimacy of the communal life in the midst of an impersonal, rationalized, urban, industrial society."[16] Ethnic identification was a way for the ethnic group to collectively cope with the new demands of life brought about by their immigration.

Over the years in the social sciences the concept of ethnic groups has been applied to those who have kept some distinctive *cultural* traits. By contrast, a racial group has referred to persons characterized by distinct *physical* traits. This has usually been skin color. But in recent years the term ethnic group has also been applied to racial groups. Often in sociological literature blacks are referred to as an ethnic group in the United States.

Ethnicity involves shared perceptions of the world; when a group holds to traditional religious beliefs, eating patterns, celebration of holidays, and so forth, they are defining and perceiving their world in the particular way of their culture. Their definitions of how others define them are also a part of their reality. For example, to define themselves as being severely restricted because of their ethnicity is to define the situation in a specific way.

Ethnicity becomes manifested ultimately in how people interact with one another. Ethnicity can be defined as the patterns of frequent association and identification with others of similar origins. These interactions become crystalized under conditions which reinforce the maintenance of kinship and friendship networks. "These are common occupational positions, residential stability and concentration, and dependency on common institutions and services." [17]

Historically, the pattern for most immigrant groups to the United States has been one of successive stages of contact, competition, and some forms of accommodation. For some immigrants (such as Protestant groups from northern Europe) accommodation led to a gradual assimilation into the dominant society. "For others (including many Africans, Latin-Americans, Orientals, and Jews) the process stopped short of full assimilation." [18]

During the great waves of immigration, people were coming in large numbers from specific towns and areas of their country origin. This meant that typically the immigrant had a kin and even village tie. Furthermore, most of those immigrants were from peasant backgrounds of living in agricultural communities of European post-feudal society. The "relationships were, for the most part, between persons who knew each other, understood their respective roles, and knew what kind of behavior to expect." [19] Greeley goes on to point out that "in the Italian neighborhoods of New York's lower east side in the early 1920s it was possible to trace, block by block, not only the region in Italy but also every village from which the inhabitants had come." [20]

Relatively few immigrants ever came from the lowest levels of their society. This was usually true because they had neither the motivation nor the money to emigrate. Therefore, all immigrant groups did not enter at the lowest occupational levels. William L. Yancey says that to understand the occupational concentrations of immigrants, it is necessary to "consider both the diverse educational occupational skills which immigrants brought, as well as the specific working opportunities which were attainable at the time of arrival."[21]

The concentration of ethnic groups into ghettos was more a characteristic of later groups than of earlier ones. In fact, most immigrants to American cities never lived in ghettos and most immigrant ghettos that did exist were the product of the largest cities and for the eastern and southern European immigrants that arrived from 1880 to 1940. "Prior to 1880, immigrant groups, mainly Irish, Canadian, British, and German, were dispersed throughout the city with concentrations only in a few points."[22]

It seems clear that ethnicity performed a valuable function for the immigrants who came to America. Many of them were coming to a country that was foreign, hostile, and alienating to them because they could not speak the language or understand the culture and institutions. Sidney Kronus says that for many of these immigrant groups a sense of consciousness and shared activity came from the church. The function of the church was not primarily to spread evangelical Christianity to the world, "but rather, to preserve the ethnic solidarity of the group."[23]

The values of ethnicity are not necessarily good. Often ethnic groups are held to be good for the individual because they provide a certain sense of belonging and of heritage. They may even be seen as good for the country because they remind us that we are a mixture of nations that makes America unique. However, ethnic groups may also be considered bad for the individual insofar as they lead to prejudice and restrict individual expression. Ethnic groups may also be seen as bad for the nation when they stress loyalty to the group and to what it can get from the system rather than from working together as Americans. Richard P. Coleman and Lee Rainwater, in their study, conclude, "We find a social level of support for the melting pot ideology and a distrust for any social movement or philosophy that could lead to an intensification of ethnic group identification."[24]

The above study also reports that while in the 1970s some Americans still strongly felt the desirability of assimilation, there were some who doubted the possibility of its realization. Those people saw neighborhoods of third and fourth generation ethnics still sticking together. They had also heard of experiences of continuous discrimination faced by some groups. The respondents in the study often denied that ethnic background made a difference in their lives, but they often believed that it entered as a factor into politics, education, and occupational success, residential segregation, and status position in general.[25]

Greeley suggests that ethnicity is one of a number of ways in which Americans can identify themselves. He says that ethnicity becomes important under several settings. First, ethnicity is important when the group is very large and has great actual or potential political and economic power (e.g., the Irish in Boston or the Italians in Philadelphia). Second, ethnicity is important when a person is a member of a small but highly visible or somewhat organized minority (e.g., blacks or Mexicans). Third, ethnicity is significant when a sophisticated group suddenly becomes conscious that it has become a minority and is surrounded by many other well organized ethnic communities. An example would be some Protestant areas in New York City.[26]

As suggested, ethnicity exists in part because of the individual's sense of identification with others like themselves. Those in a given ethnic community often develop a consciousness of each other. Frequently their cohesiveness develops because of pressures exerted against them by outsiders. In recent years this has been illustrated by Polish-Americans and Italian-Americans because of ways they feel they are being derogatorily defined. Often such negative ethnic identification does more than inhibit assimilation. It also serves as a foundation for political action. "Through a sense of ethnic community, minority members form groups to deal with an alien environment and problems forced on them by the majority."[27]

Having the birthright of ethnic membership does not ensure that a particular person will want to be defined as such. For example, many persons don't want to be thought of as Italian-American but rather as American. The Coleman and Rainwater sample found that many people when asked said they would rather identify themselves as "All-round Americans" or with no groups at all. "Catholics more than Protestants, those in the lower class more than those in the middle and upper classes, and those in lower- as compared to higher-status neighborhoods were all likely to show a reluctance to identify with any specific ethnic group."[28]

Why does ethnicity survive? It would seem after several generations that assimilation would result, but this is often not the case. Assimilation may not occur because the dominant society resists or because the minority group wants to maintain its ethnic identity. Alba suggests that ethnicity among the descendents of 19th and 20th century immigrants survives at the level of primary attachments. Therefore the search for viable elements of ethnicity has moved away from culture and toward what might be called "community."[29] But the mere persistence of ethnic neighborhoods does not indicate that most members of a given ancestry group live in such neighborhoods, "nor does it disprove that social assimilation is widespread among those outside of ethnic neighborhoods."[30]

The ethnicity of groups and of neighborhoods undergoes change. When an ethnic group improves its economic position it seeks new

St. Patrick's Day in Boston

housing, or at least housing that is new for it, and begins to move from its original location into neighborhoods that previously had been the center for another ethnic group. "Generally speaking, the first neighborhoods to be invaded are already declining, either out of physical obsolescence or because the most ambitious of its citizens are already seeking better housing for themselves."[31]

Yancey points out that ethnicity in black and Puerto Rican ghettos is quite different from that of the older ethnic urban villages found in the large city. The communities of the blacks and Puerto Ricans are removed from the best economic opportunities. They are characterized by social organizations based on relatively strong informal networks. These networks are not tied to economic opportunity. "The segregation of these new ethnics from the best economic opportunities is social as well as geographic."[32]

Kronus suggests there are two primary sources of ethnic retention and there was even some resurgence of ethnicity during the 1970s. The first was the relative lack of residential and social mobility that was experienced by a substantial proportion of urban ethnic groups. The second was the rise of white ethnic consciousness in response to the actions and demands put forth by blacks during the 1960s, when black ethnic consciousness asserted itself more forcefully than it ever had."[33] There is no evidence that ethnic segregation will disappear in the near future.

Over the years various new immigrant groups have come into the United States. These are often displaced persons escaping from their homelands for various reasons. In 1979 it was the Vietnamese and in 1980 the Cubans. Americans have mixed feelings about these groups. It appears that many who welcome them do so because they will be living in other parts of the country. The closest most Americans get to the new immigrants is seeing them on television. The poorer Americans, who often see them as competing for a decreasing number of low-skilled jobs, are often much less happy to welcome them.

With the exception of American Indians, all Americans either came themselves or are descended from immigrants. Defining ethnic groups as those who are foreign-born shrinks that percentage of the population rapidly. At the present time only about 4 percent of all Americans are foreign-born. For the most part the largest number of those defined as minority groups are the nonwhite population which makes up 16 percent of the population. Of that group three fourths are blacks and most of the rest are identified as having Spanish origins. If religion is also used as a measure of minority groups then it can be said that about 40 percent of the American population is made up of minority groups. This would include Jews, Catholics, Mennonites, blacks, Mexicans, Puerto Ricans, whites from Central and South America and the West Indies, Japanese, Chinese, and other Asiatic races."[34] Next we want to look at racial minority groups. These are groups that are set apart because of skin color, but in addition they often have language and cultural differences from the majority.

Mexicans. Mexicans, like American Indians, have had a bloody history in the United States. After the Mexican-American War ended in 1848 the number of Mexicans killed in the Rio Grande Valley was probably higher than for black lynchings during the same time period. At the end of the Mexican-American War there were about 75,000 Spanish-speaking people living in the Southwest United States.

According to the 1970 census the Mexican-origin population in the United States was almost 6.7 million, and 82 percent of them were native born. Charles Hirschman writes that even a cautious interpretation would be that at least one million persons were added to the Mexican-origin population through illegal immigration during the first half of the 1970s.[35] The official statistics for 1975 estimated the population of Mexican-origin in the United States to be about 6 to 7 million, or about one out of every 20 Americans. "To this established community of Americans with Mexican heritage is added every year an increment of 50,000 to 70,000 of legal immigrants from Mexico."[36] Furthermore, Mexicans are the largest single nationality group of legal immigrants and constitute one out of every six immigrants to the United States.

FIGURE 6–1

Illegal Aliens Apprehended in the United States, 1970–1976

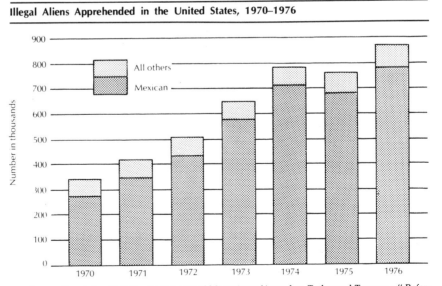

Source: Population Bulletin, "International Migrations: Yesterday, Today and Tomorrow" Reference Bureau, Inc., 32, 4 (September 1977), p. 29.

United Press International Photo

The Mexican migrant farm worker

Hirschman found that illegal entry by Mexicans into the United States was later linked to their legal migration. He says that the model pattern of legal Mexican immigration to the United States is a first venture to the U.S. as an illegal immigrant. "The first illegal trip is often necessary to acquire the credentials (an American spouse or a job guarantee to pass labor certification) necessary for legal entry."[37]

The median level of education for Mexican-Americans or Chicanos is low. For whites the median level of education is 12.1 years, for blacks 10.0 years, but for Chicanos only 8.8 years. While about 50 percent of all whites are in white-collar jobs, this is true of only 20 percent of all Mexican-Americans. They are twice as often as whites found to be employed in service positions such as domestic work, household help, and other service roles. Their median income is about two thirds of that of the United States average.

For many years Mexican-Americans have overwhelmingly contributed to one area of the work force, that of the migrant worker. They have followed the crops to most parts of the United States. Almost always they were employed at very low wages, provided with substandard housing, had to buy many necessities of life at exaggerated prices from their employers, and were generally not recognized as having any legal identity or rights. The use of the migrant worker has been greatly reduced because of agricultural mechanization. For example, until a few years ago, hundreds of Mexican migrant workers came to Michigan in the summer months to pick cherries. But the farmers now use machines that shake the cherries from the trees and relatively few workers are needed.

The substandard patterns of life for the Chicano have had great costs for them in terms of life expectancy and general health. This has been true whether they lived under the poor conditions of the Southwest or were traveling as migrant workers. Mexican Americans have a higher infant mortality rate, a shorter life expectancy, and higher mortality rates from influenza, pneumonia, and tuberculosis than do white Americans.[38]

American Indians. From the very beginning of settlement in North America there has been little concern with the rights of the native American Indian. Historically they most often have been defined as subhuman and without rights. The American treatment of the Indian has been consistently one of deceit and killing. In 1800 there were approximately 600,000 Indians but by 1850 the number was probably less than half of that. The Indians were killed by the diseases the whites brought, or killed defending their lands, or died because they were forced to leave. For example, in 1834, 4,000 Cherokees died in a forced march from their lands in Georgia to reservations in Arkansas and Oklahoma. Thousands of others died from starvation and disease.

During the 19th century well over 500,000 Indians died. They were not only killed through wars, disease, and hunger but often through a deliberate attempt to kill them. At many times and places in America there were bounties placed on Indians where the hunter was paid up to one hundred dollars for a scalp. There are still in 1980 several states where bounties exist. The dominant belief came to be that '"the only good Indian was a dead Indian." This view generally prevailed up until the 1950s when slowly it began to change. For example, most movies made before World War II treated the Indian as a "dirty redskin" who slaughtered innocent white women and children.

There are about 800,000 American Indians today and about 500,000 of them live on approximately 200 reservations. In addition, about 200,000 live in cities and another 100,000 are scattered in the Eastern area of the United States. Historically, the reservations were set up with Indian schools, but there was never any notion of allowing the Indian to maintain his own culture. Rather the schools would assimilate the Indian children into American society. For the most part their record has been a total failure. The levels and kinds of education provided the Indian have always been very poor. And even what little vocational training the Indian received took place without taking into account the actual job opportunities available."[39]

United Press International Photo

The Indian protest at Wounded Knee

There are now many Indians living in cities and towns and they are regarded as urban Indians. But they are the most powerless of all Indian groups. They not only have all the disadvantages of other urban minorities, but they also are the poorest and culturally the most distinct. So long as they live in the cities they cannot receive standard Indian services. Cities like Chicago, with fairly large Indian populations, allocate almost no community funds for urban Indians. For example in 1970, $43,000 was allocated for Indians in Chicago as compared to $401,200 for a traditional middle-class activity like the Boy Scouts.[40]

The level of education for the Indian is very low. Nationally the median level of education is only 5.3 years. On the Navajo reservation only one in five adults has finished high school. On the same reservation over half of the adults are unemployed or work only part-time. The housing is substandard as are all aspects of daily living on the reservation.

American Indians have the poorest health of all Americans. While Indians have low mortality rates for cancer and heart disease, they have very high rates for diabetes and tuberculosis. The incidence of tuberculosis among Indians is ten times higher than for the population as a whole. "Indians also have 60 times more dysentery, 30 times more strep throat, and 11 times more hepatitis than other Americans."[41]

It is estimated that nine out of ten Indian families live in housing that is far below the minimum standards of comfort, safety, and decency. About 60 percent of all Indians are under 20 years of age and the median age is only 17. The Indian infant mortality rate is 70 percent higher than the rate for infants in the population as a whole. The death rate of Indian infants 28 days old to 11 months of age is almost four times the rate of all other groups.[42]

The American Indian is unique as a minority group in that very few Americans ever encounter them or even hear much about them. Also added to this is the desire by many Indians to maintain their own culture and have as little to do with the outside world as possible. This means that there is relatively little pressure to do much for the Indian and so it can be safely predicted that very little will be done for them in the future.

American Blacks

Historically, blacks were among the earliest American settlers. Some came as free persons but most came as slaves into the Southern colonies. Blacks coming in as slaves were uniformly defined as subhuman and without human rights. The evidence for this was taken from the Bible where there are many passages related to the inferior status of blacks and slaves. At the time of the first census in 1790 there were 757,208 blacks in this country and this was about 20 percent of the total population. More than 90 percent of them were concentrated in the South.[43]

By the time of World War I there began to be a movement of blacks from the rural South to the urban North. Today about 40 percent of all blacks live in the northern United States. The mass migration of blacks from the rural South to the urban North transferred their poverty to the city. Blacks did not appear in significant proportions on the Aid to Dependent Children rolls until 1948. "The majority of blacks who migrated to the metropolitan areas of the north brought with them the legacy of the South. They were poorly educated, had few marketable skills, often were in poor health, and had entered an urban market where wage discrimination existed."[44]

In 1970 the metropolitan areas were home for over 70 percent of the black population. The comparable figures for whites is less than 65 percent. Furthermore, the central cities were home for 55 percent of the nation's blacks and only 25 percent of the nation's whites. Only about 5 percent of all suburbanites are black and they, for the most part, live in older areas characterised by industry and old housing.

"Between 1960 and 1970 the white suburban population increased by 15 million and the black by only 800 thousand."[45] (See Chapter 2.)

The movement of blacks into the city has typically been into the poorest areas. Because of racial prejudice the entrance of blacks into areas has resulted in the loss of many services. For example, many services and businesses abandon the areas where blacks have moved in. This means that blacks must go further to find services and become more dependent on public transportation.

We want to look more specifically at some social variables related to the black in America. Many of these variables are also linked with their living in urban areas. There are three general social problems that are closely interrelated—being black, being poor, and living in the city.

Education. While there has been a relative increase in levels of education for blacks, they still lag behind the white population. For example, the high school dropout rate for blacks is about 44 percent and for whites 25 percent. The rates among young blacks going on to college in 1974 were 20 percent of black men and 16 percent of black women.[46] In 1976, 24 percent of all Americans between 25 and 29 years of age had at least four years of college. This was twice what it was for blacks in the same age group. And blacks constituted less than 2 percent of all graduate students and earned less than 1 percent of the doctorates granted in 1970.[47]

Diane K. Lewis suggests that education among blacks seems to have shifted in favor of men during the past few years as there has been a greater inclusion of blacks in institutions of higher education. "Formerly, sociological studies of black communities showed that black women had higher rates of literacy and more years of schooling than males."[48]

Occupations. Blacks have always been overrepresented in low status and low income jobs. Until very recent years there were many occupations where discrimination was so powerful that blacks were completely kept out. Until recently, attempts to move blacks into higher status occupations were rare. But since the 1960s there has been a significant increase of blacks into higher status jobs. But this has remained relatively small when compared to whites because there are proportionately fewer blacks with the educational levels to meet the occupational demands.

Among young, college-educated people, black men have achieved income parity with white men, and black women slightly more than parity with white women. At higher occupational levels, among doctoral scientists and engineers, blacks under age 35 earned slightly more than whites under age 35 with the same credentials. However, blacks over 50 earned slightly less than whites over 50 with the same credentials.[49]

Lewis writes that as an aftermath of the 1960s the number of black men recruited into higher-paying, more prestigious jobs increased. But at the same time black women generally moved into the lower-status and lower-paying jobs traditionally reserved for women in the dominant society. Although the difference in earnings between black men and women has widened, the income gap between black women and white women has tended to narrow. "In 1963, 34 percent of black women were domestics, and only 10 percent were clerical workers, in 1974, 11 percent were domestics and 25 percent were clericals."[50]

Historically the labor movement has done relatively little to better the position of the black in the work force. Even though some unions have been active in the civil rights movement, at the same time local unions have not allowed blacks to become members. Most union sponsored job training programs have not been open to blacks. In the traditional craft unions the blacks have been and still are relatively few in number. They are mainly found in such unions as steel and auto workers or as state and municipal employes. These are the areas of semiskilled work rather than highly skilled and craft occupations.

In the federal government, blacks appear to do well in that they hold 15 percent of all government jobs. However, only 3 percent of those positions are the higher grade jobs in the federal classification system.

In the 1960s there was a lot of publicity about various government plans to help blacks start to develop their own businesses. But by 1970 there were only 163,000 black-owned businesses in the United States, which is only 2 percent of all businesses. "The gross receipts of all black-owned enterprises accounted for only three tenths of 1 percent of the total."[51]

There has been some improvement for the black in income in recent years. For example, the black median income as a percent of white earnings was 51 percent in 1947, 55 percent in 1960, 61 percent in 1969, and 57 percent in 1975. But this is still a long way from equality. The trends also show that, in the ratio of black to white earnings, black men in general are making slower headway in closing the income gap than are black women relative to white women. "Black men earned 64 percent of the median income of white men in 1967; 75 percent of the income of white men in 1977."[52]

Given the increasing tendency for family income to be the result of two wage earners, family income becomes an important way of looking at the economic position of the black relative to the white. In 1974, for nonwhite families the median family income was $8,265 as compared to $13,356 for white families. The income of approximately two thirds of the black families is based on the earnings of several family members, whereas only about one half of incomes for white families represent such multiple earnings.[53]

TABLE 6–1

Selected Measures of Family Income, by Type of Family and Labor Force Status of Wife, 1977

	Median income		
Type of family	Black	White	Ratio: black to white
All families	$ 9,563	$16,740	0.57
Male headed	13,443	17,848	0.75
Married, wife present	13,716	17,916	0.77
Wife in paid labor force	17,008	20,518	0.83
Wife not in paid labor force	9,697	15,389	0.63
Female-headed, no husband present	5,598	8,799	0.64

Source: U.S. Department of Commerce, Bureau of the Census, "The Social and Economic Status of the Black Population," *Current Population Reports* P–23, no–80 (Washington, D.C.: U.S. Government Printing Office, 1979), p. 190.

As mentioned earlier, the unemployment rate of blacks has generally run twice as high for whites. The employment opportunities for black men are severely limited. The high rates of unemployment and nonparticipation in the labor force suggest that numerous young blacks experience great difficulty in launching careers.[54] The proportion of unemployment ranged from 5 to 13 percent among nonwhite men between 1969 and 1975. Much of the improvement that had been registered in the late 1960s was negated.[55]

The Black and Social Class.   The black has traditionally been treated as either separate from the rest of society or at the bottom of the social class hierarchy. In the first instance they have been seen as a social caste system that operated in a separate and inferior position to the dominant white social class system. But the more recent view has been to put the black within the American social class system and by those values they are overwhelmingly placed at the bottom.

When compared with the past there is some evidence that the black middle class has expanded. But at the same time the hardcore poverty areas of the lower class have been getting worse. This may lead to problems from within the black experience in that as more blacks reach middle-class status, the black lower class may become worse off and more aggressive about its position. Tabb suggests that middle-class blacks assuming positions in the wider society will be increasingly called upon to keep the lid on things by whites "and at the same time will be under pressure from below to identify with the continuing black struggle."[56]

Tabb goes on to suggest that the growing black middle class may become convinced that the system is flexible and is willing to take talented blacks like themselves and give them full recognition. He says that if this happens American blacks will move away from the position of collectively suffering racism to the position where mobility can be achieved for a sizable but still small part of all black people. "The remainder of the black underclass may then be written off, confined to secondary labor markets, to the traditional marginal working-class role or, when in too great supply, to the human scrap heap of redundant labor."[57]

It is probable that for many blacks their lower-class position is viewed as inevitable. Coleman and Rainwater found in their study that it was not the rule for blacks of obviously low status to deny a lower-class identity. Typically they treated the question of their status indifferently or as one of the givens of their lives. Few of them looked around as did the lower-class whites to find someone lower to look down upon. "They did not make a point of being martyrs to centuries of oppression; rather, they spoke matter-of-factly as realists living in the present."[58]

Female-headed Family. The black female as the head of a family unit is much more common than among whites. This is because of higher rates of illegitimacy and lower rates of marital stability. Furthermore, the female-headed family is linked to poverty. In recent years they have become a larger component of the total black families. The female-headed family increased from 28 percent in 1969 to 36 percent in 1975 among blacks.[59]

TABLE 6–2

Percent Marital Status of Female Householders with No Husband Present, By Race, 1978

	White female	Black female
Single	0.01	0.28
Married	0.19	0.30
Widowed	0.32	0.21
Divorced	0.38	0.21

Source: Adapted from, U.S. Department of Commerce, Bureau of the Census, "Marital Status and Living Arrangements: March 1978," *Population Characteristics*, Series P–20, no. 338 (Washington, D.C.: U.S. Government Printing Office, May 1979), p. 5.

In 1973, while 77 percent of all white women who were 14 years of age and older and ever married, were married and living with their husbands, only 54 percent of the black women fell into the same category. In 1975, while only 11 percent of white families were headed by females, this was true of 36 percent of black families. "Black women, then, are more often self-supporting than white women and far more likely to carry single-handedly responsibilities for dependent children."[60] Families that have been headed by women traditionally have had incomes about one half as great as families headed by men, "and children in families headed by women are much more likely to be impoverished than children in families headed by a man."[61]

Even when marriage is a desirable relationship among blacks the sex ratio makes it more difficult than for whites. Within a marriageable age range of 25 to 64, there are 85 males for every 100 black females. There are a number of reasons for this, among which are deaths because of the Vietnam War, imprisonment, and inadequate health care. The shortage of black men contributes to the greater number of black American female-headed households. "It also permits black males to maintain their dominance in interpersonal sexual relationships, because they have the option "to move on'."[62]

The black female head of a family suffers another disadvantage relative to the white female head in that if she works she earns less. Black women high school graduates in various industrial positions earn from 70 to 86 percent of the amount earned by white women.[63] While black women with a college education earn close to what white women earn, very few of them are female heads of households.

The black woman in the mother role also suffers from special disadvantages. For example, she is more apt to have unwanted children. It was estimated that between 1960 and 1965, 17 percent of white births and 36 percent of black births were unwanted. For that time period, when the family income was under $3,000, the percentage unwanted was 27 for whites and 42 for blacks, compared to 15 and 16 percent respectively for those with incomes over $10,000.[64]

Health.   (See also Chapters 14 and 15.) Many of the health problems that blacks have are closely related to poverty. Frequently, problems are caused by environmental factors of poverty that are related to such things as alcoholism, drug addiction, and suicide. Also lead poisoning, rat-bite fever, influenza, pneumonia and tuberculosis are health disorders more common to the poor. "Race becomes a significant health variable in the United States primarily *because* racial minorities typically occupy disadvantaged socioeconomic positions."[65]

Blacks do not receive health care services that are equal to those of white Americans. Various studies show that whites have access to more physicians, a broader range of specialists, and make greater use of hospitals than blacks. "Whites are more likely to visit a physician, make use of diagnostic tests for detecting disease, receive a more thorough and competent diagnosis, and use more effective therapeutic drugs than blacks."[66]

Among whites the ratio of physicians to the population is 1:750;

among blacks the ratio is 1:3,500.[67] In 1973 whites reported 5.1 physician visits per year in contrast to 4.5 among nonwhites. And the poor and blacks are now using more ambulatory services, the evidence indicates that they require more services than they are receiving.[68]

The same general kinds of problems also exist for blacks in terms of their mental health. Furthermore, there are higher rates of mental health problems for blacks in a number of areas. Although blacks constitute about 10 percent of the population they have over 20 percent of the diagnosed hypertension. Between the ages of 25–44, hypertension kills black males 15.5 times more frequently than it does white males. "The ratio of black to white females dying from hypertension in the same age category is 17 to 1."[69]

Extent of Racial Prejudice. The black has been placed in a subordinate position in American society because of prejudice and discrimination and remains there to a great extent for the same reasons. We want to look more specifically at white attitudes in the United States at present toward blacks. For most white Americans race continues to be the most important criteria for giving low status to minority group members. For many whites a person's being black often negates any achievements of education, occupation, or income. Many whites consider *all* blacks as a group and therefore blacks are associated with undesirable residential areas.

In recent years there have been some changes in white attitudes toward blacks. From the early 1940s to the mid-1960s the proportion of national samples of whites who believed that blacks were as intelligent as whites and who said they would not be disturbed if a black with the same income and education moved onto their block rose from 35 percent in 1942 to 84 percent in 1972.[70] There also appears to have been a greater acceptance of their children bringing home black playmates by white parents from 40 percent in 1956 to 81 percent in 1971. These were for most whites abstract questions and if actually faced with the situations, the rates of acceptance would undoubtedly be much lower.

While white Americans do not approve of discrimination, they do not want complete integration either. A 1976 Harris Poll found that while only 12 percent favored "separation of the races," only 28 percent favored "full racial integration," and 48 percent chose "integration in some areas of life."

There are also some differences between blacks and whites in defining discrimination and how it can be resolved. This is illustrated in different views about an integrated neighborhood. One national study found that when an integrated neighborhood was defined as attracting both blacks and whites, those neighborhoods had a median black population of only 3 percent. Racial desegregation of urban neighborhoods typically leads to white avoidance and abandonment.[71]

Another study found that the proportion of blacks indicating they would like to live in racially mixed neighborhoods increased during the 1960s and reached 67 percent toward the end of the decade. Only 13 percent of the blacks reported that they preferred to live in an all or mostly all black neighborhood.[72] Often the blacks' desire to live in integrated neighborhoods is due less to their wanting to live with whites than to their wanting to live where the better housing is found. As Tabb points out, for the vast majority of ghetto blacks, integration can only have less and less meaning given population trends and the persistence of housing segregation. "The recent employment gains of middle-class blacks have for the most part been outside the ghetto."[73]

Attempts to Resolve Racial Conflict

In recent decades major attempts to deal with racial discrimination have occurred within the legal setting. Changes in laws can directly alter behavior and they can also have other effects. Under some circumstances laws may effect prejudice by adding moral and symbolic weight to the principles that have been embodied within the civil rights legislation. "Law contributes to the moral atmosphere that prevails within a society and may have an educational impact on its members."[74] But this has a limited effect because it is difficult to legislate morality.

In 1954 the Supreme Court overthrew the legal foundations of segregation when they ruled against the "separate but equal" doctrine that had been used to keep black children out of white schools. This was a change brought about by a legalistic approach and for the most part did not involve the general black public. But the black protest movements in the 1960s did break away from the traditional legalistic view to one of mass actions, boycotts, sit-ins, and other "civil disorders."[75]

In 1964 the Civil Rights Act provided the means to fight discrimination in employment and public accommodations. In 1965 the Civil Rights Act was passed giving rights and protection to vote. Prior to its passage only about 29 percent of the eligible blacks were registered to vote in the seven states covered by the act. But by 1972 more than 56 percent were registered to vote.[76]

For many blacks the civil rights movement was seen as representing little more than tokenism. From the point of view of the average black, not much had changed by the end of the 1960s. Unemployment remained high, schools were often segregated, and there was no indication of any new economic opportunity. Royce Singleton, Jr., says that the civil rights legislation of the 1960s has been ineffective in counteracting discrimination for two reasons. First, the new laws often

The Civil Rights Act, 1964

went unenforced because the civil rights division of the Justice Department was understaffed and underfinanced. Second, it placed the burden of litigation on the individual against whom discrimination had occurred and this was a personally and financially arduous process.[77]

The rise of the black power movement was to a great extent due to the inability of the civil rights movement to actually change the daily life of the average black. The civil rights movement was not directed at the cultural context of the black, while the black power movement was. The civil rights movement was also mainly a rural Southern movement that did not deal with the problems faced by blacks in Northern city ghettos. Moreover, the early civil rights movements were basically middle class, while the efforts of the black power groups were directed toward the black lower class.

By the early 1970s the black power movement had subsided greatly. This was due to several factors. One was the existence of new laws and administrative forces, many of which were a response to the black protest. This made it possible for many blacks to pursue their goals through existing institutional channels. Second, the ranks of the more visible and aggressive black leaders were greatly reduced by imprisonment, emigration, and assassination. Third, on the local level the white power structure was able to co-opt and to bring many black militants into government and into white political organizations. Finally, the black movement was plagued by a confusion as to whether it should pursue an assimilationist (civil rights) or a separatist (black nationalist) program.[78]

In 1972, 18 years after the Supreme Court decision which disallowed the "separate but equal" doctrine and 17 years after the 1955 decision which mandated integration "with all deliberate speed," almost a third of all black students attended public schools with 80 percent or more minority enrollment. "Sixty percent attended schools with 50 percent or more minority enrollment, and only 40 percent of minority students attended public schools with less than 50 percent minority enrollment."[79]

In recent years the concern of many whites seems to be less about the question of integration of schools and more on how it will be achieved. Various studies suggest a consensus among whites in supporting integrated schools, but major disagreements on busing. Busing is the movement of students from one school to another to achieve a more even racial balance. What this usually means is the busing of black children to white schools. A 1975 Harris Poll of adults found that only 20 percent favored busing and 74 percent were against. Among blacks only 40 percent favored busing while 47 percent were opposed.

There has been an intense reaction against busing in some cities. This has been especially true in Boston, where the 1970s have seen a general increase in racial hostilities. Elliot Zashin suggests that while it is "difficult to believe that fear, dislike, or disapproval of blacks did not underlie some of the white protests, one cannot ignore class differences and educational concerns as factors."[80]

Busing is even hard to accept by white liberals. Very few of them live in neighborhoods that have large numbers of blacks in the schools and if they do they often send their children to private schools. One study reported that 86 percent of the white liberals in their sample expressed reservations about busing. They also found that "although Jews have a tradition of liberal commitment they share in this general ambivalence about specific integration procedure."[81]

The economic factor is a powerful force in the feelings of many whites toward blacks. With the black dependency on welfare very high, many whites, especially those in the working class, feel they are being unfairly burdened with the expense. Community control of the schools is another important issue for many whites. "The incidence of disciplinary problems in public schools is highly correlated with black enrollment."[82]

When solutions to racial prejudice and discrimination are proposed the most common suggestion is through some kind of application of education. But it seems very doubtful that education has been a very effective technique for significantly changing attitudes. This appears to be true because it is very difficult for a formal educational institution to modify attitudes that are normative in the community. "Teachers themselves, for example, are very likely to share the social attitudes that prevail in the community."[83]

But Martin and Franklin go on to point out that while it is true that formal education does not dramatically reduce group prejudice in the short run, it is equally true that persons with the lowest amount of formal education tend to be most prejudiced. In the long run, formal education is favorable to more tolerant intergroup attitudes. The nature of this influence is difficult to specify. But it seems partly to be due to the greater economic security that a higher level of education usually brings, as well as the general "liberalizing effect" of education.[84]

Conclusion. It is likely that in the future many ethnic groups will become assimilated. This will occur to the extent ethnic groups wish it. As long as ethnicity is seen as something to be maintained and cultivated, full assimilation will be slowed. However, for racial groups the future is much less optimistic. There is no indication of any recent changes toward the black in terms of a reduction of prejudice. What appears to happen is that tokenism has increased somewhat. This is illustrated in television where only a few years ago there were no blacks in commercials. Today there are some blacks but they are usually aimed at a black audience or if in a group they represent careful integration. In commercials where there are half a dozen men, there may be a black, but only one.

Possibly most important to the limited chances of reducing the social problem of minority groups is the economic influence. As inflation and unemployment remain high and continue to go up, the black is hurt the most. Because they earn less, inflation causes their money to buy them even less than the white can buy. And because there is a greater demand for jobs by whites, many blacks are forced out of jobs they are "allowed" under higher employment to make room for the whites who now want those jobs.

In this chapter we have examined the concepts of racism, prejudice, and discrimination as applied to various groups. Ethnicity is a term for defining groups on the basis of certain characteristics, usually related to their countries of origin. Both Spanish-speaking Americans and American Indians were examined as racial groups in America. The major stress was placed on American blacks and a variety of social variables related to their position in society. Finally, there was a look at the legal attempts to deal with racial discrimination.

NOTES

1. Royce Singleton, Jr., and Jonathan H. Turner, "White Oppression of Blacks in America," in *Understanding Social Problems,* by Don H. Zimmerman et al. (New York: Praeger Publishers, 1976), p. 134.

2. James W. Vander Zanden, *American Minority Relations* (New York: Ronald, 1972), pp. 302–3.

3. *Ibid.,* p. 302.

4. Russell Middleton, "Regional Differences in Prejudice," *American Sociological Review* (February 1976); p. 98.

5. William K. Tabb, "Race Relations Models and Social Change," *Social Problems* (Spring 1971), p. 442.

6. Singleton and Turner, "White Oppression," p. 130.

7. Middleton, "Regional Differences," p. 102.

8. Singleton and Turner, "White Oppression," p. 131.

9. Ibid., p. 152.

10. James G. Martin and Clyde W. Franklin, *Minority Group Relations* (Columbus, Ohio: Charles E. Merrill, 1973), p. 235.

11. Richard D. Alba, "Social Assimilation among American Catholic National-Origin Groups," *American Sociological Review* (December 1976), p. 1030.

12. Thomas Fraser Pettigrew, "Race and Intergroup Relations," in *Contemporary Social Problems,* 4th ed., by Robert K. Merton and Robert Nishet (New York: Harcourt Brace Jovanovich, 1976), p. 487.

13. Martin and Franklin, *Minority Relations,* p. 233.

14. Middleton, "Regional Differences," p. 103.

15. Sidney Kronus, "Race, Ethnicity, and Community," in *Handbook of Contemporary Urban Life,* by David Street (San Francisco, Calif.: Jossey-Bass, 1978), p. 213.

16. Andrew M. Greeley, *Why Can't They Be Like Us? America's White Ethnic Groups* (New York: Dutton, 1975), p. 40.

17. William L. Yancey, Eugene P. Ericksen, and Richard N. Juliani, "Emergent Ethnicity: A Review and Reformulation," *American Sociological Review* (June 1976), p. 392.

18. Peter I. Rose, *The Study of Society* (New York: Random House, 1977), p. 508.

19. Greeley, *Like Us,* p. 38.

20. Ibid., p. 39.

21. Yancey, Ericksen, and Juliani, "Emergent Ethnicity," pp. 392–93.

22. Ibid., p. 394.

23. Kronus, "Race," p. 215.

24. Richard P. Coleman and Lee Rainwater, *Social Standing In America* (New York: Basic Books, 1978), p. 108.

25. Ibid., p. 109.

26. Greeley, *Like Us*, pp. 45–46.

27. J. Allen William, Jr., Nicholas Babchuk, and David R. Johnson, "Voluntary Association and Minority Status: A Comparative Analysis of Anglo, Black and Mexican Americans," *American Sociological Review* (October 1973), p. 638.

28. Coleman and Rainwater, *Social Standing*, p. 105.

29. Alba, "Social Assimilation," p. 1030.

30. Ibid., p. 1032.

31. Greeley, *Like Us*, p. 62.

32. Yancey, Ericksen, and Juliani, "Emergent Ethnicity," p. 398.

33. Kronus, "Race," p. 218.

34. Scott G. McNall, *The Sociological Experience*, 2d ed. (Boston: Little, Brown, 1971), p. 200.

35. Charles Hirschman, "Prior U.S. Residence Among Mexican Immigrants," *Social Forces* (June 1978), p. 1181.

36. Ibid., p. 1197.

37. Ibid., p. 1186.

38. William C. Cockerham, *Medical Sociology* (Englewood Cliffs, N.J.: Prentice-Hall, 1978), p. 35.

39. Joyotpaul and Jean Chandhuri, "Emerging American Indian Politics: The Problem of Powerlessness," in *The Fourth World*, by Leo Hamalian and Frederick R. Karl (New York: Dell, 1976), p. 145.

40. Ibid., p. 150.

41. Cockerham, *Medical Sociology*, p. 36.

42. Hanna H. Meissner, *Poverty In The Affluent Society*, rev. ed. (New York: Harper & Row, 1973), p. 65.

43. Vander Zanden, *American Minority*, p. 189.

44. Kronus, "Race," p. 206.

45. Ibid., p. 204.

46. Diane K. Lewis, "A Response to Inequality: Black Women, Racism, and Sexism," *Signs* (Winter 1977), p. 350.

47. Kronus, "Race," p. 207.

48. Lewis, "Response," p. 349.

49. Thomas Sowell, "Ethnicity in a Changing America," *Daedalus* (Winter 1978), p. 224.

50. Lewis, "Response," p. 359.

51. Kronus, "Race," p. 208.

52. U.S. Department of Commerce, Bureau of the Census, "The Social and Economic Status of the Black Population," *Current Population Reports*, P–23, no–80 (Washington, D.C.: U.S. Government Printing Office, 1979), p. 190.

53. Beverly Lindsay, "Minority Women in America," in *The Study of Women: Enlarging Perspectives of Social Reality*, by Eloise C. Synder (New York: Harper & Row, 1979), p. 322.

54. Reynolds Farley, "Trends in Racial Inequalities: Have the Gains of the 1960s Disappeared in the 1970s?" *American Sociological Review* (April 1977), p. 206.

55. Ibid., p. 193.

56. Tabb, "Race Relations," p. 440.

57. Ibid., p. 442.

58. Coleman and Rainwater, *Social Standing*, p. 209.

59. Farley, "Trends," p. 200.

60. Lewis, "Response," p. 359.

61. Farley, "Trends," p. 199.

62. Lindsay, "Minority Women," p. 327.

63. Ibid., p. 325.

64. Samual H. Preston, "Differential Fertility, Unwanted Fertility, and Racial Trends in Occupational Achievement," *American Sociological Review* (August 1974), p. 504.

65. Cockerham, *Medical Sociology*, p. 38.

66. Sidney Stahl and Gilbert Gardner, "A Contradiction in the Health Care Delivery System," *The Sociological Quarterly* (Winter 1976), p. 121.

67. Cockerham, *Medical Sociology*, p. 35.

68. David Mechanic, *Medical Sociology*, 2nd ed. (New York: The Free Press, 1978), p. 199.

69. Cockerham, *Medical Sociology*, p. 34.

70. Farley, "Trends," pp. 189–90.

71. Brian J. L. Brian and John D. Kasarda, *Contemporary Urban Ecology* (New York: Macmillan, 1977), p. 23.

72. Albert I. Hermalin and Reynolds Farley, "The Potential for Residential Integration in Cities and Suburbs: Implications for the Busing Controversy," *American Sociological Review* (October 1973), p. 608.

73. Tabb, "Race Relations," p. 440.

74. Vander Zanden, *American Minority*, p. 298.

75. Ibid., p. 320.

76. Elliot Zashin, "The Progress of Black Americans in Civil Rights: The Past Two Decades Assessed," *Daedalus* (Winter 1978), p. 247.

77. Singleton and Turner, "White Oppression," p. 156.

78. Vander Zanden, *American Minority*, pp. 321–22.

79. U.S. Department of Health, Education and Welfare, National Center for Education Statistics, "The Condition of Learning" (Washington, D.C.: U.S. Government Printing Office, 1975), p. 70.

80. Zashin, "Progress," p. 245.

81. Judith Caditz, "Ethnic Identification, Interethnic Contact, and Belief in Integration," *Social Forces* (March 1976), p. 632.

82. Kronus, "Race," p. 227.

83. Martin and Franklin, *Minority Relations*, p. 294.

84. Ibid., p. 296.

SELECTED BIBLIOGRAPHY

Alba, Richard D. "Social Assimilation among American Catholic National-Origin Groups." *American Sociological Review* (December 1976), pp. 1030–46.

Caditz, Judith. "Ethnic Identification, Interethnic Contact, and Belief in Integration." *Social Forces* (March 1976), pp. 632–45.

Farley, Reynolds. "Trends in Racial Inequality: Have the Gains of the 1960s Disappeared in the 1970s?" *American Sociological Review* (April 1977), pp. 189–208.

Greeley, Andrew M. *Why Can't They Be Like Us? America's White Ethnic Groups.* New York: Dutton, 1975.

Hirschman, Charles. "Prior U.S. Residence Among Mexican Immigrants." *Social Forces* (June 1978), pp. 1179–99.

Lewis, Diane K. "A Response to Inequality: Black Women, Racism, and Sexism." *Signs* (Winter 1977), pp. 339–61.

Middleton, Russell. "Regional Differences in Prejudice." *American Sociological Review* (February 1976), pp. 94–117.

Sowell, Thomas. "Ethnicity in a Changing America." *Daedalus* (Winter 1978), pp. 213–37.

Tabb, William K. "Race Relations Models and Social Change." *Social Problems* (Spring 1971), pp. 431–44.

Vander Zanden, James W. *American Minority Relations.* New York: Ronald, 1972.

Yancey, William L.; Ericksen, Eugene P.; and Juliana, Richard N. "Emergent Ethnicity: A Review and Reformulation." *American Sociological Review* (June 1976), pp. 391–403.

Zashin, Elliot. "The Progress of Black Americans in Civil Rights: The Past Two Decades Assessed." *Daedalus* (Winter 1978), pp. 239–62.

PART THREE

Family and Sex Based Social Problems

Chapter 7

Population

Population problems relate to relationships between the changing numbers of people and the quality of their lives. Unlike other social problems in this book, we shall treat population problems on an international level as well as in the United States. This double focus is taken because problems on an international level have great significance for American population questions. In the long run, any really significant changes in the world's population will have a major impact on American society. Future problems will probably center around the uses of natural resources basic to the survival of all populations. We will first look at population problems on the world level and second in the United States.

World Population Problems

For most of the history of mankind the increase in population was very slow. It took from the beginning of history up to the birth of Christ for the number of humans to reach about one third of a billion. It was not until about 1850 that the world's population reached the first billion. But it then took only about 75 years to add the second billion and 35 years to add the third billion. In 1965 there were an estimated 65 million persons added that year. In 1970 there were about 72 million added.[1] At the present time the population of the world is increasing at the rate of about .2 million per day and if this rate continues the population of the world will double in the next 35 years.

The dynamics of the world's population growth are determined by the various rates of births and deaths. For most of human history the rate of growth was slow because of a combination of high birth rates

TABLE 7–1

World Population Growth

	In millions		In millions
10,000 B.C.	10	1850	1,130
1 A.D.	300	1900	1,600
1650	510	1950	2,510
1700	625	1970	3,575
1750	710	1978	4,219
1800	910	1978	4,219

Source: *The World Almanac* (New York: Newspaper enterprises, 1980), p. 734.

and equally high death rates. In many parts of the world today, especially in the underdeveloped countries, population growth continues to be very high. This is the result of two factors—the unprecedented conquest of mortality and the postponement of the birth-rate decline.[2]

Deaths. Shirley Foster Hartley has pointed out that the term "population explosion" is misleading. She argues this on the grounds that it implies that an increase in the birth rate is the reason. However, this is not the case for the world as a whole. Rather, an unprecedented decline in the death rate, especially since World War II, is the main cause of the recent rapid rise in the world's population. This has happened because the death rate has responded more rapidly than the birth rate to the development and use of science and technology in such areas as "improved food distribution, a more effective social organization, and the mass application of modern public health measures: vaccines, antibiotics, sulfa drugs, and especially the use of new insecticides that brought malaria under control."[3]

We may look more specifically at death rates around the world. Basically, as suggested above, life expectancy increased as the number of threats to life were altered or reduced. Human survival is very much influenced by environmental effects. At one time animals threatened the population with direct physical dangers, but these have long been under control. The dangers in more recent times have come from lack of food, medical causes, natural disasters, and destruction by other human beings.

There have been drastic reductions in many of the environmental dangers. A number of the medical problems of the past had their base in the immediate physical environment and mortality rates were reduced by general improvements in public sanitation, especially in the cities. There have been great reductions in the number of deaths from waterborne diseases, such as cholera, typhoid, and dysentery. It was not until the 19th century that public utilities and standard sanitation procedures were introduced, reducing the death rates in urban areas which historically had the highest death rates. In the country people are much less crowded and therefore contamination from sewage is less.

In recent years it has been the widespread use of DDT to control malaria along with other improvements in safety of water supplies that helped cut the death rate. These were public health measures promoted by United Nations agencies following the end of World War II. These measures had the effect of cutting crude death rates from one half to one fourth of their traditionally high levels in many of the underdeveloped nations. This does not necessarily mean that those people who survive are healthy. They live but often suffer from many problems of health and malnutrition.

Hartley points out that changes in personal hygiene, such as the wearing and more frequent washing of cheap cotton clothes, facilitated cleanliness and this contributed to a decrease in the death rate. In the late 19th century, the medical measures of sterilization of instruments, use of masks, and disinfection probably saved more lives than all the wars of the 19th century had sacrificed. At the same time, there was also the development of immunology against some diseases.[4]

As suggested, changes in the physical environment were closely linked to the development and application of medical knowledge. The main triumph of medical technology has been the conquest of infectious disease. Around the world it has been the extension of this conquest to underdeveloped areas that has brought down the death rates. This technology has greatly reduced the spread of such diseases as malaria, yellow fever, yaws, trachoma, cholera, plague, typhoid, diphtheria, small pox, tuberculosis, and dysentery which were controlled on a mass basis at low cost.[5]

There have been other related factors that influenced the lowering of mortality. For example, there has been the increased biological knowledge that allows for the use of relatively inexpensive life-saving public health measures. As life expectancy has increased, a greater proportion of the population has survived through the child-producing years. This means that medical science has improved the chances of childbearing by lengthening the life span. At the same time better nutrition and health, at least in the more advanced societies, have lowered the age of puberty and thereby increased the possible childbearing years.[6]

Possibly the best measure of overall health and medical standards is the infant mortality rate. Two hundred years ago the chance of a child's surviving through the first year of life was much less than today. Generally in the past, one out of every four or five children would not have reached their first birthday. During much of history the chance would have been no better than one child in two or three reaching one year of age. But today the rates of infant mortality have been greatly reduced, although they do vary greatly in different parts of the world. For example, the number of deaths during the first year of life per 1,000 live births is estimated to vary from about 13 in Norway and Sweden to 259 in Zambia.

Kingsley Davis points out that the standard explanation of why the death rate has declined has been an economic one. At first the decline was restricted to those countries that experienced significant economic progress. For example, the Western world's gains in agriculture, transportation, and commerce during the 18th and 19th centuries made possible better diets, better housing, and better health care.[7] But Davis says modern technology has two aspects that reduce mortality by different means and with different historical timing. Productive technology, early in industrialization, tended to increase mortality but with time decreased it. However, this economic development did not attack the specific agents of disease. To deal with disease, the special technology of medicine arose. So in the latter half of the 19th century a rising number of medical discoveries greatly helped to lower the death rates. "Their influence was added to productive technology, which explains why mortality lessened more in the late than in the early stages of industrialization."[8]

What can be said in general about the death rates around the world at the present time? In industrial countries the death rate had reached an approximate "floor" before 1940 so that declines since that time have been relatively slight. At the present time the crude death rates are lower in many of the less developed countries which have lower proportions of older persons. "Continued mortality reductions in advanced countries are difficult and expensive because the prevailing causes of death such as cancer and heart diseases which mostly affect older people are not easily controlled."[9]

The most dramatic changes between the industrial countries of Europe and the underdeveloped countries has been the rapid reduction in mortality in the underdeveloped countries in recent years in contrast to the gradual declines over time in Europe. As late as the 1930s, mortality was so high in most Latin American countries that a newborn baby had less than a 50 percent chance of being alive at age 30. The underdeveloped countries have had such dramatic reductions because the total knowledge and resources for combating death have been applied in a very short time. By contrast, the changes in the European death rate were much slower because the methods were being developed. This also means that the increase in the average person's life span in the less developed countries has taken much less time than in the industrialized nations. It took 100 years, from 1840 to 1940, for Denmark, England, France, the Netherlands, Norway, and Sweden to raise their life expectancy from 41 to 64 years. In some of the less developed countries the same increase in life expectancy occurred in only 20 years.[10]

There is a misconception about length of life, which holds that people are living to reach much older ages than they did in the past. In the past the high infant mortality rate brought the average life expectancy down to a younger age. But as the infant mortality rate was greatly reduced this had the effect of making average life expectancy much higher. This point is illustrated by the act that in 1900, the white male, age 60, in the United States, had 14.4 years of life expectancy. In 1975, a white male of the same age in the United States had a life expectancy of only 16.8 years. All of the forces related to a decrease in the death rate have been mainly limited to the young, and still relatively little has been achieved to prolong the life of the older person.

On the world level there is no agreement as to an emergence of a definition related to an increase in population. In general, societies give support to greater life expectancy and will use methods that appear to contribute to that. However they have very different views with regard to the reduction of births as a factor in controlling population expansion. Some of the value differences can be seen in the vested interests that exist with regard to the birth rate.

Births. Historically large numbers of births have been seen as a natural and inevitable result of marriage. In fact, values supporting the production of large families have been dominant in almost all cultures. The notion that something can or should be done to control family size is recent. Values positively related to the large families were also a reflection of broader social values which came from other social institutions. Governmental concern with population size has been reflected in worry over any decline in fertility. Sometimes leaders feared that a low growth would yield few military personnel, and the traditional wisdom has been that population increase is necessary for economic growth.

What is striking about limiting the number of births in many of the industrialized countries has been the desire for the effective practice of birth control by women. Within the family women have often done this with little support or encouragement from males. Birth control has been related to women's changing views of their own sexuality as well as separating sexuality from the necessity or possibility of conception. As methods of birth control have been developed, their use has been primarily the responsibility of women. Later in the chapter we will discuss in more detail the development and reliability of birth control methods.

The age distribution of the population has a great influence on the number of births. At present the age structure of the world is very young with about half of the world's population being under 20 years of age. In the overall population picture for the future, these young

© Thomas Hopker/Woodfin Camp & Associates

Hunger and overpopulation in India

people are likely to reproduce far more rapidly than people will die. By contrast, among European nations, there are probably only 20 to 25 percent of their populations in the young age group. This means that in Europe the proportion of persons in or entering the childbearing years is much less than in the underdeveloped countries.

Having a large number of children has a number of implications for the family and society. Often large families require greater living space, but that may not be available. Food is also found to be lower in quality on the average as the number of children increases. The psychological pressures on parents increase with family size. And the more children there are, the less likely the mother is to contribute to the family income. Health is better on the average for persons in small rather than large families. "Children from large families are found to be even more deficient in academic attainment than would be predicted on the basis of IQ alone."[11]

In the long run what can affect the increase of the world population? Davis argues that if control over expansion in numbers occurs, it will be due to a rise in mortality rather than a more efficient system of birth control around the world. He suggests that as more billions with more technology struggle for the earth's resources "all-out warfare could cause not only direct casualties of unprecedented magnitude but also indirect ones from starvation, disease, and irradiation."[12]

Distribution of the Population.   Given the numbers of persons in the world, a related population problem concerns where and how they are distributed over the face of the earth. The births and deaths of persons, along with their standard of living, are effected by where they live and what natural resources are available to them.

Densities of population vary greatly and have changed over time. In America, the Indian population prior to the arrival of European settlers approximated about one person per square mile. This meant a potential of 314 human contacts in a circular area with a 10-mile radius. By 1960, the population density of the United States was about 50 persons per square mile. "That density would produce a potential of 15,700 human contacts within a circle of a 10-mile radius."[13]

At the present time there are about 60 persons per square mile in the United States. This is in contrast to about 584 per square mile in Great Britain while India has 405, Taiwan 700, and Japan 708. Within the United States there are great variations in population density. New York state has a density of 379 persons per square mile and Rhode Island has 893. By contrast, Nevada has 5.2 and Wyoming has 3.7 people per square mile. "In New York City the density is almost 26,343 persons per square mile of land, while in some parts of rural Montana the density is less than 1 person per square mile."[14]

At the present time an average of about one fourth of the population of 170 underdeveloped countries is living in urban places. By contrast almost 70 percent of the population of developed countries live in cities. Predictions are that by the year 2000 an expected 81 percent of the population will be urban in the developed countries as a whole, with 41 percent of the population urban in the less developed regions.[15] Cities are characterized by very dense populations. Probably the most densely settled area is Hong Kong with about 250,000 persons per square mile. This is over three times the density of Manhattan Island in New York City.

There is strong evidence that there are costs to persons who live in overcrowded conditions. Hartley says that, for the most part, historical examples of social and psychological aspects of overcrowding provide evidence of the ugly and undesirable potentialities of human behavior. She writes that the interpersonal pressures which result from overcrowding show a "very strong relationship with measures of mortality, juvenile delinquency, fertility, and public assistance."[16] Studies also indicate a higher incidence of schizophrenia and other psychotic and neurotic behavior in congested urban areas than in more open surroundings. The social pathology of crowded slums may be the result of the interaction of two factors: "(1) persons with behavior problems gravitate toward the slum areas, and (2) the congestion itself produces aberrant behavior."[17]

Another problem related to the distribution of the population is the availability of food. Although approximately one fourth of the world's 32 billion acres are classified as "potentially arable," only one half of that is actually under cultivation. Most of the potentially arable land not already in use requires more investment than the crop returns would be worth. Another quarter of the world's surface could be used for grazing, but would be unsuitable for cultivation. The remaining half of the land area of the world, which includes deserts, mountains, arctic wastelands, and so forth, is very limited for human use.

The land under cultivation is not producing enough food for the needs of people around the world. At least half of all people in the world are undernourished. It is estimated that even if the world's present food supply were equally distributed there would be barely enough calories to feed every person. It has been further estimated that between 10 and 20 million people, mostly children in underdeveloped countries, are dying of starvation every year.

The use of resources for food and energy are unequally distributed around the world. While 6.5 percent of the world's population lives in North America they are using about half of the world's yield of resources. The United States uses one third of the world's energy, over one third of the tin, and about one fourth of its phosphate, potash, and nitrogenous fertilizer. It also consumes one half of the world's newsprint and synthetic rubber, more than one fourth of its steel, and about one eighth of its cotton.[18]

Value commitments to various resources by different nations have a great impact on how resources are used. For example, the United States is committed to a very heavy use of beef as a basic food. For the United States to have its beef needs met means a tremendous use of grain. For example, about 20 pounds of grain are needed to produce 1 pound of beef. That same amount of grain could be used to feed nearly 20 people who are starving in other parts of the world.

Increasingly the industrialized nations of the world are interdependent rather than independent in their food production. This interdependence reflects two developments. One is that subsistence farming has declined while the growing of specialized crops has increased. Second, advances in transportation allow food to be sent long distances. This means that food can be sent to those areas that suffer from shortages created by natural disasters.

Several years ago a great deal of publicity was given to the "green revolution" that suggested breakthroughs in food production that have not materialized. In part the technological breakthrough resulted from dramatic improvement in the yield of new strains of wheat and rice. However, this required great increases in the use of fertilizers and water. But fertilizers are becoming scarce and more expensive. Many underdeveloped countries cannot afford the fertilizers nor the expensive irrigation systems that are needed.

In many of the technologically advanced nations there have been dramatic increases in production. And to some extent those increases in production of food have been shared but not to the extent of significantly improving the diets of people throughout the world. But when viewed in terms of living standards the gains made from greater productions of food have been nullified by population increase. The greater production of food has been canceled out by the increased number of mouths to feed.

The problem of the distribution of food in part is simply not enough food to go around. Only a minority of the world's people are well fed. To take from the well fed and equally distribute the world's supply of food would mean that all the people in the world would be malnourished. If the world's supply of food was distributed on the average dietary level of the population of the United States only about one third of the human race could be fed. "If India were to distribute food according to United States dietary standards, its food production could support only 90 million people, or about one sixth of its present population."[19] The consumption of food in the United States goes far beyond an adequate diet and reaches the excessive use and waste of food. There are other ecological problems related to populations and the use of resources. The rapid increases in population and the technological explosion together cause the increasing pollution of the environment. It is recognized that the increasing affluence of persons in advanced technological societies has contributed more to pollution than the simple rise in population numbers. People are not only unwilling to give up the niceties of life, but rather, having plenty, still reach out for more. A reflection of this situation is the fact that the average American daily disposes of over four pounds of solid waste.

As the population goes up the amount of waste increases. If the standard of living remains constant, twice as many people will mean twice as much garbage, whether the waste is discharged in the air, in the water, or dumped on the ground. As the number of "things" that people possess or use up increases, so does the potential destructive power of useless remains or waste. Old automobiles don't just fade away, and metal content is seldom recycled. "Pollution occurs, then, partially as a result of the population increase and the rise in standard of living. It is also a consequence of the time lag in our recognition of the problem created by people pollution and our lack of concern or inability to remedy the problems."[20] (See also Chapter 7.)

Causes. The question of what causes population increases is a central one to all those concerned with population control. To exert control assumes an understanding of causes. However, understanding causes does not necessarily mean that anything will be or can be done about them. Questions about the expansion of the world's population are often on the level of global politics, so the issues are often international ones. We will briefly look at some attempts to explain the reasons or causes of population increase.

In 1798 Thomas Robert Malthus wrote *Essay on the Principle of Population, as it Affects the Future Improvement of Society.* He argued that the major impediment to progress was the constant tendency in all animal life to increase beyond the food supply available to it. Malthus believed that for humans their ability to reason might interrupt the drive to increase the species. However, if unchecked, the population would go on doubling itself every 25 years and soon the food supply would not meet needs. Malthus saw checks that could be used. One might be that man would use his reasoning abilities which would allow him to calculate the future consequences and engage preventive measures. But Malthus did not consider contraception as a means of control. Rather he saw population control through educated reason that would lead to "moral restraint," late marriage, and the postponement of sexual intercourse. Malthus believed that other population checks would arise unavoidably. Those are checks that human beings bring on themselves through wars and other personal tragedies. They are brought on from vice and their consequences are misery.[21] But Malthus made clear that the basic relationship was between population expansion and the resources necessary for survival. His was not so much a theory of population growth as a theory of the consequences of population expansion.

Karl Marx believed there was a tendency for the human species to reproduce up to the capacity of the food supply. This meant that common ownership of the means of production could not prevent poverty but only distribute it equally. Marx argued that overpopulation could only occur under a capitalistic system of ownership because that system required unemployment or a relative surplus of labor. More recent Marxists have seen Malthusianism as a program defending the ruling class. Poverty has been blamed on capitalist industrialization and the creation of an economically helpless working class. "Malthus provided both a rationalization for an attempted solution to the social stress by blaming the problem on overpopulation."[22]

Florita Botts/Nancy Palmer Photo Agency, Inc.

The small families of some Chinese

It is doubtful that a Marxist form of government can significantly raise the standard of living for a country, since neither economic reorganization nor population limitation alone can raise the standards of human life. Increasingly, the necessity of combining population planning with economic planning is being recognized as the only possible solution. At best that would be only a partial solution.

In recent years there have been "optimum theories" about population expansion. These theories are based on arguments stating that populations are too large or too small. This implies that there is some most advantageous, or "optimum" level of persons for any given society. However, an optimum population cannot be conceived in purely economic terms. There are many other values at work at the same time in society. Hartley suggests that "optimum" should also include human welfare in general, because the abundance of things produced is being recognized as constituting only one aspect of human welfare. The material affluence in the United States has not guaranteed the physical and mental health of the population. "In many aspects of life that concern us most, and in what we call the quality of human existence, there is no way to directly measure an 'optimum' population."[23]

UNITED STATES POPULATION PROBLEMS

The population expansion of the United States has been very recent and very rapid. In 1800 there were a little over five million Americans but by 1900 the population was up to 76 million. Over the next 50 years the total more than doubled to 150 million in 1950. In 1976 the United States population was more than 215 million and it is projected that by the year 2000 it will be about 265 million.

When talking about population change for the world, the dynamics are births and deaths, but in talking about the United States alone, population change must also include immigrants. The American population growth from the very beginning was based almost completely on immigrants. In recent years the number of immigrants has played a much smaller part in population expansion. The United States from 1960 to 1975 added 32.8 million people. Of that number, 27.6 million were from an excess of births over deaths and 5.2 million from net immigration.[24]

Births. There are always some kinds of controls—social, psychological, or medical—that stop women from conceiving every time it is theoretically possible. For much of history the fertility rate was high because there was little to stop conception from taking place during ovulation if sexual relations occurred. For the most part social controls over the male to abstain from intercourse during the fertile period of ovulation have been weak or nonexistent. Therefore attempts to control births have been through various birth control methods, and those have usually been up to the woman to use.

Birth control methods, in the broadest sense, refer to the various ways used to stop either pregnancy or live births. There are a variety of birth control methods that may be applied in a number of ways. First, there is *termination* after conception. This ranges from induced abortion to ending the life of the child after giving birth. Second, there is birth control through *sterilization*, a process by which a person is made biologically incapable of reproducing. Third, there are the processes for controlling pregnancy. These include the withdrawal of the penis prior to ejaculation of sperm, or the use of a system in which the sperm is present but no ovum is available for fertilization. Last, there are the various contraceptive methods.

While most societies, preliterate and literate, past and present, have accepted large birthrates as natural and inevitable, it is also probably true that in many of those societies at various times some people have attempted to control conception. To the problems of birth control there have always been two general approaches. The first has been a mystical formula, and practices stimulating emotional responses. The second general approach has been based on rationality. This approach has centered on what a given society believed to be the processes whereby procreation occurred on the one hand, and the powers of the substances used to stimulate or defeat them on the other. Both approaches were used not only among primitive tribes but also among the civilized nations of the past. The Egyptians, the Jews, the Greeks, and the Romans all possessed beliefs about the reproductive process and some knowledge of contraceptive devices.

In most societies there was no knowledge of how conception occurred and therefore no awareness of a process that could be halted by some contraceptive measure. The rational development of birth control methods assumes the knowledge that conception occurs as a result of sexual intercourse. When this knowledge did not exist, societies had to wait to try to do something about birth control after pregnancy could be seen or the infant was born. Therefore, in primitive societies the chief method of birth control was abortion, or infanticide. A study of anthropological monographs shows that other practices were also used by some preliterate groups, for example, "delayed marriage and celibacy, both almost negligible among primitive peoples; sex taboos limiting the time and frequency of connection, pre-puberty coition, sex perversions (more or less neglected by most writers), prolonged lactation, and conception control, both magical and rational."[25]

The failure of contraceptive attempts in the past was not entirely due to ineffective methods. Because the modern techniques are effective they control conception, but even the less effective techniques of the past could have been more effective if used consistently and with care. Had such attempts been made, the population of Europe would not have risen so greatly during the 18th and 19th centuries. "We must instead say that the modern *demand* for better control has led to the *development* of more adequate techniques; i.e., has created a large market for the new, improved devices."[26]

It was not until the 19th century in the Western World, especially in England, Germany, and France, that contraceptive practices started to spread rapidly. France was the only country to use contraception as early as the end of the 18th century. This was 50 to 100 years before any other country. No other countries in the Western World experienced so early and so rapid a decline in population. In brief, in the

Western World the major reasons for the rapid spread of contraceptive practices were growing industrialization, urbanization, lessened church authority, and greater freedom for women. Norman E. Himes points out that concern with the social and economic desirability of birth control was a characteristic of the 19th century and did not exist to any extent before that time. "Medical discussion is old; the economic and social justification, the body doctrine known as neo-Malthusianism, is new."[27]

During the early years of the birth control movement it had little support. And in the first century of its history the birth control movement was more opposed than supported by the medical profession. The leading activists were not physicians. For example, Francis Place started his career as a maker of leather breeches, Marie Stokes was a botanist, and Margaret Sanger was a nurse. Organized religion was also indifferent or opposed to the birth control movement for much of its history. No major religion advocated the use of contraception prior to its popular adoption.

But the greatest resistance to the birth control movement probably came from the belief that having children was inevitable and natural. This belief assumed that nothing could or should be done—having children was the natural order of things. Most of humanity has seen

Margaret Sanger, 1932, the major force in the birth control movement

attempts to tamper with births as being like attempts to influence death—trying to alter what is believed to be beyond the power of human beings. This belief in the inevitability of birth was further supported by the fact that most of humanity has lived in patriarchal societies. Therefore, in male-controlled societies, having .babies was the woman's problem. The fact that women often had problems associated with giving birth was taken as a reflection of their "inferior" status. Men in most societies have seen the question of controlling the birthrate as one for the woman to worry about. The patriarchal male has traditionally seen sexual intercourse with his wife as his right and her getting pregnant as a measure of his masculinity. Therefore, to ask him to influence his sexual activity in some way that might affect the frequency of his wife's pregnancies was to try to influence his basic beliefs about his masculine rights as a husband. So birth control problems have traditionally been seen as problems for women to deal with if anything was to be done about them.

During the 1800s in the United States the birth control movement slowly developed in strength and influence. However, the movement was drastically restricted in 1873 with the passage of the Comstock Law. This federal statute excluded contraceptives and contraceptive information from the mails by defining them as obscene. Many states also passed statutes banning the sale and distribution of contraceptives. At that time no major social institutions supported the birth control movement. Not until 1888 was the first medical symposium on the prevention of conception presented in an American medical journal. That symposium came about as a result of an editorial in the *Medical and Surgical Reporter* that declared that while the subject demanded "discretion" for its discussion, "even so delicate a subject may be regarded with too much timidity." The editorial added that "no medical man of any experience can fail to know that the propriety and feasibility of preventing conception engages, at some time or other, the attention of a large proportion of married people in civilized lands." It went on to say that "the woman who lives in dread of her husband's sexual appetite cannot satisfy him as a wife, and, with this poison in her life, must find it hard to be a kind and wholesome mother to her children."[28]

It was not until the 1930s that the birth control movement in the United States began to take on influence through some of the institutional forces of society—principally religious, legal, and medical institutions. For example, in 1931 the Federal Council of the Churches of Christ was the first religious group to publish a report favoring birth control. During the same year support also came from the American Neurological Association, the Eugenics Society, and the Central Conference of Rabbis. In the middle 1930s there were also some important legal breakthroughs. In 1936 the Court of Appeals upheld a ruling of the District Court that contraceptives imported for a lawful purpose did not come within the restrictions of federal law. And in 1937 the American Medical Association unanimously agreed to accept birth control as an integral part of medical practice and education.

There have also been legal and governmental influences on birth control in a variety of more subtle and indirect ways than through direct intervention. Elizabeth Draper has argued that "the influence of government upon population size is immense and is by no means confined to legislation directly concerned with birth control."[29] For example, birth control is affected by government influence in many countries through the provision of family allowances and maternity benefits. Or, as in the United States, income tax allowances for children give financial encouragement or at least ease the burden on the family budget. Also, such factors as free education, vocational training, and in many countries free medical services provide for the cultural and occupational rewards and general "physical and mental well being which makes it good to live and worth having children to share."[30] Other indirect legal influences are laws providing minimum ages for marriage. In the United States these are four to six years after the female is capable of reproducing. Because most women do not have their children until after marriage, the early years of childbearing are usually eliminated. Probably no society encourages reproduction up to the limits of the biological capacity of the female. Some limits, if not in the laws then in the values of the society, are imposed on the reproductive potential of women.

Even when governments have been concerned with birth control problems, they have generally restricted themselves to policy statements and have not advocated contraceptive rights for the individual. However, in some countries explicit population policies attempting to influence birthrates became important before World War I, when many European countries appointed population commissions to investigate their declining birthrates and to develop policies they thought would reverse that trend. It has been in recent decades that first mortality and then fertility became subjects of government policy, not only to further the health and welfare of the individual citizen, but also to influence the rate of growth, size, and age structure of populations.

Birth control use is also related to certain views that are held about the sexual nature of marriage. Historically, in the vast majority of culture, sex in marriage has been important in two ways: first, as the means of reproduction, and second, as a means of satisfying the sexual needs of the husband. In the past, with few effective means for controlling conception, pregnancy frequently resulted from marital coitus. This resulted in large numbers of children, high rates of maternal and infant mortality, and a short life span for the reproducing wife. Also in the past, while women could and did receive personal satisfaction from the sexual aspect of marriage, this was not usually an expected right. In the patriarchal system sexual need was generally assumed to be a need of the man. The woman who also received sexual satisfaction was sometimes viewed by her husband (and herself) as somewhat "unnatural." "Good women," at least in terms of accepted sexual values, did not usually derive pleasure from the sexual act. Their role as sexual partner was one of duty to the husband. However, all of this has changed for many American women in that they now see their own sexual satisfaction as their right and as a goal to be achieved separately from any decision with regard to reproduction.

It might also be added that overwhelmingly the sex act in marriage is performed with no anticipation of pregnancy. An estimate based on a 6.7 average frequency of intercourse per month came to the conclusion that about 2 billion acts of sexual intercourse occurred in the United States in one year. Given the fact that 3.5 million births occur each year to married women living with their husbands, this indicates a ratio of about 1 live birth for about every 600 acts of sexual intercourse.[31]

From the previous discussion it can be seen that the emergence of a definition about birth control and the deliberate limiting of family size has been one of great controversy. Late in the chapter we shall further examine some of the social agencies and their influences on the use or nonuse of birth control methods. However, before doing so, we shall look briefly at the success of the various birth control methods.

Birth control methods. The most effective birth control methods have been oral contraception, IUDs, the diaphragm and jelly, and the condom. Less effective means are the calendar rhythm system, local chemical contraceptives, and withdrawal. But many times the failure of contraception is mistakenly attributed to the method rather than to the person using it. The fact is that reliable methods used by careful individuals are very effective in controlling pregnancy.

In recent years there have been some important changes in the use of birth control methods by many Americans. There have been important changes in the use of sterilization and abortion. In a 1970 study it was found that among older women in the reproductive years, sterilization (of themselves or their husbands) was the principal means for terminating exposure to the risk of unwanted conceptions.[32]

The methods currently in use in the United States have led to a drop in unwanted pregnancies. A nationwide study found a dramatic drop of unwanted fertility between the 1960–65 period and the 1966–70 period. There was a decline of some 36 percent in the number of unwanted births per 1,000 women years of exposure to the chance of unwanted childbearing. "We estimate that about half of the nationwide fertility decline between the two periods is due to the improvements in the control of unwanted births."[33]

Deaths. Like the rest of the industrial world, the United States has had dramatic decreases in the death rate over the past 100 years. During the 19th century there was a slow but steady rise in life expectancy. This was probably due more to superior nutrition than to breakthroughs in the control and prevention of disease. But by the end of the 19th century headway was being made in bettering sanitary conditions and controlling diseases.

When compared to most other countries the life expectancy of Americans is high. In the United States the male has a life expectancy of 68.2 years and the female 75.9 years. This is a little lower than Denmark where the comparable figures by sex are 70.8 and 76.3 years. But the rates for a country like India are only 41.9 for the male and 40.6 for the female. In recent years the overall death rate in the United States has been decreasing. In 1900, the death rate per 1,000 people was 17.2 but by 1976 had been cut almost in half to 8.9 per 1,000.

As life expectancy has increased in the United States, it has increased at a greater rate for women than for men. In 1900 the life expectancy for the male at birth was 48.2 years and for the female was 51.1 years, a difference of 2.9 years. In 1975, the white male had a life expectancy of 69.4 years and the white female 77.2 years at birth. This is a difference of 7.8 years. The greater average life expectancy of the woman has been due in part to the control of factors that were fatal in the past. This has been true especially in greatly reduced rates of maternal mortality.

Immigration. In the early history of America, immigrants were encouraged to enter the country. There were millions of persons who emigrated from Europe, and the United States took most of them. The United States absorbed 70 percent of all intercontinental migrants from 1851 to 1890, and 60 percent of those during 1890 to 1910. The large numbers that left their home countries to come to the United States are reflected in the fact that America probably has more citizens of Irish and Swedish extraction than presently reside in Ireland and Sweden, respectively."[34]

The United States welcomed immigrants as long as they were of the right sort—European and especially northwestern European. For most years the English speaking immigrants outnumbered all others, but this changed after World War I. By the end of the last century large numbers of northern and southern Europeans from Italy, Greece, and the Balkan States were coming. These people spoke different languages and held different religious beliefs. As a result, new immigration laws were passed in 1921 and 1924 that introduced the notion of national origin. By 1924 the law provided quotas, according to na-

TABLE 7–2

U.S. Immigration from Europe, 1820–1976

Country of origin	Number of immigrants (000s)	Country of origin	Number of immigrants (000s)
Germany	6,960	Spain	248
Italy	5,278	Belgium	201
Great Britain	4,863	Romania	168
Ireland	4,722	Czechoslovakia	137
Austria and Hungary	4,313	Yugoslavia	109
U.S.S.R.	3,362	Bulgaria	68
Sweden	1,270	Finland	68
Norway	856	Lithuania	4
France	744	Luxembourg	3
Greece	638	Latvia	3
Poland	506	Albania	2
Portugal	422	Estonia	1
Denmark	363	Other Europe	55
Netherlands	357		
Switzerland	347	Total	36,033

Source: Population Bulletin, "International Migration: Yesterday, Today and Tomorrow," Reference Bureau, Inc. (September 1977), p. 17.

tional origins. The numbers of each nationality in the population during the base year of 1890 were used to calculate future immigration quotas by country of origin. Only 2 percent of the base numbers were admitted in any one year. This method greatly favored the English speaking countries.

The Immigration Act of 1965 established an annual limit of 170,000 immigrants from outside the Western Hemisphere and 120,000 from within. The maximum number to be allowed from any one country in one year is 20,000 plus immediate relatives of persons already living in the United States.

The number of immigrants allowed to enter the United States from various countries was changed in 1965. During the period 1820 to 1920, 88 percent of all immigrants came from Europe. But in 1976, only 18 percent of all immigrants came from Europe. From 1820 to 1920 only 3 percent of all immigrants came from Asia, but in 1976 they accounted for 37 percent of all immigrants.[35] The total number of legal immigrants in 1976 was about 400,000. Besides that number there may be as many as two to four times that number entering the United States illegally. The vast majority of the illegal entries are Mexicans. It has been estimated that there are 8 million illegal immigrants in the United States.

The dynamics of population growth can individually or collectively be influenced by values about population change. For the most

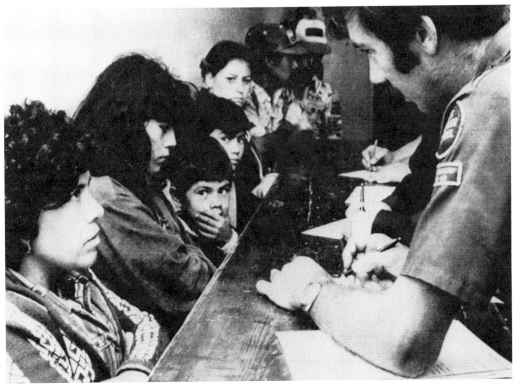

Wide World Photos

Illegal aliens being returned to Mexico

part these are values related to the "right" number of children. We will look at some social variables that reflect values about family size and influence the birth rate.

Social class. It has long been established that the lower the social class of the family, the higher the probability that the family will include a large number of children. In general this is due to values that encourage having children and economic disadvantage which results in the use of the least reliable birth control measures and limits access to knowledge about their use. About four out of every ten American families with more than five children are poor, but this is true of less than one in ten families with one or two children. There is often a cumulative effect in that poorer people have more children which makes them even poorer (see Chapter 5).

The social class difference in size of family can be seen in the use of education as a measurement of social class. One national study found that the overall relationship between education and fertility of women aged 35–44 was strongly negative. The fertility ranged from 3.9 births for women who never reached high school to 2.59 births for those who had four or more years of college.[36]

Davis argues that the birth rate tends to fall because low fertility is rewarded and high fertility is penalized. Heavy urban concentration and formal education make children nonprofitable and in fact often make them costly and troublesome. Also the skilled occupational structure makes social advancement more dependent on individual accomplishment and much less on kinship or other kinds of family ties.[37] Women are finding that having fewer children means a greater opportunity to be successful in the occupational world. Many things that are valued in American society today can be best achieved with fewer children. Often having children is recognized, at least temporarily, as giving up other desired ends.

Religion.   There are significant differences in fertility by religion. A national study found that Catholic fertility was the highest (3.64 children), Jewish fertility the lowest (2.13) and the fertility of Protestant women (2.92) fell in between. Women with no religious preference had an average of 2.76. Unwanted fertility made the greatest contribution (23 percent) to the fertility of women expressing no religious preference. "At the opposite extreme, Jewish women aged 35–44 report the lowest incidence of unwanted fertility—3 percent of their total fertility."[38]

In the United States certain religious values have been the greatest overall force against the use of birth control. This religious interest in birth control has not been common to most religions of the world. The major religions of the Eastern World do not have explicit ideologies with regard to birth control. Some aspects of some Eastern religions do encourage large families, but these religions do not object to family planning. So religious beliefs in the Eastern World have not been a major factor in resistance to population control. However, in many parts of the Western World, and specifically in the United States, religious values *have* had a major impact on population control.

Protestant groups are now almost unanimous in giving strong endorsement to birth control. This was strongly demonstrated in a statement adopted in 1961 by the General Board of the National Council of Churches of Christ in the United States. This is a federation of 25 major Protestant denominations with about 40 million members in the United States. The Protestants' point of view is based on their notion of the basic purposes of marriage. Those purposes include not only parenthood, but also the development of the mutual love and companionship of the husband and wife, and their service to society. The Protestant position is illustrated by that of the Methodist church, the largest single Protestant denomination. In 1960 it adopted the unequivocal position that "planned parenthood, practiced in Christian conscience, fulfills rather than violates the will of God."[39] It should be stressed that among almost all Protestant groups birth control methods are not just accepted, but are encouraged.

The support for birth control methods among Jews has paralleled the developments among the Protestants. The initial endorsements among Jews first appeared in 1931. Now all Jewish groups, except for the most extreme Orthodox group, endorse birth control. And even the extreme group sanctions female contraceptive methods under special health circumstances.[40] Not only do Jews accept the use of contraceptives, but all the available evidence indicates that they use contraception most effectively. It is clear that whatever problems exist in birth control methods among Protestants and Jews, they are not due to ideological rejection of birth control but rather to the limitations of birth control methods and inefficiency in using them. However, by contrast, the primary problem for Roman Catholics is the ideological position of the church, and secondarily for many, the choice and effective use of the various methods. It is therefore important to devote some attention to the Catholic position regarding birth control.

The basic theological difference between Catholic doctrine and that of Protestants and Jews relates to the basic purpose of marriage. The Catholic church believes that procreation is the primary reason for marriage, with companionship and vocation being secondary. Therefore, according to the Catholic church, birth control by any chemical or mechanical means would frustrate the primary purpose of marriage and as a result violate natural law. The position of the Catholic church can be seen more clearly by looking briefly at its position with regard to several different means of birth control.

In 1968 the Papal Encyclical ended the period of ambiguity and speculation about the Roman Catholic Church's position on birth control. It reaffirmed the traditional ban on methods of contraception other than the rhythm system. However, there has been a high level of resistance by Catholic women to the Church's teachings on birth control. Charles F. Westoff found that the proportion of Catholic women 18–39 years of age using methods of contraception other than rhythm increased from 30 percent in 1955 to 68 percent by 1970. Women not conforming in the age range 20–24 went from 30 percent in 1955 to 78 percent by 1970. It appears likely that the 20–24 age group will become very much like the non-Catholics and reach a maximum of around 90 percent.[41]

Certainly the position of the Catholic Church on birth control is tenuous. Not only are many Catholic women not paying attention but many members of the church are uncertain about the applications of the restrictions. Andrew Greeley found that only 40 percent of the priests in the United States support the Church's official teaching on birth control. Another third of the priests said that while they would discourage the use of artificial contraception they would not deny absolution to a penitent on those grounds.[42]

Working women. One of the most important consequences of the birth control development over recent decades has been the large number of married women in the work force (see Chapter 9). The development of birth control methods has been the single most important factor in the emancipation of the American woman. For almost the entire history of humanity most women have been locked in the home because of having large numbers of children. Birth control methods have allowed women to have fewer children and to have them when they want them. At the same time women have developed the willingness to turn their children over to schools and other agencies for care while they work. In general, when a woman decides to work she has fewer children.

Persons can have children or not have them as matters of choice or as events over which they have no control. But, whatever the reason, at age thirty about 1 out of every 17 married women are childless. As women get older, the childless percentage decreases but the percentage of those without children and not expecting any in the future increases. For example, for wives in the age range 20 to 24 there are 30 percent who are childless but only 13 percent expect to remain that way. But for women ages 30 to 34 there are 6 percent childless and 67 percent of them expect to stay that way.[43]

One study of women who were childless found this to be true of only 14 percent of the women who were "housewives," but true of 55 percent who were "white-collar workers."[44] There are other studies that suggest that working women desire and have smaller families than do nonworking women. Related to working is education as an influence on women having children. One study found that differences related to education operate early in the childbearing years to postpone childbearing among the higher educated. "Higher education expands non-familial interests and activities, which extend the interval between marriage and first birth."[45]

While the percentage of women not having children is small, it does represent an important change. The proportion of young women who say they want no children was only 4 percent in 1972 but that had tripled over the three previous years. Jessie Bernard writes that "although it is probably safe to say that at least nine out of ten girls who are adolescent today are going to be mothers, it is probably also safe to say that they are not going to have many babies."[46]

One writer suggests that where questions of meaning and values of "self-actualization" become more important, the notion of childbearing as a creative experience loses to other avenues of self-expression. Furthermore, the cost to females of having children may become greater than the status rewards of motherhood, where the tradeoff is motherhood versus a career. "While for many families the career and childbearing structures may combine, they remain essentially contradictory sets of obligations under modern work conditions." Teresa Donati Marciano suggests that as the number of childfree couples increase, this life style may come to be a permanent option among increasing numbers of couples, "or as a long-term option in which the choice of having a child is longer and longer delayed in the marriage cycle."[47]

There are other social forces that operate to reduce the interest in parenthood. Judith Lorber writes that with the increasing rates of divorce along with the need for more gainful employment among mothers, there is also the lack of adequate professional child care. As a result women are increasingly disenchanted with the idea of having children. Along with this is concern about overpopulation so that restrictions on the birth rate have increasing moral support.[48] She goes on to say that childbearing could become a profession and carried out with the best technology. That is, "fertility drugs for multiple births, sperm banks, embryo transfers, and uterine implants to expand the gene pool and so on. Professional breeders could be paid to salaries like today's athletes."[49]

Economic factors.   Economic assumptions are related to values about population size. For example, there has long been an assumption that growth in population is good for the economy. But while new additions to the community may bring additional revenue in taxation, the new residents also add to the costs of servicing a community. Extra sales require a greater investment in plant and equipment to expand capacity and, even though absolute profits may increase, the profit return per capital unit may not stay high for very long. Further, when an area becomes more populated with customers, it may become more populated with rival products. "This is especially true in service industries, such as motels, restaurants, and all retail outlets."[50]

The per capita costs tend to decline as city size increases to a population of about 100,000. However, beyond that point the per person costs rise with the increased size of the city. "For instance, police and fire costs per person rise, while crime rates increase even more rapidly."[51] There are mixed blessings in the encouragement of populations, and the overall cost can be quite high.

It can also be argued that slower population growth would result in lower unemployment rates since much of today's unemployment is among the young who are entering the work force for the first time. With time, lower fertility rates would spread the population out in age, and this would reduce the percentage in the youngest and most unemployable age range. This is one focus of an economic argument supporting the desirability of a decrease in population growth.

Conflicting solutions.   When we look at population in numbers in the United States there is no clear agreement that it constitutes a social problem. But even among those who see a need for reducing the growth of the population in the future, there are wide disagreements on how this should be done. Controlling family size through the various means of birth control is an area of strong disagreement. Often the argument is stated on religious or economic grounds, but there is also a family or personal dimension to it. Individuals in families frequently believe that the number of children they have is a private and very personal decision. Therefore, they resist any attempts by outsiders to suggest controls they should apply themselves. For many, having the number of children they want is seen as an inalienable right not to be interfered with by anyone or any institution.

Hartley argues that the basic question that must be dealt with regarding population is not how many people can the world feed but how well can they be fed. People can be kept alive on less than a thousand calories a day but they will live in misery and agony. She argues it is pretty hard to take as a goal the maximization of the number of people alive regardless of their level of human development. "Limiting reproduction does not in itself guarantee a better life, but allowing the present growth rate to continue reduces the possibility of improving the quality of life for the billions of persons already alive and yet to be born."[52]

In the United States there has been some shift in values .that suggest a desire to have small families. Some social pressure is developing among some groups against having large families. It used to be that middle- or upper-class couples who had large numbers of children were applauded. (The lower classes were seen as "irresponsible.") Invariably the "mother of the year," one of our many commercialized honors, was a woman with six or seven children. Yet, in 1970 one United States senator suggested that it might be more sensible to give the "mother of the year" award to a woman who had had her tubes tied and adopted two children. This symbolizes dramatically the changed attitude to family size among some social groups.

An increasing body of evidence has been emerging in the 1970s that the size of families is being reduced. One influence has been the recent trend of postponing marriage which leads to an overall older age of marriage. Because the female is more fecund in the first than in the second half of her reproductive span, the postponement of marriage tends to reduce births. Sociologically this gives women more time to educate themselves, to acquire interests not related to the family, and to develop a cautious attitude toward pregnancy. Individuals who have not married by the time they are in their late twenties often do not marry at all. And even after a woman has married, the longer a "wanted" birth is delayed the less likely she is to have that birth or a subsequent birth.

In the United States there is an increasing acceptance of the argument that little is to be gained from population expansion. One study suggests that further population growth during the next 30 to 50 years would yield no advantages and entail many costs. The costs would be

"But, Doctor, I'll be drummed out of my zero population growth chapter!"

an even more rapid depletion of domestic and international resources, increased pressure on the environment and a number of potentially serious institutional costs. "If population growth were to cease, it would purchase time, resources, and additional options: time to overcome our ignorance and to redress the mistakes of past growth, resources to implement solutions, and additional freedom of choice in deciding how we want to live in the future."[53]

Stephen Enke says that no convincing argument can be made that the United States needs more people. He says that the slower the population growth, the more opportunity to increase the capital-to-worker ratio, and the more time for improvements in technology to increase productivity. A decline in United States fertility would with time leave a population with a high proportion of employable adults.[54]

The future.   At the present time the United States birth rate is going down and the age of first marriage is going up. This can lead to a false sense of complacency about future population growth. Our population growth is still about 1 percent per year and this is twice the rate of other advanced nations of the world. But more important is the fact that we are faced with a rapid growth in the numbers of women in the heaviest childbearing years, 20–29. These numbers will be almost twice as great in 1980 as they were in 1960.[55] Because there are so many more, they can have fewer children per person but in total produce far more than in 1960.

Assuming that population expansion should be slowed down, what are the possible ways to do so? For many years the notion has been that if any control is to be exerted it must be voluntary. Traditionally these kinds of programs have attempted to make it possible for married couples to have the number of children they want. The stress has usually been on what is good for the family and especially the health of the mother and the children. The general social problem is partly based on the assumption that the number of children a couple want is the number they ought to have, whereas that number may be far greater than what is "good" for society in terms of broader social values.

The family planning movement has traditionally been conservative and placed its values within the individual family unit. Up until recent years, when the abortion movement became popular, the family planners opposed legalizing abortion. In fact, they justified contraception as a way of combatting "the abortion problem." "By concerning itself with *married* women and *family* planning, and by linking its services with *maternal* health, the family planning approach reinforced familistic ideology. It viewed women's sole concern as childrearing."[56] In fact the family planning movement had very little impact in reducing the overall population expansion through birth control of any kind.

To try to convince people that they should limit their family size for the good of the nation does not appear to work. It would probably take a very high level of education and social responsibility to control reproduction for the "common good." Clearly a society is very limited in the kinds of control it could apply. No one would seriously suggest the use of atomic war or the spreading of disease and misery to reduce population. It might be possible to introduce some kinds of control that do not imply coercion. In the United States it is not really a choice between persons producing children as they please or having state control. There are a wide range of possibilities between the two extremes. For example, possibilities include changes in the tax laws, which now encourage having children, and giving benefits to persons with none or a few children who currently subsidize, through high taxation, the large families of other people.

On the international level Davis argues that over the next 50 years very little can be expected to effectively control population growth. This he believes is not due to the lack of contraception but rather that the rewards for reproduction will remain high. In general, population policy is collective policy and the collectives with the ultimate authority are nations. Very often rivalry between nations and between groups within any one nation center around claims based on numbers of people. "With demographic competition thus built into the world's social organization, officials (whose careers depend on collective strength) resist 'weakening' their nation or group by antinatalist policies."[57]

There have been other suggestions as to possible solutions, but they are very doubtful. Some have seen space development as an answer to the world's population problem. However, at the present rate of population growth in the world we would have to put into space over 8,000 persons per hour, or 200,000 persons per day, or a grand total of 74 million persons per year. "Anyone remaining unconvinced of the absurdity of such suggestions could compute the cost."[58]

All the evidence is that something will have to be done in the future. Unless people begin to perceive the trade-offs in quantity and quality for their own children, their community, nation, and for the world as a whole, and unless they begin to sharply cut down on births, the long run solution will be death. "There is no doubt that in the long run *either birth rates must come down or death rates will go back up*."[59]

In this chapter we looked at the balance between deaths and births as determining the size of the world's population. Countries with different stages of industrial development have different kinds and degrees of population growth. In looking at population problems in the United States the means of birth control now available are very important. The control of family size is not only important to individuals, but also to such institutions as the church, government, and the economy.

NOTES

1. Shirley Foster Hartley, *Population: Quantity vs. Quality* (Englewood Cliffs, N.J.: Prentice-Hall, 1972), p. 5.

2. Kingsley Davis, "The World's Population Crisis," in *Contemporary Social Problems,* 4th ed., by Robert K. Merton and Robert Nisbet (New York: Harcourt Brace Jovanovich, 1976), pp. 272–73.

3. Hartley, *Population*, p. 9.

4. Ibid., p. 53.

5. Davis, "World's Population," p. 271.

6. Hartley, *Population*, p. 41.

7. Davis, "World's Population," p. 270.

8. Ibid., p. 271.

9. Hartley, *Population*, p. 57.

10. Ibid., pp. 57–58.

11. Shirley Foster Hartley, "Our Growing Problem: Population," *Social Problems* (Fall 1973), p. 195.

12. Davis, "World's Population," p. 302.

13. Hartley, *Population,* pp. 82–83.

14. U.S. Bureau of the Census, *Statistical Abstracts of the U.S.* (Washington D.C.: U.S. Government Printing Office, 1975) pp. 12, 25.

15. Hartley, *Population*, p. 90.

16. Ibid., p. 76.

17. Ibid., p. 86.

18. Paul R. Ehrich, Anne H. Ehrich, and John P. Holden, *Human Ecology: Problems and Solution* (San Francisco: W. H. Freeman, 1973), p. 65.

19. Hartley, *Population*, p. 112.

20. Ibid., pp. 165–66.

21. Ibid., pp. 295–96.

22. Linda Gordon, *Woman's Body, Woman's Right: Birth Control in America* (New York: Penguin Books, 1975), p. 392.

23. Hartley, *Population*, p. 297.

24. Davis, "World's Population," p. 280.

25. Norman E. Himes, *Medical History of Contraception* (New York: Gamut Press, 1963), p. 4.

26. William J. Goode, *World Revolution and Family Patterns* (New York: The Free Press, 1963), p. 53.

27. Himes, *Medical History*, p. 211.

28. Ibid., p. 289.

29. Elizabeth Draper, *Birth Control in the Modern World* (New York: Penguin Books, 1965), p. 179.

30. Ibid., p. 179.

31. Leslie Aldridge Westoff and Charles F. Westoff, *From Now to Zero* (Boston: Little, Brown, 1968), p. 24.

32. Norman B. Ryder, "The Future Growth of the American Population," in *Toward the End of Growth*, by Charles F. Westoff (Englewood Cliffs, N.J.: Prentice-Hall, 1973), p. 91.

33. Westoff, *Growth*, p. 19.

34. Hartley, *Population*, p. 64.

35. *Information Please Almanac 1978* (New York: Information Please Publishing, Inc., 1978), p. 764.

36. Charles F. Westoff and Norman B. Ryder, *The Contraceptive Revolution* (Princeton, N.J.: Princeton University Press, 1977), p. 289.

37. Davis, "World's Population," p. 299.

38. Westoff and Ryder, *Contraceptive*, pp. 281–82.

39. Lawrence A. Mayer, "U.S. Population Growth: Would Fewer Do Better?" in *The American Population Debate*, by Daniel Callahan (New York: Doubleday, 1971), p. 109.

40. Ibid., p. 111.

41. Westoff, *Growth*, pp. 26–27.

42. Andrew Greeley, "Is Catholic Sexual Teaching Coming Apart?" in *Sexuality Today and Tomorrow*, by Sol Gordon and Roger W. Libby (N. Seituate, Mass.: Duxbury Press, 1976), p. 162.

43. P. Neal Richey and C. Shannon Stokes, "Correlates of Childlessness and Expectations to Remain Childless," *Social Forces* (March 1974), p. 352.

44. S. L. N. Rao, "A Comparative Study of Childlessness and Never-Pregnant Status," *Journal of Marriage and the Family* (February 1974), p. 154.

45. Richey and Stokes, "Correlates," p. 355.

46. Jessie Bernard, *The Future of Marriage* (New York: World Publishing Co., 1972), p. 71.

47. Teresa Donati Marciano, "Variant Family Forms in World Perspective," *The Family Coordinator* (October 1975), pp. 416–17.

48. Judith Lorber, "Beyond Equality of the Sexes: The Question of Children," *The Family Coordinator* (October 1975), p. 466.

49. Ibid., p. 468.

50. Stephen Enke, "The Impact of Population Growth," in Westoff, *Growth*, p. 99.

51. Hartley, *Population*, p. 197.

52. Ibid., p. 118.

53. Ronald Ridker, "The Impact of Population Growth on Resources and the Environment," in Westoff, *Growth*, pp. 117–18.

54. Enke, "Impact of Population Growth," p. 107.

55. Hartley, *Population*, pp. 190–91.

56. Davis, "World's Population," p. 295.

57. Ibid., p. 301.

58. Hartley, *Population*, p. 200.

59. Ibid., p. 204.

SELECTED BIBLIOGRAPHY

Callahan, Daniel. *The American Population Debate*. New York: Doubleday, 1971.

Gordon, Linda. *Woman's Body, Woman's Right: Birth Control in America*. New York: Penguin Books, 1975.

Hartley, Shirley Foster. *Population: Quantity vs. Quality*. Englewood Cliffs, N.J.: Prentice-Hall, 1972.

Hartley, Shirley Foster. "Our Growing Problem: Population." *Social Problems* (Fall 1973), pp. 190–205.

Richey, P. Neal, and Stokes, C. Shannon. "Correlates of Childlessness and Expectations to Remain Childless." *Social Forces* (March 1974), pp. 349–56.

Westoff, Charles F., *Toward the End of Growth*. Englewood Cliffs, N.J.: Prentice-Hall, 1973.

Chapter 8

Illegitimacy, Abortion, and Marital Sexuality

Unlike previous chapters, each of which was devoted to one social problem, here we will be looking at three different social problems. However, these social problems do share a common base in both sexuality and a tie to marriage. Each will be discussed as a social problem in its own right with little concern with the few ways in which they overlap.

Illegitimacy

Historically the concern with illegitimacy has been linked to social control of the family and to morality. The social control factor was related to concerns with inheritance and kinship structures. Moral concerns centered around the views of illegitimacy as sinful behavior which threatened the sanctity of marriage and the family.

In the United States, both the unwed mother and her offspring have been subjected to strong moral and legal punishment. In recent years, treatment of the illegitimate child has changed both socially and legally. Legislation has been passed in all states that tends to place the illegitimate child in about the same legal status as the legitimate child. While much of the social stigma for the child had been removed, there continues to be strong criticism directed at the unwed mother.

William J. Goode argues that the most striking change in the United States over past generations about illegitimacy is that it has become a social problem rather than simply a family or a personal problem.[1] As the social problem definition emerged and gained increased support, it took on institutional characteristics. As a consequence both state and private agencies were formed to deal with both

215

illegitimate children and their mothers. Today there is commonly support for the illegitimate child, but this is far from being totally acceptable to society. In fact there are often strong sentiments against financial help on the grounds that it encourages illegitimacy.

While it is true that illegitimacy has gained recognition as a social problem it is also true that its strength or impact on society is not great. Certainly the concern with the mother's "immorality" is of much less interest today because of greater permissiveness towards all kinds of sexuality. In general, all the old questions of morality—whether they be sexual, political, or whatever—have come to be of much less interest to American society. Laws that could direct some punishment toward illegitimacy, such as those concerned with fornication, are rarely ever applied to the unwed mother.

The emergence of a definition about illegitimacy has in recent years had little to do with morality or legal controls over sexual involvement. Rather the social concern has been with the costs of illegitimacy to society. In general when there is a cry against the rates of illegitimacy this reflects mostly a financial concern. The concern is expressed in terms of welfare payments and costs to the taxpayer. We should look further at the rates of illegitimacy and attempts to deal with illegitimacy as a defined social problem.

Rates. It has been estimated that about one in every five American white women are pregnant at the time they marry. The rate is much higher for younger women. It may be that almost half of all white females in the United States who marry before 20 years of age are premaritally pregnant. Many of them marry to escape from being unmarried mothers.

There has been an increase in the number of illegitimate births in recent years. The rate of all illegitimate live births has gone from about 4 percent in 1950 to about 10 percent in 1970. However, only a small proportion of illegitimate children seem to spend a substantial period of time in families with an unmarried mother. "Perhaps 2 percent of the children born around 1970 will spend most of their childhood with a single mother."[2]

While the rates of illegitimacy continued to go up in the 1970s, the rate of increase slowed down. This was the same as the pattern for the total birth rate; both rates were increasing in number but more slowly than before. The downward trend in the increase in the illegitimacy rates applied to all age groups, except for 15- to 19-year-old white women. In 1975 there were an estimated 1 million babies born to teenagers, of which 280,000 were born to unwed mothers. By 1976 there were 1 million single-parent families in the United States, 500,000 of which were headed by teenagers.

As suggested, the traditional explanation for recognition of illegitimacy was to place responsibility on the woman. The cause was held to be a breakdown in morality and often the explanation was sin. Whatever the specific cause, the young woman got pregnant because she went against her religious or moral teachings. In more recent years a common explanation has been that young, unmarried women get pregnant because of a lack of knowledge about sex and reproduction as well as a lack of birth control knowledge.

What is somewhat surprising is that the frequency of premarital conception occurs at a time of highly effective and available means of contraception. One national sample of girls aged 15 to 19 found that nearly three out of ten girls who engage in premarital coitus become pregnant. Less than half of the teenage women who were sexually experienced used any method of contraception during their last intercourse, and less than one fifth always protected themselves. "Thus, most adolescent premarital and nonmarital intercourse is irresponsible, and a premarital pregnancy is a rather common outcome."[3]

Another study found that most young women who had coitus had used contraception at some time. But the bulk of them used it "sometimes" rather than "always." About three quarters of all who have ever used contraception rely on it only "sometimes." In fact, about

Unmarried teenage pregnancy

half of all sexually active females reported that their last sexual act was unprotected."[4]

The level of knowledge about conception and means of birth control is often very limited. A national study in 1977 found that only two in five teenagers surveyed were aware of when they were most likely to conceive. The tendency is for teenagers not to turn to contraception until after their initial sexual experiences, and this contributes to a high number of unplanned pregnancies. Melvin Zelnick and John F. Kantner found that more than half the teenagers they studied believed that a girl can become pregnant at menarche, and about 41 percent saw the time of greatest risk occurring either right before, right after, or during the menses.[5]

One partial solution would be to provide better sex education as well as to make contraception available to the young. Where these things have been attempted, there occasionally have been strong moral and religious objections to making available sex education and contraception. Often the assumed immorality of these solutions is of greater concern than the resulting pregnancies.

There are other problems related to pregnancy among teenagers. For example, when pregnancy occurs in the young adolescent, especially under the age of 16, there is a higher incidence of toxemia, anemia, contracted pelvis, prolonged labor, and a higher maternal death rate. Very young girls face an increased risk of giving birth to low birth-weight infants.[6] Infant mortality and premature birthrates are also much higher for children of young mothers.

There appears to be some relationship between the high sense of isolation of the young woman and her chances of premarital pregnancy. "In each paired comparison, a greater proportion of women high in social isolation had experienced premarital conception than was the case for their low-isolation counterparts. The greatest differentials were obtained by high and low social isolation among Catholics, where 35 percent of the highly isolated women were premaritally pregnant in contrast to only 14 percent of the wives scoring low on social isolation."[7]

There is also some evidence of effects from the parental home on the probability of premarital pregnancy. One study found that at the time of first conception, daughters from severely discordant homes more often were unmarried and without plans of marriage and more often did not live with the father of the child. Also the more discordant the parental home, the more often the woman had been living with the father of the child less than six months when she became pregnant. "The more disharmonious the marital relationship of the parents, the more often the daughter described her relationship with her male partner as unsatisfactory and disappointing."[8]

Over the past 30 or 40 years the social attitudes toward the illegitimate child have changed greatly. In many states in the past, illegitimacy of a child was marked on his birth certificate and went with him the rest of his life. But this is no longer true. Basically any blame has been taken from the child and there is a high level of agreement that the child should not be punished morally for what he or she had no control over.

There has been some institutional response to the problem of illegitimacy, especially as related to support for illegitimate children. The welfare system in many ways subsidizes illegitimacy by providing mother and child support. This is not to argue that many women have lots of illegitimate children to get "rich" off the welfare payments. The payments are at best adequate. But the fact remains that many women know that if they have an illegitimate child they can do as well or better financially as they could by working or getting married.

There are options that the state could follow other than the welfare subsidy of illegitimacy. One might be to discontinue payments after one or two children. Alternately, the children might be taken from the mother and placed for adoption. Still another possibility is that after a woman has one or two illegitimate children she be sterilized. However, whenever any of these suggestions are made, they gain little support because they are seen as interfering with the natural and civil rights of the woman. It would certainly appear that there are no foreseeable solutions to illegitimacy and while the rates may continue to go up at a slower rate they will nevertheless continue.

Illegitimacy has been positively related to another family problem in the past. About 1 out of every 14 married couples are unable to have children of their own. For many the only solution has been to turn to adoption, and most children placed out for adoption are illegitimate. Therefore, to the extent that the rate of illegitimacy goes down, the possible supply of children for adoption also goes down. A reduction in the illegitimacy rate means an increased number of married couples unable to be parents.

Illegitimacy has been a social problem when a society has a strong concern to restrict births to marriage. The stigma of illegitimacy placed on the child has for the most part disappeared in the United States. And the stigma attached to the unwed mother has also been greatly reduced. The main concern with illegitimacy as a social problem today centers around the mother often being very young and the economic dependency of many unwed mothers.

Abortion

Most cultures of the past have had some means of control over birth rates. This has been true even when there was no knowledge of effective birth control methods. Historically the means of control have been infanticide and abortion. Infanticide has been practiced by only a few cultures and has never been a practice in the United States. However, abortions have always been a part of the American society, although with strong moral and legal taboos. As a result the frequency of abortion has never accurately been measured.

Traditionally, values and attitudes about abortion have been seen as the province of religion. Abortion has long been defined by some religions as a mortal sin, to be condoned under no circumstances. Because of the strong religious pressures, laws have been passed in the United States in the past that made the availability of legal abortion practically impossible. Intertwined with the legal control was medical control. Up until recent years, in those few cases where abortion was possible it was only legal if medically approved. The doctor often was not making a decision as to medical feasibility but rather was making a moral decision for the woman. What is most striking is that the desires and rights of the woman to choose an abortion for and by herself have rarely ever existed.

The emergence of the definition of abortion as a social problem was accomplished despite strongly divergent points of view. One definition views abortion as taking life away from the fetus and therefore as totally unacceptable. The other point of view sees the woman having the right to decide whether or not she wants to carry to full term and give birth to the fetus. In this view, the choice is the woman's, and abortion is not a problem but rather a potential solution to another problem—an unwanted pregnancy.

In the past a major part of the social problem of abortion centered around the dangers that the woman encountered if she sought an abortion. These dangers were both medical and legal. Many abortions were done by quacks and hacks, and often women lost their lives as a result of abortions. Furthermore, in having an abortion, women were breaking the law and, if caught, could be legally punished. There is no way of knowing how many illegal abortions occurred in the past, but estimates range from .25 million to 1.5 million per year.

In January 1973, the United States Supreme Court overruled the existing state laws that prohibited or restricted a woman's right to obtain an abortion during the first three months of pregnancy. The states continued to have the authority to impose controls after the first three months. While this was a liberalization of previous controls over abortion, it was not an absolute right to abortion.

One effect of the right to abortion was to reduce to some extent the rates of illegitimacy. However, this may have been a short term effect. As Kingsley Davis points out, in California legal abortions were common by 1970, and the illegitimacy rate had fallen in 1971. The effect was short lived, and the rate started to climb again in 1972 and 1973. "Clearly, then, the sudden availability of abortion may temporarily affect the trend, but neither it nor the availability of contraception stops the social forces and motives leading to unwed pregnancy."[9]

The right-to-life movement

The Supreme Court decision did not resolve the issue of abortion. What it did was change around the offensive and defensive postures. Those who wanted legal abortion were put in the position of defending and protecting the new legal rights. Those opposed to abortions went on the attack to get the decision reversed or at least altered.

No sooner had the Supreme Court decision been handed down than it was under attack. Congress began to cut away at the freedom. For example, they prohibited the use of Medicaid money to pay for abortions other than when the life of the mother was in danger or where there had been incest or rape.

In general the politicians have lined themselves up with those opposing legal abortion. The politician almost always sees support of abortion as dangerous to his political future. Presidents Nixon, Ford, and Carter have all voiced moral objections to abortion. However, the main focus of opposition comes from organized religion, especially from the Catholic church. The opposition of the Church is based on the belief that life begins at the time of conception. For the Roman Catholic hierarchy, aborting the fetus is condemned as murder. Pope

Paul VI asserted that the life of the fetus takes precedence over the life of the mother. "The fetus is to be carried to term even if the pregnancy resulted from incest or rape and even if the life or mental health of the mother is in jeopardy." [10]

The antiabortion movement is made up predominantly of Catholics. As a social force the movement does not represent Catholics in general but rather the threatened church hierarchy. Linda Gordon argues that the so-called right-to-life movement repeats 19th-century antibirth-control views which linked abortion with contraception. She points out also that these groups usually oppose all kinds of social programs that would make the need for abortion less frequent. That is, child care, sex education, contraception, and so forth. "They are reacting not merely to a 'loosening of morals' but to the whole feminist struggle of the last century; they are fighting for male supremacy." [11] However, Catholic women strongly support legalized abortion as a right that women should be allowed to choose for themselves.

Shortly after the Supreme Court decision in 1973 a national study found that 52 percent of Americans favored it, 41 percent opposed it, and 7 percent were uncertain. Young people favored the change by a two to one margin, while people over 50 years of age opposed the Supreme Court decision by 49 to 44 percent. [12] A poll in 1976 showed that 76 percent of Catholics agreed with the statement: "If a woman wants to have an abortion that is a matter for her and her doctor to decide and the government should have nothing to do with it." Eighty-two percent of Protestants and 98 percent of Jews agreed with the statement. [13]

In general, various legal decisions have tended to place abortion more and more in the hands of the woman. This has been accomplished by reducing the legal control of both the doctor and the husband in the case of married women. Recent abortion decisions have favored married women and have held that a husband cannot restrain his wife from getting an abortion. Two decisions have indicated that the mother's right to privacy is more important than the father's rights, whether he is her husband or not. [14]

Rates. In 1974, the year after the Supreme Court decision, 900,000 legal abortions were performed and in 1975 there were 1 million. In recent years almost three out of every ten pregnancies were terminated by abortion. One third of all legal abortions have been performed for women under 20 years of age. Another one third of those receiving abortions were between 20 and 25 and the remainder were over 25. More than one fourth of the women were married. [15]

More than two thirds of those receiving abortions are white. However, black women are 2.2 times as likely as white women to have abortions. It has been estimated that about 70 percent of the abortions obtained legally would have been obtained illegally before decriminalization. This has meant a sharp drop in maternal mortality. A Center for Disease Control report shows a drop from 320 known abortion-related fatalities in 1961 to 88 in 1972 and 44 in 1975.[16]

FIGURE 8–1

Number of Abortions in the United States, 1973–1977

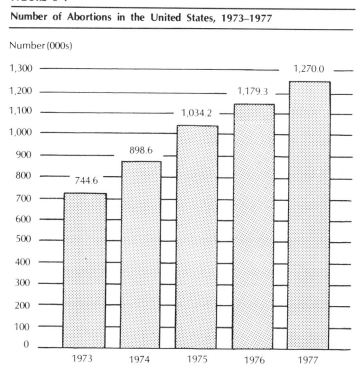

Number (000s)

Source: The Alan Guttmacher Institute, "Abortions and the Poor: Private Morality, Public Responsibility" (New York, 1979), p. 5.

As suggested, a major part of the abortion problem when it was illegal was the risks a woman took. Therefore, making abortion legal meant it could be performed by qualified physicians and under hospital conditions, thereby reducing the risk. However, even though it is now legal, most hospitals perform few if any abortions. In 1974 only one fourth of all non-Catholic general hospitals reported even one legal abortion. Fewer than one third of all private hospitals and fewer than one fifth of all public hospitals reported any legal abortions. More than half of all legal abortions were performed in nonhospital clinics.[17]

While the law makes abortion legal there is no requirement that either a physician or hospital personnel must perform them. In 1975, 11 states reported no abortions because doctors and hospitals refused to perform them. "Only 18 percent of the public hospitals and 38 percent of private hospitals in the United States reported performing even one abortion during 1975 and the first quarter of 1976."[18] Legal abortion services also vary greatly geographically. Almost half the states meet only a part of the estimated demand for abortion. In most states the majority of abortions are performed in only one or two metropolitan centers. Even in the cities, many of the abortions are performed in private clinics, and this discriminates against the poor and the pregnant teenager who lack the knowledge and the money.

As suggested, one consequence of legal abortion has been to reduce maternal mortality. In the United States today the maternal mortality rate runs about 12 deaths per 100,000 live births. By contrast, in New York City, after the first two years of the state's liberalized abortion law, the maternal death rate was 2.7 per 100,000 abortions. "The risk of death from childbirth is considerably higher than the risk of death from abortion, particularly when abortion is during the first trimester."[19] In 1975, 88 percent of all abortions were performed during the first trimester. "Even surgery for removal of tonsils and adenoids is three times as risky as legal abortion during the first 12 weeks."[20]

The arguments against legal abortion take a number of directions. First, and most important, is the argument that it stops a human life. At its extreme, this argument sees women who have abortions as "killing" their babies. A second argument is that women who have abortions will suffer a high level of guilt and this will have a harmful effect on their psyches. However, there does not appear to be any evidence to support this viewpoint. In part, this argument is based on a belief in some inherent "maternalness" in all women that cannot be inhibited without great risk. A third argument is directed at the fact that the majority of women who have abortions are unmarried. To allow them the escape from illicit pregnancy through the use of abortion is seen as subsidizing sin and approving the rejection of virtue. Many of the same people who oppose abortion also oppose illegitimacy as well as birth control for the young and unmarried. For them the problem is premarital coitus which they believe must be stopped. In a society such as ours, that is an impossibility.

The battle over legal abortion continues, and those who oppose it have not won the war of changing the Supreme Court decision, but they have won a number of skirmishes. For example, of the one million legal abortions that were performed in 1975, 300,000 were paid for by the federal government. In most cases those were financed through Medicaid funds, but that support for abortions has since been prohibited. An estimated 400,000 to 900,000 women who wanted abortions in 1977 still couldn't get them. Now, without Medicaid funds for abortions, the government may pay between $500 and $600 million for medical care and public assistance during the first year after birth. This is in contrast to the $50 million spent in 1975 for abortions. In addition "without Medicaid support for women who choose abortion, there would be an estimated 125 to 250 deaths annually from illegal and self-induced abortions as well as 12,500 to 25,000 complications requiring hospitalization."[21]

It is clear that abortion as a social problem has been responded to by strongly competing interest groups. Abortion is the kind of social problem that exists only because there is a significant group that says it is a problem. For most Americans abortion is not a social problem but rather an acceptable solution to the problem of an unwanted pregnancy. But, of course, it continues to be a social problem because of the great amount of conflict about it.

The definition of abortion as a social problem has undergone change. In general the controversy is the moral point of view against abortion in opposition to the belief that the woman has the legal right to determine the outcome of her pregnancy. The battle over legal abortion continues to be a highly emotional one.

Marriage and Sexual Problems

There exist in the United States many laws against all types of sexual behavior. But these laws are rarely ever applied. The opposition to certain aspects of human sexuality is moral. There is no form of sexual expression without some legal or moral opposition. Human sexuality as a social problem is based on morality definitions regarding deviance as sinful and sometimes as unhealthy. In this section we want to examine sexuality as a social problem, first, in terms of the different definitions relevant for women and men and, secondly, in terms of differences dependent on marital status.

Female sexuality. A brief look at some professional attitudes provides a sharp contrast to attitudes about the sexuality of females today. Up to and well through the 19th century, both moral and "scientific" criticism was directed at female sexual satisfaction. Dr. William Acton, in a standard text on the reproductive system, wrote "that the belief that women had a sexual appetite was a vile aspersion." William Hammond, Surgeon-General of the United States, wrote "the nine tenths of the time decent women felt not the slightest pleasure in intercourse"; and at the University of Basel, an eminant gynecologist named Fehling labeled "sexual desire in the young woman as pathological."

Female sexual interest was even negatively tied in with the woman's reproductive function. "In 1839 a highly successful English marriage manual written by a physician named Michael Ryan warned that female sterility was due, among other causes, to an excessive ardor of desire or 'passion excited.' . . . It is well known that compliance, tranquility, silence, and secrecy are necessary for prolific coition."[22] Sexual satisfaction for the woman was reached only by the prostitute—this attitude of past was often voiced not only by the clergy, but also by poets and physicians.

In the 19th century sexuality was often a source of conflict and tension in marriage. Sexual passion was a terror which many people devoted a great deal of energy trying to curtail. Often because of such hostility to passionate love, many Americans saw marriage as a means of restricting it. "The *Nation* [1870] editorialized that the purpose of marriage was the regulation of man's sexual appetite since it could not be repressed entirely."[23] It was often held that sexual indulgence destroyed meaningful love. In 1870 John Cowan wrote, "In proportion a woman yields to the demands of animal passion in her husband, in that same ratio he loses his love and respect for her." Within the kind of social settings that encouraged men to believe that sexual relations tended to debase a woman, the fact that a woman did not arouse sexual desire sometimes made her a good choice for a wife.[24]

The role that emerged in the United States of the stereotypical feminine woman was one who was not expected to "perform" sexually other than to simulate some modest pleasure at selected moments. Whatever sexuality the woman had, she was expected by middle age to relinquish it. "While the prevailing sex-role stereotypes allowed men to enjoy sex for as long as they wanted, women after (or even before) menopause were supposed to become completely asexual beings."[25]

The value has come to be that the only appropriate and even healthy place for female sexuality is within marriage. This view has not only been supported by religion but also has been validated by governmental and professional spokesmen. By limiting women's sexual expression to the family, the woman continues to be locked into marriage. Pepper Schwartz writes that while such reforms as child care can often be understood, any new freedoms, such as sex outside of marriage, are seen as destructive. The traditional view continues to be that the family must be preserved as it has been.[26]

Most women accept the idea that their sexual experience will be taught to them and defined for them by men. Often when their own needs do not fit the sexual patterns of their lives they may try to will themselves to be satisfied. And when there is a failure to be satisfied, the woman typically sees this to be her fault. Furthermore, the boundaries of sexual expression in marriage are usually set by what the male brings in. If he is sexually demanding the wife is sexually active; if he is not, the sexual activity usually remains at his level. Frequently in marriage if a partner is deficient in some area, there is nothing to be done other than accept the fact that one "can't have everything." Men can sometimes solve the problem by going to prostitutes, but women do not have any institutional outlet. "Thus, if the male needs less sex than the female, is unable to thrust long enough for her to experiment with her orgasmic capacity, doesn't like oral-genital contact, etc., monogamous marriage inhibits her sexual fulfillment."[27]

Sexuality has come to be an increasingly important part of marriage. In earlier cultures, including our own, marriage was not an erotic relationship but rather a social and economic institution. If there has been any significant trend it must be toward the desire and expectations that many women have about sexual fulfillment in their marriages.

By the 1970s the discrepancy between the sexual rights and aspirations of women and men had been greatly reduced. But there continues to be significant differences in sexual activity. The difference in activity is largely a function of marital status. There appears to be little difference in the sexual interest and activity of men whether married or unmarried. By contrast, unmarried women, deprived of a socially approved sex partner have a much lower incidence of sexual activity than do their married counterparts.[28]

Many of today's books written about sex emphasize the sexual problem centering around the woman's achievement of orgasm. Attention is directed at the need for extended foreplay so that actual coitus does not start until the woman is near her sexual peak; the couple may then reach "the ultimate summit of mutual orgasm."

There has come to be a great deal of stress on ability to sexually perform for both men and women. Because for many women there is a new-found knowledge and acceptance of their sexuality, they may sometimes tend to overemphasize performance and pleasure. For example, some may feel that multiple orgasms are a necessary part of any sexual encounter and feel deprived when that does not happen. Certainly the level of anxiety can be high for both women and men about the quality and variety of their sexual lives, and, even when that does not lead to problems, it can interfere with sexual pleasure and the enjoyment of a loving relationship. Constantina Safilios-Rothschild writes that many women are setting rigid rules of performance for men and feel cheated when the man is not able to "deliver the goods."[29]

The problem that typically causes women to seek clinical help is that of frigidity. Frigidity is usually defined as the failure of the woman to be sexually aroused or to reach orgasm in sexual relations. The definition implies several possible dimensions. One indicates an incapacity to function sexually, which is sometimes attributed to biological causes. But most of the evidence indicates that the causes of frigidity are primarily psychological rather than physical. Masters and

Johnson found that for most women, failure to reach orgasm was due to repressed expression of their sexual identity because of ignorance, fear, or authoritarian direction. These kinds of influences led to the initial inhibiting failure of their sexual functioning. The authoritarian influence was reflected in the fact that of 193 women who had never achieved orgasm, 41 percent were products of rigidly religious backgrounds. Eighteen were from Catholic, 16 from Jewish, and 7 from fundamentalist Protestant backgrounds.[30]

In the clinical work of Helen Singer Kaplan, she has also found the background of the women to be closely related to sexual problems. She says that constrictive upbringing is an extremely important and highly prevalent source of the types of conflict which lead to sexual dysfunctions. "Again and again the histories of patients who have sexual problems reveal that an extremely punitive and moralistic attitude prevailed in their families during childhood. Especially religious families imbue their children with serious sexual conflicts."[31]

The causes of frigidity may be due to negative socialization to sex, or may be the result of the female's feelings for her sex partner. For example, some women become frigid if they develop a dislike for their husbands; for them the necessary condition of love has been destroyed. For many women one of the most frequent causes of orgasm failure is a lack of complete identification with their marital partner. "The husband may not meet her expectations as a provider. He may have physical or behavior patterns that antagonize. Most important, he may stand in place of the man who had been much preferred as a marital partner but was not available or did not choose to marry the distressed woman."[32]

In some instances frigidity seems to have been caused by guilt and shame which have been inculcated in the frigid woman early in her life and which she unconsciously has been reiterating to herself for many years. The frequency of frigidity is difficult to estimate. In the *Redbook* study of the female, it was found that 7 percent of the women had not achieved orgasm in marital coitus. However, the failure to achieve orgasm does not necessarily mean that the woman is frigid; some women may achieve sexual satisfaction in marriage without orgasm. They may find the act pleasurable to themselves and their husbands because of psychological satisfactions.

Male sexuality. The social stresses in the male development toward sexuality focus on physical pleasure and expression. The boy growing up tends to see his sexuality in terms of genital sensations, penis size, and on "making it" and "making out." Therefore his stress is typically on pleasure from physical activity rather than from interpersonal concerns.

Often the self-perception that men have of themselves has important effects on their sexual performance. Many men are affected by a

Courtesy of the Institute for Sex Research, Inc., photo by Dellenback

Alfred C. Kinsey, the pioneer of sex research

notion of being "cool," to control a number of emotional feelings and expressions. This coolness can affect other areas of their lives. Such is sometimes the case in the sexual area, where being in control means to be cool and where you know exactly what you are doing in lovemaking so you will be a successful lover. Often the male must be cool and in control so that he is sure he makes all the right moves and that his partner reaches her sexual orgasm. Concern may not really be for her sexual pleasure but rather for affirmation that he is a technically good lover, and therefore manly.[33]

A number of years ago the Kinsey study found that impotency in the male was less common than many experts had believed. "There is a rare male never able to have intercourse for anatomical or physiological reasons." Kinsey found impotence in less than one percent of the males under 35 years of age, and of this group only a small number had lifelong impotency. Impotency increases as the male ages, but not at a rapid rate; of males 70 years of age, only 27 percent have become totally impotent."[34]

There are some social variables related to the occurrence of impotency in men. One frequent factor in the onset of impotence is related to the incidence of acute ingestion of alcohol or to a pattern of excessive alcohol use. Another variable, as with frigidity in the woman, is the influence of religious orthodoxy. After clinical treatment, Masters and Johnson report there was a 67 percent failure to immediately reverse symptoms of primary impotent men, "and a 50 percent failure to reverse symptoms of secondary impotent men influenced by religious orthodoxy."[35]

Kaplan writes that in her clinical experience she would estimate that about 10 percent of the patients seeking relief from sexual dysfunction were found to have early diabetes, use narcotics, abuse alcohol, have neurologic disease, severe depression, and other physical contributory causes. She says that the clinician "must remain alert to such physical factors which may play a role in the sexual complaints of as many as 20 percent of his patients."[36]

Impotency for the male has generally more important implications than frigidity for the female. The impotent male cannot usually indulge in sexual relations, while the frigid female can, and sexual potency is usually more closely linked to masculinity than sexual desire in the woman is to feminity.

Sexual problems. Sexual problems, whether for the female or male, are in most instances learned. As suggested, strong negative attitudes learned while growing up may result in negative sexual socialization. In other instances, sexual problems do not emerge until adulthood, and they may be a result of marriage. There is evidence that the most common problems for older couples who seek sexual counseling are boredom and satiation. Wives and husbands often complain of an inability to turn one another on. Because their responses are often not the same as in the past this can cause frustration, anxiety, and sometimes impotency and frigidity. The sanctity of marriage as the only outlet for sexual expression may at the same time be the setting for destroying sexual interest and ability.

The changing views about female sexuality over recent decades were greatly influenced by Freud. In Freud's view, female sexuality was curtailed by what he defined as the infantile nature of women. Freud tried to push women from their "immature" interest in clitoric sexual response to the "mature" nature of vaginal sensations. What this meant was that the woman's sexual satisfaction increasingly was dependent on the male. But the recent evidence from the work of Masters and Johnson clearly shows that all orgasms are clitoric and the woman does not need a male sex partner to achieve sexual satisfaction.

Therapy for sexual problems

In recent years sexual problems for both women and men have come to be defined as responsive to clinical help. What is new about the methods is to not deal with the assumed psychological causes of the sexual problems. Trying to get at the causes of sexual malfunctioning in the past had very limited success. The new approach is usually to ignore complex causes while trying to bring about relief of the symptoms and to help the individual achieve sexual awareness and competency which had been lacking.

Modern methods of sexual therapy take a social approach to treatment. Therapists try to provide alternative ways of looking at things. Often the approach is to let persons know they are normal and okay—that they are not sick or perverted. This approach is opposed to the treatment by many traditional psychiatrists who believe that any sexual problem is simply a manifestation of broader problems. However, this is often impossible to demonstrate reliably. There continues to be competition in both defining the problematic nature of sexual dysfunctions as well as ways to treat them.

Extramarital sex.   Extramarital sex is a social problem for many who view it as harmful to the individual and to society. From a social point of view extramarital sex is often seen as threatening the strength of marriage, undercutting the family, and threatening the "moral fabric." The person, especially the woman, who engages in extramarital sex does so, it is often assumed, because of problems or will have problems as a result of her activities.

In the United States, the prevalent attitudes and values are that all sexual activity after marriage will be restricted to the marriage partner. In the past, the male might discretely indulge in sexual relations outside of his marriage. Sometimes he was expected to, because of sexual needs that could not be met by the good, nonsexual woman he married. But only under rare circumstances was the wife expected to ever have a single sexual outlet outside of marriage. The traditional double standards have changed to the extent that both partners are expected to restrict their sex needs to marriage and any extramarital "rights" of the husband are not much greater than those of the wife.

What a person will do sexually is basically determined by the strength of his or her moral values about certain behavior. One grows up over the years learning sexual values from others. Morality develops in the individual through another "person" who confronts him in himself. George Simmel wrote that it is by means of the same split through which the ego says to itself "I am" and confronts itself as a knowing subject within itself as a known object—it also says to itself "I ought to."[37] This "I ought to" in the person can become very powerful and to go against it can be extremely painful. But to others the "I ought to" may never have been strong, or may have lost much of its strength over time.

The various agencies of society present to the individual in varying degrees moral beliefs from the time they are born. As children grow up, they are presented with a wide range of sexual prohibitions. These come from the family, religion, school, government, and so forth. What they are all doing is defining areas of acceptable sexuality and vast areas of unacceptable sexual expression. For many persons, growing up sexually becomes something viewed negatively and often seen as wrong. Extramarital sex becomes a social problem for many persons in society because society says it is wrong and to go against those sanctions is often to go against the severe strictures of society.

It has been seen that in most societies women have fewer opportunities for extramarital sex than men, and even where the opportunity for women exists, they have lower incidences and frequencies than men. It must be recognized that this is due to cultural differences and not biological ones. That is, the evidence clearly indicates that if women are given the opportunity without strong social and psychological restrictions, many find extramarital sexual involvement attractive and enjoyable. In those countries where strong progress has been made toward social equality of the sexes, evidence indicates increased incidence of extramarital sex among married women which approximates the male pattern. This appears to be the pattern of an increasing number of American women—especially among the more highly educated.

Part of the past value system controlling extramarital sexual activity has been a variety of sanctions against such activity. While in the past the major taboos against extramarital activity were part of the religious context of sin, this has changed and extramarital activities are now sometimes defined as "sick" behavior. Adultery is often presented within the psychiatric jargon as being immature, narcissistic, and neurotic.[38]

The belief that marriage is the only legitimate and healthy place for sexual expression is validated by religious, educational, and governmental institutions as well as by spokesmen from all the professions. Certainly the view continues to be that the family is woman's greatest satisfaction and whatever she may achieve in the job market or elsewhere is not to threaten her commitment to her marriage and her children. As Schwartz writes, to do otherwise would mean that woman's liberation had "gone too far." "Reform, such as with chil-

"There must be a limit to permissiveness."

dren, can be understood, but new freedoms, such as sex outside of marriage, are destructive and the work of 'radicals.' "[39]

Monogamous sexual values are further reinforced by the personalized attitudes that individuals have with regard to sex. The female is generally conditioned to believe that love is a precondition for sexual behavior. Most middle-class males, during their early years, are socialized to believe that love, marriage, and sex go together. But they rapidly become resocialized by their peers that love in many instances has little to do with sexual pleasure. By contrast, the belief is that if a woman is in love, she gets married if possible, and then the relationships of marriage, love, and sexual outlet are usually seen by her as inseparable. The male often views his wife as his exclusive sexual property; any tampering with her is viewed as a severe threat to something he feels very possessive about. For both partners, the exclusive, ego-centered nature of the love relationship implies that the spouse is not interested in any other age-peer of the opposite sex in any romantic or sexual way. If one shows a romantic or sexual interest in someone else, this may be viewed as catastrophic to the ego-relationship of marriage. But even in this area, male and female differences continue. Many men feel that adultery on the part of the woman is an irreparable blow to the marriage because it threatens their exclusive rights to her. Women are less inclined to see male adultery in the same extreme way. The husband who has what is seen by the wife as a single sexual encounter may be forgiven; however, if he has an affair of some length, the wife is more threatened because, to her, a lengthy affair implies that her husband must care about the other woman—thus, the "other" woman becomes an emotional threat.

The stated attitudes against extramarital coitus are strong; yet the behavior patterns indicate that a number of individuals deviate from these norms. The extent to which behavior deviates from the stated values indicates the weakness of the values in effectively influencing behavior. This deviance also raises questions about the total acceptance of monogamy, with exclusive and total sexual satisfaction being achieved through the marital partner.

When the Kinsey studies on the female were first published in the early 1950s the American public was very surprised by the statistics on extramarital coitus. Kinsey found in his sample that by age 40, 26 percent of the married women and 50 percent of the married men had had extramarital coital experience.[40] In the *Redbook* national study, it was found that 31 percent of the women had extramarital coitus. However, the average age of the women in that sample was about 35 years, somewhat younger than the women in the Kinsey study. So a projection of a few years to equalize the age variable makes it likely that this extramarital rate will be higher than Kinsey's. In the *Redbook* study, the differences by age groups of the women clearly point to this suggestion. Of the women under 25 years of age, 25 percent had had an extramarital coital experience. This was true of 29 percent of the women 25–29, 35 percent of those 30–34, 38 percent of those 35–39, and 37 percent of those past age 40. The key group may be that of 25–29; and as they move to age 40 their rate will continue to increase, as will the under 25-year-old group coming behind them. Ultimately the rate of extramarital coitus for women under age 30 may be around 50 percent.

TABLE 8–1

Number and Percent of Women Who Had Extramarital Relations by Length of Marriage

	Had Extramarital Relations	
Length of marriage	Number	Percent
Less than 1 year	87	12
1–4 years	968	21
5–10 years	1,669	30
Over 10 years	2,030	38

Source: "October Sex Quiz," *Redbook Magazine* (December 1974).

One striking finding in the *Redbook* study was that extramarital sex *as a single event was not the common pattern.* The average number of times a woman had sexual relations with each extramarital partner was almost six times. Only 17 percent of the women had limited themselves to one sexual experience. By contrast, one third had extramarital coitus more than ten times with each partner. Therefore, extramarital coitus was not usually an isolated event but clearly implied a willingness to maintain a series of experiences with the sexual partner. Extramarital coitus frequently implied a conscious planning, and this fits the pattern of increasingly greater sexual aggressiveness for women.

In a study of extramarital sex by the writer, some relationships between categories of women and the likelihood of extramarital sex were examined. It was found that the single variable most predictive of extramarital sex was the low rating of the marriage. Yet, there were also a number of women who rated their marriages very good and had extramarital coitus. The general set most predictive of a high rate of extramarital sex was women with a low-rated marriage who are sexually liberal, and who live a liberal life style. The data did suggest that for some, extramarital sex may serve a positive function in marriage. "We would speculate that in those marriages where the couple can isolate extramarital sex from the emotional interaction of marital sex the less threatening will that behavior be to the overall satisfaction within marriage."[41]

There are a variety of reasons why people have sexual experiences outside of marriage. Some reasons, which may also operate in various combinations, are: (1) looking for variation in sexual experience, (2) retaliation or getting even because their spouse had an extramarital affair, (3) rebellion against the traditional values of monogamy, (4) looking for new emotional experiences, (5) developing a friendship, (6) partner encouraging them to have an affair, (7) proving they can still be sexually attractive with age and, (8) hedonistic values of wanting to do so because it is fun and enjoyable.

It seems clear that a significant number of both husbands and wives seek and find sexual partners outside of marriage. It also seems clear that this cannot be attributed in all cases to a series of changing circumstances, especially in the case of the woman who has more than one partner and plans on continuing her extramarital sexual experience. While no stated changes in the attitudes toward extramarital coitus have been made, it is obvious that the old norms no longer exert effective control over many married people. Most significant is the indicated behavioral change in the sexual experience of wives; the philandering of husbands has generally had latent acceptance, but the philandering of wives has not, past or present.

It would appear that extramarital sexual relationships are seen as much less severe a social problem than in the past. This is true even though the frequency of extramarital sexual relationships has increased. It is that the behavior is seen as less wrong and less significant by society. Furthermore, the agencies of defining morality for society are not as strong as they once were in their positions against extramarital sex. Nor are they listened to as much at the present time as they were in the past.

The personal sexual problems are usually centered around frigidity in women and impotency in men. Extramarital sex is a social problem in that the general moral values of society see it as inappropriate in a society that values sexual monogamy. Often the problem is based in the lack of agreement between the moral values and how people actually behave.

NOTES

1. William J. Goode, "Family Disorganization," in *Contemporary Social Problems,* *4th ed.* by Robert K. Merton and Robert Nisbet (New York: Harcourt Brace Jovanovich, 1976), p. 521.

2. Mary Jo Bane, "Marital Disruption and the Lives of Children," *Journal of Social Issues* (Winter 1976), p. 109.

3. Roger W. Libby, "Adolescent Sexual Attitudes and Behavior," in *Sexuality Today and Tomorrow*, by Sol Gordon and Roger W. Libby (N. Scituate, Mass.: Duxbury Press, 1976), p. 175.

4. Melvin Zelnick and John F. Kantner, "Sex and Contraception among Unmarried Teenagers," in *Toward the End of Growth*, by Charles F. Westoff (Englewood Cliffs, N.J.: Prentice-Hall, 1973), pp. 12–13.

5. Ibid., p. 9.

6. Clara Johnson, "Attitudes toward Premarital Sex and Family Planning for Single-Never-Married-Teenage Girls," *Adolescence* (Summer 1974), p. 255.

7. H. Theodore Groat, Arthur G. Neal, and Lynn Meadows, "Social Isolation and Premarital Pregnancy," *Sociology and Social Research* (January 1976), pp. 193–94.

8. Nils Uddenburg, "Mother-Father and Daughter-Male Relationships: A Comparison," *Archives of Sexual Behavior* (January 1976), p. 75.

9. Kingsley Davis, "The World's Population Crisis," in Merton and Nisbet, Contemporary Social Problems, p. 240.

10. Nadean Bishop, "Abortion: The Controversial Choice," in *Women: A Feminist Perspective, 2d ed.*, by Jo Freeman (Palo Alto, Calif.: Mayfield Publishing Co., 1979), p. 66.

11. Linda Gordon, *Woman's Body, Woman's Right: Birth Control in America* (New York: Penguin Books, 1975), p. 415.

12. Gwynn Nettler, *Social Concerns* (New York: McGraw-Hill, 1976), p. 241.

13. Bishop, "Abortion," p. 66.

14. Miriam Aberg, Patricia Small, and J. Allen Watson, "Males, Fathers, and Husbands: Changing Roles and Reciprocal Legal Rights," *The Family Coordinator* (October 1977), p. 330.

15. Bishop, "Abortion," p. 72.

16. Ibid., p. 73.

17. Edward Weinstock et al., "Abortion Needs and Services in the United States, 1974–1975," *Family Planning Perspectives* (March–April 1976), p. 58.

18. Bishop, "Abortion," p. 75.

19. Nettler, *Social Concerns*, p. 243.

20. Bishop, "Abortion," pp. 75–76.

21. Ibid., p. 75.

22. Morton M. Hunt, *The Natural History of Love* (New York: Alfred A. Knopf, 1959), p. 319.

23. Bryon Strong, "Toward a History of the Experimental Family: Sex and Incest in the Nineteenth-Century Family," *Journal of Marriage and the Family* (August 1973), p. 458.

24. Ibid., p. 464.

25. Constantina Safilios-Rothschild, *Love, Sex and Sex Roles* (Englewood Cliffs, N.J.: Spectrum Books, 1977), pp. 108–9.

26. Pepper Schwartz, "Female Sexuality and Monogamy," in *Marriage and Alternatives* by Roger Libby and Robert N. Whitehurst (Glenview, Ill.: Scott, Foresman, 1977), p. 235.

27. Ibid., p. 237.

28. Barbara Payne and Frank Whittington, "Older Women: An Examination of Popular Stereotypes and Research Evidence," *Social Problems* (April 1976), p. 492.

29. Safilios-Rothschild, *Love, Sex*, p. 125.

30. William H. Masters and Virginia E. Johnson, *Human Sexual Inadequacy* (Boston: Little, Brown, 1970), p. 230.

31. Helen Singer Kaplan, *The New Sex Therapy* (New York: Quadrangle, 1974), p. 148.

32. Masters and Johnson, *Inadequacy*, p. 235.

33. Robert R. Bell and Wendy L. Jones, "The Adult Sex Role and Resistance to Change" (Paper presented to National Council on Family Relations, New York, October 1976), p. 14.

34. Alfred C. Kinsey et al., *Sexual Behavior in the Human Female* (Philadelphia: W. B. Saunders Co., 1953), p. 213.

35. Masters and Johnson, *Inadequacy*, p. 213.

36. Kaplan, *Sex Therapy*, p. 69.

37. Kurt H. Wolff, ed. and trans., *The Sociology of George Semmel* (New York: The Free Press of Glencoe, 1950), p. 99.

38. Robert R. Bell, Stanley Turner, and Lawrence Rosen, "A Multivariate Analysis of Female Extramarital Coitus," *Journal of Marriage and the Family* (May 1975), p. 375.

39. Schwartz, "Female Sexuality," p. 235.

40. Kinsey, *Sexual Behavior*, p. 416.

41. Bell, Turner, and Rosen, "Analysis," p. 384.

SELECTED BIBLIOGRAPHY

Bell, Robert R.; Turner, Stanley; and Rosen, Lawrence. "A Multivariate Analysis of Female Extramarital Coitus." *Journal of Marriage and the Family* (May 1975), pp. 375–85.

Bishop, Nadean. "Abortion: The Controversial Choice." In *Women: A Feminist Perspective*, 2d ed., by Jo Freeman. Palo Alto, Calif.: Mayfield Publishing Co., 1979, pp. 64–80.

Gordon, Linda. *Woman's Body, Woman's Right: Birth Control in America.* New York: Penguin Books, 1975.

Groat, H. Theodore; Neal, Arthur G; and Meadows, Lynn. "Social Isolation and Premarital Pregnancy." *Sociology and Social Research* (January 1976), pp. 189–98.

Kaplan, Helen Singer. *The New Sex Therapy.* New York: Quadrangle, 1974.

Payne, Barbara, and Whittington, Frank. "Older Women: an Examination of Popular Stereotypes and Research Evidence." *Social Problems* (April 1976), pp. 488–501.

Schwartz, Pepper. "Female Sexuality and Monogamy." *Marriage and Alternatives*, by Roger Libby and Robert N. Whitehurst. Glenview, Ill.: Scott, Foresman, 1977, pp. 229–40.

Winstock, Edward et al. "Abortion Needs and Services in the United States, 1974–1975." *Family Planning Perspective* (March–April 1976), pp. 56–59.

Chapter 9

Sex Roles and Sexism

There have been few societies where most of the female members have had complete equality with the males. Long lost in antiquity are the roots of sex discrimination. This is the focus of the social problem to be dealt with in this chapter. While women have always had secondary status, any strongly developed opposition to that position has been rare. In recent years, articulate and aggressive women have attacked American social institutions that not only support, but are often based in part, on sexism.

In the later 1960s in the United States a new militancy seeking female equality or liberation emerged. The United States has had a long history of feminism that has brought about many significant social changes. But the new militancy has been much more aggressive and demanding than anything that had gone before. To a great extent this was because the female liberation movement had developed out of such militant movements of the 1960s as civil rights, student protests, and the politically radical left.

In this chapter we want to examine briefly the historical background of social definitions of women's roles in society. (A historical look helps show how women's roles in society have undergone change and how they are a part of an emerging definition.) This will also involve examination at the present time of women's roles in the family and in the work force.

HISTORICAL BACKGROUND AND EMERGENCE OF A DEFINITION

Almost all societies of the past have been patriarchal, meaning in effect that women have had second-class status. If we go back to early Greek civilization, it can be seen that the powers the Greek husband had over his wife were no less than what he had over his children. If they had no children, he could divorce her. The dowry of the wife became the husband's property during his lifetime and he had the rights to any separate earnings she might acquire. She was under his jurisdiction almost entirely and could not even leave the house without his permission. By contrast, the early Roman wife stood in a position of complete social equality to her husband and was seen as having dignity and honor both within the family and the state. She was both honored and subordinated. She was highly respected, and yet she was given no tangible legal rights.

Whatever status the woman had gained during the Roman period she began to lose with the rise of Christianity. In that period a tendency developed to increasingly restrict the woman's legal and social rights. Women were given no special position or recognition in early Christian teaching. Jesus expressed no new ideas with respect to the position of women. The apostle Paul advocated that women take a subordinate position to man and over time this became the dominant attitude among early male Christian leaders. Therefore, the status accorded to women was a step back compared to what they had had in Rome. Eventually women were excluded by Christians from any offices. Still less were they men's equals in private life. Married women were held to be subject to their husbands.

Christianity developed an obsession with sexual matters which also placed a great strain on women. Treated by the Saxons as property, women by the Middle Ages often were seen as the source of all sexual evil. It was argued that sexual guilt really rested in women because they tempted men who would otherwise have remained pure. The combined views of woman as inferior to man and as repository of sin has placed her at a level of inferiority from which she has never completely recovered in the eyes of traditional Christian thought. With time, and due to Christian influence, she also came to be legally defined as inferior. In the English common law the husband's rights over the wife's personal property were almost unlimited. After the end of the 13th century the common law put the absolute property in the wife's chattels with the husband. She was not even permitted to make a will without the husband's consent. In many respects, up until the 20th century the woman had a status not too different from that of a slave. This was the general state of affairs that existed at the time the American colonies were founded and developed.

Women continued to be treated in many respects as second-class persons. They received very little formal education because it was commonly believed that girls were unfit in brain and character to study seriously. It was argued that girls should be taught how to run a household, and, if suitable, how to display the graces of a lady. However, near the end of the 18th century there were voices being heard that no longer accepted the traditional definition of the woman. And if helplessness was one common female adaptation to the world around her, for other women a new militancy was coming to be an alternative. For a few women there was the choice of either barricading themselves in the home with the myth of frailty or to struggle to get outside the home and find some new identities.

In 1792, the first comprehensive attack on marriage as it then existed and the way in which it subjugated women was made by Mary Wollstonecraft in a book called *A Vindication of the Rights of Women*. She did not want to do away with marriage but rather to correct some of the inequalities that existed. She argued that women should have increased social and economic rights as well as greater education so that in marriage they would not have to be submissive, but rather equal to their husbands. Women were also being heard in other areas of protest. In general, in the 18th and 19th centuries when voices of protest were heard they were from women. It was primarily women who fought against slavery, against child labor, and against the development of slums. They also fought for schools, libraries, playgrounds, and legislation to protect children. Women have historically been the social conscience of American society.

During the 19th century great changes occurred in the United States. Industrialization meant a change in life patterns, as the productive unit shifted from the family to the individual going away from the home to work. For some women, where the home had been the setting for all their work, the chance to work in a factory appeared like freedom. Hard work for 12 hours a day, or more, had been normal for most American women and their tasks had been heavy, endless, and unpaid. For many of them the early factory system represented a semiskilled and repetitive job which demanded less physical exertion.

In the decades prior to the Civil War in the United States a changing definition of women had developed on the part of men. The "sinful" nature of women came to be stressed less by men, and women came to be seen as more spiritual. The new explanation for their exclusion from politics came to be not because they were inferior, but rather because of their superiority. They were seen as not so much sinful but as too good for the world. As a result, their moral value placed them above the nasty business of politics and making money. The men turned over to them the matters of "culture" and the rearing of children. Women were encouraged to believe that their sex gave them a distinct function that was different from and better than the mere getting of money. It is doubtful that very many men really believed that what women did was important. The really important world was their world—the man's world of money making and politics. So they could keep women out of their world and feel morally superior about it at the same time.

Despite all the forms of resistance, the women's rights movement did develop and grow. The factor of industrialization continued to remove many women from the home and freed many of them from the functions they had performed in the past. There were a mumber of landmarks in the movement. For example, in 1833 Oberlin was the first men's college in the United States to admit women, and four years later Mount Holyoke, the first women's college, was opened. The first Woman's Rights Convention was held at Seneca Falls, New York, in 1848. The first to speak out in public for women's rights were Fanny Wright, the daughter of a Scotch nobleman, and Ernestine Rose, the daughter of a rabbi. There was great hostility toward those women. The first was referred to as "the red harlot of infidelity" and the second as "a woman a thousand times below a prostitute."[1] The declaration that came out of Seneca Falls brought forth an outcry of revolution and insurrection directed at the women and the hostility was so great that some of the women withdrew their signatures.

The major force in the growth of the feminist movement in the 1800s was the slavery issue. So the concern that turned many women into pioneer reformers was less an attack on sexual bondage than an assault on the slavery of the blacks. In their seeking to free the slaves many radical women became more conscious of their own lack of freedom. "Through helping others, they learned to help themselves. The destiny of American women and American Negroes had been interacting, and still is."[2]

Any attempts to change the roles of women have been met by strong resistance from men. From their position of great power they often defined women who were seeking change as a social problem. These women were often defined as unnatural and socially destructive—destructive against the social order as it had long existed to overwhelmingly favor men. In the past, almost all men and women were against the women's rights movement.

The man was, of course, a double standard male who saw his way of life being threatened and the possibility of some of his conveniences being taken away from him. The man had no desire to change his world but only to increase his rights as a male. On economic grounds he found his world ideal. A subjugated wife, even if cranky, was simpler and cheaper to deal with than an equal before the law who could leave with her property if she wanted or who could sue for redress if mistreated. From the business point of view the woman's low position made good sense to him. So any plea for female education or reform in marriage was often linked with atheism, socialism, abolition, teetotaling, sexual immorality, and other despicable forces by the male.

During the early part of this century there developed an increasing concern about women working outside the home. In some instances the concern was that working was bad for women. However, the movement for protective labor legislation came from male workers who wanted to restrict the competition of women and children. This was different from the more humanitarian impulses of middle-class reformers to protect women and children. Politically the liberals tried to protect women while the conservatives wanted to keep women free as a source of cheap labor. In 1908 the Supreme Court unanimously supported the freedom-of-contract doctrine which gave women special protection.[3] The special protection also served to keep women out of many occupations.

The most dramatic change in the image of women came after World War I. This resulted from the upsurge in women's employment outside the home. The 1920s saw the emergence of the white-collar class in the United States, and women were a large part of it. For example, over twice as many women entered the labor force during that decade as during the previous one. But the major event, and one that had been fought for many years, was the passing of the 19th Amendment to the Federal Constitution in 1920. It read that the "rights of citizens of the United States to vote shall not be denied or abridged by

Suffragettes to see President Wilson in 1913

Historical Pictures Service, Inc., Chicago

the United States or by any state on account of sex." This was an important landmark in the fight for women's rights. However, it did not bring about any great changes in the political life patterns of women.

The 1920s were a period of great change in the roles and rights of American women. That decade saw a revolution in morals that was most vividly reflected in the behavior of women. During the 1920s women discarded many taboos. For the first time women began to smoke and drink in public. As recently as 1918 it was considered daring for a New York hotel to permit women to sit at the bar. But during the 20s, despite prohibition, both sexes drank in public. In the years since the 20s there have been few alterations in the position of women that were not first evident during that decade.

Once women had the legal right to vote in 1920, they found that this did not lead to legal equality. This was because there could be no real sex equality until women actually participated on an equal basis with men in politics, occupations, and the family. Actually, in the 1920s, the grip of the traditional political machines became even stronger with women voting. This was because the female relatives of every man connected with the political machines were registered to vote. For many of those city bosses the vote of the women was merely a multiplication factor. In fact, women refused to vote against antifeminists in Congress, and sent them back with increased majorities as their representatives. While the women had the vote, they generally continued to use it as their men told them to.

Since 1920 the number of women who have attained positions of power in the federal and state governments have been unbelievably few. There have been only five women elected state governors. Two women have held cabinet rank in the federal government and only six have served as ambassadors or ministers. At the present time the United States has one female senator. And while women hold about one fourth of all jobs in the federal civil service, they hold only 2 percent of the top positions. Before its passage the right to vote was seen by many as a potentially great shift of political power to women. But any special power block among women in politics has been very rare.

In recent years in the United States there have been a number of changes in the attitudes toward women. In one study, college freshmen were asked if they believed "the activities of married women are best confined to the home and the family." In 1967, among males, 61 percent answered "yes," but by 1972 the number had dropped to 39 percent. Among women the percentages over the same period dropped from 38 percent to 18 percent.[4] A Harris Poll found that nationwide support for the women's movement had risen 17 points from 1971 to 1975, from 42 percent to 59 percent, and more of the support came from men.[5] Certainly the stated acceptance of greater female rights and opportunities has increased. But that is often not translated into any meaningful action.

American Women Today

From the point of view of traditional society, women as a social problem exists on several levels. For some, women are seen as being "unnatural" in their desires to have the same rights as men. They are seen as being destructive to marriage and the family by rebelling against those roles. The argument against women in these areas is often seen as very fundamental. For them not to actively fulfill their traditional roles of wife and mother is to define them as destroying the basic fabric of society. And for many sexists, it is not only that they are destroying marriage and the family but are entering the occupational world where they do not belong. We want to examine these social problems attributed to women within the context of social change.

Wife role. The most modern and democratic view of the wife role is within the family setting of basic role equality. This type of marriage is usually not an association of complete equals but rather is based on the notion of the development of some role specializations within marriage. In different areas, both partners recognize that authority is vested in the role or in the interests and abilities of only one of them. This recognition allows each one to defer to the other in different areas of competence, without loss of prestige. The division of labor in marriage is not based on a belief of complete differences between the husband and wife roles and often, if conditions demand, one partner can temporarily take over the role of the other. But even in this setting various duties are sex assigned. While a husband might take over the washing of laundry if his wife is ill, as soon as she is well she takes it over in most cases. Even the most democratic marriage is generally one where the husband has more privileges and does more of the things important and interesting to society and the wife is typically left with undesirable and unpaid housework.

While in the past very few women saw any real alternative to marriage this has changed somewhat. At least among the younger generation, marriage in the future for them is not seen as inevitable. One study showed 14 percent of the young women questioned rejected marriage for a variety of reasons.[6] There has also been some recent evidence that marriage is seen as more significant by men than by women. This is more true the more successful the man. One study reports that "among males, those with the highest levels of intelligence were the least likely to remain single, whereas females with the higher levels of intelligence were the most likely to do so."[7] For many highly intelligent women the option of an occupation has taken over from the traditional one of marriage.

The breadwinner role of the man is basic to both his and his wife's image of his appropriate family role. Frequently his family success is not given on the basis of his roles as husband and father but rather as provider. Often the man feels he has no option or little freedom with regard to his job. His breadwinner role is rooted in his job security. But there is nothing inherently satisfying in the work of many men. A great amount of man's work "is monotonous and/or psychologically unrewarding, at best: at its worst, it is dangerous to the man as well as to others in society."[8]

An examination of power in marriage indicates differences for wives and husbands. It has been observed that women are often caught up in a vicious circle because of their economic dependence upon their husbands and their lack of contact with the work world, and their being tied down to the house restricts, to a great extent, the kind of decisions over which they can claim expertise and, ultimately, control. "Women, therefore, as a 'class' have not had the chance to obtain the 'resources', skills, and expertise that would allow them a share in most important types of family power."[9]

In most marriages power relationships continue to be dominated by men because as husbands they have more resources than their wives. Women have been socialized to function less autonomously during their courtship years and often see themselves as less able than men to make the best decisions. "The legal system supports the husband's superior power, giving him the right to decide on family residence, surname, and places on him the responsibilities for supporting the family."[10]

In any social system people attain prestige or status in various ways. Historically, status has often been given to individuals on the basis of their family rather than their individual achievement. Most often, in recent times, the wife has gotten her community status from her husband. Anne Statham Mache points out that women traditionally have been evaluated more on whom they associate with than on their own personal successes. Often women want to remain married to desirable men because much of their social worth depends on having a desirable mate. "The more successful they are at maintaining the marriage, the better they feel about themselves."[11]

For the nonworking housewife the husband's income is the only reward that a woman personally enjoys. It may be that the vicarious success a woman is alleged to get from her husband's success is more myth than reality. There is some evidence that a husband's success makes the nonworking housewife feel less adequate in contrast. But the tendency for housewives to unfavorably compare themselves to their husbands may be most true of highly educated women because they have the personal skills to do well for themselves.[12]

As suggested, the role of the wife is often legally defined in ways separate from the role of the husband. For example, if the husband moves for his occupation and his wife refuses to go with him, in a number of states she would be guilty of desertion. Or, in over one third of the states, if a couple live separately by mutual agreement, the wife's domicile still legally belongs to the husband. The laws are such that if a woman marries a man who is a resident of a different state she cannot vote or run for office in the state where she lives.[13]

In some instances marriage may be characterized by equality of roles. But when this appears to happen, often the inequality of what gets done in the home is not overcome. For most women an important part of their marriage role overlaps with their role as housekeeper. One study found that husbands of full-time housewives were more likely to evaluate their marriages in a positive way then were husbands of working wives.[14] Furthermore, husbands of working wives when compared with husbands of housewives were in poorer health and were not only less content with marriage but also with work and life in general. "The implications of these findings are that men whose wives work are subject to greater stress than men whose wives are not working, and they appear to be having more difficulty coping effectively with this pattern of family living."[15]

Mother role.   One major basis of limiting the parental role to mother during the first years of life has been because of feeding. For most of human history the mother and infant could not be separated because of prolonged breast feeding. In this century this has drastically changed with new methods of feeding infants. Joan Huber states that the baby's survival, no longer dependent on the ability of the mother to breast feed, cannot be overemphasized. "Techniques of food sterilization have shattered the ancient dependency of a baby on a lactating women."[16] There was a sharp decline in breast feeding from about 80 percent of firstborn babies in the late 1920s to about 25 percent in the early 1960s.[17] There has been a constant attempt to pursuade women to believe in some great superiority of breast feeding both for themselves and their babies. But this is often a part of a conservative argument to keep the woman in the home.

Alice S. Rossi has pointed out that for the first time in the history of any known society, motherhood became a full-time occupation for adult women in the United States.[18] In the past that was an impossibility because the woman had many more things to do and more children to look after. Full-time motherhood came about as the result of technological development and economic affluency. Once full-time motherhood came about, women were told how important it was, and the fact that mankind had previously functioned without it was generally forgotten. It seems clear that continuous mothering, even in the first few years of life, is not necessary for the healthy emotional development of the child. What is more important is the nature of the care rather than who provides it.

For many years, whatever direction the argument took, it was to rationalize the woman becoming a mother and staying at home. The message was that mothers belonged at home to provide their children with a hearty breakfast and see they looked respectable when they went off to school. And she should be at home to welcome them when they returned from school in mid-afternoon. Those values came to be the conventional wisdom of a good mother. By the 1950s, "women's investment in their children's human capital seemed so natural that most people forgot it was a comparatively recent development."[19]

The mother role is of course interrelated with the roles of wife and housekeeper in the traditional family setting. One study of the division of household tasks found a negligible impact made by the presence of young children. While they sometimes altered the content of household work, their presence did not influence the division of household work. "In other words, although there was some evidence that older children played a small role as suppliers of household labor, the needs of preschoolers appeared to have no effect on who did what in the house."[20]

Housekeeper role. This role is not filled in any significant way by other family members. Household work can often be time consuming and, whatever the level of achievement and performance, it rests almost entirely with the wife. One researcher observes that with the exception of childcare, women have few reactions one way or another to their daily tasks. "Moreover, they do not feel especially pressured and rarely challenge the household division of labor. One gets a picture analogous to Blauner's assembly line workers who 'turned off' their minds while on the job."[21] Catherine White Berheide also found that about 80–95 percent of the over 60 representative household tasks covered in her study were done primarily by women and that when the married women worked they typically did not do a smaller proportion of the household work.[22]

The United States Bureau of the Census classifies the housewife, along with "student" and "looking for work" as temporary statuses of conditional respectability and low economic prestige. Regardless of the propaganda, housework is basically low-status work. This is reflected in a number of ways. Our society rewards occupational efforts with money and yet housework is not within the money economy. In fact, it is not always defined as real work. Many women who do not hold income-producing jobs will say they don't work—only take care of a house. Among women who work for money, domestic work is at the bottom of the occupational hierarchy. Lower-class young women prefer to work in offices and factories rather than to hire out and care for children and a house. Because they cannot get domestic help, many middle-class women must do their housework themselves. The low-prestige occupation of housework has become common to many educated women.

There are a variety of different costs for many women who pursue the housekeeper role. Even those who do not find it menial or degrad-

Mike Jaeggi

The exception not the rule

ing may feel isolated from the ongoing stream of human activity which validates their identity and sense of worth. It may confirm a sense of powerlessness. "The woman who is being 'sheltered' and provided for at home is not only financially dependent but lacks psychological leverage as well."[23]

One study found that, overall, housewives appeared to be comparatively dissatisfied with their lives. In general, they see their lives as less interesting than their husbands and generally as worse than those of women who do have jobs. They also tend to be more dissatisfied with themselves and their lives than either full-time or part-time workers. Many of them want to work and often for reasons apart from any economic necessity.[24]

The value of "housewife" may vary with the different levels of the social-class system within which the position occurs. The position of the upper-class housewife may be much more highly valued in the overall social structure than the position of lower-class housewife. Joan Acker goes on to suggest that it may be that the value of this position rises as its functions become more symbolic and less utilitarian. "Or, to put it another way, the value may rise as functions become centered more around consumption and less around productive activities."[25]

In a study by Linda Burzotta Nilson there is evidence of some prestige in being a housewife when compared with some other options. There are many who will give higher prestige to being a housewife than they will to many working-class occupations. Being a housewife has about the same prestige as the skilled clerical jobs that are filled by millions of women. Only the higher white-collar jobs and professions bring women higher prestige, and those require formal training or experience.[26] Marriage without employment can still be a woman's avenue for higher status, though not as high as the husband's in most cases.[27]

Traditional female roles in the family have been discussed for the middle class. However, there are some sharp differences among women in the lower-middle and lower social classes. Most of those women continue to live in a world that is patriarchal—at least when the male is present. For many there is little in marriage that is shared between the husband and wife. For example, Mirra Komarovsky found in her study of a working-class group that the husband and wife shared little other than the immediate daily tasks. "The impoverishment of life and of personality curtails the development of shared interests."[28]

In the lowest social-class levels, frequently the husband participates very little and the wife carries the responsibility for the home and the children largely by herself and seldom participates with her husband in anything "collective" because she is basically grounded in the home. She is neither a joiner nor a participant. She may be quite religious but is much less likely to attend church regularly than her middle-class counterpart. She is virtually isolated from life outside the confines of her family and neighborhood.

Yet with all the restrictions on the life of lower-class women, there does not appear to be a high degree of status frustration among them. They expect to be housewives—that is their reason for being and there is no real alternative. Komarovsky found in her study hardly a trace of the feeling of low prestige that educated housewives attach to that role. Rarely did she find a woman saying, "I am just a housewife." The women did have discontent, but it was not caused by a low evaluation placed on domesticity; rather, it was from the frustrations of being a housewife. When some of the women did show a dislike for housework, they often felt guilty about their dislike of what they saw as the normal female responsibility. "Unlike some college-educated housewives who detest housework, our respondents never say that they are too good for it, that housework is unchallenging manual labor."[29]

There is some recent evidence to suggest that working-class women do not have quite the idealized view of housework that is sometimes suggested. Myra Marx Ferree found that working-class women who are full-time homemakers are less likely to be satisfied in general than those women who have paid jobs. "Full-time housewives are more apt to be dissatisfied with the way they are spending their lives, to feel they have not had a fair opportunity in life, and to want their daughters to be 'mostly different' from themselves. Less educated women may be happier at home than other women are, but they are not happier at home than if they are working."[30]

MALE-FEMALE DIFFERENCES

Before looking at women in the work force and in occupational careers it is necessary to examine the basic differences between males and females. This is important because so much of the discrimination against the female has been and continues to be rationalized on the grounds of unchangeable, physical differences. It is argued here that almost all significant differences between the sexes can be explained on the basis of differential socialization and that the biological differences have been greatly exaggerated insofar as the differential behavior patterns attributed to them.

Historically, women have been defined as different (implying inferior) on many grounds. In general, the arguments have been based on alleged biological differences. "Anatomy becomes destiny" because little can be done to change anatomy. When a society refuses to allow women to do many things, they don't. Then their not being trained to do those things is taken as proof that they can't.

It is obvious that men and women are somewhat different as sexual beings and often perform in complementary ways. However, there is no inherent reason for believing that either sex is dependent on the other for sexual satisfaction. Heterosexuality, as well as homosexuality or solitary sexuality, are adaptations to sexual needs that are made by individuals. The fact that the vast majority of adults prefer heterosexuality as a means of expression is because they have been socialized to do so.

The ideal of femininity plays an important part in politicizing the sexuality of women. It often does so by justifying women's sexual repression and passivity based on a "natural" or biological cause. This view has made it possible for women to be admired when they can make themselves sexually attractive but at the same time have only been allowed to hint at the sexuality that is within. As a result many women have become experts in sexual teasing, "learning how to use sex as a commodity and come to be viewed and view themselves as sex objects."[31]

Probably the most important biological difference between the man and woman is the differential reproductive burden. The man is needed only to provide the sperm and he doesn't even have to be present to do that, while the woman in a normal pregnancy and birth must carry the fetus for nine months. In the past, the pregnancy period of the woman led to many restrictions being placed on what she could do. However, it seems clear that most women, who have no pregnancy complications, can work at most jobs with no more than a loss of a week or two for the birth of the child. So there is no reason why many women, if they choose, cannot pursue a career at the same time that they have children. It is common to argue that time off for pregnancy interferes with a career for women. Yet many men must also take time off from a career for illnesses and other reasons and this does not usually affect their careers. Or some flexibility could be set up to allow women to use vacation time to have children. The point is that there is little that is inherent in the birth experience for women that *necessarily* must restrict them in the ways that they have been restricted socially in the past.

Another common argument for differential treatment of women centers around the fact that the *average* woman is not as strong as the *average* man. That is, she has been excluded from certain jobs because it has been argued that she does not have the strength to perform them. The range of physical strength among women is as wide as it is among men. This means there are some women who are stronger than some men. Strength, by sex, is not an absolute difference, but a relative one. Many times men are rejected from jobs because they are not strong enough. "Men only" becomes irrelevant; the job requirement should be simply the strength to qualify. In that way work would be available to individuals on the basis of abilities, skills, strengths, and motivation, regardless of sex. A woman might be turned away from a job because she was not strong enough but some men would also be turned away for the same reason.

From the time of birth infants are treated in different ways if they are female or male. A basic part of early socialization is to direct aspects of their growth along the lines of gender. Research shows that as infants, girls are expected to be and are trained to be quieter, more passive, and more controlled—to be "nicer" babies than boys.[32]

There are also important differences in the social learning of young

Elizabeth Hamlin/Stock, Boston, Inc.

J. Berndt/Stock, Boston, Inc.

Being socialized for different sex roles

children as they interact with their peers. For example, there are different types of social skills developed by girls and boys. The game requirements of boys may initially encourage them to develop nonexclusive friendships and once these are formed they further the tendency of boys to interact in large groups.[33] By contrast, girls tend to interact in small groups. "Girls tend to engage in more intimate behavior than boys and dyads are conducive to intimate behavior."[34]

It has also been argued that because women do have some physical differences, this results in personality differences based upon their being female. A psychoanalytic view is that there are personality types that represent femininity. Yet there are no personality qualities found in women that are not also found in men. Once again it is a question of relative differences rather than absolute ones. And whatever it means to be a woman is dependent on the socialization experience and what the individual personality brings to bear. Any combination of so-called female personality traits if applied to male and female samples would find them in some men and absent in some women.

Many personality qualities get sorted out very early in life and are socialized into one sex or the other. For example, many women have a strong need to compete and achieve but that need is directed toward the traditional goals that are most readily available to females. Also the evidence supports the notion that aggressive personality traits are more commonly valued in men and passive personality traits valued in women. At very young ages acts of aggression are more often given support for male children than for female children. And males more often come to believe that their aggressive behaviors will be rewarded. The forces of socialization are tremendously important in channeling the personality characteristics of females and males in some very different directions.

The early influences have a great impact on the direction the person will take later in life. The values are different by sex and provide a background out of which adult role choices will be made. One study of college students found that men emphasized such categories as being capable, logical, and self-controlled. They valued the cerebral and self-directed person. By contrast, the women emphasized the categories of forgiving, helping and loving. "The male value strictures facilitate ambition, self-sufficiency, and accomplishment in the workaday world. By comparison, women seem self-harmfully idealistic and dependent on other people for their raison d'être."[35]

The above study also indicated sex differences in pressures felt by college students. Thirty-five percent of all the women and 19 percent of the men often felt close to collapse. "Whereas the most frequent cause given by men is worry over course work and exam pressures, women most often cite trouble in their personal relationships with men and with members of the parental family."[36] This also indicates how much longer women are locked into their families as significant others than are men.

An important part of the assumed difference between males and females has been a part of the American historical heritage. Basically, the difference has been intellectualized to not only be inevitable but also desirable. The most powerful intellectual influence has been that of Freud. The propaganda that women should marry early and breed often has prevailed. The psychologists and psychiatrists have replaced clergymen as the authorities. In this century the belief came to be that it was best for a woman to become a mother, not because God said so, but because Freud said so. Freud's view of women was to define them as inferior human beings. The castration complex and penis envy, two ideas basic to his thinking, were based on the belief that women are inferior to men. Freud's view of women reflected the time in which he lived. In his middle-class world there were highly conservative beliefs about the proper roles for men and women in marriage and society. Those views have little validity for the kind of world that exists today. But the Freudian view has continued to be perpetuated. For many years American women have been told and thus controlled through Freudian followers that there can be no greater destiny for women than to fulfill their traditional femininity. Women have been told to pity the neurotic, unfeminine, unhappy women who have wanted to be poets or physicians.[37]

Freud's followers generally have seen women in the same image as he did—as inferior and passive. They have argued that women will only find *real* self-fulfillment by affirming their "natural" inferiority. Some of his followers write that for women there must be a willingness to accept dependence on the male without fear or resentment and that they must not admit of wishes to control or master, to rival or dominate. "The woman who is to find true gratification must love and accept her own womanhood as she loves and accepts her husband's manhood. The woman's unconscious wish to possess the organ upon which she must thus depend militates greatly against her ability to accept its vast power to satisfy her when proffered to her in love."[38]

In recent years both Freudian and some other psychiatric interpretations have lumped the increased employment of women with many social and personal problems. Women working outside the home has been linked with increased divorce, more crime and delinquency, and increased alcoholism and schizophrenia among women. American society has also been inundated with the psychoanalytic viewpoint that believes that any conflict in personal or family life must be treated on the individual level. "This goes with the general American value stress on individualism, and American women have increasingly resorted to psychotherapy, the most highly individualized solution of all, for the answers to the problems they have as women."[39] The psychiatric influence has been such that any problem is seen as individually based rather than socially determined. As a result, many women who have felt miserable and unhappy as housewives have determined themselves to be at fault or inadequate rather than recognizing that in many cases they are victims of social situations that cause their problems.

Not only the Freudian view of women but most psychiatric and some psychological approaches have been on the level of individual responsibility. The common model has been that women's destined roles are significantly different from men's. Her traditional role is always based on traditional assumptions of her adult meaning being based in the home, as secondary to her husband and as a mother. When women have broken away from that model they have usually been seen as a problem. They may be seen as representing a social problem because they are failing to do what society holds to be appropriate for them. Or they constitute a social problem for themselves because they are fighting against what is "natural" for them. It has only been recently that significant recognition has been given to a new dimension of women as a social problem. That is the inability to provide and encourage women to move out of their traditional roles and into new ones. Many women have the desire and motivation to seek new roles but society blocks them or makes it very difficult. This is what constitutes the social problem for those women seeking equality as adult human beings.

The problem is that American society continues to hold stereotypes about what women should do. Many women are caught in a double bind. On one hand they find many restrictions and taboos still operating against them as they seek equality of rights with men in work, marriage, family, sexuality, and so forth. On the other hand, women have often been so effectively socialized to traditional female roles that to seek sex-role equality can sometimes result in guilt, anxiety, and uncertainty. For this dimension of the social problem to be resolved, barriers against equality need to be removed and women must have the opportunity to feel natural about their rights to equality.

Women and Work

In 1900 about 20 percent of all American women were employed outside the home. However, their social visibility was not great and there often appeared to be fewer women working than were in fact. They were not very visible because they were concentrated at the low status levels of society. Typically they were unmarried young women from working class families, poor widows, or married women from low-income and immigrant groups. In the middle class even the single women usually did not work.[40]

Female labor today is, as it has been for decades, a marginal section of the labor force. In this respect the current increase of women in the work force cannot be interpreted as real progress because the provisional status of female labor has not been greatly altered. A sharp economic depression would probably see women lose most of what they have gained in the work force. Furthermore, women have a weak position in the labor force because they have less education than their husbands and can be subjected to greater physical coercion.[41]

About nine out of ten women work outside the home at some time during their lives. In general, marriage and the presence of children tend to limit their employment, while widowhood, divorce, and the decrease of family responsibility tend to bring them back into the work force. The necessity of supporting children has a strong influence on women entering work. The labor-force participation rates of women with preschool children in 1971 shows the variations. Among the married mothers, 30 percent were working, but this was true of 41 percent of the separated mothers and 62 percent of the divorced mothers. And the rates of all married versus all divorced women working was 41 and 70 percent respectively.[42] The percentage of women in the work force with children shows a very significant increase. In 1950, 21 percent of women with children worked but by 1974 it had increased to 51 percent. Even among those least likely to work, married women with preschool children, there were 34 percent in the work force.[43]

Rates.   The percentage of the work force being female has steadily increased over the years. In 1900 only 18 percent of all workers were women and in 1940 it was 25 percent. The sharpest increase in labor-force participation among women came in the 1960s, from 37.1 percent in 1960 to 42.8 percent in 1970. However, the rate of increase slowed down in the early 1970s and there is little increase projected for 1980 to

1990. Jessie Bernard writes, "We may, in fact, have reached some kind of limit at just under half—46 percent—by 1980. The projected increase between 1980 and 1990 is only from 45.6 to 45.9 percent."[44] Put another way, in 1972, 40 percent of all married women were in the work force. Among the married women the highest rates of participation in the labor force were where the husband's income did not represent poverty levels, but rather the lower range of middle-income levels. The rate then declined as the husband's income reached higher levels. About two fifths of all married women and many single women as well were both homemakers and workers.

There have been changes in the work patterns over the life cycle of women. In 1900, if the woman worked at all during her lifetime, it was usually only before marriage and children, and the proportion employed declined steadily with age. But in 1970 more than half (54 percent) of all women between the ages of 45–54 were in the labor force. This was proportionately as many women as in the 20–24 age group. The projected rate for the older group is 58 percent in 1990. Even among women 55–64 years of age "the increase in labor force participation has been phenomenal, rising from 18 percent in 1940 to 43 percent in 1970 and projected to be 46 percent by 1990."[45]

Between 1960 and 1975 married women with children under the age of six more than doubled in rates of labor-force participation. The

TABLE 9–1

Percent of Married Women in the Labor Force, by Presence and Age of Children and Woman's Age and Race: United States, 1960 and 1975

	Percent in labor force					
	All married women with husband present			*Black married women with husband present*		
Presence and age of children, and age of woman	*1960*	*1975*	*Percent change 1960–1975*	*1960**	*1975*	*Percent change 1960–1975*
Total	34.7	44.4	28	46.7	53.7	15
No children under age 18 ...	38.3	43.9	15	52.6	47.5	−10
Woman aged 16–34	62.4	77.2	24	69.7	70.0	0
Woman 35 and over	34.3	35.5	3	49.2	42.5	−14
Children aged 6–17	42.7	52.3	22	56.3	61.8	10
Children under age 6	23.3	36.6	57	35.3	54.0	53
Aged 3–5 only	29.2	41.9	43	48.1	60.0	25
Under age 3	20.0	32.7	64	29.6	49.9	69

*Black and other races for 1960.

Source: Population Bulletin, "Marrying, Divorcing and Living Together in the U.S. Today," Reference Bureau, 32, 5 (Washington, D.C.: U.S. Government Printing Office, October 1977), p. 11.

increases were from 15 to 33 percent among women with children under three years of age, and from 25 to 42 percent among women with children between the ages of three and five. Over that 15 years the largest percentage increase of women working occurred among those women who in the past were deemed least likely to work.[46]

Of those mothers who worked (with at least one child under 14 years of age), 46 percent of the children were cared for in their own homes, with 15 percent looked after by their fathers, 21 percent by other relatives, and 9 percent by maids, housekeepers, or babysitters. Another 16 percent of the children were cared for outside their own homes, about half by relatives. Thirteen percent of the children were looked after by their mothers while they worked, and 15 percent had mothers who worked only during school hours. Eight percent of the children were expected to care for themselves, while only 2 percent of the children were in group care, such as day-care centers, nursery schools, and after-school centers.[47]

Large numbers of women in the workforce are playing the role of breadwinner. Forty-two percent of all women in the labor force support themselves or themselves and their children. Added to this is another 16 percent of all women who work because their husbands' incomes are too low.[48]

TABLE 9–2

Percent of Women (16 years and older) in the Work Force by Marital Status, 1975

	Percent
All women	45
Divorced	73
Married, husband absent	55
Married, husband present	43
Widowed	25
Never married	57

Source: U.S. Department of Labor, *U.S. Working Women: A Chartbook* (Washington, D.C.: U.S. Government Printing Office, 1975).

It is often assumed that the economic position of the working woman has greatly improved. But such is not the case. In fact, because of segregation of women into low-status, low-paying jobs, their position has not changed. Women's overall relative full-time median earnings fell from 61 percent to 56 percent of men's between 1960 and 1974. Also the rates of unemployment for women have been increasing.[49] Income of women is also influenced by their age. For example, the average hourly earnings of married women under 25 are about 85 percent of those of men at the same age. But by age 35 the ratio has dropped to 60 percent and it continues to drop with increasing age.[50] This is a reflection of the fact that the older the woman, the less her chance of being in a prestigious and well-paying occupation.

Whether one looks at gross incomes, particular occupations and work settings, or at other factors related to income levels, the results are constant—women earn less and are less likely to acquire positions where the rewards will be greater. "Moreover, the higher the position the female obtains, the greater the absolute salary differential between herself and her male colleagues. The more prestigious the occupation (e.g., physics) and the more prestigious the setting (e.g. Harvard) the greater the disparity."[51]

In some occupational areas women's positions have lost ground in recent years. This appears to be the case in higher education. Between 1972 and 1975–76 the number of women who were chief executive officers in institutions of higher education decreased from 162 to 148. Women presidents fell from 11 percent to 3 percent and the proportion of tenured women faculty dropped from 17 percent in 1971–72 to 13 percent in 1974–75. "In 1959–60 the median salary of women in four-year institutions was 84.9 percent of the median salary of men; in 1965–66, 83.4 percent; in 1971–72, 82.5 percent; and in 1974–75 even lower."[52]

TABLE 9–3

Percent of Married Women (Husband Present), By Occupation, 1955–1977

Occupation	1955	1965	1970	1975	1977
Profession, technical and kindred workers	10.5	14.7	15.4	17.6	17.1
Farmers and farm managers	0.7	0.2	0.2	0.3	0.2
Managers and administrators	4.6	4.7	4.7	5.7	6.0
Clerical and kindred workers	25.4	30.2	33.6	35.0	35.5
Salesworkers	9.4	8.1	7.1	6.8	6.5
Craft and kindred workers	1.3	1.3	1.3	1.6	1.6
Operatives and kindred workers	21.8	17.5	16.3	12.5	12.9
Private household workers	6.3	5.1	3.5	2.2	1.9
Service workers, except private household	12.8	15.5	17.6	16.5	16.4
Others	7.2	2.8	0.3	1.7	1.8

Source: Adapted from U.S. Department of Commerce, Bureau of the Census, *Statistical Abstract of the U.S., 1978* (Washington, D.C.: U.S. Government Printing Office, 1978), p. 405.

There are other forces that affect the entrance into certain occupations as well as the earnings of women. Even when controlling for education and experience, often thought to account for income differences between the sexes, the differences in salaries continue. In fact, the salary differences may become even greater with increased education and experience on the part of women.[53] Furthermore, sex segregation on the job helps keep the women's wages down. When women compete only with other women, their wages are considerably lower than when they compete with men. "It appears that women earn less not only because they are in low-paying occupations, but they also earn less because they are in women's jobs."[54]

One of the social forces in the improvement of income for men in the United States has been through the labor movement. However, women have proportionately gained far less through unions than have men. While 28 percent of all male workers belong to unions, only 10 percent of all female workers do. Women are underrepresented in unions mainly because of their occupational distribution. Few women have ever been in the skilled crafts where unions started.[55] Over the years, with few exceptions, labor unions have never been strong or early advocates of job equality for women. "Most unions have upheld sex segregation, creating separate seniority rosters for men and women and ratifying different wage scales for the two sexes."[56]

Education is also related to women working. The more education women have the more likely they are to be in the work force. In March 1970, the rate for all wives who had 11 years or less of education was 34 percent. This compared with 44 percent of those who had completed high school and 47 percent of the wives with one year or more of college. The more education they bring to their jobs the higher the earnings. But when compared to men with the same education and type of job, they earn less.[57]

There have been a number of studies that look at women working and how this is related to marriage. Alan Booth found that the wife's employment had little effect on marital discord and feelings of stress by the husband. "If anything, husbands whose wives are employed enjoy a happier marriage and are under less stress than men who are married to housewives."[58] On the other hand, there is evidence that the husband's attitude about his wife working affects her feelings about her job. Paul J. Andresani found that the greatest conflict was when the woman's husband had an unfavorable attitude toward her working. This was even more upsetting for the woman than having young children or her own attitude toward the propriety of women working. "This is especially noteworthy since well over half of the women who worked perceived their husbands as being unfavorably disposed to their working outside the home."[59]

As suggested, the major concern with women working is the alleged effect on their children. The assumption has long been that for healthy and desirable development of the child and adolescent the mother should remain at home. For the woman to not do so is seen as "causing" all kinds of problems for the children. However, research does not support this assumption. Very few studies show any meaningful differences between children of working mothers in general and the children of nonworking mothers. Rossi writes that children of working mothers are no more likely than children of nonworking mothers to become delinquent, to show neurotic symptoms, to feel deprived of maternal affection, to perform poorly in school, to lead narrow social lives, and so on.[60]

Another study found that adolescents' perception of parental interest, parents' help with school and personal problems, and closeness to parents were largely unrelated to mothers' employment status. This serves as evidence against the belief that parents are more likely to reject their children or deny them emotional support because the mother is working. Margaret M. Poloma points out that while there is no evidence from existing research that working mothers as a group are better mothers than those who do not work, the data suggest that professionally employed women perceive their employment as making them better mothers than they otherwise would have been.[61] One article reports that after examining 24 studies, it was found that there were no differences between the children of mothers who work and mothers who do not work.[62]

Women have often been so well socialized to believe they should stay home and care for their children that, for many, going to work leads to feelings of guilt. Women who enjoy working may have to pay for their satisfactions. They may feel guilt by believing their satisfaction was bought at the expense of their children's welfare. Also, women who work have to deal with the amount of time they can give to their children. The working woman often finds that time is at a premium for her and she has to make decisions as to its allocation. As a result, a great deal of stress may be placed on the quality of the time spent with children rather than the quantity. Many working mothers devote their undivided individual attention to their children in the relatively short time they have with them.

Career women. We now look more directly at women who pursue occupations in the same way as most men, that is, as a potential life work that will be long range for them and to which they will have a commitment. In the past most American women have been interested in jobs and not in careers. This is the primary reason why the United States, with one of the highest proportions of working women in the world, ends up with a very small proportion of its women in such professions as medicine, law, and the sciences.

An absolute requirement for entering most careers is that the individual have the formal education necessary for qualification. Therefore, it is important to look at women in higher education and how they fare as compared to men. In general, in most families there continues to be a somewhat greater stress on the boy going to college than the girl. However, once girls enter college, their chances of staying in are the same, about four out of ten who enter. However, the reasons for dropping out are different. Boys are more apt to leave school because of academic problems or difficulties in their personal adjustment, while the most common reason for girls' dropping out is to get married.

Education is the major means for entrance into the high status and better paying occupations. As with men, women have also increasingly used education as a means of upward social mobility. But women still trail behind men in receiving degrees in higher education. In 1970, women received 41.5 percent of all bachelor's degrees, 39.7 percent of master's degrees and 13.3 percent of the doctor of philosophy degrees.[63]

What kind of occupations do women enter? Of all the women in the work force a large number of them fall into low-skilled clerical jobs. But the women who enter professional careers tend to go into teaching, nursing, social work, and related occupations. These are commonly seen by both men and women as occupations appropriate to the "special" qualities of women. However, the definition of what is appropriate work for men or women changes over time. For example, during the colonial period elementary school teaching was seen as a male occupation, supposedly because women did not have the necessary stamina of mind to educate the young. One rarely hears of an American woman dentist, but 75 percent of the dentists in Denmark are women and dentistry is considered to be a female occupation in some South American countries.

From a very early age most young girls are channeled toward certain occupations as possibilities for their futures. As they grow older women have traditionally been directed toward jobs "natural" to their femaleness. For example, jobs that call forth nurturant service or emotional behavior are most favored. Also positive values are placed on jobs that allow women to be neat and clean, to work in congenial surroundings and to do work during the daytime. Greer Litton Fox describes this as the "nice girl" construct. This value keeps women out of men's way. "By limiting women's power and degree of participation in the public world, by channeling women into certain jobs, by limiting the expression of female sexuality, and by providing a ready justification for punishment, the nice girl construct can be seen to facilitate the hegemony of men in a sex-stratified world."[64]

When we look at the kinds of jobs that women do we can clearly see their lower prestige relative to men. For example, 98 percent of "stenographers, typists and secretaries" are women. Eighty-nine percent of "waiters and waitresses" are women. By contrast, 4 percent of all craft workers are women. Women are in low-paid industries like knitting (65 percent) and apparel manufacturing (81 percent). Men are in high-wage manufacturing such as transport equipment (88 percent)

"No, I'm not a career girl. Are you a career boy?"

and machinery (84 percent). "Women sell clothing and notions whereas men sell cars and appliances on commission."[65]

Whether an occupation is subordinate or autonomous determines to what extent it will be sex-typed. A large proportion of female jobs are subordinate to male jobs—for example, nurse to doctor or secretary to executive. When male jobs are subordinate they are not usually subordinate to female labeled jobs. Jobs that are relatively autonomous (truck driver, salesman) are typically male. Women are less often self-employed than men even when both are doing the same work.[66]

Whatever the specific occupation it is clear that if women are given the chance to pursue satisfying careers they pursue them just as consistently as men. For example, the percentage of law degree holders who are in practice is similar among women and men, and figures for female and male doctors are also alike.

While women comprise over 40 percent of the entire labor force, they constitute only 8 percent of the nation's physicians, 4 percent of the lawyers, 5 percent of the physical scientists, and 12 percent of the social scientists. It is of interest that in a study of women in *Who's Who*, 31 percent of the physicians were women as were 45 percent of the eminent social scientists. This would suggest that women who compete successfully in "masculine" professions perform at exceptional levels of competency.[67]

Within any occupation women are not equally distributed across the hierarchy. In contrast to comprising about 75 percent of all federal workers in the four lowest employment brackets, only 3 percent of those employed in the four highest grades are women. Women are not evenly spread through the various federal agencies. Rather, they are concentrated in those agencies that perform social service functions. "Women comprised 58.0 percent of the employees of the Department of Health, Education and Welfare but only 17.6 percent in the Department of Transportation."[68]

The cultural definitions of the professions as linked to one sex or the other are often based on what are believed to be special characteristics of one sex. In illustration, many times women are thought to be good elementary school teachers because as females they are believed to have compassion, sympathy, and feeling for children that men do not have. Or as Cynthia F. Epstein points out, in the same way that it has been argued that blacks "have rhythm" and are therefore good jazz musicians, so women are said to have "intuition" and a gift for handling interpersonal relations and are therefore encouraged to become social workers. The image of women also includes some non-characteristics: "lack of aggression, lack of personal involvement and egotism, lack of persistence (unless it be for the benefit of a family member), and lack of ambitious drive."[69] The career woman who is seen as having many of the above characteristics often has been viewed as the antithesis of the feminine woman.

In some occupations consisting of a large proportion of women, men have replaced them in the positions of power and influence. For example, the decline in the percentage of female elementary school principals has been very great. In 1928, 55 percent of the principals were women; in 1948, 41 percent; in 1958, 38 percent; and in 1968 the figure was reported to have dropped to 22 percent.[70] The assumption seems to be that while the woman can be a teacher she is not qualified to be an administrator. In many occupations there appears to be a distinction made where women can be the professional field workers, whether it be teachers, social workers, or nurses, but when it comes to administration those positions should be filled by men.

There have been several studies trying to determine the role of the woman's occupation in her own social status. Nilson found that the husband's occupational status alone does not determine the social standing given to his wife. She found that people take the occupational attainments of both a husband and a wife into roughly equal account in assessing the wife's social standing.[71]

Another study suggests that the wife is no longer a mere extension of her husband. Often, outside the home, married spouses go their separate ways. It is not necessary for people to evaluate both spouses equally because often individuals don't make contact with both. "The family continues to provide the emotional support to partners, to act as an economic unit to some extent, and to pass on status benefits to children, but members of society may be evaluating adults as individuals rather than the family as a unit when status assignments occur."[72]

Predictions about the future and women's chances in the work force are not encouraging (see Chapter 3). In part, this is because of changes taking place in the social needs of the labor force. For example, in 1980 22 percent of the labor force was needed for manufacturing, but by the year 2000 only 2 percent of the population will be needed. There will be a severe shortage of these kinds of jobs. Some suggest the answer is better education to qualify for better jobs. But we now have 80 percent of all college graduates taking jobs previously filled by workers with lower educational credentials. "Between 1972 and 1985 over 22 million people with college degrees will compete for about 18 million openings for high status jobs."[73] In this buyers market the squeeze will be tighter on women than on men.

One common myth about employment is that women—far more than men—leave their jobs or take more time off. But the evidence indicates that women workers have favorable records of attendance and labor turnover when compared to men employed at the same job levels and under similar circumstances. A Public Health Service survey of time lost from work by persons 17 years of age and over because of illness or injury shows an average of 5.6 days lost by women and 5.3 days lost by men during the calendar year.

There have been some recent gains by women as related to pregnancy and work. In November 1975, the Supreme Court ruled that mandatory laying-off by the employer of women during the last three months of pregnancy and the first six weeks following childbirth is in violation of the Fourteenth Amendment.[74] But there are still many restrictions placed on the pregnant woman working and the woman often cannot control how much time she wants to take. This is usually decided for them by their employer.

Because the career woman, whether married or single, is filling a social role with a great amount of social confusion, she is often defined by others in a variety of ways. For example, many housewives see the career woman as a threat to themselves. "The career woman is often seen as a competitor for their husbands (the working woman, though deprecated, also seems more glamorous—and often is, because she usually takes care of her appearance and is more interesting). The career also provides an alternative model to the domestic life and may cause the housewife to question her own choice of life style."[75] If the career woman is married and is a mother and gives the appearance of being happy and satisfied with her life, she often becomes a severe threat to the woman who has rejected a career and is not very happy with her life.

Many men react to career women with confusion. If the woman is attractive, they cannot quite cope with her as a nonsexual being. Because so many men are geared to women primarily as sexual objects, they find it very difficult to see them as something more. It is probably also true that many American men are uneasy in the presence of highly intelligent women in a way which they would not be with very intelligent men. But most men probably react to career women as potential threats to themselves and in this sense their opposition is not ideologically based but rather based on vested interest.

Very often women who choose both marriage and career find their situation one where the norms are confused and unclear. There are no clear guidelines for them to apportion time and resources between the two major role responsibilities. The ability to handle the roles of wife, mother, and career person is still for the most part a matter of individual adaptation. So while fewer career women today are spinsters, among those who marry there is a high rate of divorce. "The proportion of divorced professional women is substantially higher than that of professional men."[76]

Often female business executives do not marry. In one study of women with successful careers in business half of them had not married. And even those who did marry had remained single until at least age 35. The marriage rates among female doctorates has been similiar. "Women who received doctorates in 1957–58 were studied several years later when many were in their 40s, and even by then only 55 percent had married."[77]

There is some evidence that marriage favors some career women. Married women surpass single women on some measures of professional achievement. For example, married women academics publish as much as their male colleagues and more than single academic women. However, a sizable minority of professional women avoid the conflict of family and professional roles by not marrying. There is also a relatively high divorce rate among professional women. And some professional women do marry but minimize family obligations by remaining childfree. However, the majority of professional women do marry and the majority of those who do marry also have children.[78]

In conclusion, historically women have been seen as a social problem when they went against their "natural" destiny and refused to be totally devoted wives and mothers. It was in their failure to be full-time mothers that they were seen as a severe problem. However, these attitudes have greatly changed and while women's past "failures" are still seen as social problems this is not so strong as a few years ago. There has come to be a new focus on women as a social problem. For many, the problem is the inability and lack of opportunity for women to have equal opportunities with men. The new focus on women as a social problem is on sexism in America.

There has emerged in recent years a much greater conscious attempt to bring about changes for greater equality of American women.

This chapter looked at the changing meanings and significance of the traditional roles of wife, mother, and housekeeper. An examination was made of the different socialization of girls and boys and levels of difference that exist between the sexes. While women have greatly increased their number in the work force in recent years, the kinds of jobs they get continue to be limited, as does their share of the economic rewards.

NOTES

1. Betty Friedan, *The Feminine Mystique* (New York: W. W. Norton, 1963), p. 86.
2. Anshen Sinclair, *The Emancipation of the American Woman* (New York: Harper and Brothers, 1965), p. 37.
3. Joan Huber, "Toward a Sociotechnological Theory of the Women's Movement," *Social Problems* (April 1976), p. 378.
4. Jerold M. Starr, "The Peace and Love Generation: Changing Attitudes toward Sex and Violence among College Youth," *Journal of Social Issues* 30 (1974), p. 30.
5. *The New York Post* (May 14, 1975), p. 35.
6. Cynthia Fuchs Epstein, "Sex Roles," in *Contemporary Social Problems*, 4th ed., by Robert K. Merton and Robert Nisbet (New York: Harcourt, Brace Jovanovich, 1976), p. 450.
7. Riane Tennenhaus Eisler, *Dissolution* (New York: McGraw-Hill, 1977), p. 75.
8. Nona Glazer-Malbin, "The Captive Couple: The Burglar of Gender Roles in Marriage," in *Understanding Social Problems*, by Don H. Zimmerman et al. (New York: Praeger Publishers, 1976), p. 276.
9. Constantina Safilios-Rothschild, *Toward a Sociology of Women* (Livingston, Mass.: Xeros College Publishing, 1972), p. 2.
10. Glazer-Malbin, "Captive Couple," pp. 274–75.
11. Anne Statham Macke, George W. Bohrmstedt, and Ilene N. Bernstein, "Housewives' Self-Esteem and Their Husbands' Success: The Myth of Vicarious Involvement," *Journal of Marriage and the Family* (February 1979), p. 16.
12. Ibid., p. 56.
13. Eisler, *Dissolution*, p. 78.
14. Ronald J. Burke and Tamara Weir, "Some Personality Differences between Members of One-Career and Two-Career Families," *Journal of Marriage and the Family* (August 1976), p. 280.
15. Ibid., p. 285.
16. Huber, "Women's Movement," p. 374.
17. Alice S. Rossi, "A Biosocial Perspective in Parenting," in *The Family*, by Alice S. Rossi, Jerome Kagan, and Tamara K. Hareven (New York: W. W. Norton, 1977), pp. 5–6.
18. Alice S. Rossi, "Equality between The Sexes: An Immodest Proposal," *Daedalus* (Spring 1964), p. 615.
19. Huber, "Women's Movement," p. 377.
20. Catherine White Berheide, Sarah Fenstermaker Berk, and Richard A. Berk, "Household Work in the Suburbs: The Job and Its Participant," *Pacific Sociological Review* (October 1976), p. 505.
21. Ibid., p. 510.
22. Ibid., p. 504.
23. Myra Marx Ferree, "Working-Class Jobs: Housework and Paid Work as Sources of Satisfaction," *Social Problems* (February 1976), p. 433.

24. Ibid., p. 436.

25. Joan Acker, "Women and Social Stratification: A Case of Intellectual Sexism," in *Changing Women In a Changing Society,* by Joan Huber (Chicago: University of Chicago Press, 1973), p. 180.

26. Linda Burzotta Nilson, "The Social Standing of the Housewife," *Journal of Marriage and the Family* (August 1978), p. 546.

27. Ibid., p. 547.

28. Mirra Komarovsky, *Blue-Collar Marriage* (New York: Random House, 1962), p. 155.

29. Ibid., p. 55.

30. Ferree, "Housework," pp. 434–35.

31. Constantina Safilios-Rothschild, *Love, Sex and Sex Roles* (Englewood Cliffs, N.J.: Prentice-Hall, 1977), pp. 2–3.

32. Greer Litton Fox, " 'Nice Girl': Social Control of Women through a Value Construct," *Signs* (Summer 1977), p. 809.

33. Donna Eder and Maureen T. Hallinan, "Sex Differences in Children's Friendships," *American Sociological Review* (April 1978), p. 247.

34. Ibid., p. 283.

35. Sharon L. Sutherland, "The Unambitious Female: Women's Law Professional Aspiration," *Signs* (Summer 1978), p. 791.

36. Ibid., p. 785.

37. Friedan, *Mystique,* pp. 15–18.

38. Ferdinand Lundberg and Marynia Farnham, "Women: The Last Sex," in *The Family and The Sexual Revolution,* by Edwin Schurr (Bloomington: Indiana University Press, 1964), p. 230.

39. Rossi, "Equality between The Sexes: An Immodest Proposal," p. 613.

40. Frieda Shoenberg Rozen, "Women in the Workforce: The Introduction for Myth and Reality," in *The Study of Women,* by Eloise C. Snyder (New York: Harper & Row, 1979), p. 80.

41. Glazer-Malbin, "Captive Couple," p. 275.

42. Ruth A. Brandwein, Carol A. Brown, and Elizabeth M. Fox, "The Social Situation of Divorced Mothers and Their Families," in *Women in a Man-Made World,* 2d ed., by Nona Glazer and Helen Youngelson Waehrer (Chicago: Rand McNally, 1977), p. 352.

43. Rozen, "Women in the Workforce," pp. 80–81.

44. Jessie Bernard, *The Future of Motherhood* (New York: Penguin Books, 1974), p. 150.

45. Ibid., pp. 193–94.

46. Elizabeth M. Almquist, "Women in the Labor Force," *Signs* (Summer 1977), pp. 844–45.

47. Women's Bureau, *1969 Handbook of Women Workers,* 204 (Washington, D.C.: U.S. Department of Labor, 1969), p. 49.

48. Rozen, "Women in the Workforce," p. 86.

49. Glazer and Waehrer, *Man-Made World,* pp. 303–4.

50. Rozen, "Women in the Workforce," p. 87.

51. Laurel Richardson Walum, *The Dynamics of Sex and Gender: A Sociological Perspective* (Chicago: Rand McNally & Co., 1976), p. 150.

52. Marion Kilson, "The Status of Women in Higher Education," *Signs* (Summer 1976), p. 937.

53. Patricia A. Yopopenic, Linda Brookover Bourques, and Donna Brogen, "Professional Communication Networks: A Case Study of Women in the American Public Health Service," *Social Problems* (April 1975), p. 495.

54. Gail L. Zellman, "The Role of Structural Factors in Limiting Women's Institutional Participation," *Journal of Social Issues* (Summer 1976), p. 37.

55. Rozen, "Women in the Workforce," p. 91.

56. Epstein, "Sex Roles," p. 429.

57. Elizabeth Waldman and Anne M. Young, "Marital and Family Characteristics of Workers, 1970," *Monthly Labor Review* (March 1971), p. 46.

58. Alan Booth, "Wife's Employment and Husband's Stress: A Replication of Refutation," *Journal of Marriage and the Family* (November 1971), p. 649.

59. Paul J. Andresani, "Job Satisfaction among Working Women," *Signs* (Spring 1978), p. 606.

60. Rossi, "A Biosocial Perspective in Parenting," p. 56.

61. Margaret M. Poloma, "Role Conflict and the Married Professional Woman," in Safilios-Rothschild, *Sociology,* p. 191.

62. Thomas C. Tavleggia and Ellen M. Thomas, "Latchkey Children," *Pacific Sociological Review* (January 1974), p. 31.

63. Kilson, "Status of Women," p. 938.

64. Fox, "Nice Girl," p. 817.

65. Rozen, "Women in the Workforce," p. 84.

66. Epstein, "Sex Roles," p. 424.

67. Louise M. Bachtold, "Women, Eminences and Career-Value Relationships," *Journal of Social Psychology* (April 1975), p. 191.

68. Lee Sigelman, "The Curious Care of Women in State and Local Government," *Social Science Quarterly* (March 1976), p. 591.

69. Cynthia F. Epstein, *Woman's Place* (Berkeley: University of California Press, 1970), p. 22.

70. Ibid., p. 10.

71. Nilson, "Social Standing," pp. 589–90.

72. Dana V. Hiller and William W. Philliber, "The Derivation of Status Benefits from Occupational Attainments of Working Wives," *American Sociological Review* (February 1978), p. 68.

73. Eisler, *Dissolution,* p. 97.

74. Rossi, "Perspective," p. 21.

75. Epstein, "Sex Roles," p. 120.

76. Ibid., p. 98.

77. Marilyn Peddicord Whitley and Susan P. Paulson, "Assertiveness and Sexual Satisfaction in Employed Professional Women," *Journal of Marriage and the Family* (August 1975), p. 574.

78. Kay Richards Broschart, "Family Status and Professional Achievement: A Study of Women Doctorates," *Journal of Marriage and the Family* (February 1978), p. 72.

SELECTED BIBLIOGRAPHY

Almquist, Elizabeth M. "Women in the Labor Force." *Signs* (Summer 1977), pp. 843–55.

Andrisana, Paul J. "Job Satisfaction among Working Women." *Signs* (Spring 1978), pp. 588–607.

Berheide, Catherine White; Berk, Sarah Fenstermaker; and Berk, Richard A. "Household Work in the Suburbs: The Job and Its Participants." *Pacific Sociological Review* (October 1976), pp. 491–518.

Burke, Ronald J., and Weir, Tamara. "Some Personality Differences Between Members of One-Career and Two-Career Families." *Journal of Marriage and the Family* (August 1976), pp. 279–87.

Ferree, Myra Marx. "Working Class Jobs: Housework and Paid Work as Sources of Satisfaction." *Social Problems* (February 1976), pp. 431–41.

Friedan, Betty. *The Feminine Mystique.* New York: W. W. Norton, 1963.

Huber, Joan. "Toward a Sociotechnological Theory of the Women's Movement." *Social Problems* (April 1976), pp. 371–87.

Oakley, Ann. *The Sociology of Housework*. New York: Pantheon Books, 1974.

Macke, Anne Statham; Bohrnstedt, George W.; and Bernstein, Ilene N. "Housewives' Self-Esteem and Their Husbands' Success; The Myth of Vicarious Involvement." *Journal of Marriage and the Family* (February 1979), pp. 51–57.

Nilson, Linda Burzotta. "The Social Standing of the Housewife." *Journal of Marriage and the Family* (August 1978), pp. 541–48.

Chapter 10

The Elderly

In the 1960s and 1970s old age was "discovered" as a social problem. At one time the elderly were respected and had significant influence within American society. But for many years, and up until recently, they were generally ignored. For example, there was very little interest in the biological and social sciences in understanding the implications of aging either for the individual or for society. The basic social problem with regard to the elderly is what their place in society should be. In what way are they able to be fully functioning citizens?

To the extent that aging means an eventual loss of health and often social skills, it is an inevitable problem and one everyone must ultimately deal with if they live long enough. While many kinds of losses are inevitable, societies can vary in their contributions to how individuals deal with them. In general, the present cultural values in the United States do not contribute a great deal to a relatively easy adjustment to aging. Our interest in this chapter is to look at how and why aging is a social problem in contemporary American society.

There are problems in defining who are elderly and when old age starts. Old age has started at various times during different historical periods as well as in different societies. Unlike the transitions into young adult status that have been recognized in many societies there is rarely a ritual ceremony for the entrance into old age. It may also be noted that in most societies, including the United States, there are few legal distinctions made in the rights of people during their adult years. Throughout life the adult retains the same political rights, and civil law makes no distinctions between the rights of a person aged 40 or one of 70. From the perspective of legal definitions the aged are not looked upon as a class apart from other adults. The concept of "old" has a number of dimensions. It can refer to psychological and sociological factors as well as the physical changes in the body and related health problems. Therefore, a person may be old in some ways but not in others. These kinds of discrepancies can lead to problems for the aging individual who does not define himself as old but is required to interact within a social structure which often sees him as a dependent, nonproductive member of society. Often there is a struggle, with society defining the individual as elderly and the individual not willing to accept the definition.

Generally, old age is a real ordeal for both men and women. Susan Sontag writes that growing older is mainly an ordeal of the imagination. It is, as she sees it, a social pathology that afflicts women more than men. Often women experience growing older with a great deal of distaste and even shame. "This equating of well-being with youth makes everyone naggingly aware of exact age—one's own and that of other people. Most people in nonindustrial societies are not sure how old they are. People in industrial societies are haunted by numbers. They take an almost obsessional interest in keeping score cards of aging, convinced that anything above a low total is some kind of bad news."[1]

In physical change the most obvious indication of aging is the appearance of the skin, which tends to dry out and to wrinkle. And as the person ages the tendons, the skin, and the connective tissues lose their elasticity. There may also be a hardening of blood vessels and stiffening of joints. Many of the health problems that are faced by the elderly are due to a general decline in the circulatory system. The person's capacity for sight and hearing are often reduced and the brain begins to shrink. The heart, lungs, kidney, and bladder begin to operate at reduced levels of efficiency.

The process of biological aging does not vary in any important way for males and females insofar as any different patterns of sex hormone change. It is the reactions to aging, by sex, that do vary. These reactions are closely related to the varying role obligations of the sexes and to cultural values. "The decline in energy and strength is a greater source of conflict for the male. The decline in physical attractiveness that accompanies aging is, or at least has been, a greater source of conflict for females in our society."[2]

The defining of aging is further confused because it often has different meanings and implications for men and women. Very often aging has an earlier impact on women. Inge Powell Bell argues that women must endure the specter of aging much sooner than men because the cultural definition of aging gives men a decided psychological, sexual, and economic advantage over women. "The multimillion dollar cosmetics advertising industry is dedicated to creating a fear of aging in women." She goes on to point out that a man's wrinkles do not define him as sexually undesirable until possibly his late 50s. "For him sexual value is defined much more in terms of personality, intelligence, and earning power than physical appearance."[3]

The fear of aging among many women has a real basis in the fact that society deprives them of many rights when they are defined as old. As a result many women often distort their age, hoping to delay society's categorical stigma. Even professional women, who presumably have roles which should not be threatened through middle age, are much more likely than men to feel their advancing age is a serious impairment to them. Bell points out that in the listings of the Directory of the American Psychological Association, "women are ten times as likely to omit their age as men."[4]

While aging usually implies physical changes, how people see themselves as well as their social changes greatly influence their view of aging. One difficulty is that old age is the only stage in the life cycle that shows systematic social losses rather than gains. This is because the major adult tasks and roles are finished and so their responsibility for self and others decreases and their dependency on others may increase. Irving Rosow points out there is severe alienation from major adult roles because of widowhood and retirement. This is reflected in a loss of rewards because of a decline in income and an increase in illness and physical handicaps.[5]

The influence of youth values affects everyone in the aging process. Certainly both men and women are prone to periods of depression about aging. But men appear to panic less about aging than do women. There is a double standard about aging that denounces women with special severity; society is much more permissive about aging in men. Men are "allowed" to age in ways women are not, and often they receive positive supports and status related to aging. Sontag argues that for most women aging means a humiliating process of gradual sexual disqualification. This is because women are considered maximally eligible in early youth and after that their sexual value steadily decreases. They are old as soon as they are no longer very young. But what makes men desirable to women is generally not tied to youth. "On the contrary, getting older tends (for several decades) to operate in man's favor, since their value as lovers and husbands is set more by what they do than how they look."[6]

There are also differences by social class among women and their reaction to aging. Anxiety appears to be more common and more acute among middle-class and wealthy women than among working-class women. The economically disadvantaged women are more fatalistic about aging and cannot afford to fight the long cosmetic battle. So aging is more a social judgment than a biological eventuality. "Far more extensive than the hard sense of loss suffered during menopause is the depression about aging, which may not be set off by any real event in a woman's life, but is a recurrent state of 'possession' of her imagination, ordained by society—that is, ordained by the way this society limits how women feel free to imagine themselves."[7]

Women generally see little reason to look forward to old age. While some may look forward to the new role of grandmother they generally do not see that as a role of an old person. Simone de Beauvoir, in her study of aging, observes she has never come across one single woman, either in real life or in books, who had looked forward to her own old age cheerfully. "In the same way no one ever speaks of a 'beautiful old woman'; the most one might say would be a 'charming old lady.' "[8]

For many people, as they get old their lives are destined to be lonely. This loneliness can take a variety of forms. The loneliness can come from living in "aged" communities, from retirement, or from the loss of friends and/or spouse. It is basically an inevitable result of a society that teaches its members from childhood on that old people are, for the most part, irritable, worthless, and strange. "It is no wonder that the young treat the old with such callousness and that the old regard the young with suspicion and anger. Nor is it astonishing that the old regard each other as senile, troublesome, and useless."[9]

One study found that for women to live in rural areas and to be widowed posed a double jeopardy to the quality of life in their later years. Three out of four older rural widows experienced varying degrees of loneliness, for which there was no single cause. Even frequent interaction with children, peers, and others did not necessarily correlate with decreased loneliness. Often, if the rural widows perceived their health as poor and felt tied down because of transportation difficulties they showed the greatest risks for loneliness.[10]

The view of general society is often that the elderly are somehow vaguely defined and should not force themselves on society as a clearly defined group seeking special recognition and dispensations. The very fact of using such words as *elderly*, *old*, and *the aged* is often seen as being insensitive and unfair. In their place many would have our society use such euphemisms as "senior citizen" and "golden years." All this really shows is that the truth of old age is to be camouflaged by the use of synonyms that fool no one.

In general, the American public views growing old as a negative experience. For example, 69 percent of the general population believe that the best decade of one's life to be during the 30s or younger while 83 percent say it is in the 40s or younger.[11] However, older people often view themselves in a more positive way than do the general public. For example, while only 31 percent of old people report that they spend a lot of time "sitting and thinking," there are 62 percent of the public who believe this to be common behavior of most people over 65. Less than 10 percent of the old people say "not enough to do" is a very serious problem for them, yet nearly 40 percent of the public offered that view of the old.[12]

Joseph Kovacs/Stock, Boston, Inc.

Old age can be a very lonely time

This social attempt sometimes to try and pretend that old age does not really exist has other consequences. It means that we do not know a great deal about the social and psychological factors of being old. When compared to old age, we know far more about the subculture of youth. It may be that many do not want to admit to a subculture of the aged, with its implications of segregation and alienation. In some respects, the aged have much in common with youth. Both groups have high unemployment, their bodies and personalities are undergoing change, and they are both heavy users of drugs. Both groups are very much concerned with time. But while youth figures time from birth, the elderly figure back from an estimated time of death.

Given the social values against recognizing the elderly it is understandable that defining old age is difficult. Certainly one cannot talk about old age as something that arrives on a given birthday. Rather the entrance into old age is through a transition stage and this is usually during the 60s. Before age 60 very few people would be defined as elderly, and once they enter their 70s very few would not be defined as elderly. It is during the 60s that the significant changes in life patterns and styles usually associated with old age take place. The usual age for computing old age in the official records is that of 65. In 1870 about 3 percent of the American population was 65 years and over. In 1900 it was 4.1 percent and in 1970 was 9.8 percent. It is estimated that by 2025 about 17 percent of the population will be 65 years and over.[13]

There is a common misconception that people are now living much longer than they did in the past. This confusion appears to come about because an infant born in 1900 could at that time expect only to live to be about 50 years of age, but an infant born in 1975 could expect to live about 70 years. However, this difference is almost entirely due to a sharp reduction in infant mortality. In 1900 many infants and young children died, lessening the average life expectancy for all their peers. But a more meaningful comparison is the life expectancy that persons at age 65 still have ahead of them. Today, the average life expectancy for a man 65 years of age is 14 more years. In 1900 the 65-year-old man had 13 years of life expectancy ahead of him. Although we have prolonged life in general, creating a large group of the aged, we have not prolonged the life of the aged.

Today in the United States, on each day, about 5,000 people turn 65 while about 3,600 who are 65 and older die. The result is a net increase in the 65 plus population of about 1,400 persons each day or about 500,000 each year. In general, the new older Americans are healthier, more vigorous and active, and better educated than their predecessors. A person who reaches age 65 in fairly good health has a fair chance of living another 15 years—13 years for men and 18 for women.[14]

Life expectancy has had different implications for men and women. Over the years women have continued to outlive men at increasing rates. Around 1940 the life expectancy for women was 4.3 years more than for men, but by 1973 this had increased to 7.4 years. In the United States life expectancy at birth is 74.0 years for females and 66.6 years for males. By age 65, the difference in life expectancy decreases to 3.5 years. The sex ratio also changed over the years. In 1900, among people 65 and over, there were 102 males for every 100 females. By 1966 the ratio in that age group had dropped to 76.6 men for every 100 women. But among people 75 and older the ratio of women is even greater—100 women for every 73 men. By 1985, in the group beyond 75, the ratio is stronger in the United States than in most other countries. This may be because mortality of men reflects the different burdens of the roles men and women are expected to perform in American society. For example, American men have high rates of heart attacks that are clearly related to the demands and tensions of the economic system.[15]

There has been some expansion in the range of old age. For ex-

TABLE 10–1

Years of Life Expected at Birth, By Year of Birth and Sex

Year of birth	Male	Female
1900	46.3	48.3
1920	53.6	54.6
1940	60.8	65.2
1960	66.6	73.1
1970	67.1	74.7
1977	69.3	77.1

Source: "U.S. Department of Health, Education, and Welfare," *The World Almanac* (New York: Newspaper Enterprises, 1980).

ample, almost 9 million Americans have passed their 75th birthday; this is compared to less than 1 million at the turn of the century.[16] There are over 1 million Americans 85 years and older. It is also estimated there are about 13,000 Americans past the age of 100. It is further estimated that the number of people over 80 will nearly double over the next 20 years. Often these people become a special problem because they have the lowest incomes and require the most medical and nursing care.

What are some of the options to the elderly in how they live their lives? We first examine the importance of kinship for the elderly person. In the past, in many societies including our own, the extended family has been responsible for the care of the aged. Very often the elderly maintained control of the family until their death so they were never really dependent on their children. An examination of some of the early families to settle in New England shows that the father often maintained control over his sons until they were well into middle age and he was well into old age. That was part of a patriarchal system that not only gave authority to the male but even more to the older male. However this has greatly changed and the extended family has been greatly altered, while at the same time the high value and authority accorded the elderly has been greatly reduced.

At the present time the importance of kinship is greatly confused. Our society has set up other institutions to care for the aged. These usually have been under the institution of government: for example, Social Security and Medicare. Often the elderly turn to their kin to look after them in a social and psychological sense, if not in an actual physical way. Kinship carries with it special demands. When the ties of kinship are the strongest they are based on positive concern, which is a function of its permanence, love, and obligation. Implied is a sense of duty and very often there is no guarantee of positive rewards or satisfactions for the kin.

It should be stressed that most old people do live in families, either as a married couple or as relatives of the family head. Because there are more widowed women, living alone or living with someone other than the spouse is more usual among women than among men. "Thirty-one percent of aged women and 16 percent of aged men report that they live with someone other than a spouse; this usually means they live with adult children." [17]

Helena Znaniecki Lopata, in her studies of widows in Chicago, did not find among them exchanges of support from any relatives other than children. She found that relatives contributed very little to the emotional support systems of the widows. This meant that the widow, by choice or force of circumstances, was a relatively independent woman. For the widow, there was an almost total absence of male relatives, "including father and brother, in the emotional support system." [18]

Not only is there a greater closeness between parents and their adult children but this closeness tends most often to be with the daughter. Almost all studies show that women are more involved in kin affairs of all types than are men. Yet, in spite of the stronger linkage in the kinship interaction of women, more older men than women actually live in families. This is because women tend to live longer than men, there are more nonmarried women (including widows) than single men, and mobile older women probably are more self-sufficient than older men.

There have been significant changes in the United States in dependency by age. In 1900, for every 100 persons of working age there were a total of 94 dependents. Of those, 86 were young dependents and 8 were old. By 1970, for every 100 working persons there were 91 dependents of whom 72 were youth and 19 aged. If there is zero population growth by 2025 the dependency ratio could drop to 77, of whom 30 (about 40 percent) would be aged dependents. "From a society oriented to supporting children and the young, the United States would then have to shift emphasis to the support of the old." [19]

As parents get older and turn to their adult children, this often implies for all parties an important role reversal. During their previous adult years the parent had been responsible for their children and now their children have become responsible for them. Older persons, because of different levels of ability, find themselves in different relationships with their children. But ultimately the older persons gave much less than they received when in a dependent status with their adult children.

The number of older people who live with their children in the United States is quite high. One third of all people who have living children do live with them. Such joint households are usually two generational, though, not three-generational households, with children in them. Usually the middle-aged couple have one of their parents move in with them after the grandchildren have left home. This kind of family is different from the common model because it is made up of elderly and middle-aged adults. There has been very little research into this kind of family—its structure and needs.

Moving in with children usually happens when there are limited options. It is often action taken only when there is not enough money to live alone or where health is so poor that self-care is impossible and, to a lesser extent, when the elderly person is widowed. In general, this is not a solution older people take if there are any other possible options.

Even when the elderly do not move in with their children they will often move so as to live close to them. There are a number of studies that show that the great majority of older Americans who have children live within one half hour's driving distance of at least one child. Moreover, they see one another quite frequently. One nationwide sample found that 65 percent of the elderly had seen at least one child in the 24-hour period prior to the interview.[20]

When the elderly have frequent contact with their children there can be problems. Studies indicate that often the relations between young adults and their parents are characterized by frequent contact, affection, and an obligation to help out in time of need. It is when obligation to help becomes the dominant element in the relationship that trouble frequently enters. If actual aid enters the relationship it can weaken the affectionate and enjoyable aspects of it. It is quite possible that the shifting of the help patterns from the older to the younger creates the basis for problems because it is something neither is used to.

Another study of older parents not living with a child found that 52 percent had seen a child within the past 24 hours and 78 percent had seen one within the last week.[21] Adult children who live near their parents often provide a number of patterns of help. They are the primary source of care for immobilizing illnesses. However, when children are not available there are a variety of acceptable substitutes. These may include relatives, neighbors, and friends. But this flexibility for help does not apply to older people getting financial aid. This kind of help is limited to adult children or to various organizations. Neighbors and friends are unconditionally excluded from financial assistance.[22]

Problems between the elderly and their children can be related to other factors. Because they are of different ages their interests may vary. The things one age group holds to be important may not be important to the other. For example, they may often have sharp differences in religious values, political beliefs, and so forth. This means that these topics can be a source of conflict if they see much of each other. To minimize conflict they may avoid discussion of those topics. When this happens the two generations are often thrown back on their family ties, and the demands placed on those ties strain them or cause them not to be satisfying to all concerned. The important point is that for many possible reasons the relationships between the elderly and their adult children may not be satisfactory and often lead to problems that the emotional bond cannot overcome.

While the discussion has been about the elderly turning to their children, this is not an option available to all older persons. For example, 8 percent of all persons over age 65 have never been married. Furthermore, not all the married persons who ever had children have surviving children. Of the noninstitutionalized population over 65 about 25 percent do not have any children.[23] While some of these persons may have siblings to turn to, many older persons may in effect have no kinship structure. Certainly as the extended family of cousins and aunts and uncles continues to shrink, it means fewer kinship relationships available to persons at all ages.

The stress has been on the need of many older people to have involvements with their children. But at the same time there is, for most elderly people, a strong need to maintain independence. There is a fear among many people as they get older that they will have to be dependent on others. As a result there is a great concern with retirement plans that provide independence. Today many people as they get older are inclined to use their money rather than simply to accumulate it. One aspect of this is the smaller interest today in the idea of "building up an inheritance" for children. More and more the older people are coming to believe they have the right to spend their own money on their own needs.

Most older persons who are living as heads of households are living alone. And the great majority of older primary individuals are women. This is true for three reasons. First, there are more widows than widowers because of different life expectancies. Second, because women tend to marry men older than themselves they increase their chances of being survivors. Third, the rates of remarriage are greater for males then females. Therefore, many older women are required to adapt to a drastically new way of life—living alone.

The research also shows that as people get older they change their residence much less. James E. Montgomery has suggested that the anchoring variables "include limited income, declining health, a strong sense of place, and an unwillingness to face adjustment problems occasioned by moving." This often implies the elderly will have less contact with their adult children, who are subject to far more movement. The younger generation increasingly enter occupations that insist on moving them a great deal. And a difference exists in the symbolic importance of the home. For many in the older generation

TABLE 10–2

Percent of Persons Living Alone, By Marital Status, Age, and Sex, 1978

	Male	*Female*
Total Living Alone	100.00	100.00
Marital status		
Married, spouse absent	14.5	5.9
Widowed	17.2	57.3
Divorced	23.7	14.4
Single	44.7	22.5
Age		
Under 25 years	13.7	7.2
25–34 years	26.4	9.9
35–44 years	13.0	4.4
45–64 years	24.3	26.9
65 years and older	22.7	51.7

Source: Adapted from U.S. Department of Commerce, Bureau of the Census, "Marital Status and Living Arrangements: March 1978," *Population Characteristics*, Series P–20, no. 338 (Washington, D.C.: U.S. Government Printing Office, May 1979), p. 5.

the home has been "the old homestead" in the sense that they have lived there for many years, reared their children there, and have a strong emotional identification with it. Therefore to leave is to tear out important roots of the past. This is not only true for the home but also the neighborhood and community. But the younger generation, often moving every few years, rarely develops these emotional bonds to any house.[24]

Homes are also important to the elderly because often as they get older they are more and more dependent on them. Older people leave their houses less. It has been estimated that persons over 65 spend 80 to 90 percent of their lives in their homes. In society, only small children, the chronically ill, and those institutionalized for law violations are so restricted to house and neighborhood. Other studies indicate that with increasing age the life space used continues to diminish. If people become old and enfeebled or ill, their life space becomes reduced to an apartment, to a room, and ultimately to a bed with four restraining walls.[25]

There has been a trend in recent years for many older people to give up their homes and move to new locations after their children have grown up. Many of them move to retirement areas in such states as Arizona, California, and Florida. This raises problems for many because they may move many miles from their adult children and other relatives. Yet, one study found that postretirement migration did not lead to greater family isolation for the aged than if they had remained in their home communities. Gordon L. Bultena and Douglas G. Marshall point out, "Many of the migrants who presently see their children only infrequently were unlikely to have much greater contact with them had they retired instead in their homes." What frequently happens is that personal interaction between the aged and their children is increasingly tied to holiday and vacation periods. They found that "older persons who retire to Florida and Arizona typically find this as convenient a locale for receiving or initiating family visits as was their previous residence in the Midwest."[26]

Studies indicate that most older persons do not wish to live in retirement communities, many cannot afford to do so, and the health of many will not permit it. "But the leisure-oriented who possess the health, the money, and the desire seem to find these communities highly satisfactory."[27] The community setting provides expanded opportunities for friendships. The proportion of friendships among the elderly appears to be related to the number of peers who live nearby.

A retirement community in Florida

As previously suggested, the values of the elderly are often more rigid than for younger persons, and, therefore, they can, in the community of peers, find persons who share their values. The retirement communities provide some protection against social change and the threat of conflicting values and beliefs. One effect of this is to even further isolate the elderly.

At age 65 and over about 5 percent of the population are institutionalized. However, a majority of people who enter nursing homes do so following a period of time in the hospital and many eventually return to their homes. Simply being old sharply increases the probability of institutionalization. While the elderly constitute 10 percent of the general population they make up 45 percent of the total institutionalized population.[28]

Being institutionalized is usually linked to health problems (see Chapter 15). In a study of 92 institutions for the aged about 50 percent of all staff are classified as being in medical occupations. Even the personal care services that make up the bulk of the treatment provided by the institutions for the aged are cloaked in the medical symbol of the practical nurse.[29] It has been found that the mortality rate during the first year after institutionalization is significantly higher than the rate of those who stay in their accustomed surroundings. "Separation from home contributes to the appearance and mortality of many a severe disease."[30]

Social relationships are important to us at all ages. As people become older they find their social relationships altered and often ended through death. The loss of consistent and satisfying relationships can have harmful effects on the individual. One study of older people found that low social interaction is strongly related to depression. Marjorie Fiske Lowenthal found that the majority of those who lost a confidant were depressed and gaining a new one did not help much. This suggests the importance of the stability of relationships.[31]

One striking factor is the impact of the loss of a confidant as against never having had one. It has been found that life-long loners tended to have average or better morale and to be no more prone to mental illness in old age than anyone else. But those who have tried and failed to establish social relationships are especially vulnerable to hospitalization for mental illness. Persons who have had close relationships but voluntarily reduced their social activity are often the healthiest and happiest. What appears to be important is that reduction of interaction was the choice of the individual. A study in Great Britain, Denmark, and the United States found it is not an absolute degree of isolation that leads to feelings of loneliness in old age, "but rather becoming socially isolated relative to a prior degree of social engagement."[32]

The need of the individual for significant others is very strong in

FIGURE 10–1

Distribution of Elderly Population

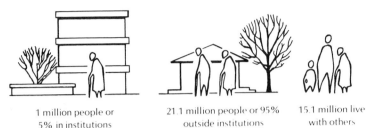

1 million people or 5% in institutions	21.1 million people or 95% outside institutions	15.1 million live with others	6 million live alone

Source: U.S. Department of Health, Education and Welfare Public Health Service *Health Highlights 1976–1977.* (Washington, D.C.: U.S. Government Printing Office, 1978), p. 13.

old age. This is increasingly so as the presence of kin, especially spouses for widows, decreases and other persons become important. There have been a number of studies that show the importance of friends as confidants, as significant others, and as contributing to the older person's general happiness and satisfaction with life.

There are differences in how women and men are able to cope with the loss of a confidant. First, women are more likely to have a confidant than are men. The Lowenthal study shows this to be especially true for those under 65 where nearly three fourths of the women but only half the men reported that they had a confidant. Among those elderly people who were still married the men were more likely to name their wives as confidant than were women to name their husbands. Women were about twice as likely as men to mention a child or another relative, and more likely to name friends.[33] Men have traditionally learned that if they must reveal very much about themselves the appropriate confidant is their wife. Self-revealing to others is often not seen as appropriate masculine behavior. Therefore men have fewer options of people to reveal to and if they no longer have a wife it may be especially hard for them to develop a confidant relationship.

Old persons find themselves increasingly in what Zena Smith Blau refers to as major role exits; that is, exiting from their major roles of work and marriage. This is the time in life when friends would be very valuable to help compensate for the demoralizing effects of major role exit. But it is at this time in life that friendship opportunities are fewer than ever before. Over the life cycle, friendships are often of minor significance in adulthood compared to work and marriage. But they could be an effective substitution for the loss of those roles. A single intimate friendship can be an effective "buffer" against demoralization from the three major kinds of social losses that beset older people: loss of a spouse, retirement, and diminished social participation. "Indeed, the morale of people who are more isolated in old age, but who have one intimate friendship, is as high as that of people with increased social participation. One intimate friendship is as effective as several less intimate ones for safeguarding morale after the role exit."[34]

Retirement

There is conflict in American society about defining old age and what should be done about it. There are really no legal definitions that specifically deal with old age. This means that definitions of old age are only indirectly based on other kinds of definitions. This is often the case of attributing legally far more meaning to ages of retirement than are there in actuality. For example, forced retirement from a place of work is a decision by the employer and has no legal basis of its own.

The occupational role is usually the most important adult role filled by the male. Therefore, when he leaves that role it will usually indicate a sense of loss and the need for adaptive behavior. In part this can be understood in that there are strong similarities between retirement and unemployment. The implications of retirement for the wife will be discussed shortly. Among men, the one who has the greatest trouble adjusting to retirement is the one who identifies himself most closely with the bread-winning role.

In many societies the accumulated experience of the older worker was valued, but in modern society that is generally not the case. Very often the new methods of industry demand younger workers with new knowledge and techniques. In an industrialized society skills can become obsolete quite rapidly. Often the worker is retired as soon as possible because he is technologically obsolete. This can threaten the individual's self-esteem. More than that is that retirement lessens the opportunities for daily social interaction and is demoralizing in that way. The formal work role carries with it a variety of informal relations and affiliations. "Retirement may signify the loss of several group affilitions such as the work group, the union or occupational associations, work-connected recreational groups, and the like."[35] Often when people feel a strong loss of self-esteem they start to feel worthless and lonely. This may lead them to withdraw even more from social contacts. "Even were they to be accepted by those who are still working, they may no longer want to be around successful people, because they will then feel all the more like failures."[36]

American society does little to provide a smooth transition into old age. The adjustments older persons make are usually achieved on their own and not through new and significant roles being available. In this sense, the older person's life is "roleless" and unstructured by society.

Their loss of former roles is not balanced by new ones. Often, the old tend to hang on to their middle-age role identities because they see nothing ahead. In the transition to old age the lack of new groups and new roles emphasizes the absence of positive social growth which had been a part of the earlier stages of life.[37]

The rates of older persons in the work force has undergone significant change in recent decades. In 1900, 67 percent of the men and 8 percent of the women over age 65 were actively employed. By 1974, only 24 percent of the older men remained employed as did 10 percent of the women. In general, the older persons who continue to work today are in part-time jobs, agricultural labor, or are self-employed.[38]

The point is that retirement means not only the loss of the job but also the interpersonal relationships linked to it. Daily interaction with friends at work is over. The retired man who returns to work can only be a visitor and quickly discovers that the work world continues without him. The shared interests and concerns that supported his friendships with fellow workers receive less reinforcement. This is especially true when the friend remains at work and continues to have work-related experiences the retiree cannot share. "Whether work-based friendships will survive retirement may depend heavily upon whether alternative bases for shared experiences exist or can be developed."[39]

Blau found that the retired man often experienced not only loneliness but also self-denigration. The loss of his work and social relationships leads him to question the very meaning of his own existence. And he often feels regret—that in the past he had failed to cultivate other interests besides his work. "Thus he has neither resigned himself to his difficulties nor has he been able to resolve them. And his inability to do so gives him a sense of inadequacy—'there is something wrong with me.'"[40]

There is evidence that often older persons share the common denigrating values about the elderly, but *not* when applied to themselves. They usually exempt themselves from any invidious comparisons. Rosow found they stigmatize others while resolutely disassociating themselves from the stigmatized category. While only one third of the sample regarded persons over 65 as still productive and useful, five sixths felt they were still useful themselves.[41] Another study found that as long as they maintained their health older people tended not to regard themselves as "old." Many believed that they made a "better appearance" than others their age. "It may be that each old person's unfavorable image of 'other old people' serves as a negative reference group by which he or she—by being different—is able to accentuate the positive and thus to reconstruct reality."[42]

There may be an attempt at "passing" that characterizes the aged as a quasiminority group. Often middle-aged and older people will try to deny their advancing age. In her study Patricia L. Kasschau found

Reprinted by permission *The Wall Street Journal*

"Now that I've retired, I have time for all the things I dreamed of doing,
but I forget what they were!"

there was a reluctance on the part of some older people to label an experience as discriminatory on the basis of their age. To do so would be an admission that other people consider one "old." Rather than admit old age one would often deny discrimination.[43]

A major part of the American work ethos has been to ingrain it as basic to the male's personal and social reality. Regardless of satisfaction reached in the work, the employment itself is likely to have high emotional significance for any man reared in the United States. So even though men are expected to retire at a certain age, many of them find this inconsistent with their images of masculinity. Retirement deprives a man of the respect accorded the breadwinner in the American family and constrains him to a role similar to that of women.

Various studies indicate that when persons are asked whether they would rather go on working or retire, the reasons given for either choice are usually negative. When they say they want to continue working, often it is because they fear poverty if they stop work; if they wish to discontinue working, it is often because of poor health. But in neither type of situation do they look forward to retirement as a way of life that is pleasurable, they tend not to see either work or leisure as a form of self-fulfillment because neither one nor the other is freely chosen.

Retirement is an arbitrary decision to have people leave the work force. It is arbitrary because it picks a specific age, and generally that age cannot be altered to fit different cases. This means that some persons are forced out of their occupations when they still have the ability to give a great deal, while others hang on long after they have nothing to give simply because they are not old enough to retire. There is also discrimination based on age that occurs well before retirement. In the United States about half the states have laws that forbid all discrimination on the basis of age. Yet, various employers give semiofficial instructions to agencies that result in age discrimination. For example, one study of eight large cities found that employment agencies fixed the upper age limit as 35 and one third at 45. It was also found that 97 percent of the advertisements in newspapers set 40 as the limit.[44] So job discrimination against the aged and increasingly against the middle aged is already a fact. Yet, while nearly 40 percent of the long-term unemployed are over 45, only 10 percent of the federal retraining programs are devoted to men of that age. To add to the problems it is also often difficult for older people to get bank loans, home mortgages, or automobile insurance.

The level of income after retirement is often a major problem. Economists estimate that for retirees to maintain their preretirement lifestyle within reasonable limits, they need a retirement income equal to 60 to 70 percent of their earnings immediately preceeding retirement. But this is a goal beyond the reach of most older Americans. On the average they have half the income of their younger counterparts.[45] For individuals and families over age 65 earnings make up only 30 percent of aggregated money income. The other two main sources are retirement benefits (37 percent) and income from assets (25 percent).

Differences in age among old people determines how much they can earn and still receive full Social Security benefits. Persons 72 and over can earn any amount of money and still receive full Social Security benefits. But persons under age 72 can earn only $5,000 without losing any benefits. (Only earned income is counted, not pensions, dividends, and so forth.) If the person earned more than $5,000 in a year, $1 of benefits could be withheld for each $2 earned.[46]

Over the years there has been an absolute gain in the financial resources of the elderly. But it may be a situation of relative deprivation. Their various social benefits have increased at a rate slower than that of the nation as a whole. For example, income standards are substantially higher for younger generations while Social Security benefits have grown at only one third the rate of net income of younger persons. "Thus, while the aged are better off in relation to their predecessors, they remain substantially disadvantaged in comparison with their younger counterparts."[47]

There is some argument that restrictions on job opportunities and other activities of the aged are justified because of inabilities on their part. While certainly some older people are handicapped in what they can do, this is not true for most. For example, studies show that the elderly are able to memorize and recall new information, but they need more time than younger people. Their responses are apparently slowed down by anxiety.

Simone de Beauvoir has suggested that society takes an ambiguous view of aging with regard to doctors, lawyers, and professional men in general. She suggests this is especially true for doctors because, for a certain period of time, age adds to their value. It is thought to bring experience, and a person with a long career behind him is preferred to a novice. But later the picture changes. "The old doctor is looked upon as worn out, in biological decline, and as one who has therefore lost much of his ability. And above all he is thought to be out of date."[48]

With the general displacement of many unskilled and semiskilled jobs in American society this has reduced the job chances for many older people. For example, one common job in the past was elevator operator but this position has pretty much disappeared. There are some new jobs that draw upon older people; for example, security work. But the number of new positions are not replacing the ones being lost and aged population is increasing in total size.

Marriage and the Elderly

As the number of elderly in the United States has increased the number of them married has also increased. Past the age of 65 there are 72 men for every 100 women and past the age of 75 there are 64 men for every 100 women. In 1976, 77 percent of all men past 65 were married but this was true of only 47 percent of the women. When women pass age 75, 70 percent of them are widows.[49]

As couples grow older and they move into retirement their marriages undergo changes. They very often go through basic role changes they are neither prepared for or want. The movement into new roles calls for new adjustments and often this implies resolving

FIGURE 10–2

Percent of Persons 65 Years and Older, by Marital Status and Sex: March 1978

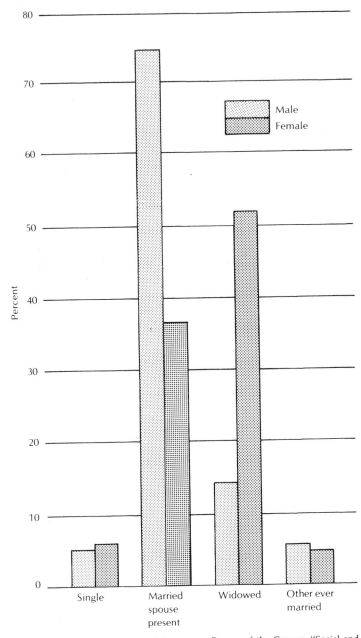

Source: U.S. Department of Commerce, Bureau of the Census, "Social and Economic Characteristics of the Older Population: 1978," *Current Population Reports* P–23, no. 85 (Washington, D.C.: U.S. Government Printing Office, 1979), p. 3.

conflicts with roles being left behind. It often means relinquishing the former rewards and abandoning the portion of one's self that had been invested in the previous role. For the man this may mean leaving his occupational role and for the woman it can be leaving an active mother role. Rosow found in his research that whatever role adjustments a couple made, they were independent of their private definitions as a couple. "Those that worked out a satisfactory adjustment did so on a purely personal basis, while many others, of course, did not find any satisfactory pattern."[50]

As married couples move through middle age they are typically confronted with major role changes. There is the loss of an active parental role as the children leave home and greater focus is placed on their marriage roles. Beth Hess has found considerable evidence that for the elderly with surviving spouses the marital relationship not only remains paramount but is enhanced by the children's leaving after adolescence. She suggests that possibly there was nowhere for marital satisfaction to go but up given the fact that marriages with adolescent children show the greatest signs of stress.[51]

The literature on postparental marriages suggest that couples turn to one another for companionship as well as psychic satisfaction. Often the couples who are unable to adapt to the major role stress in marriage will drop out before old age through divorce, separation, and desertion. For the very poor, where marital adjustment is much more problematic, and where there is lower life expectancy, there is even less probability of them experiencing long-term intact marriages.[52]

In many respects remaining married into old age has positive gains. Among the married there is the positive effect of psychological well-being among the elderly, especially when they are compared to the divorced and widowed. There is also some reason to suspect that overall levels of marital satisfaction and adjustment may be higher for the elderly than the married people in the intermediate stages of the family life cycle.[53]

Gary R. Lee found that marital satisfaction was positively related to morale among elderly married people and that this relationship was markedly stronger for women than for men. However, being married for older people was not at all an unmixed blessing. This was true because those whose marriages were less happy were much more likely to have much lower morale.[54]

Among elderly couples whose marriages survive, the one partner whose health typically goes first is the husband. Therefore, men more often than women depend on their spouses for health care in varying degrees. This can range from maternal nurturing to terminal nursing care. One study found that 40 percent of the elderly women had nursed their husbands for over a year. "Not only does this kind of health problem severely curtail many kinds of marital interaction, it also reduces the wife's freedom of action."[55]

We have discussed some of the implications of retirement for the husband, but it is just as important to look at the consequences of retirement for the elderly wife. The occupational retirement of the husband has many implications for the marriage relationship. What is especially important in contemporary American society is that retirement is a new form of social life, in that it is different from previous patterns of old age and has not achieved any specific institutional integration. "Past societies have had numbers of aged people, but these were not retired persons. They remained integrated in traditional institutional orders through work and kinship roles and relationships.[56] Our interest here is with the impact of retirement on the marriage roles—the man retires from his occupation and spends most of his time at home with his wife.

Wilma Donahue suggests that in the normal life cycle a woman has often experienced two or three "retirements" by the time her husband is facing his first retirement. What Donahue means by "retirement" experiences of the woman are that many left jobs for childrearing and thus had experienced that retirement experience during early adulthood. Women also experience retirement in other activities: for example, when their children grow up and leave the parental home, women experience another retirement from an essential function and have to make adjustments to the cessation of the maternal role. Yet in some cases the woman may find it more difficult to accept her husband's retirement than it was to accept her own retirements. Several studies show that a significant proportion of women do not want their husbands to retire because they believe that they will have more housework to do, "that their daily routine will be disrupted, that they do not want their husbands home all day, and that they will have to live on a lower income."[57]

As pointed out, one very common problem associated with aging is that the woman becomes a widow. In 1970 there were over 6 million widows and 1.5 million widowers in the United States. "By 1985 the number of older unmarried females is expected to rise by about 3 million and the number of unmarried males by about 700,000."[58]

For the aging woman widowhood has long been considered her major role transition. It has also been a common practice among gerontologists to compare widowhood for women to retirement for men. Typically the conclusion is that widowhood for women is less significant than retirement for men. But there is no evidence that widowhood for the woman is easier to take than retirement for the man.[59]

When a woman is past 50 years of age widowhood usually is a permanent status, although not necessarily a role she prefers. Only 5 percent who become widowed after age 55 ever remarry. This is in sharp contrast to widowers, most of whom remarry if they are under 70.[60] These differences in remarriage rates for widows and widowers are due to: (1) more widows so there are far fewer potential mates and (2) men can, with far greater social approval than women, marry someone younger.

There are two changes occurring that affect the marital status of the elderly. One is that more and more older people are getting divorced. Second is some evidence of change in remarriage for the widowed. One writer states that the increase in remarriage among people 65 and over has been dramatic. From 1960 to 1973 the number of brides 65 and over has more than doubled and the number of grooms almost doubled. "More than 35,000 marriages now occur annually in which one of the participants is 65 or over."[61]

There is evidence that losing a spouse through death may contribute to a shorter life for the survivor. It may be that some persons lose the will to live after the spouse's death if he or she was highly significant to them. In this sense it is possible that widowhood has deleterious consequences for the survivor. Another factor may be that persons with poor health risks tend to marry one another. Or a widowed individual may have shared an unfavorable environment with the deceased spouse that contributed to both deaths.[62]

There is also evidence that when the husband is the survivor he has more problems than when the wife outlives the husband. In part, this can be explained by the lower degree of involvement in family and friendship roles that older men have. Also for them there is the double loss of work and spouse, and usually they had very limited involvement in housekeeping and cooking compared to women. As a result they are less able to cope with being on their own.[63]

There are several factors that may lessen the problems for the couple after the husband's retirement. When the household activities are contrasted before and after retirement, often the home in which the husband has retired is more likely to show increased activity on the part of the husband and decreased involvement by the wife than it did before retirement. One study found there were two factors which tended to lessen the possibility of upsetting family balance even though there was a change in task distribution. First, the retired husband did not share tasks with his wife any more than he did when he was working. Second, those jobs which the retired husband did "appeared to be masculine or marginal in orientation rather than those which would have a significant influence on the self-conception of the wife. The supposed invasion by the retired husband thus became more of an emancipation from tasks which the wife could have relinquished at any time the husband was willing to accept them."[64]

Lillian E. Troll suggests that what happens after retirement is that the husband shifts from his instrumental role of good provider to the more expressive one of helping around the house. At the same time his wife moves from a relatively less expressive good homemaker role to a more expressive caring role with her husband. The retired husband winds up sharing the household tasks, but whether or not he feels good about that is dependent on his values. If, as is true of many working-class husbands, he sees housework as demeaning then he may feel devalued. However, this does not seem very common among middle-class men.[65]

Where the social limitations on the elderly are the strongest is with regard to sexual behavior. For many younger people the idea of sexual relations between elderly people is shocking and even disgusting. Sometimes the elderly accept the sanctions against their sexuality. They may become ashamed of their desires or deny having them. He refuses to be a lecherous old man in his own eyes (or a shameless old woman in hers). They fight against their sexual drives to the point of thrusting them back into their unconscious minds. These kinds of values not only hurt the elderly but also others. The widespread denial of sexuality in older people can make it difficult to correctly diagnose many of their medical and psychological problems. It may also distort interpersonal relations in marriage, or disrupt relationships between children and parents thinking of remarriage.

For women, the first strong feeling of aging usually occurs at the time of the menopause. But while this represents the end of her childbearing years, it does not mean the end of her sexual interests or abilities. The menopause does not occur all at once but may represent a transition over many months. The menopause may start as early as age 35, but it more commonly begins sometime between 45 and 47, and it may not occur until the early or even middle 50s. The majority of women, about four fifths in fact, pass through this period without any ill effects whatever and, so far as regular health is concerned, without even being aware of it. Masters and Johnson found no reason why the menopause should be expected to slow down the female's sexual capacity, performance, or drive. The healthy aging woman normally has sex drives that demand resolution—there is no time limit drawn by the advancing years to female sexuality."[66]

As the woman moves into older age, her sexual activity shows some decrease, usually due to two main causes: (1) her own decrease in sexual interest and (2) the fact that a large number of older women have no spouse or have a spouse with little or no sexual interest and/or ability. Cornelia Christenson and John Gagnon found that for married women at age 55, 89 percent were coitally active; by age 60 the rate was 70 percent, and by age 65 the rate was 50 percent.[67] Also at age 65, of the married women, 25 percent were actively involved in masturbation; and of women of the same age no longer married, 33 percent were engaging in masturbation.

The major limiting factor on the older woman is not lack of sexual interest but rather the lack of a sexually active partner. Christenson

Bruce Davidson/Magnum Photos, Inc.

Old age and loving

and Gagnon found that "in terms of both incidence and frequency of coitus the relative age of the husband was a strongly determining factor: The wives with husbands younger than they showed higher figures and those with older husbands considerably lower ones, at successive ages for the females."[68] Masters and Johnson came to essentially the same conclusion—that the sexual activity of women at 70 years of age and over was greatly influenced by male attrition.[69] In the Christenson and Gagnon sample, there was not a single case of a woman at 65 or over involved in postmarital coitus.

For the male, the central problem of aging is the fear of impotency. A male at any age may have temporary impotency. It may occur only on occasion or for varying periods of time. In almost all cases, impotency is believed to be caused by psychological factors such as overwork, anxiety, fear, and fatigue. For the male in a temporary state of impotency, the inability may contribute to his problems and intensify his impotency. He worries about his inability to have an erection, and, as a result, the worry contributes to even greater difficulty. Generally, the cure for impotency is rest and mental relaxation—which for most men may be easier said than done.

Generally speaking, as the male grows older his fear of impotency becomes increasingly important. Masters and Johnson state that there is no way to overemphasize the importance that "fear of failure" plays in the aging male's withdrawal from sexual performance. "Once impotent under any circumstances, many males withdraw voluntarily from any coital activity rather than face the ego-shattering experience of repeated episodes of sexual inadequacy."[70]

What appears to be most significantly related to active marital sexual expression in old age is whether there has been an overall pattern of active sexual interaction during the marriage. When the male is stimulated to high sexual output during his formative years and a similar level of activity is established for the 31–40-year age range, his middle-aged and involutional years usually are marked by constantly recurring physiologic evidence of maintained sexuality. But what is of great importance in the research of Masters and Johnson is that the "male over 50 years old can be trained out of his secondarily acquired impotence in a high percentage of cases. If he is in adequate health, little is needed to support adequacy of sexual performance in a 70- or even 80-year-old male other than some physiologic outlet or psychologic reason for a reactivated sexual interest."[71]

Nearly everyone has a varying number of years without a partner after the death of the spouse. The elderly person without a spouse is assumed to have little or no sexual interests. Society tends to see them, as they do an elderly person with a sick, feeble, or impotent spouse, as persons to be shunted off with the suggestion that continence and self-control should be exercised as seemly virtues for the aging members of the community. Many elderly people do have sexual relationships when they can but many probably suffer from a sense of guilt because they were socialized to believe that sex outside of marriage was wrong.

Problem Areas

In concluding this chapter it is useful to look briefly at some of the problems related to the elderly. These are problems not only for the older person but also for society because it must provide means for dealing with them. This is especially true since the extended family takes less responsibility for the elderly.

Low incomes.   Most of the aged do not become poor until after they retire when their incomes may drop as much as 50 to 66 percent. These are typically middle-class working people and it is probably harder for them to cope with their new poverty than it is for people who have been poor all their lives.[72] These persons contribute to the expanding population of poor people among the elderly. And while the elderly constitute about 10 percent of the population they make up about 20 percent of the total poor.

Anywhere from one third to one half of the aged are poorer, are employed less, work in lower-status occupations, have less education and poorer health than similar proportions of the non-aged population. And too, the aged, like certain minority groups, tend to be concentrated in rural areas and in the central city and are underrepresented in the suburbs. But this should not be taken to mean that large numbers of elderly are totally dependent on society. Actually, the overwhelming majority of the elderly can take care of themselves reasonably well. "Only 5 percent of aged Americans live in institutions; perhaps another 5 percent remain bedridden at home."[73]

Medical problems. For many elderly people their physical health is related to their low incomes. The elderly are the most uniformly undernourished segment of the population. Their high rates of malnutrition are related to low income, problems of getting to stores and lack of knowledge about proper nutrition. In 1972 over 40 percent of the noninstitutionalized elderly population had some limit to normal activity because of a chronic condition as compared to only 13 percent of the general population. Heart disease, rheumatism, and arthritis are the most common afflictions of the aged. Chronic conditions increase substantially with age and it is common for people to have multiple chronic conditions. Persons over 65 have nearly two and one-half times as many restricted activity days as the general population.[74]

On the average the elderly visit physicians 50 percent more than the rest of the population. They have health care and medical costs nearly four times greater than for younger persons. They also have over twice as many bed and hospital days. One study reported 83 percent of the elderly persons questioned had had no hospitalization during the previous year.[75] Ultimately death does occur and the leading causes among the elderly are diseases of the heart, cancer, and strokes, in that order. Together they account for almost three fourths of all mortality.[76]

As will be discussed in Chapter 14 there are clear limits on what can be done to prolong the life of the elderly. Medicine can do very little for the illnesses that are associated with aging, and even less about the process and experiences of aging itself. Medicine cannot cure cardiovascular disease, most cancers, arthritis, advanced cirrhosis, nor even the common cold.[77]

A large number of elderly Americans (close to a million) are living in nursing homes or convalescent facilities supported by Medicare. In fact, as a new growth industry, nursing homes now provide more beds than do hospitals. These kinds of facilities are in part a social means for handling the aged outside of their children's homes. There is no agreement that this is a satisfactory solution. On one hand, it does take the elderly away from a private home where they may not be able to look after themselves or where their demands are seen as too

much for others. But on the other hand it puts them in a highly segregated setting of aged and often ill persons. This means that their
lives are distorted and frequently very repressive and sad. Often the
big event in many of these homes is when one of the patients dies.
Their world becomes not only institutional, but also very fixed in that
they are all basically alike. Unfortunately there may be no really good
social solution to caring for the dependent aged.

As people get older not only do they suffer increasingly from
physical problems but also mental ones. In fact, sometimes the two are
closely related. Aging brings about in some people both physical and
mental changes that are reflected in mental health problems. The most
obvious illustration is senility. The rate of mental illness among the
aged is about 236 per 100,000 population. By contrast, the rate is about
76 per 100,000 in the 25–34 age group.[78]

Suicide rates. The most vivid measurement of problems among the
elderly is reflected in their suicide rates. In the United States about 22
out of every 100,000 people in their 40s kill themselves. This figure
continues to rise with age, and at 80 it reaches 697 in every 100,000.
"Some old people kill themselves after neurotic depressions that have
not yielded to treatment, but most of these suicides are the normal reaction to a hopeless, irreversible situation that is found to be un-
bearable."[79]

As suggested, aging is an inevitable condition of survival and
while there may be some individual variation the body ultimately undergoes deterioration. In American society there is also a kind of social
deterioration in the loss or major alteration of significant social roles.
Aging is becoming an increasingly greater social problem because
more people are in the older age group and there are limited and often
unsatisfactory ways for them to live the later years of their lives. This
social problem will continue because little can be done to prolong life
or significantly affect medical changes through improvement. Furthermore, the social roles and position of older people will probably continue to lose significance so that the sense of personal and social loss
with old age will continue to become more intense.

NOTES

1. Susan Sontag, "The Double Standard of Aging" in *Sexuality Today and Tomorrow;*
by Sol Gordon and Roger W. Libby (N. Scituate, Mass., Duxbury Press, 1976), p. 351.

2. Betty Yorburg, *Sexual Identity* (New York: Wiley, 1974), p. 46.

3. Inge Powell Bell, "The Double Standard" in *Marriage and Families,* by Helena Z.
Lapata (New York: Van Nostrand, 1973), p. 216.

4. Ibid., p. 219.

5. Irving Rosow, *Socialization to Old Age* (Berkeley: University of California Press, 1974), p. 23.

6. Sontag, "Double Standard," p. 353.

7. Ibid., p. 354.

8. Simone de Beauvoir, *Old Age* (London, Great Britain: Cox and Wyman, 1972), p. 277.

9. Suzanne Gordon, *Lonely in America* (New York: Touchstone, 1976), p. 193.

10. Vira R. Kivett, "Loneliness and the Rural Widow," *The Family Coordinator* (October 1978), p. 392.

11. Joseph Harry and William De Vall, "Age and Sexual Culture among Homosexually Oriented Males," *Archives of Sexual Behavior* (May 1978), p. 200.

12. Matilda White Riley and Joan Waring, "Age and Aging," in *Contemporary Social Problems*, 4th ed., by Robert K. Merton and Robert Nisbet (New York: Harcourt Brace Jovanovich, 1976), p. 398.

13. Ethel Shanas and Phillip M. Hauser, "Zero Population Growth and the Family Life of Old People," *Journal of Social Issues* 30 (1974), p. 89.

14. *Information Please Almanc 1978* (New York: Information Please Publishing, Inc., 1978), p. 668.

15. Zena Smith Blau, *Old Age in a Changing Society* (New York: New Viewpoints, 1973), p. 4.

16. *Information Please Almanac 1978*, p. 668.

17. Shanas and Hauser, "Zero Population," p. 85.

18. Helena Z. Lopata, "Contributions of Extended Families to the Support Systems of Metropolitan Area Widows," *Journal of Marriage and the Family* (May 1978), p. 362.

19. Shanas and Hauser, "Zero Population," p. 83.

20. Gordon F. Strieb, "Older Families and Their Troubles: Familial and Social Responses," *The Family Coordinator* (January 1972), p. 13.

21. Lillian E. Troll, Sheila J. Miller, and Robert C. Atchley, *Families in Later Years* (Belmont, Calif.: Wadsworth, 1979), pp. 86–87.

22. Rosow, *Socialization*, p. 67.

23. Streib, "Older Families," p. 13.

24. James E. Montgomery, "The Housing Patterns of Older Families," *The Family Coordinator* (January 1972), p. 39.

25. Ibid., p. 37.

26. Gordon L. Bultena and Douglas G. Marshall, "Family Patterns of Migrant and Nonmigrant Retirees, *Journal of Marriage and the Family* (February 1970), p. 92.

27. Montgomery, "Housing Patterns," p. 43.

28. Cary S. Kart and Barry L. Beckhaus, "Black-White Differentials in the Institutionalization of the Elderly: A Temporal Analysis," *Social Forces* (June 1976), pp. 901–2.

29. John F. Myles, "Institutionalization and Sick Identification among the Elderly, *American Sociological Review* (August 1978), p. 509.

30. Ivan Illich, *Limits to Medicine* (London: Marion Boyars, 1976), p. 83.

31. Majorie Fiske Lowenthal and Clayton Haven, "Interaction and Adaptation: Intimacy as a Critical Variable." *American Sociological Review* (February 1968), p. 20.

32. Jaber F. Gubrium, "Marital Dissolution and the Evaluation of Everyday Life in Old Age," *Journal of Marriage and the Family* (February 1974), p. 107.

33. Lowenthal and Haven, "Interaction," p. 28.

34. Blau, *Changing Society*, pp. 71–72.

35. Ibid., p. 32.

36. Gordon, *Lonely in America*, p. 177.

37. Rosow, *Socialization*, pp. 127–28.

38. *Information Please Almanac 1978*, p. 671.

39. Beth Hess, "Friendship" in *Aging and Society*, vol. 3 by Matilda White Riley, Marilyn Johnson, and Anne Foner (New York: Russell Sage Foundation, 1972), p. 365.

40. Blau, *Changing Society*, p. 28.

41. Rosow, *Socialization*, pp. 88–89.

42. Riley and Waring, "Age and Aging," p. 395.

43. Patricia L. Kasschau, "Age and Race Discrimination Reported by Middle-Aged and Older Persons," *Social Forces* (March 1977), p. 731.

44. de Beauvoir, *Old Age*, p. 227.

45. *Information Please Almanac 1978*, p. 671.

46. Ibid., p. 678.

47. Rosow, *Socialization*, p. 160.

48. de Beauvoir, *Old Age*, p. 385.

49. *Information Please Almanac 1978*, p. 671.

50. Rosow, *Socialization*, p. 59.

51. Hess, "Friendship," p. 310.

52. Ibid., p. 311.

53. Gary R. Lee, "Marriage and Morale in Later Life," *Journal of Marriage and the Family* (February 1978), p. 132.

54. Ibid., p. 137.

55. Troll, Miller, and Atchley, *Families*, p. 45.

56. Wilma Donahue, Harold L. Orbach, and Otto Pollak, "Retirement: The Emerging Social Patterns" in *Handbook of Social Gerontology*, by Clark Tibbits (Chicago: University of Chicago Press, 1960), p. 334.

57. Ibid., pp. 371–72.

58. Barbara H. Vinick, "Remarriage in Old Age," *The Family Coordinator* (October 1978), p. 359.

59. Diane Beeson, "Women in Studies of Aging: A Critique and Suggestion," *Social Problems* (October 1975), p. 54.

60. Troll, Miller, and Atchley, *Families*, p. 69.

61. Vinick, "Remarriage," p. 359.

62. Carol J. Barrett, "Women in Widowhood" *Signs* (Summer 1977), p. 861.

63. Vinick, "Remarriage," p. 360.

64. John A. Ballweg, "Resolution of Conjugal Role Adjustment after Retirement," *Journal of Marriage and the Family* (May 1967), p. 281.

65. Troll, Miller, and Atchley, *Families*, p. 64.

66. William H. Masters and Virginia E. Johnson, *Human Sexual Response* (Boston: Little, Brown, 1966), pp. 246–47.

67. Cornelia Christenson and John H. Gagnon, "Sexual Behavior in a Group of Older Women," *Journal of Gerontology* (July 1965), p. 352.

68. Ibid., p. 352.

69. Masters and Johnson, *Response*, p. 245.

70. Ibid., pp. 269–70.

71. Ibid., pp. 262–63.

72. *Information Please Almanac 1978*, p. 671.

73. Time Magazine, "Country of Young," in *Family in Transition*, by Arlene S. Skolnick and Jerome H. Skolnick, (Boston: Little, Brown, 1971), p. 436.

74. Myles, "Institutionalization," p. 509.

75. *Information Please Almanac 1978*, p. 671.

76. Leon Bouvier, Elinore Atlee, and Frank McVeigh, "The Elderly in America," in *Readings in Aging and Death: Contemporary Perspectives*, by Steven H. Zarit (New York: Harper & Row, 1977), p. 36.

77. Illich, *Limits to Medicine*, p. 82.

78. de Beauvoir, *Old Age*, p. 493.

79. Ibid., p. 276.

SELECTED BIBLIOGRAPHY

Beeson, Diane. "Women in Studies of Aging: A Critique and Suggestion." *Social Problems* (October 1975), pp. 52–59.

Blau, Zena Smith. *Old Age in a Changing Society.* New York: New Viewpoints, 1972.

de Beauvoir, Simone. *Old Age.* London, Great Britain: Cox and Wyman, 1973.

Gubrium, Jaber F. "Marital Dissolution and the Evaluation of Everyday Life in Old Age." *Journal of Marriage and the Family* (February 1974), pp. 107–13.

Lee, Gary R. "Marriage and Morale in Later Life." *Journal of Marriage and the Family,* (February 1978), pp. 131–39.

Medley, Morris L. "Marital Adjustment in the Post-Retirement Years." *The Family Coordinator* (January 1977), pp. 5–11.

Montgomery, James E. "The Housing Patterns of Older Families." *The Family Coordinator* (January 1972), pp. 37–46.

Rosow, Irving. *Socialization to Old Age.* Berkeley: University of California Press, 1974.

Strieb, Gordon F. "Older Families and Their Troubles: Familial and Social Responses." *The Family Coordinator* (January 1972), pp. 5–91.

Troll, Lillian E.; Miller, Sheila J.; and Atchley, Robert C. *Families in Later Years.* Belmont, Calif.: Wadsworth, 1979.

Chapter 11

Homosexuality

Probably for most of history homosexuality has been so well hidden it could be ignored by society. In the Western world, over the past 100 years, when all forms of human sexuality were highly repressed homosexuality was usually hidden. For it to become a social problem there has to be social awareness and some public disclosure of its existence. Once these conditions existed there could be no doubt it would be a social problem because it went so strongly against the moral values of society. Values strongly based in religious morality became translated into laws. For example, a passage in the Book of Deuteronomy states: "He that lieth with a man as with a woman is an abomination unto the Lord." With time these kinds of proscriptions have been largely formalized in the law, with criminal penalties attached to homosexual acts.[1]

In recent years in the United States there has been an increasing amount of public awareness of and reaction to the problem and for the most part it has centered on the male homosexual. However, while our first focus in this chapter will be with the male homosexual, the second part will deal with the female homosexual or lesbian.

Male Homosexuality

Historical view. In antiquity homosexuality was widely prevalent in most countries of the eastern Mediterranean, and to this day it is more prevalent there than in other parts of the Western world. Homosexuality was common among some early Greeks, in part because their values about beauty resulted in the idealization of the slim body of the young man. But with the rise of Christianity homosexuality became more and more taboo. As the years passed the homosexual was seen increasingly as the ultimate in depravity and excessive self-abuse. During the Dark Ages and the Middle Ages homosexuality was thought to be a supernatural state of mind. It was attributed to possession by devils, and the cure was exorcism by bell, book, and candle.

Until well through the 17th century in England no special role was given to the homosexual, but toward the end of the 17th century the belief developed that homosexuality was a condition characterizing certain persons and not others.[2] In other words, being a homosexual was seen as a broad social role rather than as simply a sexual act. It was a fairly complex role, built around the homosexual's desire and activity. This appears to be the way homosexuality is viewed in most of the Western world today, even though countries do vary in their definitions of homosexuals. A majority of European countries do not prohibit homosexual acts between consenting adults.

Emergence of a definition. In the United States the frontier way of life isolated men from women for long periods of time. Under those conditions many men turned to one another for sexual satisfaction and homosexuality was often taken for granted. Homosexuality also appears to have been common among the soldiers of both the North and the South during the Civil War, "and there are accounts of male prostitutes who followed the armies."[3]

Many societies have fallen between the extremes of permissiveness and restrictiveness in dealing with homosexuality. In fact many societies have been permissive informally while being restrictive formally. There is evidence that in societies where homosexuality is highly restricted persons turn to either homosexuality *or* heterosexuality, but that in the activities where there are no strong social sanctions against homosexuality, the activities of the males are less apt to be either homosexual or heterosexual and more often bisexual. It must also be recognized that cultures are rarely consistent in their definitions of homosexuality, but very often are characterized by internal disagreements. In other words, in any given society there are different people with different views of homosexuality. For example, homosexuals see their activity as a legitimate minority practice while many psychologists see it as a type of illness and law enforcement agencies see it as a crime.

The American laws about homosexuality come out of the same background as did most American laws about sexual behavior. They come from the English common law, with strong religious moral overtones. For the purposes of the legal discussion homosexual behavior is defined as sexual behavior between two persons of the same sex. This sexual behavior can consist of simple touching, kissing, petting, stroking the genitalia, oral-genital contact, and anal intercourse (for the male).

None of the 50 states defines homosexuality as a crime per se; "the diverse limitations imposed by the states are aimed at punishing the acts employed by homosexuals to achieve sexual gratifications."[4] While it is no crime to be a homosexual there are certain acts commonly performed by homosexuals that are against the law. In most states, oral-genital and anal sexual acts are against the law, even if performed by heterosexual couples and in private.

The homosexual has no legal outlet for his sex need satisfaction and so whatever he does is illegal. There are many laws passed to protect persons or property against the invasion of others. But this does not appear to be the case with regard to the laws against homosexuality. Such laws are passed not to protect persons or property against the "dangers" of adult homosexual activity but rather to enforce the cultural taboos against homosexuality. However, this is not to say that a definite majority of Americans no longer believe that homosexuality is "bad" and no longer believe that it should be controlled. Most Americans *do* take a negative view, but this doesn't affect the logic of the legal position one way or another.

The United States Supreme Court has in effect refused to deal with legal questions about homosexuality. In 1976, they ruled by a vote of six to three to uphold the constitutionality of state antihomosexual laws. The court did not pass on the wisdom or propriety of such legislation but only that the states had the right to regulate the private consensual activity of adults.[5]

Given the laws against homosexual activity, how restrictive or harsh are the legal controls? In theory the laws are very harsh. For example, a number of states provide a maximum penalty of ten or more years in prison for some homosexual offenses. The penalties range from a maximum of one year in New York for a crime against nature with a person over 18 years of age where consent was given, to life imprisonment for the same situation in Nevada. Four states privide a five-year maximum for sodomy, while four other states provide a five-year minimum for the same charge. Not only do the penalties vary widely by states, but there is also a wide variation in how homosexual crimes are defined. For example, some states use the term *sodomy,* others *crimes against nature,* and still others *buggery.* This also means that the state courts define the same types of homosexuality in different ways and mete out different kinds of punishment. For example, some states have defined these laws as applying only to intercourse per anus (the common-law meaning of sodomy), while other states have held the laws to include fellatio. Twenty states have sodomy laws which have been framed to enlarge the common-law definition.[6] Furthermore, in some states an individual may receive the same penalty for a single homosexual experience that he would receive in other states for a continuous record of homosexual experience. All of this means that the laws are confused, and therefore their application varies widely over time, by location, and by who is doing the applying. This leaves a great deal of discretion not only to the courts but also to the police.

The legal controls over social problems are applied on two levels. One is the level of abstraction as presented through the formal legal codes and laws and interpreted through the courts, and the other is the use and application of the laws by the police. As suggested, there is confusion in the formal laws with regard to homosexuality and confusion in how the courts interpret those laws. This means, as is often the case with legal confusion and changing legal views, that the police make many interpretations in applying the laws. The police know what range of legal possibilities they have, and they can choose within that range on the basis of a number of factors they see as important. Furthermore, laws may or may not be applied because of a lack of police manpower, because of the belief that police efforts are needed elsewhere, or because the police feel that homosexuality is not an area of great importance and so leave it alone. It is also true that the police sometimes use homosexuals as informants and will therefore leave those homosexuals alone. In general the police do not bother homosexuals unless they define them as constituting a public nuisance. A legal study in Los Angeles found that even when the police knew that homosexuals were cohabiting they usually would not initiate any action. In part that was a practical decision because the law was unenforceable in private situations, since it was almost impossible to arrest persons for private homosexual activity without exceeding search and seizure limitations.[7] Generally the police leave homosexuals alone if they are in private or in clubs unless there are complaints of soliciting or lewd conduct. Actually, decorum is common to the places frequented by middle-class and upper-middle-class homosexuals.

In many cities it has been a common practice for the police to use "entrapment" methods to apprehend homosexuals. There has often been disagreement between the police and the homosexual as to what constitutes "entrapment." Police have generally argued that it is only entrapment if the decoy officer makes a clear and unequivocal solicitation of the person and arrests the person when he agrees. But most homosexuals consider it to be entrapment if the decoy uses any dress, gestures, or language that lure the homosexual in any way into a solicitation. However, the trend in many large cities has been for the police to give up almost all entrapment methods. The New York police publicly announced abandonment of their entrapment procedures, and this was reflected in a decline in arrests of homosexuals from about 800 in 1965 to about 80 in 1969. The "hands-off" policy toward the homosexual often reflects the views of political leaders but not the feelings of the police. Police officers often reserve a special contempt for deviants: cases of unprovoked beatings of homosexuals are a part of the record of most large police departments.[8]

The police have always been responsible for determining who gets arrested as having committed a homosexual act. Legally both persons engaging in the homosexual act, whether sodomy or oral intercourse, are guilty. But the police often arrest only the active person. The police tend to see the man who receives the sex act as "queer," while they often see the man who performs the sex act as suspect but as having an understandable tendency toward sexual opportunity. To the police the crux of the matter is that the man who brings the other man to orgasm is the "real" homosexual while the man who is brought to orgasm is not. The police may feel that seeking an orgasm is not really blameworthy even in a homosexual situation but that being interested in bringing another male to orgasm is unmitigated perversion.

Most arrests for homosexual activities take place in public facilities. The persons apprehended are almost always consenting adults in a parked car, public restroom, movie theatre, public park, in an alley, or in some similar place. In most of the cases the persons are strangers to one another.[9] It is the relatively public setting that makes them subject to arrest. If they were in a hotel or apartment their chances of arrest would be very slight.

There have been recent attempts to liberalize the laws about homosexuality. In 1973 eight states (Illinois, Connecticut, Colorado, Oregon, Ohio, North Dakota, Delaware, and Hawaii) had done away with their penalties against private sexual relationships, both homosexual and heterosexual, between consenting adults. In some states various discriminations are maintained. For example, Kansas has reduced sodomy penalties for homosexual adults from felonies to misdemeanors but allows heterosexuals, married or unmarried, to perform oral or anal sex without any legal restraint.

It is not suggested that there is any strong trend in the United States in the direction of more liberal laws about sexual behavior in general and homosexuality in particular. The sodomy laws are indicative of the possible legal trends with regard to homosexuality. In the period from 1951 to 1965 Arizona, California, New Hampshire, New Jersey, and Wyoming increased their penalties against sodomy. During the same period Arkansas, Colorado, Georgia, Illinois, Nevada, North Dakota, New York, Oregon, and Wisconsin lessened their penalties.[10] These changes do not indicate any very strong liberal trend with regard to homosexuality. One common fear is that if the laws were liberalized there would be a sharp increase in homosexuality. John H. Gagnon and William Simon have suggested that greater tolerance of homosexuality through the reform of sex laws would not increase the incidence of homosexuality even if it encouraged those males who had not, due to fear of the law, engaged in homosexual contact to enter into such relationships. "At the same time, there may be a countertendency. The lowering of sanctions and the decrease in stigma may reduce the barrier between the homosexual and heterosexual world, and this may allow some persons in the homosexual world to develop an interest in heterosexual adjustments."[11]

One often reads estimates or statements made about how many homosexuals there are in the United States. There can be no accurate figure given because homosexuality is in most instances very well hidden and there are no national samples of homosexuals to provide a reliable rate. It seems certain that the figure is nowhere as high as some homosexual groups would suggest. It may be that roughly 25 percent of all American men have had at least one homosexual experience, but no more than 3 percent of all men beyond the age of 15 would define themselves as mainly or completely homosexual.[12]

Causes. It is doubtful whether any other social problem has been subjected to as many attempts to explain its causes as has homosexuality. It appears that because homosexuality has been traditionally seen as so "abnormal" there has been a great need to explain it, in part so that "normal" sex can be more securely understood. Homosexuality has presented a challenge to the developing personal and social sciences of the past 100 years. There have been attempts to explain homosexuality by biologists, geneticists, physiologists, psychiatrists, psychoanalysts, psychologists, social psychologists, sociologists, and others. The body of literature in this area is so vast that it can only be very briefly mentioned here.

The beliefs about the causes of homosexuality have changed over the years. A hundred years ago, when homosexuality was seen as a vice, it was attributed to depravity, excessive "self-abuse," satiation, and the hedonistic search for new sensations. The cure at that time was public censure and private penance. "Seventy years ago, when homosexuality was regarded as a form of moral and neurological degeneracy, the cause was attributed to the 'bad seed' of one's ancestors, and there was no cure because it is impossible to reverse heredity."[13]

The attempts to explain the "causes" of homosexuality may be placed into three general groupings: medical, psychological, and social. In earlier days homosexuality was seen as sinful and evil behavior. Later it was viewed as moral degeneracy. But neither of those approaches is now given serious consideration. As we shall see there is a basic conflict of values among the definers of the causes of homosexuality.

Medical explanations. Under this heading we may briefly consider several medical approaches. For example, there has long been an attempt to explain homosexuality on the grounds of inborn characteristics; that is, the person is seen as having been born with traits or forces that would make him become a homosexual. However, no research of any significance supports this approach. Another medical approach has been in terms of hormone treatments for believed deficiencies. But almost uniformly hormonal studies have failed to find any differences between homosexual and heterosexual individuals, as have various studies of body structure, genital anatomy, and brain injuries failed. "Studies showing any positive findings in these areas have been poorly done, have had too few subjects or a poor selection of subjects, or have been contradicted by other studies."[14] In recent years there has developed a small body of research indicating that hormonal imbalance may be involved in the explanation of at least some homosexuality. "But there are many questions still to be answered about the role of hormones in homosexuality."[15]

There is an implicit assumption in the medical view of homosexuality and that is that man has an inborn instinct or tendency to be heterosexual. Therefore any variation from heterosexuality is unnatural and to be treated as a sickness. But scientific studies of other cultures or of animals do not lend any support to an instinctual theory of human sexuality. "Human sexual behavior varies widely and is dependent on learning and conditioning."[16]

The more common medical approach to homosexuality is reflected in the tendency to label it as a "disease" or an "illness." This is in part a reflection of a trend in society to apply the concept of illness to many personal and social problems. The view that homosexuality is a disease implies several consequences. The first is that those in whom the condition exists are sick persons and should be regarded as medical problems and as primarily a medical responsibility. The second is that sickness implies irresponsibility or at least diminished responsibility. It has been argued that homosexuality does not fit the criterion of using symptoms to determine whether a disease exists because in many cases it is the only symptom and the person is healthy in all other respects. There are cases where psychiatric abnormalities do occur, and if they occur with greater frequency in the homosexual, this may be because they are products of the strain and conflict brought about by societal pressure and not because they are causal factors. It appears that the disease approach does little to explain the causes of homosexuality and contributes little to understanding homosexuality.

Psychiatric explanations. Probably the best-known theories about the causes of homosexuality have been developed by psychiatrists. This is particularly true of the psychoanalytic theories, which assert that homosexuality is a form of mental sickness. The psychoanalytic approach is to try to affect the causes of the "sickness" in the homosexual or to help him accept his "sickness" and live with it. Basically the psychoanalytic and psychiatric approach to homosexuality has been to define it as a manifestation of some sexual abnormality and some disturbed personality development.

Psychiatry has played a major role in defining how the homosexual is viewed both by society in general and by those interested in seeking professional "treatment." During the 20th century psychiatry has been the major force in stereotyping the homosexual. Under the guise of a value-free medical model many psychiatrists have translated the rhetoric of religion into the rhetoric of mental illness. Defining homosexuals as mentally ill has often served only to degrade the homosexual as inferior to the heterosexual because health (heterosexuality) is better than illness (homosexuality).[17]

Beginning in the 1940s and continuing to the present psychiatry has played a major part in the defining of many social problems. And because psychiatry is a medical specialty it has enjoyed the tremendous prestige and influence that medicine has in general in the United States. This means that most of the professional opinion about homosexuality that gets presented through the mass media has been psychiatric. Therefore, most Americans view homosexuality as a sickness that can be dealt with through various medical cures. The fact that very few committed homosexuals want psychiatric help or that among those who do that few are significantly influenced to change is lost to the general public. The psychiatric record in significantly helping or changing homosexuals in any way is very limited.

Given the general assumption that homosexuality is undesirable, the psychiatric approach has traditionally been to try to eliminate it. The psychiatrist has sought to reverse the patient's homosexuality and to bring his sex life into conformity with conventional, heterosexual norms. "Although there have been numerous claims of success by therapists, those claims are not supported by systematic scientific research." More often than not, after "successful" therapy the individuals either revert to their homosexual activities or "in robotlike fashion and with a supercilious air akin to that often found among religious converts, they function as heterosexuals. In neither case, however, do they usually convey the slightest impression of ease, happiness, naturalness, or contentment."[18]

One of the basic problems with psychiatrists' generalizations about behavior is the biased nature of their samples. The basic question is how psychiatrists who see only a small number of disturbed homosexuals can reach conclusions about all homosexuals, the vast majority of whom do not come in for treatment. "The few studies that have compared nonpatient homosexuals and nonpatient heterosexuals have not borne out the theory that homosexuals are sick or even different, except for sexual preferences."[19]

There is some evidence of changing views about homosexuality among psychiatrists. In 1973 the American Psychoanalytic Association's board of trustees voted unanimously to remove homosexuality from the category of mental illness. The new official definition uses the term *sexual orientation disturbance* for "individuals who are disturbed by, in conflict with, or wish to change, their sexual orientation." The trustees hasten to add that "the diagnostic category is distinguished from homosexuality which by itself does not necessarily constitute a psychiatric disorder."[20]

The removal of the label of mental illness from the homosexual was accomplished with a great deal of conflict among psychiatrists. There was immediately a movement to have the label restored. Joann S. DeLora and Carol A. B. Warren point out that the same type of backlash can be seen in the legal and religious spheres. "When homosexual acts in private were removed from the purview of the law in California, fundamentalist Christians started a movement to have the law revived."[21] This is a pattern common to many social problems whether they be homosexuality, abortion, drugs, and so forth. That is, any significant change can rarely be taken as an overall victory, but only a temporary gain that may soon be lost.

In the area of psychology there are a number of practicing behavioral therapists who work with homosexuals. Many of them are more influenced by prevailing cultural opinion than by the philosophy of their training in their treatment of homosexual clients. For example, 13 percent in one study indicated a willingness to change a person's sexual orientation against their wishes. "Therapists share many biases concerning homosexuality, notably that it is less good, more tense, less dominant, less masculine, less rational, and more passive than heterosexuality."[22]

Many homosexuals are involved in satisfying and meaningful social relationships that serve to make their world orderly, intelligible, and integrated. There is no scientific evidence that homosexuality in and of itself is abnormal. Homosexuals do not invariably want to change their sexual orientation or to be treated for it in any fashion. Many homosexuals enjoy their sexual orientation and their relationships. "Furthermore, no demonstrable harm to the rest of society due to the existence of a cadre of homosexuals within its ranks has been shown."[23]

Social explanations.   There is a psychological assumption that social theories of homosexuality make. This assumption is that there is nothing innate in the sex drive of the individual other than the need for tension release. Therefore, the objects toward which the sex drive is directed are a result of social learning. "Young male mammals who have not been previously conditioned will react to any sufficient sexual stimuli, whether these are autoerotic, heteroerotic, or homoerotic in character, and moreover may become conditioned to any of these

A relationship

stimuli."[24] Consequently homosexuality, like heterosexuality, is learned through one's social experiences with regard to the sex drive. This means that there is no "natural" sexual pattern, but rather there are sexual patterns that one learns in order to satisfy the drive. Whatever the causes for the direction by which one seeks to satisfy the drive, it is satisfied within a dynamic social setting that may variously reinforce or undercut that direction over time.

One writer has argued that not until the sociologist sees homosexuals as representing a social category, rather than a medical or a psychiatric one, will we begin to ask the "right questions about the specific content of the homosexual role and the organization and functions of homosexual groups."[25] This approach recognizes that the sexual inclinations of the committed homosexual are a part of a continuing role and not simply a series of specific sexual activities. The role of the homosexual is not peculiar to himself but is shared with other homosexuals. The very nature of their particular deviance draws homosexuals into interaction with one another. It has been pointed out that the homosexual's sexual object choice has dominated and controlled the views about him and led to the assumption that his sexual choice determines all other aspects of his life. "This prepossessing concern on the part of nonhomosexuals with the purely sexual aspect of the homosexual's life is something we would not allow to occur if we were interested in the heterosexual."[26] Of course, homosexuals vary widely in the degree to which their sexual commitment is the major focus for organizing their lives.

The view of homosexuality as a social role implies a "naming process" for both the homosexual and for others who define him as such. As Mary McIntosh has pointed out, the "naming process"—the social labeling of deviants—operates as a means of social control in two ways. First, it provides a clear-cut and recognized dividing line between permissible and nonpermissible behavior. Second, it helps to segregate the deviants from others and thus restricts their practices and rationalizations to relatively confined groups. Often the deviant sees his social role as a condition which he cannot control. Given this view, the homosexual often sees his homosexual role as justified because he cannot move back into the heterosexual world completely. But it is suggested that the homosexual should be seen as playing a social role rather than as having a condition.[27]

What can be said sociologically about the causes of homosexuality? The concern with the basic causes of homosexuality may be overdone. Even if the causes could be distinguished, that knowledge would have limited application to influencing or even understanding the *development* of homosexuality. This is true because often the reason for starting to move toward some form of deviant behavior has little to do with the influences that occur once the start is made. For example, the initial reason for taking drugs may have little relevance to the developing patterns that change the drug user into a drug addict. There is a tendency to think of causes as discrete and set in time rather than as diffuse and changing over time. The research data on homosexuality clearly show it to be a complex phenomenon not only in its manifestations in individual and social experience and behavior but also "in its determination by psychodynamics, biological, cultural, situational, and structural variables. An 'either-or' position with respect to any one of these variables simply does not account for the extraordinary diversity of the phenomena to be accounted for."[28]

There is a need to question some of the assumptions made about the causes of homosexuality and the directions that homosexuality takes, because often the discovery of homosexuality in a person is taken as clear evidence that major psychopathology exists. "When the heterosexual meets these minimum definitions of mental health, he is exculpated: the homosexual—no matter how good his adjustment in nonsexual areas of life—remains suspect."[29] The image of the homosexual often presented to society is that of the homosexuals the medical practitioner encounters, and these are almost always people with severe problems. On this point Wardell Pomeroy, a practicing psychologist, has said that if his concept of homosexuality were based on what he has seen in his practice he would also think of it as an illness. "I have seen no homosexual man or woman in that practice who wasn't troubled, emotionally upset, or neurotic. On the other hand, if my concept of marriage in the United States were based on my practice, I would have to conclude that marriages are all fraught with strife and conflict, and that heterosexuality is an illness."[30]

The homosexual subculture is found in the large cities of the United States. There are undoubtedly some variations among the different cities with regard to the size and complexity of the subculture. But there are patterns that are common to all cities, and these are the focus of interest in this section. One of the problems in trying to study a deviant subculture is that so much of it is hidden, not only from the broader society but often even from many of the deviants themselves.

The homosexual subculture or the gay community is not a unified, cohesive group, since homosexuals come from very diverse social backgrounds. Barry Dank and Carol Warren have each studied what they refer to as gay communities. Both researchers found that while homosexuals have a common sexual identification, that does not eliminate their economic, political, religious, ethnic, and educational differences. "Gay life styles are the product of both the individual's own unique social background and personality, and the nature of his interaction with other homosexuals."[31] Warren found these variables to be related to types of homosexual relationships. She observes that short-term relationships were based on different criteria than were long-term relationships. "Gay men select their lovers according to general rules of ethnic, racial, age, and class similarity, although there are exceptions. The short-term sexual relationship, on the other hand, is based more on strictly sexual preferences."[32]

Other researchers have talked about a much more secret world for some homosexuals. This is embodied in cliques and communities that are generally middle class (with some blue-collar members), and it is relatively older than the overt gay subculture, including men in their late 20s to their 50s. It is also nonactive and relatively conservative in its political views. "They keep their homosexuality secret from most straight friends, co-workers, and family."[33]

What does the homosexual subculture mean in the broadest sense? The subculture implies a continuing group of individuals who share some significant activity and begin to develop a sense of a bounded group possessing special norms and a particular language. These individuals engage in various social activities that reinforce a feeling of identity and provide a way of institutionalizing the experience, wisdom, and mythology of the collective.[34] It is within the context of the subculture in relation to the broader society that homosexuals are able to develop working solutions to problems of sexual performance and psychological gender which cannot be understood in the perspective of the heterosexual world.

One study found that if the person perceived others as defining him as homosexual and reacting to him as such, his self-definition incorporated the homosexual stereotype. When there were highly negative feelings there was bitterness and a withdrawal to a homosexual group. The societal reaction and the self-definition produce stress and need for some kind of adaptation. For some homosexual individuals there is a heightened awareness of their deviation and a hypersensitivity to the responses of others. The author of this study writes: "the findings of our analysis show that association in homosexual groups was caused by perceived societal rejection."[35]

Of course, all deviant subcultures represent structures built around that which makes their members deviant. The deviance becomes a highly significant role for the individual. This is similar to the complex activities that are built around the person's other major roles such as sex role, occupational role, or role as a family member. But for the deviant, as well as for others who know him as a deviant, the role of the development of the deviant commitment to homosexuality is of major importance in the organization of the homosexual's overall life style. The homosexual may organize his friendship, leisure time, and occupational adjustments around the homosexual community. The subculture becomes a socialization setting not only for the new homosexual but also for those who have been in the subculture for a while. Once individuals enter that life their personal and social identities as homosexuals are continually being defined through their interaction with one another. Of course, different people are involved in different degrees within the subculture and are therefore differentially influenced by it.

However great the homosexual's degree of involvement in the subculture, it must always be recognized that that involvement is only one important influence on his life style. The subculture presents one set of variables, which interact with many other variables, "such as personality dynamics and structure, personal appearance (including body build, gestures, demeanor), age, and occupation, to produce these attitudes, self-concepts, and behavior. Most accounts of gender identity and sex roles in male homosexuals focus on personality traits and psychodynamics and ignore the important contribution of the shared perspectives of homosexual subcultures."[36]

Bisexuals.   Because a special sexual choice sets homosexuals apart it is important to look more specifically at the direction the sexual activity takes. That is, there is a need to examine the range of homosexuality both as a sexual act and as a sexual role. One basic distinction that is made is between the bisexual and the homosexual. Bisexuals are persons who have both homosexual and heterosexual experiences. Some persons are bisexuals because they believe that the sexual act is the thing that one does and that the gender of the partner doesn't really matter. The sexual experience, not the sexual partner, is what matters. But other bisexuals may be caught in conflict because they are bothered by their inability to make a clear choice to go one way or another. Many of these seek out the homosexual subculture because they see it as providing them with a rationale for their homosexual inclinations.

In an extensive study of male homosexuals, Martin S. Weinberg and Colin J. Williams reported that 56 percent said that they had engaged in sexual relations with a female. But only 11 percent reported doing so within the six months prior to completing the questionnaire. Of that same group 50 percent reported having had homosexual relations about once a week or more while 24 percent reported having had homosexual relations once a month.[37]

DeLora and Warren argue that a bisexual identity is a relatively new phenomena and that many scientific observers as well as participants in the gay world deny the viability of a truly bisexual identity. They go on to argue that the most important aspect of bisexuality today is that it is becoming institutionalized as a lifestyle and identity. As with many beliefs, bisexuals can become almost religious in their ideology. They stress the universality of human love and the naturalness of sexual expression or love for everyone. "In this they are sometimes bitterly opposed by both the advocates of traditional morality and the older members of the gay subculture."[38] It seems likely that the actual number of bisexuals of this sort are small. But because they are often highly visible in the entertainment world they seem much more common than they are in fact.

Homosexual subculture. One of the characteristics of the homosexual subculture is a high degree of sexual promiscuity. The amount of promiscuity makes it very difficult to estimate the number of sex partners of the adult male homosexual. Many homosexuals estimate that they have had hundreds of sex partners, and some even place their estimates in the thousands. In his sample of adult male homosexuals Paul H. Gebhard found that two thirds had had over 75 sex partners. He points out that part of the reason for the large numbers is that some homosexuals are as interested in sexual activity for its own sake as in achieving orgasm.[39]

DeLora and Warren describe a common setting for the highly promiscuous sexuality of some homosexuals. This is often found in the Turkish baths or steam baths that proliferate in urban areas of the United States. These are places where men who want inexpensive sex can gain access to dozens or even hundreds of potential sex partners. "Many steam baths have an 'orgy room' designed to entertain multiple participants in sexual encounters. All have private rooms in which potential sex partners can sit or lie in wait."[40]

Highly important to any deviant subculture is what takes place when an individual enters and is accepted by the subculture. In the life cycle of the individual this is a crucial "naming stage." Within the homosexual subculture this stage is referred to as "coming out"— presenting oneself as being homosexual at least to the extent of wanting to function at times within the subculture. "This process often involves a change in the symbolic meaning of the homosexual category for the homosexually oriented individual. What for him was previously a category for the mentally ill, perverts, and so forth, now becomes a socially acceptable category."[41]

When the homosexual first comes out, his decision may release a great deal of sexual energy. During the initial period after coming out he may pursue sex quite indiscriminately and with great vigor and enthusiasm. At this time the young homosexual often throws himself totally into the homosexual life. He frequently wants to become totally involved because he is not part of a subculture in which he feels comfortable.

During the coming out stage there is often a tendency to "act out" in public places in a somewhat effeminate manner. Many young males (between 18 and 25) go through a crisis of femininity. Some, in a transitory fashion, wear female clothing, known as "going in drag." However, "the tendency is for this kind of behavior to be a transitional experiment for most homosexuals, an experiment that leaves vestiges of 'camp' behavior, but traces more often expressive of the character of the cultural life of the homosexual community than of some overriding need of individual homosexuals."[42]

Gebhard found that deep emotional involvements were commonly reported among homosexuals. In his sample 81 percent said that they had loved another male, and 63 percent had loved more than one male."[43] As suggested, finding a permanent partner was a goal of many homosexuals. The proportion who pursued this goal increased after about age 30, when finding a steady mate became a significant concern.[44] As the homosexual's competitive ability on the sexual market decreases, a more permanent relationship becomes even more desirable to him.

It is clear that an increasing number of homosexual couples want to make their relationships legitimate. In one case, *Baker* v. *Nelson* (Minnesota, 1972), one such couple challenged the restrictions on homosexual marriages, arguing that "the right to marry without regard to the sex of the parties is a fundamental right of all persons and that restricting marriage to only couples of the opposite sex is irrational and invidiously discriminatory." The court disagreed, affirming the traditional position that marriage "is the state of union between persons of the opposite sex."[45]

Of all the personal factors that might worry the homosexual probably none is more psychologically upsetting for many than aging. Because such great importance is attached to appearing youthful and attractive in order to compete successfully, the homosexual often worries about losing his youth. In some of the subcultures aging may occur at

Homosexual marriage to legitimize the relationship

Mimi Forsyth/Monkmeyer Press Photo Service

around age 30, and men past that age may be seen as "senior citizens." It is very common for the homosexual to try to postpone getting old by imitating the young. One observer writes that the middle-aged homosexual grows long "what is left of his hair, wears beads, body shirts, western vests, and peace emblems, studies the head's manner of movement and speech, and goes right on getting high on alcohol, because he considers drugs unsafe."[46]

Gagnon and Simon have suggested that aging is a life-cycle crisis that the homosexual shares with the heterosexual in our youth-oriented society. They point out that while American society in general places an extremely high emphasis on youth, the homosexual community places an even greater stress. But the homosexual has fewer resources with which to meet the crisis of aging than does the heterosexual. "For the heterosexual there are his children whose careers assure a sense of the future and a wife whose sexual availability cushions the shock of declining sexual attractiveness. In addition, the crisis of aging comes later to the heterosexual, at an age when his sexual powers have declined and expectations concerning his sexuality are considerably lower."[47]

Militancy is usually based in the subculture because that is the source of organizational structure and force. However, some homosexuals have been involved in the new militancy in various ways that are only partly related to the homosexual subculture. But basic to the new homosexual militancy is some organization. This is necessary so that homosexuals can present their case collectively and not as isolated individuals. Up until recent years almost all homosexuals in the United States were extremely secretive, and the last thing they wanted was any kind of public exposure. As a result they had no way of presenting organized resistance to the forces against them in the broader society.

Among homosexuals the militant movement is usually known as the "homophile" movement. Edward Sagarin has pointed out that no group so large in number and so completely stigmatized has remained unorganized so long.[48] No homophile organization appeared in America until after World War II. Sagarin suggests that several factors inhibited earlier organizing among homosexuals. First, before World War II the attitude in the United States was negative to social change with regard to sex and particularly with regard to homosexuality. Second, the concealment of the homosexual encouraged him *not* to organize. Third, there was no structure for the exchange of ideas and values which could lead to an organization. Finally, there were no leaders primarily because those who had the intellectual respect that might allow them to be leaders had the most to lose by giving up their anonymity.[49]

But these restrictions changed in many respects, and the greater sexual permissiveness of society created a climate that made possible the emergence of the homophile organizations. The generally new attitudes toward sex meant that even the highly taboo area of homosexuality could be discussed. The 1960s and 1970s saw the discussion of homosexuality even in the most conservative of mass media—television. At the present time there are homosexual groups which conduct programs to educate the public to a better understanding and tolerance of homosexuality.

The one thing all the homosexual groups have in common is the willingness of their membership to identify themselves as homosexual and to seek an end to social discrimination against the homosexual. These aims are reflected in the slogans: "Out of the closets and into the streets" and "Gay is good" and in the general revolutionary rhetoric of the militant young.[50]

Also basic to the homophile movement is the changing concept that the homosexual has about himself. The homosexual organizations try to bolster their members' feelings that they are "as good as anybody else"—which means "as *well* as anybody else."[51] The groups argue that homosexuality is neither a sickness nor a mental disturbance and that talking about cures is therefore irrelevant. "Anyone who suggests cure, according to Mattachine leaders, must be a charlatan or a quack."[52] For them the slogan might be "gay is good" in the same way that "black is beautiful." This is also seen in the belief that "cure" is irrelevant.

Probably few, if any, homosexuals are able to so immerse themselves in the homosexual subculture as to cut themselves off from the broader society. Being members of the homosexual subculture does not remove homosexuals from the social influences of society. Even if the role of homosexual becomes the major role for some persons in the subculture, it is not the only one. Such persons will probably have to interact or be defined according to broader society in some significant areas of their nonsexual behavior. But probably most homosexuals feel that they must hide their homosexuality on many if not most occasions, and this builds a strain in making sure that they are filling the proper role in a given social situation.

As mentioned at the start of the chapter, engaging in homosexual acts is against the law, and there is always the danger of getting caught. The greater the success of the homosexual in the "straight" community, the greater his anxiety about getting caught. The fact that his homosexual secret is "criminal" means that any exposure may lead to legal consequences—and this increases his personal anxieties. Although most homosexuals are able to avoid exposure, the potential for exposure is always there.

Weinberg and Williams provide some evidence of the homosexual's willingness to let his sexual preference be known. Thirty percent of their respondents reported trying to hide their homosexuality from *all* heterosexuals; 20 percent said that they tried to hide it from a few heterosexuals or none; and about one fifth of their sample could be considered overt homosexuals. As to social interactions, about half was with other homosexuals, and only a small number said that they socialized only with other homosexuals. "Sixteen percent state that they are not really known homosexuals, and an additional 29 percent that they are not part of any homosexual group. While 30 percent attend homosexual bars and clubs once a week or more, 34 percent never or almost never attend."[53]

In recent years there has been some concern with the homosexual from a combined legal and medical perspective. That concern has centered on the possibility of his being a high carrier of venereal diseases. Up until the late 1950s there were no standard reports on male-to-male transmissions of venereal disease. In fact, the American Social Health Association, which accumulates such data from 120 health departments each year, did not request that information until 1967. However, as early as 1955 there had been scattered reports which indicated an increasing spread of syphilis by homosexuals. One recent finding showed that only 7 percent of male patients with gonorrhea admitted to homosexual contact as compared to 57 percent of male patients with syphilis. There would appear to be no logical reason why the percent of homosexuals should be so much lower among patients with gonorrhea than with syphilis. One reason why venereal disease rates are higher among homosexuals is that their sexual contact rates are twice as high as those of heterosexual patients. That is, homosexuals averaged twice as many sexual contacts as did heterosexual males. E. Randolph Trice found that venereal diseases are usually spread by homosexuals who prefer anal intercourse. Another study concluded that "syphilitic infection is most likely to occur in the male homosexual in the age group 15 to 29, who is apt to be highly promiscuous, and whose sexual preference is anal sodomy."[54]

How do the institutions of religion, government, and the military treat the homosexual? In recent years some religious groups have accepted the homosexual, but for the most part organized religion has rejected him and part of the reason for the rejection of homosexuality by religion may be that religious groups have often had to deal with it in their own ranks. When a lay person is found to be a homosexual it usually means silent shunning, and if a clergyman is found to be a homosexual it means a transfer to a different location. But given the changing nature of some religious groups—their increasing concern with personal and social problems—there will probably be a liberalizing of many church policies with regard to homosexuality. But the changes will probably come from a few of the leaders and not from the more conservative congregations. One change was a resolution advocating equal rights for women and homosexuals, passed in March 1975 by the governing board of the National Council of Churches. At the same time the board made it clear that the stand did not imply that homosexuals should be eligible to serve as ministers.[55]

In 1972 San Francisco passed the first civil rights legislation for homosexuals. By a vote of ten to one the Board of Supervisors expanded the city's job discrimination ordinance to include prohibitions against discrimination on the basis of sex or sexual orientation by companies doing business with the city.[56]

The federal government has long had a policy of not hiring homosexuals as well as a policy of getting rid of homosexuals discovered after hiring. This has been done on the ground that the homosexual is a security risk because he would be subject to blackmail and other forms of extortion. A chairman of the Civil Service Commission has said that a person who proclaims publicly that he engages in homosexual activities would not be suitable for federal employment. However, the same chairman went on to say that homosexual tendencies alone were not sufficient cause for denial of employment. "In other words, it's all right to have homosexual tendencies but it isn't all right to exercise them, even in private with consenting adults."[57] However, the liberalizing influence has been affecting federal employment policies. The Federal Appeals Court in Washington, D.C., recently declared that a government agency could not dismiss a homosexual employee without first proving that his homosexuality would significantly influence the efficiency of the agency's operations. In 1971 one United States District Court ordered the defense department to restore security clearances to two declared homosexuals. The court ruled that the Bill of Rights prohibited the government from subjecting homosexuals to "probing personal questions." Furthermore, the government could not withhold security clearance for refusal to answer such questions."[58]

Finally, one United States institution that has always taken a highly repressive view toward homosexuality is the military, although historically armies have not only tolerated homosexuality but have on occasion encouraged it. It is possible that the strongly repressive policies of the American military establishment are an overreaction to the homosexual permissiveness of the military in other societies.

The rates of homosexuality in the armed forces are difficult to estimate. One study of the army shows that from 1960 to 1967 only 8 out of every 10,000 soldiers were discharged for reasons of homosexuality. Of course, this number represents only those homosexuals whom the Army found out about and processed for discharge.[59] A study of homosexuals who had been in the military services found that only about one fifth of them reported difficulties during their military experience.[60] Apparently a definite majority of homosexuals are able to complete their military careers without being in trouble on that score.

What about general public opinion? Even the medical profession is far from unanimous in its acceptance of more permissive views toward the homosexual. In a recent sample of doctors 68 percent agreed that discreet homosexual acts between consenting adults should be permitted without legal restrictions, while the rest felt they should not. This is a much more liberal position than that of the general public. A Harris poll reported that 63 percent of the nation considered homosexuals "harmful to American life." Respondents in a study of traits attributed to the male homosexual found them: "sexually abnormal," 72 percent; "perverted," 52 percent; "mentally ill," 40 percent; and "maladjusted," 40 percent.[61] In a 1970 study based on a nationwide random sample two thirds of the respondents regarded homosexuality as "very much obscene and vulgar," and less than 8 percent endorsed the view that homosexuality was not at all obscene and vulgar. Substantial majorities of the respondents agreed that homosexuals should be allowed to work as artists, beauticians, florists, and musicians, but almost equally substantial majorities did not believe that they should be permitted to engage in occupations of influence and authority. "Three quarters would deny to a homosexual the right to be a minister, a school teacher, or a judge, and two thirds would bar the homosexual from medical practices and government service."[62]

Female Homosexuality

It was suggested that often strong negative feelings are directed at the male homosexual by the general public. By contrast, when the female homosexual (or lesbian) is mentioned there is often vague, almost puzzled, reaction by many people. That is, people are aware that such women exist but have never come in contact with them, so their awareness is abstract and not based on experience. Also, by contrast with the male homosexual, relatively little has been written about the lesbian and she has rarely been presented through the mass media. So for most Americans the level of knowledge as well as the level of experience is low.

The female homosexual should be discussed separately from the male homosexual because, even though there are some similarities among homosexuals of both sexes, the differences are probably greater than the similarities. The basic similarity is that both male and female homosexuals choose members of their own sex as sex partners. But once that is recognized, the similarities are generally not very great. Basically the male homosexual is a male and the female homosexual is a female in terms of the basic roles by which others see them and they see themselves. And the choice of a same-sex partner generally does not significantly change these basic roles for either men or women. Within the homosexual setting males are more apt to develop and depend on subcultural involvement than are females. That is, the social context of being a homosexual is more complex and developed for the male than for the female.

Historical background.   While there are many historical references to male homosexuality there are relatively few references to female homosexuality. The Talmud of the ancient Hebrews regarded the practice of lesbianism as a trivial obscenity and the woman was punished by a priest. There is some evidence that lesbianism was common in the harems of Egypt and India, where women were herded together and often saw no men other than the husband they shared. Each wife was expected to wait her turn to be sexually satisfied by the shared husband. But many may have turned to one another for sexual release. It may have been that the husband knew of the homosexuality but was willing to overlook it rather than to have his wives' sexual frustrations create problems for him.

The first real advocate of female homosexuality in the Western world was Sappho, who lived in the 6th century B.C. She was born and lived most of her adult life on the island of Lesbos. Sappho had several affairs with men and was the mother of one child. She was one of the first persons to argue for the rights of women. Sappho appears to have fallen in love with many of her female students, and she wrote sensuous poems for them. Those poems later won her great respect, and she came to be known among the Greeks as the Tenth Muse. Basically the belief that developed on Lesbos was that the admiration of beauty could not be separated from sex, and as a result many women took sexual delight in one another. The word *lesbian* has become a universal generic term for the female homosexual.

Given the high repression of all forms of sexual behavior in the early days of the American colonies there is little evidence that lesbianism existed at that time and if it did it must have been very well hidden. In the early written records of the United States there is little reference to female homosexuality. In fact, in American literature, the female homosexual is ignored throughout the 19th century except possibly for some suggestion in the novels of Oliver Wendell Holmes. Lesbianism appears "for the first time in American literature in explicit fashion in the expatriate writing of Henry James and Gertrude Stein."[63]

The laws that exist with reference to the female homosexual are much simpler and less restrictive than those that exist for the male homosexual. Basically the reason is that in most societies homosexuality among men has been seen as far more threatening in both scope and complexity. It is also important that with few exceptions the legal controls over sexual behavior developed in all societies have been the work of men. In many respects the laws about sexual behavior have been aimed at protecting their interests. For example, in prostitution the male customer is usually protected. In extramarital relationships the woman has more to lose and is more severely condemned than the man. Few laws have been directed against the lesbian because men have rarely ever seen her as a threat. When men have thought about her they have always felt superior to the lesbian and have seen no need to legally constrain her.

Much of the American legal system came from the common law of England, and it can be seen that the English legal view of the female homosexual is close to that found in the United States. At no time in England was homosexual behavior between women prohibited by law. This has probably been a reflection of the relative unimportance of women in society. When the criminal law of England was recently reformed to allow private homosexual relations between consenting adults, lesbians were never taken into consideration because there were no laws against them in the first place.

In many states the sex laws do not apply to lesbians, but in some states the laws for female homosexuals are similar to those for the male homosexual. For example, in New York it is not illegal to be a female homosexual, but it is illegal to perform a homosexual act. Yet, rarely do the women run into trouble with the law because most homosexual arrests are made for public behavior. Lesbians are rarely "cruisers" and don't hang around public toilets, where the majority of male arrests are made. According to Kinsey, from 1696 until 1952 there was not a single case on record in the United States of a sustained conviction of a female for homosexual activity. Kinsey also found that of his total sample of several hundred women who had had homosexual experience only three had had minor difficulties and only one had had serious difficulties with the police.[64]

For the most part the police do not consider lesbians as a threat because lesbians keep to themselves, are not as promiscuous as male homosexuals, and rarely solicit others. The UCLA study in Los Angeles found that "decoy enforcement is considered too degrading for policewomen. However, entertainment licenses have been revoked as the result of observation of lewd conduct in lesbian bars by male undercover officers."[65] The same study goes on to say that the police view lesbians as much less aggressive than male homosexuals. Their behavior is much less conspicuous than that of male homosexuals and less likely to offend the public. Thus, "there are a minimal number of complaints concerning female activity."[66] However, the police seem to have been picking up more female homosexuals in recent years. In New York City the police have picked up women for "loitering," a charge applied "for soliciting another for the purpose of engaging in deviate sexual intercourse."

TABLE 11–1

Number and Percent of Women by Age Who Have Had Sexual Experience with a Woman

	Sexual experience			
	Yes		No	
Age	Number	Percent	Number	Percent
Under 20	86	15	485	85
20–24.............	509	12	3,793	88
25–29.............	596	10	5,069	90
30–34.............	327	9	3,139	91
35–39.............	166	10	1,561	90
40 and over	286	14	2,051	86
Totals	1,970	12	16,098	88

Source: "October Sex Quiz," *Redbook Magazine* (December 1974).

These arrests are probably the most militant lesbians, who are insisting on their rights in all areas, including that of soliciting sex partners if they choose to do so. In a study of active lesbians in Philadelphia one fourth said that they had been arrested by the police, but usually on a drug or solicitation charge. Twenty percent said that they had experienced physical aggression from the police. But some of these women were a part of other militant and deviant subcultures, and therefore their encounters with the police were often not simply a result of lesbian activities. The women may be lesbians, political militants, female militants, and so forth, and may come into contact with the police in various roles or combinations of roles.[67]

As mentioned it is hard to estimate with any accuracy the frequency of male homosexuality, but it is even harder to estimate the frequency of female homosexuality. Most lesbianism is undiscovered because it is less overt. The differences also contribute to a misconception shared by many that female homosexuality is less common than it is in fact, and that makes estimating the rates even more difficult. There are several other reasons for underestimating the number of lesbians. First, an effeminate male is often associated with homosexuality, whether or not he is a homosexual. But masculine women are not usually defined as homosexual. Therefore, the defining of visual characteristics varies for men and women. Second, male homosexuals are much more apt to gather in public places, and the public is therefore more aware of them than it is of the lesbians it rarely sees. Third, the male is promiscuous and seeks out his sexual partners openly and aggressively—ways that are not common for the lesbian. He is therefore seen in his sexually seeking role. Finally, male homosexuals are more open and aggressive and are therefore given much more publicity in the newspapers.

The best estimates suggest that possibly 15 percent of American females have at least one homosexual experience. In the *Redbook* study of married women 12 percent said they had had a homosexual experience since the age of 18. For the majority that had happened only once and 60 percent described the homosexual experience as unpleasant or repulsive. DeLora and Warren estimate that only about 2 percent of all females define themselves as mainly or completely homosexual.[68]

Causes.   Most theories about homosexuality have been developed to explain the male homosexual. Often such theories are applied to the female homosexual as a kind of afterthought. The failure to study female homosexuality is not due only to the fact that fewer lesbians turn to psychiatry for therapy. The truth is that psychiatric studies almost invariably emphasize male behavior. This is another reflection of society's traditional view that what men do is more important than what women do.[69] However, some lesbians believe that their sexual orientation is a problem that should be taken to the psychiatrist.

The biologically oriented theories of female homosexuality are usually the mirror image of those for males. Usually implied is the assumption that sexual orientation is influenced by the same genetic and/or hormonal factors and that lesbians show a biologically caused shift toward maleness. However, most female homosexuals have normal sex hormones after puberty and there is little evidence of difference in body build between heterosexual and homosexual women.[70]

The limitation of the hormonal approach is reflected in a survey of the literature that was unable to find any concrete clinical reports on actual attempts to successfully "cure" lesbianism through the use of estrogens or by antiandrogen treatment. "Clinical evidence suggests that in most cases the variation of androgen levels in adulthood does not change sexual orientation."[71]

Over the years the traditional psychoanalytic view of female homosexuality has been dominant in defining them as pathological. But for the most part what research was done by analysts used highly atypical samples such as lesbians in prisons and emotionally disturbed women in therapy to support their psychodynamic approach.[72]

One study characterizes as sexist the belief that women who are dissatisfied with the traditional feminine roles of wife and mother are by definition sick and need to be cured. "It is, in fact, the very fallacy that, in the past, allowed psychotherapists to do many of their female clients more harm than good. The interpretation is doubly hazardous to lesbians, insulting not only their homosexuality, but their womanhood as well."[73] The study also points out that the well-meaning therapist is often stymied by the paucity of practical or theoretical literature concerning the lesbian and especially the mentally healthy lesbian. The lack of nonjudgmental material is said to have had a great deal to do with the failure of the helping professions to be supportive of lesbians. "Furthermore, many members of the helping professions continue to speak in terms of curing the lesbian of her current sexual preference. Such treatment of the lesbian can create rather than solve problems."[74] Some lesbians have been helped by feminist therapists who can provide an open therapeutic environment for lesbian women.

Implied in most theories of homosexuality is that whatever the alleged causes they are out of the hands of the individual. To a great extent this is a denial that the individual might choose homosexuality. Many persons cannot accept the notion of a choice of homosexuality—it simply defies their value commitments and is seen as a threat to the family. Yet, choice is often involved. One study found that half of the lesbians explained their homosexuality as free-choice behavior, another one fifth believed it to be innately determined, and one seventh saw it as a result of negative childhood or heterosexual experiences.[75]

Mark Friedman, clinical psychologist, states that his research on lesbians shows them to score higher than a control group in autonomy, spontaneity, orientation toward the present (as opposed to obsession with the past or anticipation of the future), and sensitivity to their own needs and feelings. Another study comparing lesbians with a control group found the lesbians to be more independent, resilient, bohemian, and self-sufficient. Still another study, quoted by Friedman, found that lesbians scored higher than the controls on both goal direction and self-acceptance.[76]

There have been many attempts to find psychological factors that would differentiate homosexual from heterosexual women. For the most part they have been unsuccessful. There has been a failure to discriminate lesbians from heterosexuals on the basis of projective tests, no differences in problem drinking, personal adjustment, defensiveness, and self-confidence or self-acceptancy. Actually some studies that do find differences between the two groups find some that favor the adjustment of lesbians. Lesbians have been reported to be more independent and dominant, to tend more toward self-confidence, and to appear to be more independent, inner directed, accepting of aggression, and satisfied with their work than matched heterosexual women. "In other instances, there are indications that lesbians exhibit tendencies toward more depression, suicide attempts, and alcohol abuse."[77] Ferguson and Finkler suggest that for some lesbians the ability to confront and resolve their deviancy may result in a more well-defined sense of identity and greater self-acceptance.[78]

It seems probable that most lesbians follow a pattern of growing up similar to that of most heterosexual girls. The notion that "extreme" or "special" socialization causes homosexuality is not substantiated by the available research. All the women that Gagnon and Simon studied reported some heterosexual dating and mild sex play during their high school years. "Only two carried it to the extent of intercourse, although a larger number indicated that they had experi-

Alex Webb/Magnum Photos, Inc.

A couple

mented with heterosexual coitus after homosexual experiences."[79] It appears that by high school age many young homosexuals, both male and female, are aware of schoolmates like themselves.

Simon and Gagnon have provided the best sociological explanation for the development of female homosexuality. They argue that in most cases the female homosexual follows a conventional pattern in developing her involvement with sexuality. They go on to say that the organizing event in the development of male sexuality is puberty, while the organizing event for females is the period of romantic involvement that culminates in marriage for most. For females the "discovery" of love relations precedes the "discovery" of sexuality while the reverse is generally true for males. "The discovery of their homosexuality usually occurred very late in adolescence, often even in the years of young adulthood, and the actual commencement of overt sexual behavior frequently came at a late stage of an intense emotional involvement."[80] What Simon and Gagnon are saying in part is that for women, training in love comes before training in sexuality. And for most women, including most lesbians, the pursuit of sexual gratification is something distinct from emotional or rational involvement and is not particularly attractive; "indeed, for many it may be impossible."[81] So lesbian women may have fewer partners because they have internalized the sociosexual norms of combining love and sexuality just as have heterosexual women.[82]

The above argument suggests that in one sense the female homosexual should be defined somewhat differently than the male homosexual. They both choose sex partners of the same sex, but there are often differences in what is wanted from and with the partner. The male most always wants the partner primarily for sexual activity, while this is often much less true for the female. This is not to argue that the lesbian does not have a strong sexual interest, but rather that her sexual interest is often a part of an interpersonal interest. A lesbian, then, is a woman who feels a strong and recurring need to have sexual relations with another woman within an interpersonal context.

As is true for many other social problems there can be problems for lesbians when they define themselves as deviant. The self-naming process for the female homosexual sometimes leads to fear and anxiety. Del Martin and Phyllis Lyon have suggested that every lesbian must face an identity crisis. This occurs during that period of life when she is at odds with the society in which she lives. Martin and Lyon report a discussion involving 20 lesbians between the ages of 25 and 32 in which it was revealed that only two had not attempted suicide when they were teenagers.[83] Fear plays a big part in the life of most lesbians, and often the fear is justified. "Lesbians are subjected to reprisals from all quarters of society: friends, family, employers, police, and government."[84]

In general, the causes of female homosexuality, like those of male homosexuality, are seen as complex and varied. As Ethel Sawyer points out, homosexuals are coming to be viewed as people who emerge as special kinds of social beings because of their intrinsic motivations, individual adaptations, and childhood conflicts. But along with this the homosexual is also coming to be viewed as a product of the total and ongoing environment, which includes the family, "peer groups, various legal and societal penalties and sanctions, and subcultural expectations, all of which help to shape the homosexual as he exists in American society."[85] And as is the case with the male homosexual there is little reason to believe that the strongly committed female homosexual is very often going to be totally reoriented from complete homosexuality to complete heterosexuality. There seems little likelihood of any "cure" for female homosexuality in the sense of changing the nature and the object of the lesbian's sexual desires.

The subculture is much less important for female homosexuals than it is for male homosexuals. The main reason for this difference is the women's greater desire for privacy. In general the women are much less aggressive in all ways than are the men. However, for some women the lesbian subculture does exist and does have meaning.

The evidence suggests that for homosexual women their "coming out" occurs two or three years later than for homosexual men. This reflects the differences in sexual socialization for women and men regardless of gender orientation. In American society men learn earlier to cope with their own sexuality without its having to be legitimated through love. But women, and apparently many homosexual women, learn to articulate their sexual needs at a later age than men.[86]

What can be said in a general way about the lesbian subculture? For the individuals who participate in it, the subculture serves a number of functions. First, it provides a means for making sexual contacts as well as for expediting those contacts, though it is nowhere the "flesh market" of the male homosexual subculture. However, physical appearance does play a part in the interaction within the lesbian bar. For example, considerable emphasis is placed on youth, and the younger lesbians are often critical of the appearance of older lesbians. Joanne Long reports that on many occasions young lesbians referred to the one bar that attracted older lesbians as the "wrinkle room." She reports that it is fairly common for attractive women to pair off with unattractive ones. But some of the most unattractive lesbians, especially those who are obese, are often forced to settle for unattractive lovers because they are rejected by the other women. "In general, however, physical attractiveness is not as important in the lesbian subculture as in the heterosexual society."[87]

The lesbian subculture also provides a source of social support. It is a place where the lesbian can express her feelings or describe her experiences because she is interacting with others like herself. The subculture also "includes a language and an ideology which provides each individual lesbian with already developed attitudes that help her resist the societal claim that she is diseased, depraved, or shameful."[88] It can be seen that these ends of the lesbian subculture are basically no different than those of the male homosexual subculture, rather, the difference is one of degree, with the subculture generally being less important to lesbians than to male homosexuals.

Reasons have been suggested for the lesser involvement of women in the homosexual subculture. One is that the woman who makes a commitment to homosexuality is not as removed or as alienated from conventional society as is the man. Her sexual choice and her patterns for pursuing it are less recognized and recognizable to the broader society. A second reason is that the forces of repression that result in differences between males and females during the ages when sexual activity is initiated may also help the female to handle subsequent sexual restrictions more easily than the male is able to. "More females than males should therefore be able to resist quasipublic homosexual behavior which increases the risks of disclosure; further, lesbians should be better able to resist relations that involve sexual exchange without any emotional investment."[89]

As with male homosexuals, the "passive" and "active" roles of female homosexuals have been exaggerated. The stereotype has been that the "active" sex partner who performs the sex is the "dyke" while the "passive" partner who receives sexual stimulation is the "femme." Lesbians do not often define themselves with such simplicity. In the Philadelphia sample, half of the female homosexuals defined themselves as "gay" and half as "bisexual." The distinction appeared to be that the "gay" women had completely rejected men as sex partners while the "bisexual" women had *almost* completely rejected men.

It appears that a large proportion of lesbians have had some heterosexual experiences. Martin and Lyon comment that at least three fourths of the lesbians they knew had had heterosexual intercourse more than once. These experiences took place within a marriage situation, while dating, as experiments conducted out of curiosity, or as tests of sexual identity. "For the majority of those women the experience was good, erotically; that is, orgasm was achieved and there was a pleasurable feeling. But there was not the emotional involvement which was present in the lesbian sexual relationship."[90] Long found that among the women she studied it was a "cardinal sin" to have sexual relations with a man. "Bisexual women are generally rejected in the lesbian subculture. Men are given almost no place in the lesbian world and are seen in all ways as intruders."[91]

There are some differences between female and male homosexuals and their heterosexual experiences. One study found that more than half of the lesbians had experienced heterosexual intercourse at least once in their lives, whereas only one fifth of the homosexual men had. In the year prior to the study, twice as many homosexual women as men had had at least one heterosexual intercourse experience. Furthermore, most lesbians gain their first sexual experience heterosexually, but none of the men had their first heterosexual experience before their first homosexual experience.[92]

Phillip W. Blumstein and Pepper Schwartz write that contrary to classical psychosexual theory many women go from an identification with heterosexual behavior to one with homosexual behavior, even after a quite satisfactory period in the first category. And there are some women where there is no coherent gender pattern, alternating randomly between males and females. "And, of course, there are many kinds of women fitting between the two polar types."[93] The authors stress that the behavior of persons with a bisexual identification is amazingly diverse and that their day-to-day life styles vary greatly from one to another. "Not only are the paths of bisexuality many and diverse, but they are processual and dynamic, involving sometimes abrupt changes and at other times gradual shifts from one stage to another."[94]

Another characteristic of lesbians that distinguishes them from male homosexuals is that they are much less promiscuous. One study found that homosexual men had 15 times as many sex partners during the course of their lives as had lesbians. "During the year preceding the study, the lesbians had had an average of 2 different partners; the homosexual males, by contrast, had an average of 16."[95]

There appears to be little question that lesbians in general have a high desire for permanent relationships. This is a pattern generally common to women, regardless of the type of sexual partner. The lesbian, like the heterosexual female, places a higher stress on interpersonal involvement than on sexual outlet. As a result homosexual relationships between females tend to be more affective, to take place under more stable conditions, and to be viewed in terms of a total relationship. Men are far more likely to see homosexuality simply as a means of sexual gratification and as a casual impersonal act. Long found that the overwhelming emphasis among lesbians was to meet new women in the hope of developing permanent relationships rather than simply of obtaining sex. Many women go to the lesbian bars in the hope of finding a lover. Since there is so much pressure among the women to find mates the lesbian bar might be called a "mate market." This is in sharp contrast to the male homosexual bar which is much more a "sexual market."[96]

Siegrid Schafer's study found that about four fifths of the lesbians and three fifths of the homosexual males had steady relationships at the time of the study. But nearly twice as many women as men live together and almost all lesbian women spend all their free time with their respective partners. It was also found that most of the homosexual males renounced sexual fidelity.[97]

It was suggested that aging was crucial for the male homosexual in many ways, including an increasing desire for more durable relationships. It appears that aging is less traumatic for the lesbian because she does not operate in a setting as competitive as that of the male homosexual. There is some irony in the fact that in a society in which the decline in physical attractiveness that comes with aging is generally more crucial to and resisted more by women, the reverse may be true among female homosexuals. This difference is also explained in part by the greater stress homosexual females place on interpersonal factors. In general it would appear that aging is easier for the female homosexual to handle psychologically than it is for the male homosexual.

One area in which there is a great difference between male and female homosexuals is with regard to children. Many lesbians not only want children but have them. Often lesbians will have children from a marriage and keep them after divorce. A woman would have to be quite openly homosexual before the court would refuse to give her custody of the child, because children are almost always placed with the mother. Actually there is no law against placing a child with lesbians, and any refusal by the courts probably would be on the ground of a poor moral atmosphere in the home. There has been some pressure in recent years to allow lesbian couples to adopt children. It is doubtful whether this will occur where the women openly state that they are lesbians. However, there have been moves in some places to allow single women to adopt, and this will enable lesbians who do not identify themselves as such to adopt children. It would also appear that lesbians who have children to take care of find it somewhat easier to adjust to the aging process.

Unlike the situation of male homosexuals, no occupations are stereotyped as being lesbian occupations. About the only prediction that might be made is that lesbians would be found more commonly in those occupations in which women are isolated from men through physical separation or other restrictions against heterosexual interaction. Occupations are important to lesbians because they are not dependent on males as breadwinners. Lesbians appear to be more seriously committed to work than are most women, and one reflection of this is that they tend to have relatively stable work histories.[98] Martin and Lyon believe that most lesbians make it a practice to keep their private lives completely separate from their work, even though they may be aware of the presence of other lesbians where they work. "Consequently most lesbians observe an unspoken moral code of not exposing one another, a sort of mutually protective loyalty pact."[99]

Like the male homosexuals, but to a much lesser extent, lesbians have developed militant organizations to push for what they believe to be their rights. The largest lesbian organization, the Daughters of Bilitis, was founded in 1955. It derives its name from some 19th century song lyrics that glorified lesbian love. The organization has its headquarters in San Francisco, and in 1969 there were four official and five probationary chapters. The organization's purpose is to explore changing some laws that are believed to discriminate against the lesbian, but it also maintains social clubs where some counseling takes place. The organization is generally known by its initials, DOB, and it has a few honorary male members whom it calls Sons of Bilitis, or SOBs.[100]

Sidney Abbott and Barbara Love argue that the radical lesbian is no longer ashamed of her commitment to a lesbian way of life and she has come to realize that most of her problems are due to social repression rather than to unhealthy traits in her personality. They point out that the homosexual movement is different from most other social movements because of the ease of concealment. "As a social move-

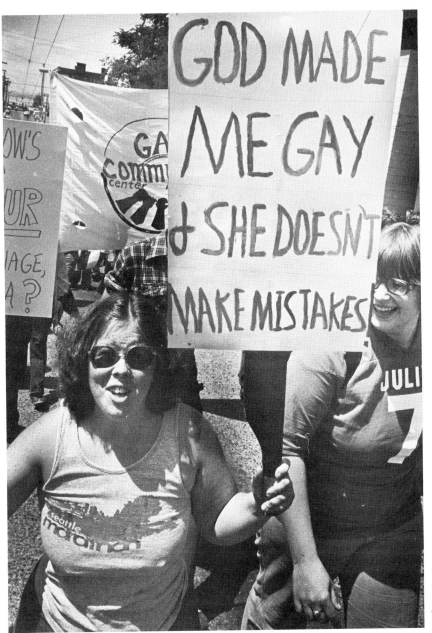

The gay movement

ment fighting for acceptance, lesbians and male homosexuals will have to find a way to mobilize the many homosexuals who still feel they cannot afford to 'come out' in the open."[101] DeLora and Warren write that the typical lesbian feminist tends to scorn the traditional feminine styles of seductive dress, make-up, and use of body language. And they also are very likely to scorn the uniform of the butch lesbian bar community.[102]

The new militancy of some lesbians is not so much a result of their feeling that discrimination against them has been increasing as that they should do something about the wrongs they fell they have long suffered. There is also some evidence of overlap between the militant lesbians and some factions of the militant women's liberation movement. This should not be surprising because the female homosexual is a member of two minority groups—she is a woman and a homosexual.

It seems quite likely that in the future, lesbianism, if not more common, is going to be much more open. This would seem to be an inevitable part of women's achieving greater equality. As women attain rights to sexual expression closer to those of the male, those rights are going to be directed in a number of different directions. As society moves toward a single sex standard for both males and females the consequences will cut across all areas of sexual expression. Therefore, women will have greater equality both heterosexually and homosexually.

There are changes occurring in the United States toward the treatment of homosexuals of both sexes. This is true even though public opinion has not changed much. For example, in San Francisco if a homosexual feels he is receiving undue police harassment he is encouraged to go to the police department's community relations division, which will usually straighten the matter out. And the State Liquor Authority of New York lifted its traditional ban on homosexual bars, and various state courts decided that "intrasexual" dancing, touching, and even kissing were not necessarily disorderly so long as they refrained from touching one another upon primary sex organs.[103] The National Institute of Mental Health recommended the repeal of laws against private homosexual acts between consenting adults and a reassessment of bans by employers against hiring homosexuals. Yet, this recommendation came at the same time that a CBS poll found that two thirds of all Americans regarded homosexuals with "disgust, discomfort, or fear."[104]

The future of the homosexual in America is difficult to predict. This is because there is such a wide gulf between some professional belief and argument for greater tolerance and freedom and the prevailing feeling of contempt and disgust found among most Americans. If the homosexual, through his subcultural support and strength, chooses to become increasingly militant for his rights, one of two things will probably happen. He might be able to make the general population more tolerant of his sexual choice, but more likely, if he becomes militant he will antagonize more "middle Americans" and find the resistance to him even greater.

Homosexuality is a social problem similar in some ways to abortion, drug use, and pornography. They all represent a choice of behavior that society does not allow the individual to make for himself. It is an activity that society says can only have one choice and to go against that choice is to be morally wrong and therefore sinful or sick. The only way that homosexuality can cease to be defined as a social problem is for society to reduce its moral condemnation. It is certainly not going to cease being a problem because homosexuality will disappear. The vested interests with regard to homosexuality are rarely ones of financial gain as with crime, drugs, prostitution, and so forth. But rather they are the vested interests of a traditional morality that insists on defining what is proper and right for others.

Male homosexuality has become much more open in American society. Over the years there has been an attempt to explain homosexuality as first sin and later as mental illness. There is no agreement as to the causes of homosexuality nor as to any possible "cures." Often the problem for the homosexual is to live his or her life with minimal conflict and stress due to the dominant society with antihomosexual beliefs. Male homosexuality appears to be more common than female homosexuality.

NOTES

1. Debora Phillips, Steven C. Pischer, Gerald A. Groves and Ratan Singh, "Alternative Behavior Approaches to the Treatment of Homosexuality," *Archives of Sexual Behavior* (May 1976), pp. 223–24.

2. Mary McIntosh, "The Homosexual Role," *Social Problems* (Fall 1968), p. 188.

3. Wainwright Churchill, *Homosexual Behavior among Males* (New York: Hawthorn Books, 1967), p. 57.

4. "The Consenting Adult Homosexual and the Law," *UCLA Law Review*, University of California at Los Angeles (March 1966), p. 658.

5. Donald E. J. MacNamara and Edward Sagarin, *Sex, Crime, and the Law* (New York: The Free Press, 1977), p. 133.

6. Gilbert M. Cantor, "The Need for Homosexual Law Reform," in *The Same Sex: An Appraisal of Homosexuality*, by Ralph A. Weltge (Philadelphia: Pilgrim Press, 1969), p. 85.

7. *UCLA Law Review*, "Consenting Adult," p. 689.

8. *Newsweek* (Oct. 27, 1969).

9. MacNamara and Sagarin, *Sex, Crime*, p. 137.

10. Cantor, "Law Reform," p. 83.

11. John H. Gagnon and William Simon, "Sexual Deviance in Contemporary America," *The Annals* (March 1968), pp. 116–17.

12. Joann S. DeLora and Carol A. B. Warren, *Understanding Sexual Interaction* (Boston: Haughton Mifflin, 1977), p. 270.

13. Churchill, *Homosexual Behavior,* p. 89.

14. Wardell Pomeroy, "Homosexuality," in Weltge, *Same Sex,* p. 12.

15. Robert E. Gould, "What We Don't Know about Homosexuality," *New York Times Magazine* (February 24, 1974), p. 58.

16. DeLora and Warren, *Interaction,* p. 274.

17. Barry M. Dank, "The Homosexual," in *Outside USA,* by Patrician Keith-Spiegel and Don Spiegel (San Francisco: Rinehart Press, 1973), p. 227.

18. Churchill, *Homosexual Behavior,* p. 252.

19. Gould, "What We Don't Know," p. 59.

20. Ibid., p. 13.

21. DeLora and Warren, *Interaction,* p. 273.

22. Phillips et al., "Alternative Behavior," p. 225.

23. Ibid., p. 224.

24. Churchill, *Homosexual Behavior,* p. 95.

25. McIntosh, "Homosexual Role," p. 192.

26. William Simon and John H. Gagnon, "Homosexuality: The Formulation of a Sociological Perspective," *Journal of Health and Social Behavior* (September 1967), p. 179.

27. McIntosh, "Homosexual Behavior," pp. 183–84.

28. Evelyn Hooker, "Male Homosexuals and Their 'Worlds' " in *Sexual Inversion,* by Juelil Marmor (New York: Basic Books, 1965), p. 86.

29. Simon and Gagnon, *op. cit.,* p. 180.

30. Pomeroy, "Homosexuality," p. 13.

31. Dank, "The Homosexual," p. 279.

32. Carol A. Warren, *Identity and Community in the Gay World* (New York: Wiley, 1974), p. 75.

33. DeLora and Warren, *Interaction,* p. 277.

34. William Simon and John H. Gagnon, "Femininity in the Lesbian Community." *Social Problems* (Fall 1967), p. 217.

35. Ronald A. Farrell and James F. Nelson, "A Causal Model of Secondary Deviance: The Case of Homosexuality," *The Sociological Quarterly* (Winter 1976), p. 118.

36. Hooker, "Male Homosexuals," pp. 44–45.

37. Martin S. Weinberg and Colin J. Williams, *Male Homosexuals* (New York: Oxford University Press, 1974), pp. 99–100.

38. DeLora and Warren, *Interaction,* p. 286.

39. Paul H. Gebbard et al., *Sex Offenders* (New York: Harper & Row, 1965), p. 344.

40. DeLora and Warren, *Interaction,* p. 329.

41. Dank, "The Homosexual," p. 275.

42. Simon and Gagnon, "Femininity," p. 147.

43. Gebhard, *Sex Offenders,* p. 347.

44. David Sonenschein, "The Ethnology of Male Homosexual Relations," *Journal of Sex Research* (May 1968), p. 80.

45. Lenore J. Weitzman, "Legal Regulation of Marriage: Tradition and Change," *California Law Review* (July–September 1974), p. 1235.

46. Tom Burke, "The New Homosexuality," *Esquire* (December 1969), p. 308.

47. John H. Gagnon and William Simon, *Sexual Conduct* (Chicago: Aldine, 1973), p. 357.

48. Edward Sagarin, *Odd Man In: Societies of Deviants in America* (Chicago: Quadrangle, 1969), p. 79.

49. Ibid., p. 81.

50. Weinberg and Williams, *Male Homosexuals,* p. 28.

51. Sagarin, p. 103.

52. Ibid., p. 103.

53. Weinberg and Williams, *Male Homosexuals*, pp. 98–99.

54. E. Randolph Trice, "Venereal Disease and Homosexuality," *Medical Aspects of Human Sexuality* (January 1969), pp. 70–71.

55. J. L. Simmons, *Deviants* (Berkeley, Calif.: Glendessary Press, 1969), p. 11.

56. Del Martin and Phyllis Lyon, *Lesbian Women* (New York: Bantam Books, 1972), p. 228.

57. Lewis I. Maddocks, "The Law and the Church versus the Homosexual," in Weltge, *Same Sex*, p. 101.

58. Martin and Lyon, *Lesbian Women*, p. 216.

59. William M. Sheppe, "The Problem of Homosexuality in the Armed Forces," *Medical Aspects of Human Sexuality* (October 1969), p. 72.

60. Simon and Gagnon, "Femininity," p. 180.

61. Simmons, *Deviants*, p. 29.

62. Warren, *Identity*, p. 158.

63. Donald W. Cory, *The Lesbian in America* (New York: Citadel Press, 1964), p. 48.

64. Alfred C. Kinsey et al., *Sexual Behavior in the Human Female* (Philadelphia: W. B. Saunders, 1953), p. 584.

65. *UCLA Law Review*, "Consenting Adult," p. 693.

66. Ibid., p. 740.

67. Joanne Long, "The Lesbian Bar—A Public Institution," unpublished paper, 1975.

68. DeLora and Warren, *Interaction*, p. 270.

69. Gould, "What We Don't Know," p. 59.

70. Heino F. L. Meyer-Bahlburg, "Sex Hormones and Female Homosexuality: A Critical Examination," *Archives of Sexual Behavior* (March 1979), p. 110.

71. Ibid., p. 103.

72. March R. Adelman, "A Comparison of Professionally Employed Lesbians and Heterosexual Women on the MMPI," *Archives of Sexual Behavior* (May 1977), p. 194.

73. Janet S. Chafetz, Patricia Sampson, Paula Beck, and Joyce West, "A Study of Homosexual Women, *Social Work* (November 1964), p. 716.

74. Ibid., p. 722.

75. K. D. Ferguson and Deana C. Finkler, "An Involvement and Overtness Measure for Lesbians: Its Development and Relation to Anxiety and Social Zeitgeist," *Archives of Sexual Behavior* (May 1978), p. 226.

76. Mark Friedman, "Homosexuals may be Healthier than Straight," *Psychology Today* (March 1975), p. 30.

77. Ferguson and Finkler, "Involvement," p. 212.

78. Ibid., p. 226.

79. Gagnon and Simon, "Sexual Deviance," pp. 259–60.

80. Ibid., p. 251.

81. Simon and Gagnon, "Homosexuality: The Formulation of a Sociological Perspective," p. 214.

82. Siegrid Schafer, "Sociosexual Behavior in Male and Female Homosexuals: A Study in Sex Differences," *Archives of Sexual Behavior* (September 1977), p. 362.

83. Martin and Lyon, *Lesbian Women*, p. 27.

84. Ibid., p. 205.

85. Ethel Sawyer, "The Impact of the Surrounding Lower-Class Subculture on Female Homosexual Adaptations," *Society For the Study of Social Problems*, San Francisco, Calif. (August 1967), p. 2.

86. Schafer, "Sociosexual Behavior," p. 357.

87. Long, "Lesbian Bar."

88. Gagnon and Simon, "Sexual Deviance," p. 262.

89. Simon and Gagnon, p. 219.

90. Martin and Lyon, *Lesbian Women*, p. 88.

91. Long, "Lesbian Bar."
92. Schafer, "Sociosexual Behavior," p. 358.
93. Philip W. Blumstein and Pepper Schwartz, "Bisexuality in Women," *Archives of Sexual Behavior* (March 1976), p. 172.
94. Ibid., p. 180.
95. Schafer, "Sociosexual Behavior," p. 359.
96. Long, "Lesbian Bar."
97. Schafer, "Sociosexual Behavior," p. 363.
98. Gagnon and Simon, "Sexual Deviance," p. 270.
99. Martin and Lyon, "Lesbian Women," p. 90.
100. Sagarin, *Odd Man In*, p. 89.
101. Sidney Abbott and Barbara Love, "Is Women's Liberation a Lesbian Plot?" in *Woman in Sexist Society*, by Vivian Gornick and Barbara K. Moran (New York: Signet Books, 1971), p. 613.
102. DeLora and Warren, *Interaction*, p. 285.
103. Burke, "New Homosexuality," p. 308.
104. *Washington Post* (October 25, 1969), p. 8.

SELECTED BIBLIOGRAPHY

Blumstein, Phillip W., and Schwartz, Pepper. "Bisexuality in Women." *Archives of Sexual Behavior* (March 1976), pp. 171–81.

Churchill, Wainwright. *Homosexual Behavior Among Males*. New York: Hawthorne Books, 1967.

DeLora, Joann S., and Warren, Carol A. B. *Understanding Sexual Interaction*. Boston: Houghton Mifflin, 1977.

Farrell, Ronald A., and Nelson, James F. "A Causal Model of Secondary Deviance: The Case of Homsexuality." *The Sociological Quarterly* (Winter 1976), pp. 109–20.

Gagnon, John H., and Simon, William. *Sexual Conduct: The Social Sources of Human Sexuality*. Chicago: Aldine, 1973.

McIntosh, Mary. "The Homosexual Role." *Social Problems* (Fall 1968), pp. 182–92.

Meyer-Bahlburg, Heino F. L. "Sex Hormones and Female Homosexuality: A Critical Examination." *Archives of Sexual Behavior* (March 1979), pp. 101–19.

Phillips Debora; Pischer, Steven C.; Groves, Gerald A.; and Singh, Ratan. "Alternative Behavior Approaches to the Treatment of Homosexuality." *Archives of Sexual Behavior* (May 1976), pp. 223–28.

Schafer, Siegrid. "Sociosexual Behavior in Male and Female Homosexuals: A Study in Sex Differences." *Archives of Sexual Behavior* (September 1977), pp. 355–64.

Warren, Carol A. B. *Identity and Community in the Gay World*. New York: Wiley, 1974.

Weinberg, Martin S., and Williams, Colin J. *Male Homosexuals*. New York: Oxford University Press, 1974.

PART FOUR

Health Based
Social Problems

Chapter 12

Alcohol

The origins of alcohol use go back into prehistory. It has been established that breweries flourished in Egypt almost 6,000 years ago, and there is even some evidence that Stone Age humans made alcoholic beverages. The use of alcohol has appeared in varying degrees in most societies throughout recorded history and traditionally played an important symbolic as well as pharmacological role in many social, religious, and medical practices and customs. For hundreds of years there has been controversy over the value and use of alcoholic beverages. Probably in most societies the issue has not been whether or not alcohol should be used, but rather who should use it and where, when, and under what conditions it should be used. In various cultures alcohol has been used as a means of social facilitation, to celebrate or commiserate, as a part of religious ritual, to try to psychologically "escape," and for many other purposes.

Alcohol has been used in the United States from the start. In colonial America there was general acceptance of some alcoholic beverages, such as rum, beer, wine, and cider. Contrary to what is generally believed the Puritans were not against the use of alcohol—but they did punish drunkenness. Yet there were condemnations of alcohol during the early colonial period, when Increase and Cotton Mather both preached against the "demon rum." But in general during that period drinking was common among most adult men and was not seen as either a personal or a social problem.

Historically in the United States it was not until the westward movement that a widespread concern with heavy drinking began to develop and that it first came to be defined as a social problem. The new social problem of heavy drinking was the result of a combination of factors. First, there was the general social disorganization and lawlessness that were a part of the western frontier. Second, there was the developing industrialization, urbanization, and heavy migration that were expanding and transforming the cities. Third, there was an increasing availability of rum in the East. Finally, there was an increase in the frontiersmen who wanted a strong, cheap, and potable liquor.

Emergence of a Definition

The campaign that developed against drinking was based on moral disapproval and sought total prohibition of alcohol. In the early 1800s a new definition of the drinker emerged which pictured him as an object of social shame. Some observers argue that after the 1850s the patterns of American drinking became extreme, most people being either heavy drinkers or abstainers. By the 1870s rural and small-town America had developed middle-class morals that included the dry attitude of abstinence and sobriety. Joseph R. Gusfield suggests that "moral persuasion, rather than legislation, has been one persistent theme in the designation of the drinker as deviant and the alcoholic as even further debased."[1] Well into the 20th century the alcoholic was viewed as a sinner. This definition affected how the family of the alcoholic was viewed. Seventy five years ago the members of an alcoholic's family were usually viewed as innocent victims of a self-indulgent, irresponsible, weak, and sinful person. The heavy drinker was someone the family should hide and the clergy reform.

The antidrinking view reached its peak of power and influence in January 1920, when national prohibition was enacted. It may have been that drinking was so much a part of society that it could not be legislated out. During prohibition even many nondrinkers saw drinking or nondrinking as a matter of individual choice. As a result, ignoring and circumventing prohibition became increasingly acceptable to large numbers of Americans. Many powerful pro-alcohol forces with a vested interest in the sale of alcohol were also anxious to have prohibition repealed. In general since the repeal of prohibition there has developed on the broadest social level in the United States a basic indifference to alcohol. People do become concerned about problems resulting from drinking—alcoholism, drunken driving, adolescent drinking, and so forth. But there does not appear to be any general strong opposition to the use of alcohol because it is immoral or bad, especially when it is used in moderation.

The views of various societies toward alcohol cover a wide range. It has been argued that there may be a universal tendency for valuations of alcoholic beverages to become polarized in any given society. "At one extreme liquor, wine, and beer are glorified in song, poetry, and drama as keys to ecstasy and sublimity; at the other extreme, they

Historical Pictures Service, Inc., Chicago

Prohibition—Federal agents destroying liquor in 1921

are viewed as perverters of human morality and the chief causes of the ills of society as well as of the sorrows of individuals."[2] It has also been suggested that there are three general ways in which a society can influence its rates of alcoholism. One is the extent to which a society creates tensions in its members that would lead them to alcohol as a possible source of reducing their tensions. Second are the kinds of attitudes that a society develops in its members toward drinking. Third is the degree to which a society provides means of tension reduction other than alcohol.[3]

The ways in which different cultures use alcohol may be closely related to various social institutions. Alcohol may be used at a variety of social functions, including religious functions. When alcohol is used in a religious setting, it centers around ceremonial functions. For example, Roman Catholics use wine in Holy Communion. Alcohol may be used at a Bar Mitzvah or a wedding. Often alcohol is used hedonistically—to show solidarity between friends and relatives. And in some societies alcohol is used in a utilitarian way—to gain some advantage over another person or for medicinal purposes.

There are other social differences in drinking patterns. For example among some groups alcohol may be drunk moderately with meals while among others it is drunk after meals. It appears that heavy drinking after meals is most conducive to drunkenness. This is illustrated in a comparison of American Jews and Italians, who often drink with meals and in the home, to American Irish, who are more likely to drink outside the home and not at meals. "Among the first, a majority of adults use alcohol and report having done so since childhood but the rate of alcoholism is quite low; while among the latter, childhood drinking is less likely, and alcoholism rates are much higher."[4]

Conflicting Solutions

As there developed a greater and greater social awareness of drinking in the United States it came to be defined within a variety of frames of reference based on different values and vested interests. The various vested interests have played a part in determining how it came to be defined as a social problem, its seriousness, and what should be done about it. Those groups which have seen the use of alcohol as sinful and immoral have represented one kind of vested interest. Another has been those who see it leading to medical and interpersonal problems. But there have been other vested interests that have supported the use of alcohol, for example, those involved in its manufacture and sale. There have also been many who believe drinking represents an individual right and should be the choice of the person and not controlled by any social agencies.

The emergence of various laws with regard to alcohol use have given power to the courts and the police. In this area the police usually have a high degree of discretion in whether or not to arrest someone who has been drinking. They can overlook or pick up, they can book him for drunkenness or some related charge, or let the person go. The police have been given the legal responsibility to apply what are essentially moral sanctions against drinking. Dealing with alcohol in all its ramifications is an important part of police work. This is work that employs many and is therefore a vested interest to that occupation.

Many individuals have had a strong vested interest in the use of alcohol. Often individual drinking leads to a personal investment in its use. That is, the person develops a dependency or a sense of need that is met by its use. He therefore often rejects any attempt to define his use of alcohol in negative terms or any attempts to take his source away from him. Very often the alcoholic has spent years constructing a system of denial to others that he needs alcohol. Implied is that he accepts the general negative definitions but denies he personally is so defined. Often his drinking is associated with behavior that affects relationships with others and they find this undesirable. Furthermore, the use of alcohol may mean the individual feels he needs it to perform in some of the basic functions in life. All of this contributes to the possibility of a high vested interest in alcohol by those who use large amounts.

As suggested, in the past the heavy drinker or alcoholic was usually defined on the basis of internal factors, that is, factors which he, the person, was responsible for. He was sinful, personally defective, or willfully self-destructive. But the most accepted explanation of cause today is within the context of illness—whether due to mental health problems or sometimes physical reasons for turning to drink.

It should be stressed that the vast majority of those who use alcoholic beverages stay within the limits of the culturally accepted drinking patterns and drink predominantly as an expression of their social learning. But some drinkers suffer from alcoholism, and this may be defined as a complex chronic illness although it is not very well understood. According to the American Medical Association alcoholism is a form of drug dependence characterized by preoccupation with alcohol and loss of control over its consumption, usually leading to intoxication once drinking has started. The alcoholic has a high tendency to relapse and usually suffers physically, emotionally, occupationally, and socially because of his addiction. And too, the very size of the problem—the large number who are alcoholics—makes the question of causes and cures extremely difficult to determine.

Many believe that alcohol is a stimulant but in fact it is a protoplasmic poison with a depressant effect on the nervous system. If alcohol is taken in large enough quantities it can render a person unconscious, and in the past alcohol was sometimes used as an anesthetic. As alcohol is absorbed into the system, it functions as a continuous depressant of the central nervous system. What appear to be stimulation effects are the result of the depression of inhibitory control mechanisms. "Alcohol is thought to exert first its depressing action on the more primitive parts of the brain responsible for integrating the activity of other parts of the central nervous system, thereby releasing the higher centers from control."[5] In general the drunker people get the less control they have physically, psychologically, and socially.

As a medical problem alcoholism is outranked only by mental illness, heart diseases, and cancer. Furthermore, it is estimated that 20 percent of the people in state mental hospitals are there because of alcoholic brain disease and that 50 percent of the people in prisons have committed their crimes in association with alcoholic consumption. Alcohol also contributes enormously to breakdown and welfare costs. In total, alcoholism is very costly to American society. Alcohol dependence was identified in 1973 by a government study as "without question, the most serious drug problem in the United States."[6]

TABLE 12–1

Alcohol Related Deaths

Disease	Number of deaths (per year)
Heart and blood vessel disorders	1,000,000
Cancer	350,000
Alcohol alone	200,000
Accidents	120,000
Influenza and pneumonia	60,000
Diabetes mellitus	34,000
Cirrhosis of the liver	24,000

Source: Joel Fort, *Alcohol: Our Biggest Drug Problem* (New York: McGraw-Hill, 1973), p. 108.

The most striking result of alcoholism is death. It has been estimated that alcohol-related problems are the cause of more than 85,000 deaths in the United States each year. This would include about half (30,000) of the annual highway fatalities. There are other costs. It is estimated that the life expectancy of alcoholics is about ten years less than that of nonalcoholics. Because alcohol has a large number of calories but little in the way of nutrients, over time alcohol destroys liver cells and builds up scar tissue (cirrhosis of the liver). Alcohol is also related to a number of heart problems. And about one fourth of all suicides are alcohol related.

Whatever the causes of alcoholism, becoming an alcoholic takes time. This is true because repeated ingestion of alcohol results in tolerance so that a higher level of alcohol is needed in the bloodstream to produce a given level of intoxication. Thus, both physical and psychological dependence may result from prolonged use. It has been found that psychological dependence occurs in about 10 percent of all users and that the development of physical dependence requires the consumption of large amounts of alcohol over a period of about 3 to 15 years or more. "In the dependent individual, even a few hours of abstinence precipitates the beginning of the alcohol withdrawal syndrome, a syndrome similar to that following withdrawal of barbiturates or other depressant drugs."[7]

The label alcoholic is a social definition. Society provides definitions of drinking, with assessments made as to frequency and the costs for the individual and for society. Yet, the generally accepted definition of an alcoholic is based on a social definition which describes a stereotyped physical condition. The alcoholic is usually seen as one who has an uncontrollable need for alcohol and whose need must be met to avoid severe withdrawal symptoms. These are typically uncontrollable trembling, nausea, heavy perspiring, and a rapid heartbeat.

Institutionalization of Alcohol Use

Heavy drinking or alcoholism is clearly defined as a social problem in the United States. There may still be some disagreements as to the significance of social drinking and whether or not that constitutes a social problem. In this area society shows mixed values, but social drinking is generally seen as acceptable. Drinking may be seen to reduce tension and contribute to sociability. It is also seen as lowering sensitivity, efficiency, and caution. It has been argued that in a complex society these influences can be socially dangerous because a complex society puts strong emphasis on self-control and on inhibitions and repressions of aggression and irresponsibility. Alcohol releases those inhibitions and can wreck regularity of behavior. "The need for imagination and perception, for control over responses, for timing and balance, is greatly increased by the complex culture; just to get things done is a more delicate task, and the penalty for not getting things done has far greater social implications than in the simpler society."[8]

Probably in all societies some controls over drinking have developed, and in most societies the controls are at least in part built into the legal systems. In many societies, including our own, there are elaborate legal controls over who may sell alcoholic beverages, where they may sell, to whom, and under what circumstances. But our main interest is in the controls over people who are using alcohol. And the legal view of the drinker is closely related to the social view of his use of alcohol and the effects it is believed to have on him. As suggested, whether or not drinking alcoholic beverages is a social problem is culturally defined. In the United States the use of alcohol is generally defined as a problem when the user is defined as an alcoholic or as an excessive and problem drinker, or when he commits offenses related to the influence of alcohol. This last would include such things as driving an automobile while under the influence of alcohol or being drunk and disorderly.

Large numbers of persons are arrested for public drunkenness. There are about two million arrests each year on this charge, and this accounts for about one out of every three arrests made in the United States. These arrests place a very heavy burden on the criminal justice system. The laws provide maximum jail sentences ranging from a few days to six months. The most common maximum sentence is 30 days. It also appears that many of those arrested have a history of prior drunkenness arrests.

© John Penzari

A police officer giving a sobriety test

An area of great social concern has been drinking and driving. One study points out some of the social variables that are related to driving and the use of alcohol. This study found that persons with higher education and in more prestigious occupations were more likely to drive and drink.[9] There was also evidence to suggest that certain social and cultural factors affect behavior after drinking. The middle-class person learns to behave "properly" even after consuming a good deal of alcohol. This can extend to his driving, where he may give the appearance of being well in control and not attract attention from the police. By contrast lower-class persons may not have such proscriptions, and as a result their driving may be more erratic. "Moreover, both groups may respond differently when stopped by police officers; specifically, middle-class persons may not only appear to be in greater control, their demeanor may be more acceptable to the officer." [10]

It has been estimated that there are about 800,000 alcohol-related motor vehicle accidents annually in the United States and that they account for about 30,000 deaths. Along with the deaths goes injuries and immeasurable property damage, loss of wages, and medical and insurance expenses. [11] The effects on the drinking driver are physical ones due primarily to the depressive action of alcohol on the nervous system. This in turn affects perceptions, motor responses, and emotional states.

Drinking and driving is something that elicits a great deal of social reaction but relatively little in legal controls and punishments. The typical penalty for driving while under the influence of alcohol is no penalty at all. With multiple offenses, the suspensions of the person's license often occurs but it has been estimated that as many as one half of all those drivers with a suspended license continue to drive.

For many Americans drinking and driving both appear to be inalienable rights. Often the man believes he has the right to drink and also the same right to drive his car. To deprive him of using those two rights together may be seen by him as a violation of his rights. For example, if the police make arrests of individuals for drunk driving when they leave a bar at closing time that is often defined by many as sneaky and inappropriate by the police.

It seems clear that the criminal justice system is ineffective in deterring drunkenness or in meeting the problems of the chronic alcoholic offender. What the legal system does in effect is remove the drunk from where he can be publicly seen, sobers him up, and provides him with food, shelter, emergency medical service, and a brief period of forced sobriety. Built into the arrest system is inherent discrimination against the homeless and the poor. "Due process safeguards are often considered unnecessary or futile. The defendant may not be warned of his rights or permitted to make a telephone call. And although coordination, breath, or blood tests to determine intoxication are common practices in driving-while-intoxicated cases, they are virtually nonexistent in common drunk cases." [12]

Robert Strauss concludes that experience in the United States and in many other parts of the world clearly shows that any attempts to deal with the problems of alcohol by legislating change have been ineffective unless laws can be made to reflect normative forces of behavior. "In the United States, drinking customs reflect the beliefs and values of many national, regional, ethnic, and social groups." [13]

We have suggested a relatively high rate of drinking in the United States, and now we may look more specifically at some rates of drinking and alcoholism. Millions of persons may be variously classified as light drinkers, moderate drinkers, heavy drinkers, problem drinkers, and alcoholics. A recent estimate is that there may be as many as nine million adult problem drinkers with millions more on the verge of having serious drinking problems. Of that nine million about four million are problem drinkers and five million alcoholics. The Department of Health, Education, and Welfare defines a heavy drinker as one who consumes at least one half ounce of alcohol nearly every day with five or more drinks per occasion once in a while.[14] The figures suggest that about one in every ten people who drink any alcohol are afflicted with drinking problems or alcoholism. The World Health Organization defines alcoholism as "a chronic behavior disorder manifested by repeated drinking of alcoholic beverages in excess of dietary and social uses of the community and to the extent that interferes with the drinker's health or his social and economic functions."[15]

Economic costs.   A major concern of society is the economic cost of alcohol use. But society generally has an ambivalent view toward alcohol because on the one hand there are vast profits made from it by business as well as by governments through taxation. Yet, on the other hand there are also costs paid by business, citizens, and governments. For example, it is estimated that nine billion dollars is lost annually in business and industry due to alcohol use. This figure reflects economic losses in terms of absenteeism, sick leave, job accidents, and missed or late work commitments.

Overall the economic cost of alcohol related problems has been put at about 25 billion dollars. In terms of medical costs more than 8 billion dollars has been estimated as the annual cost of alcohol related health and medical problems. This comprises 12 percent of all adult health expenditures and 20 percent of the total adult expenditures for hospitalization. Some other studies suggest about one third of all male patients in general hospitals are problem drinkers even though most of them are not there for treatment of their drinking problems.[16]

The family.   The effects of the alcoholic on the family have long been a strong social concern. The impact of the alcoholic on the family is usually a gradual one, and the response of various members of the family to the alcoholic is influenced by their respective personality structures and family roles. Actions directed toward the alcoholic are influenced by the past effectiveness of those actions. The family members' views of the alcoholic are affected by the broader cultural definitions of alcoholism as evidence of weakness, inadequacy, or sinfulness; "by the cultural prescriptions for the roles of family members; and by the cultural values of family solidarity, sanctity, and self-sufficiency." Alcoholism in the family "poses a situation defined by the culture as shameful, but there are no cultural prescriptions which are effective or which permit direct action not in conflict with other cultural prescriptions."[17] This is in contrast to such family crises as illness or death where there are cultural definitions and expectations of behavior that family members may draw on.

In most states where drunkenness may be used as a ground for divorce, no distinction is made between aggrieved husbands and aggrieved wives. However, in some states such distinctions are made. For example, in Kentucky a wife may be granted a divorce from her husband on the ground of drunkenness only if his condition has been "accompanied by a wasting of the husband's estate and without any suitable provision for the maintenance of the wife or children. A husband, however, can be granted a divorce from his wife on the ground of her mere drunkenness alone, without the necessity of showing any additional factors."[18]

Alcoholism can greatly affect the interpersonal relationships within the family. For the alcoholic the roles of spouse and parent are usually drastically influenced and the roles of all family members undergo change. These changes help explain why alcoholics are more frequently divorced or separated than are nonalcoholics. It also frequently explains why wives, husbands, and children of alcoholics have relatively higher rates of physical, emotional, and psychosomatic illnesses. The emotional relationships are affected because frequently the alcoholic demands a great deal of emotional support from other family members but can offer little in return.

Social interaction is usually based on the ability to predict the others' behavior in various situations. For example, if a wife and husband come together for dinner they know quite well how the other will behave. But one of the consequences of alcoholism is often to undercut the ability to predict the other's behavior. The alcoholic husband may not come home for several days or the alcoholic wife may pass out in bed for the evening. Often this kind of inability to predict leads to confusion, anger, and frustration in dealing with an alcoholic.

Because in most cases the husband is the alcoholic the sexual nature of marriage is affected by the husband's drinking. The wife may avoid sex under these circumstances because she finds his condition unattractive. And because of his preoccupation with alcoholism, or because of impotence resulting from the sedative effects of alcohol, the alcoholic is often an unsatisfactory sex partner. The relationship between alcohol usage and sexual impotence in the male is a strong one. Masters and Johnson found that impotence that developed in the male in his late 40s and early 50s was more closely associated with excessive alcohol consumption than with any other single factor. The sexual tensions and desires of the truly alcoholic male simply disappear as he deteriorates physically and mentally.[19]

Over the years there have been many beliefs concerning the effects of alcohol on sexual behavior. Alcohol does not have a specific aphrodisiac effect. Small doses such as used in much social drinking may release inhibitions enough to cause a temporary increase in sexual interest and drive. However, larger doses of alcohol rapidly depress the person's behavior in general, including his sexual response. Chronic alcoholism or even habitual heavy drinking frequently seriously impairs the sexual response of both men and women, but most especially men. "Presumably this is a consequence of the neurological damage and the generally debilitating effects of alcoholism.[20]

We have some evidence on how people view the use of alcohol as related to their sexual experiences. Throughout this book references have been made to the *Redbook* study where over 100,000 women in the United States responded to a questionaire about their sexuality. The study was done in 1974 and the respondents are a biased sample, in the direction of being well educated, living in urban areas, and being willing to answer and mail back the questionaire. Ninety percent of the women said they had had sexual relations while under the influence of alcohol. But of that group only 12 percent said they did so often. When asked if the use of alcohol contributed to the sexual experience 31 percent said "yes"; 14 percent, "no"; 38 percent "sometimes"; and 17 percent "can't say."

Among women there can also be a relationship between the uses of alcohol and pregnancy. Joan C. Martin reports in one sample of pregnant women, whose ages ranged from 15 to 49, about 54 percent of the women were light to heavy drinkers, with "heavy" defined as consumption of at least one ounce of alcohol daily.[21] She goes on to point out that various studies show a pattern of altered growth, morphogenesis, and mental retardation in infants and children with mothers who were alcoholics or heavy alcohol users during their pregnancy. The children were undergrown, exhibited a failure to thrive, and tended to score in the retarded range on developmental and motor tests. "Some of the morphological defects included small eyes, hip dislocations, aberrant creases on the palms, and heart defects."[22]

As would be expected, children may be more affected by living with an alcoholic than are other family members. Often the social nature of the child is being developed in a social setting characterised by conflict and social disapproval. Furthermore, the children frequently model their behavior on roles that are being filled in a distorted fashion. The nonalcoholic parent may try to fill both parental roles and not be successful at either.

Parents' drinking can affect their children in other ways. Children coming from homes where a parent is an alcoholic have a greater chance of being an alcoholic in their adult life than children coming from nonalcoholic families. The alcoholic parent in effect teaches the child the role of being an alcoholic. Also parents may contribute to their children's future drinking patterns by their views toward the use of alcohol. This is especially true when the use of alcohol is compared

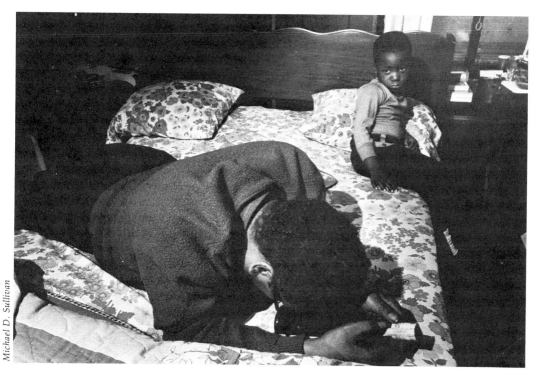

Michael D. Sullivan

The effects of the alcoholic parent on the child

with drug use. One study found that a majority of parents considered hard liquor less dangerous to the future health and safety of their children than most drugs. Only 16 percent felt it to be a greater threat than marijuana.[23]

The family with an alcoholic member often suffers some shame, knowing that society generally defines alcoholics as weak and shameful persons. Even though the family may have no responsibility for the alcoholism it still must suffer some stigma because of the alcoholic member. The family is stigmatized in basically the same way that it gains prestige in the community because of some personal success of the father. But alcoholism is deviance, and in its efforts to handle the problem the family labors under the imputation of blame. It often feel guilty, ashamed, inadequate, and, above all, isolated from social support. Often friends contribute to the feeling of shame. Frequently when the wife consults friends about her alcoholic husband the friends discount her concern and tell her the situation is really not so bad. This may contribute to her tendency to deny that a problem exists and can also add to her guilt by making her remorseful over her "disloyal" thoughts about her husband.

Other Social Variables Related to Drinking

The young. There are some social factors other than in the family related to drinking. One important area of interest is drinking among young people. Generally the concern is not so much with whether they drink but rather with whether they drink to a degree defined as socially excessive. For the most part the drinking patterns of the young can be predicted from the drinking patterns of their parents. In most cases in the United States the first drinking experience among the young occurs in the home under parental supervision. Among the various social groups those with the lowest risk of developing alcoholism are those in which drinking is learned at an early age in a context of complex social and ceremonial activities supervised by persons who themselves drink safely.

A common pattern for many teenagers is to learn about alcohol from observing their parents and other adults drink. Teenagers often drink at home in the presence of and with the encouragement of their parents. They often describe such at-home use of alcohol as "tasting" or "sipping," whereas its use with their peers is described as "drinking" meaning the consumption of entire glasses or bottles of wine, beer, or whiskey. One study of high school students states that about one third to one half of the boys and one fourth of the girls drink to an extent that would be recognizable as a pattern of moderate drinking in an adult. "Little of the drinking that teenagers do is high-frequency/high-quantity, and an average of only about 3 percent can be characterized as 'problem' drinkers." Straus writes that the family is the most frequent setting and family members the most frequently companions at the time of earliest exposure to alcohol. About half of those who drink report having some experience or taste of alcohol by the age of ten.[24]

In the United States most adolescents at some time enter social situations in which there is a temptation to experiment with alcoholic beverages. This may be because they are curious or because their parents include them in their drinking habits or behavior patterns. Because the peer group is very powerful among adolescents and the pressures to conform and thereby achieve one's identity are so great, the introduction of drinking as a positive force is very hard for the individual to resist. Also, drinking is defined as adult behavior and the adolescent often wants to be seen as an adult, he will turn to drinking because he thinks it will give him adult status. Studies of high school students have found that anywhere from one third to four fifths have had some experience with the use of alcohol.

A Harris Poll shows that among seventh graders 63 percent of the boys and 54 percent of the girls have at least tried alcoholic beverages. By the time they have graduated from high school, 93 percent of the

FIGURE 12–1

Alcohol Use Among Junior and Senior High School Students

Percentage of heavy drinkers

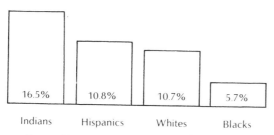

| 16.5% | 10.8% | 10.7% | 5.7% |
| Indians | Hispanics | Whites | Blacks |

Source: U.S. Department of Health, Education and Welfare, Public Health Service, *Health Highlights, 1976–77* (Washington, D.C.: U.S. Government Printing Office, 1978), p. 25.

boys and 87 percent of the girls have experimented with alcohol. The proportion of high school students who drink increased at each level in the early 1970s. "While causal relationships have yet to be demonstrated, adolescent alcohol use is related to sexual activity, use of other drugs, automobile accidents, and poor school performance."[25]

Probably only a small percentage of adolescents are alcoholics. But reports in the 1970s clearly indicated an increase in drinking among high school students. And this was related to an increase in problems. Intoxication is a special problem for adolescents because their reaction to alcohol is complicated by lack of experience in dealing with its effects and by the fact that much of their drinking occurs in public. "When adolescents do become intoxicated they are, therefore, likely to get involved in other difficulties and be highly visible."[26]

Male-female differences.   Fewer females than males drink, and when women do drink they consume less than men. There may be as many as four male alcoholics for every one female. Gallup, in 1974, found that 76 percent of men and 61 percent of women used alcohol. Comparisons over time suggest that the prevalence of use among women is increasing more rapidly than among men.[27] One may predict that the rates of drinking and alcoholism among women will come closer to those of men. This expectation is predicated on women's achieving greater equality in the United States. One consequence of equality is the right and opportunity of women to acquire the socially undesirable problems of men. For example, if many men drink because of occupational pressures, then as women become increasingly involved in these occupations they too will probably turn more and more to alcohol. One measure of the achievement of total sexual equality will be the equalization of alcoholism rates among men and women.

Studies show that not only do men drink more alcohol than women but they also do it more frequently, in greater quantities, in bars rather than at home and with friends rather than family members. Men are much more likely to drink beer, to be heavy or problem drinkers, and to abstain from drinking for health or financial, as opposed to moral, or religious reasons or "lack of desire."[28] Carolyn Becker goes on to conclude that heavy or "escape" drinking is still more an integral part of the male drinking role and women are more apt to express strong values aginst drinking. But both sexes displayed features of social-mindedness and ego-involvement in their drinking patterns.[29]

Race differences. Most of the studies suggest that male alcoholism rates are higher for blacks than for whites, but one study of drinking behavior on the national level found that white and black men varied little in their rates of drinking. However, black women had much higher proportions of both abstainers and heavy drinkers than did white women.[30] Blacks in the United States have higher death rates from alcoholic disorders than do whites. In 1970 the rates of death per 100,000 related to alcohol were almost twice as high for black males (44.8) and females (14.9) as for whites (22.9 and 7.8). The differentials are even more striking at the younger ages. "The death rate for ages 15–34 was 16.7 for black males and 2.3 for white males.[31]

George D. Lowe found that adults in black society are more accepting of teenage drinking than are whites. The use of alcohol by youth is controlled more by adults in the black community.[32] Black teenagers are more likely to drink at home with the family than are white teenagers. But Paul C. Higgins found that race seems to make little difference in drinking behavior for male teenagers when controlling for class or church attendance. For females, black teenagers still drink at home.[33]

Lowe found that the black alcoholic was not self-motivated to enter treatment programs. While black alcoholics had low admission rates to all programs they were especially underrepresented in the purely voluntary treatment programs. "The black alcoholic is more likely to view admission as punishment than as treatment and is unlikely to admit himself into any program."[34]

Social class. In general, the higher the social class the greater the probability of drinking. One study found that in a lower social class group 52 percent abstained from the use of alcohol. But in the middle class abstinence was 34 percent and 21 percent for the upper class.[35] Another study found that the incidence of drinking for both sexes increases with each year of college. There was also a rise in drinking

GIFT COUNSELOR

"**Ms. Peabody, 'a nice bottle of booze' is not the answer to** *everyone's* **gift problem.**"

among all college students with the greatest increase occurring for women drinkers.[36]

Drinking is much less visible in the middle class than in the lower class, because among the middle class there is a high rate of drinking at home and therefore less visibility on the street while under the influence of alcohol. In general the public defines the middle-class drinker in much less harsh terms than it does the lower-class drinker. The middle-class drinker, unless he clearly shows otherwise, is believed to be a good provider and is generally believed to be able to handle his drinking. In effect the lower-class drinker is condemned as much for being lower class as he is for being a drinker.

In the middle class a particular system of norms and behavior patterns related to drinking has developed. Permissive drinking goes with a notion of cosmopolitanism, and abstinence is often seen as a negative judgement of a life style. To drink socially is to be cosmopolitan and often carries with it the implication that one is emancipated from traditional Puritan values. The person who doesn't drink is often looked down upon as a "square"—as one who lacks sophistication. Hence, it is often the case that the use of alcohol is important, not in itself but as symbolizing a certain life style. The style is sometimes reflected in what one chooses to drink. A martini (very, very dry) is a sign of sophistication while a "7 & 7" is more common or lower middle-class.

Another study has found differences by social class and driving a car while under the influence of alcohol. In a random sample of drivers in Iowa, of the group which admitted to driving after having consumed at least three drinks, 33 percent were in the lowest prestige occupations, while 46 percent were in the highest prestige occupations. It was also found that better educated people were more likely to drive and drink than poorly educated persons.[37]

The evidence indicates that there is proportionately more drinking in urban and suburban areas than in small towns and more in small towns than in rural areas. The rate of drinking in the large cities may be double that found in the farming areas. Another study suggests that the greater the degree of nervous stimulation, the greater difficulty in establishing primary relationships along with greater opportunities for alcohol consumption in urban areas converge to generate together the confirmed prediction that urban communities will have higher proportions of alcohol users.[38]

One of the lowest social levels is that of the "skid rows" found in most large cities. On skid row most of the inhabitants are heavy drinkers or alcoholics. They appear to show little interpersonal concern, and they cooperate on occasion primarily because this is more effective than not cooperating. One purpose for cooperating is to facilitate getting alcohol. When they don't individually have enough money to buy a bottle of wine, a number of skid row inhabitants may pool their resources as a "bottle gang." Generally they meet, pool their money, get a cheap bottle of wine, drink it, and split up once the bottle is empty.

The drunkenness of the skid row alcoholic tends to be prolonged and steady. He is dependent not so much on a large intake of alcohol as on a constant intake. For many skid row residents the term sobering up means more than just clearing the system of alcohol. It also refers to "coming down," a change in perspective from optimism to pessimism.[39] Jacqueline Wiseman observes that the life of the skid row man is neither as sexless nor as homosexual as has often been portrayed. There are also some women on skid row. "If the woman has enough money, or shelter for two, they would share resources and dispel their mutual loneliness. Such women usually have clerical jobs, are well past middle age, and have 'been around.' Most of these liaisons last anywhere from one night to six months."[40]

"Cures"

For centuries there have been attempts to cure alcoholism. The attempts have been closely linked to what has been believed to be the cause. When it was believed that people became alcoholics because they were possessed of the devil or were committing a sin it was the church that tried to cure them. But the problems of drinking have for the most part been removed from religion and placed in the hands of medical clinics. So the tendency to handle drinkers through protective and welfare agencies, rather than through police or clergy, has become stronger.

With the increased use of drugs in recent years there has been an interest in the relationships between alcohol use and drug use. Some research indicates that while a user may be able to distinguish subjectively between the effects of alcohol and the effects of barbiturates it is very difficult for the observer to tell the difference on the basis of the user's behavior. One serious problem has been that heavy alcohol users are sometimes resistant to the effects of barbiturates, minor tranquilizers, and anesthetics although the cross-toleration does not significantly affect what constitues a lethal dose, so many overdose deaths occur due to the mixing of these drugs in chronic users.

There has developed the establishment of detoxification centers. Many experts argue that these should replace the police station as the first detention for drunkards. If this were done the drunkard would be brought to a public health facility by the police and kept there until sober. After that the decision to continue treatment would be left to the individual. There has also been some work with "in-patient programs" where the patients are given high-protein meals with vitamin and mineral supplements and appropriate medication to help cut down on withdrawal symptoms. In these settings bath and laundry facilities are also available, as are basic clothing and limited recreation facilities. For any continued success, "aftercare" programs are also needed. There is little reason to believe that the chronic drinker will change a long-term pattern of drinking after a few days of sobriety and care at a public health unit. It has been suggested that a network of aftercare facilities should be expanded to include halfway houses, community shelters, and other forms of public housing.

Alcoholics Anonymous. The approach of Alcoholics Anonymous is by far the best known attempt to help the alcoholic stop his drinking. This group is important not only in itself but also because it has served as a model for many attempts to deal with other problems; programs to deal with the drug addict, the chronic gambler, and so forth have been modeled after Alcoholics Anonymous. This means that the public image of the organization is high and that the organization is generally seen as the only really successful way to treat alcoholism. Therefore, it is useful to look at how it operates and to examine its successes and failures.

Alcoholics Anonymous (AA) was founded by a medical man and a stockbroker as a result of a chance meeting they had in 1935. The stockbroker, through some kind of mystical experience, had stopped his own drinking and wanted to share his new sobriety with others. Initially there was a 12-step program to stop drinking. Some of the steps were: you admit you are licked; you get honest with yourself; you talk it out with someone else; you make restitution to the people you have harmed; you try to give of yourself without stint, with no demands for reward; and you pray to whatever God you think there is, even as an experiment, to help you do these things.[41]

The various Alcoholic Anonymous groups are very powerful and pervasive subcultures. Basically one enters AA because he believes he has been a deviant through his alcoholism and wants to give up that deviant role. He does so by joining a powerful subculture made up of persons with similar motivations. He is rewarded for making the changes by persons in the same situation who confirm his new "self in transition." "When these conditions are met, transforming a deviant identity is encouraged."[42] One supporter of the AA approach says that the subculture provides a way of life "which is more realistic, which enables the member to get closer to people, which provides one with more emotional security, and which facilitates more productive living. Thus, the AA group becomes an important new reference group—a new point of orientation."[43] The high value and importance of conformity in the subculture is a major value in AA. It is argued that when the alcoholic seeks help it is the great strength of AA that he is interacting with persons who have been through the program and have stopped drinking. So the subculture says, "Come on in, do what we say, and you can be like us—people who no longer drink."

A basic belief of AA is that there are no ex-alcoholics. This is because, according to AA, alcoholism cannot be cured and the person who has stopped drinking must therefore give constant vigilance to his own urge to drink as well as to the like urges of other AA members. For AA members there are only alcoholics in control (for the time being) of their temptations and never ex-alcoholics. In the jargon of the group, such persons are referred to as dry or sober alcoholics.

The subculture of the AA members develops in a number of other ways. For example, a ritualism of behavior develops. Initially all members were called by their first names as a means of protecting their identity, but this now continues as a ritual. As is true of all subcultures, the members of AA develop a language of their own which contributes to their sense of solidarity and exclusiveness. The language often has meaning in reference to the special experiences that the members have in common or have actually shared. It includes, for example, such phrases as "nickel therapy" for "phoning another AA member to avert a 'slip' " and "the guy upstairs" for "God as you perceive him."

Alcoholics Anonymous sees alcoholism as a disease that is arrested when a person stops drinking and erupts again if he or she resumes

A convention of Alcoholics Anonymous

drinking. AA refuses to consider alcoholism as a symptom rather than a disease. Sagarin says that if it did there would be more need for psychotherapy and much less need for AA. As a result the organization has become, almost by nature and in spite of itself, antitherapy. At its meetings and in its publications AA strongly denounces those who argue that alcoholics are psychopathological or that they have behavior disorders in any way similar to those of manic-depressives and persons with obsessions.[44]

An important part of the AA subculture is the pressure for honesty about oneself, which is reflected in a strong need to confess. Edward Sagarin suggests that the great need to confess brings about a catharsis "similar to that produced by religious confessions and psychoanalysis."[45] This contributes to the high sense of personal and spiritual commitment of the AA member. The subculture not only influences his behavior and interaction with others but, more important, becomes his reason for being. This appeal to the alcoholic often appears to transcend many social factors. AA is found in prisons, in hospitals, in small towns and large cities, and among the rich and the poor. In fact there are AA branches in several police departments, and other branches that cater especially to priests.

There is disagreement about the success of Alcoholics Anonymous. It is quite likely that more contemporary alcoholics have reached sobriety through AA than through all other agencies combined. However, while the AA plan works for some it does not work for many, and there is no clear understanding of why it works when it does. A critical view is that of Sagarin, who states that many of AA's claims and assumptions about its success are unproven, obviously self-serving, and of doubtful validity. "They may be not only wrong but actually harmful. Some of these claims are: that alcoholism is a disease; that it is incurable but can be arrested; that AA has had a 50 percent success rate with its members; and that only an alcoholic can understand—or help—another alcoholic."[46] But another observer has suggested that the major contribution of AA has been not only in rehabilitating alcoholics, but also in dramatizing that alcoholics can be helped. "By virtue of their interest, they have made work with the alcoholic legitimate."[47]

It has been suggested that one possible consequence of arresting or halting deviance is that stopping the undesirable may have undesirable consequences. It is possible that the results of halting a deviance may be worse than the deviance itself. But more often there are negative consequences that tend to be ignored in light of the fact that the primary problem has been solved. For example, possible consequences for the individual who stops drinking are loneliness, frustration, and other difficulties. This is especially true if the individual became an alcoholic because of personal problems. When he stops drinking these problems are refocused, and he is therefore in the same situation as when he originally developed his alcoholism. And because AA does not accept the approach of psychotherapy the alcoholic usually has not been helped with his original problems.

The alcoholic who goes on the wagon may also create problems for his family. In many cases his wife has been managing the family, and with his continuing sobriety he usually wants to return to his former family roles. There is often resistance by both the wife and the children. The wife/mother has been both parents for so long that it takes time to get used to the idea of consulting the father on problems and asking for his opinions. Often the father tries too hard to manage this change overnight.

Joan K. Jackson found that if a man's sobriety comes about because of AA he very often commits himself so totally to AA activities that his wife sees little of him and feels neglected. And as she worries less about his drinking, she may push him to cut down on some of his outside activities. But this can be dangerous because AA activity is correlated with success in Alcoholics Anonymous. The wife also learns that even though her husband is off alcohol she is by no means free of alcoholics. "In his Twelfth Step work, he may keep the house filled with men he is helping. In the past her husband has avoided self-searching; and now he may become excessively introspective, and it may be difficult for her to deal with this."[48]

In conclusion it can be said that alcoholism in the American society is related to the degree to which alcohol is used. In general social drinking that is individually controlled is not viewed as social problem and in fact may even be given some positive social value. The social problem is associated with the heavy drinker and the alcoholic. And even when there is agreement that this is a problem there is little agreement on what to do about it. Most medical persons define alcoholism as a psychological problem that should be treated through some form of physical and psychological therapy, whereas Alcoholics Anonymous defines it as a disease that can never be cured. Although alcoholism refers to something that most people would agree is a social problem there is limited knowledge and high disagreement on what should be done about it. But alcoholism is at the level of an institutionalized social problem because there is little social question that it is and many groups vie to control it. There are also many strong norms and laws as well as clearly defined roles related to the alcoholic and those he interacts with in a variety of social settings.

The use of alcohol has always been common to American society. But over the years there developed a strong antidrinking viewpoint. There are a variety of laws related to drinking with probably the greatest concern the mixing of drinking and driving automobiles. There is no strong agreement as to the causes of alcoholism. Alcoholics often have a variety of problems related to marriage, family, and work. Alcoholics Anonymous is a well known attempt to deal with alcoholism that has helped some but does not work for all.

NOTES

1. Joseph R. Gusfield, "On Legislating Morals: The Symbolic Process of Designating Deviance," *California Law Review* (January 1968), p. 63.

2. Edwin M. Lemert, *Human Deviance: Social Problems and Social Control* (Englewood Cliffs, N.J.: Prentice-Hall, 1967), p. 73.

3. Robert F. Bales, "Cultural Differences in Rates of Alcoholism," in *Deviant Behavior and Social Process* by William A. Rushing (Chicago: Rand-McNally, 1969), p. 283.

4. U.S. Department of HEW, "Alcohol and Health," Rockville, Md.: Public Health Service (1974), pp. 15–16.

5. Helen H. Nowlis, *Drugs on the College Campus* (New York: Anchor Books, 1969), pp. 85–86.

6. "Drug Use in America, Problem in Perspective," Second Report of the National Commission on Marijuana and Drug Abuse (Washington, D.C.: U.S. Government Printing Office, March 1973), p. 143.

7. Nowlis, *Drugs*, p. 87.

8. Seldon D. Bacon, "Alcohol and Complex Society," in Simon Dinitz et al. *Deviance* (New York: Oxford University Press, 1969), p. 206.

9. Harvey Marshall and Ross Purdy, "Hidden Deviance and the Labelling Approach: The Case for Drinking and Driving," *Social Problems* (Spring 1972), p. 542.

10. Ibid., p. 543.

11. Robert Straus, "Alcoholism and Problem Drinking" in *Contemporary Social Problems*, 4th ed., by Robert K. Merton and Robert Nisbet (New York: Harcourt Brace Jovanovich, 1976), p. 206.

12. *The Task Force Report*, "Drunkenness Offenses," in Dinitz et al., *Deviance*, p. 247.

13. Straus, "Alcoholism," pp. 214–15.

14. Joan C. Martin, "Drugs of Abuse during Pregnancy: Effects Upon Offspring Structure and Function," *Signs* (Winter 1976), p. 365.

15. Richard S. Shore, "The Alcoholic," in *Outsiders USA*, by Patricia Keith-Spiegel and Don Speigel (San Francisco: Rinehart Press, 1973), p. 229.

16. Straus, "Alcoholism," p. 210.

17. Joan K. Jackson, "The Adjustment of the Family to the Crisis of Alcoholism," in *Deviance: The Interactionist Perspective*, by Earl Rubington and Martin S. Weinberg (New York: Macmillan, 1968), pp. 52–53.

18. Leo Kanowitz, *Women and the Law* (Albuquerque: University of New Mexico Press, 1969), p. 97.

19. William H. Masters and Virginia E. Johnson, *Human Sexual Response* (Boston: Little Brown, 1966), p. 268.

20. Helen Singer Kaplan, *The New Sex Therapy* (New York: Quadrangle, 1974), p. 89.

21. Martin, "Pregnancy," p. 358.

22. Ibid., p. 365.

23. Sandra Stencel, "Resurgence of Alcoholism," *Editorial Research Reports* 2 (December 26, 1973), p. 990.

24. Straus, "Alcoholism," p. 210.

25. Paul C. Higgins, Gary L. Albrecht, and Maryann H. Albrecht, "Black-White Adolescent Drinking: The Myth and the Reality," *Social Problems* (December 1977), p. 215.

26. Straus, "Alcoholism," p. 204.

27. Ibid., p. 189.

28. Carolyn Becker and Sidney Kronus, "Sex and Drinking Patterns: An Old Relationship Revisited in a New Way," *Social Problems* (April 1977), pp. 482–83.

29. Ibid., p. 494.

30. George D. Lowe and G. Eugene Hodges, "Race and the Treatment of Alcoholism in a Southern State," *Social Problems* (Fall 1972), pp. 245–46.

31. Ibid., p. 250.

32. Ibid., p. 247.

33. Higgins et al., "Black-White," p. 220.

34. Lowe and Hodges, "Race," p. 247.

35. Erich Goode, *Deviant Behavior* (Englewood Cliffs, N.J.: Prentice-Hall, 1978), p. 285.

36. Becker and Kronus, "Drinking Patterns," p. 483.

37. Marshall and Purdy, "Hidden Deviance," p. 542.

38. Charles W. Peek and George D. Lowe, "Wirth, Whiskey, and WASPs: Some Consequences of Community Size for Alcohol Use," *The Sociological Quarterly* (Spring 1977), p. 218.

39. Jacqueline Wiseman, *Stations of the Lost* (Englewood Cliffs, N.J.: Prentice-Hall, 1970), p. 15.

40. Ibid., p. 36.

41. Milton A. Maxwell, "Alcoholics Anonymous: An Interpretation," in *Alcoholism*, by David J. Pittman (New York: Harper & Row, 1967), p. 216.

42. Earl Rubington and William S. Weinberg, *Deviance: The Interactionist Perspective* (New York: Macmillan, 1968), p. 323.

43. Maxwell, "Alcoholics Anonymous," pp. 218–19.

44. Edward Sagarin, *Odd Man In: Societies of Deviants in America* (Chicago: Quadrangle, 1969), p. 47.

45. Ibid., p. 37.

46. Ibid., p. 45.

47. Morris E. Chefetz and Harold W. Demone, Jr., "Alcoholics Anonymous," in Dinitz et al., *Deviance*, p. 272.

48. Jackson, "Adjustment," p. 64.

SELECTED BIBLIOGRAPHY

Becker, Carolyn, and Kronus, Sidney. "Sex and Drinking Patterns: An Old Relationship Revisited in a New Way." *Social Problems* (April 1977), pp. 482–97.

Higgins, Paul C.; Albrecht, Gary L.; and Albrecht, Maryann H. "Black-White Adolescent Drinking: The Myth and the Reality." *Social Problems* (December 1977), pp. 215–23.

Lowe, George D., and Hodges, D. Eugene. "Race and the Treatment of Alcoholism in a Southern State." *Social Problems* (Fall 1972), pp. 240–51.

Marshall, Harvey, and Purdy, Ross. "Hidden Deviancy and the Labelling Approach: The Case for Drinking and Driving." *Social Problems* (Spring 1972), pp. 541–53.

Straus, Robert. "Alcoholism and Problem Drinking." In *Contemporary Social Problems*, 4th ed., by Robert K. Merton and Robert Nisbet. New York: Harcourt Brace Jovanovich, 1976, pp. 183–217.

Chapter **13**

Drugs

In recent years a great interest has developed in the "drug problem." Drug use is often presented as a major social problem that is undermining the morality of society and destroying many members of the younger generation. The definition of drugs as a social problem occurs within the context of passionate response frequently based on limited knowledge. This is true whether the view is that all drugs are evil and dangerous or that drugs are the way for the individual to find his true identity. In this chapter, our interest is in the various types of drugs and their consequences as well as in the social settings in which drugs are used.

Drugs have been a part of most cultures in the world. The evidence indicates that only a few societies have been without mind-altering drugs. The American society places great stress on the use of drugs under many circumstances, but it also makes many strong distinctions between the kinds of drugs to be used and the circumstances under which drugs may be used. However, this has not always been true in the United States. For many years certain remedies that had narcotic contents of 5 to 10 percent were sold over the counter without any controls. Through such wonder-working medications as Mrs. Winslow's Soothing Syrup, D.R. Cole's Catarrh Cure, and Perkins' Diarrhea Mixture, large amounts of opium, codeine, and cocaine were fed to children as well as adults. Also, every well-equipped home had a rosewood chest, an earlier version of today's medicine cabinet, with its ball of opium and its bottle of paregoric. It is estimated that by 1863 addiction in the United States ran as high as 4 percent of the population.[1] By 1900 there were institutions of different types for the treatment of drug addiction at various locations around the country. Before the attempt to suppress the drug trade started in 1915, the drug addicts were mostly scattered throughout respectable society.

EMERGENCE OF LAWS

There had been some initial concern with the possible dangers of drug use as early as the 1830s. But for the most part during the 19th century the problem of drug dependence was handled through continuous availability and consumption of the drug. The discomforts of abstaining from drugs were seen as just another set of aches and pains that could be eliminated by the use of drugs that were seen as the panacea for all ills. Early in this century estimates suggest there were between 200,000 and 500,000 drug addicts in the United States. Most of them were addicted to patent medicines available in any drugstore. Their addiction was defined as basically a medical problem and generally did not interfere with their personal effectiveness. "But by legislation that made opiates unavailable except through illegal channels, and by subsequent vilification of the drug user, addicts were transformed into criminals."[2]

The first law that tried to control drug addiction was the Boylan Law, passed by the New York legislature in 1904. The Harrison Narcotic Law, enacted in 1914, was modeled on the Boylan Law, but it omitted the important measures that were concerned with the physician's role in treating addiction. The Harrison Act was designed to control the production, manufacture, and distribution of addictive drugs by making it necessary to register all transactions in such drugs and by specifying that only physicians could prescribe them.

The Federal Narcotics Bureau played a major role in the emergence of drug use as a social problem. By focusing on the judicial decisions, they were able to circumvent the lobbies of physicians and pharmacists and create a new class of criminals—the addicts. The Treasury Department drew up regulations based on early court decisions that instructed doctors when and when not to give narcotics. "The judgment had been made that addiction was essentially not a disease, but a willful indulgence meriting punishment rather than medical treatment."[3] The social reality of what came to be the social problem of drugs was shaped by specific individuals and interest groups. There were specific moral entrepreneurs who agitated to have their "evil" become institutionalized through the passage of laws. Alongside those were the special interest groups such as pharmacists, physicians and the Narcotics Bureau that shaped the social problem.[4]

Over the years the Harrison Act has been supplemented by a number of other antinarcotics statutes under which the unauthorized possession, sale, or transfer of drugs has been severely punished.

Rather than constituting a rationally planned program for dealing with the narcotics problem, this legislation has mainly represented an emotional response to periodic crises. During this period the Federal Narcotics Control Board came up with what it saw to be the solution to drug use. That solution was compulsory treatment, and the board's successor since 1930, the Bureau of Narcotics in the Treasury Department, still considers compulsory treatment the only road to complete cure.[5]

In 1937, marijuana was added to the list of drugs controlled under the Harrison Act. The States were all urged to pass similar legislation and they all did, usually without any knowledge of what they were legislating against. During this time marijuana was described as leading inevitably to moral degeneracy. So legislators hurried to express their adversion to "degeneracy by increasing penalties for those found to have marijuana in their possession as well as for those trafficking in it."[6]

During the 1950s there was a piling up of drug offenders in the federal prisons. During that period the number and proportion of drug offenders in such prisons had more than doubled and the average length of sentences served increased almost fourfold. Furthermore, addicts received no treatment in federal or state prison. During the Nixon administration (early 1970s) new drug legislation was introduced. It returned almost exclusively to the punitive approach, and no provisions were made for the treatment of drug offenders but only for their imprisonment. Enforcement officials were given sweeping powers to violate civil rights. But opposition to the Nixon administration's proposed law did bring about some significant modifications. Among them were provisions for federally supported community treatment facilities and for continuing research. Subsequently the National Institute of Drug Abuse was established "thereby guarding against total domination of the program by the perspective of law enforcement personnel."[7]

Having seen that the legal system with regard to drug treatment in the United States was a failure both in not treating the addict as a medical problem and in not controlling the distribution of drugs, one might question why the system continues. One explanation is that using heavy criminal sanctions to control drug addiction rather than to treat the addict as a sick person may continue because the drug laws are primarily symbolic rather than instrumental in their effect. The severe treatment of addicts is evidence that policymakers may be more interested in expressing disapproval than in controlling the problem effectively. In fact the constant publicity given to various drugs by politicians and some of the police have sensationalized many drugs and stimulated curiosity about them. New drug laws have almost always been enacted on the basis of anecdotal, unscientific, and illegal testimony. Their enactment has often occurred in a climate of hysteria which may have been consciously developed and reinforced through the mass media. For example, laws against the use of LSD were passed with little medical, sociological, or scientific testimony. Often politicians are against drugs in the same way that they are against sin. That is, drugs are something safe to be against and in fact being against them may win votes because most people are against drugs—at least when used by others.

A commonly heard argument is that there should be drug reforms, but the argument almost always takes it for granted that the current policies are still desirable. In other words the legal view of drugs, rather than the medical approach taken in other countries, is rarely questioned by politicians. But some experts, who receive little attention, state that what is needed is an absolute reversal of the present attitudes and laws. These experts argue that the addict will get his drugs no matter how hard the law enforcers try to stop him and the major social problem is not the use of drugs but the kinds of things addicts do to get them.

The use of drugs is a social problem because they are now legally forbidden as well as socially condemned. Upholding the law has largely taken precedence over understanding this social problem. It is important to recognize that the harms associated with drug use are very much a product of social policy rather than of the pharmacological effects of the drugs. So social policy has to be a major factor in sustaining the definition of drug use as a social problem.

It must be recognized that the highly restrictive laws with regard to drug addiction have been enacted in a society that is quite permissive about drugs in general. In fact the American public places a high positive value on the use of "legitimate" drugs. In the United States drugs are usually acceptable and approved when they are seen to relieve some kind of pain, illness, or disability or, more generally, to help bring a person from some negative state toward a condition seen as "normal." More and more drugs are seen as legitimately used not only in reducing physical pain but also in alleviating mental anguish.

About 60 percent of the patients who appear in general practitioners' offices or clinics do so for largely nonspecific medical reasons. "Patients seek the help of a physician because they are lonely, depressed, anxious, dissatisfied or unhappy."[8] This means that a great many of them will be treated through drugs. In 1971 physicians wrote 230 million prescriptions for various drugs with psychoactive agents, less than 30 percent of which were written by psychiatrists. "During 1970, 5 billion doses of tranquilizers, 3 million doses of amphetamines and 5 million doses of barbiturates were produced in the United States. About one third of all Americans between the ages of 18 and 24 used a psychoactive drug of some type."[9] While the legitimate drugs help many there are dangers of overdependence, and even more serious, there is danger of death. There are, for example, approximately 3,000 deaths per year resulting from overdoses of barbiturates.

There are sex differences in the use of medically prescribed drugs. One nationwide study found that 20 percent of the women surveyed reported the use of physician-prescribed tranquilizers or sedatives in the previous year. Women are about twice as likely as men to have these drugs prescribed. This is a reflection of the fact that women have traditionally visited physicians more; for example, for child birth and depression. Therefore women have been prescribed these drugs more often than men. It is also likely that many male physicians see drugs as "appropriate" for women because they define women as more emotional than men and the drugs are supposed to alter emotional behavior. Tranquilizers and sedatives also appear to be more commonly taken by persons of middle or older ages.

Often physicians who prescribe drugs have no special qualifications to deal with psychological problems. Frequently the treatment is given to alleviate symptoms and does not get at the root of the problem. As Arnold Bernstein and Henry L. Lennard have pointed out, when drugs are given to a middle-aged woman who is upset about her child's rebellion or to an elderly man who is isolated from children or community, the problems are being masked. "The drugs decrease the anxiety of unhappiness of the individual but, more important, they decrease the amount of trouble his anxiety, misery, or unhappiness is causing others." [10]

Another danger from the legitimate use of drugs is that along with the widespread and intense belief in the power of medicine, there is often a tendency to ignore the limitations and the side effects of drugs. Many of the drugs physicians prescribe have side effects of which they are unaware or simply ignore. It may be that as many as three fourths of all physicians learn about a new drug from the advertisements of the manufacturer. These advertisements often gloss over or ignore many possible side effects. This lack of medical knowledge influences about 1.5 million people who are admitted each year to hospitals for drug side effects.

There is also some indication that with the breakdown of the traditional patient-doctor relationship and an increasing amount of medical specialization, people depend more on medication than on physicians. The patient often sees the physician simply as the one who prescribes the drugs that will take care of his problem. Once the patient has the medication, he sometimes uses it excessively or indiscriminately. There are some patients who use medication as a kind of magical protector and depend on medication rather than people to handle certain emotional drives and needs.

There are other kinds of problems related to the great amount of

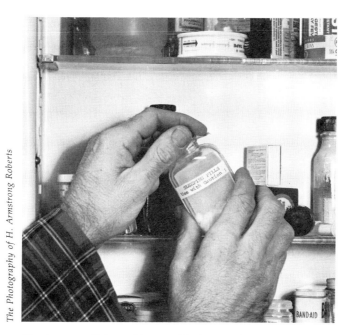

The home medicine cabinet and legitimate drugs

medically prescribed drugs. For example, it has been estimated that the overuse of antibiotics in the United States had led to new and resistant strains of bacteria that may cause up to 100,000 deaths per year. Other examples of legal drug abuse are forcing mental patients to take powerful tranquilizers so they don't trouble the staff or the use of amphetamines to slow down the "hyperactive" child.

Adult society, with its use of many kinds of drugs, has socialized many of the younger generation to the use of drugs. The generation that is sometimes now looking for new experiences in drugs received its orientation in a society that had been using various pills for adjustment to its psychic problems. Over the years, barbiturates and nonaddictive drugs have been finding their way into the hands of many adults, and this had been increasingly reflected in accident and suicide statistics. In one sense the medicine cabinet in the middle-class home has been a socializing experience that in some ways predisposed children toward experimentation with drugs.[11]

Illegal drugs are believed to provide a wide range of benefits. At one extreme, the believers in drug use see the psychedelic compounds, such as LSD and mescaline, as a way of counteracting the "depersonalization," "commercialization," and "inhumanity" of modern American society. For such people the use of drugs is a modern means to mystical experience and to the great "inward journey of self-

exploration and self-discovery." At the other extreme, those who oppose drug use see it as self-indulgent, degenerate, and both psychologically and physiologically damaging. "Drug use is viewed as a
'symptom'—either of profound psychological problems or of some
fatal weakness in the moral fiber of American youth. It is a form of
moral depravity, and it must be ruthlessly stamped out, its users
thoroughly punished, and the young indoctrinated in the 'hazards' of
drugs."[12]

The defining of "good" and "bad" drugs in the United States is
constantly undergoing some change. But those who argue the advantages of illegal drugs have a limited audience because power groups
have little interest in expanding the legal use of such drugs. (There is
some change with marijuana which will be discussed later.) No one is
arguing for social acceptance of hard drugs. The legal production and
sale of addictive drugs would mean little in the way of profit so the
possible power brokers are not motivated to move in that direction. In
other words the only way that vast profits are to be made is to keep
hard drugs illegal.

The American system has been attacked on the ground that the
legal approach to drug addiction has failed. Obviously the laws have
failed in that they have not eliminated drug addiction. Actually they
have contributed to the narcotics problem. The addict, because he is
cut off from any legal supply of drugs, must seek out illegal drug
sources. The strong demand of addicts for the satisfaction of their drug
needs means that huge profits can be made on the illegal market.
Because there are great profits to be made, illegal activity is seen as
worthwhile by the drug sellers. The traffic in illegal drugs has been estimated to gross billions of dollars per year. Narcotics smuggling and
distribution are big businesses for the crime syndicates. Yet, as has
been pointed out, at the beginning of the century little illegal profit
was being made from drug sales. Therefore, it seems clear that the
illegal view of drugs that has developed since 1914 has been the major
factor in creating the highly profitable criminal business of selling illegal drugs.

Before looking at the various kinds of drugs and their use and consequences, it is necessary to define some terms. The word *narcotic* is
used to refer to opium and the various painkilling drugs that are made
from opium, such as heroin, morphine, paregoric, and codeine.
These, as well as other opiates, are taken from the juice of the poppy
fruit. Several synthetic drugs, such as Demerol and Dolophine, are
also classified as narcotics. The *opiates* are widely used in medicine to
kill pain. Cocaine, made from cacao leaves, and marijuana are legally
classified as narcotic drugs although they are not narcotic in chemical
makeup. Pharmacologically the term narcotic is applied to a drug
which, in most people under most circumstances and at the right level

of dosage, will produce sleep and relieve pain. However, from the legal point of view the term narcotic has been applied to almost any drug assumed to be habit forming or addictive. The general public has gone even further in its definition of the term narcotic, using it to refer to any drug which is socially disapproved. The term *drug* refers to any chemical substance that alters mood, perception, or consciousness. The social and legal settings define the nature of drug use. The term *drug addiction* refers to a state of periodic or chronic intoxication brought about by the repeated use of a drug of either a natural or a synthetic nature.

TYPES OF DRUGS

In this section our interest is in examining various types of drugs. However the *hallucinogens* are one group that cuts across several categories of drugs. In this group are included such drugs as LSD, mescaline, psilocybin, and marijuana. These drugs have a hallucinatory effect and influence the user's perception of the world both within and outside of himself. The drugs are not addictive, although under some personality conditions they may become habit forming. This group is also sometimes referred to as the psychedelic drugs. The black market for the sale of hallucinogens is loosely organized, with friends often supplying one another and covering their mutual costs, rather than being an organized network of pushers.

Variations in the effects of drugs on the individual may be related to how they are taken. The injection of the drug directly into the vein delivers the total dose immediately, and this produces a rapid maximum response of minimal duration. Smoking and inhalation cause rapid but less efficient delivery of the dose because a quantity of the drug is destroyed during burning or escapes into the air and does not reach the lungs. Oral ingestion produces different effects, according to the system in which the drug is dispensed. Generally oral ingestion diminishes but prolongs the effect of drugs.

Barbiturates.   The first barbiturate appeared in 1903 and was called barbital (Veronal). Barbiturates are classified among the general depressants. They are not specific in effect and are capable of depressing a wide range of functions. Their influence on the central nervous system ranges from a mild sedation to coma, depending on the level of dosage. At moderate dosage levels the barbiturates often produce loss of inhibition and euphoria, much as does alcohol (also a depressant). The drugs depress other functions, such as nerves, skeletal muscles, smooth muscles, and cardiac muscles. Barbiturates are estimated to be the cause of about 3,000 deaths per year.

Barbiturates are under the regulation of the Bureau of Narcotics

TABLE 13–1

Drug Use, by Type of Drug and by Age Group, 1977 (Current users are those who used drugs at least once within month prior to this study. Based on national samples of 1,272 youths, 1,500 young adults, and 1,822 older adults. Subject to sampling variability; see source)

Type of drug	Percent of youths (12–17 years)		Percent of young adults (18–25 years)		Percent of older adults (26 years and older)	
	Ever used	Current user	Ever used	Current user	Ever used	Current user
Marijuana and/or hashish	28.2	16.1	60.1	27.7	15.4	3.2
Inhalants	9.0	0.7	11.2	*	1.8	*
Hallucinogens	4.6	1.6	19.8	2.0	2.6	*
Cocaine	4.0	1.0	19.1	3.7	2.6	*
Heroin	1.1	*	3.6	*	0.8	*
Other opiates	6.1	0.6	13.5	1.0	2.8	*
Stimulants†	5.2	1.3	21.2	2.5	4.7	0.6
Sedatives†	3.1	0.8	18.4	2.8	2.8	*
Tranquilizers†	3.8	0.7	13.4	2.4	2.6	*
Alcohol	52.6	31.2	84.2	70.0	77.9	54.9
Cigarettes	47.3	22.3	67.6	47.3	67.0	38.7

*Less than .5 percent.
†Prescription drugs.

Source: U.S. Department of Commerce, Bureau of the Census, *Statistical Abstract of the U.S., 1978*, (Washington, D.C.: U.S. Government Printing Office, 1978), p. 123.

and Dangerous Drugs, Department of Justice. The federal laws provide for a strict accounting of drug supplies by the manufacturer, distributor, and seller, and they limit the refills of the prescription, at the discretion of the physician. This means that barbiturates can be obtained legally only through a physician. The illegal manufacture and dispensing of barbiturates can lead to fines as high as $10,000 and prison sentences of up to 5 years. Those convicted of selling the drugs to persons under 21 years of age can be fined $15,000 to $20,000 and can be sentenced to 10 to 15 years in prison. To be in possession of these drugs illegally can bring a fine of from $1,000 to $10,000 and/or imprisonment of 1 to 3 years. There are also state laws that control the illegal use of barbiturates.

Amphetamines. Amphetamines, which were first produced in the 1920s for medical use, stimulate the central nervous system and are best known as a means to fight against fatigue and sleepiness. They are sometimes used to limit appetites in medically-controlled weight reduction programs. The most commonly used are amphetamine (Benzedrine), dextroamphetamine (Dexedrine), and methamphetamine (Methedrine). These drugs are also known under the slang terms of pep pills and "bennies."

The amphetamines produce effects resembling those resulting from the stimulation of the sympathetic nervous system, that part of the nervous system which has major control over bodily functions. There is a high potential for psychological dependence in some individuals if they use amphetamines regularly over a period of time. The psychological dependence appears to be a function of the drugs' ability to bring forth feelings of energy, initiative, self-confidence, and well-being. After a period of usage many people find it very difficult to meet the demands of life without this uplift. There is some evidence that women are more apt to use amphetamines than are men. By contrast men use hallucinogens more often.

There is little doubt that amphetamines can improve a person's performance on a wide variety of tasks, especially those involving an element of fatigue or boredom. They are in a way "superman" drugs because they can increase the capacity for simple physical and mental tasks, and because they increase intelligence, as measured by simple tests, by an average of up to eight points. However, highly coordinated tasks like playing golf or flying an airplane are unaffected in quality, though they can be prolonged beyond the normal duration. One of the most dangerous uses of amphetamines is "speeding." This is a series of injections, each of which is followed by a general climax of intense feelings and bodily sensations.

The amphetamines have undergone a strong reevaluation in recent years and their use is now seriously questioned. For many, after extended usage there are such withdrawal symptoms as severe depression, fatigue, anxiety and extreme irritability. And recent evidence indicates that they may not even be effective for most of the medical problems for which they are prescribed. For example, they are ineffective in fighting obesity. Many physicians have more or less abandoned amphetamines as a therapeutic tool.[13]

Cocaine.   The effects of the use of cocaine are very similar to those of the amphetamines. As the popular usage of the amphetamines has decreased, however, the use of cocaine has increased. At the present time cocaine is the fastest growing illicit drug being used in the United States. Erich Goode says it is the most fashionable, chic, and prestigious of all the illegal drugs and that there has developed a kind of cocaine *mystique*. It is very expensive and can run four times the cost of heroin.[14]

The most commonly described effect of cocaine is exhilaration, a sense of elation and well-being. There is also a sense of increased energy and the suppression of fatique. Cocaine does not produce tolerance so there is no need to increase the dose over time to achieve the same high. "It does not produce a physical dependency, or addiction: there are no withdrawal symptoms. However, if one steps up the dose one can experience a number of extremely unpleasant side effects.[15]

Marijuana. Marijuana is a drug found in the flowering tops and the leaves of the Indian hemp plant. The plant grows in mild climates in countries all over the world. The marijuana plant is a relative of European hemp and looks like a scrawny, six-foot nettle. The term marijuana has become synonymous with cannabis and all of its products and derivatives, including the natural and synthetic tetrahydrocannabinols. The substance cannabis is derived from the resin exuded by the female hemp plants. This substance has been used by humans throughout recorded history. It is the leaves, stems, and flowering tops that are dried and chopped to produce the marijuana common to the United States and Mexico. The chopped-up product is usually rolled and smoked in short cigarettes or in pipes, and may be taken in food. The smoke from marijuana is harsh and smells like burnt dried grass, and the rather sweetish aroma is quite easy to identify.

At one time in the United States extracts of cannabis were used almost as commonly for medicinal purposes as is aspirin today. Cannabis could be purchased without a prescription, and it was often prescribed by physicians for the treatment of a broad range of medical conditions, from migraine headaches and excessive menstrual bleeding to ulcers, epilepsy, and even tooth decay. Many medical reports were written about the use of cannabis but hardly ever did they refer to any intoxicating properties of the drug. "Rarely, if ever, is there any indication that patients—hundreds of thousands must have received cannabis in Europe in the 19th century—were 'stoned' or changed their attitudes toward work, love, their fellow men, or their homeland." [16]

Well before the Marijuana Stamp Act of 1937, the use of cannabis in general medicine was already declining. This was because there had always been problems in prescribing the drug. It is insoluble in water and cannot be injected intravenously for rapid effect. Moreover, the delay before it begins to take effect when given by mouth—one or two hours—is no longer than with many other drugs.

How common is the use of marijuana in the United States? It is by far the most commonly used drug; about one in four adolescents report having smoked it. Its use increases with age. While only about 10 percent of all 14-year-olds report having smoked it, the figure rises to about 50 percent among 18-year-olds.[17] Its use has also increased over recent years. For example, successive Gallup Polls conducted between 1967 and 1974 indicated that the percentage of college students who had tried marijuana increased from 5 percent in 1967 to 55 percent in 1974. The studies suggest that from one half to three fourths of students in many colleges have tried marijuana at least a few times and most of those who have tried it continue to use it at least occasionally.[18] Marijuanna is often used at least occasionally by many middle-class adults.

There may be some social factors related to certain young people using marijuana. For example, with reference to religious affiliation, Jews and Catholics have been found to be slightly more apt to use it than are Protestants. One study reports that initiation of use was related to such variables as sex and religion. However, among those having ever used it, those social categories had no predictive power with regard to extent of use. Also stopping the use of marijuana was not related to aging per se, "but to the entry that most people made eventually into significant social statuses."[19] For many their marijuana use occurred at a stage in life where it was a part of a general life style.

TABLE 13–2

Marijuana Use, by Characteristics and Residence of User, 1974 and 1977

Characteristic	Percent ever used		Percent current user		Characteristic	Percent ever used		Percent current user	
	1974	1977	1974	1977		1974	1977	1974	1977
Youths, 12–17 years . . .	23	28	12	16	Adults (18 years and over	19	25	7	8
Male	24	33	12	19	Male	24	30	9	11
Female	21	23	11	13	Female	14	19	5	6
White	24	29	12	17	White	18	24	7	8
Black and other	17	26	9	12	Black and other	27	27	8	8
12–13 years	6	8	2	4	18–25 years	53	60	26	28
14–15 years	22	29	12	15	26–34 years	30	44	8	12
16–17 years	39	47	20	29	35 years and over	4	7	*	1
Northeast	26	35	14	21	Northeast	22	29	7	11
North Central	21	29	11	19	North Central	17	24	7	8
South	17	19	6	7	South	13	17	5	4
West	30	36	19	22	West	29	32	11	11
Large metro. areas† . . .	27	37	14	22	Large metro. areas† . . .	24	30	9	11
Other SMSAs‡	22	28	11	16	Other SMSAs‡	20	26	8	9
Nonmetro. areas	18	18	10	10	Nonmetro. areas	12	16	4	4

*Less than 5 percent.
†Comprises 25 largest standard metropolitan statistical areas (SMSA) as of 1970.
‡Standard Metropolitan Statistical Area (Census Bureau).
Source: U.S. Department of Commerce, Bureau of the Census, *Statistical Abstracts of the U.S., 1978,* (Washington, D.C.: U.S. Government Printing Office, 1978), p. 123.

The effects of marijuana vary not only among different individuals but also with a given individual over time. The wide variety of responses to marijuana seems to be more closely related to personality differences and the cultural setting in which it is used than to any specific property of the drug itself. The effects of the drug also vary as one learns to smoke in the most effective manner and then becomes sensitized. In most individuals these effects are pleasurable at low dosage levels and unpleasant at higher dosage levels.

More specifically the effects of marijuana include a euphoric state accompanied by motor excitation and mental confusion. These reactions are frequently followed by a period of dreaminess, depression, and sleep. The only notable physical changes brought about by marijuana are slight increases in the heart rate and the dilation of the blood vessels in the conjunctivas, which results in the common "red eyes" of the marijuana smoker. This is probably the most efficient way of detecting whether someone is stoned. Marijuana has usually been found to inhibit the expression of aggressive impulses by pacifying the user, "interfering with muscular coordination, reducing psychomotor activities, and generally producing states of drowsiness, lethargy, timidity, and passivity. Only a very few marijuana users have been arrested and convicted for such violent crimes as murder, forcible rape, aggravated assault, or armed robbery."[20]

Intellectually, the use of marijuana tends to increase imagination but reduce concentration. For example, intelligence test scores are slightly lower or unchanged, "and if attention is held, say in a game of poker, an expert player can more than hold his own against other good players. Jazz musicians claim that they can play more excitingly under the influence than without; in simple—but musically sterile—laboratory tests of note identification and beat duration, their performance is worse on the drug."[21] What often happens is that the person "thinks" he is better at performing tasks than he is by any objective criterion. This is a result of the psychological lift and optimistic interpretation marijuana generally induces in the user.

It appears that a person who is accustomed to the effects of marijuana can compensate for any impairment of mental and physical functioning. This view is supported by the testimony of smokers who say that a marijuana high is much more manageable than alcohol intoxication. In driving tests it has been found that in terms of total scores, subjects performed no worse when they were stoned on marijuana than when they were sober. "They did show somewhat more speedometer errors when under the influence of marijuana. In contrast, after consuming the equivalent of about six ounces of 86-proof whiskey, there was a marked impairment in all measures of the driving simulator test."[22]

There have been a number of studies examining the relationship between marijuana use and school performance. Steven R. Burkett found very apparent relationships between the use of marijuana and low school performance, low grades, and the feeling that school was "meaningless." The use of marijuana by both males and females was related to a general withdrawal from the immediate school situation, "i.e., a withdrawal characterized by a genuine dislike for school, and/or the perceived irrelevance of the educational process as experienced thus far."[23]

Burkett further found that low-achieving middle-class youth were more likely to experiment with and/or use marijuana regularly than were high-achieving middle- and lower-class youth.[24] On the college level recreational users of marijuana are often average or better-than-average students. They are more often found among students in the humanities and the social sciences rather than among students in the "hard" sciences or in professional schools. However, the heavy users tend to be disengaged from conventional ties and most sharply alienated from most of the dominant values in American society.[25]

Many people argue that sexual experiences while under the influence of marijuana are more erotic and exciting. It may be that the loss of inhibitions induced by marijuana makes them feel that such is true. It is not known whether marijuana actually makes for a physiological heightening of sexual response or whether this impression may be explained on psychological grounds. Some people claim to be more receptive to and more interested in erotic behavior and to more effectively lose themselves in the sexual experience after smoking marijuana. Some also claim that the orgasm is more prolonged and pleasurable.

The women respondents in the *Redbook* study were asked if they had ever had sexual relations while under the influence of marijuana. Of the total response group 40 percent answered "yes." But there were wide variations by age. For example, for women under 20 years of age, 69 percent had had the experience. By contrast, for women 25–29 years of age it was 40 percent and for those 35–39, it was 28 percent. When the women who had used marijuana were asked if it had contributed to their sexual experiences 33 percent said "yes," 11 percent "no," 10

TABLE 13–3a

Number and Percent of Women Who Ever Had Sexual Relations While Under the Influence of Marijuana, by Age

Age	Yes		No	
	Number	Percent	Number	Percent
Under 20 years	408	69	186	31
20–24 years	2,423	56	1,904	44
25–29 years	2,304	40	3,383	60
30–34 years	1,127	32	2,361	68
35–39 years	478	28	1,244	72
40 years and over	583	25	1,741	75
Totals	7,323	40	10,819	60

Source: "October Sex Quiz," *Redbook Magazine* (December 1974).

TABLE 13–3b

Number and Percent of Those Women Who Ever Had Sexual Relations While Under Influence of Marijuana and Contributed to Sexual Experience, by Age

| | Contributed | | | |
| | Yes | | No | |
Age	*Number*	*Percent*	*Number*	*Percent*
Under 20 years	255	63	149	37
20–24 years	1,390	58	1,021	42
25–29 years	1,010	44	1,287	56
30–34 years	325	29	795	71
35–39 years	103	10	371	90
40 years and over	60	10	514	90
Totals	3,143	39	4,337	71

Source: "October Sex Quiz," *Redbook Magazine* (December, 1974).

percent "sometimes;" and, 46 percent "can't say." By age there was also a wide difference with 63 percent of those under 20 years of age saying "yes" but only 10 percent of those women past age 40 who had ever used marijuana.

There have long been many claims about the use of drugs and sexual experience. In most instances there has been no evidence that drugs act as any kind of aphrodisiac. But in recent years there has been some claim that *amyl nitrate* enhances the intensity and pleasure of orgasm. This drug is a vasodilator that is sometimes prescribed to relieve the pain of angina pectoris. In theory the drug which is popped during the height of sexual arousal acts by increasing the vascular response of the genitals. But there is serious question about the use of this substance. There is no scientifically valid data to support the aphrodisiac claims and the use of the drug is medically dangerous. "Coronary occlusions, some resulting in death, have been reported to follow the use of amyl nitrate during intercourse."[26]

Conflicting Solutions

There has often been confusion over the "expert's" views about marijuana. Generally reliable authorities have publicly taken opposite views regarding it, not only on moral and social policy grounds, but also on the basis of the supposedly "hard" scientific facts. This confusion is reflected in the fact that of several thousand publications on marijuana being published only a few actually meet the standards of scientific investigation. They are often ill-documented and ambiguous, emotion-laden and incredibly biased, and can, in general, be relied upon for very little valid information.

There is also a great deal of difference between public opinion and the views of many experts. In general, public opinion is based on erroneous beliefs. The common belief is that marijuana is addictive, debilitating, and inevitably leads to other addictions. The differing view of physicians, psychiatrists, and sociologists have not greatly altered its popular image. According to current definitions, marijuana is a social problem since it is contrary to social values. It is a social problem because of moral values rather than any strong medical evidence that it is dangerous to physical or mental health.

There is no evidence that marijuana is a drug of addiction. There is also no evidence that marijuana has a direct causal relationship with criminal behavior in the sense that it leads the user to commit criminal acts. Most authorities have dismissed the lurid charges that have been a part of the traditional "marijuana menace." The current medical thinking is that tolerance and physical dependence do not develop and withdrawal does not produce any abstinence syndrome. Although the use of marijuana is not seen as a cause of crime, it is often associated with illegal acts. The link between the use of marijuana and that of hard drugs can be overdone. It is obviously true that many drug addicts started out on marijuana, but many of them also started out on cigarettes, alcohol, and milk.

The failure to link in a causal way the use of marijuana with drugs of addiction is a fact that many young persons are fully aware of. The attempt by authorities to present a causal link where none exists makes them suspicious and skeptical of statements that are true. For example, when the Federal Bureau of Narcotics writes "that it cannot be too strongly emphasized that the smoking of marijuana is a dangerous first step on the road which usually leads to enslavement by heroin" many persons know that scientific knowledge does not support this kind of assertion and they often become distrustful.

There have been many statements attempting to link marijuana use to various kinds of anti-social behavior. But by itself marijuana does not lead to acts of violence, juvenile delinquency, or aggressive behavior. Nor is there any conclusive evidence that physical damage or disturbances of bodily processes are due to high uses of marijuana. "There is very little evidence as to the long term effects of heavy use of marijuana on the body. Although it appears that the long term consumption in moderate doses has no harmful effects."[27]

Many studies link the use of marijuana mainly to the young. Burkett found that marijuana use was centered primarily within a sector of youth who at least temporarily had withdrawn from conventional adult sponsored activities.[28] This represents a gap from the adult world and places an overwhelming stress on peer relationships. Marijuana use is tied to peer involvement, both in terms of the amount of time spent with friends and association with others who use marijuana. Burkett writes that "these findings suggest that the peer group provides the context within which its members receive a certain degree of support and 'protection' for their action."[29]

Another study states that attitudes toward drug use as well as actual use are far more strongly influenced by the beliefs and practices of intimate friends than by parental beliefs and practices. One study of high school students found that in "no other aspects except age, sex, and race did best friends resemble one another so closely as in illegal drug use."[30] Another study says that the predictibility of marijuana use/nonuse is a function of only a few variables, and the number of friends who use marijuana is the best single predictor. "The influence of friends' use on respondents' use/nonuse is probably a reinforcing rather than a controlling effect."[31]

It is doubtful that very many who use marijuana see it as being deviant behavior. And many of those who use it to be deviant feel a sense of satisfaction with being different. The setting in which they may see their use of marijuana as making them different is one where they are more willing to try exciting things and to experiment. The rest of the world may be seen as too conventional. It is doubtful that many marijuana users see themselves as a part of a social problem. They do not accept the moral and legal definitions of marijuana use that make it a social problem. The broad social situation is one which includes various publics that say marijuana use is a social problem while at the same time the users of marijuana are generally indifferent and basically unaffected by those definitions. The only time users are really affected is when they run into the law, and that is happening less and less.

Among those who use marijuana for any length of time, it is often a part of a broader life style. In general, the life style is more radical or permissive than is defined as acceptable by the larger social groups. For example, marijuana users are more likely than nonusers to have premarital sexual relations and at a younger age. They are more apt to have a variety of partners and to experiment in a wider variety of sexual experiences than are nonusers. It is often within this generally more permissive life style that values toward marijuana use emerge. One of the values, as suggested, is that marijuana use is a positive life experience and not a social problem.

Life styles can vary in types and drug use is usually a part of the more extreme kinds of counter-culture groups. One study of a counter-culture community examined the patterns of marijuana use. It was found that regular marijuana smokers often smoked alone but in addition there were spontaneous gatherings where smoking was a very important part. Don H. Zimmerman found that persons in the group possessing marijuana were expected to share it and when it was

Magnum Photos, Inc.

Sharing marijuana

shared there was the expectation it would be a social event with talk or common activity. Within the limits of the marijuana available the persons could smoke as much as they desired and they were free to get as stoned as they wanted. There were no social sanctions controlling the amount of marijuana an individual could properly consume.[32]

Laws. Up until recently the sale of marijuana was a felony under federal law, and the penalty for possessing the drug was 2 to 10 years' imprisonment for the first offense. For the sale or transfer of the drug a first offense could bring a 5- to 20-year sentence and a fine of up to $20,000. However, a great amount of pressure emerged in the late 1960s to ease the severity of the punishments. Beginning in 1966 the proportion of defendants ultimately convicted declined gradually, as did the percentage of defendants who were incarcerated and the average length of their sentences. "This response reflected an attempt to mitigate the harshness of the law as applied to this new user population."[33]

The former laws were changed, and possession of marijuana was reduced to a misdemeanor. Special treatment was set up for first offenders, and their records could be wiped clean after satisfactory completion of a probationary period. After a series of hearings Congress passed the Comprehensive Drug Abuse Prevention and Control Act, and in October 1970 the President signed it into law. Many of the states also eased their laws.

In 1973 some of the states started to decriminalize the possession of small amounts of marijuana. In 1973 Oregon abolished criminal penalties for possession of an ounce or less of marijuana and made it a civil offense similar to a traffic violation that carried a maximum fine of $100. In 1977 it was no longer a criminal offense in ten states and there were bills pending in a number of other states. Goode estimates that within a few years "marijuana possession will no longer be a crime in at least half the states."[34]

In the past the arrests of marijuana users have been limited and selective. In most criminal offenses the likelihood of detection is greatly influenced by citizen complaints and victims who contact the police. However, citizens play a very minor role in determining whether or not drug violations are detected. Arrests for drug offenses almost always arise from police initiated contacts with the person arrested. In marijuana arrests it is estimated that about two thirds occur spontaneously without any investigation. Usually these arrests are made by patrol officers in their routine policing of public areas and after a seizure of less than one ounce of marijuana.[35]

In many situations the marijuana user has been arrested for other reasons. It may be that he comes to the attention of the police because of race, appearance, or his behavior toward the police. This has meant that arrest rates for marijuana use have very much been at the discretion of the police. Often arrests have not been due to police interest in getting drug users but in seeking arrests in other areas and getting the marijuana violations as a secondary charge.

One of the functions of laws against criminal behavior is deterrence. If laws are effective, they are intended to deter people from engaging in the behavior due to the consequences of getting caught. But Robert F. Meier found that the perceived certainty of punishment showed no effect on the use or nonuse of marijuana. He found that the factors, legal or extralegal, that appeared to functionally inhibit marijuana use were age, fear of physical consequences of such use, and beliefs that marijuana use was immoral.[36]

Emerging Social Institutionalization

In general the views of society have remained hostile toward the use of marijuana. One writer has observed that much of the hostility comes from people who have never examined the facts. He suspects that "what makes them dislike cannabis is not the belief that the effects of taking it are harmful but rather a horrifying suspicion that there is a source of pure pleasure which is available, for those who have not earned it, who do not deserve it."[37] This would help to account for some of the hostility of many older people who consider marijuana to be a part of a hedonistic society they deplore. Some people see the use of marijuana as a result of a manipulative society's control over the young. They believe that an evil, criminal influence is at work to get the young to use marijuana. This fits a theory of society which holds that there are the corrupted and the corrupters. These people see healthy youngsters being corrupted by a few psychologically disturbed and economically motivated individuals.[38]

Undoubtedly the greatest resistance to marijuana use comes from the older members of society. The attitude to marijuana is a value area in which the amount of generational conflict is very great. In part this is reflected in the fact that few people past age 50 have ever used marijuana. One study reported that only 9 percent of the over-50 generation agreed with the statement that "most people who use marijuana lead a normal life." By contrast half the young adults (18 to 25) considered most marijuana users to be normal. Another study asked parents what they would do if they found that their teenage children were smoking marijuana. Forty-seven percent said that they would try to stop them through persuasion and reason, 23 percent said that they favored a punitive approach. "Interestingly, 9 percent of the latter group felt so strongly about the matter that they were willing to report their own child to the police. A considerable number, 35 percent, indicated they were uncertain about what to do."[39]

Goode argues that marijuana is shedding its deviant and criminal status and is moving into the realm of conventionality. He argues that the reason for its becoming conventional is because of who the users are, rather than in the nature of the drug's use and its effects. Increasingly the users have been the sons and daughters of the affluent and respectable. In general, the higher one's education, the greater the likelihood of using marijuana.[40] It is certainly true that marijuana use has lost much of its stigma but it still appears to be some distance from becoming conventional. It still cannot be legally purchased and for many there continues to be some threat of legal or moral problems. It may also be that the general interest in marijuana is decreasing and there is less concern with making it more conventional.

Drugs of Addiction

The drugs of addiction are seen as much more severe and dangerous social problems than marijuana. The addictive drugs are clearly institutionalized in American society. That is, with few exceptions they are seen as bad. However the questions of what to do about them are far from being resolved.

Drugs of addiction are also called opiates. These are drugs with pain-killing and euphoria-producing properties and include chemicals which are derived from or are the equivalent of opium. The best known are morphine and heroin. The term narcotics is also often used to describe the opiates. Addiction implies a physical dependence that is far more than just habit or some vague emotional craving. The morphine or heroin addict's organism depends on a regular supply of the opiate just as a normal organism depends on a regular supply of important vitamins. In this section our interest is mainly in heroin and morphine. Both can be purchased in the United States only in illegal markets. Therefore, people who become addicted to heroin are engaged from the first shot in what they know to be an illegal activity. The second most common drug of addiction is morphine, which is similar in its effects to heroin. But many people who become addicted to morphine develop their addiction unknowingly, often through its medical use as a pain killer. In fact a number of physicians become addicted to morphine, a drug they have access to. Often the morphine addict, with no legitimate sources from which to get the drug, may get pushed into the illegal drug market to meet his addiction.

Morphine and heroin are depressants, and this is contrary to the misconception that addicts are dangerously "hopped up." Actually these drugs produce a general lowering of the activity of the nervous system and other bodily activity. Also, no known organic diseases are associated with chronic opiate addiction, though these are often found with alcohol addiction, cigarette smoking, and even chronic overeating. Although opiate use does produce such effects as pupillary constriction, constipation, and sexual impotence, none of these conditions need be fully disabling, nor are they usually important. The great danger with drugs of addiction does not lie in what they do to the organism but rather in their behavioral and social consequences for the person. The extreme physical and psychological need for such drugs means that the addict will usually do almost anything to meet his needs, and this is often what is most harmful.

There have been recent changes in the patterns of heroin use. Before 1970 it was rare for anyone to use heroin more than five or six times without becoming addicted. But in the 1970s heroin became more and more a drug in a pattern of multiple drug use, especially among young drug users. It is still rare for someone to use heroin occasionally without becoming addicted if he uses no other drugs, but the terms heroin addict and heroin user are no longer synonymous. "It may be that mixing other drugs, especially barbiturates, with heroin during the initial stages of heroin use makes the road to addiction slower, but no less sure."[41]

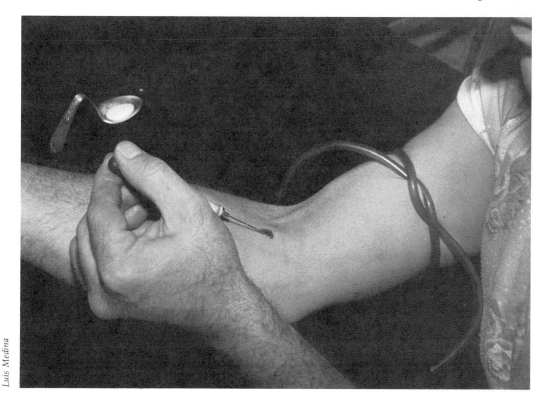

Luis Medina

A heroin addict

There are other dangers to the use of the heroin. For example, there have been studies of babies born to heroin addicts. Women constitute from one fourth to one half of the heroin addicts in the United States and about 80 percent of them are in the childbearing years. Once pregnant there is a high prematurity and stillbirth rate. Between 55 and 90 percent of all offspring develop withdrawal symptoms within 24 hours after birth. "These include evidence of central nervous system irritability with restlessness, shrill crying, cyanosis, vomiting, diarrhea, and convulsions. The mortality rate for untreated infants who develop these symptoms is high."[42]

The federal laws have changed very little with regard to heroin. Where the laws have changed it has not been in reducing the seriousness of heroin use but to provide some assistance to the states for research and experimental treatment programs.

Who are the heroin addicts? They are most heavily concentrated in slum areas of the largest metropolitan centers. It has been estimated that about 40 percent of the nation's addicts live in New York City.

Daniel Glaser suggests that the typical addict was, before addiction, a person of greater aspiration than others of his background. For example, drug addicts in Chicago and Puerto Rico had higher educational achievement than nonaddicts of similar ethnic descent. He goes on to say that the list of addicts he accumulated in New York City suggested four or five male addicts to one female, "perhaps because females have more attractive job and marital opportunities than unskilled males find in the city."[43]

"Causes" of drug use.   In this section our interest is in the "causes" of drug addiction. By this is meant not only why persons become drug addicts but also how addiction takes place. Our first interest is in the process of drug addiction. There is a great difference between using something that is addictive and using something that becomes habit forming. A habit is primarily mental and emotional—the smoker's desire for a cigarette, the drinker's desire for a cocktail. However, addiction is as physical, as urgent, and as implacable as a person's need for water. One study of young addicts suggested that three conditions were necessary for them to emerge as addicts: first, a psychological and predisposing inadequacy; second, a crisis that occurred in their lives; and third, a timely offer of drugs. Of course, those same conditions might have led the young person to get drunk for the first time, but what appears to be crucial is a state of readiness and the availability of the drug. When one first takes drugs there may be some positive feeling in one's reactions to the drugs, but this seems to last only during the early stages of addiction. "In the later stages, a reversal of effects occurs, in which the drug is no longer taken primarily to obtain positive pleasure but rather to avoid the negative effects of withdrawal."[44]

As suggested, some persons who get started on morphine may unknowingly wind up as addicts. But other persons do make conscious moves toward addiction. It takes deliberate acts to become addicted to heroin, and a first step may be taken because of a feeling of uselessness and despair. But the addict must see some hope through his involvement in drugs; to him, if to no one else, they offer some improvement to his present condition. It would seem that few nonaddicts could ever anticipate what it means to become an addict. For most who try narcotics there is undoubtedly an exaggerated expectation of what they will gain and an unrealistic anticipation of what the costs will be. It is often only when it is too late that an accurate understanding develops.

The most difficult question is why people consciously turn to the drugs of addiction, especially in light of all the negative publicity about those drugs. The availability of drugs does not seem to be an important factor in drug addiction. Almost all studies show that people who become drug addicts do so because of personality factors rather than the availability of the drugs. That is, drug addiction is a symptom of some need rather than a disease. Some persons see the use of drugs as a means of finding their sense of identity. A part of personality training may derive from socialization experiences to the use of drugs. One study pointed out that users of drugs of addiction, in contrast to nonusers, had been ill more often as children, had been taken more often to a physician, and had been given more medications.[45]

There is no single cause for addiction, as there is no single type of addict. For example, the physician who becomes an addict is very different from the lower-class black who is a part of a subculture composed of delinquents and addicts. "However, individuals in certain socioeconomic categories run a relatively greater risk of encountering and using narcotics than do those in other categories. Also, it seems likely that of those individuals in the high-risk categories it is the more troubled or the more disadvantaged, situationally, who are especially likely to take up drugs."[46]

Sociologically, studies clearly show a relationship between poverty and drug addiction. Addiction comes in settings where many other social problems also exist. The slum areas in which addiction develops are also characterized by high rates of delinquency, dropping out of school, truancy, unemployment, family disintegration, poverty, and so forth. However, most drug addicts are adults, not adolescents.

Drug addiction "cures."   The great concern with drug addiction as a social and psychological problem has resulted in many attempts to find solutions. At the same time there is often indifference or even hostility to the drug addict. Most Americans probably believe that the drug addict could cure himself if he would only put his mind to it. They believe that for some reason—being lazy, or sinful, or irresponsible—he will not take the responsibility of curing himself. But persons who work with drug addicts know that addiction is very powerful and that severe methods are often needed if the addict is ever to be cured. When a person stops taking drugs his most difficult problem—the problem of staying off drugs—is usually just starting.

Stopping addiction often means major life style changes. So, often in the early phases of an episode of cure the drug abstainer may show considerable ambivalence about where he stands in the addict and nonaddict social situation. The tendency to relapse occurs if he develops an image of himself as socially different from nonaddicts, and actual relapse occurs when he redefines himself as an addict. It is at this point, when the old values and old meanings he experienced as an addict are still immediate and the new ordering of his experience without narcotics not well established, that the ex-addict seems most vulnerable to relapse.

One problem for the ex-addict is the adjustment to his new role of how others view him. The addict has established an image of himself in the eyes of others who knew him as an addict—members of his family, social workers, law enforcement officers, physicians, and so forth. Through their gestures the nonaddicts indicate their doubts about the addicts's right to participate in their worlds. And the former addict is highly sensitive to the nonaddicts's cues. The nonaddicts have their expectations about the abstainers's future conduct. In general they exhibit skepticism concerning their "cure" and future success. Often when abstainers become addicts again, they have redefined themselves as addicts and consequently have taken the actions necessary for relapse.

In recent years there have emerged a variety of programs which attempt to deal with drug addiction. Some are detoxification programs, designed to reduce need gradually and thereby return the addict to a drug-free state. There have also been civil commitment programs which combine drug treatment with incarceration. And there have been two approaches we want to discuss in some detail: the use of therapeutic communities such as Synanon; and the methodone treatment programs, which attempt to keep the addict functioning in the community without having to steal to get his heroin.

Synanon's approach has received a great deal of publicity through the mass media although it has only been tried on a small number of drug addicts. The methods are dramatic and therefore prone to evoke interested response and some sensationalism. Synanon had its origins in Alcoholics Anonymous, in that its founder was a member of AA and was an ex-alcoholic (but not an ex-drug addict). Not long after its start the organization left Alcoholics Anonymous and became fully involved with drug addicts, and Synanon was founded in May 1958. One writer points out that it is ironic that the dominant person in Synanon was never a drug addict, which contradicts the Alcoholics Anonymous type of slogan, "Only an addict can help an addict."[47]

Admission into a Synanon house appears to have two principal functions. First, the newcomer is forced to admit, at least on the verbal level, that he is willing to try to conform to the norms of the group he is entering. He knows that the members will tolerate no liking for drugs or drug addicts. From the moment he enters the house he is tested as to his willingness to conform to all the demands made on him by the members of Synanon. For example, he has to have his hair cut off, give up all of his money, and sever all family ties. Second, the admission process seems to weed out those who simply want to rest for a few days, to get a free place to stay, or to keep out of the hands of the police. So the new person is expected to want to completely stop his drug addiction. "This means that he must say that he wants to quit using drugs once and for all, in order to realize his potentials as an adult; he must not indicate that he merely wants a convenient place in which to go through withdrawal distress so that he can be rid of his habit for a short time because he has lost his connection, or for some other reason."[48]

The most difficult requirement for the addict entering Synanon is that he must withdraw "cold turkey"—simply stop using drugs without any medical help. If he is able to stop he must live in the community for a minimum of two years. The main feature of the actual treatment is the seminars, where the members meet in small groups several times a week and subject each other to extreme criticism, abuse, and ridicule. The members of each seminar are rotated so that all members of the community come under fire from one another. What this means is that Synanon is like "a mental institution, prison, or a 19th century American utopian community in that one's entire life is lived within its walls. Like monks and nuns, the members give themselves over to the place, but the keys to the doors are always in their hands."[49]

What is fairly unique to the Synanon approach is that the addict is treated almost as a nonhuman and is made to feel completely worthless. This technique is the opposite of the therapy approach in which the subject is told that the basis of his problem is his lack of feeling as to his own self-worth. In that kind of approach, the most common one, the subject is made to believe that he is a worthwhile person and that his problem comes primarily from the fact that he has failed to realize that. But at Synanon just the opposite occurs as the addict's self-contempt and self-hate are developed. The lowness of his worth is drummed into him from the very beginning. The newcomer starts by cleaning out toilets and works his way up to doing the dishes. And at every point those above him are constantly demeaning him to insure his continued humility and abasement.

Synanon has a clearly stated program for distributing status symbols to members in return for their conformity to the values of the community. The Synanon experience is organized into a career of roles that represent stages of graded competence. And at the peak are those roles that might later be used in the broader society. Because the member does not have the status of "inmate" or "patient," as in a prison or hospital, he can achieve any position in the status hierarchy. But no member can go up the status ladder unless his "attitude" is correct, no matter what degrees of skill he might have. So any success must be achieved within the context of total conformity to the values of the Synanon program, and individual initiative is of negative value.

The Synanon program usually evokes strong support or severe criticism. It has been argued that Synanon reaches only a small number of addicts and doesn't work for many of those. But the leaders of Synanon do not claim to "cure" drug addicts. The contribution that this program makes is that it helps some to stay away from drugs. The statistics on dropouts suggest that the group relations method does not begin to have effect until newcomers are fully integrated into the antidrug, anticrime value system that is Synanon. This means that great time and expense are needed to help those few who are able to stay on and be aided.

It has also be argued that in reality the members have substituted a dependence on Synanon for their dependence on drugs. Therefore, it has been suggested that Synanon should be seen as a protective community rather than as a truly therapeutic community aimed at the eventual reintegration of the patient with the outside world. A more critical view has been taken by Edward Sagarin. He suggests that because Synanon is so hostile to the outside world the members develop no real will to get out. Therefore, it may be that Synanon has modified the Alcoholics Anonymous type statement "once an addict always an addict" to "once an addict to narcotics, always an addict to Synanon." It is a convenient modification, one similar to AA's statement that "alcoholism cannot be cured," and one which performs the same function; to keep the individuals tied to the organization, thus preserving its present state and insuring its further growth.[50]

This discussion has been to present a radical and highly authoritarian way of dealing with certain types of alcoholics. As suggested, it has had limited application of success because many could not accept the demands of participation. And there has also been recently an expose of Synanon as guilty of severe malpractice procedures which has made the whole approach subject to severe questioning.

Methadone. One attempt at curing drug addiction has been the methadone approach. This approach is based on the fact that one drug can sometimes be substituted for another without producing increased addiction. This approach was used a number of years ago with heroin before it was recognized as a drug of addiction. Heroin was then substituted for morphine. Methadone is a synthetic opiate which is less active than heroin. It is given to the drug user in decreasing doses. Much of the early work with this approach was done in New York City where applicants were voluntarily hospitalized for six weeks after being examined by physicians and psychiatrists. They were given methadone after their discharge and were then usually still dependent on methadone but no longer dependent on heroin.

When methadone was first introduced it was to provide treatment for the metabolic deficiency. The analogy was often made to insulin treatment for diabetics. And like the diabetic the methadone-maintained patients were expected to need treatment for the rest of their life. Methadone was viewed as good for the patient because dirty hypodermic needles and the threat of hepatitis would be eliminated. It was seen as good for society because low cost methadone would obviate the addict's need to steal.[51]

Leo Choplin/Black Star

Treatment in a methadone program

Methadone is as potent a painkiller as morphine and heroin, and its other effects are also similar. For major purposes, all three drugs are interchangeable, and all are highly addictive. Another common characteristic of heroin and methadone is that neither is known to cause organic damage—neither appears to cause cancer, cirrhosis, deformed fetuses, or to destroy brain cells. One important difference between heroin and methadone is the timing of effect. Heroin peaks and fades away rapidly, and after four to six hours the user wants and needs more. Oral methadone peaks more slowly and lasts longer. "As a general proposition, a dose once every 24 hours is sufficient, and methadone variations are under development to make it effective for three days."[52]

Methadone treatment is seen by many as a means of allowing an addict to live a "normal" life. Because it is longer lasting the addict can take his methadone in the morning and work comfortably all day, unlike the heroin addict who may need several fixes in that time. There is also some evidence that methadone programs relieve many family strains and improve family relationships. "As an interim measure, methadone programs offer immediate social rewards for the married addict living with his family. The gain in this respect may offset any failure to accomplish a complete 'cure' of the addiction."[53] Yet, methadone has no attraction for at least half of the addicts on the streets. In fact there is evidence of a good deal of cheating by addicts on methadone programs. One study reported that 50 percent of the methadone users admitted to using some heroin for special crises or special kicks.[54]

A study by Paula Holzman Kleinman found that real changes among those in a methadone program was limited. She discovered that changes were limited to those who were retained in the program for more than three years, and that changes both in heroin use and criminal behavior occurred within the first year after entry for treatment and did not develop further in succeeding years. She found that even in that group changes were minimal. "Fully 25 percent of the patients in this group had worked at no time during their more than three years of treatment and while the level of crime dropped, it did not drop below the rate in the onset-to-entry period."[55]

The methadone approach is still highly controversial and has drawn especially strong opposition from law enforcement groups because in most cases it does not resolve the addiction problem but substitutes a legal drug for an illegal one. This is what bothers many law enforcement agencies—because their vested interest is in drug addicts and not in what makes them addicts. Another point of view is that methadone has helped to alleviate the addiction problem by allowing the addict to function without the results of increased addiction, thereby helping him to become a more productive member of society.

In conclusion, drug use, particularly in the addictive area, can be seen as an institutionalized social problem in the United States today. There is little serious disagreement that drug use is a problem. In addition the means of getting money for drugs is also recognized as a serious problem. There have developed strong laws on drug use and sales, and bureaucracies have been established to apply those laws. As with other social problems there is a constant struggle to provide "solutions" for drug abuse, solutions that at best have done very little to resolve the social problem.

America is a drug-using nation with some drugs being legal and others illegal. A rough distinction can be made between the addictive and nonaddictive drugs. Marijuana, a nonaddictive drug, has undergone a change toward much greater acceptance in the United States in recent years. With addictive drugs such as heroin, a major problem is the illegal cost of getting the drug, which results in other social problems such as crime and violence. The various attempts to "cure" the drug addict have had limited success.

NOTES

1. Marie Nyswanger, "History of a Nightmare," in *The Addict*, by Dan Wakefield (New York: Gold Medal Books, 1963), p. 21.

2. John A. Clausen, "Drug Use," in *Contemporary Social Problems*, 4th ed., by Robert K. Merton and Robert Nisbet (New York: Harcourt Brace Jovanovich, 1976), pp. 144–45.

3. Charles Reasons, "The Politics of Drugs: An Inquiry in the Sociology of Social Problems," *The Sociological Quarterly* (Summer 1974), p. 398.

4. Ibid., p. 399.

5. Nyswanger, "Nightmare," p. 24.

6. Clausen, "Drug Use," pp. 168–69.

7. Ibid., p. 169.

8. Arnold Bernstein and Henry L. Lennard, "The American Way of Drugging," *Society* (May 1973), p. 16.

9. Ibid., p. 14.

10. Ibid., p. 22.

11. Helen H. Nowlis, *Drugs on the College Campus* (New York: Anchor Books, 1969), p. x.

12. Ibid., p. xi.

13. Erich Goode, *Deviant Behavior* (Englewood Cliffs, N.J.: Prentice-Hall, 1978), p. 244.

14. Ibid., p. 246.

15. Ibid., p. 246.

16. Solomon H. Snyder, *Uses of Marijuana* (New York: Oxford University Press, 1971), p. 13.

17. LaMar T. Empey, *American Delinquency* (Homewood, Ill.: Dorsey Press, 1978), pp. 149–50.

18. Clausen, "Drug Use," p. 154.

19. James R. Henley and Larry D. Adams, "Marijuana Use in Post-Collegiate Cohorts: Correlates of Use, Prevalence Patterns, and Factors Associated with Cessation," *Social Problems* (Spring 1973), p. 519.

20. Nowlis, *College Campus*, p. 96.

21. Peter Laurie, *Drugs: Medical, Psychological, and Social Facts* (Baltimore: Penguin Books, 1967), p. 85.

22. Snyder, *Uses of Marijuana*, p. 63.

23. Steven R. Burkett, "School Ties, Peer Influence, and Adolescent Marijuana Use," *Pacific Sociological Association* (April 1977), p. 190.

24. Ibid., p. 194.

25. Clausen, "Drug Use," p. 163.

26. Helen Singer Kaplan, *The New Sex Therapy* (New York: Quadrangle, 1974), p. 94.

27. *Non-Medical Use of Drugs, Interim Report of The Canadian Government's Commission of Inquiry* (Middlesex, England: Penguin Books, 1971), p. 133.

28. Steven R. Burkett and Eric L. Jensen, "Conventional Ties, Peer Influences, and the Fear of Apprehension: A Study of Adolescent Marijuana Use," *The Sociological Quarterly* (Autumn, 1975), p. 532.

29. Burkett, "School Ties," p. 195.

30. Denise Kandel, "Adolescent Marijuana Use: Role of Parents and Peers," *Science* (September 14, 1973), p. 1070.

31. Robert F. Meier and Weldon T. Johnson, "Deterrence as Social Control: The Legal and Extra Legal Production of Conformity," *American Sociological Review* (April 1977), p. 299.

32. Don H. Zimmerman and D. Lawrence Wieder, "You Can't Help But Get

Stoned: Notes on the Social Organization of Marijuana Smoking," *Social Problems* (December 1977), p. 203.

33. *Marijuana: A Signal of Misunderstanding. The Official Report of the National Commission on Marijuana and Drug Use* (New York: New American Library, 1972), p. 133.

34. Goode, *Deviant Behavior*, p. 213.

35. Weldon T. Johnson, Robert E. Petersen, and L. Edwards Wells, "Arrest Probabilities for Marijuana Users as Indicators of Selective Law Enforcement," *American Journal of Sociology* 83 (1977), p. 693.

36. Meier and Johnson, "Deterrence," p. 302.

37. Alastair MacIntyre, "The Cannabis Taboo," *New Society* (December 1968), p. 848.

38. *Marijuana: A Signal of Misunderstanding. The Official Report of the National Commission on Marijuana and Drug Use,* pp. 116–17.

39. Ibid., p. 147.

40. Goode, *Deviant Behavior*, p. 215.

41. James V. Delong, "The Methadone Habit," *New York Times Magazine* (March 16, 1975), p. 92.

42. Joan C. Martin, "Drugs of Abuse During Pregnancy: Effects Upon Offspring Structure and Function," *Signs* (Winter 1976), p. 364.

43. Daniel Glaser, Bernard Lander, and William Abbott, "Opiate Addicted and Non-Addicted Siblings in a Slum Area," *Social Problems* (Spring 1971), pp. 511–12.

44. Edwin M. Schur, *Crimes Without Victims* (Englewood Cliffs, N.J.: Prentice-Hall, 1965), pp. 128–29.

45. Nowlis, *College Campus*, p. 24.

46. Schur, *Crimes,* pp. 128–29.

47. Edward Sagarin, *Odd Man In: Societies of Deviants in America* (Chicago: Quadrangle, 1969), p. 143.

48. Rita Volkman and Donald R. Cressey, "Differential Association and the Rehabilitation of Drug Addicts," in *Deviance,* by Earl Rubington and Martin S. Weinberg (New York: Macmillan, 1968), p. 411.

49. Sagarin, *Odd Man In,* pp. 143–44.

50. Ibid., p. 158.

51. Paula Holzman Kleinman, Irving F. Lukoff, and Barbara Lynn Kail, "The Magic Fix: A Critical Analysis of Methadone Maintenance Treatment," *Social Problems* (December 1977), p. 208.

52. Delong, "Methadone," p. 16.

53. June S. Clark et al., "Marriage and Methadone: Spouse Behavior Patterns in Heroin Addicts Maintained on Methadone," *Journal of Marriage and the Family* (August 1972), p. 501.

54. Walter R. Cuskey and William Krasner, "American Way of Drugging," *Society* (May 1973), p. 48.

55. Kleinman et al., "Magic Fix," p. 212.

SELECTED BIBLIOGRAPHY

Bernstein, Arnold, and Lennard, Henry L.   "The American Way of Drugging." *Society* (May 1973), pp. 14–25.

Burkett, Steven R.   "School Ties, Peer Influence, and Adolescent Marijuana Use." *Pacific Sociological Review* (April 1977), pp. 181–201.

Clark, June S., et al.   "Marriage and Methadone: Spouse Behavior Patterns of Addicts Maintained on Methadone." *Journal of Marriage and the Family* (August 1972), pp. 496–502.

DeLong, James. "The Methadone Habit." *New York Times Magazine* (March 16, 1975), pp. 16, 78, 80, 86, 90, 92–93.

Glaser, Daniel; Lander, Bernard; and Abbott, William. "Opiate Addicted and Non-Addicted Siblings in a Slum Area." *Social Problems* (Spring 1971), pp. 510–21.

Johnson, Weldon T.; Peterson, Robert E.; and Wells, L. Edwards. "Arrest Probabilities for Marijuana Users as Indicators of Selective Law Enforcement." *American Journal of Sociology* 83 (1977), pp. 681–99.

Kleinman, Paula Holzman; Lukoff, Irving F.; and Kail, Barbara Lynn. "The Magic Fix: A Critical Analysis of Methadone Maintenance Treatment." *Social Problems* (December 1977), pp. 208–14.

Martin, Joan C. "Drugs of Abuse During Pregnancy: Effects Upon Offspring Structure and Function." *Signs* (Winter 1976), pp. 357–68.

Meier, Robert F., and Johnson, Weldon T. "Deterrence as Social Control: The Legal and Extra Legal Production of Conformity." *American Sociological Review* (April 1977), pp. 292–304.

Reasons, Charles. "The Politics of Drugs: An Inquiry in the Sociology of Social Problems." *The Sociological Quarterly* (Summer 1974), pp. 381–401.

Snyder, Solomon H. *Uses of Marijuana.* New York: Oxford University Press, 1971.

Zimmerman, Don H. and Wieder, D. Lawrence. "You Can't Help But Get Stoned: Notes on the Social Organization of Marijuana Smoking." *Social Problems* (December 1977), pp. 199–207.

Chapter 14

Physical Health

Usually when we think of physical health problems, we think of injuries or diseases of the body that are treated in various medical facilities. Normally medical importance is placed on physical symptoms and their treatment. However, many physical health problems are also a part of a social setting. Within that setting they are defined. The meaning of health problems derives from the way people react to them and how they treat each problem. Physical health, then, is a social problem not only because of its cost and demands on society in general but also because of social implications for the individual patient and those who deal with him. Our main interest in this chapter is to look at how health problems are defined and treated within American society. We will first look at the patient, and then at the physician and the hospital.

SOCIAL DEFINITIONS OF ILLNESS

The social definitions of health and diseases are often shaped by the social context in which they occur. Some kinds of physical conditions may be defined as a social problem in one society but not in another.

David Mechanic points out that in some societies the obese woman is an object of envy and desire while in other societies obesity is defined as a physical and emotional disease. In some societies supernatural powers are attributed to the epileptic, "while in others the epileptics are regarded as not only ill but also as objects of scorn and social prejudice."[1]

The social definition of the health problem and what should be done about it has undergone significant change over time. What has happened in recent times has been the ascription of natural disease to many areas of human behavior not previously defined in that way. The new definitions often designate as pathological and responsive to scientific treatment what used to be seen as a consequence of personal choice or of an irrevocable state of sin and genetic inferiority.[2] In the past, medicine labeled people in two ways. There were those for whom cures could be attempted and those who were beyond any help. In either case diagnosis could lead to stigma. There may also be for the physician a third way of diagnosis and that is often the making of value judgements of a social nature rather than simply a medical one. "Diagnosis may exclude a human being with bad genes from being born, another from promotion, and a third from political life."[3]

What is most striking is that over the years the scope of defining all sorts of social conditions under the jurisdiction of the medical establishment has come about practically without question. One major consequence of this has been to draw more and more types of social deviance under the classification of "illness." As Eliot Friedson points out, this has been quite independent of demonstrated and accurate conceptions of etiology or of efficient and reliable methods of treatment. Increasingly, whatever else it may be, illness has come to be a type of deviance. Deviance from a set of norms representing health or normality. "In human society, naming something an illness has consequences *independent* of the biological state of the organism."[4] For example, persons diagnosed as having cancer define themselves and are defined by others within a social and personal context triggered by the diagnosis. The definition of cancer leads to a wide variety of social reactions that can go far beyond the physical nature and consequences of the physical health problem.

It has been common in sociological literature on deviance and of social problems not to deal with physical health as a problem. Friedson argues that the exclusion of medicine and illness from these sociological considerations stems in part from the belief that the illness approach of medicine is so authoritative that one has no choice but to adopt it. This implies that there is some special sanctity to biological conceptions of illness that rule them out of sociology's purview.[5] But this is simply one social construction of reality. On another level, there are important and significant questions for sociologists regarding physical health.

One major problem for the sociologist in examining illness as social deviance or as a social problem centers around the changing definitions of health labels. There is generally much greater social acceptance of problems defined as ill-health than to other forms of negative labels and possibly even to having no label at all. And the conditions are more acceptable when defined as involuntary rather than voluntary. Being defined as having a health problem is often "better" than being defined as a criminal or political deviant. It is even better than being called lazy. For example, in the world of work where many people may be bored, they often want to hear "that physical illness relieves them of social and political responsibilities."[6]

The current concern with health problems in present American society is closely linked to the tremendous cost of health care. People are constantly being made aware of these costs because of the inadequacy of society to deal with them. There is also a strong concern with health care because people have unrealistically high expectations of what medicine can achieve. New "medical breakthroughs" are constantly being publicized, but in the long run they have very little impact in reducing health problems.

The concerns about health in American society are also influenced by the heavy stress on health problems. Very little is said about the generally good health of individuals and there are no agencies to publicize the fact that most people are quite healthy. "No one takes public notice of the truth of the matter, which is that most people in this country have a clear, unimpeded run at a longer lifetime than could have been foreseen by an earlier generation."[7] For the medical establishment to constantly stress the threat of illness over good health is like the military establishment constantly stressing war over peace—it leads to larger and larger expenditures.

It is commonly assumed that most health problems originate from within the person making him responsible for his own bad health. Over 99 percent of the population is born healthy; they are made sick either as a result of personal misbehavior or environmental conditions or both. Many illnesses arise from the kind of society we have chosen to live in. For example, various dangers from work situations, environmental influences, and dangers from technological creations are sources of major health problems.

It should also be noted that most physical health problems in society are not serious ones. Much of the total illness in the population consists of self-limited conditions that have very little affect on longevity and mortality. "Mild upper-respiratory conditions are the most frequent type of illness and contribute significantly to work and school absenteeism, although for the most part they are not disabling."[8] Whatever the severity of illness, Americans very often define themselves as "not feeling well." One study found that 95 percent of those surveyed considered themselves to have been unwell during the two weeks prior to the interview. Another study found only 5 percent of the respondents considered themselves free of symptoms while 9 percent claimed to have suffered from more than six different symptoms in the two weeks prior to the interview.[9]

The state of medical knowledge at the present time in the United States is such that there are virtually no diseases for which medicine cannot provide some treatment. But this often means caring for the symptoms rather than curing or preventing the illness. It has come to be a basic obligation of medicine to provide increased comfort, to relieve pain, and to alleviate anxiety. Of course, these efforts are almost always time-consuming and expensive. But these procedures constitute the vast bulk of medical practice as it is currently carried out in the United States.

The Patient

The person comes to be defined as a patient when he defines himself as having some kind of medical problem and he seeks out help. Ultimately his definition as a patient comes from the medical establishment. Medicine has the authority to label one person's complaint as an illness while denying that claim to another. As a result "medicine may be said to be engaged in the creation of illness as a social state which a human being may assume."[10] When the person becomes a patient he is often reduced to an object. It is his body that is being repaired and he is often no longer considered a person to be healed. Ivan Illich writes that even if he is allowed to participate in the repair process, he acts as the lowest apprentice in a hierarchy of repairmen. "Often he is not even trusted to take a pill without the supervision of the nurse."[11]

There have been some changes in the role of the patient. In recent years, in some states, the "rights" of patients have been drafted into law. Greater emphasis has been placed on the patient's "right to treatment," "right to information," "right to privacy and confidentiality," and "right to be allowed to die" rather than be kept alive by artificial means. However, in most instances the great mystique of medicine makes the patient's position very weak. This is because he is outside the privileged body of information, diagnosis, and treatment that makes up the medical mystique. Medical knowledge is assumed to be beyond the comprehension of the patient.

There is sometimes conflict between the patient and the physician or hospital as to what the appropriate patient role should be. Very often the patient wants time, sympathetic attention, and concern for himself as a person. "The physician on the other hand views time as a precious commodity, given the number of patients he has to see and his interest in making what he thinks is a suitable income."[12] When this happens, it is rare that the patient's wants are met because the doctor holds the power.

We want to examine some of the variables that are related to the patient role. Age is related to whether or not a person is likely to be a patient. In part this occurs because the severity of medical problems varies by age as do the patient seeing the physician. For example, children and adolescents are more apt to see a physician than the severity of their symptoms would require. By contrast, older adults, between the ages of 35 and 64 visit a doctor less often than recommended.[13] It also seems that men are less apt to see a doctor when they experience symptoms of illness than are women. If the extent of knowledge about symptoms of an illness is considered, it appears that women generally know more about health matters than do men and are therefore more apt to seek help. For many men there is a "macho" quality that sometimes suggests they shouldn't seek medical help because it isn't the manly thing to do.

Social class.   Social class, as usually defined by educational and occupational levels, is related to health knowledge and medical treatment. In general, people in the lower social classes have higher frequencies of feeling sick and are disabled more and for longer periods of time. In part this difference exists because lower-class people are comparatively ignorant of the nature, extent, and character of bodily functions. They are also more prone to think and describe their experiences with illness in folk notions that are still exploited by patent medicine advertisements with such expressions as "qualities of blood" and the necessity to "purge the system." They are more prone to use, if not folk remedies, then at least traditional patent remedies for many of their ailments."[14]

The life style and knowledge of medical care also contributes to the problems of the lower class. Very often their occupations are physically dangerous to them. Their eating habits often center around "junk foods" which are usually fattening and low in nutritional value. They very often do not get appropriate exercise. Housing conditions can lead to problems because of lack of protection from the physical environment. Often they lack access to medical help even when they need it.

William C. Cockerham points out that many persons in the lower social classes tend to deny the sick role. They may do this only because they do not have the chance to enjoy the secondary gains common to the middle class, but also because the functional incapacity of the poor may make them less likely to be able to earn a living or to survive under conditions of poverty. "Therefore, persons living in a poverty environment might work, regardless of how sick they might be, so long as they feel able to perform some of their work activities."[15]

The kinds of medical care that the lower class gets is different from the middle class. Most often the medical help they receive is at the charity clinic or out-patient clinic at a hospital. In such clinics a number of medical practitioners are concentrated in one place, and often their facilities are inadequate and unattractive. Courtesy is sometimes seen as impractical because of the pressure of time and

Luis Medina

A public health clinic

often because the patients are seen as having much lower status than the medical personnel caring for them. The poor, as welfare cases, are often not treated as fully adult and as self-responsible persons.[16]

Freidson writes that the traditional clinic is generally staffed by practitioners who devote such a small proportion of their professional practice to the task that the patient's chance of seeing the same person on successive visits is very unlikely.[17] The quality of the physician in public clinics is low because they are often young doctors, or foreign ones who are as yet unable to get into lucrative practices. One study in New York city pointed out the lack of adequate outpatient care facilities that led to a chronic health care crisis. The reasons for the poor health care facilities were: (1) the low status of such facilities, which led to low levels of medical skills and therefore did not attract ambitious and higher qualified doctors; and (2) the fact that those facilities largely served the poor who used emergency rooms and outpatient clinics as substitutes for the family doctor.[18]

Another problem more common to the lower than middle class derives from a particular view of health and medical care. A common middle-class value supports the practice of preventive medicine where the person seeks medical means of stopping something from happening. But among the lower class this is much less common and medical care is something to be sought out when one is sick and not before. Cockerham writes that preventive medicine is largely a middle-class concept which provides a "patient with an elaborate structure of routine prenatal and postnatal care, pediatric services, dental care, immunization, and screening for the presence of disease."[19]

Cancer. We want to say something specifically about cancer as a medical problem. It is special in the tremendous impact it has on society. The word cancer has come to be one of the most frightening

If you believe everything you hear, you probably
think everything can give you cancer. And that no
matter what you do, cancer's going to get you.
You're wrong.
Let the American Cancer Society help you get
the facts. Call or write your local unit for their free
pamphlet, "You Can Control the Risk of Cancer."
And stop running scared.

Call **800-572-1080**
American Cancer Society

The great American fear—cancer!

words in the American language. The word usually brings forth such responses as "hopelessness," "death," "pain," and "terrible fear." To a great extent the fear about cancer has been a product of the mass media. In part this has resulted from efforts to raise funds for cancer research. The fear is built around the belief that cancer is usually a debilitating and killing disease.

As discussed with reference to other social problems, the American belief is that we can come up with solutions to anything if we really try. The great frustrations and confusion result when large scale efforts are made and no real solutions come about. In recent years billions of dollars have been put into cancer research and no significant breakthroughs toward cancer control have been made. Furthermore, all the evidence suggests there are no major breakthroughs likely in the foreseeable future. Therefore, fear of cancer is compounded—not only are we afraid of the disease itself, but we also fear our inability to do anything about it. "Survival rates for the most common types of cancer—those which make up 90 percent of the cases—have remained virtually unchanged over the last 25 years."[20]

A striking fact about cancer is that while it is the most feared disease in the United States, people will still do many things that increase the probability of their getting cancer. For example, alcohol is a strong "risk factor" in cancer of the mouth, pharynx, larynx, and esophagus. But an even more powerful risk factor is smoking. John H. Knowles estimates that "if cigarette smoking was to be eliminated completely, a 20 percent reduction in death due to cancer would result."[21] There are many reasons why people continue to smoke even though they increase their chances of cancer. One reason is that many refuse to link cancer risk factors to themselves. So long as they see that some people smoke all their lives and never get cancer, they will often put themselves into that group. They won't recognize the fact that there isn't room for everyone there. When smoking begins among the young, there is much less tendency to link it to future death which is perceived as far off in the future.

But society, and various values, are also responsible for the continuation of smoking and resultant cancer for tens of thousands. Primarily the values are economic ones. In some states, such as Virginia and North Carolina, tobacco sales are a major source of state income. When the decision comes to income versus health, income wins. In effect the tobacco industry takes the position that cancer is acceptable for society because it provides jobs and income. It is seen as more important to keep tobacco workers employed (to say nothing of preserving the millions of dollars of corporate profits) than to possibly reduce the incidence of cancer.

THE MEDICAL SYSTEM

We have to ask how much impact the medical system has on people's health. The best estimates suggest that the medical system—which includes doctors, drugs, and hospitals—accounts for about 10 percent of the usual indices for measuring health. These indices are: whether you live at all (infant mortality), how well you live (days lost due to illness), and how long you live (adult mortality). The other 90 percent of health indices are determined by factors over which the medical system has little or no control. These influences come from individual life style (smoking, exercise, worry), social conditions (income, eating, physiological inheritance), and the physical environment (air and water quality). "Most of the bad things that happen to people are at present beyond the reach of medicine."[22]

A large percentage of deaths that are due to cardiovascular disease and cancer are "premature" in that they occur in relatively young individuals and are related to the individual's bad habits. Heart disease and strokes are related to dietary factors, cigarette smoking, potentially treatable but undetected hypertension, and lack of exercise. Cancer is related not only to smoking but also probably to diets rich in fat and refined food stuffs, certain drugs or the inhalation of a wide variety of noxious agents.[23] There is also some evidence that cancer may be related to stress.

The health problems of the individual consist mainly of illnesses that are acute and benign. They are either self-limiting or subject to control through a few dozen routine interventions. As Illich points out, "for a wide range of conditions, those who are treated least probably make the best progress."[24] Today there is a much more acute awareness of the risk of disease and this is associated with the apprehension that a minor illness may turn suddenly into a killing disease. There is a higher expectation that all kinds of disease can be treated effectively. However, for many diseases and illnesses only the symptoms can be treated. The person may be allowed to live more comfortably and with less pain, but the causes remained untouched.

In general the extent of medical knowledge has made no great jumps in developing the technology of infectious disease since 1950. Most successful new interventions have been for relatively uncommon illnesses. As a result "we are left with approximately the same roster of common major diseases which confronted the country in 1950."[25]

In industrial societies the leading causes of death, as well as the main health hazards, are the degenerative diseases that are associated with aging. There are many chronic infections that go up sharply with middle age. There are also the new classes of medical problems, alcoholism, and obesity. The conditions of modern life are related to diseases such as lung cancer, coronary heart disease, and peptic ul-

TABLE 14–1

The Ten Major Causes of Mortality, United States, 1900 and 1976

	1900		1976	
Rank	Rate (per 100,000 population)	Disease	Rate (per 100,000 population)	Rank
	1,719.1	All causes	917.8	
1	202.2	Influenza and pneumonia	34.3	5
2	194.4	Tuberculosis	1.7	19
3	142.7	Gastroenteritis	0.9	21
4	137.4	Diseases of the heart	472.1	1
5	106.9	Cerebrovascular diseases	91.0	3
6	81.0	Chronic nephritis	*	
7	72.3	All accidents	45.2	4
8	64.0	Cancer and other malignant neoplasm	174.7	2
9	62.6	Certain diseases of early infancy	11.1	10
10	40.3	Diphtheria	0.0	—
25	11.0	Diabetes mellitus	17.1	6
19	12.5	Cirrhosis of the liver	14.4	7
15	22.9	Bronchitis, emphysema, and asthma	12.3	8
26	10.2	Suicide	12.1	9

*No comparable classification.

Source: *Environment* (March 1980), p. 14.

cers. Among the young the leading cause of deaths are accidents, heart disease, cancer, homicide, and suicide. For those under 25 years, "accidents are by far the most common cause of death, with homicide and suicide the next leading causes."[26]

What are the leading causes of death and what can be said about decreasing them in the future? In 1974 cardiovascular disease was the cause of 39 percent of all deaths. In general, there is no decisive, conclusive technology with the power to end, reverse, or stop this disease. The actual pathogenic conditions which cause the disease are not known. Cancer accounted for 19 percent of all deaths in 1974. Available medical technologies deal with its treatment through surgery, radiation, or chemotherapy. Some cancers can be cured, others controlled. As yet, we cannot prevent the disease. Cerebrovascular disease accounts for 11 percent of all deaths. There is no therapy for preventing or reversing arteriosclerosis or the class of strokes which result from this condition. Kidney disease accounted for 10.4 percent of all deaths in 1974. For the major types there is no effective treatment. While there may be some help through early treatment, in most cases kidney lesions develop gradually and unobtrusively and once established are not reversible.[27]

The Physician

We want to look at the unique professional position physicians have in the American occupational system. Before looking specifically at the profession we may look at the number and distribution of doctors in the United States. The number of physicians has a great deal to do with how the profession is viewed. In the mid-1970s there were over 350,000 doctors actively practicing medicine in the United States. They made up less than 10 percent of the total health manpower. However, physicians have the power to control both the conditions of their own work and the conditions of most of the other members of the health profession as well.[28]

In 1960 there were 1.5 doctors per 1,000 population and by 1979 this had increased to about 2.0 per 1,000. This has had no effect in decreasing the cost of the physician for the patient. In fact, one estimate suggests that every time a new doctor begins practice the nation's medical bills go up another $250,000 a year. The reason is that the typical physician generates that much additional business in lab tests and hospital admissions. Medicine is a sellers' market because the customer has no bargaining power. He initiates only one decision—to see the doctor. The sellers (doctors and hospitals) then take over and decide what services the patient needs. They do not ask him what he wants, but rather order him to buy the services. Being unable to diagnose his own illness, the patient has little choice but to obey the doctor.

It is the strong control over his own profession that contributes greatly to the very high status of the physician. For many years in the United States the physician has ranked, without competition, at the top of the professions. The preeminence of the medical profession is evidenced not only in high prestige but also its recognized authority. The physician's knowledge about illness and its treatment is considered to be both authoritarian and definitive. "Medicine's position today is akin to that of state religions of yesterday—it has an officially approved monopoly of the right to define health and illness and to treat illness."[29]

The physician is therefore the ultimate expert on what is health and what is illness. He is the expert on how to attain the former and cure the latter. The medical perspective leads him to see the world in terms of health and illness, and the public is also inclined to turn to him for advice on all matters related to health and illness regardless of any real competence.[30] The practice of medicine is also frequently a moral enterprise and often leads to values of good and evil. For example, medicine has the authority to label one person's complaint a legitimate illness, to declare another sick although he may not complain, and to refuse another the social recognition of pain, disability, and even death. "It is medicine which stamps some pain as 'merely subjective,' some impairments as malingering, and some deaths—though not others—as suicides."[31]

Freidson argues that while the person is treated with sympathy rather than punishment for being ill, he is expected to get rid of what has been defined as bad. While ideally the person may not be judged, his disease is judged and his "disease" is a part of him. True moral neutrality exists only when a person is allowed to be or do what he wants without question from others. "Clearly, the physician neither approves of disease nor is neutral to it. When he claims alcoholism is a disease, he is as much a moral entrepreneur as a fundamentalist who claims it is a sin."[32]

The patient is usually put in the position of not being able to understand the expert. The rationale for this situation is that the patient lacks professional training and is therefore too ignorant to understand the information he might receive. Often he is defined as being too upset by his illness to be able to use medical information in a manner that would be rational and responsible. This perspective suggests that giving information to the patient does not help him. "Thus, the patient should not be treated like an adult, but rather like a child, given reassurance but not information."[33]

Another relatively unique characteristic of medicine as a profession is that its everyday practice is carried out in privacy. In the other high status professions work goes on in the publicity of the court, the church, the lecture hall, and often in the office. By contrast, the work of the doctor is typically conducted in the closed consulting room or bedroom. "Furthermore, the physician usually renders personal services to individuals rather than to congregations or classes."[34]

The practice of medicine then is one of extreme private control. This implies that it excludes others or determines the extent to which other occupations are to be a part of the medical system. For example, the individual practitioner can and does refuse to enter into referral or corroborative relationships with those of whom he does not approve. The result of this professional monopoly by physicians has been to define most health problems as "illness" that require specific and immediate diagnosis and treatment. Health care is activated by the demands of persons defining themselves as "sick" and asking for medical verification. Doctors have an "incentive to do something because they are paid to do so and because patients accept the definition of the situation as one of sickness requiring medical activism, prescriptions, operations, and so forth."[35]

We usually think of medical treatment as constituting the bulk of medical practice. The profession does treat the illnesses that people take to it, but it is also motivated to discover illnesses of which the layman may not be aware. "One of the greatest ambitions of the physician is to discover and describe a 'new' disease or syndrome and to be immortalized by having his name used to identify the disease."[36]

The medical practice. Most physicians operate as individual entrepreneurs and sell their services on a fee-for-service basis. There has been, in recent years, some trend toward group practices, especially among more recent medical school graduates. At present about 60 percent of all American physicians are in office-based practices. Another 25 percent are in primarily hospital-based practices, mostly as residents and interns.[37]

A practice is usually built up by pleasing one patient who tells his friends who pass it on to their friends. The positive side of this method is that it is built on the sense of security and good feeling the patient has for the doctor. On the negative side, patients are often unable to judge the technical quality of medical care. Frequently patients are pleased because they get what they want rather than what might be medically best for them. Freidson suggests that "much of the excessive prescribing of antibiotics, barbiturates, tranquilizers, and other drugs must be ascribed to pleasing the patient or to giving in to him out of sheer weariness."[38]

One of the most striking changes in the medical profession in recent years has been the increased percentage of doctors in specialized practices. By the mid-1970s about 85 percent of all doctors were in specialties and about 30 percent of all doctors were in the surgical specialties. It is ironic that even the general practice of medicine has become a specialty calling for several years of specialization so that one can enter into something called "family medicine" of "community medical care."

Robert R. Alford suggests that optimal medical services could be rendered if one fifth of all physicians were in the consulting specialties instead of four fifths, which is the current proportion. The overelaboration of specialists has led to a fragmented pattern of care and one not always particularly responsive to human problems motivating much medical concern. Alford goes on to say that the medical profession faces the dilemma of maintaining a united front vis-a-vis outside threats and at the same time finding some viable method of dividing up the body and the spoils among themselves. "The more they squabble, for example, over whether orthopedic or general surgeons have jurisdiction over the fractures, the more they expose to the general public the mundane origins of the allegedly scientific basis for specialties."[39]

Probably of all the medical specialties, the one most exaggerated is that of surgery. Americans have the highest rate of elective or optional surgery in the world. There are over 14 million such operations each year and this number is double the rate per capita for England and Wales. There is no surgery that does not have some risk. More than 90

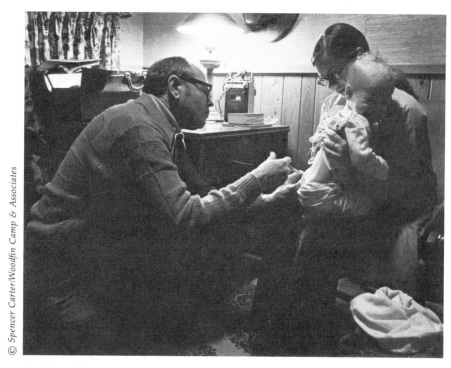

A thing of the past—a physician making a home visit

percent of all tonsillectomies performed in the United States are technically unnecessary and even this operation has some risk. One patient in a thousand dies directly as a consequence of the operation and sixteen in a thousand suffer from serious complications. Furthermore, all lose valuable immunity mechanisms becase of tonsillectomies.[40]

Given the high professional standing of the physician, how does the public view the doctor? The doctor has long been viewed by Americans as the repository of vast knowledge and the most respected of all professionals. In recent years the doctor increasingly has come to be seen by many as motivated by economic greed. So the view of the physician has undergone some general social change. One study says that a generation ago children in kindergarten had painted the doctor as a white coated father figure. "Today, they are just as apt to paint him as a man from Mars or a Frankenstein." Illich writes that this new mood of suspicion toward the medical profession has caused medical and pharmaceutical companies to triple their expenses for public relations.[41]

Aaron Wildavsky found that three quarters to four fifths of the population, depending on the survey, were satisfied with their doctors and the care they were getting. However, one third to two thirds think the system that produces those results is in bad shape. "The rich don't like waiting, the poor don't like high prices, and those in the middle don't like both."[42]

In recent years there has been increased publicity given to medical problems and inequalities. A few years ago one rarely heard critical comments about the physician or hospital care. But today, there is frequent exposure to the public of medical inadequacies. It is not only the dangers related to such unnecessary surgery as tonsillectomies and hysterectomies but also with such things as bad drug prescriptions. There are about 30,000 deaths every year caused by bad reactions to antibiotics and other drugs prescribed by physicians. A major reason for this is the incompetency of some doctors. Once they receive their license they can practice for the rest of their lives without ever being further examined as to competency. The most conservative estimates would suggest that at least 5 percent of all doctors are incompetent to practice medicine.

The increased critical feelings toward physicians is also reflected in the increased number of malpractice suits. There is an estimated 20,000 or more malpractice suits brought against doctors every year and the number has been steadily rising. "In New York, for example, the number of suits filed against physicians rose from 564 in 1970 to 1,200 in 1974; in the past decade, the average award for a malpractice suit grew from $6,000 to $23,000, with far more very large awards being made than in the past."[43] But many suits are delayed or remain unsettled for long periods of time and usually the real financial gain is not to the victim but to others. "Between 16 and 20 percent of every dollar paid in malpractice insurance went to compensate the victim, the rest was paid to lawyers and medical experts."[44]

Ivan Bennett argues that the fear of litigation has created an unhealthy adversary situation between the physician and the patient. What this often means is that the doctor practices defensive medicine. He orders more technology, such as extra tests and x-rays, to protect himself or the hospital against future law suits. He may also stay away from complex and difficult procedures that could benefit the patient but that also involve risk.[45]

Illich argues that with the transformation of the doctor from an artisan exercising a skill on patients he knew personally to a technician applying scientific rules to classes of patients, malpractice acquired an anonymous, almost respectable status. Often this has come to mean that what could before have been considered an abuse of confidence and a moral fault can now be rationalized into the occasional breakdown of equipment and operators. "In a complex technological hospital, negligence becomes 'random human error' or 'system breakdown'—callousness becomes 'scientific detachment'—and incompetence 'lack of specialized equipment.' "[46]

Medical training. The most difficult stage of becoming a doctor is getting into medical school. In the United States medicine is a laissez-faire enterprise. In 1975, there were 114 medical schools with 10 more in the process of development. The total entering freshman medical class in 1975–1976 was 15,295, 24 percent of whom were women. To get into medical school has become increasing competitive in recent years and there are about ten generally qualified applicants for every available position.[47]

The academic medical centers are usually free to pursue their own objectives. There are no national plans or objectives that give direction to the training and distribution of medical generalists and the various specialists. This means that the specialists that get turned out have no logical relationship to what is needed by society for better medical practice. This is illustrated by the high excess of surgical specialists and the lack of general or family practitioners.

In recent years the medical establishment has been strongly influenced by the influx of foreign medical school graduates. They now represent each year almost 50 percent of the new American medical manpower pool. These doctors very often come into the lower status medical centers for their residency training. They usually go into hospitals not affiliated with academic centers and fill posts that American medical school graduates find undesirable. Yet, foreign medical graduates have generally chosen specialty careers in a way undistinguishable from that of their American counterparts. Many of the foreign doctors who come for their advanced training want to stay when they finish because of the great amounts of money they can earn in the United States. This contributes to the "brain drain" of the countries they come from. Many of those countries start out with a very low physician to population ratio and this is further exacerbated by their loss of doctors to the United States.

American Medical Association (AMA). There is no trade union or guild organization in the United States any more powerful than the AMA. By the end of the 19th century the AMA had gotten state legislature to set strong controls over who could practice medicine by setting up licensing requirements. The tests were prepared, administered, and judged by the medical profession. This resulted in a sharp decrease in the number of doctors and a number of medical schools were closed. The result of this was to give the medical profession virtual monopoly over all levels of health care.

The AMA became a classic prototype of economic monopoly, and for many years the ratio of physicians to the population declined. By the 1950s it stabilized at the present low level. The AMA continued to make the same argument against any increase in the output of doctors by insisting that training more doctors would reduce the quality of doctors. By the 1960s there was some shift in this position and some admission that there was a doctor shortage.

Jeffrey Lionel Berlant argues that the AMA is perhaps the strongest trade union in America. Like any trade union, it derives its power from its ability to restrict the number of those who engage in it as an occupation. It restricts admission by controlling admission to medical school and by restricting the legal rights to practice by licensing requirements. The members of the medical licensing commissions are virtually always physicians."[48] It is also the case that a major source of the power of the AMA over individual physicians lies in the fact that no other professional association of any significance in the United States provides the doctor with an alternative to membership in his local medical society and this kind of membership is critical to his career.[49]

The AMA has consistently opposed any governmental participation in the organization and control of medical practice. In 1920, it officially opposed any subsidies for health centers, group medicine, and diagnostic clinics by states or national government. "After World War I, it opposed compulsory insurance plans financed by the government, continued its opposition through the Truman administration, and was unsuccessful only in 1965 against Medicare and Medicaid."[50]

In recent years there have been changes in the views of the American public toward the medical profession. The AMA has never been as successful as it might wish in garnering favorable public opinion for the medical profession.[51] Thomas suggests that nothing has changed so much in the health-care system over the past 25 years as the public perception of its own growth. In part, this is due to an increasing concern with health problems. "To some extent, the propaganda which feeds the obsession is a result of the well intentioned efforts by particular disease agencies to obtain public money for support of research and care in their special fields.[52]

In recent years the AMA has been losing membership and is constantly being subjected to criticism for its conservation political stance. But this does not mean that physicians are losing power. Physicians in private practices and the voluntary hospitals still constitute the core of the health system. All the federal, state, and local programs which occupy the time and energy of reformers are still on the periphery of the health system. "Almost none of the reports from numerous commissions ever mention invading the territory of the private physician and the voluntary hospitals."[53]

While the power of the AMA has decreased somewhat, it is still a highly formidable organization. With its organization, influence and financial strength, it will likely remain a very important influence in future legislative battles in the health sector. It will also continue to be very instrumental in the shaping of the overall direction of the medical profession. Friedson argues that American society can no longer depend on the medical profession and its system of self-regulation to provide a responsible system of health care. He believes that some kind of legal system is needed to provide a set of requirements that will stimulate the medical profession to provide a set of responsible care. The balance of power must shift so that the patient is in a position of sufficient independence to be able to exercise choice and have a voice in the organization, presentation, and substance of the care he gets."[54]

Hospitals

The functions of the hospital have changed over a period of time. The identification of hospitals with pestholes appeared under early Christian influences because they were dormitories for travelers, vagrants, and derelicts. "Until the late 18th century the trip to the hospital was taken, typically, with no hope of return. Nobody went to the hospital to restore his health. The sick, the mad, the crippled, epileptics, incurables, foundlings, and recent amputees of all ages and sexes were jumbled together."[55] As late as the 19th century, medicine was a relatively unimportant institution and it was humble before the majesty of religion and law.[56]

Since the end of the 19th century, three big changes have occurred in hospitals. First, medicine became a science in terms of applying the scientific method to seek out medical knowledge and to develop successful techniques for treatment. Second was the development of med-

TABLE 14–2

Inmates of Long-Term Care Institutions, by Type of Institution and Age: 1976

Type of facility	Total*	65 years old and over		
		Total	65 to 79 years	80 years and over
Number:				
Total	1,550,100	1,027,850	390,720	637,130
Nursing homes	1,182,670	989,340	368,370	620,970
Physically handicapped	37,780	2,280	1,360	920
Psychiatric	65,400	4,540	3,890	650
Mentally handicapped	189,210	5,690	4,370	1,320
All other	75,060	26,010	12,740	13,270
Percent:				
Total	100.0	100.0	100.0	100.0
Nursing homes	76.3	96.3	94.3	97.5
Physically handicapped	2.4	0.2	0.3	0.1
Psychiatric	4.2	0.4	1.0	0.1
Mentally handicapped	12.2	0.6	1.1	0.2
All other	4.8	2.5	3.3	2.1

*Total includes persons who did not report on age.

Source: U.S. Department of Commerce, Bureau of the Census, *Current Population Reports*. Series p–23, no. 69. (Washington, D.C.: U.S. Government Printing Office, 1977), p. 10.

ical technology and the discovery and use of antiseptic measures in the hospital to help curtail infections. Third was a significant improvement in the quality of hospital personnel.[57] After World War II, the base of knowledge and technological development made great strides. The hospital, with its expensive and complex equipment, along with technicians and consultants became the center of the medical system.

Today, in the United States, medical care centers around the short-term general hospital. The voluntary hospital represents 50 percent of all U.S. hospitals. Typically these have been characterized by emphasizing high quality care for the higher social classes and allowing access to their facilities to lower-class patients primarily through clinics and teaching programs.[58]

For the physician the hospital constitutes a major work setting. The hospital provides the facility which every practice must, in one way or another, have available. "The every-day practitioner who does not or cannot personally hospitalize his patients and supervise their care in hospitals must be prepared to see his patients transfer to practitioners who can see them through the hospital."[59]

In recent years, hospital costs have come to be a major social and health problem. In 1965 the United States spent about $39 billion in medical outlays of all kinds (hospital bills, physicians fees, lab tests).

By 1979 the total was up to $206 billion and this constituted 9.1 percent of the gross national product. It is estimated that at the present rate of increase, medical costs will double every five years, a rise far in excess of inflation. The problem of rising medical costs is basically the cost of hospital care. Prices of even the most routine facilities and treatments are staggering. For example, in 1969, Massachusetts General Hospital charged $80 a day for a semiprivate room. In 1979, the bill was $189 a day.[60]

Bennett argues that much of the complexity and increasing costs of present medical care comes from the use of half-way technologies. The use of measures that merely palliate the manifestations of major diseases where the underlying mechanisms are not yet understood and for which no definitive control or cure has yet been devised. "The recent history of medicine is replete with evidence that each time a major disease has been controlled, the definitive technology has been cheaper and simpler than the technologies devised before the disease was understood."[61] But often the increased cost is due to medical uncertainty and the doctor often deals with his uncertainty by doing more. The doctor's simple rule for resolving uncertainty is often to seek care up to the level of the patient's insurance, a rule reinforced by the high cost of malpractice. The patient is anxious, the doctor insecure."[62]

High hospital costs are also linked to inefficient hospital management. One illustration is that hospitals are usually not used for out-patient treatment (where there are no overnight stays). But probably one-third of all hospital procedures could be done just as effectively and more economically this way. Also very few hospitals allow the patient to practice selfcare—everything must be done for him at a high cost. It is often the case that hospitals compete against each other with expensive equipment that gets limited usage.

The very nature of the hospital makes it an expensive place. Given the way they function they must maintain complex facilities, such as emergency rooms, 24 hours a day, even though those facilities may be used only sporadically. They are also labor intensive and the general ratio is 2.64 employees for every hospital bed. The costs of labor at all levels has gone up sharply. For example, wages and benefits now take 70 percent of the budget of New York Hospital-Cornell Medical Center, versus 35 percent only 20 years ago. The introduction of expensive machinery raises rather than lowers labor costs. "For example, if a hospital buys a CAT (computerized axial tomography) scanner, a kind of super x-ray machine, it must also hire highly trained, highly paid technicians to run it."[63] The bureaucracy of the hospital also adds to the high cost. "The cost of administering the patient, his files, and the checks he writes and receives, can take a quarter out of every dollar on his bill."[64]

Time Magazine writes in 1979 that the total payments to doctors and hospitals will come to more than $3,500 for a typical family of four. They go on to say that the system could hardly have been better designed to fan inflation than if that had been its purpose. "It has in effect repealed for medicine the last vestiges of the law of supply and demand, a free market equivalent of the law of gravity, and made health care a market of weightlessness; what goes up and keeps going up."[65] At the same time that the costs go up, the pressure continues on the individual to seek medical and hospital care. For example, regular medical checkups have been promoted for many years, although there is serious question as to their value. This has contributed to the constantly increasing percentage of the population who are admitted to hospitals.

Medical professions in general, and the doctor in particular, have a commitment to finding illness in the patient. Friedson points out that since the doctor believes that the work he does is all for the good of the patient, he assumes that it is better to impute disease than to deny it and risk overlooking or missing something. This position is in contrast to the legal sector. There it is assumed that it is better to allow a guilty man to go free than to mistakenly convict an innocent man. "In short, the decisive rule guiding the medical activity of practitioners is to be safe by diagnosing illness rather than health."[66]

Drugs are a major part of the total cost of medical care. In the United States, the volume of the drug business has grown by a factor of 100 during this century. At present about 20,000 tons of aspirin are consumed each year, almost 225 tablets per person. Drugs for the central nervous system are the fastest growing part of the pharmaceutical market and make up about 30 percent of the total sales. Illich says that the age of new drugs began with the discovery of aspirin in 1899. He suggests that regardless of all the talk about many new drugs, that some experienced clinicians believe that less than two dozen basic drugs are all that will ever be desirable for 99 percent of the total population.[67]

The hospital as an institution. While hospitals vary in size, they generally are large institutions involving personnel and technology that can be very complex. There are about 2.8 million health workers of all types employed by the hospitals. Over the years the structure of the hospital staff has changed. For example, at the turn of the century, the ratio of supportive personnel to doctors was about 1 to 2, but now it is as high as 15 to 1.

In the larger hospitals there has come to be a hierarchy of prestige and authority among paramedical workers. For example, the nurses are higher than the attendants and technicians. This hierarchy is also likely to reflect the social origins of the workers. "In the grossest comparison between physicians and paramedical workers, the latter are to a disproportionate degree women and less valued ethnic, racial and religious groups in the United States."[68] The word paramedical has come to refer to occupations organized around the work of healing but directly controlled by physicians. The paramedicals are characterized by a lack of autonomy, responsibility, authority, or prestige.[69]

Friedson goes on to point out that in the hospital physicians generally communicate extensively only with those who are subject to their prescription, order, or direction. In fact, physicians are apt to be very poorly informed about any institutional and occupational resources that rest outside their jurisdiction. "They are likely to be suspicious of the value of all that lies outside their domain. Their commitment leads them to depreciate the importance of extra medical services."[70] As the dominant profession, the physician is jealous of his prerogative to diagnose and forecast illness. While he doesn't want anyone else to give information to the patient, neither is he himself inclined to do so. "A number of reasons are advanced—difficulty of being sure about diagnosis—the physician's own busy schedule."[71]

What is most important is the fact that all the work done by the other occupations in the hospital and in any way related to the service of the patient are subject to the order of the physician. The medical profession alone is held to be competent to diagnose illness, treat or direct the treatment of illness, and evaluate the service. Without authorization by the physician, little can be done for the patient by the paraprofessional. The patient's medication, diet, excretion, and recreation are all subject to medical orders. In general, without medical authorization, paramedical workers are not supposed to communicate anything of significance to the patient "about what his illness is, how it will be treated, and what the chances are for improvement."[72]

As earlier mentioned once a physician is licensed to practice there is very little control over his competency. There are some regulatory devices established in the hospitals but these are limited. The hospitals do have some initial control over physicians by providing staff admitting privileges. Once the physician is admitted, there is very little control over the quality of medicine practiced. As Friedson points out, about all that is left to concerned members of the medical practice "is exhortation and, it is hoped, instruction by means of articles in professional journals that may or may not be read and that, if read, may or may not influence behavior."[73]

The hospital patient.   Once patients accept admission to the hospital, they have very few rights and privileges. Basically the hospital strips patients of adult responsibility and places them in a highly dependent position. Hans O. Mauksch says that the entire process of admission demonstrates this dependency. Everything patients bring with them to the hospital is surrendered at the time of admission. This includes even medications which patient's physician has prescribed and

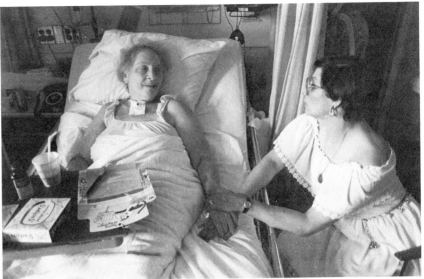

Michael Weisbrot and Family

The restricted world of the hospital patient

trusted the patient to take on his own must be given up. As a result "the hospital as an anonymous agency has become the interloper, the power wielder, which can withhold from the patient."[74] There are few other social institutions that make the individual more dependent than the hospital. Once the patient is in the hospital the very nature and architecture of the hospital make it very difficult for a patient to develop a community of interaction with other patients.

One result of the high dependency forced on patients entering the hospital is the feeling of alienation. One study found that patients were alienated from their usual lives and reduced to largely impersonal statuses in the hospital. This was brought about by stripping them of all their personal things, controlling their resources, and restricting their mobility while in the hospital. Cockerman writes that this inner isolation from others, along with the uncertainty that often goes with feelings of illness, can create for patients a sense of inadequacy and inability to control their lives. This attitude of incompetency is made even more intense by the patients having to assume "an institutional role like the sick role, in which he or she is officially dependent and excluded from decision making."[75]

Another problem with hospitals is that hospitals are dangerous places. Obviously danger is associated with what is brought in by the patient and also from infections that can be picked up from other patients. There is also the danger of accidents. It has been estimated that 7 percent of all patients suffer compensable injuries while hospitalized. "The frequency of reported accidents in hospitals is higher than in all industries but mines and high-rise construction."[76] It has been established that one in every five patients admitted to a typical research hospital acquires an iatrogenic disease, sometimes trivial, usually requiring special treatment, and in one case in thirty leading to death."[77]

Death is one of the dominant concerns of the hospital. But basically the values of the hospital are to do all they can to postpone death. Death is often viewed as the ultimate failure. It is often seen as something that could be avoided, at least for a little longer, if the health care system functioned more efficiently. In part the problem is based on the current technological emphasis that centers around the success story of healing. Therefore, the patient whose disease cannot be cured, the human being who is dying, is perceived to be a failure of the health professions. "The hospital and its culture considers death in some way one of its own taboos. In the hospital patients do not die, they expire. Patients do not die on the operating table; rather, the patient is lost on the table."[78]

In the hospital, whatever else death and dying means, it also means more work. David Sudnow found that for a dying patient to be in the ward meant that soon the body would have to be cleaned, wrapped, pronounced, and discharged. The family would have to be told. "These activities, and the work requirements they entailed, provided the situational frame of interpretation around such states."[79]

One study of intensive care units (ICU) shows how medical personnel react to various kinds of deaths in the hospital. The ICU had the reputation among hospital personnel as an especially dramatic and tense work setting. It was often a hectic environment and the atmosphere was highly charged with tension. "Patients are fearful; concerned family members haunt the corridors, waiting apprehensively for news."[80] It was found that in order to maintain the necessary emotional detachment while caring for critically ill and dying patients the ICU personnel developed several techniques. The most apparent were humor, escape into work, language alternatives and rationalization.[81]

For the ICU staff there was usually no emotional response when an elderly person died. However, the patient's age was the most important factor affecting the balance detachment and concern. Emotional overtones were visible among the ICU staff whenever a child was introduced to the unit." Sudnow also found this to be true in the hospitals he studied. He found that usually death was treated with little notice. But when a child died, special measures were felt to be necessary. "Nurses have been known to break down in tears when a child died."[82]

Increasingly the hospital in the United States has come to be the place where people go to die. Over the past 25 years the percentage of

Americans who die in hospitals has increased by one third. More and more people die in the hospital because it is the place to receive care which cannot be received at home. Often a person with a terminal illness will be sent home but when death becomes close they return to the hospital. In part this is done to prolong life and in part to make death less physically painful. About one half of all deaths occur in large general hospitals but an increasing number are occuring in nursing homes. "Probably, fewer than one third of the deaths in American society take place at home, at work, or in public places."[83]

Philippe Arries has pointed out that death in the hospital is no longer the occasion of a ritual ceremony where the person dying presides among assembled relatives and friends. Death has come to be a technical phenomena presided over by the physician and the hospital personnel. The final experience of dying does not directly involve the patient because in most cases they have lost consciousness.[84]

In recent years there have been significant changes in views about death. One is that it is much more openly discussed and recognized than it was a few years ago. There has also been legislation allowing persons to refuse certain types of treatment. There is growing interest in euthanasia, "as evidenced by increasing numbers of persons who have joined organizations advocating the legality of 'mercy killing.' "[85]

Part of the difficulty of changing views toward death is that the physician has a strong sense of an ethical duty to preserve life. It is at least arguable that so long as patients are legally competent to make a decision to die, they have the right to do so. But what happens when the patient is not legally competent because of being comatose or insensable due to pain or drugs? "At the present time there is no answer to this question and no policy, other than the decision of a physician to terminate treatment made on a case-to-case basis."[86]

Another related problem is the responsibility of the physician to tell the patient and/or his family about the seriousness of the illness. One study found that 90 percent of the doctors preferred not to tell cancer patients that their condition was terminal. In discussing their diagnosis with the patient the use of euphemisms was the general rule. "Patients would be told they had a 'lesion,' a 'mass,' or perhaps a 'tumor,' but terms like 'cancer' and 'malignancy' were avoided."[87]

The Economic Costs of Illness

As suggested earlier one of the major concerns with medical care in the United States is its astronomically increasing cost. It has reached a point where only a very few citizens would be able to pay for a serious medical problem without some kind of medical insurance plan. In the

United States we have no unified health care system. By contrast, in Great Britain, most physicians are paid through tax revenues. Because they don't derive income from their patients they can emphasize preventive medicine rather than treatment. However, the British method has failed to reduce health disparities because living conditions and life styles could not be equalized. "The physical environment of poverty and poor nutrition continued to adversely affect lower-class health."[88]

In the United States starting with Blue Cross in the 1930s, and continuing through the postWorld War II, has been the trend for employers to provide medical insurance for their workers and private insurers have picked up the bulk of the hospital and doctor bills. In 1965 Medicare was provided for those over 65 and Medicaid assistance for the poor. There are still gaps in the coverage. For example, the 20 percent or so of the bill that the typical Medicare patient must pay can be a severe burden. And there is always the threat of a long illness. In 1975 about 90 percent of all hospital care was paid through third-party systems, 37 percent by private health insurance, and 53 percent by the government.

The use of third-party reinbursements make procedures (drugs, tests, injections, surgery) profitable. And they penalize the doctor who takes the time to listen and to explain to the patient. The doctor's office fee is the same for a short or a long encounter with the patient. So the conscientious doctor will earn less than his counterpart who runs an injection mill.[89]

Medicare and Medicaid are paid for through Social Security taxes. In 1965 when these plans were put into action many problems emerged. Alford writes that the problems besetting Medicaid were epitomized in New York city, where the costs of welfare and Medicaid payments doubled between 1965 and 1969.[90] These programs turned out to be a financial "boon" to organized medicine and to hospitals. They grossed three times more in 1976 then in 1965. It allowed them to pass excessive demands for payment on to insurance companies instead of to the patients themselves."[91]

There have been many attempts in recent years to introduce on the federal level national insurance plans. At this time there is no plan even close to legislative passage. Even if one is passed, it will probably not change the structure of medical care, because organized medicine has a professional monopoly on medical knowledge, techniques, and procedures. "They can define most clearly and authoritatively what health care should entail in the United States."[92]

Certainly money is needed to relieve the drain on the individual for medical costs. But money may not be the answer to significant improvements in health. There is very little that medical attention or care can do for some conditions, for example, fatal wounds resulting from homocide or automobile accidents, or advanced cases of cirrhosis of the liver from alcoholism, or lung cancer from smoking. It is possible that we may be reaching the point where there is no longer a significant relationship between spending money on health and getting results. "It has been suggested that the complete eradication of heart disease, cancer, and stroke would extend the average life expectancy at birth by only six or seven years."[93]

There also tends to be little overlap in interests or procedures between the medical establishment and public health interests. The issues that influence health, such as nutrition, family size, population density, environmental mobility, poverty, racism, unemployment, housing, and so forth are rarely taken into consideration in any overall calculation of how to directly better health conditions.[94] It seems clear that we are likely to have medical health problems well into the future. The conditions related to physical health problems are not going to change nor is there going to be a more equitable and conscientious approach to dealing with the patient by the physician.

In American society ill health is a personal and social problem. There is a social expectation that illness should be curable by medical experts. Yet, we are far from the point where medical technology can cure many illnesses. As long as we seek medical care to solve health problems, medical costs will also be a problem.

Because all of us will have health problems at some time this is a problem area with which we can all readily identify. The medical profession decides what is illness and what will be done about it. The role of the patient is influenced by age, sex, education, social class, and so forth. The physician has the most powerful professional role of any, and almost totally dominates the entire medical health field. Hospitals have come to be highly complex, specialized, and tremendously expensive. We are involved in a great amount of value conflict as to the ways and means to cover the costs of health care.

NOTES

1. David Mechanic, *Medical Sociology*, 2d ed. (New York: Free Press, 1978), p. 26.
2. Eliot Freidson, *Professional Dominance: The Social Structure of Medical Care* (Chicago: Aldine, 1970), p. 6.
3. Ivan Illich, *Limits to Medicine* (London: Marion Boyars, 1976), pp. 90–91.
4. Eliot Friedson, *Profession of Medicine* (New York: Dodd, Mead & Co., 1973), p. 208.
5. Ibid., p. 214.
6. Illich, *Limits*, pp. 122–23.
7. Lewis Thomas, "On the Science and Technology of Medicine," *Daedalus* (Winter 1977), p. 43.

8. Mechanic, *Medical Sociology*, p. 185.

9. Illich, *Limits*, p. 222.

10. Friedson, *Profession*, p. 205.

11. Illich, *Limits*, p. 235.

12. Leon Eisenberg, "The Search for Care," *Daedalus* (Winter; 1977), p. 238.

13. William C. Cockerham, *Medical Sociology* (Englewood Cliffs: N.J.: Prentice-Hall, 1978), p. 67.

14. Friedson, *Profession*, pp. 287–88.

15. Cockerham, *Medical Sociology*, p. 102.

16. Friedson, *Professional Dominance*, p. 197.

17. Ibid., p. 198.

18. Robert R. Alford, *Health Care Politics* (Chicago: University of Chicago Press, 1975), p. 102.

19. Cockerham, *Medical Sociology*, p. 69.

20. Illich, *Limits*, p. 24.

21. John H. Knowles, "The Responsibility of the Individual," *Daedalus* (Winter 1977), p. 62.

22. Aaron Wildavsky, "Doing Better and Feeling Worse: The Political Pathology of Health Policy," *Daedalus* (Winter 1977), p. 105.

23. Knowles, "Responsibility," p. 62.

24. Illich, *Limits*, pp. 79–80.

25. Thomas, "Science," p. 37.

26. Knowles, *Limits*, p. 61.

27. Thomas, "Sciences," p. 39.

28. Cockerham, *Medical Sociology*, p. 115.

29. Friedson, *Profession*, p. 5.

30. Ibid., p. 147.

31. Illich, *Limits*, p. 145.

32. Friedson, *Profession*, p. 253.

33. Ibid., p. 142.

34. Ibid., p. 91.

35. Alford, *Health Care*, pp. 195–96.

36. Friedson, *Profession*, p. 252.

37. Mechanic, *Medical Sociology*, p. 384.

38. Friedson, *Professional Dominance*, p. 71.

39. Alford, *Health Care*, p. 198.

40. Illich, *Limits*, p. 112.

41. Ibid., p. 225.

42. Wildavsky, "Doing Better," p. 105.

43. Renee C. Fox, "The Medicalization or Demedicalization of American Society," *Daedalus* (Winter; 1977), p. 13.

44. Illich, *Limits*, p. 31.

45. Ivan L. Bennett, "Technology as a Shaping Force," *Daedalus* (Winter 1977), p. 132.

46. Illich, *Limits*, p. 30.

47. Mechanic, *Medical Sociology*, pp. 379–80.

48. Jeffrey Lionel Berlant, *Profession and Monopoly* (Berkeley: University of California Press, 1975), p. 180.

49. Friedson, *Profession*, p. 28.

50. Berlant, *Monopoly*, p. 259.

51. Ibid., p. 285.

52. Thomas, "Science," p. 43.

53. Alford, *Health Care*, p. 195.

54. Friedson, *Professional Dominance*, p. 215.

55. Illich, *Limits*, pp. 156–57.
56. Friedson, *Profession*, p. 248.
57. Cockerham, *Medical Sociology*, p. 171.
58. Ibid., p. 173.
59. Friedson, *Profession*, pp. 109–10.
60. *Time Magazine* (May 28, 1979), p. 22.
61. Bennett, "Technology," p. 129.
62. Wildavsky, "Doing Better," p. 108.
63. *Time Magazine*, p. 23.
64. Illich, *Limits*, p. 50.
65. *Time Magazine*, p. 23.
66. Friedson, *Profession*, pp. 255–56.
67. Illich, *Limits*, pp. 74–75.
68. Friedson, *Profession*, p. 53.
69. Ibid., p. 49.
70. Friedson, *Professional Dominance*, p. 151.
71. Ibid., pp. 141–42.
72. Ibid., p. 141.
73. Ibid., p. 101.
74. Hans O. Mauksch, "The Organizational Context of Dying," in *Death: The Final Stage of Growths*, by Elizabeth Kubler-Ross (New York: Prentice-Hall, 1975), p. 18.
75. Cockerham, *Medical Sociology*, p. 186.
76. Illich, *Limits*, p. 186.
77. Ibid., p. 32.
78. Mauksch, "Organizational Context," p. 10.
79. David Sudnow, *Passing On: The Social Organization of Dying* (Englewood Cliffs; N.J.: Prentice-Hall, 1967), p. 170.
80. Robert H. Coombs and Lawrence J. Goldman, "Maintenance and Discontinuity of Coping Mechanicism in an Intensive Care Unit," *Social Problems* (Winter 1973), p. 343.
81. Ibid., p. 346.
82. Sudnow, *Passing On*, p. 171.
83. Cockerham, *Medical Sociology*, p. 287.
84. Phillipe Aries, *Western Attitudes toward Death* (Baltimore: Johns Hopkins University Press, 1974), p. 88.
85. Cockerham, *Medical Sociology*, p. 296.
86. Ibid., p. 297.
87. Ibid., p. 291.
88. Ibid., p. 40.
89. Eisenberg, "Search," p. 243.
90. Alford, *Health Care*, p. 9.
91. Cockerham, *Medical Sociology*, p. 210.
92. Ibid., p. 214.
93. Ibid., p. 215.
94. Knowles, "Responsibility," p. 3.

SELECTED BIBLIOGRAPHY

Alford, Robert R. *Health Care Politics.* Chicago: University of Chicago Press, 1975.
Cockerham, William C. *Medical Sociology.* Englewood Cliffs, N.J.: Prentice-Hall, 1978.
Eisenberg, Leon. "The Search for Care." *Daedalus* (Winter, 1977), pp. 235–46.
Friedson, Eliot. *Professional Dominance: The Social Structure of Medical Care.* Chicago: Aldine, 1970.

Friedson, Eliot. *Profession of Medicine*. New York: Dodd, Mead & Co., 1973.

Illich, Ivan. *Limits to Medicine*. London: Marion Boyars, 1976.

Mechanic, David. *Medical Sociology,* 2d ed. New York: Free Press, 1978.

Thomas, Lewis. "On the Science and Technology of Medicine." *Daedalus* (Winter, 1977), pp. 35–46.

Wildavsky, Aaron. "Doing Better and Feeling Worse: The Political Pathology of Health Policy." *Daedalus* (Winter, 1977), pp. 105–23.

Chapter 15

Mental Illness

All societies have had to face the problem of some members being unable or unwilling to meet minimal standards of conduct. Individuals may be unable to function for various reasons. These include mental health problems which limit the functional ability of the individual. Mental health problems have become a common explanation in the behavior of those who are able to meet the minimal demands of society but who suffer some personal limitations or create problems for society.

During the 13th and 14th centuries, persons who were mentally ill were called witches and were tortured and persecuted. Frequently they were blamed for many of the social and individual problems of the time. Lealon E. Martin writes that witch hunts during that time "were awesome displays of mob violence marked by mass psychosis."[1] Many societies in the past have defined the mentally ill as possessed by the devil, and as a result they were frequently tortured and killed.

The 18th century saw changes in views of mental illness with the emergence of increasing medical and scientific explanations of behavior. From the 1840s on there were asylums built in the United States for the mentally ill. Prior to that time the poor and insane were usually ignored. If they made a nuisance of themselves they were treated as criminals and put into criminal institutions where treatment was usually degrading and inhuman. Often the institutions were built in outlying areas so they would be out of sight.

DEFINING THE PROBLEM

An important part of modern day views of mental illness and its treatment is found in the definition of mental illness itself. In general, mental illness is socially defined not by how frequently certain traits or behavior appear in the overall population, but rather on the basis of ideal behavioral norms a society believes in and upholds. Probably all definitions of mental illness assume some notion of what positive mental health should be, but there is no single, generally agreed upon definition. Therefore, the definitions stress why a mental health problem exists rather than describing the nonproblematic conditions of positive mental health.

Basically any definition of mental health problems assumes that in some way the individual is not normal. These definitions locate basic mental health problems in the person's private emotional self. In some way the self has been altered, repressed, or wrongly developed. A definition of mental disorder then denotes a significant departure from normal cognitive and emotional functioning for the individual. The impaired person may not see himself as ill even though he may be aware of himself as feeling very poor and miserable. Often in cases of serious mental illness, the person does not regard himself as ill.

Technically, mental illness is whatever relevant professionals define it to be. Classifications of mental illness are set up, added to over time, and sometimes even reduced by the professionals. For example, in recent years some mental health professionals have decided that homosexuality is no longer a form of mental illness. As a result, the symptoms which previously defined the illness remain unchanged, but the psychiatric interpretation of those symptoms has altered.

There is a close link between defining a mental illness and costs in treating it. The big business of mental illness is reflected in the fact that about 5,000,000 persons every year seek psychiatric help. Over the years the government has become highly committed to funding medical definitions of all kinds of deviancy. This contributes to the support of thousands of professionals who function as psychoanalysts, psychiatrists, clinical psychologists, social workers and in many other related occupations.

Sociological definitions of mental illness suggest that the values of society are reflected in how people are defined and treated. Like other forms of deviancy, mental illness becomes visible when others recognize a person's limitations in making proper responses in his network of interpersonal relations. The evaluation of particular behavior always depends on the frame of reference of those evaluating it. "Whether a deviant act is seen as evidence of 'crime,' 'corruption,' 'illness,' and so on, will be contingent on the criteria with which the evaluator operates and how he applies them."[2]

David Mechanic has written that while it is clear that mental illness is a social problem it is not clear which social problems fall within the domain of mental illness. He points out that delinquency thrives in certain areas of large cities and that to define delinquents as children in need of psychiatric care may lead us away from looking at the conditions and social forces which contribute to that delinquent behavior and its definition by others. Increasingly, in recent years, the concepts of mental illness and mental health have come to be used ambiguously to include a wide range of social problems. These psychiatric definitions implicitly suggest that the mentally ill individual is at fault, although many of his problems are a direct result of the organization and patterning of the community itself.[3] Therefore to understand many aspects of mental illness it is necessary to go beyond the individual and look at the social conditions that influence them.

Eliot Freidman argues that mental illness is a social definition which is supplied or controlled by the physician. Once the application of this definition has been made, it contributes to the problem in a very significant way. In other words, some illnesses, once defined, may never become undone, since they will always have some impact on the individual. To have been defined as mentally ill stigmatizes the normal status of the individual. "If one is diagnosed as having a *stigmatized* illness, being cleared of it is not possible; simply having been suspected of it is stigmatizing."[4]

Models of Mental Illness

We want to look more specifically at how mental illness has been defined in terms of models used by various approaches or disciplines. The models of mental illness that are constructed not only offer specific definitions of mental illness but they also give each approach a rationale for the treatment of the mentally ill.

Medical model. The medical model of mental illness rests on the general medical model which traces the cause of problems to diseases found in the individual. Clearly this approach is from physical medicine. Definitions of normality are based on the absence of disease, and abnormalities are seen as reflecting the presence of certain symptoms of disease. The assumption that mental health is a form of deviance based in sickness or disease places the care of the ill in the hands of the medical profession.

Since medical models of mental illness locate the cause of such problems within the individual treatment is directed toward that cause with the assumption that the symptoms can be alleviated or eradicated. When mental illness is seen as a disease, that often allows strong control to be exerted on the life of the individual. Often the repression of individual idiosyncracies can be justified and even called a humanitarian effort.

This approach is a part of what Peter Conrad calls the "medicalization" of certain social problems or forms of social deviance. To medicalize is to define behavior as a medical problem of illness and to mandate or license the medical profession to provide some type of treatment for it. Examples of this in recent years have been alcoholism, drug addiction, and treating of violence as a genetic or brain disorder. Conrad writes that this is not a new process, that the medicalization of mental illness can be traced back to at least the 17th century. But in recent years the above problems along with such things as hyperactive behavior in children have become defined as medical problems both in etiology "or explanation of the behavior and the means of social control and treatment."[5]

Conrad argues that the medical record of many kinds of problems is a central question for society. He says that in the last analysis medical social control may be the central issue because it is the de facto agent of the status quo. While the medical profession may not have entirely sought this role, its members have in general been unconcerned and unquestioning in their acceptance of it. "With the increasing medical knowledge and technology it is likely that more deviant behavior will be medicalized and medicine's social control will expand."[6] This is a reflection of the unparalleled power that the medical profession has to define its own area of concern. There are no other professions or institutions that are seriously taken as alternatives to medicine in the defining of mental health problems and possible solutions.

Psychiatric models.   While psychiatrists are less apt to use a disease model of mental illness they are the major part of the medical establishment controlling diagnosis and treatment of the mentally ill. In recent years psychodynamic theory has had a pervasive influence over the psychiatric treatment of mental patients in the United States. The basic assumption of this model is that behavior is dominated by unconscious processes which can contribute to inappropriate social functioning and psychological distress. Treatment is seen as resting on repeated and intensive exploration between the therapist and the patient. Often a psychoanalytic model assumes that the basic unconscious processes can be discovered and remedied. This form of treatment is very expensive, since a single therapist can treat relatively few patients. "Psychoanalytic theory requires private practice and rich patients."[7]

In general psychiatrists and other mental health professionals not only emphasize bizarre behavior and personal suffering but they frequently see illness in terms of failure of persons to adjust adequately to their social surroundings or to fit into a recognized social group. This approach often assumes there is a uniformity about society against which the individual's behavior can be measured. However, there are extensive subgroup differences in both values and behavior in various communities and it is often impossible to decide whether a person's behavior is bizarre or whether he is responding to his subgroup values rather than the assumed dominant cultural values.[8]

The psychiatric view of deviance often fails to appreciate the extent to which nonconforming behavior results from learning processes where persons in various communities quite normally develop attitudes, values, and behavior patterns that are illegal or disapproved of within the larger society. "No doubt, some deviants suffer from profound psychological disorders, but just as it is irresponsible to argue that all deviant behavior is acquired through normal learning processes, so it is irresponsible and shortsighted to conceive of all behavior we disapprove of as sick."[9] Yet, the psychiatrist is rarely going to look seriously at his problem from a social perspective. Rather, he will approach his problem from the viewpoint of changing the patient rather than changing the society.

In American psychiatry the approach has been strongly influenced by psychoanalysis and a variety of neo-Freudian influences. By contrast, the basic orientation of most European psychiatrists has been strongly organic and they have used limited disease concepts to describe psychiatric disorders. "When American psychiatrists talk about

"I'm beginning to think you were better off when your hostility was suppressed..."

Reprinted by permission The Wall Street Journal

diseases they use this concept in a much wider sense than their European counterparts, including a variety of problems in living that many European psychiatrists could not regard as disease."[10]

The psychoanalytic model leads to certain basic assumptions about causes and solutions in mental health problems. Those who hold to a psychoanalytic view believe that treating symptoms without getting at the assumed internal causes will only lead to the appearance of new symptoms. However, this assumption is not supported by the available evidence. Often the only effective way of dealing with a problem is to deal only with the symptoms. The psychoanalytic model has long made assumptions about mental disorders that cannot be tested. Moreover, those trained in the psychoanalytic model are inclined to treat patients, rather than evaluate the model. Very often its predictions based on the psychoanalytic model appear autocratic and narrow. For example, as Peter E. Nathan and Sandra L. Harris point out, according to psychoanalytic theory a "person whose childhood was chaotic and disordered should have developed a psychosis, or at least a disabling neurosis."[11]

William C. Cockerham writes that one of the most striking criticisms of the psychoanalytic model is that it is based for the most part on myth. The advocates of the model are required to accept the dogma coming from the unproven assumptions of Freudian thought in much the same way that persons living in the Middle Ages accepted on faith the idea that mental illness was caused by the devil. There is no evidence that the human personality has the Freudian tripartite structure consisting of the id, ego, and superego. Those are simply basic assumptions of the psychoanalytic model. Furthermore, this viewpoint portrays persons as being propelled by instincts and does not take into account individuals's ability to determine their own behavior.[12]

Psychotherapy.   The term psychotherapy covers a range of activities based on a wide variety of theories and ideas. In practice the term may refer to little more than a social relationship between a therapist and a patient that is built around an attempt to improve the patient's perspective or psychological condition. But for most patients this is not a feasible approach because of the relatively long term and intensive relationship that is required.[13] Martin observes that almost any method employed by a general physician, psychiatrist, or clinical team to help a person to adjust better to life or to remove or alleviate his mental problems may be psychotherapy.[14]

Implied in psychotherapy is the belief that the therapist can bring about significant change in the patient. Whatever theories or whatever techniques they use, therapists attempt to bring about beneficial changes in the patient's attitudes and symptoms. "All psychotherapies are concerned with using the influence of the therapist to help patients to unlearn old, maladaptive response patterns and to learn better ones, but they differ considerably in their specific goals and methods."[15]

In most instances patients seek out the therapist with the implicit belief or hope that the therapist can help them. In receiving the patient the therapist must try to develop the patient's trust, confidence or faith. "Many therapists feel that in the absence of such an attitude little can be accomplished; and there is some evidence that this state of mind in itself can have important therapeutic effects."[16] Often the belief that something will help may bring about greater positive change than any special therapeutic technique.

There are certain basic assumptions that go into any approach to therapy. As the treatment moves along the therapist instructs the patient to follow certain activities based upon whatever theory the therapist adhers to. Whatever the specific nature of the theory, all implicitly inform the patient that the therapist knows what is wrong and can select the treatment to successfully deal with the problem. Often when the therapist is not successful in bringing about change, the fault is said to rest with the resistance of the patient to cooperate rather than any inadequacy in the therapist's theory or method.

In recent years there has been a great increase in the use of group therapy. This makes therapy available to many more and at lower costs. It is assumed that something is gained by the individual in being a part of a group therapy program. The organization and conduct of group therapy varies widely. Usually it is characterized by factors such as comfortable environment and regular sessions, with the therapist serving as a catalyst. There is also usually "permissiveness of verbal expression, lack of unnecessary restrictions, an hour or hour-and-a-half meeting once a week, and uninhibited critical evaluation of reaction to group interactions."[17] As with individual psychotherapy the leader in group therapy has full confidence in his ability to know what should be done. However, the long-term success rates of group therapy are far from impressive.

Drug treatment.   Drug treatment does not refer to a theory of mental illness but rather to a way of dealing with the problem. Drugs are used to change undesirable symptoms; i.e., reduce anxiety, nervousness and so forth. It was in the 1950s that the great breakthrough in the so-called mind drugs and their use in dealing with mental illness occurred. There emerged the use of several drugs for specific problems. Tranquilizers came to be used for excited and overactive patients while antidepressants were used with the withdrawn, apathetic, or deeply depressed patients. But none of these drugs cure any disorders. At best they allow the patient to respond more efficiently to the therapist and the world around him.

The major tranquilizers have come to be the dominant form of treatment in mental institutions and they often make the patient more responsive to other forms of therapy. For the most part they make the patient easier to handle and less of a problem for institutional staff. Tranquilizers for the outpatient can be self-administered and are much less expensive than various forms of therapy. However their therapeutic value is highly questionable and their greatest advantage may be that they create a kind of "medicinal strait jacket" that controls the behavior of the patient.

TABLE 15–1

Number and Percent of Mental Health Patient Care Episodes by Inpatient and Outpatient Services, by Year

Year	Inpatient services		Outpatient services	
	Number	Percent	Number	Percent
1975	1,791,201	28	4,618,272	72
1973	1,679,608	32	3,569,724	68
1969	1,678,371	47	1,894,451	53
1965	1,565,525	59	1,071,000	41
1955	1,296,352	77	379,000	23

Source: Adapted from *The World Almanac* (New York: Newspaper Enterprise, 1980), p. 958.

In addition to tranquilizers there are two other categories of therapeutic drugs; (1) antidepressants or psychic energizers, especially the amphetamines which temporarily greatly enhance the patient's view, and (2) sedative or sleep-assisting agents such as the barbiturates. At the present time mind drugs may figure in every third or fourth drugstore prescription. Probably in most cases they are taken more on faith than upon specificity.[18] It is clear that the use of drugs can have powerful effects on the behavior of the individual. Many times drugs may be used to reduce the threat of dangerous behavior by individuals to themselves or to others. But in other circumstances drugs may be used to control the patient for the convenience of others. Often this happens without patients' knowing what is being done to them. Therefore a basic issue is whether patients should ever be given psychopharmacologic agents without their consent. This has come to be a confused legal question. Philip Berger points out that while the exact legal mechanism varies from state to state it is common to force drugs on highly disturbed psychiatric patients who refuse medications.[19]

In general what can be said about the various therapies and the use of drugs in successfully dealing with mental health problems? Over the past 25 or 30 years, therapeutic approaches have not changed significantly. While new drugs may provide transient symptomatic relief it is unlikely that they alter the underlying processes of these illnesses. In short, there is no real technology available for the treatment of "functional illness, psychoneurosis, or the various forms of social maladaptation. It seems safe to say that nothing much has happened since 1950 to alter the situation one way or another."[20]

Social approaches to mental illness. In contrast to the theories that view mental illness as a part of the individual and lodged within the mind, there are social reaction theories. These theories view mental illness and the mental patient as a relationship between the individual and society. It is argued that societal reactions are always involved in mental illness and hospitalization if only in terms of self-other attitudes and definitions. "Social reaction theorists emphasize that the course of illness and stabilization of behavior around particular deviant behavior patterns which may depend on the way others react to the person in question."[21]

One societal reactive approach has been the use of *labeling theory*. This is the belief that some diagnoses of mental illness made by psychotherapists are pigeonholes into which various behavioral symptoms are placed. The argument is made that persons are not schizophrenic because they manifest symptoms of a disease but rather because they are persons who violate accepted standards and are therefore defined as schizophrenic. Mechanic argues that there is little evidence to suggest that such labeling is powerful enough to be a major influence in producing chronic mental illness. Furthermore, "some patients get well rather quickly and stay well, while others, such as schizophrenics, tend to be chronically ill; the theory of labelling does not explain why such differences occur."[22]

There have also been attempts to deal with some mental health problems on the broader community level. There has emerged a general community psychology movement based on the belief that social conditions and institutions have to be taken into account in dealing with individual mental health problems. The Mental Health Facilities Act of 1963 made funds available for building and staffing comprehensive health centers in the United States. In 1964, the National Mental Health Act was passed and three years later the National Institute of Mental Health was established. As a result some federal funds were made available for research and training as well as to help subsidize community health services. The services are very restricted in what they can do because funds are limited and there is little attempt to deal with the prevention of mental illness.

The Frequency and Distribution of Mental Illness

It is estimated that at any given time between 20 and 32 million Americans need some kind of mental health care and that does not include 6 million defined as mentally retarded. In 1976 about 32 million Americans received treatment of some kind for mental health problems.

However, if one looks only at the more serious forms of mental illness the evidence suggests that about 10 percent of the American population suffer and about one-seventh of those ever receive any type of psychiatric treatment.[23]

When compared to all other types of health problems mental health is the most common. Mental illness strikes more often, attacks more people and requires more prolonged treatment. It also causes more suffering by the individual and for his family and friends. It wastes more human resources, takes up more buildings and other facilities. It consumes more of the personal finances of the individual and his family and the use of public taxes than any other disease.[24] We want to look at the rates of mental illness and how these are related to a variety of social factors.

Sex differences. Most of the studies of the frequency of mental disorder by sex indicate that: (1) There are no consistent differences by sex in rates of functional psychosis in general and in schizophrenia in particular. However, depressive disorders are generally higher for women. (2) Rates of neurosis are consistently higher for women regardless of time and place. (3) Rates of personality disorders are consistently higher for men regardless of time and place.[25]

The higher rates of neurosis among women in society are in part a result of how women are defined relative to men. In general men are able to reject more of the sex role stereotypes without viewing themselves as sick and without being hospitalized than are women. Many personality characteristics attributed to women such as "passivity" and "dependence" are also used to define the woman as having some degree of a mental health problem. Some of the factors that make up the stereotype of female personality characteristics are also used to define women as having a mental health problem (see Chapter 9).

Marital status. The evidence consistently suggests that married women tend to be in poorer mental health than married men in modern Western industrial society. Most of the evidence suggests that married women who work outside the home are in somewhat better mental health than married women who do not. Overall, there is fairly strong evidence that the main reason married women tend to have poorer mental health than married men is because of the traditional roles they usually occupy.[26]

Anne Statham Macke has found that while marriage can increase a woman's general happiness it can at the same time increase her susceptibility to certain types of mental illness. "Marital roles continue to be important sources of identity for most women, so being successfully married should increase a woman's happiness and her self-esteem."[27] Another study found that adjusted wives seemed to better fit the traditional role of the submissive woman and maladjusted wives the common stereotype of the unhappy, castrating shrew.[28]

However, marriage can also function as a protective barrier for both the wife and husband against external threats. While marriage cannot stop economic and social problems from invading life, it can sometimes help people fend off certain psychological assaults that such problems might otherwise cause. Leonard I. Pearlin argues that even at a time when marriage is often a fragile relationship, it often has the capacity to protect people from the full impact of external strains.[29]

What are the rates of mental illness among the various marital statuses? In general mental illness is highest among those who have been married but no longer are—the widowed, separated, and divorced. Pearlin and Joyce S. Johnson found that the presently married were the most free of depression, the formerly married the most burdened by it, and the never married fell between those extremes. "Among the groups making up the formerly married category, the separated are outstandingly most susceptible to depression, with no appreciable difference existing between the divorced and widowed."[30] Studies indicate that women who have never married reported fewer mental health problems than married or separated women. A national study showed that "divorced or separated women had significantly higher depression scores than did married, single, or widowed women."[31]

When mental health rates are compared by sex and marital status the married women tend to have much higher rates of mental illness than married men. However, when single men are compared with single women, divorced men with divorced women, and widowed men with widowed women, it is found that those women do not tend to have higher rates than their male counterparts. "In fact, if there is a difference, it appears to be that women in these categories tend to have lower rates."[32]

Walter R. Gove also found that the married of both sexes have lower rates of mental illness than the unmarried. He suggests that the relationship may be due to both the nature of the roles of the unmarried and the selective processes which keep some unstable persons from marrying. In general, at least in terms of mental illness, being married is considerably more advantageous to men than it is to women, "while being single, if anything, is slightly more disadvantageous to men than to women."[33]

Occupation. As suggested there is some evidence that working outside the home by married women has some positive association with better mental health. Rosabeth Moss Kanter writes that intensive studies of depressed women have shown that women who worked outside the home while depressed were less impaired in their functioning than housewives, and that this was not a function of differences in severity of the illness—"that there was something protective in the work situation."[34]

Among men the research indicates a relationship between mental health and work such that unemployment among persons previously steadily employed in stimulating work may be related to increased incidence of psychological disorders.[35] For most men working is very closely related to their self-image as a successful adult. Therefore, to lose their jobs is to undercut their basic self-image and this can lead to a variety of mental health problems.

Types of Mental Illness

As previously suggested mental illness is often subjective, and hence professionals themselves do not agree in particular cases. One study found that when various evaluators were used, there was an agreement of 68 percent in diagnosing schizophrenia, 69 percent in manic depression psychosis, and 70 percent in mental deficiency. In general the agreement on schizophrenia, anxiety states, and neurotic depression are the lowest.[36]

There are also different medical diagnoses in different countries. There have been substantial differences in reported rates of varying diagnoses in the United States and Great Britain which suggest that psychiatrists in the two countries have quite different diagnostic conceptions. For example, in 1956, the first admission rates for schizophrenia were 56 percent greater in American public and private mental hospitals than in England and Wales. "Conversely, there was a relative scarcity of patients diagnosed as 'manic depressive' in the United States."[37]

The diagnosis will determine the treatment plan. This concerns not only methods of treatment but also whether they will be an outpatient or an inpatient. For example, in 1973, of all outpatients receiving treatment about 16 percent were dignosed as schizophrenic while this was true of 32 percent of all inpatients.[38] We want to look more specifically at some of the classifications of mental illness.

Neuroses. Since neurotic behavior does not involve a break with reality, these people typically recognize and share the definition of the internal nature of their problem, and they do not distort reality to explain it, as does the psychotic. Furthermore, no matter how disturbed, depressed or anxious they may be, the neurotic retains the ability to recognize that his functioning is impaired. "By definition, the symptomatic behavior of the neurotic is the same behavior exhibited by the normal person under grossly stressful conditions."[39]

For the most part the emotional problems rest in the feelings of the individual who begins to suffer from a neurosis. The individual may be bothered, frequently or continually, by feelings of anxiety, by fears or depression. There can be various reactions, such as disassociation from life or environment and obsessive compulsions to do something.[40] Anxiety is the chief characteristic of neurosis. "When the intensity of anxiety is so great that it produces symptoms that markedly impair the individual's ability to interact with others or carry out normal activities, it is appropriate to label the resulting state a neurosis."[41]

Psychosis. A psychosis can be termed a severe form of mental disease where the person's ability to function is extensively disorganized. The person often experiences feelings alien to himself, shows aberrant behavior, and suffers from distortions of reality.

The incidence of manic depression is about the same as the incidence of schizophrenia, about 300 cases per 100,000 population. It is estimated that about 1,500,000 persons are being treated for depression at any given time.[42] Schizophrenia results in more than 900,000 episodes of care each year. This figure understates the actual prevalence because it includes only hospital and clinic reports. A conservative estimate would place the likely total at about 2 million acute psychotic episodes each year.[43]

The incidence of schizophrenia has been nearly constant over the past hundred years in the United States. Schizophrenia is less frequent among professionals and highly educated people than it is among those in unskilled and semiskilled occupations and those with relatively low educations. "This finding appears to be due in part to the tendency of persons rendered ineffective by schizophrenia to drift downward or at least to fail to advance in occupational status."[44]

Schizophrenia contributes overwhelming to the population hospitalized for mental illness. About 60 percent of all patients under 65 years of age occupying beds in mental hospitals in the United States are diagnosed as schizophrenic. At present about 200,000 patients are hospitalized in the United States as diagnosed schizophrenics, while another approximately 400,000 are either patients in outpatient clinics or are not being treated at all. The chances that a person will be hospitalized for schizophrenia in his lifetime have been estimated at one in a hundred.[45]

However, many who are hospitalized as schizophrenic are there briefly before being released back into the community. The common pattern for a person who is schizophrenic is to have several episodes of fairly severe symptoms with periods of relative normalcy in between. There appears to be a decline in the tendency for episodes to occur following the first hospitalization.[46]

There are several forms of treatment used in dealing with the schizophrenic. The traditional psychoanalytic (Freudian) view of the causes of schizophrenia is that the disorder represents fixation or regression to the most primitive levels of psychosexual development. The belief is that as a result the schizophrenic fails to develop important personality structures, "especially certain defensive ones, which

Bill Bridges/Globe Photos, Inc.

A catatonic schizophrenic

permit adequate response to ordinary environmental stress."[47] But psychoanalysis has not been effective against any of the major mental disorders including schizophrenia.

There is considerable disagreement among investigators about the causes of schizophrenia. The theories of conditions believed to be causal range from totally biological to entirely social. There is strong evidence that genetic factors play a part in some schizophrenia. For example, studies indicate that about 10 percent of children with one schizophrenic parent and almost half of those with two schizophrenic parents develop schizophrenia. But that can only explain some cases. In general the cause of the disease remains unknown.

A few years ago, some cases of schizophrenia were linked with causes in the brain, so that between 1948 and 1955, an average of about 1,000 patients a year received a prefrontal lobotomy. This was surgery where a section of the brain was removed. But with the advent of tranquilizing drugs the use of neurosurgery for schizophrenia has become increasingly rare. "Surgery has no value in some of the most common kinds of schizophrenia, while in others it is actually harmful."[48]

In the 1950s drug therapy came to be the common means of treating schizophrenia. But the drugs do not cure schizophrenia and the withdrawal of drugs often leads to the full recurrence of the patient's psychotic symptoms. However, maintenance dosages of the drug usually enable the patient to leave the hospital and in some cases do productive work. Even for patients who remain hospitalized, drugs have often meant a happier, more interesting life and more hope for eventual release.[49] Basically drug therapy has allowed for the manageability of schizophrenia but has not much changed the disease itself.

The Psychiatrist

The psychiatrist is first trained in medicine and then specializes in psychiatry. The psychiatrist has far more influence and power than the psychologist in defining mental illness and controlling the means of treatment. Furthermore, the psychiatrist, probably more than any other doctor, occupies a social as well as a scientific role. His judgments have social influence well beyond the medical context and the psychiatrist's view of disease, "more than that of his nonpsychiatrist colleagues, will reflect the particular center where he has been trained."[50]

American psychiatry became very much involved in mental health policy following World War II. The profession of psychiatry became most intensively involved in public policy issues during World War II, initially through participation in selective service screening of draftees. Between January 1942 and June 1945, an estimated 1,875,000 men among the 15 million men examined were rejected for service because of alleged psychiatric disabilities."[51]

The medical background of psychiatrists, with its great prestige and implications of medical responsibility, has allowed them to maintain a powerful position relative to the other mental health professionals. Very often this has given the psychiatrist the power to control the work of others. Sometimes this leads to a great deal of resentment because the other professions regard themselves as equally qualified "if not more expert than the psychiatrist in assessment and treatment."[52]

While psychiatrists are medically trained, the medical profession in general has little contact with psychiatry during their training. Clinical training in psychiatric diagnosis and treatment is often an elective rather than a required course in the undergraudate medical curriculum. This training is rarely included in the residency training program for internists and pediatricians, the groups that have largely replaced the general practitioner. Often the physician in general practice will avoid treating mental health problems they are unaware of by treating symptoms only by the free use of tranquilizing drugs.[53]

American psychiatric treament follows the pattern of private practice. The discrepancy between the provision of private and public services in psychiatry has not existed in most European countries. For example, in England most of the available psychiatric manpower is in mental hospitals dealing with severe mental illness of an acute character and with chronic disability.[54] In the United States there has been some improvement in recent years in the staffing of mental hospitals, "but the bulk of the services continue to be distributed in a private fee-for-service basis and too little attention of American psychiatrists is devoted to the problems of lower-status psychotic patients."[55]

Like almost all other medical specialities, psychiatry is overwhelmingly made up of men. This has meant that psychiatrists have used male definitions of the mental health problems of women to decide which one had problems and why, what should be done for women, and when and if they should be released from treatment.[56] While there have been a few more women entering psychiatry in recent years they have become disproportionately involved in "women's work" psychiatry—they deal mainly with preadolescent children and women.

Psychiatrists, in participating in the involuntary confinement of individuals as mentally ill through criminal proceedings, act as agents of social control by utilizing the police power of the state.[57] This power is used both at the time of the court hearing and at the time when there is consideration for release after some period of confinement. In fact, "the psychiatrist is the only courtroom participant who can take away the defendant's right to trial."[58]

As suggested, the middle and upper class make up the overwhelming number of all psychiatric patients. One reason for this is that middle-class people have more favorable attitudes toward psychiatry and greater knowledge to correctly identify psychiatric disorders than lower-class people. This leads them to enter psychiatric treatment with less severe problems for shorter periods of time. The greater intellectual sophistication of the middle and upper classes makes them more likely to initiate hospitalization for themselves. "The lack of such

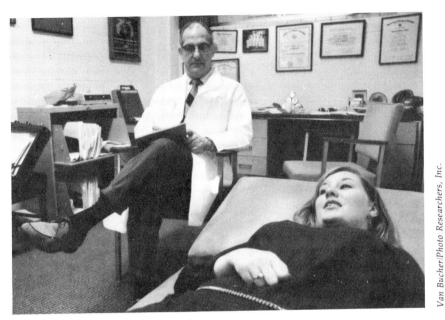

One kind of treatment—psychoanalysis

sophistication among the lower classes makes social control agents more likely to initiate hospitalization."[59] Gove and Patrick Howell point out that persons from the higher social classes are more likely to seek professional help despite the fact that the lower classes manifest more symptoms of mental illness.[60]

Regardless of social levels, others will seek help for a person whose behavior has become unacceptable. Many patients come to the attention of mental health professionals only during the course of an unmanageable crisis. Often without such an emergency the wife's or husband's problem is likely to be ignored. "Many people are willing to tolerate deviance or ignore it until someone actually makes a complaint about it and forces society to act against the deviant."[61]

Sometimes the individual comes to see himself as having a psychiatric problem because his behavior is in radical contrast to what he sees as normal functioning. But on other occasions people recognize their problems as psychiatric only after others in their environment make this connection. "In short, the recognition of mental illness generally takes place in community contexts."[62]

Richard James Bord points out that what one "sees" as a psychiatric problem is mainly a function of what one is ready and capable of "seeing." He suggests that it seems reasonable that the more the general public is "educated" into the psychiatric perspective, the more incidences of mental illness will occur. "Not only will relatively innocuous behaviors, e.g., the depressed, neurotic, be more labeled by others as indicating mental problems, but those engaging in such behaviors are more likely to view this as evidence of a personal problem."[63]

In the United States today, once persons have accepted the label "mentally ill," they are culturally predisposed to expect relief from psychotherapy and to look to a psychiatrist for this relief.[64] There are very few choices among experts they can turn to in help. For example, in the past people who felt they had problems of a mental nature would often turn to the clergy, but this has become much less frequent. Increasingly, psychiatry has a monopoly in providing care for those who seek help for mental health reasons.

When people go to the psychiatric profession for help, they cannot expect to get much optimistic reassurance. Doctors and other health workers are even less able to assure happiness for the person than they are able to assure good health. Very often all the psychiatrist can do is to reduce the symptoms or help them live a little better with their problem by putting them on drugs. But in both cases the problem remains with the person.

Every year there are many Americans who are involuntarily committed for mental health reasons. There are two types of involuntary commitment. First are those concerned with criminal offenses where insanity is claimed as a defense for criminal behavior. Second are those which are civil or noncriminal in nature. In the criminal case, if insanity is established the person is relieved from criminal responsibility. For the civil action there must usually be the finding that the mental disorder is of such a degree or character that if the individual in question were allowed to remain free they would constitute a danger to self, others, or property.[65]

One study of a New York state community found that a common aspect of commitment cases was the inability of patients to take care of themselves in an appropriate manner. A large number of the patients, according to the doctors, were incapable of adequate social functioning, "unable to assess their own need for care, bizarre in affect and behavior, and seemingly out of contact with reality. The investigator felt that those patients if left alone would get themselves into serious difficulty and they required supervised care."[66]

There can often be severe conflict between the person being defined as mentally ill and their perceptions of themselves. Persons who suffer from mental illness often fail to recognize or to accept the definition that they are mentally ill and require treatment. Hence, they may be unwilling to seek psychiatric help or to cooperate in their care. It is the assumption that such patients may be a threat that leads all states to provide legally for their involuntary commitment to psychiatric facilities. But the decision of the court rests on determining if the patient's condition is sufficiently serious to require care and treatment for his own welfare, the welfare of others, or the welfare of the community. There is the implicit assumption that there are recognizable criteria for deciding when an illness requires care and treatment and when such treatment serves the welfare of various parties.[67] It is the psychiatrist who is assumed to have such knowledge.

Whatever the decision-making process, whether by the individual, relatives, or the community, it usually takes a good deal of time. However, as soon as people are found in need of care or help they can be placed in mental hospitals, which may also involve other losses of freedom. In 40 states such persons can lose the right to vote. In almost half of the states they lose the right to hold political offices, and in many states they can be divorced.

The Mental Hospital

In the Western world various kinds of institutions have been used to care for the mentally ill. For example, in ancient Greece, mental patients were taken to temples and there were treated by attempts to eliminate the causes of their disorders. At that time, it was believed that mental illness was caused by demons or divine spirits. "Incantations as well as pharmaceuticals, herb compounds, and juices were used to treat patients."[68]

In the United States, a rapid influx of immigrants accompanied the development of industrialization and urbanization. This led to an increased tendency to hospitalize those who could not adapt to new circumstances. Hospitalization was assumed to both help the patient and to protect the rest of society.

The early 1900s saw the great buildup of mental institutions in the United States. Mostly these were built and operated by county and state governments. During this period of time, there was a systematic age bias in that older persons were disproportionately hospitalized; over the years the percentage of elderly hospitalized has continued to increase. The view which continued well into the 20th century was that the mentally ill and the mentally incompetent were to be sheltered from the outside world and kept from harming themselves and others. They were provided with some help and treatment but it was usually minimal. Very often the hospitals functioned as places for incarceration rather than for treatment.

Each year from the building of the first state mental hospitals up until 1955, there were nearly 600,000 persons confined in state and county hospitals for the long term care of the mentally ill and most of those hospitals had been built in the later part of the 20th century. For the most part, those hospitals provided little more than custodial care for the ever increasing number of patients.

TABLE 15–2

Selected Statistics on State and County Mental Hospitals

Year	Total admitted	Deaths in hospital	Residents at end of year	Expense per patient
1955	178,003	44,384	558,922	$ 1,116.59
1960	234,791	49,748	535,540	1,702.41
1970	393,174	30,804	338,592	5,435.38
1976	413,559	10,922	170,619	13,634.53

Source: Adapted from "National Institute of Mental Health," *The World Almanac* (New York: Newspaper Enterprises, 1980), p. 241.

Up until the mid-1950s there were few outpatient clinics available for psychiatric patients. Neither did a majority of the general medical hospitals admit severely ill psychiatric patients. The view toward mental illness was pessimistic because each year the number of patients admitted to hospitals increased, while very few were discharged. "People sat year after year on benches or on the floor doing nothing, while their physical health deteriorated as well. The psychiatrists charged with the care and treatment of these patients were baffled. Both cause and therapy were quite unknown and untaught in medical schools."[69]

The use of institutionalization and care within the medical institutions underwent a drastic change in the mid-1950s with the development of the drugs (tranquilizers). As a result, there has been a steady decline in the use of mental institutions as the main centers for the care and treatment of the mentally ill. Many patients were released much sooner and were treated as outpatients. There have also been other changes in that older persons are most often placed in alternative settings such as in nursing homes. However, patients who are leaving the mental health institutions are by no means free of all psychiatric symptoms, and most continue to receive treatment. Changes in patterns of treatment are reflected in statistics which show that in 1955, 77 percent of all mentally ill patients were receiving treatment as inpatients, but by 1971 this had dropped to 43 percent with the other 57 percent being outpatients.

Many patients who in the past would have been kept in the mental hospital are now returned to the community after a relatively short period of time. "Most patients leave the hospital within a year, and the average stay is not more than a few months."[70] At present more psychiatric patients are being treated in general hospitals and are not counted in state tabulations. Other patients are in nursing homes and still others have been administratively discharged to "welfare hotels" and rented rooms with dubious effect on their mental and physical well-being.[71]

Leon Eisenberg argues that when figures from all institutions are combined, the frequency of hospitalized cases for psychiatric problems in the general population has hardly changed at all since the mid-1950s. However, the length of stay in the institution has been dramatically shortened. What has increased has been the demand for outpatient care. "Over the same period, official counts of the number of out-patient's episodes of care provided for the mental health facilities has increased five-fold."[72] We want to look at some of the social variables related to hospitalization for mental health problems.

Age.   When patients under 18 years of age are admitted, it is often because of acute, temporary reactions to stressful situations. Over the past 25 years there has been a great increase in the first admission rates for the very young. This is a reflection of the young, more than any other age group, being significantly affected by changes in society. The amount of change in admission rates decreases with greater age. But it should be kept in mind that the older age groups had the highest rates and therefore less room for change than the younger.

Between the ages of 26–65, schizophrenia and alcoholic disorders account for over 50 percent of all patients admitted to state and county mental institutions. There are relatively few major disorders that show during the childhood years and psychoses do not usually show until late adolescence. But from then until early middle age the incidence steadily goes up. Over the next 20 years, the psychoses of middle age are often manic depression and involuntional melancholia. For those over age 65 the most common diagnosis is organic brain syndrome.

Sex.   In 1968, adult women made up 60 percent of the patients in general psychiatric wards, 61 percent of the population in private hospitals and 62 percent of the population in outpatient clinics. A pattern of frequent and recurring hospital commitments, as well as longer stays appear to characterize the career of the female psychiatric patient. In 1971, although more men than women were admitted to state and county hospitals, women were kept much longer and this was especially true for women over 35.[73] The two sexes differ little in rates of diagnosed schizophrenia, but women are twice as likely as men to be treated for depressive disorders. Women also have higher rates for the treatment of psychoneurosis. "Men, on the other hand, are four times more likely to be treated for alcoholic disorders."[74]

Marital status.   Gove and Terry Fain found a direct causal link between marital status and length of hospitalization. They found that even if the patient's family would like to help, unmarried patients are less likely to have an acceptable place to return to and this can increase the length of hospitalization.[75] There is also a relationship between marital status and the onset of institutionalization. Involuntary commitment, in comparison to voluntary admission, is higher for the never married, next the disrupted and estranged (separated, divorced, and widowed), and least for the married.[76]

Race.   There are proportionately more blacks than whites in mental institutions. In general, blacks will more often be diagnosed as needing hospitalization and whites more often as best suited for psychotherapy. Nathan reports that middle-class white psychiatrists record fewer symptoms for black patients than for whites. Instead, the psychiatrists focused on the most dramatic and striking behavior among the blacks. Often the blacks emerged from the diagnostic process appearing more disturbed and more pathological than the whites who showed the same behavior. It was also found that the behavior which caused the hospitalization of white females was usually labeled "neurotic" while essentially the same behavior for black women was called "schizophrenic.'[77]

Social class.   One study found that the rate of hospitalization for the lower-class males was higher than for all other groups. The high incidence in the lowest social class may be explained by the fact that those persons were the ones in closest contact with the courts, welfare workers, and other officials who could refer them for hospitalization. Moreover, they were the less likely to be protected, tolerated, or financially supported by their families."[78] Another study found that low income tends to be associated with both a history of abnormality and a longer duration between the manifestation of symptoms and hospitalization."[79]

Diagnosis and treatment.   As earlier suggested psychiatric diagnoses tend to be unreliable classifications. Within many hospitals and clinics the psychiatrists who are responsible for diagnosis have only brief contact with patients. The psychiatrist is oriented toward looking for pathology and not for good health. Often when they assess persons for working-class or minority group backgrounds they mistake differing life styles for pathology.[80] Mechanic writes that in his experience over a three-month period of studying two mental hospitals, he never observed a case where the psychiatrist advised the patient that he did not need treatment. "Rather, all persons who appeared at the hospital were absorbed into the patient population regardless of their ability to function adequately outside the hospital."[81]

Generally speaking, the treatment that is given in a mental hospital is not likely to be specific to the diagnosed mental disorder. Rather, if a treatment is given at all, a cycle of therapies tends to be given across the aboard to the entire entering group of patients. The medical work-up is used more to learn if there are contraindications for the standard treatments than to find indications for them.[82] Actually, in mental hospitals there is very little treatment that can take place and patients seem to get better to the extent that they repress symptoms and conform to their daily routines.

Very often psychiatric institutions for the care of the mentally ill can be seen as institutions of social control as well as providing medical facilities. This is reflected in the fact that the length of the patient's hospitalization will be closely related to the dangerousness of the patient to themselves and to others. When this happens the hospital is functioning primarily as a holding institution rather than a medically servicing one. Often the concern with controlling the dangerous patient precludes any attempt to deal with their psychiatric problems.

Many mental institutions can be described as *total institutions*. A total institution is a place of residence where a large number of like-situated individuals are cut off from the wider society for fairly long periods of time and together lead an enclosed, formally administered round of life.[83] The central features of total institutions are that people are not treated as individuals but in groups and are required to do the same things together. Their activities are tightly scheduled as officially imposed from above. Often the hospital life requires the patient to adapt in a way detrimental to his future adjustment to the world outside. "The career of the mental patient is irreparably harmful to his future reputation."[84]

John F. Myles observes that at the heart of the general model of total institutions is the systematic manipulation of the client's self-identity. This means the social reconstruction of the self which is inherent in the process of becoming an inmate. "In the context of mental institutions, this implies adoption of a definition of self which is con-

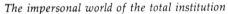

The impersonal world of the total institution

Zalesky/Black Star

ditioned by the patient or sick role."[85] Often the inmates become dependent on the hospital and may find it difficult or impossible to leave. "The inmate gradually learns the sick role, to reduce aspirations, and to find friends within the hospital instead of outside. The longer he stays at the hospital, the less likely he is to leave."[86]

The role of the patient in a total institution undergoes rapid change from his previous roles. The patient is no longer looked upon as a father, or an employee, or a customer, but rather a patient. His ability to play everyday social roles may atrophy from disuse.[87] From the perspective of the hospital the patient must become socialized to a "patient role" and accept the definition of his symptoms placed on him by the hospital staff and other patients. If the patient tries to reject the psychiatric definition of his illness the psychiatrist is apt to report that the patient is a poor treatment risk.[88]

It has been found that there is a progressive increase over time in the hospital of the proportion of patients who appear apathetic about life outside the hospital. In general, the longer the stay in the hospital, the less the contact between patients and their relatives.[89] Life for the patient that is significant tends to be more and more centered on what occurs in the total institution. For many, that setting comes to be the dominant force in their lives.

Goffman points out that in the outside world the individual can hold objects of self-feeling—such as his body, his immediate actions, his thoughts, and some of his possessions clear of any contact with alien and contaminating others. But once he is in the total institution those territories of the self also are violated. "The boundary that the individual places between his being and the environment is invaded and the embodiments of the self profaned."[90]

Mechanic observes that sometimes patients find their hospitalization experience a relief. The community situation from which they come is often one characterized by extreme difficulty and great personal distress. Therefore, many patients in mental hospitals report that hospital restrictions do not bother them. They may appreciate the physical care they are receiving and feel that the hospital, despite restrictions, enhance their freedom rather than restricts it.[91]

As suggested, the total institution can come to be of overriding importance in the life of the patient. If a patient is offered a discharge and declines it, it is commonly said that this proves he is still ill—and in fact, too ill to leave. But there may be good reasons why he comes to choose not to leave. He has already suffered the stigma of being a mental patient and in this reduced status has even poorer prospects in the outside world than he did before he came in. "Furthermore, by the time he is ready to be discharged he is likely to have learned the roles in the hospital."[92]

J. K. Wing writes that the staff and inmates in total institutions have fundamentally different points of view, and they may come to view each other in narrow and hostile stereotypes. There is usually a great social distance between the two sides and little movement between them. The patient quickly learns that decisions about admission and discharge are made by authority and the individual has little say about them. For staff, the amount of patient contact with noninstitutional life is strictly rationed as a privilege to be given to the patient.[93]

In conclusion, the most striking change in the treatment of mental illness as a social problem in recent years has been through the use of drugs rather than through institutionalization. Again it must be stressed that drugs may allow the patient to more readily cope with the *symptoms* of their mental illness but not with its *causes*. Given the more complex demands of modern society, the incidence of the social problem of mental illness likely shall increase. From a broad social perspective, mental illness and its definition as a social problem will continue indefinitely because as with many other social problems, there is no evidence to support hope for cures now or in the future.

The definitions, as well as treatments, of mental illness have undergone change. The medical field of psychiatry is still the dominant force in these definitions. The major change in treatment came in the mid-1950s with the introduction of the various "mind drugs." Those drugs sharply reduced the number of patients institutionalized and their length of stay. Mental illness rates are related to some degree to a variety of social variables; that is, sex, marital status, occupation, and so forth. In general the types of mental illness are the neuroses and the psychoses.

NOTES

1. Lealon E. Martin, *Mental Health: Mental Illness* (New York: McGraw-Hill, 1970), p. 9.

2. David Mechanic, "Some Factors in Identifying and Refining Mental Illness," in *Mental Illness and Social Process*, by Dr. Thomas J. Scheff (New York: Harper, 1967), pp. 25–26.

3. David Mechanic, *Mental Health and Social Policy* (Englewood Cliffs, N.J.: Prentice-Hall, 1969), pp. 31–32.

4. Eliot Freidman, *Profession of Medicine* (New York: Dodd, Mead & Co., 1973), pp. 260–61.

5. Peter Conrad, "The Discovery of Hyperkinesis: Notes on the Medicalization of Deviant Behavior," *Social Problems* (October 1975), p. 17.

6. Ibid., p. 20.

7. Mechanic, *Mental Health*, p. 8.

8. Ibid., p. 2.

9. Ibid., p. 5.

10. David Mechanic, *Medical Sociology*, 2d ed. (New York: Free Press, 1978), p. 102.

11. Peter E. Nathan and Sandra L. Harris, *Psychopathology and Society* (New York: McGraw-Hill, 1975), p. 21.

12. William C. Cockerham, *Medical Sociology* (Englewood Cliffs, N.J.: Prentice-Hall, 1978), p. 227.

13. Mechanic, *Mental Health,* p. 48.

14. Martin, *Mental Health,* p. 43.

15. Jerome Frank, "The Dynamics of the Psychotherapeutic Relationship," in Scheff, *Mental Illness,* p. 169.

16. Ibid., p. 195.

17. Martin, *Mental Health,* p. 48.

18. Ibid., p. 45.

19. Philip Berger, Beatrix Hamberg, and David Hamberg, "Mental Health: Progress and Problems," *Daedalus* (Winter 1977), p. 270.

20. Lewis Thomas, "On the Science and Technology of Medicine," *Daedalus* (Winter 1977), p. 42.

21. William A. Rushing and Jack Esso, "Status Resources and Behavior Deviance as Contingencies of Societal Reaction," *Social Forces* (September 1977), p. 135.

22. Mechanic, *Mental Health,* p. 47.

23. Cockerham, *Medical Sociology,* p. 219.

24. Martin, *Mental Health,* p. 125.

25. Cockerman, *Medical Sociology,* p. 235.

26. Walter R. Gove and Michael R. Geerken, "The Effect of Children and Employment on the Mental Health of Married Men and Women," *Social Forces* (September 1977), p. 75.

27. Anne Statham Macke, George W. Bohrnstedt, and Ilene N. Bernstein, "Housewives' Self-Esteem and Their Husbands' Success: The Myth of Vicarious Involvement," *Journal of Marriage and Family* (February 1979), p. 51.

28. Beth L. Fineberg and Joseph Lawman, "Affect and Status Dimensions of Marital Adjustment," *Journal of Marriage and Family* (February 1975), p. 158.

29. Leonard I. Pearlin and Joyce S. Johnson, "Marital Status, Life-Strains and Depression," *American Sociological Review* (October 1977), p. 714.

30. Ibid., p. 706.

31. George Levinger, "A Social Psychological Perspective on Mental Dissolution," *Journal of Social Issues* (Winter 1976), p. 42.

32. Walter R. Gove, "The Relationship between Sex Roles, Marital Status and Mental Illness," *Social Forces* (September 1972), p. 43.

33. Ibid., p. 43.

34. Rosabeth Moss Kanter, "Work in the New America," *Daedalus* (Winter 1978), p. 55.

35. Berton H. Kaplan, John C. Cassel, and Susan Gor, "Social Support and Health," *Medical Care* (May 1977), p. 47.

36. Mechanic, *Medical Sociology,* p. 108.

37. Ibid., p. 109.

38. National Institute of Mental Health, "Statistical Note 92" (Washington, D.C.: 1973).

39. Nathan and Harris, *Psychopathology,* p. 259.

40. Martin, *Mental Health,* p. 24.

41. John A. Clausen, "Mental Disorders," in *Contemporary Social Problems,* by Robert K. Merton and Robert Nisbet (New York: Harcourt Brace Jovanovich, 1976), p. 111.

42. Berger, Hamberg, and Hamberg, "Mental Health: Progress," p. 263.

43. Leon Eisenberg, "The Search For Care," *Daedalus* (Winter 1977), p. 240.

44. Clausen, "Mental Disorders," p. 125.

45. Berger, Hamberg, and Hamberg, "Mental Health: Progress," p. 261.

46. William W. Eaton, Jr., "Mental Hospitalization as a Reinforcement Process," *American Sociological Review* (April 1974), p. 258.

47. Nathan and Harris, *Psychopathology*, p. 187.

48. Ibid., p. 199.

49. Ibid., p. 202.

50. Mechanic, *Medical Sociology*, p. 115.

51. Ibid., p. 55.

52. Mechanic, *Mental Health*, p. 7.

53. Eisenberg, "Search" p. 240.

54. Mechanic, *Mental Health*, p. 58.

55. Mechanic, *Medical Sociology*, 473.

56. Phyllis Chesler, *Women and Madness*, (New York: Avon Books, 1972), p. 62.

57. Henry J. Steadman, "The Psychiatrist as a Conservative Agent of Social Control," *Social Problems* (Fall 1972), p. 269.

58. Ibid., pp. 263–64.

59. Allan Horwitz, "Social Networks and Pathways to Psychiatric Treatment," *Social Forces* (September 1977), p. 86.

60. Walter R. Gove and Patrick Howell, "Individual Resources and Mental Hospitalization: A Comparison and Evaluation of Societal Reaction and Psychiatric Perspectives," *America Sociological Review* (February 1974), p. 89.

61. Cockerham, *Medical Sociology*, p. 243.

62. Mechanic, *Mental Health*, p. 23.

63. Richard James Bord, "Rejection of the Mentally Ill: Continuities and Further Developments" *Social Problems* (Spring 1971), p. 507.

64. Frank, "Dynamics," p. 1717.

65. Cockerham, *Medical Sociology*, p. 246.

66. Mechanic, *Mental Health*, p. 125.

67. Ibid., p. 127.

68. Martin, *Mental Health*, p. 7.

69. Berger, Hamberg, and Hamberg, "Mental Health: Progress," p. 263.

70. Mechanic, *Mental Health*, p. 80.

71. Eisenberg,"Search," 240.

72. Ibid., p. 240.

73. Chesler, *Madness*, p. 121.

74. Clausen, "Mental Disorders," p. 116.

75. Walter R. Gove and Terry Fain, "The Length of Psychiatric Hospitalization," *Social Problems* (February 1975), p. 416.

76. Rushing and Esso, "Status Resources," p. 132.

77. Nathan and Harris, *Psychopathology*, pp. 45–46.

78. William Rushing, "Two Patterns in the Relationship between Social Class and Mental Hospitalization," *American Sociological Review* (August 1969), p. 533.

79. Gove and Howell, "Individual Resources," p. 91.

80. Clausen, "Mental Disorders," p. 113.

81. Mechanic, *Medical Sociology*, p. 27.

82. Erving Goffman, *Asylums* (New York: Doubleday, 1961), p. 361.

83. Ibid., p. viii.

84. Mechanic, *Mental Health*, pp. 88–9.

85. John F. Myles, "Institutionalization and Sick Identification among the Elderly," *American Sociological Review* (August 1978), p. 509.

86. Eaton, "Mental Hospitalization," p. 252.

87. J. K. Wing, "Institutionalization In Mental Hospitals," in *Mental Illness*, Scheff, p. 221.

88. Mechanic, *Medical Sociology*, p. 31.

89. Wing, "Institutionalization," p. 234.

90. Goffman, *Asylums*, p. 23.
91. Mechanic, *Mental Health*, p. 89.
92. Goffman, *Asylums*, p. 379.
93. Wing, "Institutionalization," p. 220.

SELECTED BIBLIOGRAPHY

Berger, Philip; Hamberg, Beatrix; and Hamberg, David.   "Mental Health: Progress and Problems." *Daedalus* (Winter 1977), pp. 261–76.
Bord, Richard James.   "Rejection of Mentally Ill: Continuities and Further Developments." *Social Problems* (Spring 1971), pp. 496–509.
Chesler, Phyllis.   *Woman and Madness.* New York: Avon Books, 1972.
Cockerham, William C.   *Medical Sociology.* Englewood Cliffs, N.J.: Prentice-Hall, 1978.
Gove, Walter R., and Fain, Terry.   "The Length of Psychiatric Hospitalization." *Social Problems* (February 1975), pp. 407–19.
Martin, Lealon E.   *Mental Health: Mental Illness.* New York: McGraw-Hill, 1970.
Mechanic, David.   *Medical Sociology,* 2d ed. New York: Free Press, 1978.
Nathan, Peter E., and Harris, Sandra L.   *Psychopathology and Society.* New York: McGraw-Hill, 1975.
Steadman, Henry J.   "The Psychiatrist as a Conservative Agent of Social Control." *Social Problems* (Fall 1972), pp. 263–71.

PART FIVE

Criminal Based Social Problems

Chapter 16

Juvenile Delinquency

The concern with juvenile delinquency is fairly old. This is because all societies have recognized that certain kinds of behavior are wrong because they are defined as harmful at least to some. Out of this protective view emerged the social concern with criminal norms and laws, and various means for protecting the innocent and punishing or trying to change the guilty. But early in the history of mankind there probably also developed the recognition that not all persons who did wrong could be defined and treated in the same way. Over the centuries one such variation related to the age of the individual wrongdoer, while others were related to his mental competence as determined by either mental ability or mental illness. The problem of age and individual responsibility has been confused during the transitional years between childhood and adulthood. In some primitive societies this was not a problem because they defined people as children, with few rights and obligations, until they reached a certain age and then defined them as adults if they passed the tests to which they was subjected at that time. In the United States it is the pattern that a child up until 10 or 12 years of age is defined as prerational and is not usually held responsible for his or her actions. For example, an 8-year-old child who kills someone is not held responsible. In most situations, by age 18 the individual is held responsible for what he does (assuming mental competence and in some cases an absence of mitigating circumstances). During the period of adolescence the individual is only partly responsible. Juvenile courts as well as various types of detention centers have been set up to work with those whose behavior is based on only partial individual responsibility.

EMERGENCE OF A DEFINITION

Up until about the 14th century in Europe the child was not seen as significantly different from the adult. Rather children were viewed as miniature adults and their world was not a special one of childhood but rather a version of the adult world. In general, children were not seen as very different or in need of special protection. Children took their chances with life from a very young age. In many European towns during the 17th and 18th centuries, children were found abandoned and dying on the streets, on doorsteps or in garbage dumps. Even the deliberate killing of infants was often viewed in about the same way many view abortion today.[1]

The literature of the Middle Ages and the Renaissance is full of assertions about the sexual abuse of children. For example, some people believed until as late as the 19th century that veneral disease could be cured by having intercourse with children. Furthermore, throughout the Middle Ages and as late as the 17th century children were involved in activities that if done today would define them as delinquents. To illustrate, as soon as they could talk children used obscene language and gestures. "Many engaged in sex at an early age, willingly or otherwise, they drank freely in taverns, if not at home; few of them ever went to school, and when they did, they wore sidearms, fermented brawls, and fought duels."[2]

In general in the early American colonies anyone over the age of fourteen was judged an adult, although some colonies made some exceptions. For example, in Pennsylvania, only those over the age of sixteen could be whipped for noncapital offenses. But there were some offenses that applied only to children—rebelliousness, disobedience, or playing on public streets. In some colonies the penalty for rebelliousness against the father was death.

Many children came to the colonies without any family. Large numbers of homeless children were rounded up in the cities of England and indentured to the colonies as workers. The purchase of black children as slaves was common in America until nearly through the 19th century.

The methods that were used to control children have almost always been severe and in general, obedience to the parents and other adults was valued highly. Harsh punishments were used to ensure that obedience. As La Mar T. Empey points out, a large percentage of the children living in the 18th century would by today's standards be considered battered children. The basic belief in rearing children was to control them through severe beatings. "Beating instruments included whips, heavy rods and cudgels, and the 'flapper'—a paddle with holes in it so that it would raise blisters. Beatings began in infancy and were a regular part of the child's life."[3]

Until the end of the 19th century the young offender was either seen as outside the law or treated as a criminal. Children under the age of 7 were believed to be incapable of criminal intent. But from 7 to 14 they were believed capable of intent and were subject to the same laws as adults.

Before the Civil War in America a few states had passed laws that required children to attend school and that prohibited those under 12 years of age from working. Laws also provided that the work day of a child over 12 was to be limited to 10 hours. "Although such laws were supposed to provide some protection for the young, they proved largely unworkable. Employers ignored them; many children worked rather than attending school; and parents even joined in circumventing the law."[4]

The first significant shift in the legal definitions of juvenile behavior occurred in 1870 in Boston where for the first time separate court hearings were held for juveniles. The last part of the 19th century was one of increasing protest against the continued confinement of children of all ages with adult criminals. Most of the outcry came from the Northern states because in the South the reformatory movement had never caught on. In the South, children continued to be tried as criminals and confined to harsh adult prisons.[5]

The first juvenile court was established in Cook County, Illinois in 1899. Within a few years most of the states had founded juvenile courts or some equivalent. New laws came into being specifying that those under 18 years of age were treated outside the criminal law. In general the purpose of criminal courts has been to administer justice and to see that offenders pay for their crimes. By contrast, juvenile courts were designed to "help children in trouble" and to "rehabilitate" them.

By the early 1900s there were large numbers being defined as delinquents and they were overwhelmingly males. The ratio at that time was about 50 males for every female juvenile delinquent. This was largely due to the much stronger social controls exerted over the lives of girls. Their lives were far more restricted than those of boys and the chances to be delinquent were not nearly as great.

Over space and time the behavior of adolescents has varied widely, as has the definition of that behavior. And some of the features of delinquency which are so pervasive in the United States and which have come to be taken for granted as inherent in the idea of delinquency may be absent in other cultures. It is probable that delinquent groups have different stresses in different societies and that those stresses could be related to differences in the various social systems of which the subcultures are a part. This also helps to emphasize the point that there is nothing inherent in an activity which makes it delinquent. Furthermore, our own society's definition of delinquency has varied over time. For example, school truancy was at one time defined as a more serious form of delinquency than is the case today. Or one of the most common types of delinquency today—the stealing of automobiles—did not exist 50 years ago.

But whatever specific acts are defined as delinquent, the general concept of delinquency has probably been close to universal. "In every society known to us, a certain number of minors have also been transgressors. And, when troubled by the delinquency in their midst, members of every society have sought to account for that phenomenon. The threat posed by 'ungovernable youth' has provoked a multitude of reactions and led to a variety of explanations."[6] Few areas of human behavior have been more extensively studied than that of delinquency. Part of the reason for this is that personal alarm competes with the economic cost. "In a culture where the cash nexus has much to do with shaping morals, 'experts' feel heavy pressure to find a remedy, cut the loss, declare war on crime, and stamp it out. Moral and financial accounts are to be settled simultaneously."[7]

High rates of juvenile delinquency appear to be a characteristic of industrialized societies. Not only are the rates high, but statistics from European nations, Japan, the United States, and those filtering out of Russia, China, and some of the developing nations suggest great increases during the 60s.[8] This is probably so because industrialization frees many of the young from the work force and also places high values on the possession of many material things.

Sociologically, any study of delinquents must start with the recognition that they in effect are "second-class citizens" because they have only partial rights in society. And most adolescents, whether delinquent or nondelinquent, often seek adult status with all the rights and privileges they see as going with that status. Adolescents, being neither children nor adults, and having few defined roles available to them in the overall culture, have created a loose cultural system to provide some role meanings for their adolescence. This means that there are certain conflict points with the dominant adult cultural system. And the inconsistency of adult definitions of adolescent behavior has also contributed to the emergence of various delinquent values. The very fact that the adult views the adolescent with indecision as to appropriate behavior means that the adolescent is treated one way on one occasion and a different way on another. Since adolescents often desire decisiveness and some precision in role definitions, they may try to create their own roles. When they do, they often demand a high degree of conformity by other adolescents as "proof" of the rightness of their definitions.

As a result of the vast amount of research, almost every social variable believed to have negative consequences has been linked to delinquency. In one sense the concern about delinquency becomes a rallying point around which one may aim at a variety of assumed causes. This means that often attention is directed at delinquency not so much because it is a problem in itself as because it is seen as the result of other problems of deviance that various groups are concerned about. For example, one may study the relationship of delinquency to broken homes because the delinquency is seen as further proof that broken homes are bad and the broken home is the area of deviance where the concern rests. This approach may also be found in studies attempting to causally link delinquency to poverty, racial conflict, and so forth.

One major difficulty in any study of delinquency is the various legal meanings of the term. The laws in the different states are very general and often quite vague. For example, in the state of Illinois a delinquent is described as an "incorrigible" growing up in "idleness," "loitering" in the streets at night without a proper excuse, or guilty of "indecent" or "lascivious" conduct. New Mexico, as another example, exceeds Illinois in vagueness by making "habitual" infraction a necessary condition for the definition of delinquency. Furthermore, delinquency does not refer only to crimes committed by juveniles, because the statutes are so broad that they allow juvenile authorities to assume control over all types of adolescents engaged in all kinds of misbehavior. In some cases the laws empower the juvenile court to take jurisdiction of adolescents who show vague conditions, such as "immorality," as well as of those who are involved in specific areas of misconduct.

In general, the legal definition of a juvenile delinquent is a person under 18 years of age who either commits an adult crime or transgresses into areas which society considers beyond his or her physical, mental, or moral capabilities.

Rates. In 1975 there were about 33 million juveniles in the United States between the ages of 10 and 17. During that same year there were about 1.7 million arrests. If each arrest represented one juvenile, the percentage of those arrested would be 5.1 percent. The rates of arrest vary by age. Delinquency is relatively low at age 10, but increases steadily thereafter, reaches its peak at age 16, and then, at age 17, begins to decline sharply.[9]

Juveniles are overrepresented in the population of all persons who are arrested for crimes. Persons under 18 years of age constitute less than 20 percent of the population but are arrested for 44 percent of the seven serious felonies that make up the FBI's Crime Index Offenses. (Criminal homicide, forcible rape, robbery, aggravated assault, burglarly, larceny-theft, and motor vehicle theft.) "Juveniles are arrested for 48 percent of all property crimes; 55 percent of the arrests for motor vehicles; 53 percent for burglary and 46 percent for larceny."[10] Juveniles are overrepresented among those who get arrested. When compared to older persons, they are more visible and less skillful in carrying out crimes.

It has been estimated that over one million delinquency cases, not counting traffic offenses, are handled by the juvenile courts in one year. But because some children appear in court more than once the actual number of individuals involved would be less. Only about three percent of all children between the ages of 10 and 17 appear in court. Actually less than half of those who are listed as court cases are actually tried in court. The rest of them are handled unofficially. Over the years there has been an increase in the number of delinquency cases reaching the court. For example, between 1960 and 1973 the number of delinquency cases increased from 510,000 to 1.14 million.[11]

The number of juveniles apprehended for delinquent charges are only a small part of all those who commit delinquent acts. Some indication of the overall rate of delinquent acts committed can be determined through self-report studies. All of those studies indicate that the amount of undetected law violation is great. It seems that almost all children by their own admission have broken the law at some time or another and sometimes repeatedly. Truancy and drinking would rank first, with anywhere from half to two thirds of all adolescents having committed them. Defying parents and fornication rank second.[12]

One study found that 88 percent of the teenagers in the sample confessed to committing at least one chargeable offense in the three years prior to being interviewed. But less than 3 percent of the offenses were detected by the police. "Only 22 percent of the youngsters ever had any contact with the police, only 9 percent in the three years prior to the survey; and less than 2 percent of the sample had ever been under judicial consideration."[13]

There are many adolescents in detention centers and in adult jails. It may be as many as one quarter of all juveniles are held in detention awaiting a court hearing. The National Council on Crime and Delinquency estimates that more than 100,000 children a year who have not been convicted of any crime are held in jails and detention centers.[14] There are a number of factors that enter into the decision of whether or not a juvenile will receive a sentence to correctional facilities. The evidence suggests that, along with prior record and seriousness of offense, social disadvantage, psychiatric disturbance, and family neglect also play key roles.[15]

Children under the age of 12 are less likely to be detained than are adolescents. Yet, in 1971, 3 percent of the nation's detention centers were holding children under 6 years of age; "9 percent were holding children from 6 to 8; and 43 percent of all detention centers were holding children from 9 to 11."[16] But many of the children are not delinquent. They are often placed in detention centers because they are neglected or abused and there are no other facilities for their care.

Delinquency is a social problem with little struggle between vested interest groups. Delinquency does not provide a profit for any business interests nor do other institutions want to gain control of detecting and detaining them. The vested interests are the legal agencies that deal with delinquency. This includes the police, the juvenile courts, and the various detention and control services. Around these vested interests have developed elaborate bureaucracies and one of their major interests is in acquiring as much of the public dollar as possible. These interests therefore stress the great amount of juvenile delinquency and the complex and costly means of dealing with it. We want to look in more detail at the police and the courts.

Police.   Regardless of the variety of vested interests, the real agent defining most delinquents is the police. Police come upon adolescents doing something that is against the law, and they must decide whether the lawbreaking youth should be treated as a "bad one" needing court attention or as a "good kid" who needs only a strong lecture. Other agencies may enter if the police define him as needing the attention of the court. For example, "someone must decide whether a youth should be sent to a training school or placed on probation. Someone must judge whether a training-school inmate should be turned loose on parole this week, next month, or at some other time." [17]

When police respond to delinquent actions, they are usually responding as more than just police. They are often responding as individuals who have strong moral values about what they feel to be correct adolescent behavior. Because many police come out of lower middle-class backgrounds, they usually believe that the adolescent should be seen and not heard, and this in itself may determine whether or not an arrest takes place. In general the police tend to see the adolescents they come in contact with as being of two general categories. First, there are those they see as "good kids" who do not usually cause any trouble, and second, there are the "troublemakers," who constitute most of the adolescent groups the police have contact with. The police may even make further distinctions. For example, among the good kids they may distinguish between the "quiet, studious kids who never cause any trouble" and the "good kids who cut up a little and need to be warned."

Joseph R. Gusfield observed that juveniles apprehended by the police received more lenient treatment, including dismissal, if they appeared contrite and remorseful about their violations than if they did not. "This difference in the posture of the deviant accounted for much of the differential treatment favoring middle-class 'youngsters' as against lower-class 'delinquents.' " [18] Marcia Garrett says that there

Wide World Photos

A policeman searching a teenager

is a good deal of evidence that police assess the delinquent potential of a boy by the image the boys project in their behavior. And often boys as a means of situational self defense will present a respectful and cooperative posture to the arresting officer.[19]

A number of other factors determine how the police will react to potential delinquents and how they will treat them. It has been suggested that other than the previous record of the youth the most important factor is his behavior toward the police. In the opinion of police themselves, the demeanor of apprehended juveniles was a major determinant of their decisions in about half of the juvenile cases they processed. The actual cues that the police used to decide the demeanor of the juvenile were quite simple. When juveniles were contrite about their wrongs, respectful to the police, and fearful of the sanctions that might be employed against them, they were usually seen by the police as basically law-abiding or at least "salvageable." By contrast youthful offenders who were fractious, obdurate, or who appeared nonchalant in their encounters with police were likely to be viewed as "would-be tough guys" or "punks" who deserved the most severe sanction—arrest.[20]

The animosity that police officers tended to show toward recalcitrant or aloof offenders appeared to come from two sources. The first was indifference about their transgressions. The second was the feeling that the youths did not accord the respect that the police believed they deserved. Because the police saw themselves as honestly and impartially performing a vital function that deserved respect from the community they often attributed the lack of respect shown them by the juveniles to the latter's immorality.[21]

There is evidence that many police respond to adolescents in terms of stereotypes. For example, compared to other youths, blacks and other boys whose appearance matches the delinquent stereotypes are more often stopped and interrogated by police. This occurs even when there is no evidence that an offense has been committed. Also, when arrested, boys fitting the stereotypes are usually given more severe dispositions for the same violations than those who do not fit the stereotypes.[22] Therefore, becoming a delinquent, like becoming a criminal, often depends on factors that may have little or nothing to do with the illegal act itself.

Garrett found that the arrest of some boys was related to the nature of the stereotype they seem to fit. He found that the police had a delinquent stereotype that involved elements of demeanor and appearance. For example, unkempt appearance, resentment, and lack of deference to authority were associated with an image of how a delinquent looked and acted.[23]

The courts. The philosophy of the juvenile court is that it should act in the best interests of the child. A major value has been that the court should act as parents should act. In theory "the focus in juvenile courts is on the future psychological, physical, emotional, and educational needs of children, as opposed to punishment for their past misdeeds."[24] In practice, according to Empey, the juvenile justice system functions like a large funnel by screening out significant numbers of individuals near the point of entry. "First the police screen out large numbers of the children they apprehend, and then the courts repeat the process with the remainder."[25]

TABLE 16–1

Actions At Intake By Type Of Offense Charged (Percentages) Among Delinquents

Type of offense	Dismiss	Action taken	
		Informal handling	Formal handling
Status	26	36	38
Misdemeanor	33	34	33
Property	39	34	35
Person	16	32	51

Source: Mark Creekmore, "Case Processing: Intake, Adjudication; and Disposition" in Rosemary Sarri and Yeheskel Hasenfeld. *Brought to Justice? Juveniles, the Courts, and the Law* (Ann Arbor: University of Michigan National Assessment of Juvenile Corrections, 1976), p. 127.

The statutes of the juvenile court usually start by defining a delinquent as one who has committed any act which, if it were committed by an adult, would be a crime. Most states go on to prohibit other behaviors including such things as incorrigibility. In practice the judge has great discretionary power with respect as to how juvenile proceedings are conducted and whether a child falls under the definition of being a delinquent. "The presumption is that the needs of the child, not the seriousness of offensive behavior, should determine disposition."[26] The dispositions handed down by the juvenile court, ranging from probation to institutionalization, are deprivations of freedom that a child experiences as punishment. Albert K. Cohen writes that neither the court nor anyone else knows enough about the causes and treatment of delinquent behavior to really diagnose and prescribe behavior. "Regardless of rhetoric or intentions, the juvenile court administers punishment."[27]

Naomi Feigelson Chase argues that where family courts do exist they fail to come to grips with the really serious juvenile crimes. A part of the history of the family court has been its inability to deal seriously with real problems. "The history of the child-welfare movement shows that punishment doesn't punish, that incarceration doesn't rehabilitate, and that social work, at least the kind we practice, is a failure, too."[28]

Causes of Juvenile Delinquency

We want to look at several theoretical attempts to explain the cause of at least some delinquency. The earliest sociological theories of delinquency came out of efforts to explain the characteristics and the spatial distribution of gangs in cities. "These, in turn, were related to research and speculation concerning structural and growth processes of cities and the influence of different, and sometimes conflicting, cultures in the American melting pot."[29] Ever since the publication of Shaw's famous studies, many American sociologists have argued that the most serious forms of male juvenile delinquency can be described as distinctively subcultural ways of life. During the same general period, Thrasher's work on gangs had a great influence. In essence Thrasher saw the delinquent subculture as the way of life that would be developed as a group became a gang. Thrasher saw crime and delinquency as being attractive to the boy who saw being a good boy as dull. They were attractive because one could be a hero in a fight. Fun, profit, glory, and freedom was a combination hard to beat, particularly for the inadequate conventional institutions that formed the competition.

Subcultures. Cohen examined what he called a delinquent subculture, which he saw as a system of beliefs and values brought about through the process of verbal interaction among young men in similar circumstances. Their circumstances were alike by virtue of their like positions in the social system, and the subculture constituted a solution to problems of adjustment for which the established culture provided no satisfactory solutions. The problems were for the most part problems of status and self-respect which arose among working-class children because of their inability to meet the standards and expectations of the established culture. The delinquent subculture, with its characteristics of nonutilitarianism, malice, and negativism, provided an alternative status system and justified, for those who participated in it, hostility and aggression against the source of their status frustration. Basically Cohen argued that many working-class boys were forced to develop the delinquent subculture as a way of recouping the self-esteem destroyed by the dominating institutions of the middle class. Rather than concentrate on the gang and its development over time, Cohen focused on the delinquent subcultures.[30]

David Matza also recognized that subculture is the central idea of the dominant sociological view of delinquency.[31] He suggested that the sociological theorists have a remarkably similar picture of the delinquent. That is, they see the individual as committed to delinquency because of his membership in a subculture that requires the breaking of laws. "The sociological delinquent is trapped by the accident of

An adolescent gang

Richard Younker

membership, just as his predecessors were trapped by the accident of hereditary defect or emotional disturbance. The delinquent has come a long way under the auspices of positive criminology. He has been transformed from a defective to a defector."[32]

Matza goes on to suggest that the subculture of delinquency is a delicately balanced set of precepts doubly dependent on extenuating circumstances. Both performing and abstaining from delinquent acts are approved only under certain conditions. Matza is saying that the delinquent subculture is really of two minds regarding delinquent actions, one which allows members to gain prestige by behaving illegally and another which shows the impact of conventional precepts of legal conformity. Matza believes that the subculture of delinquency is more dependent on and integrated into the conventional society than are most other deviant subcultures. Therefore, he says that the key to the analysis of the subculture of delinquency may be its high degree of integration into the wider society rather than its slight differentiation.[33]

A basic part of Matza's theory is the concept of neutralization. The concept suggests that modern legal systems recognize the conditions under which misdeeds may not be penally sanctioned, and that these conditions may be unknowingly duplicated, distorted, and extended in customary beliefs. So the delinquent's neutralization proceeds along the lines of the negation of responsibility, "the sense of injustice, the assertion of tort, and the primacy of custom."[34] The theory of neutralization is also an explicit denial of Cohen's thesis of a delinquent subculture. The neutralization view suggests that most delinquents are not following a different or subcultural set of norms. Rather, they are basically adhering to the conventional norms while accepting many justifications for deviance. Matza also introduces the concept of "subterranean values" to show that the values behind a large portion of juvenile delinquency are far less deviant than is commonly indicated. Subterranean analysis requires the exploration of connections between local deviant traditions in a subculture and a variety of traditions in conventional society. "Subterranean tradition may be defined by specification of key points along the range of support. It is deviant, which is to say that it is publicly denounced by authorized spokesmen. However, the tradition is viewed with ambivalence in the privacy of contemplation and in intimate publics by most conventional citizens."[35] The subterranean values are close to the old code of conduct for "gentlemen of leisure." There is high emphasis on daring and adventure, the rejection of disciplined work and labor, a desire to obtain things of luxury and prestige through the show of masculinity. It is only the form of expression that differs—the form being labeled 'delinquent.' In essence, it is not the values that are deviant but only the forms of expressing them.

Labeling.   In recent years one of the dominant positions in attempting to explain the emergence of self awareness as a delinquent has been through labeling theory. This view is that the juvenile is presented with social definitions of himself as a delinquent and that he often comes to accept those definitions. These influence both his self-image and his future behavior. So the individual becomes caught up in a delinquent role as a result of the new definition and expectations others have of him. "From this perspective, then, the operations of the social control system are instrumental to the movement of individuals from nondelinquent to delinquent self-images."[36]

This conceptual view argues that because he is being labeled and sanctioned by power and control agents of society, the juvenile will emerge with a "spoiled" or deviant public image. This negative image will make it very hard for him to maintain that he is not a delinquent. Stress is placed on who it is that defines the juvenile as delinquent and that a spoiled self image emerges if he is defined by power groups in society. Implied is the belief that a juvenile who engages in similar forms of behavior but does not come into contact with an official agency of social control "is not so abruptly, ceremoniously, and publicly cast into the category of deviant."[37]

The argument that official labeling by power groups in society will force a public identification as a delinquent by the individual is based on the assumption that official intervention publicizes the delinquent behavior. But even more important is that the public sanctions provide significant legitimation of the definition of the juvenile as delinquent. But many members of the public are unaware of the behavior or do not see the behavior as serious. Yet, they are assumed in labeling theory to take the official definition seriously and sanction the behavior as delinquent. Unless the individual has to deal directly with persons or agencies who take seriously his being a delinquent, it is questionable how much that definition will have meaning for him.

Many adolescents over time will accept the definition of being a delinquent. One study found variations by class, race, and social standing as to the impact of official labeling on the individual's self-evaluation as a delinquent. However, there was "a persistence for those who have been officially labeled as delinquent to think of themselves and to feel thought of by others as delinquent more often than those who have not been so labeled."[38] But as the authors go on to point out, alterations in a self-concept are not facile nor immediate but rather require the reorganization of a fairly fixed value structure in order to fit the newly acquired self-definition. "Such a reorganization takes time and, in the case of labeling theory, involves a move from a conforming to a delinquent orientation."[39] Prior to the change in self image there is a period of flux where the individual is losing old, conforming values and beginning to adopt the new, delinquent ones.

"Such a period represents a negative socialization, a moving away from a position of conformity into one of delinquency."[40]

The basic assumption in most of the literature on labeling theory and delinquency assumes that the individual perceives the degree and extent of his public identity and how it has been spoiled by the actions of legal authorities. The assumption is that ultimately the delinquent boy will realize it is no longer possible for him to maintain a public image of being a "good boy."[41]

One study found at the time of the disposition of their case only a small proportion of youths perceived any significant change in their interpersonal relationships with friends or family. In addition only a small proportion anticipated any difficulties in completeing school. About half expected increased police surveillance and felt that they may have endangered their chances to obtain desired employment in the future.[42] For these youths there was a minimal sense of "spoiled" identity in their interpersonal relationships but much more in their anticipated relationships with formal agencies.

Another study examined the relevance of how significant others' reactions to the juveniles affected them. In general, if the significant others negated or diminished the importance of the official sanction, the official intervention was weakened or totally avoided. There was a significant relationship between the juvenile's delinquent behavior and the attribution to the juvenile of a delinquent identity by each of his significant others. That is, the delinquent identification by the juvenile was significantly related to the delinquent identification of the juvenile by mother, father, and friend.[43] This study also found that the juvenile had already come to an identification of self as delinquent before the arrest. The official labeling was not necessary to produce a deviant self-identity. The juvenile had already acquired a spoiled identity.[44]

The actors in areas of social problems like all actors achieve a sense of self through social definitions. To a great extent the power of the definers make a great deal of difference in how the person and related others accepted as significant the "spoiled identity." When the courts say a juvenile is a delinquent, related institutions such as the schools accept that definition. As a result their treatment of the individual may be within that context. However, the individual's or his friends' acceptance of his definition as a delinquent may be a different matter. He can be negatively affected by the definition and have a real sense of spoiled identity. However, there are other possibilities—he may be indifferent to the definitions or may actually find them positive for his self image. Labeling does not always have the negative consequences that are generally assumed.

Institutionalization of Delinquency

From the previous discussion it can be seen that in many respects delinquency has become institutionalized in American society. This is effected especially through the legal procedures of the police and the courts. In this section we want to look at the institutionalized relationships of delinquency and other institutions of society.

Family. Many attempts have been made to associate delinquency with family factors. The most common variable studied has been that of the broken home. In part this has been a reflection of the "sacred" view of the family, which assumes that any disturbance of the family leads to all kinds of problems for the children. Often in the past the purpose of such studies has been to make a moral point rather than to shed any objective light on the relationship. However, in recent years there have been some studies that show relationships between delinquency and the broken home.

Roland J. Chilton and Gerald E. Markle found that proportionately more children who come into contact with police agencies as well as juvenile courts on delinquency charges live in disrupted families than do children in the general population. "In addition, the study suggests that children charged with more serious misconduct more often come from incomplete families than children charged with less serious delinquency."[45] Another study found that among female delinquents those from single parent or totally broken homes were more likely to be confined when they had one prior offense than those who had a comparable offense record but were fom intact homes."[46]

Studies also show relationships between how parents treat their children and the probability of delinquency. Gary F. Jensen found that "the neutral or isolated child is more likely to be a delinquent than the child who is loved by and attached to his parents even when delinquent patterns 'outside the home' are scarce or absent."[47] Viewing the relationship from another perspective, researchers have found that the parents of delinquent boys are more sanctioning of antisocial behavior than are the parents of nondelinquent boys. In this study mothers of delinquent boys were seen by their sons as highly sanctioning. The mothers sanctioned delinquency by their antisocial expectations, their insistent discipline, and a cold hostile attitude. "Fathers sanctioned delinquency by their insistent discipline, and by serving as antisocial models."[48]

Foster and his co-workers found that the delinquent youths they interviewed did not feel that their contact with a law enforcement agency had resulted in any significant social liability in terms of interpersonal relationships. They did not perceive any negative effects whatever on the attitudes of their friends toward them. The boys felt that their parents had relatively fixed opinions of them which were developed before they got into trouble. "The parents appear to expect their boys to get into trouble. Likewise, the parents who consider their children basically good continue to believe so despite what happened with the police."[49]

Religion. Religious values and institutions have traditionally been seen as the antithesis of all kinds of "badness"—including delinquency. A part of the American stereotype sees the boy who goes to church and participates in religious activities as a good boy. Frequently various types of religious therapy and orientation have been used as means for dealing with delinquency. Yet, it is also clear that often those who get in trouble also appear to be religiously active. Therefore, the question of the relationship between religious involvement and delinquent behavior may be raised.

A study of high school students found that those who often attended church were slightly more likely than infrequent attenders to express respect for the police, and were slightly less likely to agree that law violation was all right if you did not get caught. But this study also found that students who believed in the devil and in a life after death were just as likely to commit delinquent acts as were students who did not hold these beliefs. And students who attended church every week were just as likely to commit delinquent acts as were students who attended church rarely or not at all.[50] The authors conclude that the church is "irrelevant to delinquency because it fails to instill in its members love for their neighbors and because belief in the possibility of pleasure and pain in another world cannot now, and perhaps never could, compete with the pleasures and pains of everyday life."[51] Another study found that for white males, nonwhite males, and white females there was a moderate positive relationship between church attendance and one's respect for the juvenile court system.[52]

Schools. The high school years are the years in which delinquency is most apt to occur. The high school is crucial if for no other reason than that it has control over the adolescent for so many hours of the day. It brings the young together for functions that extend far beyond those of the formal school system. Undoubtedly a great deal of delinquency either occurs in the school or is planned there. Furthermore, various types of delinquent acts are specifically related to the school, for example, truancy and school vandalism. And other, more general delinquent acts, such as assault, intimidation, shakedowns, rapes, and so forth, often occur within the school.

Almost all high schools operate on the basis of such middle-class values as deferred gratification, interpersonal courtesy, respect for the individual and property, and hard work. But for many high school students those values are of no importance, and they are in high school only because they must remain there until they are old enough to legally quit. For many of these young people the attractions of life are outside the school. Studying so as to get a good job is not even a part of the real world many young boys know. What is prestigeful and important to them are the lower-class values of toughness and immediate, hedonistic pleasures. Therefore, for many lower-class boys, both black and white, the future world implied in the high school system is meaningless and seems to stand in the way of the immediate pleasures and status symbols that are important to them. In most cases it is lower-class students whom the school defines as troublemakers because from the school's point of view they go against the school's values and norms most often.

Those students who are defined as delinquent by the schools are also defined as such by the police. In fact, when the police officially define a student as delinquent, the school often defines him the same way and at the same time. The "official" delinquent is seen by the school as "disruptive" and as being bad for its reputation. So contacts between the adolescent, the police, and the school will have major significance for the adolescent's career as a delinquent within the school system.

Another way in which the school sees itself as combating delinquency is through athletic programs. The assumption seems to be that physical prowess and high energy can be channeled from delinquent acts into organized athletics. And one study did find that there were fewer delinquents among athletes than among nonathletes. The study found that the association was most marked among boys who were blue-collar low achievers; that is, boys who came out of the lower middle class and were not successful in school often became either delinquents or athletes. There is a possibility that athletics attracts the most conforming types of boys. "Stated differently, the negative relationship between athletic participation and delinquency may not be the result of the deterrent influence of athletics at all, but rather to selection of conformers into the athletic program."[53] Organized sports in the United States not only place great stress on *conformity* but also tend to stress conservative, traditional values. The players are constantly told that what matters is the team's winning and not the individual performance. But they learn that one gains far more by being a star on a mediocre team than by being a mediocre player on a great team. Athletes will usually accept extremely authoritarian control by the coaches not only over their athletic activities but often over many other aspects of their lives. Given these considerations, it may be that those boys who choose sports over a delinquent career may have qualities that allow them to be severely controlled and regimented.

Social class.   For the most part the discussion in this chapter has centered on delinquency in the lower-middle and lower classes. Most of the studies of the past have seen delinquency as rooted primarily in the lower class. In recent years there has emerged a strong awareness that delinquency in the middle class is much greater than has generally been recognized. But to say this is not the same as to say that delinquency arrests are as high in the middle class as in the lower class. One obvious reason is that the middle-class young person has less need for some delinquency because he has many more material possessions; for example, he is more apt to have legal access to a car.

Most of the studies in recent years investigating undetected delinquency seriously question the traditional beliefs about delinquency being much more common within the lower class. The studies suggest that the relation between social class and law abiding behavior is either small or nonexistent. In general, it appears that children from the various social classes are more alike than different.[54] Garrett writes that self-report studies demonstrate that delinquent behavior is more evenly distributed over the social classes than official statistics indicate. However, "studies of victimization suggest that more serious traditional crime occurs more frequently in the lower class than in middle- or upper-class residential areas."[55]

Garret also found differences by social class in some of the violations of delinquents. He found that beer and liquor violations, curfew violations and male-female sex relations were characteristic of boys from all social classes. "However, lower-class boys are expected to be slightly more involved in these as well as other offenses than are other boys. For most violations, middle-class boys are seen as less delinquent than those from working-class backgrounds."[56] One researcher points out that delinquency creates for many slum youth something called a "mobility trap." During childhood and early adolescence the boys are able to feel like "big shots." But later delinquency records and school problems that usually occur reduce their status opportunities regardless of ability. In time the delinquent behavior may also be a trap, in part because of strong sanctions against those who persistently violate felony laws, and partly because persistent heavy opiate usage and desperate hustling, create eventual physical debilitation in many cases.[57]

Female delinquency. The delinquency of girls has always been less in number and in severity than that of boys. The sex of the individual has a great deal to say about the direction of their behavior. And like most significant areas of life where there are different sex roles, this is also true with delinquency. The psychological and sociological worlds associated with sex roles have historically offered wide differences in the potential for delinquency.

There has not been much research into female delinquency when compared with studies made of male delinquency. This has been true because there has been much less interest in female delinquency and because female delinquency is believed to be a minor problem as compared to male delinquency. In part this view is justified, because the number of male delinquents is far greater than that of female delinquents. In recent years the ratio of boys to girls appearing in juvenile courts has been about four to one. However, sex ratios vary by different types of delinquency. Boys tend overwhelmingly to be arrested on charges involving stealing and mischief of one sort or another, "while girls are typically brought before the court for *sex offenses* and for *'running away,' 'incorrigibility,'* and *'delinquent tendencies,'* which are often euphemisms for problems of sex behavior."[58] This means that most of the girls who are defined as delinquent are so defined because of their moral behavior rather than for legal reasons. For most of them their wrong is that they are sexually promiscuous by society's moral standards for girls.

The most common arrest for girls is for larceny (13 percent), but that figure is well behind the rate for boys (33 percent). The arrests made for traditional serious crimes are still predominantly male, typically young males, not females. There is only one offense, running away, where girls (57 percent) are arrested more frequently than boys (43 percent). This difference may be due at least in part to the traditional double standard where society and the police are more concerned with unsupervised girls than unsupervised boys. Looking at the overall picture, in 1975, arrests of females at all ages constituted only about 16 percent of all arrests in the United States.[59]

There seems to be some evidence that when girls are a part of a delinquent subculture, they are in a male subculture. When this happens, a girl is largely dependent for her status on the boy with whom she is identified. However, in some instances delinquent girls do develop a separate subcultural group. This may be for the purpose of sexual activities, drug addiction, or as counterparts of the male gangs. In general when girls are involved in delinquent subcultures, their activities are as varied as those of any male member. James F. Short, Jr., found that drug-using girls seem especially caught up in a vicious cycle of unsatisfactory interpersonal relations. But even the drug nonusers "appear to be swept along by limited social and other abilities, and experience which limits opportunities to acquire those skills or to exercise them is acquired."[60] Girls in the lower class generally have low status in social activities which are important to boys. This is a reflection of a male-dominant view of the sexes. So the girl in the delinquent boys' gang has a second-class membership and has little direct influence on activities defined as important by the male members. Cohen has argued that the subculture of the boys' delinquent gangs is really inappropriate for the adjustment problems of lower-class girls. At best this subculture is "irrelevant to the vindication of the girl's status as a girl, and at worst because it positively threatens her in that status in consequence of its strongly masculine symbolic

Luis Medina

A juvenile girl and a male gang

function."[61] It would appear that most girls who become a part of the boys' delinquent gangs do so because they are willing to accept second-class membership. It would also seem that when delinquent girls do violate the norms of society, it is not because of ignorance of or hostility to the norms. Rather they are motivated toward deviance because they want to maintain status within the subculture.

Freda Adler argues that the female gang member entered the gang gradually, and at first she was peripheral to the male-centered gang activity. Sex was, of course, offered and accepted, as were drugs, but her activity in that role was incidental to the main operations.[62] She goes on to say that by the mid-1960s the police were reporting an increase in arrests of girls for being gang lookouts, carrying weapons, and generally aiding in gang warfare. "By the 1970s, girls had become more highly integrated in male gang activity and were moving closer to parallel but independent, violence-oriented, exclusively female groups."[63]

One researcher suggests that one important difference between the delinquent female and her male counterpart is related to the extent to which girls possess resources that they may manipulate for their own ends in the adult world. "Specifically, adolescent females are more than capable of competing successfully with adult females through the use of promise of sexual rewards."[64] The adolescent boy has little of value, whether morally or legally acceptable, to the broader society. But what the adolescent girl has is prized by many adults, though legally and morally prohibited. She is therefore in the position of being wanted, and knowing this she can negotiate other ends that are desirable to her.

At the same time the female has more freedom to pursue some activities that are not legally available to the male. For example, the adolescent female who is not old enough to drive can get an older male to take her places. By contrast the adolescent male restricted to his age peers may often steal a car. It may also be easier for the adolescent girl to drink illegally when with an older male. In general the adolescent girl has more social agencies helping her satisfy many of her needs than does the adolescent boy.

As indicated, almost all discussion of female delinquency stresses its sexual nature but says little about other aspects. There is little data on what the delinquency of the female delinquent actually consists of, except that it usually involves sexual misconduct of some kind. Whatever other delinquent aspects of her life there might be are generally overlooked. But it does appear that sexual delinquency is often used by her as a form of bargaining and even social control. One important research question might be: If one put aside all female delinquency directly and indirectly related to sexual activity, what would be left? It might be that the findings would show that generally female delinquency *is* really sexual delinquency. If this is true then it is possible that the rates of female delinquency will decrease if the degree of premarital sexual freedom continues to increase and what is seen as sexual deviance continues to decrease. On the other hand, one might also speculate that as boys and girls become more alike in their behavior patterns more girls will become delinquent in areas usually associated with males, such as physical aggression, truancy, stealing, and so forth. This would be consistent with the argument that as females achieve greater equality with males, this will be reflected in all areas including deviance and social problems.

Adler suggests that the movement for greater female equality may be having a twofold influence on female juvenile crimes. First, girls are more involved in drinking, stealing, gang activity, and fighting. These are behaviors traditionally associated with the male role. Second, there are increases in the total numbers of female deviance. The departure from the safety of traditional female roles and the testing of uncertain alternative roles coincide "with the turmoil of adolescence creating criminolgenic risk factors which are bound to create this increase. Between 1960 and 1972 national arrests for major crimes showed a jump for boys of 82 percent and for girls, 306 percent."[65]

The process whereby the girl gets arrested and brought to the courts is somewhat different from that of boys. For example, whereas the law enforcement agencies apprehend the majority of delinquent boys, a much greater percentage of delinquent girls are brought to court by referral from schools, social agencies, and relatives. Etta A. Anderson points out that female criminals and delinquent girls often receive "chivalrous treatment." They are given special "protection" but that often really means they receive harsher treatment than males. The feeling of law enforcement and court persons was that the female delinquent needed to be detained for her own safety and well-being. "Perhaps the best documented fact concerning the 'protective' treatment of delinquent girls is that they are detained and institutionalized for status offenses much more frequently than boys."[66]

TABLE 16–2

Estimated Number and Percent Distribution of Delinquency Cases Disposed by Juvenile Courts, by Sex, United States, 1958–1974

Year	Boys		Girls	
	Number	*Percent*	*Number*	*Percent*
1958	383,000	81	87,000	19
1962	450,000	81	104,500	19
1966	593,000	80	152,000	20
1970	799,000	76	252,000	24
1974	927,000	74	325,700	26

Source: National Center for Juvenile Justice, *Juvenile Court Statistics, 1974* (Pittsburgh: National Council of Juvenile Court Judges, 1977), p. 14.

The ratio of boys to girls appearing before juvenile courts has dropped to about 4 to 1. This may be the lowest ratio of any country and the figure represents a decrease from the 50 to 1 ratios early in the century. There is also some evidence that when girls receive sentences they serve longer periods of time. In one study, some of the reasons given by the staff for keeping girls incarcerated included the ideas that girls need to be "kept occupied" and they may not be able to "resist temptation" if released. It is also the practice of juvenile courts and detention homes to force females to undergo pelvic examinations and submit to extensive questioning about their sexual activities—regardless of the offense with which the girl is charged."[67]

In conclusion, regardless of the social class level of delinquents most of them grow up and leave their delinquency behind. It is important to recognize that delinquency, unlike many other forms of deviance, is restricted to an age range. While a boy might become a homosexual, a drug addict, an alcoholic, and so forth during adolescence and remain that type of deviant for the rest of his life, he cannot remain a delinquent. When he reaches his early adult years he can enter the straight world or the deviant one of criminality. It may be that some of the forces that make delinquency attractive to some adolescents are the very forces that contribute to their wanting to leave the delinquent subculture. The delinquent subculture often gives the boy the sense of being an adult—something he very much wants. But when he becomes an adult, he no longer needs the subculture for that status and in fact may find that continuing in it will cost him something in his newly achieved adult recognition.

Juvenile delinquency is clearly recognized as a social problem in the United States. There have been changes over time in defining kinds and groups involved in delinquency, for example, the historical pattern of limiting delinquency mostly to the lower class and to males. There is some disagreement among social agencies on how to deal with delinquency, but the difference is mainly in style rather than substance. There are also clear and well established bureaucratic structures such as the police, the courts, and the detention facilities which deal with delinquency.

Over the years there has been a somewhat changing definition of juvenile delinquency. In the United States the laws are often vague and contradictory from one state to another. The police play a crucial role in what behavior will be defined as delinquent and whether or not the individual will be apprehended. The juvenile courts are set up as courts of equity to deal with the lesser responsibility expected of adolescents as compared to adults. There are several different schools of thought in attempting to explain the causes of delinquency. The delinquency rates of girls have always been much lower than those of boys but the difference has shown some decrease in recent years.

NOTES

1. LaMar T. Empey, *American Delinquency* (Homewood, Ill.: Dorsey Press, 1978), p. 28.

2. Ibid., p. 71.

3. Ibid., p. 41.

4. Ibid., p. 88.

5. Ibid., p. 90.

6. Bernard Rosenberg and Harry Silverstein, *The Varieties of Delinquent Experience* (Waltham, Mass.: Blaisdell, 1969), p. 3.

7. Ibid., p. 4.

8. Freda Adler, *Sisters in Crime* (New York: McGraw-Hill, 1975), p. 87.

9. Empey, *Delinquency*, p. 131.

10. Ibid., p. 123.

11. Ibid., p. 118.

12. Ibid., p. 147.

13. Jay R. Williams and Martin Gold, "From Delinquent Behavior to Official Delinquency," *Social Problems* (Fall 1972), p. 213.

14. Naomi Feigelson Chase, *A Child Is Being Beaten* (New York: McGraw-Hill, 1976), p. 158.

15. Empey, *Delinquency*, p. 459.

16. Ibid., p. 466.

17. Peter G. Garabedian and Don C. Gibbons, *Becoming Delinquent* (Chicago: Aldine, 1970), p. 4.

18. Joseph R. Gusfield, "Moral Passage: The Symbolic Process in Public Designations of Deviance," *Social Problems* (Fall 1967), p. 179.

19. Marcia Garrett and James F. Short, Jr., "Social Class and Delinquency: Predictions and Outcomes of Police-Juvenile Encounters," *Social Problems* (February 1975), p. 381.

20. Irving Piliavin and Scott Briar, "Police Encounters with Juveniles," in *Deviance: The Interactionist Perspective* by Earl Rubington and Martin S. Weinberg, (New York: Macmillan, 1968), p. 145.

21. Ibid., p. 142.

22. Ibid., p. 143.

23. Garrett and Short, "Social Class," p. 369.

24. Charles Zastrow, *Introduction to Social Welfare Institutions* (Homewood, Ill.: Dorsey Press, 1978), p. 195.

25. Empey, *Delinquency*, p. 120.

26. Albert K. Cohen and James F. Short, Jr., "Crime and Juvenile Delinquency," in *Contemporary Social Problems*, 4th ed., by Robert K. Merton and Robert Nisbet, (New York: Harcourt Brace Jovanovich, 1976), p. 51.

27. Ibid., p. 51.

28. Chase, *Child Beaten*, p. 139.

29. James F. Short, Jr., *Gang Delinquency and Delinquent Subcultures* (New York: Harper & Row, 1968), p. 133.

30. David J. Bordua, "Delinquent Subcultures: Sociological Interpretations of Gang Delinquency," in *Deviant Behavior and Social Process* by William A. Rushing, (Chicago: Rand McNally, 1969), p. 28.

31. David Matza, *Delinquency and Drift* (New York: Wiley, 1964), p. 21.

32. Ibid., p. 60.

33. Ibid., p. 61.

34. Ibid., p. 64.

35. Suzanne S. Ageton and Delbert S. Elliott, "The Effects of Legal Processing on Delinquent Orientations," *Social Problems* (October 1974), p. 88.

36. John R. Hepburn, "Official Deviance and Spoiled Identity," *Pacific Sociological Review* (April 1977), p. 163.

37. Ageton and Elliott, "Legal Processing," p. 88.

38. Ibid., p. 88.

39. Ibid., p. 89.

40. Jack Donald Foster, Simon Dinitz, and Walter C. Reckless, "Perceptions of Stigma Following Public Intervention for Delinquent Behavior," *Social Problems* (Fall 1972), p. 203.

41. Ibid., p. 207.

42. Hepburn, "Official Deviance," p. 170.

43. Ibid., p. 175.

44. Roland J. Chilton and Gerald E. Markle, "Family Disruption, Delinquent Conduct, and the Effect of Subclassification," *American Sociological Review* (February 1972), p. 98.

45. Charles W. Thomas, "The Effect of Social Characteristics on Juvenile Court Dispositions," *The Sociological Quarterly* (Spring 1977), p. 248.

46. Gary F. Jensen, "Parents, Peers, and Delinquent Action: A Test of Differential Association Perspective," *American Journal of Sociology* (November 1972), p. 244.

47. Curt Gallenkamp, "Parents and Their Delinquent Sons," *Dissertation Abstracts* 29 (1968), p. 3085.

48. Foster, et al., "Perceptions," p. 204.

49. Trovis Hirschi and Rodney Stark, "Hellfire and Delinquency," *Social Problems* (Fall 1969), p. 207.

50. Ibid., p. 213.

51. Paul C. Higgins and Gary L. Albrecht, "Hellfire and Delinquency Revisited," *Social Forces* (June 1977), p. 956.

52. Walter E. Schafer, "Participating in Interscholastics and Delinquency: A Preliminary Study," *Social Problems* (Summer 1969), p. 47.

53. Empey, *Delinquency*, p. 155.

54. Garrett and Short, "Social Class," p. 368.

55. Ibid., p. 372.

56. Daniel Glaser, Bernard Lander, and William Abbott, "Opiate Addicted and Non-Addicted Siblings in a Slum Area," *Social Problems* (Spring 1971), p. 520.

57. Cohen and Short, "Crime," p. 86.

58. Empey, *Delinquency*, p. 125.

59. Short, *Gang Delinquency*, p. 6.

60. Albert K. Cohen, *Delinquent Boys* (Glencoe, Ill.: Free Press, 1955), pp. 143–44.

61. Adler, *Sisters*, p. 98.

62. Ibid., p. 99.

63. Gerald Marwell, "Adolescent Powerlessness and Delinquent Behavior," in Rushing, *Deviant Behavior*, p. 43.

64. Adler, *Sisters*, p. 95.

65. Empey, *Delinquency*, p. 354.

66. Etta A. Anderson, "The 'Chivalrous' Treatment of the Female Offender in the Arms of the Criminal Justice System: A Review of the Literature," *Social Problems* (February 1976), p. 353.

67. Ibid., p. 353.

SELECTED BIBLIOGRAPHY

Ageton, Suzanne S., and Elliott, Delbert S. "The Effects of Legal Processing on Delinquent Orientations." *Social Problems* (October 1974), pp. 87–99.

Anderson, Etta A. "The 'Chivalrous' Treatment of the Female Offender in the Arms of the Criminal Justice System: A Review of the Literature." *Social Problems* (February 1976), pp. 350–55.

Empey, LaMar T. *American Delinquency*. Homewood, Ill.: Dorsey Press, 1978.

Foster, Jack Donald; Dinitz, Simon; and Reckless, Walter C. "Perceptions of Stigma Following Public Intervention for Delinquent Behavior." *Social Problems* (Fall 1972), pp. 202–9.

Garabedian, Peter G., and Gibbons, Don C. *Becoming Delinquent*. Chicago: Aldine, 1970.

Garrett, Marcia, and Short, James F., Jr. "Social Class and Delinquency: Predictions and Outcomes of Police-Juvenile Encounters." *Social Problems* (February 1975), pp. 368–81.

Hepburn, John R. "Official Deviance and Spoiled Identity." *Pacific Sociological Review* (April 1977), pp. 163–79.

Higgins, Paul C., and Albrecht, Gary L. "Hellfire and Delinquency Revisited." *Social Forces* (June 1977), pp. 952–57.

Thomas, Charles W. "The Effect of Social Characteristics on Juvenile Court Dispositions." *Sociological Quarterly* (Spring 1977), pp. 952–57.

Williams, Jay R., and Gold, Martin. "From Delinquent Behavior to Official Delinquency." *Social Problems* (Fall 1972), pp. 209–28.

Chapter 17

Crime

Crime is a concept which is created with the existence of laws. When a law is passed and its breach is defined as a criminal offense, the possibility of crime develops. In our society there are two major categories of law: criminal law and civil law. In this chapter we shall be dealing with offenses under criminal law. (Civil law concerns noncriminal acts in which the state performs as arbitrator between the parties.) Criminal law prohibits certain acts and sets forth punishments for violators. People who commit these acts and are charged with the offense face the common legal process under criminal law: arrest, trial, and (if convicted) punishment. There are two components of a criminal act: (1) a commitment of the proscribed act and (2) a response of the legal system.

In all societies some kinds of behavior have been defined as crimes. Even in preliterate societies certain kinds of behavior violated the accepted beliefs as to appropriate behavior. The evidence has been that all societies have found it necessary to control certain kinds of behavior. "Serious violations of the law are universally understood and are, therefore, in that sense, intrinsically criminal."[1] In all societies it has been a crime of some magnitude to kill another person although there have been great variations in the punishment of killing and in situational factors which would mitigate the offenses.

The development of a written language allowed for the codification of laws. This meant that right and wrong, punishment and permissiveness and the degree of social vengeance became more specific and understood. Over time many laws have been created and have become a part of the code. Many times laws lose their significance for a society and rather than being repealed continue on the books. They may not be applied but they are there for some possible future time.

At any given time a very small portion of the laws may actually be in use.

Laws give predictability to society and allow for order among its members. The laws, along with informal rules of conduct such as norms, allow people to anticipate what they should do and what can generally be expected of others. For example, traffic laws allow us to feel reasonably confident about which side of the street people will drive along, on what color light they will stop and go, and at what speed they will drive. In other words, laws give order to what would otherwise be complete anarchy. Laws also give order to proper conduct and persons are often controlled because of the fear of what might happen if they do not conform. In this sense law serves as a deterrent. Of course, no laws function as a deterrent for all people. And sometimes laws have effects that extend beyond their legislative intent. Laws may generate crime. For example, laws against the legal sale of drugs lead to illegal sales and to other illegal acts committed to get money to buy the illegal drugs.

Regardless of the laws that exist on the books the most important aspect of laws is the way they are enforced. Laws can be passed for a variety of reasons. While they may be designed to control specific behavior, they may also be enacted for moral reasons. Many laws against sexual behavior are seen as moral deterrents and are expected to get people to change their values and to conform. As we shall see, the laws that are enforced tell us a lot about the bases and distribution of power in society. The power to define and enforce definitions of right and wrong is held by specific elite groups in society.

THE EMERGENCE OF A DEFINITION

The laws of the land define a wide variety of human actions as criminal. But these vary widely in significance and social concern. Over time in the United States, there has been an emergence of new and stronger definitions of crime as well as a decreasing concern in some areas. In general, social concern has remained high toward such crimes as assault, murder, and rape. Where there has been an increasing concern with crimes, it has often been in the economic area, for example, embezzlement and fraud. These activities have been threatening to some persons in power, and therefore the laws have been tightened. However, there are many activities which are also crimes but to which power groups pay little attention. Such is the case in the areas of white-collar crime which does not threaten power groups.

The vested interests of society play a major role in defining the significance of crime. Economic interests often overlap with political ones, so that graft and political corruption continues to be a major source of criminal activity but little is done about it. The ability of the power groups to take care of themselves is no better illustrated than in the Watergate scandals where there were few convictions and even those persons convicted received minor punishments.

Another area of shifting definitions of crime is morality. The power block of persons who once had a great amount of influence over legislated morality has been reduced. This reduction is reflected in the diminished influence of organized religion in legislative action concerning behavior the religious groups believe to be morally wrong. The laws have been eased, or even eliminated, in such traditionally moral areas as abortion, nonaddictive drug use, sexual rights among consenting adults, no-fault divorce and so forth.

Crime rates. People have an interest in the extent to which members of society abide by their laws. They are often concerned with the rates of violation at a given time and in the change in the rates over time. There are various ways of looking at crime in a society. For example, it is possible to focus on crimes as committed acts or on persons who commit the crimes, the criminals.

All acts defined as violations of laws do not have the same chance of being discovered when committed. The characteristics of acts influence whether or not the behavior is discovered, reported, or recorded. Some offenses are more likely to be discovered than others. For example, street crimes are more apt to be uncovered than white-collar crime. Or if there is a victim the crime is more apt to come to the attention of authorities than if there is not. "Victimless activities, e.g., prostitution and gambling, are less likely to come to official notice."[2]

In any official crime statistics there are limitations since a great deal of crime is never reported. Those crimes that are really successful are never heard of. The old cliché that there is "no such thing as a perfect crime" is not true. Furthermore, there may be an unwillingness to prosecute. Many embezzlements are covered up and don't get on the records. And much of all reported crime remains unsolved. In fact, the number of arrests that are made may have little to do with how much crime is being committed.

Reported criminal statistics describe a process and the reported rates may stop at various stages along the way. Criminal statistics tell about complaints received which are crimes known to the police. Figures may refer to persons arrested or prosecuted for various crimes. The figures describe officially defined groups but not the total number of people who have committed acts defined as criminal. "Much crime is not discovered; if discovered, not reported; if reported, not recorded. Different kinds of offenders and offenses have different but largely unknown probabilities of becoming officially known."[3]

The notion of whether or not there is a crime problem derives from criminal statistics. Spector found that the evidence for a crime

A bank robber in lower Manhattan

problem was not that there was a high rate of crime or that the rate was higher than it had been. Rather, the evidence was that there were many individuals and groups complaining about various aspects of crime. The so-called "crime problem" as a social problem "is generated and sustained by the activities of complaining groups and institutional responses to them."[4]

The most commonly used statistics are the Uniform Crime Reports published annually by the Federal Bureau of Investigation (FBI). The reports rely on statistics submitted by each state and from every city with a population over 10,000. These statistics are submitted by the local police and do not report all crimes. The rise in reported crimes can mean several things and are often misleading. But even with their limitations they are the best statistics available.

It appears that political and social organization in police departments affect the number of crimes reported to the FBI. For example, when reformers take office there is often a dramatic increase in the crime rate. This is because crimes previously ignored are recorded and the police more actively seek out crime and make arrests. But usually as the new reform administration settles into office the reported crime rate drops off. The drop in crime demonstrates to the voter that the new officials have been effective. "The amount of crime reported to the FBI is also influenced by the professionalism and the fiscal resources of police departments."[5]

There are a variety of reasons as to why people do not report crime. Sometimes the offender is related or is a friend and the victim does not want to press charges. Sometimes the victims are afraid the police will find something out about them. On other occasions crimes are so trivial they are not worth the time and effort of appearing in court. The seriousness of an offense is one of the most important factors in whether or not a crime will be reported. Crimes involving the use of weapons or where there is extensive personal injury are reported more often than those in which weapons were not used or which involved minor injury. Once the police respond, their decision to file a report is influenced by the seriousness of the complaint, "the complainant's preference for police action, deference toward police, social status, and the relational differences between complaint and subject."[6]

It is clear that the FBI statistics underrepresent the extent of crime. There are other sources of information about crimes. For example, victimization surveys and anonymous questionnaires give a picture of the amount and distribution of crime that is quite different from the official statistics. And the official crime rates show little or nothing about the actual behavior from which the rates are constructed. A robbery may be listed as an event but tells nothing about the nature of the persons or the circumstances under which it occurred.

Recognizing the limitations of the available crime statistics, what can be said about crimes? The National Criminal Information Center estimated for a given year that there were approximately 37 million

TABLE 17–1

Estimated Occurrence of Crimes by Time in the United States

Serious crimes	19 each minute
Larceny—theft	1 every 6 seconds
Burglary	1 every 10 seconds
Auto theft	1 every 32 seconds
Aggravated assault	1 every 70 seconds
Robbery	1 every 71 seconds
Forcible rape	1 every 10 minutes
Murder	1 every 26 minutes

Source: Charles Zastrow, *Introduction to Social Welfare Institutions* (Homewood, Ill.: Dorsey Press, 1978), p. 178.

victims of successful or attempted crimes. Of that number about 55 percent were individuals, 41 percent were households and 4 percent were businesses. The most common victimization did not involve the direct use of threat or violence. The single most common crime was personal larceny (40 percent). This involves such acts as stealing money, picking pockets, or property loss where force was not involved. The next most common loss was household larceny (20 percent). Burglary ranked next (17 percent) which involves unlawful entry but not direct confrontation between victim and criminal. "Thus, such violent crimes as assaults (11 percent), robbery (3 percent), or rape (0.4 percent) rank relatively low in terms of overall frequency."[7]

Crime can also be estimated in terms of its economic costs. When the budgets of all the various kinds of local police, sheriffs, public-safety and federal law enforcement agencies are added together the total budget of the crime-fighting industry approaches the size of the Pentagon budget, which is annually around $75 billion.[8] As another illustration of the cost we can look at one specific crime—the theft of automobiles. About one million automobiles are reported stolen every year. It can be roughly estimated that the stealing and fencing of automobiles is a $2 billion a year business.[9]

Another important point about crime rates is that a number of crimes are committed by the same person. In the period from 1970 to 1974 the percentage of repeaters, by types of crime were as follows: auto theft, 79 percent; robbery, 79 percent; forgery, 73 percent; murder, 68 percent; gambling, 65 percent; rape, 65 percent; assault, 65 percent; narcotics, 59 percent; and embezzlement, 28 percent.[10]

Some Social Correlates of Crime

The commission of crimes is not randomly distributed among people. That is, certain social variables are related to high or low crime rates. Various social settings place persons in situations where they are more or less apt to engage in crime. In other words, there are influencing situational factors.

Sex.   We know that not only do men commit far more crimes than do women but they are also more vulnerable as victims. The only exception is the obvious one of rape. Otherwise, when the overall rates are compared or when families and males of the same age are contrasted, the chances that a male will be victimized, especially in a violent crime, are much greater. "Not only are they more vulnerable to assault and robbery, but three out of four murder victims are male."[11] Much of the social world we live in is still sex segregated. In the most highly dense crime areas men are more common and they are in the more specific situations where crimes are apt to be committed. Crimes are far more common among men than women. The crime and the delinquency rates for males greatly exceed that for females in all nations, all communities within the country and in all age groups. They have also been greater for all periods of history where organized statistics are available and for all types of crime (with the exception of a few peculiar to women, such as prostitution).[12] For example, in specific crimes, males commit 42 percent of all auto thefts, 93 percent of all robberies and 68 percent of all larceny. These crimes, as well as almost all others, are much more closely related to the roles that men play. Not only are they more apt to be in situations where those crimes occur but they are more apt to be a part of male lifestyles.

TABLE 17–2

Selected Arrest Categories by Sex and Percent of Female Arrests, 1977

	Number		Percent of female arrests
	Males	Females	
Murder and non-negligent manslaughter	14,032	2,384	14.5
Robbery	110,489	8,851	7.4
Aggravated assault	184,293	27,238	12.9
Burglary	404,638	25,860	6.0
Larceny—theft	656,619	306,898	31.8
Motor vehicle theft	119,071	10,492	8.1
Other assaults.............................	324,080	52,192	13.9
Fraud	127,725	69,552	35.2
Vandalism.................................	120,542	15,721	8.4
Prostitution and commercialized vice..........	22,670	53,212	70.1
Drug abuse offenses	462,154	74,415	13.8

Source: Adapted from "1977 Uniform Crime Reports," *The World Almanac* (New York: Newspaper Enterprises, 1980), p. 125.

One exception to the wide difference between men and women in crimes appears to be murder and aggravated assault. In those categories the rates of men are not significantly greater than those of women, although both are rising. These are primarily crimes of passion in which well over half of the victim-offender relationships are interpersonal as opposed to the economically motivated offenses. "It would appear that the liberated female criminals, like their male counterparts, are chiefly interested in improving their financial circumstances and only secondarily in committing violence. . . ."[13]

But in recent years the rates of increase of some crimes among women, relative to men, have been striking. During the period between 1960 and 1972 the number of women arrested for robbery rose by 277 percent, while the male figure rose 169 percent. "Dramatic differences are found in embezzlement (up 280 percent for women, 50 percent for men), larceny (up 303 percent for women, 82 percent for men), and burglary (up 168 percent for women, 63 percent for men).[14] However, caution should be taken in interpreting these high percentage increases because the base numbers were quite small. As a result, a relatively small increase in the number of cases, as compared to men, shows a very dramatic increase.

We will shortly look at some of the attempts to explain crime but at this point something may be said of explanations of female crime. There have often been attempts to come up with sexual explanations of female crime. One assumption has seen women turning to crime for purely sexual reasons regardless of whether or not the crime itself is a sex offense. "That is, the female criminal's behavior is explained in sexual terms which include such notions as penis envey; female promiscuity; and the physiological inferiority of women."[15]

Some criminologists describe the woman offender as the recipient of more lenient or "chivalrous" handling in the justice system than her male counterpart. However, there appears to be little evidence to support this contention. A common view of "chivalry" is that the male offender supposedly "takes the risks" for the woman, who goads him into committing crimes. "This goading is often accompanied by seduction and/or manipulation of the man by the devious woman, who will see to it that she is protected in the justice system by allowing the man to 'take the rap.' "[16] These kinds of myths tend to hang on even though there is no evidence to support them.

Age. In general, those persons under 18 years of age are treated as delinquents. This depends upon different laws or the different application of laws (see Chapter 16). There are differences in the rates and types of crime committed by juveniles and adults. For example, in arrests for major crimes in the United States in 1974 only 17 percent of all aggravated assault was committed by persons under 18 years of age. By contrast, that group committed 49 percent of all larceny and 55 percent of all auto thefts.[17] But the young are represented in crime statistics in another way in that they are most apt to suffer from personal crimes. Rape, robbery, assault, and larceny are most commonly committed on the young. "After adolescence or young adulthood, the risks of victimization decrease steadily."[18]

The young are not as likely as older persons to be involved in white-collar crime, professional theft, or syndicated crime. In most instances the young come to the attention of the police for property crimes, vandalism, and specifically juvenile offenses such as running away. Among adults in general, the older the age range the less the involvement in crime. This is especially true in aggravated assault or in prostitution. Older people involved in crime are more often in professional crime or white-collar crime.

TABLE 17–3

Victimization from Selected Crimes Against Persons, for the Population 12 Years and Over and 65 Years and Over, by Race: 1977 (Rate per 1,000 population)

Crime	Persons 12 years old and over			Persons 65 years old and over		
	Total	White	Black	Total	White	Black
Crimes of violence.................	33.9	33.0	41.9	7.5	7.0	13.4
Rape and attempted rape.........	0.9	0.9	1.0	0.1	0.1	—
Robbery and attempted robbery ..	6.2	5.4	13.0	3.4	3.0	7.9
With injury	2.2	1.9	5.2	1.9	1.8	3.4
Without injury	4.0	3.5	7.9	1.4	1.1	4.4
Assault	26.8	26.8	27.9	4.0	3.9	5.6
Aggravated	10.0	9.6	13.9	1.2	1.0	2.7
Simple	16.8	17.2	14.0	2.8	2.8	2.8
Personal larceny	97.3	98.2	90.0	23.6	23.1	26.9

Source: U.S. Department of Justice, Law Enforcement Assistance Administration, National Criminal Justice Information and Statistical Service, unpublished data from the National Crime Survey.

Race. In 1975, of the total number of arrests in the United States, 25 percent were black; for serious crimes they constituted 33 percent of all arrests.[19] Blacks, far more than whites, are also the victims of crime. For example, while blacks constitute only about 11 percent of the population, approximately 52 percent of all murder victims in the United States are black. The persons who suffer most are black males. "Black women, in fact are almost as likely as white men to be victims. It underscores the excessive vulnerability of black people to crimes."[20] Given that most of the crimes committed by blacks are against blacks, the cause is not prejudice but rather the disproportionate number of blacks living in low socioeconomic areas where crime rates are the highest.

Blacks also appear to be more severely treated by the court system. For the same offenses, blacks are more likely than whites to be sentenced, and of those sentenced, to receive longer sentences. Also, of all persons convicted of homicide and sentenced to death, a significantly higher proportion of blacks than whites actually have been executed. If the black commits the crime on the white, the punishment is more severe. Convicted black rapists whose victims were white were more often sentenced to death than defendants of any other racial combination of defendant and victim.[21]

Social class. Persons in the lower socioeconomic classes are more apt to commit burglary, larceny, robbery, and assault. The middle-class criminal is more often involved in white-collar crime, embezzlement, and shoplifting. Lower-class persons' crimes are more easily noticed and reported to the police. Therefore, they are more often apprehended and convicted. Moreover, the middle class not only get caught less for their crimes but when they do get caught they have some advantages. They have resources, knowledge, and connections which can get them out of ever being prosecuted or get them more lenient treatment. Because the middle-class person who commits a crime shares many of the values and speaks the same language as the police and the courts, he gets treated as one of them. Often the lower-class person stands out because of his difference and as a result is treated differently and often more harshly.

Social class is associated with crime in another way. Criminal behavior and police awareness are linked to certain areas of the city. The lower-class lives in poor high-crime areas. William J. Chambliss found that the location of the vices in the ghettos and slums of the city may well contribute to a variety of types of crimes. As a result, ghetto residents often have a disdain for law and law enforcers. One thing they learn is that all crime is not equal in their area. "Their day-to-day observations that criminal syndicates operate openly and freely in their areas with complete immunity from punishment, while persons standing on a corner or playing cards in apartment are subject to arrest, cannot help but affect their perception of the legal system."[22]

Ethnicity.   Various ethnic groups have over the years had a high rate of involvement in crime. This was usually caused by their earlier years of settlement in the United States and crime for some of them was a means of social mobility. At certain times various ethnic groups were viewed as "natural" criminals. For example, the early Irish immigrants were once seen as a criminal class but have long since acquired respectability. There were some groups, such as the Chinese and Southern Italians, who came with living patterns that were criminal in the new cultural context. But with time, the new values were assimilated and the activities defined as criminal were greatly reduced.

Over the years the trend has been that some new immigrant groups get involved in crime. In the United States today the highest rates of crime and delinquency are for the newest arrivals (many from Puerto Rico and Latin American countries) or for those with the longest history of cultural conflict and deprivation (for example, native Americans and blacks). But some groups that have especially low crime rates today, such as American Jews, once had high rates. "Conversely, American Orientals, long noted for low rates of crime and delinquency, in some places now evidence higher rates, in response to declining cultural isolation, changed economic conditions, and deterioration of established patterns of community social control."[23]

It is difficult to examine crime in the United States without making use of the common social categories which describe them. This is because crimes vary so much. The commonly used categories which follow are often arbitrary and there are overlaps between them, with some crimes falling in more than one category.

Conventional crime. Included here are less serious crimes such as theft, robbery, petty larceny and burglary. These are often the crimes committed by the young and unskilled. Planning conventional crime is not nearly as sophisticated as organized crime among professional criminals. Only a small percentage of conventional crime ever leads to an arrest. There are a vast amount of goods stolen from a wide variety of stores for the purpose of personal use or subsequent sale. These kinds of crimes are violations of the laws protecting private property. The persons who are involved in them are usually isolated individuals in that they work alone and are not a part of any criminal subculture.

To illustrate this level of criminal activity we may look briefly at shoplifting. There have been some samples of shoppers that suggest that as many as 5–10 percent of all customers in a large department store will steal before they leave the store. "Shoplifters cost retailers between 60 and 100 million dollars annually."[24] One study found that the sanctions that are imposed on the working- and middle-class amateur shoplifter were intense and often humiliating but were short-lived. This was because only the shoplifters and a few intimates knew of the incidents and they were rarely arrested or imprisoned. But while the shoplifter's social world remained stable, it was unlikely that their cognitive world could remain so. "Professional security guards attempt to force a criminal definition of shoplifting on him or her."[25]

The above study found that the motivation to shoplift was commonplace and the same as normal shopping—the acquisition of goods at minimal cost. It was found that the decision to steal was an inverse function of the perceived risks associated with stealing. "Shoplifters reported that the low risk of apprehension was an important determinant of their behavior."[26] However, the amateur shoplifter represents a relatively small part of the overall loss. A great deal is stolen by professional shoplifters and even more by employes.

Organized crime. Organized crime is carried out by large, well-organized groups of criminals who operate in fairly well-defined areas such as gambling, loan-sharking, drugs, and prostitution. They have connections with the police and other agencies that provide them with protection. In general, their market is among respectable people who do not want to see the laws enforced so they can get the goods that organized crime provides.

Organized crime is modeled on basic bureaucratic principles. Organized criminals develop a large organization which seeks to be as efficient as possible to achieve maximum profit. It is bureaucratic in that there is a division of authority, responsibility and labor. People fill roles that are interrelated and are rewarded for their efficiency in doing their jobs. Their basic activities are either stealing goods or providing illegal goods and services.

In some instances organized crime approximates the military or bureaucratic model and has a table of organization and a chain of command. Alternatively, it may be more like a holding company where one group has financial interests in and therefore some measure of control over a number of operating firms. On other occasions it resembles a franchise system where the central office advances capital and sets people up in business with some degree of independence and shared profits. "In other cases, it is more a matter of interlocking directorates or of a cluster of family business with feudal overtones."[27]

Organized crime has a tremendous amount of power and influence in the United States. The Knapp Commission found organized crime to be the single biggest source of police corruption. This was achieved through control of the city's gambling, narcotics, loan-sharking, and illegal sex-related enterprises such as homosexual after-hours bars and pornography.[28]

Chambliss discovered that, once established, the effect of organized crime on the entire legal and political system was profound. He found that maintenance of order in organized crime groups required the use of extra-legal procedures because the law could not always be relied on to serve the interest of the crime syndicate. To make discipline and obedience certain it was often necessary to enforce the rules of the syndicate in extra-legal ways. To avoid detection of those procedures the police and the court system have had to be kept from discovering the events that the organized crime group did not want discovered. "In actual practice, policemen, prosecutors, and judges who are *not* members of the cabal must not be in a position to investigate those things that the syndicate does not want investigated."[29]

There has long been controversy over the extent to which organized crime actually exists. Since the early part of the century there have been pictures of national crime syndicates presented first as the Mafia and later as La Cosa Nostra. There is some argument that the Mafia is not an organization but rather a method of executing a criminal enterprise. This argument contends that the Mafia is an attitude not an organization, that it is a pattern of social obligations operating through a network of friendship and kinship.[30] There does not seem to be much question that these groups do exist but the extent of their organization and influence is not reliably known.

Certainly the evidence suggest that the position taken by the FBI under J. Edgar Hoover was erroneous. The FBI has a long history of failure in dealing with organized crime. For many years, the answer to this failure by Hoover was to deny that organized crime existed. It seems likely that Hoover was so concerned with maintaining the image of the strength of the FBI that he didn't want to do battle with organized crime because it would have tarnished his image.

Professional crime. Professional crime is organized crime and the acts are ones of calculation, tradition, and sometimes opportunism. It does not usually involve violence. Typically the professional criminal is a safe-cracker, con-man, pick-pocket, check-forger, hijacker of property, and handler of stolen goods. They earn their living by what they do and often take pride in the abilities and skills they need to be occupationally successful.

Many professional criminals are functional members of organized crime. This is due to the nature of the business which requires a great need for cooperation among criminals. "In narcotics, importers and distributors and dealers have to live together. In stolen goods, the thief and the fence must have an understanding to do business. In gambling, the bookie and the loan-shark are intimately allied."[31] But many professional thieves work on their own or have relationships with other criminals only on certain occasions.

Albert K. Cohen and James F. Short, Jr., point out that the details of social organization vary greatly, being adapted to the special requirements of the task at hand, the nature of the competition or the special requirements of the job. The criminal trades do have certain problems they share in common based on the fact that they are criminals. They must develop the skills necessary to be able to evade, neutralize and somehow reduce the costs of arrest, prosecution, and imprisonment. Many do know one another but the community of professional criminals is sometimes vague. "A community of interest generates a community of sentiment and solidarity but, like most human communities, it is loose, imperfect, and vulnerable."[32]

It is probable that for all types of crime, the professional criminal is the least apt to get caught. In part, this is because his activities are not impulsive but rather are carefully planned. Often he prefers not to enter a crime unless the "fix is in" where he has made a deal with the police. He often has a defense attorney on the stand-by in case he is caught. In those cases where he is caught, the aim is for minimal punishment, and because he rarely engages in violence his punishment is often minimal.

White-collar crime. These are the crimes of people who break the law as a part of their day-to-day business activity. White-collar crime includes a wide variety of actions, such as: the businessperson who has inside knowledge which allows her to turn a high profit; the druggist who sells drugs without prescription; or the medical doctor who takes some payment in cash and never reports it on his income tax. These kinds of acts are usually ignored by society and by the courts. Furthermore, the people who do them consider themselves to be law abiding and respectable citizens.

"I tried everything—tax incentives, kickbacks, payoffs,
loopholes—and they all worked."

The amount of money involved in white-collar crime is unknown
because there is no way of knowing how much white-collar crime actually takes place. However, it is clear that the amount of money lost
through white-collar crime is enormous. For example, it is estimated
that employes steal as much as 15 billion dollars a year from their employers. Or that banks probably lose at least five times as much money
to crooked employes as they do to bank robbers. But most people do
not view these kinds of crime as being real crime. The traditional
crimes, such as robbery and rape, are seen as far more serious than
white-collar crimes. One study found that people believed that selling
marijuana was more serious than such white-collar crimes as "manufacturing and selling autos known to be dangerously defective,"
"knowingly selling defective used cars as completely safe," "a public
official accepting bribes in return for favors" and "fixing prices."
Price-fixing was considered to be among the least serious of the crimes
ranked.[33]

Stanton Wheeler has written that over the past quarter century
sociological research has changed and that we now know more about
those persons whose jobs depend on the existence and importance of
crime and much less about criminal offenders. And the one particular
area of criminality that is almost totally neglected is the illegal activity
within large-scale corporate industrial society.[34] Wheeler goes on to

say that three different but related areas of activity have been neglected. First, the wide range of types of corporate illegal activities. Second, those forms of criminal activity that have gained increased importance with changing technology and the new methods of handling money. This would include stock manipulation, marketing of stolen securities, and forms of theft that depend on the computer and credit card, as well as new patterns of embezzlement. Third, and perhaps the most important and thus far least examined, bribery and fraud, "engaged in by public officials or by large-scale entrepreneurs."[35]

Homicide.   In Chapter 7 we will examine various forms of violence. In this section we are only interested in violent personal crimes. These crimes include assault, robbery, and forms of homicide that are activities in which physical injury is inflicted or threatened. These crimes violate the individual's right to live with personal safety. The chances of a person at age 12 or older being a victim of a violent crime is about 1 in 33. The chances are that between 2 and 3 out of 100 persons will be attacked. The most common assault is simple assault which does not involve the use of a weapon and does not result in serious injury. In 1973 the chances were "about 7 in 1,000 that a person would be robbed; about 2 in 1,000 that the person would be injured during a robbery; and about 1 in 10,000 that a person would be murdered."[36]

Homicide tends to occur in the context of a quarrel or where insult or jealousy is clearly present. Whatever weapon is used, the carefully planned and highly rational killing is a rarity in the United States. Homicide seldom occurs in highly public places. "The usual site is a home or other nonpublic place. The bedroom and the kitchen are common scenes of attack."[37]

One study of criminal homicide shows the interactional nature of the crime. It was found that criminal homicide was a collective transaction that involved an offender, victim and sometimes various kinds of audiences. Many victims either directly participate in their destruction by throwing the first punch or firing the first shot or contribute to the escalation of some conflict that results in their death. Criminal homicide is the end result of an intense interchange between the offender and the victim. The transactions that result in murder involve a joint contribution of the offender and the victim escalating to a confrontation in which at least one, but usually both, attempted to establish or save face at the other's expense by standing steady in the face of adversity. "Such transactions additionally involved a consensus among participants that violence was a suitable if not required means for settling the contest. . . ."[38]

David F. Luckenbill found that such transactions usually occurred in nonwork or leisure time settings. They tended to occur between six p.m. and two a.m. and especially on the weekends. Almost half were at home, 15 percent in a tavern, 15 percent on a street corner or "turf" and 12 percent while the participants drove or "cruised" in a car. In over 60 percent of the cases the offender and the victim were related by marriage, kinship, or friendship. "In the remaining cases, while the offender and victim were enemies, mere acquaintances, or complete strangers, at least one, but often both were in the company of their family, friends, lovers, or co-workers."[39]

Criminal homicide, according to Luckenbill, does not appear to be as one-sided an event as is generally assumed. Instead, the murder is the outcome of a dynamic interchange between the offender, the victim, and in many cases, bystanders. The offender and victim develop lines of action shaped in part by the actions of others and directed toward saving or maintaining face and reputation. Violence is seen as an accepted means for resolving questions of loss of face or character.[40]

Victimless crime. The victimless crimes are those where there are voluntary transactions, exchanges, and relationships in which none of the involved parties feel they are a victim. These include a range of sexual activities between consenting adults such as homosexuality and prostitution. Also included are: the illegal sale of liquor and cigarettes, the sale and use of drugs and pornography, gambling, drunkenness, vagrancy, disorderly conduct, and traffic violations. Most of these are victimless crimes in that no one is a victim until made so by arrest, and in most instances the people who commit such acts do not view themselves as criminals.

In recent years there has been a reduction of legal interest in victimless crimes as evidenced by the greater freedom for many kinds of sexual behavior and for the use of marijuana. In part, the change has been due to more liberal values and also the fact that over time, the cost of controlling such crime has been very high and efforts at control have limited results. There is some disagreement about how victimless many such crimes really are. While the act itself may be victimless, related activities may have a victim. For example, the use of drugs may involve robbery to get money or a prostitute may be the victim of white slavery.

Conflicting Solutions

As earlier suggested, there have been changing definitions of what constitutes crime and the severity of treatment appropriate for offenders. Vested interests influence the definitions of crime and prescriptions for punishment. A basic part of all attempts to deal with crime is found in the beliefs and assumptions held about why crime occurs or why specific individuals commit crimes. We want to look briefly at some attempts to explain crime. These are theories that offer suggestions about the causes of crime.

Psychiatric theories. Most of these theories have their basis in psychoanalytic theory which means they try to explain crime in terms of motivation and personality. Basically these views see crime as motivated from within the individual through impulses of some basic biological nature. These impulses are seen as constantly threatening to come forth, and society provides the means of controlling them. Basically, the person is seen as biologically antisocial and society must constantly fight to control those urges. Criminal behavior results when the forces of society are too weak to control those powerfully aggressive and destructive tendencies. The view does not see the individual learning to be a criminal but rather looks at how some people are able to control their criminal forces while others are not. These theories really do not explain why some means of personally controlling the basic urges are criminal while others are not.

These views basically hold that all people are born criminals but that most people learn socially to control their criminal biological impulses. In general, the assumption is that humans are innately aggressive, and while the veneer of civilization has prevented total chaos, it does not really change the basic fundamental human nature. Variations of this theory see some persons suffering from illness or personality defects which remove their moral inhibitions on certain kinds of crimes. The treatment patterns suggested by this theory have been individualized psychiatric treatment or counseling, group therapy or guided group interaction, and self-help groups. Generally they have not been effective. "In study after study, differences of outcomes between groups subject to these treatments and control groups have turned out to be nonexistent or negligible."[41]

Conflict theories. The conflict explanation of crime argues that crime emerges when individuals or loosely organized small groups have limited power are seen as threatening by larger and often well-organized blocks which have much more power. The basic assumption of the conflict position is that crime is first and foremost a political event. Certainly in all societies some institutions work to the relative advantage of some groups of society more than others. This means that some get most of the rewards while others may do most of the work for relatively little. Different segments of society have differential access to the resources and opportunities.

In every modern society institutions place the power to regulate, maintain and modify the social order in the hands of some minority. The legal system is one of the institutions that the powerful members of society use to secure their own interests and to perpetuate their values. Those in power are able to maintain their power by control of the legal institution. They thereby control what, who, and under what circumstances, something is criminal. For example, street crime continues to be strongly watched and punished while white-collar crime is mostly ignored. Attempts to treat some of their activities of the powerful minority as criminal are usually blocked by that power. So attempts to strengthen the law against political graft, price fixing, and so forth, rarely get anywhere.

The Marxist criminologists see differential control in society of the means of material production as the key determinant and primary object of the social conflicts that are found in law and crime. Marxist thought starts with the proposition that practically everyone in capitalistic society is brutalized by the insecurity of having to live in a system that rewards greed and is destructive of generosity and cooperation. "Crime is intrinsic to capitalism. Class differences in both the behavior and labeling of crime are attributed to class difference in opportunities and power within the legal system designed to facilitate rather than stop the exploitation of workers by the bourgeoisie."[42]

For conflict theorists the source of crime rests in the social system. As a result, the individual has little to say about his criminality or lack of it. Rather, he is a victim of his society. If this is true it would appear that criminality is a natural outgrowth of all modern societies and not just capitalism. The theories also do not deal with the fact that often crime does involve some individual choice and that criminals sometimes come from levels of society that according to the theories would seem unlikely if not impossible.

Anomie.   The theory of anomie suggests that people's aspirations are reflected in their definitions of success and failure. The aspirations are mainly set for them by cultural goals. In the United States, success is defined mainly in terms of material success. But different racial, class, and ethnic groupings are widely different in their ability to realize their aspirations by those means the culture defines as legitimate. "Where the disjunction between 'culture goals' and 'institutionalized means' for their achievement is great, a condition of anomie develops—that is a breakdown of the regulative norms—and people turn to whatever means will work."[43]

Anomie theory sees crime as a product of culture and social structures. While it talks about disjunctions between goals and means, the theory does not specify the conditions in society that determine choices among the possible responses. Also, as Cohen and Short point out, there is a great deal of crime that does not make sense as an alternative, albeit illegal, means to the acquisition of material goods. For example, violence or illegal tactics used by militant minorities do not fit.[44]

Differential association.   This theory argues that criminal behavior is learned in interaction with other persons and through the dynamic process of exchange one is affected. "Such learning includes the specific direction of values, attitudes, motives, drives, and rationalizations of criminality, as well as techniques of committing crime."[45] Criminality is a learned sequence through associations with persons following criminal behavior patterns. So whether or not a person decides to commit a crime is based on past and present learning experiences through close contact with others.

No theory of criminology is able to pull together everything that is relevant to the nature or causes of criminal development. Cohen and Short argue that probably the theory of differential association comes closer than any other single theory to making sense of the greatest range of facts about crime.[46] This theory recognizes the interactional nature of learning crime. And while structural factors have a strong influence, the individual is very much an actor in his criminality or lack of it.

Institutionalization

As suggested, crime and criminality become institutionalized through the emergence of laws and their application through the legal process. In this section we want to look at the institutional agencies that represent vested interests and how they deal with crime. These agencies, the police and the courts, have become institutionalized themselves. They are powerful bureaucracies with clearly defined roles and norms that are self-perpetuating institutions. Both the police and the courts need the continuation of crime for their own survival. So any "war" on crime is never pursued with the hope or the expectation of total victory. Often the hope is only enough victory to justify their institutional expansion a little more.

Police. Until the early 19th century the police as we know them today did not exist. Before that time societies depended on other social institutions such as the church and the family for social control. It is probable that police were organized as a result of fear. The establishment of the London Police came from the inability of other institutions to handle the emergence of urban crime. However, Richard L. Block argues that fear is not the basis for continuing support for the police in modern times. Yet, when extreme fear of crime does become widespread it often becomes the dominant basis of support for the police.[47]

In the United States the police started in the major cities. The first city police force was in New York, which was soon followed by Boston and Philadelphia. These forces were created in the 1830s and 1840s. By the 1870s all the major cities had full-time police forces. However, the early police forces did not prove to be too successful. Usually the police were drawn from the least educated segments of the society and were poorly trained and poorly paid. Very quickly the police became the instruments of political corruption and were used for personal gain and political advantage.

In the 20th century the police on all levels have emerged as a social institution with strong vested interests in their own survival. The social problem of crime became the reason for being and for continuance. The basic mandate under which the police are supposed to work is to enforce the law and maintain order. Law enforcement includes crime prevention, crime detection, and the apprehension of criminals. To maintain the order means to settle disputes between citizens who make charges against one another. The police are also expected to control such personal disorders as created by drunks and such structural disorder as caused by traffic jams. "The means for enforcing the law and maintaining order are those that exist within the framework of due process and protection of individual rights."[48]

The crime-fighting business of which the police are the major part is a very big business. It is a vast enterprise employing hundreds of thousand of persons. There are over 211,000 men and women employed in 40,000 public law enforcement agencies in the United States. The costs to maintain those agencies are over $1 billion a year. During each year more than one million persons are admitted to 10,000 county and city jails and other places of forced confinement. There are well over 200,000 inmates housed in state and federal prisons in the United States. There are thousands of judges, probation, and parole officers, and hundreds of thousands of prison and jail administration and guard personnel employed full-time by the crime control apparatus.[49]

Who are the police? In general, they come out of lower-middle-class or working-class backgrounds. A study of New York City police found them to be quite alike in religious, class, and ethnic backgrounds. Their educational background was high school and they were overwhelmingly white and Catholic. "The consequence of this selective recruitment is the creation of a body of men whose backgrounds and values fall within a very narrow range."[50]

One study found that when a person enters the ranks as a police officer he often breaks many ties with civilian society. This isolation leads the police officer to feel set apart from others. His world as a police officer is distinct from the outer world. Furthermore, solidarity among police often derives from their belief that this occupation is unusually dangerous.[51] The police subculture has been described as highly secretive, defensive, and distrustful of the society being policed. But often within the police force there may be little cooperation between various departments and between various individual officers above the level of two-partner teams. "This combination of solidarity against the outside world and independence within the police force lays a heavy burden on the individual officer and his closest partners in their relations with citizens."[52]

Often the police are placed squarely in the middle of two basically conflicting sets of demands. On the one hand, their job obligates them to enforce the law at times with discretion. But at the same time, considerable disagreement exists over whether or not some acts should be subject to legal sanctions. The conflict is heightened because often some influential persons in the community insist that all laws be rigorously enforced while others demand that some laws not be enforced, at least against themselves. "Faced with such a dilemma and such ambivalent situations, the law enforcers do what any well-managed bureaucracy would do under similar circumstances—they follow the line of least resistance."[53]

An important part of both the police and the public image of their job is danger. Whenever a police officer is killed on the job it receives a great deal of publicity. This appears to create an image of danger far greater than exists in reality. Actually, the danger for the police is not as high as it is in some other occupations. The death rate for police is 33 per 100,000. By contrast, miners are killed at a rate of 94 per 100,000, agricultural workers, 55, and construction workers, 76.[54] Furthermore, the number of suspects killed by the police is six times greater than the number of police killed.

As suggested, the problem of police corruption has been around as long as there have been police forces. In New York City investigations have occurred on the average of once every 20 years since before the turn of the century. But very little happens as a result. The conditions exposed by one investigation seem substantially unchanged when the next one makes its report.[55] The dishonest police officer is very often greatly influenced by the corruption of others—politicians, businesspersons and private citizens. The police officer is inherently no more resistant to temptation than anyone else but his position exposes him to tremendous pressures. "The most common are political influence; acceptance of gratuities or bribes in exchange for nonenforcement of laws, particularly those related to gambling, prostitution, and liquor offenses, which are often extensively interconnected with organized crime; the fixing of traffic tickets; minor thefts; and occasional burglaries."[56]

The Knapp Commission found that in New York while corruption was widespread it was not uniform in degree. They found that police fell into two basic categories—"meat-eaters" and "grass-eaters." The meat-eaters were those police who aggressively misused police power for personal gain. The grass-eaters simply accepted the payoffs that happened their way. The meat-eaters got the huge payoffs that made headlines but they were a small percentage of all corrupt police. The vast majority of police on the take did not deal in large amounts of graft. "And yet, grass-eaters are the heart of the problem. Their great numbers tend to make corruption 'respectable.' They also tend to encourage the code of silence that brands anyone who exposes corruption as a traitor."[57]

A common belief presented by the police in dealing with corruption is the "rotten-apple" theory. This is that any officer found to be corrupt must promptly be denounced as a rotten apple in another wise clean barrel. It is never admitted that his individual corruption may be symptomatic of underlying disease. This doctrine is based on two premises. "First, the morale of the Department requires that there be no official recognition of corruption, even though practically all members of the Department know the truth; secondly, the Department's public image and effectiveness require official denial of the truth."[58]

The police strongly resent and resist any attempts by any outside groups to inevestigate charges of corruption or police brutality. They especially resist various attempts at civilian boards of review. It is not only a resistance to any outside group but also the contempt that many police feel for any civilian groups. Yet, to resist any kinds of attempts by outside investigations means they are always subject to the charge of whitewashing their activities.

The police and the community.   For most people, over the course of their lives, the police represent their entire contact with the law. In dealing with the community the police have a wide degree of discretion in the application of laws. There are many laws on the books, and the police can often decide which ones to apply, where, and under what circumstances. Therefore, the police are often in a position of deciding what is and what is not lawful behavior. The police encounter citizens in the community under a wide variety of roles. The different roles that the citizen fills influences how the police react to him. The police may see him as suspect, offender, complainant or informant. And often it is the setting in which the police encounters the citizen that affects how they react to that citizen. Seeing him in the slums, in a middle-class neighborhood, in a bar and so forth, influences the policeman's reactions. Similarly, the area of behavior he is engaged in makes a difference to how the police react. In many situations, such as of gambling, prostitution or traffic violations, there may be strong community pressures against enforcement of laws. In other areas the police may have little ability to attempt full law enforcement, such as white-collar crime.

In some areas there is a climate of isolation between the police and the community. This is especially true in slum neighborhoods where there are often values supporting what the police see as illegal behavior. "In such neighborhoods a policeman tends to see only the bad and to have contact with residents only when they have committed an offense. He may come to feel that the problems he is to deal with are unsolvable and that he has no support or cooperation from the community. It is easy for the man who feels himself to be an outcast to react by disregarding standards of ethics and laws."[59]

When the policeman comes into contact with a citizen it is almost always the police officer who initiates the direction of the interaction. The policeman must make some determination of what action to take. If he is to carry out his mission the policeman must maintain control over the interaction. "He cannot permit his authority to be challenged or he will lose the initiative. Thus, challenges to his authority are a threat to which he will probably react by escalating his claims to authority."[60] James R. Hudson goes on to argue that the ability to claim a given identity in an interaction involves bargaining. But the power is not equally distributed in police/citizen encounters. The police have one mechanism that can alter any negotiation over status claims, the power to arrest. By placing a citizen under arrest the policeman shifts the interaction from police/civilian to police/suspect. "Arrest gives the police officer much greater protection of his role identity at the same time it strips certain identities held by the civilian."[61]

Yet, even though the community has given the police the power and the mandate to enforce laws, many citizens do not feel any need to give them active support in carrying out that mandate. Often an arresting policeman will find degrees of hostility among observers of his action. The police can become further alienated from the community because a part of their mandate is to enforce the moral norms. Often they must curb the illegal sale of alcohol, break up card or crap games, and arrest prostitutes. It is, of course, the citizen who is seeking out those services. As a result, he is often very unhappy when the policeman is doing his job.

One study found few groups in society which have a strong sense of support for the police. Little relationship was found between social class and support for the police either among whites or blacks. There was no relationship between fear of crime and social class among blacks, and only a weak relationship among whites. It was concluded that neither fear of crime nor support for the police can be explained to any great extent by the social class structure. This study goes on to say that when there is citizen support for the police it is based on good and respectful police work. But the "negative effect of fear of the police in support for the police was far stronger than the positive effect of fear of crime."[62]

Another study found that the majority of complaints filed against the police were not concerned with the actions taken but rather with the policeman's lack of explanation. The citizens were objecting less to what was being done in field interrogations than to how it was done. At the same time police officers complained most frequently about the lack of respect given them by citizens. Such respect was a decisive factor in determining whether a citizen was arrested or not.[63]

A policeman providing protection on the subway

We know that a number of factors go into a person's chances of being arrested. To commit a crime is not enough, it must be brought to the attention of the police and they must take action. In other words, any given arrest for any given crime must be selected by the police out of a wide range of crimes committed by a wide range of people. Self-report studies show that persons who admit to various crimes, but who have not been apprehended, are quite different from those arrested and convicted for the same behavior.[64]

As suggested, the police have strong notions about crime and criminals which effect their actions. Many policemen believe there are certain groups in society that are inherently criminal. "This anticipation of law violating behavior underlies much of the discretionary treatment accorded the black and the poor."[65] The arrests and prosecution of delinquents, shoplifters, and homosexuals have been shown to be motivated more by stereotyped appearance of the offender than by evidence of actual criminal behavior. It is also true that "facial stereotypes of the murderer, robber, and traitor have been found to influence jury evaluations of guilt for each of these criminal categories."[66]

The police can and do use a great deal of discretion in making an arrest after detaining a suspect. One study found that only 14 percent of all confrontations between citizens and police resulted in arrests. This suggests that the rest were decided by the detaining officer to be innocent of any major offense.[67] The police also have values about making arrests as reflected in the belief that making "good pinches" is not easy and making "fake work" (making minor crime arrests where no evidence would suggest to an astute observer that a more serious crime has been committed) is not highly regarded. "Since good pinches are the basis of police esteem it follows that minor crime arrests will be avoided except where they expedite the achievement of arrest for serious crimes."[68]

The police are one part of the institutional structure to deal with crime. Another part is the court system and the means of dealing with criminals after they are prosecuted. In the process of behavior being defined as criminal the police determine whether or not a crime has been committed and make the arrest. The court determines the punishment or treatment. Those responsibilities are assigned to other agencies by the courts.

The formal function of criminal courts is to administer justice according to the laws and their interpretations. The court's function is also to see that offenders are made to pay for their crimes. The court must establish that the charge brought against the person fits the legal definition of his activity. If the person is found guilty the court must fit the punishment within minimal and maximal penalties that are prescribed by the law. With that legal range the court has some discretion in what punishment it can hand down. However, the realistic goals of the court may be somewhat different from the ideals. The courts are very often concerned with bureaucratic administrative goals based on maximum production as well as their own career advancement. The concern over backlogs and crowding in jails awaiting trial has often led to an assembly line production in the criminal courts.[69]

Judges can be elected or appointed to office. Whichever way it is done, there is no guarantee against incompetence and corruption. The common assumption typically is that simply by virtue of being an attorney a person is competent for any judgeship. The judge hears the case from other lawyers in the positions of prosecutor and defense. Very often the prosecuting attorneys are in office for their own political ambitions and see their positions as a means to some other end.

The defense are criminal lawyers who generally come from lower social class backgrounds than do lawyers in civil practice. Criminal lawyers as a group have attended less prestigious law schools than did those in civil practice, and criminal lawyers generally make less money than do those in civil practice.[70]

When a criminal case is brought into court it is ideally an adversary process where the prosecution and defense represent the two sides in the criminal justice system. Representing the "people" is the prosecutor and representing the accused are defense attorneys who may be private attorneys, court appointed or public defenders. However, very often instead of being adversaries they are cooperating bureaucrats who must get their job done in what they each see as the most efficient manner. They know that jury trials are slow and costly and slow down production. "By establishing a case's 'worth,' the cooperating attorneys save additional time that might be spent quibbling over what penalty a defendant should receive."[71]

There is often plea bargaining between prosecuting and defense attorneys. The defense agrees to a plea of guilty in return for a lesser charge. In that way the case can be handled rapidly. A guilty defendant who pleads guilty to receive a lesser sentence than he deserves gets a better deal than the innocent defender who is found guilty. The innocent person faces pressure to make a deal and plead guilty in the interest of saving time and avoiding possible incarceration.[72]

There are other important factors that enter into the punishment a person can receive in a criminal court. It is clear that all persons are *not* equal in the eyes of the court even if they are charged with the same crime. There have been many studies of sentencing that demonstrate the importance of criminal histories and how and where the offense was carried out. The social background of the defendant also makes a difference. Independent of the financial ability to retain a private attorney, the higher status person usually gets a more lenient conviction. The leniency of legal treatment of middle- and upper-class persons is often influenced by notions of punishment and deterrence. "The offender is to suffer not only proportionately to the severity of his crime, but also that he will weigh the advantages and disadvantages of a repeated offense."[73] And the assumption often is that the higher social class person does not need that lesson so strongly made as does the lower-class defendant.

As Swigert and Farrell go on to argue, the decision to punish, for both the rich and the poor, is a calculus of loss and pain. The lower-class defendant, often with minimal status in his community, little occupational prestige and a personal life often characterized as disorganized, enters the court with little to lose other than loss of freedom by being imprisoned. "The higher status person, on the other hand, simply as a result of arrest is said to suffer greatly."[74] Certainly, if community involvement and occupational commitment are important they do have more to lose than the person without these commitments.

If the defendant is found guilty some course of action is prescribed for him. The use of prisons as a form of punishment is fairly recent in human history. It appears that the extensive use of imprisonment as a penalty did not occur until the 13th century in England. Before that time all criminals were mixed regardless of age or sex and the primary concern was custodial. By the beginning of the 18th century there was the commonly accepted belief that inflicting pain on the offender had an intrinsic value of its own. This belief was a kind of psychological hedonism, which maintained that a person calculates the pleasures and pains of any anticipated actions. He then governs his behavior by choosing the action which will bring him the greatest balance of pleasure minus the pain.

Since the early 1800s in the United States, prisons and jails have become more specialized. Jails have come to be used for those receiving short sentences and for those who are awaiting trial. Over the years separate institutions have been built for special groups; for example, for confining the young, keeping women separate from men, and holding those judged to be criminally insane. There are also prisons defined by degrees of security—maximum, moderate, and minimum.

There has been a historical progression in beliefs about how criminals should be treated. Initially the treatment of crime was through strong punishment and death. But more humanistic beliefs along with recognition that those methods were not successful led to a reduction in severity. That is when prisons came to be seen as the means of punishment. But today it is generally recognized that prisons are failures. They usually function to dehumanize the person and attempts to rehabilitate them have largely failed.

In general, the correctional system involves three different types of agencies which are designed to correct and punish. First are those that incarcerate by locking people up in jails and prisons. Second are systems for monitoring convicted offenders by local, state or federal probation officers. Here the offender is free from imprisonment but is required to report periodically to his probation officer and he must meet any requirements set up for his probation. Third are parole boards which administer and supervise the activities of persons who have been released from prison.[75]

In prisons the correctional administrator's main concern is with controlling those who have been sentenced until they serve their time. This is handled with bureaucratic concern especially with an eye to minimizing costs and any kinds of conflict. This means that rehabili-

The small world of a prison cell

tation programs are minimal since correction agencies are largely concerned with maintaining control over their charges.[76]

The more specific objectives for imprisonment are: First, to reform criminals so they will no longer commit crimes; Second, to incapacitate criminals so they cannot commit crimes for a period of time and thereby protect society; Third, to provide social retribution for the victim; Fourth, to serve as a warning to the general public, thereby having a deterrent effect.[77] Usually these objectives are total failures or at least failures in part. Often the prison has totally different consequences for the individual. These prisoners often learn new criminal techniques; they come to label themselves as criminal, and they may become so well accustomed to the prison that they are unable to deal with the outside world.

One major commitment to the notion of punishment is that it will serve as a deterrent, not only for the offender, but for others who might commit a similar act. Deterrence refers to a particular relationship between the existence, or perception, of legal sanctions and subsequent behavior.[78] One major limitation with the notion of deterrence is the assumption the person will enter a rational process of recognizing the threat of getting caught and weighing it against the anticipated benefit of his possible actions. In areas such as violent crime, which is frequently committed in high anger and on impulse, there is no time for rationally assessing the consequences. By contrast, the commission of such crimes as kidnapping may be far more responsive to the effect of deterrence because it requires a period of rational premeditation.

Recently students of crime and delinquency have tended to downgrade deterrence in favor of other objectives, particularly treatment and rehabilitation. "In recent years, however, a growing body of research provides evidence that the swiftness and certainty of punishment—and, to a lesser extent, its severity—have a tangible effect on crime rates. However, the deterrent effects that have been demonstrated are generally large."[79]

What are some of the other options to imprisonment? One is parole. As suggested it is basically a conditional release where the person continues to fill an indeterminant sentence or one that is unexpired. While on parole the person is still considered to be under custody. The assumption of parole is that it both punishes and treats the offender. Success of parole is hard to measure but parole violations have been claimed for 35 to 80 percent of all cases.

Probation is seen as somewhat different from parole in that the person is viewed as being under treatment but no longer being punished. Probation is granted by the courts and involves the suspension of a sentence and gives the person freedom but under the supervision of a probation officer.

There have also been experimentations with community-based corrections. For example, work release where prisoners are allowed to work for pay outside the prison but return at night or for other periods of time. Evaluations have been mixed. There is also the use of prerelease furloughs which allow a prisoner to take some brief release time from prison as he gets near the end of his sentence. There have also been halfway houses that are defined as intermediate between the prison and the community. All of these attempts have had mixed reviews and none of them seem to represent any real way for the future.

But there will continue to be great concern with present prison systems and attempts to find alternatives to imprisonment. This concern comes out of several considerations. First, there is a growing disillusionment with treatment in any institutional setting. Second, current research suggests that alternatives to incarceration produce results not very different from putting the person in prison. Third, many believe that incarceration simply leads to stigmatization and discrimination. Finally, court processing and incarceration are tremendously expensive.[80]

Serious crimes, those seen as a threat to persons and their property, are overwhelmingly viewed as a special problem. Those crimes that are not seen as threatening to the individual or to power blocks in society are often ignored. In recent years there has been an increase in the fear of crime by Americans, especially those living in big cities. How much of this is a product of a real increase in crime and how much a product of mass media and the propagandists of the legal institutions is difficult to assess. Whatever the case, people believe there is an increase in the crime rate. It also seems clear that there is no solution for the problem of criminal behavior and that attempts to resolve the problem through traditional methods have failed. Crime, like so many social problems, has to be recognized as a basic part of our society and something we have to live with.

Crimes are common in the United States although there is no accurate knowledge of the rates. Crimes can be divided into the categories of: conventional, organized, professional, white-collar, homicide, and victimless crimes. Crimes have become institutionalized through the emergence of laws and the legal process. The police play the crucial role in defining what acts will constitute crime in that they often make the choice to arrest or not to arrest. Imprisonment can be seen as performing several functions: (1) to reform the criminal; (2) to incapacitate the criminal; (3) to provide social retribution; and, (4) to warn the public and thereby be a deterrent.

NOTES

1. Charles Wellford, "Labeling Theory and Criminology: An Assessment," *Social Problems* (February, 1975), p. 335.

2. Lois B. DeFleur, "Biasing Influences on Drug Arrest Records: Implication in Deviance Research," *American Sociological Review* (February, 1975), p. 89.

3. Albert K. Cohen and James F. Short, Jr., "Crime and Juvenile Delinquency," in *Contemporary Social Problems*, 4th ed., by Robert K. Merton and Robert Nisket (New York: Harcourt Brace Jovanovich, 1976), p. 56.

4. Malcolm Spector and John I. Kitsuse, "Social Problems: A Re-Formulation," *Social Problems* (Fall 1973), p. 158.

5. Alan Booth, David L. Johnson, and Harvey M. Choldin, "Correlates of City Crime Rates: Victimization Surveys versus Official Statisitcs," *Social Problems* (December, 1977), p. 188.

6. Ibid., pp. 187–188.

7. LaMar T. Empey, *American Delinquency* (Homewood, Ill.: Dorsey Press, 1978), pp. 173–74.

8. Thomas Plate, *Crime Pays* (New York: Ballantine, 1975), p. 4.

9. Ibid., p. 23.

10. U.S. Department of Justice, *Uniform Crime Reports* (Washington, D.C.: U.S. Government Printing Office, 1975), p. 49.

11. Empey, *Delinquency*, p. 180.

12. Cohen and Short, "Crime," p. 61.

13. Freda Adler, *Sisters In Crime* (New York: McGraw-Hill, 1975), p. 16.

14. Ibid., p. 16.

15. Etta A. Anderson, "The 'Chivalrous' Treatment of the Female Offender in the Arms of the Criminal Justice System: A Review of the Literature," *Social Problems* (February, 1976), p. 352.

16. Ibid., p. 352.

17. Federal Bureau of Investigation, *Crimes in the United States* (Uniform Crime Reports (Washington, D.C.: Government Printing Office, 1975), pp. 188–89.

18. Empey, *Delinquency*, p. 178.

19. Information Please Almanac, 1977 (New York: Information Please Publications, Inc., 1978), p. 783.

20. Empey, *Delinquency*, p. 184.

21. William J. Chambliss, "Vice, Corruption, Bureaucracy and Power," in *Official Deviance*, by Jack D. Douglas and John M. Johnson (Philadelphia: Lippincott, 1977), p. 328.

22. Ibid., p. 328.

23. Cohen and Short, "Crime," p. 62.

24. Robert E. Kraut, "Deterrent and Definitional Influences on Shoplifting," *Social Problems* (February, 1976), p. 358.

25. Ibid., p. 359.

26. Ibid., p. 365.

27. Cohen and Short, "Crime," p. 89.

28. Knapp Commission, "Police Corruption In New York City," in Douglas and Johnson, Official Deviance, p. 277.

29. Chambliss, "Vice," p. 327.

30. Francis A. J. Ianni, "The Mafia and the Web of Kinship," *The Public Interest*, (Winter 1971), p. 83.

31. Plate, *Crime Pays*, p. 8.

32. Cohen and Short "Crime," p. 87.

33. John F. Galliher and James L. McCartney, *Criminology* (Homewood, Ill.: Dorsey Press, 1977) p. 383.

34. Stanton Wheeler, "Trends and Problems in the Sociological Study of Crime," *Social Problems* (June 1976), p. 525.

35. Ibid., p. 528.

36. Empey, *Delinquency*, p. 176.

37. Stuart Palmer, *The Violent Society* (New Haven, Conn.: College and University Press, 1972), p. 43.

38. David F. Luckenbill, "Criminal Behavior as a Situated Transaction," *Social Problems*, (December 1977), p. 177.

39. Ibid., p. 178.

40. Ibid., p. 185.

41. Cohen and Short, "Crime," p. 96.

42. Austin T. Turk, "Class, Conflict, and Criminalization," *Sociological Focus* (August 1977), p. 215.

43. Cohen and Short, "Crime," p. 73.

44. Ibid., p. 74.

45. Ibid., pp. 72–73.

46. Ibid., p. 73.

47. Richard L. Block, "Fear of Crime and Fear of Police," *Social Problems* (Summer 1971), p. 100.

48. William B. Sanders, "Criminal Justice and Social Control," in *Understanding Social Problems,* by Don H. Zimmerman et al., (New York: Praeger Publishers, 1976), p. 329.

49. Palmer, *Violent Society*, pp. 81–82.

50. James R. Hudson, "Police-Citizen Encounters That Lead To Citizen Complaints," *Social Problems* (Fall 1970), p. 182.

51. Ibid., p. 183.

52. Marcia Garrett and James F. Short, Jr., "Social Class and Delinquency: Predictions and Outcomes of Police-Juvenile Encounters," *Social Problems* (February 1975), p. 369.

53. Chambliss, "Vice," pp. 310–11.

54. Sanders, "Criminal Justice," pp. 329–30.

55. Knapp, Commission, p. 273.

56. "President's Commission on Law Enforcement and the Administration of Justice," in Douglass and Johnson, *Official Deviance*, p. 255.

57. Knapp Commission, pp. 272–73.

58. Ibid., p. 274.

59. President's Commission, p. 263.

60. Hudson, "Police-Citizen," p. 183.

61. Ibid., p. 190.

62. Block, "Fear of Crime," p. 100.

63. Mary Glenn Wiley and Terry L. Hudik, "Police-Citizen Encounters: A Field Test of Exchange Theory," *Social Problems* (October, 1974), p. 120.

64. Harvey Marshall and Ross Purdy, "Hidden Deviance and The Labeling Approach: The Case for Drinking and Driving," *Social Problems* (Spring, 1972), p. 541.

65. Victoria Lynn Swigert and Ronald A. Farrell, "Normal Homicides and the Law," *American Sociological Review* (February, 1977), p. 19.

66. Ibid., p. 17.

67. Wiley and Hudik, "Police-Citizen Encounters," p. 119.

68. David W. Britt and Charles R. Tittle, "Crime Rates and Police Behavior: A Test of Two Hypotheses," *Social Forces* (December, 1975), p. 449.

69. Sanders, "Criminal Justice," p. 328.

70. Galliher and McCartney, *Criminology*, p. 241.

71. Sanders, "Criminal Justice," p. 338.

72. Ibid., p. 339.

73. Swigert and Farrell, "Normal Homicides," p. 27.

74. Ibid., p. 27.

75. Sanders, "Criminal Justice," p. 345.

76. Ibid., p. 328.

77. Charles Zastrow, *Introduction to Social Welfare Institutions* (Homewood, Ill.: Dorsey Press, 1978), pp. 189–90.

78. Robert F. Meier and Weldon T. Johnson, "Deterrence As Social Control: The Legal and Extra Legal Production of Conformity," *American Sociological Review* (April 1977), pp. 293–94.

79. Cohen and Short, "Crime," p. 93.

80. Ibid., p. 94.

SELECTED BIBLIOGRAPHY

Adler, Freda. *Sisters in Crime.* New York: McGraw-Hill, 1975.

Anderson, Etta A. "The 'Chivalrous' Treatment of the Female Offender in the Arms of the Criminal Justice System: A Review of the Literature." *Social Problems* (February 1976), pp. 350–55.

Block, Richard L. "Fear of Crime and Fear of Police." *Social Problems* (Summer 1971), pp. 91–101.

Booth, Alan; Johnson, David R.; and Choldin, Harvey M. "Correlates of City Crime Rates: Victimization Surveys versus Official Statistics." *Social Problems* (December 1977), pp. 187–97.

Britt, David W., and Tittle, Charles R. "Crime Rates and Police Behavior: A Test of Two Hypotheses." *Social Forces* (December 1975), pp. 441–50.

Hudson, James R. "Police-Citizen Encounters that Lead to Citizen Complaints." *Social Problems* (Fall 1970), pp. 179–93.

Luckenbill, David F. "Criminal Behavior as a Situated Transaction." *Social Problems* (December 1977), pp. 176–86.

Turk, Austin T. "Class, Conflict, and Criminalization." *Sociological Focus* (August 1977), pp. 209–19.

Wheeler, Stanton. "Trends and Problems in the Sociological Study of Crime." *Social Problems* (June 1976), pp. 525–33.

Chapter 18

Violence: Homicide, Sexual, and Family

Violence probably has been a part of the human condition from the beginning. To some degree it was necessary to survive in a hostile environment. But even as the physical environment was tamed, violence continued to be high. In the 20th century there have been by conservative estimates close to four million homicides and 25 million suicides around the world. Assault and rape have been committed in even greater numbers. And while there is no way of knowing how many have been killed through war the total has to be in the hundreds of millions.

In the United States violence has long been socially supported. It is no exaggeration to say that violence played a major part in the settlement of America. In the past some argument could be made for violence as the white settlers took the country away from the Indian and learned to control the hostile environment. But for many years there has been no social need for violence. However, violence values have continued to be prized and followed by many Americans. In this chapter we want to look at three general categories of violence and how they fit the American value system.

HOMICIDE

Societies vary greatly in their homicide rates. Studies suggest that the median rate for nonliterate societies was somewhat lower than for literate societies. In general, societies where there is little or no homicide are characterized by being very cooperative and noncompetitive. They usually stress the importance of the society over the individual. The

Indians of the Southwestern part of the United States had such societies.

Crosscultural studies suggest that in the vast majority of non-literate societies homicide victims and offenders are rarely if ever strangers. "When victims and offenders have never met, the offender is nonetheless likely to be familiar with the victim's characteristics or with the characteristics of individuals like the victim."[1] Even in far larger and more complex industrial societies homicide victims and offenders are likely to know one another.

Among modern societies there is a wide range in the homicide rates. For example, the countries of northern Europe, such as Belgium, Iceland, Ireland, the Netherlands, and Norway have very low homicide rates. At the other extreme, countries in Latin America, such as Colombia, Mexico, and Nicaragua have high homicide rates. These are countries with strong traditions of violence.

Often the view of violence in a society is influenced by war. During the Vietnam War, the murder and nonnegligent manslaughter rate in the United States more than doubled. "This rapid increase was somewhat more remarkable because it followed a period of almost monotonic decline in the homicide rate since the record-keeping began in 1933."[2] This same study of combatant nations also found substantial postwar increases in their rates of homicide. There were no such increases in the noncombatant nations also studied. It was concluded that postwar increases were more frequent among nations with large numbers of combat deaths. "The presence of authorized or sanctioned killing during the war had a residual effect on the level of homicide in peacetime society."[3]

Violence is used in this chapter to mean behavior that is consciously directed toward another to bring about physical injury. There can also be violence toward property. Violence can be defined as socially legitimate or illegimate. Legitimate violence is usually socially approved as a part of institutional behavior, for example, among the military or the police. Forms of violence are also legitimate in many sports, such as ice hockey or football. By contrast illegitimate violence is not supported by any social institution and tends to be behavior related to individuals or small groups. Often it is behavior that is directly or indirectly related to the institutions that have social sanctions to respond to violence or sometimes to initiate violence against others, For example, the police may raid a place they suspect of illegal gambling operations.

Violence is often confused with aggression. While violence is an act that causes damage, aggression involves a wide range of assertive and intrusive behavior. Aggression can include both overt and covert attacks against people. It can include such defamatory acts as sarcasm, self-directed attacks, and dominant behavior. "Aggression may lead to violence, but it may also find an outlet in business competition, legal debate, and sports—all legitimate modes of conduct."[4] But our main interest is in that kind of aggression that is directed at another person in terms of physical harm and that goes against the legal and/or moral values of society.

There are also legal distinctions made about violence. For example, assault is an attempt to injure or kill someone. Murder is a form of aggravated assault. Robbery through the taking of someone's property by the threat of violence or through intimidation accounts for about 40 percent of all reported crimes of violence. There is also noncriminal homicide. This is excusable homicide which is accidental or justifiable, for example, a police officer shooting someone trying to escape. Self-defense is also a form of noncriminal homicide. By contrast, criminal homicide is murder and this implies intentionally causing death or doing so in the course of a felony such as robbery. There are two degrees of manslaughter. Voluntary manslaughter, or first degree murder, where death results from an act that can be assumed to lead to another's death, or where the intent caused severe injury to another person. Involuntary manslaughter, or second degree murder, applies when the act is less directly related to the death. There may also be "criminally negligent homicide" which often means the reckless or negligent use of a motor vehicle.

Rates.   The violent crimes of murder, robbery, aggravated assault, and forcible rape make up about 10 percent of all crimes reported. The rest of the reported crimes are ones against property. According to the FBI reports, one American is murdered every 27 minutes; forcibly raped every 10 minutes; subjected to aggravated assault every 76 seconds; and robbed every 82 seconds." There is evidence of an increase in reported crime. There were 17 percent more crimes reported for 1974 than for 1973 and the national crime rate has risen by 32 percent since 1967.[5]

In recent years the type or direction of violence has been undergoing change. In the mid-1970s personal violence took a divergent course from collective violence. That is, personal violence continued to rise at a high rate and to be increasingly perceived as socially threatening despite strong efforts to reduce it. Since 1961, the incidence of all serious crimes has more than doubled. While personal violence was increasing, the incidence of most forms of collective violence subsided subtantially during the same period. By the late 1970s collective violence was no longer viewed as a significant issue. "Riots in ghettos became very rare; violent student demonstrations became very infrequent."[6]

Who is it that gets killed in the United States? About one third of the killings involve people connected in intimate relationships. About 12 percent of all homicides in the United States involve one spouse

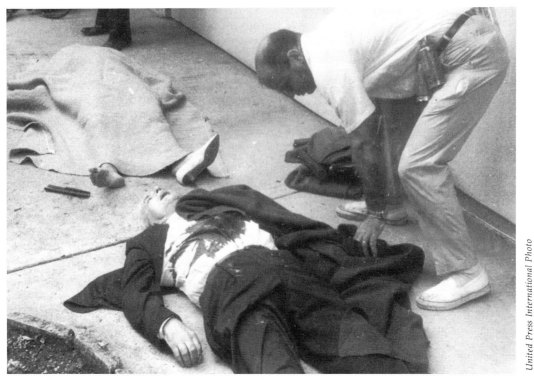

United Press International Photo

Who gets killed? This man shot by police after he had killed his wife and two teenage daughters.

killing another, 3 percent a parent killing a child, and in 8 percent the killing is done by some other relative. Added to this, about 7 percent that come out of a romantic triangle or a lovers quarrel. Roughly another one third come out of arguments that take place between individuals who know one another. The last third are homicides committed during the commission of a felony and these are almost always stranger-stranger relationships.

The ultimate means of dealing with violence is with violence and this has long been a part of American tradition. Since 1930 in the United States between 4,000 and 5,000 persons have been legally executed. Electrocution, hanging, gassing, and shooting of the offenders have been the methods used. For a few years capital punishment was not being used in the United States and was not common in the 1970s. However, even though capital punishment is now legal in some states, the overall legitimacy of capital punishment is very much up in the air.

Who are those who commit crimes of violence? First, they are usually men and usually their victims are other men. About three quarters of all homicides are committed by men and about three quarters of their victims are men. When women kill they also tend to kill men. About three quarters of all persons killed by women are men. Men are much more likely to kill their friends and companions while women are more likely to kill their husbands or lovers. Erich Goode explains these differences by the observation that men are very concerned about the evaluations made of them by other men. "Women, too, are extremely involved in the judgments made by the men closest to them in their lives; other women matter less to them."[7]

Alcohol.   Most murders are committed by persons without criminal records. And even though about 30 percent of all homicides are committed during the course of a crime they are usually not premeditated. There is a close link between the use of alcohol and violent crimes. In general, the more violent the crime, the greater the possibility that the offender was involved in heavy drinking. One study reported that in 60 percent of all violent criminal homicides the killer had been drinking prior to his attack on the victim.[8] Another study found intoxicants present in over one half of the encounters that terminated in violence. That study suggested two major implications of intoxication. First, what had been established as self-other identities of the persons may have become challenged and this led to an identity threat. Furthermore, the movement from a pretense to an open awareness context is often encountered in drinking situations. As a result the established rituals of demeanor or deference may be neglected or threatened. Second, intoxicants may have an impact on the actor who perceives a threat to his identity. "Unable to retaliate with lucid verbalization, the intoxicated paticipant may resort to some other techniques of establishing his identity and saving face."[9]

Murder is more frequent in large cities than in small town and rural areas. However, by geographical region, the South is the most dangerous place to live from the viewpoint of being violently killed by others. The six states with the highest rates of homicide are all Southern states. Those states continue to hold to the traditional values of violence more so than other areas of the United States. Physical reaction or violence are more apt to be an accepted way of responding to various kinds of situations in the South.[10]

There also appears to be an interrelationship between social class, race, and violence. "Blacks are more likely to fight than whites, and the poor are more likely to fight than the nonpoor."[11] There is some suggestion that this is due to a subcultural violence theme, that people coming from black and poor backgrounds are socialized to use violence and therefore turn to it more often as a part of their lives.

In most instances violence is an interpersonal event. However, individuals can do violence to themselves. Persons may self-inflict pain or kill themselves. But when violence occurs with another, it is not accidental and it is the result of some sense of severe frustration. The frustration typically manifests itself in anger and the striking out toward the other. Criminal homicide is generally an intensely personal crime directed against those who are perceived as strong threats. "Victims tend to be perceived as sources of blockages in the offender's attempts to carry out adequately their social roles."[12]

As suggested, most homicides occur between persons who know each other. This means that typically the murder results from interaction between them. Interaction between any two people can vary greatly in its intensity of good or bad feeling. When hostility is felt in interaction, attempts can be made to resolve the differences, or there may be a temporary withdrawal of the participants. But in some instances withdrawal is not really an option psychologically or socially. The force for resolution can become overpowering. When this is the case continued interaction can become hostile, aggressive and sometimes violent.

Often, in situations where violence occurs there are audiences, and these can have a significant impact on the direction the confrontation takes. The audience can goad the persons on or make it very difficult for either to walk away or to reach any peaceable resolution. In other instances the audience may provide support for some face-saving tactics. But support from the audience can often have negative consequences. John R. Hepburn found that when the person perceived that he had the support of the audience, his opposition to the person he was confronting was greater. The self-conception and public identity of the individual is heightened by the audience's acceptance of his claim for deference and prestige. As a result he may continue to escalate the hostility. "The use of violence is more apt to occur when what ego perceives is also perceived by the audience as an acceptable and available alternative."[13] The individual feels his choice of action is one the audience supports.

Hepburn found that among people in lower socioeconomic statuses the personal state of mind was very important to the possibility of violence. He suggests that it is the cost of failure that accounts for so many acts of violence by persons of that social class level. They appear to have fewer positive self-identities. Added to this is the greater acceptance of violence as normative behavior. As a result lower socioeconomic status persons, "with few positive identities, who adhere to the subculture of violence consider their self-esteem and public identities to be of crucial significance. A threat to the identity of such a person is a grave threat."[14]

Theories of Violence

The attempts to explain why some people engage in violence while others do not can be seen in several theories. These theories attempt to show how or why violence emerges.

Psychoanalytic theories.   These theories view the individual in terms of innate or learned impulses and reactions. Society is seen as a controlling agent, channeling the expression of impulses or reactions in appropriate ways or suppressing them altogether. Violence is evidence of breakdown in this system of social control. Psychoanalytic theories have limited value for the sociological understanding of violence, since they focus on the individual and innate impulses while largely excluding the view of group influences and social learning.

Subculture of violence.   This theory is the opposite to the psychoanalytic one in that it views violence as learned behavior. Violence is seen as a part of a subculture where it is accepted and even encouraged. The values of the subculture support violence under a variety of conditions. Where such values prevail, the assumption is that violence is learned through the limitation of others or in social rewards for violent behavior.

This theory as proposed by Marvin E. Wolfgang and Franco Ferracuti argues that violence results from the adherence to a set of values which supports and encourages its expression.[15] Those values are seen to be in conflict with but not totally in opposition to those of the dominant culture. "It is said that within the subculture, various stimuli such as a whistle, a slightly derogatory remark, or the appearance of a weapon in the hands of an adversary are perceived differently than in the dominant culture; in the subculture they evoke a combative reaction."[16]

Howard S. Erlanger argues that at the present time we do not know how important a deviant value system is in explaining violence in the United States. Furthermore, if it exists, it is not clear whether such a value system can be found predominantly within the black or low-income white communities or whether it can be said to be relatively independent of social structure. "But there is enough evidence to conclude that these groups are not *characteristically* different from the dominant society in their rate of approval of the use of physical aggression."[17]

There is certainly no clear understanding of what causes violence. In some instances the police encourage violence by their own use of violent methods and violence toward the police is a threat they constantly keep the public aware of. Violence is presented as a factor which makes their job more dangerous and this danger can often be translated into dollars for hiring more police, for the purchase of more equipment, as well as higher economic rewards for police.

Gun control.   There are few societies in the world where it is as easy to get a gun as in the United States. It is also clear that one major cause of homocide is the availability of guns. It would seem logical that one way to reduce homicides would be to make the acquisition of guns much more difficult. However, it is not that simple. The attempts to establish gun control laws represent a vivid illustration of how vested interests enter into defining whether or not a social problem exists. Does the legal availability of guns constitute a social problem? The reactions are strong, different, and sometimes violent.

The views about the private possession of guns goes far back in American history. But from the very beginning there have been controls over firearms. For example, Massachusetts, as early as 1692, passed legislation which prohibited carrying "offensive" weapons in public. In 1813, Kentucky passed the first American law prohibiting the carrying of concealed weapons. In 1911 there was enacted in New York the most restrictive gun law, the Sullivan Law which required a license to possess a handgun.

Today, many Americans own their own guns. One national study asked if the person had in their home or garage any guns or revolvers. This study, done in 1973, found that just under one half had guns. This was consistent with a poll done in 1959. This study suggested there had been no widespread increase in the proportion owning a gun although there has been a general belief that such was the case. However, there was an increase of those owning hand guns. In 1959, 32 percent of all who own guns had handguns but this was up to 42 percent in 1973.[18] How accurate these reported figures are there is no way of knowing. General estimates of privately owned firearms in the United States range from 90 to 200 million.

Ownership of a gun varies a great deal among Americans. The ownership of weapons is highest in rural areas and small towns and decreases as city size increases. The belief that the big city is where gun ownership is highest is not true. Gun ownership is disproportionately high in the South. And in the South whites are about 10 percent more likely to own firearms than are non-whites. Also gun owners are disproportionately Protestant and middle class.[19] Gun ownership is more common among older Americans who live in areas that continue to place high value on the ownership of guns.

For some boys in the United States learning about guns is a natural part of their socialization. One study found it is usually the father who introduces his sons to guns and does so at an early age. The combined factors of sex and region of the country account for much variation in children's being introduced to guns. Southern males are the most likely to be introduced to guns and Southern females the least likely. "Southerners are more likely to be raised in homes with guns, more likely to have some familiarity with a weapon, and more likely to have been introduced to guns at an earlier age than non-Southerners."[20]

A major part of the value system that justifies the having and using of guns is hunting. At one time guns were important to the survival of Americans to hunt the game they needed for food. But it has been several hundred years since that was true. Hunting comes to be

"Saturday night specials" on sale at a truck stop in Tennessee

justified for many Americans as a sport and this is based on all sorts of rationalizations. But the bottom line in hunting has to be the sense of something gained by the hunter from killing. This is the case because the reasons given other than the pleasure of the kill do not make sense. The pleasure of being outdoors or of stalking game could be achieved without killing the game. To say that hunting is to thin out the deer herds is illogical because it is a very inefficient way of doing so because often the wrong deer by age or sex are killed. For many Americans hunting is a way of legitimately killing, whatever the rationalization they offer.

In general the police strongly support gun control laws because they have a lot to lose by the availability of guns. For example, in 1974, 95 of the 132 local, state, and federal police officers killed on duty were slain by handguns. These guns are also responsible for many other deaths. About 68 percent of all homicides in the United States were committed through the use of firearms. Over one half of all homicides involved handguns, and about 25 percent of all cases of assault were committed with the use of a firearm.[21]

Since 1938, the vast majority of Americans have favored some kind of action for the control of firearms sold to civilians. For example, in one study, 75 percent of the total sample said they would favor "a law which would require a person to obtain a police permit before he or she could buy a gun."[22] Among those who do not own guns the support for stricter controls is almost unanimous. In the cities, about 90 percent of all nonowners favor stricter controls. "While most of the people who are opposed to gun control own guns, it is also true that most of the people who own guns are *not* opposed to gun controls."[23]

But despite the overwhelming support stated for gun control no laws get passed. This is true in spite of the highly emotional reactions to the gun slayings of the Kennedys and Martin Luther King. For the most part this is because those who want stronger gun controls are not strong in their feelings nor are they organized. By contrast, the forces against gun control are very committed, wealthy, and well organized. They argue that people have the right to carry arms which is based in a historical setting that has little relevance to today's world. The major force against gun controls is the National Rifle Association which can get out as many as 500,000 letters when needed. They have also made effective efforts to defeat candidates who have supported gun controls. This group vividly represents the ability of a small minority to dominate the majority in legislative action through organization, dedication, and money.

Violence has long been a part of the American tradition. There are a variety of legal meanings for violence so that some, at least under certain conditions, are acceptable to society. The trend in recent years has been away from collective violence and more to personal violence. In general violence is most commonly committed by men against men. And in roughly two thirds of all killings the individuals are not complete strangers and may even know each other quite well.

Rape

Over the centuries there has been change in the definition of forcible rape. In many instances in the past rape was seen as justifiable, appropriate, and the right of many men. It has only been in recent years that the view has come to be that rape is no longer a right for men. In the past rape has been viewed as appropriate in the "spoils of victory" during war, in marriage if the wife resists, or against women defined as inferior because of class, caste, or race. Rape continues to be seen as right or at least acceptable by some men under various circumstances.

Legally rape is divided into two categories—forcible and statutory. Statutory rape refers to cases in which the female is under the age of 18 (or in which the court determines that the female is mentally incompetent or mentally ill). Forcible rape is characterized primarily by the presence of force or threat of force. In either case, rape is illegal sexual intercourse performed by a man on a woman over whom he has no sexual rights. In the eyes of the law, violence in sexual intercourse *is* permissible, but sexual relations with a woman who is not one's property is not legal. "From their inception rape laws have been established not to protect women, but to protect women's property value for men."[24]

The victim.   There can be no way of knowing how many rapes occur in the United States. While rape accounts for about one in seventeen of the total number of all violent crimes, it is probable that over 90 percent of all rapes go unreported. There has been a rise in the report of rapes, but this may not be a reflection of an increase in actual rapes. It may be that women are more willing to report a rape than was true in the past. There are differences among women in reporting rape. For example, the older the woman, the greater the likelihood that she will report a rape. "Higher educated women with professional occupations tended to report cases of rape far more than women who were less educated and who had less than professional occupations."[25]

It appears that the rapist is a man not very different from men in general. He is average in personality, appearance, intelligence, and sexual drive. What is more striking is that the rapist is not usually a stranger. One study of patterns of rape victimization revealed that 48 percent of the rape victims knew the offender. Another study by victims of rape found that 8 percent were raped by men they knew and with whom they had had intimate relations. Another 12 percent were raped on dates and 23 percent were raped by acquaintances. Less than half of the victims (41 percent) were raped by total strangers.[26] Diane Herman suggests that very often rape evolves out of a situation in which "normal" males feel a need to prove themselves to be "men" by displaying dominance over females.[27]

The younger the woman, the greater are the chances that, if rape occurs, she will know the person involved. In a study of 259 rape victims at the Philadelphia General Hospital, 58 percent of the rape victims under the age of 18 were assaulted by a relative or an acquaintance. "When the victim is a child, she is likely to be sexually attacked by her father—6 of the 13 children were raped by their fathers."[28]

Sexual aggression and dating.   There is evidence that sexual aggression is fairly common in the dating and courtship stages. In the 1950s two sociologists found a high frequency of attempted force in sexual relations not only while dating, but also while going steady and engaged. In the mid-1970s one of the authors repeated that study. It was found that sexual aggression in dating and courtship continued to be a common experience for college females. About 50 percent of the coed respondents reported being physically offended at some level of erotic intimacy during the academic year studied. The authors go on to say that the normative pattern of sexual aggression for males, and its frequent escalation into offending force, has not been disturbed in recent years by the move to greater sex role equality. "In fact, from high school through college, sexual offending aggression is shown to be an experience of the majority of females."[29]

The above study found that the most dramatic change from 1957 to 1975 was that male sexual aggression showed *greater* disregard for the nature of the paired relationship. The recent study suggested, that for many males, the female becomes a suitable sexual target regardless of the stage of premarital intimacy, including the most casual and impersonal. "It may be that impersonality in the sexual encounter is one of the most dominant of the new sexual folkways, regardless of the much publicized quest for 'meaningful relationship.' "[30]

One common myth concerning rape is that "it just happens." However, the evidence that most rape occurs with men known to the victim refutes that myth. Studies also report that about half of all rapes occur in the victim's or the rapist's home. Possibly another 15 percent occur in automobiles. In these familiar situations the overwhelming number of rapes are premeditated. In one study, 71 percent of all reported rapes were prearranged and another 11 percent were partially planned. Only 18 percent were impulsive acts.[31]

The use of alcohol has a high association with all crimes of violence, including that of rape. Sexual aggression, especially where force is used, as well as against young children, often involves drunkenness. In one study, in about 40 percent of all acts of male sexual aggression against adult women, the offender was classified as drunk. "Exactly two thirds of all aggressive sexual offenses against young girls, or child molestation, involved drunkenness."[32]

The rapist.   What is the rapist's self image? In many cases he feels that what he did was his right as a male. Often the rapist shows no shame or guilt for his actions. While he will typically defend his actions on the basis of his "powerful" male sexual needs, that is not actually the case. First, he has no stronger sexual drives on the average than any other man. Second, whatever his sexual drive, it can be controlled in the same way that most men place limits on their sexual urges. In any case the male myth of a strong driving need for sexual outlet is a rationalization and a fantasy. Very often the motive for committing rape is not basically sexual. Far more often his actions are based in contempt for women or a need to show power and domination. The factor of contempt for women is reflected in the fact that rapes are often accompanied by attempts by the male to sexually humiliate the victim. For example, urinating on the victim, anal intercourse, and ejaculation in the victim's face and hair.[33]

There are other myths that influence the male's self image during and after rape. For example, some men see the intimacy of the sex act as leading to a sense of intimacy even though it occurred under force.

Sometimes the rapist after the act behaves as if he had grounds for establishing a personal relationship with his victim. Often the rapist believes the victim is acting out her objection to save face and to prove she is "good." This male myth has its roots in the egotistical belief of some males that all resistance on the part of the female is a subterfuge. This myth helps males to rationalize the rape by pretending to themselves that deep down the woman really wanted it.

There are other myths that allow men to blame their victim. There are myths that hold that if the woman is in certain situations she has to accept responsibility for whatever happens. For example, if a woman allows herself to be picked up while hitchhiking or accepts several drinks in a bar, she is believed to be making herself available for sexual intercourse. Under these circumstances the male often feels she has no right to resist and if rape does occur she gets what she deserves. This male view is that there are many situations that women should not enter, and if they do and rape results, it is their own fault. This is like a person walking down a dark street and being blamed for being mugged because he shouldn't have gone down the street.

Power. The factor of power is very important to rape. That is, a major part of many rapes is the male's chance to express his power over the woman and receive some sense of satisfaction from his greater power. Often the pleasure comes not from the sexual act but from being able to exert power—to be able to dominate and often show contempt for the female by the dominance. This is often the case in rape by adolescent males who are at a stage of life where their sense of power is new and uncertain. For some of them rape becomes a means of showing their new manly power. The evidence suggests that among young adolescents there is more apt to be group rape as well as an increased level of violence and humiliation toward the female.[34]

There is other evidence of the importance of power and aggression for the male commiting rape. This has been shown to be a characteristic of homosexual rapes in male prisons. Rapists in prison are often men with little or no history of homosexual behavior and do not consider themselves homosexual. They equate their actions with those of the aggressive heterosexual male. Sexual release is rarely the primary reason for the rape. Rather, the main motive is often the need of the male to exercise control and dominance over another person. In this situation it is another male who is frequently seen as weak, vulnerable, and like a woman. Often the motives in heterosexual and homosexual rape are the same.

The sexual maltreatment of children is probably as negative and repulsive a form of behavior as conceivable to most Americans. Persons who might tolerate most forms of deviance would take a strong position against child sexual molesting. However, estimates suggest that 80,000 to 100,000 children are sexually molested every year. In the majority of the cases the molester is known to the child and in about one fourth of the cases is related to the child. There is some evidence that most incest occurs in intact families and never comes to the attention of authorities.

When incest takes place all the evidence suggests it is overwhelmingly between father and daughter. One study in Chicago found 164 cases of father-daughter incest and only two cases of mother-son incest. "Incest appears to follow the general pattern of sexual abuse of children, in which 92 percent of the victims are female, and 97 percent of the offenders are males."[35]

Rape and marriage. With a few recent exceptions, the concept of "marital rape" does not exist legally. In the eyes of the law a woman cannot be raped by her husband because the crime of rape is legally defined as forcing sexual intercourse on someone other than the wife of the person accused.[36] But if rape is defined as man having sex with a woman by force and against her will, then marital rape does occur. How many times this occurs no one knows, but it must be millions of times every year.

Given the social values about the husband's sexual rights to his wife, it is probable that most women who are physically forced to have sexual intercourse by their husbands do not define it as rape. The belief in the sex rights of the husband is a powerful one and one that continues in many marriages. This contributes to the fact that rape in marriage is rarely reported even as cruel behavior. When it is reported, sexual violence is usually a part of more extended physical violence by the husband.

Richard J. Gelles suggests that if rape is viewed as an act of violence and power, then men who have few social and psychological resources are most apt to use marital rape to coerce, intimidate, and dominate their wives. Sometimes the rape of wives grows out of the male's lack of verbal skills and inability to argue equally with his wife. Sometimes it is the husband's means of demonstrating how he can dominate his wife despite his failure in other areas. "In addition, since rape can be a degrading experience, some husbands may use this act to humiliate their wives and thus gain a degree of power and control over their spouse."[37]

Men who believe in a double standard of sexual rights and see their wives as their personal sexual property often find it especially difficult to deal with rape if their wife is the victim of another man. In part, for some men, rape is an offense that one man commits against another. It can be an attack made on his private property. Often the husband whose wife has been sexually violated may not only question his own masculinity but may also feel that his wife contributed in some way to her own victimization or enjoyed the experience. "His self-esteem is thus lowered not only by the rapist but by his wife's presumed complicity."[38]

United Press International Photo

Picketing for better treatment of rape victims

Conflicting solutions.   The social and legal views about rape are undergoing change. Various women's groups have fought to get better protection and treatment for the rape victim. There are attempts to break down the past mistreatment of rape victims and to gain stronger legal support for them. The male legal system has perpetuated its own myths about rape and has protected the man. This has been done by not taking the victim seriously or blaming her in various ways for the rape. These institutionalized values are only beginning to be questioned and forced to change. We can see the extent of the traditional institutional ways of dealing with rape by looking at the legal procedures in rape cases.

Legal treatment.   Very often police have not believed the rape victim or have found ways of blaming her. The police typically come out of a social class background that supports the traditional views about women and rape. Women often report that their honesty is questioned when they report rape to the police. After rape her first contact is usually the police and they can make it very difficult for her. Some officers have asked victims questions like "How many orgasms did you have?" The police have a great deal of power in deciding whether a crime has been committed, and very often in rape charges, they decide the case is unfounded.

When a rape case gets to the courts it often runs into indifference or even harrassment. Because rape is legally a serious crime, a high level of evidence is required for conviction. The evidence required is often far more than in other serious crimes. Proving rape is frequently very difficult because there are no witnesses to support the victim's testimony. Rape is also different from other criminal cases in that special rules of evidence may be used in court. The courts are not interested in whether or not intercourse occurred but rather in whether there was consent at the moment of coitus. But the courts generally have not regarded the word of the complainant as sufficient. By contrast there is no collaboration required by the court for physical assault.[39]

Rape is one of the few crimes where the victim is often as much on trial as the accused. The victim often comes under trial by having her past questioned. Defense attorneys frequently attempt to get acquittals for their defendants by tarnishing the image of the victim in the eyes of the jury. In some states the complainant's past sexual conduct can be introduced in the trial but not the defendant's, even if he has been guilty of past sexual offenses.[40]

Courts will usually refuse to convict a man of rape if they believe there was any complicity by the woman, and complicity can be defined in very broad terms. As a result of these biases the rate of conviction in rape cases is lower than for any other violent crime. It is clear that the woman charging rape who enters the legal system which is defined traditionally by males is not equal in the eyes of the law.

Legally rape is divided into the categories of statutory and forcible. Forcible rape implies actual violence or the threat of violence. The rapist is not very different from the average man although very often the use of alcohol may be a contributing factor. Power is very important to the rapist, often more than any sexual drive. The police and the courts have traditionally not taken rape as seriously as similar crimes of violence.

Family Violence

Over the centuries men have had the rights of exerting physical controls or punishments over members of the family. It was generally assumed that if the male decided the woman needed physical punishment, it was his right to provide it. This was also clearly the case with regard to children, and for centuries the common view was "spare the rod and spoil the child." We want to look at family violence first with reference to marriage and second with reference to children.

Marital violence. In the early days of American settlement there was an acceptance of physical punishment used within the family. In 1874, the Supreme Court of North Carolina stated "if no permanent injury has been inflicted, nor malice, cruelty nor dangerous violence shown by the husband, it is better to draw the curtain, shut out the public gaze, and leave the parties to forget and forgive." Based on this ruling, a lower court twelve years later decided that a criminal indictment could not be brought against a husband unless the battery led to permanent injury, endangered life and limb, or was malicious beyond all reasonable bounds. Short of these extremes the courts would not interfere.[41]

The practice and acceptance of violence in marriage is high in the United States today. In one large representative sample it was found that between one fourth and one fifth of the adults questioned felt it was acceptable for spouses to hit each other under certain circumstances. Another sample of college students found that 16 percent reported that their parents used physical force to resolve marital conflicts during the previous year.[42]

The wife who is a victim of her husband's violence in the home is often treated socially in the same way as when she is sexually violated. She is frequently blamed and charged with actions that "forced" him to beat her. The woman is often seen as a nagging wife who has driven her husband past all endurance and he reaches the limits of his patience and hits her.[43] Some presume that a pattern of interaction must lead to violence by the husband. It comes to be seen as the only recourse for him. When the end is defined as inevitable, then the wife is easy to blame for leading her husband to that end. The fact that violence does not have to be the end of any process is usually ignored. As a result the beaten wife can become another example of blaming the victim.

Gelles, in his research, found that the decision of whether or not to stay with an assaulting spouse or to try and do something about the marriage is not related just to the extent of the severity of the physical assault. Often the victim cannot leave because there are complex subjective meanings to intrafamilial violence. The woman may feel a strong sense of commitment to or entrapment in the family. And sometimes violence between the mates is viewed as normative.[44]

Family violence is often something learned as a child and carried into the adult years. Gelles found that women who observed spousal violence in their family or orientation were more likely to be victims of conjugal violence in their family or procreation. "In addition, the more frequently a woman was struck by her parents, the more likely she was to grow up and be struck by her husband."[45] It is possible that the more experience that a woman has with violence the more she is inclined to approve of the use of violence in the family. She may grow up with the expectation that husbands are "supposed" to hit wives. "It could be argued that women who grew up in surroundings which included and approved of family violence are more likely to marry a person who is prone to use violence."[46]

Child abuse.   In recent years there has been a great amount of coverage in the mass media about child abuse. Because of the much greater public awareness along with professional interest, it might be thought that it is a new social problem. However, the evidence suggests that child abuse is not new and it is probably not increasing. "Child abusers and abused children were among the 'missing persons' of official statistics and social problems/social policy literature prior to the 1960's."[47]

TABLE 18–1

Violence as Cause of Childhood Death
(deaths per 100,000 population aged 5–14 years)

	1965	1976
Deaths from all causes	42.2	35.7
Violent deaths	19.6	19.6
Automobile accidents	8.9	8.7
All other accidents	9.8	9.4
Suicide	0.3	0.5
Homicide	0.6	1.0

Source: U.S. Department of Health, Education, and Welfare, Public Health Service, *Health Highlights 1976–1977* (Washington, D.C.: U.S. Government Printing Office, 1978), p. 7.

The ultimate form of child abuse, that of infanticide, has been found in many cultures of the past. Infanticide practices were based on values and beliefs that defined which children should or should not survive. In antiquity, any child who was physically defective or cried too much might be killed. Throughout history boys have been considered of greater value than girls so overwhelmingly the female infants were the ones put to death.

James Garbarino argues that for child abuse to occur there are two necessary conditions. First, for abuse to occur within the family there must be cultural justification for the use of force against children. Second, a culturally defined concept of children as the property of their parents and the parents having legitimate use of physical force seems to be an essential condition of child abuse.[48] These are conditions that generally rest in the patriarchal authority of the father.

The label of child abuse is often applied to different actions of parents or guardians toward their children. The act of physically beating a child is not the same as inadequately feeding a child or of abandoning him. In general the term child abuse refers to physical abuse with the level of beating or hitting seen as painful and dangerous and having relatively long term effects on the child.

Rates.   No one knows how much child abuse there is. This, like so much violence, occurs within the privacy of the home and never gets reported. Some estimates of child abuse and child neglect place it as high as 10 million cases per year. It has been estimated that between 200,000 and 250,000 children in the United States need protective services. Of that group 30,000 to 37,000 may be badly hurt by their parents each year.[49] It has also been estimated that one out of every four cases of child abuse ends in the child's death.

As suggested, children may be abused in various ways. Beyond those who are physically abused there may be another 60,000 being held in homes or detention centers. There are a further estimated 300,000 children defined as so hyperactive that they are placed by authorities on drugs to keep them in school.[50] In a majority of cases reported to authorities the children are victims of neglect rather than abuse. In a study of children as suspected victims in 1972, almost three fourths of them were considered cases of neglect. Of all the reported abuse and neglect cases about 70 percent were confirmed. "For every 1,000 children under 18 in the United States, 1.71 cases of abuse and 4.45 of neglect were suspected, brought to the attention of protective services, and confirmed."[51]

Neglect.   Child neglect more often refers to what has *not* been done rather than what has been. The specific types of physical neglect include child abandonment or letting the child live in filth, unattended, and without proper nourishment. It may also include educational neglect if the child remains absent from school or medical neglect if no attempt is made to provide necessary medical care for the child.[52] Neglectful parents are often physically and emotionally drained. They frequently have health problems, are socially withdrawn or isolated, are frustrated or lack hope for the future. They often have had emotionally deprived early childhood experiences. They are generally less emotionally disturbed than abusive parents but are like them in having been socially isolated when young.

One study of maltreatment in Florida found the rate to be highest for children under the age of four and it declined with advancing age. This study found the mother to be the most frequent abuser followed by both parents, and then by the father. "A sizable proportion of suspected abuse and neglect was attributed to stepparents and mothers' boyfriends."[53]

Child abuse is often not spread around among the children in the family. Frequently, one child is singled out to be the primary target of the abuse. This often happens if the child is viewed as mentally slow or as a potential delinquent by the parents. In situations where there is marital conflict the child may be picked because of resemblance to the disliked spouse. Or the abused child may cry more, be hyperactive or demand more parental care. The child may be punished more because of being illegitimate or because the marriage was the result of unwanted pregnancy.[54]

One study reports that in general boys and girls are about equally abused but there are differences by age. Under the age of 12 there are more boys abused, but beyond that age teenage girls being abused outnumber the boys. As children, girls are considered more conforming than boys and as a result less force is used against them. "When girls become adolescents, however, parents' worries about their dating and sexual behavior are more likely to cause arguments and lead to more use of force against them."[55]

In the past it was generally assumed that there was much more violence in the lower class than in the middle class. But recent available data does not necessarily bear out the contention. What may happen is that lower-class families have fewer resources and less privacy and are more apt to contact public agencies, such as the police, which compile domestic statistics. Middle-class families have greater access to support services. "These differences make lower-class family violence more visible as police or emergency room statistics, and therefore more available to researchers."[56]

The parents. There have been a number of studies in recent years that examine the background of parents that abuse their children. One study found that maltreating parents had little basis for "rehearsing" the role of caregiver. In almost every aspect of rehearsal they seemed deficient—from having been maltreated as children to not having pets on which to "practice." There is repeated mention made of their lack of knowledge and unrealistic expectations about children and of their lack of childrearing knowledge.[57]

It has also been found that incompetence in the role of caregiver is associated with stress. Very often abusing parents see themselves as impotent in the face of forces internal and external to the family. The abusive families were characterized by great demands for adjustment, by events "which disrupt roles and relationships thereby requiring potentially stressful psychosocial and behavior accommodations."[58] Very often the patterns followed by abusing parents is deliberate, calculated and consistent punishment without apparent causes for doing so.

The possibility for child abuse may be far greater than what actually takes place. There is some reason to believe that about 25 percent of all families in the United States are in danger of being "abuse prone." This is due to some combination of childrearing, ignorance, unrealistic expectations concerning children, propensity toward violence, psychotherapy, presence of a "special" child, and so forth. One study found that 22 percent of the adults sampled said they thought they "could at some time injure a child" and nearly 16 percent had actually come close to injuring a child in their care.[59]

The long range costs for the abused child can be very great. Some studies have found that children reared in a family setting where there was physical violence, such as spouse beating or child abuse, were later likely to commit physically violent acts themselves, such as rape, murder, and assault. Furthermore, it has been found that "many abusive parents were simultaneously engaged in spouse beating, and their children were rapidly accumulating criminal records for committing physically violent acts."[60]

In general, childrearing patterns of punishment are related to child abuse. First, the use of physical punishment is common in American child rearing practices. Studies suggest that in excess of 90 percent of all parents employ physical force in the upbringing of their children. "One quarter reported spanking infants before the age of 6 months and almost half were spanking by the time the child was 12 months of age."[61] Other studies suggest that as late as the last year of high school, over half the parents used physical punishment or its threat as a means of disciplining their children, and "these respondents were college-bound students, not high school dropouts/troublemakers."[62]

According to various national polls both parents and teachers in the United States favor the use of corporal punishment. There are a number of states that not only permit the use of corporal punishment in the schools but prohibit any local school board from banning it. "Gallup polls have shown that 62 percent of parents, believe in 'modest' use of corporal punishment and 65 percent of elementary teachers agree."[63]

Where the social values allow for the use of some physical punishment it is easy for parents or for teachers to extend its use. Often the parents report that child abuse was an extension of punishment. Frequently the parent in providing discipline oversteps the limits and loses control of the situation. "Just as 'normal' sanctioned discipline is an attempt to restore authority, abuse is a more desperate attempt to do so."[64]

The social reaction to child abuse is often a confused one. It is clear that most Americans approve of the use of physical discipline. But the question is how much physical discipline? When one gets to damaging the child or creating long term pain, it would generally be argued that that is too much. But that clearly leaves a range of physical punishment between those extremes, and it is within this range that people vary in their judgments. The law doesn't help matters very much because it is unclear as to the limits of acceptable physical punishment. In general, it requires strong evidence such as a severely battered child to gain the attention of the public, and, even then, the legal system is reluctant to interfere with the families' rights.

The law. With the increased publicity given to child abuse in recent years there has been some evidence of a reform movement in child care. This movement has led to new social work roles, such as protective workers and child advocates. But today, as it was in the late 19th and early 20th centuries, the social work industry has its most direct consequences for the children of the urban poor.[65]

In the late 1960s, primarily in response to the growing national concern about child abuse, all states adopted child abuse reporting laws. Those laws are essentially a case-finding device. The laws require that professionals (such as physicians, social workers, nurses, etc.) must report suspected cases of child abuse to specified social agencies. The agencies to which reports are made are usually the county welfare department, the county sheriff, or the local police department. "The laws provide penalties for failure to report and also grant civil and criminal immunity to the professionals required to make such reports."[66]

One shift in thinking is that often the abusing parents are defined as "sick" rather than criminally malicious. The consequences of using the sick label for abusers is reflected in two results. One is the low rate of prosecution of the offenders. Second, the changes in reporting statutes channel reporting toward the "helping services" rather than the police. Even when prosecution does occur convictions are obtained in only five to ten percent of the cases. "And even in these cases, sentences are shorter for abusers than for other offenders convicted under the same law of aggravated assault."[67]

The thrust of most of the recent reform movement has been to try to educate parents not to maltreat their children. But that has not changed the position of children within society nor has it made them able to secure treatment for themselves. To think that people will be reached through some kind of education is unrealistic. The values toward child abuse for many parents have often been socialized from their own childhood and those values are not going to be influenced by some external value system that has little meaning and may never influence the parent.

As suggested earlier in the chapter, domestic violence is something the police would like to avoid. Not only is it often difficult for the police to deal with but it can also be dangerous for them. Domestic violence not only endangers the lives of family members but accounts for a high percentage of the deaths and injuries sustained by the po-

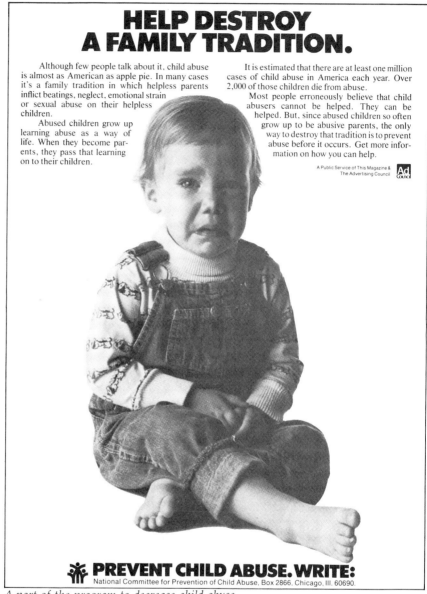

HELP DESTROY A FAMILY TRADITION.

Although few people talk about it, child abuse is almost as American as apple pie. In many cases it's a family tradition in which helpless parents inflict beatings, neglect, emotional strain or sexual abuse on their helpless children.

Abused children grow up learning abuse as a way of life. When they become parents, they pass that learning on to their children.

It is estimated that there are at least one million cases of child abuse in America each year. Over 2,000 of those children die from abuse.

Most people erroneously believe that child abusers cannot be helped. They can be helped. But, since abused children so often grow up to be abusive parents, the only way to destroy that tradition is to prevent abuse before it occurs. Get more information on how you can help.

A Public Service of This Magazine &
The Advertising Council

PREVENT CHILD ABUSE. WRITE:
National Committee for Prevention of Child Abuse, Box 2866, Chicago, Ill. 60690.

A part of the program to decrease child abuse

lice while answering calls. In 1974, one out of every five police officers killed in the line of duty died while trying to break up a family fight.[68]

Most courts and social agencies are not well prepared to deal with family abuse. The courts are often influenced by various myths as to the causes of family violence and as a result they are often ineffective in dealing with violence. Child abuse is very often an "embarrassment" to the legal agencies. They do not feel adequate in handling it and will often avoid responsibility whenever possible.

Conclusion.   All three areas of violence discussed are based in part on myths. These are the myths of the rights of physical expression that are a part of the value system of many American men. Furthermore, the problem of violence is further confused because it can cover a wide range of activities, some of which clearly have social approval, some of which clearly do not, and a lot that falls in between. There is some indication that in recent years some forms of violence are coming to be defined legally as less acceptable than in the past. This is true with regard to rape and child abuse. But the power groups of society are far from being in complete agreement even in these areas. As a reflection of this, laws and the courts tend to be inconsistent in their decisions and ineffective in controlling these problems.

There has long been an acceptance of the male's right to the use of some violence in the family setting. The wife who is a victim is often treated as if it is her fault. In recent years there has come to be a much greater awareness of child abuse. Because it is usually hidden from the authorities the rates are not known but it is believed to be fairly frequent. Often the parents who abuse their children were themselves abused as children.

NOTES

1. Stuart Palmer, *The Violent Society* (New Haven, Conn.: College and University Press, 1972), p. 15.

2. Dane Archer and Rosemary Gartner, "Violent Acts and Violent Times: A Comparative Approach to Positive Homicide Rates," *American Sociological Review* (December 1976), p. 937.

3. Ibid., p. 961.

4. Amital Etzioni, "Collective Violence," in *Contemporary Social Problems*, 4th ed., by Robert K. Merton and Robert Nishet (New York: Harcourt Brace Jovanovich, 1976), p. 680.

5. Federal Bureau of Investigation, "Uniform Crime Reports For the United States" (Washington, D.C.: U.S. Department of Justice, 1973), p. 1.

6. Etzioni, "Collective Violence," p. 678.

7. Erich Goode, *Deviant Behavior* (Englewood Cliffs, N.J.: Prentice-Hall, 1978), p. 411.

8. Ibid., p. 278.

9. John R. Hepburn, "Violent Behavior in Interpersonal Relationships," *The Sociological Quarterly* (Summer 1973), p. 425.

10. Goode, *Deviant Behavior*, p. 415.

11. Howard S. Erlanger, "The Empirical Status of the Subculture of Violence Thesis," *Social Problems* (December 1974), p. 285.

12. Palmer, *Violent Society*, p. 44.

13. Hepburn, "Violent Behavior," p. 426.

14. Ibid., p. 426.

15. Marvin E. Wolfgang and Franco Ferracuti, *The Subculture of Violence* (London: Tavistock Publications, 1967), pp. 95–113.

16. Erlanger, "Empirical Status," p. 280.

17. Ibid., pp. 289–90.

18. James D. Wright and Linda L. Marston, "The Ownership of the Means of Destruction: Weapons in the United States," *Social Problems* (October 1975), p. 94.

19. Ibid., p. 95.

20. Alan Marks and G. Shannon Stokes, "Socialization, Firearms, and Suicide," *Social Problems* (June 1976), p. 628.

21. Federal Bureau of Investigation, "Uniform Crime Reports" (Washington, D.C.: U.S. Department of Justice, 1975), p. 20.

22. Wright and Marston, "Ownership," p. 103.

23. Ibid., p. 104.

24. Diane Herman, "The Rape Culture," in *Women: A Feminist Perspective*, by Jo Freeman (Palo Alto, Calif.: Mayfield Publishing Co., 1979), p. 44.

25. Goode, *Deviant Behavior*, p. 426.

26. Richard J. Gelles, "Power, Sex, and Violence: The Case of Marital Rape," *The Family Coordinator* (October 1977), p. 341.

27. Herman, "Rape Culture," p. 45.

28. Gelles, "Power," p. 342.

29. Eugene J. Kanin and Stanley R. Parsell, "Sexual Aggression: A Second Look at the Offended Female," *Archives of Sexual Behavior*, 6 (1977), p. 75.

30. Ibid., p. 76.

31. Herman, "Rape Culture," p. 51.

32. Goode, *Deviant Behavior*, p. 278.

33. Herman, "Rape Culture," p. 45.

34. Ibid., p. 48.

35. Judith Herman and Lisa Hirschman, "Father-Daughter Incest," *Signs* (Summer 1977), p. 736.

36. Gelles, "Power," p. 339.

37. Ibid., p. 342.

38. Herman, "Rape Culture," p. 45.

39. Ibid., p. 55.

40. Ibid., p. 56.

41. Del Martin, *Battered Wives* (New York: Pocketbooks, 1977), p. 33.

42. Suzanne K. Steinmetz, "The Use of Force for Resolving Family Conflict: The Training Ground for Abuse," *The Family Coordinator* (January 1977), p. 20.

43. Martin, *Battered Wives*, p. 6.

44. Richard J. Gelles, "Abused Wives: Why Do They Stay?" *Journal of Marriage and the Family* (November 1976), p. 659.

45. Ibid., p. 662.

46. Ibid., p. 663.

47. Gelles, "Power," p. 135.

48. James Garbarino, "The Human Ecology of Child Maltreatment: A Conceptual Model for Research," *Journal of Marriage and the Family* (November 1977), p. 725.

49. Martin, *Battered Wives*, p. 24.

50. Naomi Feigelson Chase, *A Child is Being Beaten* (New York: McGraw-Hill, 1976), p. 153.

51. Saad Z. Nagi, *Child Maltreatment In the United States* (New York: Columbia University Press, 1977), p. 35.

52. Charles Zastrow, *Introduction to Social Welfare Institutions* (Homewood, Ill.: Dorsey Press, 1978), p. 93.

53. Nagi, *Maltreatment*, pp. 38–39.

54. Zastrow, *Introduction*, p. 95.

55. Chase, *Child Beaten*, p. 104.

56. Martin, *Battered Wives*, p. 55.

57. Garbarino, "Human Ecology," p. 724.

58. Ibid., p. 724.

59. Ibid., p. 725.

60. Steinmetz, "Use of Force," p. 19.

61. Garbarino, "Human Ecology," p. 726.

62. Steinmetz, "Use of Force," p. 20.

63. Chase, *Child Beaten*, p. 38.

64. Steinmetz, "Use of Force," p. 21.

65. Chase, *Child Beaten*, p. 60.

66. Zastrow, *Introduction*, p. 91.

67. Stephen J. Pfohl, "The 'Discovery' of Child Abuse," *Social Problems* (February 1977), p. 321.

68. Martin, *Battered Wives*, p. 15.

SELECTED BIBLIOGRAPHY

Erlanger, Howard S. "The Empirical Status of the Subculture of Violence Thesis." *Social Problems* (December 1974), pp. 280–91.

Gelles, Richard J. "Abused Wives: Why Do They Stay?" *Journal of Marriage and the Family* (November 1976), pp. 339–47.

Gelles, Richard J. "Power, Sex and Violence: The Case of Marital Rape." *The Family Coordinator* (October 1977), pp. 659–68.

Hepburn, John R. "Violent Behavior in Interpersonal Relationships." *The Sociological Quarterly* (Summer 1973), pp. 419–29.

Herman, Diane. "The Rape Culture" in Jo Freeman, *Women: A Feminist Perspective*. Palo Alto, Calif.: Mayfield Publishing Co., 1979, pp. 41–63.

Nagi, Saad Z. *Child Maltreatment in the United States*. New York: Columbia University Press, 1977.

Palmer, Stuart. *The Violent Society*. New Haven, Conn.: College and University Press, 1972.

Pfohl, Stephen J. "The 'Discovery' of Child Abuse." *Social Problems* (February 1977), pp. 310–13.

Martin, Del. *Battered Wives*. New York: Pocketbooks, 1977.

Steinmetz, Suzanne K. "The Use of Force for Resolving Family Conflict: The Training Ground for Abuse." *The Family Coordinator* (January 1977), pp. 19–26.

Name Index

Subject Index

This book has been set VIP in 10 and 9 point Palatino, leaded 2 points. Part numbers are 20 point Optima Bold and part and chapter titles are 30 point Optima Bold; chapter numbers are 36 point Optima Bold. The size of the maximum type page is 33 by 46½ picas.